ATHLETIC SCHOLARSHIPS

4TH EDITION

Thousands of Grants—and over $400 Million—
for College-Bound Athletes

ANDY CLARK AND AMY CLARK

Karen Breslow
General Editor

D1545309

WITHDRAWN

☑®
Checkmark Books®
An imprint of Facts On File, Inc.

ATHLETIC SCHOLARSHIPS 4th Edition: Thousands of Grants—and over $400 Million—for College-Bound Athletes

Copyright © 2000, 1994 by Alan Green

Checkmark Books
An imprint of Facts On File, Inc.
11 Penn Plaza
New York, NY 10001

Library of Congress Cataloging-in-Publication Data
  Clark, Andy, 1958-
  Athletic scholarships: thousands of grants—and over $400 million—for college-
  bound athletes/Andy Clark and Amy Clark; Karen Breslow, general editor.—4th ed.
  p.cm.
Includes bibliographical references and index.
ISBN 0-8160-4309-4 (alk. paper)—ISBN 0-8160-4308-6 (alk. paper)
1. Sports—Scholarships, fellowships, etc.—United States—Directories. 2. Universities
and colleges—United States—Directories. I. Clark, Amy Holsapple. II. Breslow,
Karen. III. Title
GV351 .G52 2000
796'.079'73–dc21   00-22078

You can find Facts On File on the World Wide Web at http://www.factsonfile.com

Layout by Erika K. Arroyo
Cover design by Cathy Rincon

Printed in the United States of America

MP FOF 10 9 8 7 6 5 4 3 2 1
(pbk) 10 9 8 7 6 5 4 3 2 1

This book is printed on acid-free paper.

CONTENTS

ACKNOWLEDGMENTS

We would like to thank our three children: Andy, Aaron, and Amelia. The oldest just turned seven and Amelia is two. In their own special way, each helped us complete this book.

The student-athletes who use this book deserve respect and recognition. You are the ones who really put in the effort to compete in sports and to succeed academically. We wish you success in all your endeavors!

This book was definitely a team effort! We really appreciate and thank all of those wonderful contacts at the colleges and universities who were kind enough to provide the valuable information necessary to compile this book. Two other team members are also to be thanked. Gary M. Krebs, former associate editor at Facts On File, Inc., provided an incredible level of support throughout the project. Traci Cothran did a very thorough job of copyediting, which really enhanced the accuracy of the information. Thanks again, team!

INTRODUCTION

You do not need to be a football hero to win an athletic scholarship. This book details over $400 million of athletic scholarship aid (with even more that is not specified) available in sports from Alpine Skiing to Wrestling . . . and everything in between. It also provides information that will enhance your chances of obtaining an athletic award to help defray the cost of a college education.

Each year, the nation's colleges and universities award millions of dollars in grants-in-aid to student-athletes. And each year, a significant percentage of available assistance is not awarded—partly because recruiters and coaches, with limited budgets, are unable to locate qualified students, and partly because qualified students are either unaware of all the potential opportunities or uncertain about how to go after them.

Undoubtedly, the easiest way to win an athletic scholarship is to be a star, particularly in "major" sports like football or basketball, which get considerable coverage in local newspapers. The word on top "talent" is never kept secret and an outstanding high school or junior college athlete will find the mailbox overflowing, the telephone ringing off the hook, the stands filled with interested coaches and, where permitted by association rules, a long line of recruiters waiting to ring the doorbell.

But if you are not a star, if you are an average or above-average athlete, you may never see or hear from a recruiter, despite the fact that you may be scholarship material. As such, you will have to actively look for financial aid. The problem, though, is that most student-athletes do not know how to go about it, and the majority of campaigns end up haphazard and often unproductive.

This book explains the process that is often used in awarding athletic scholarship aid and it provides the essential tools needed to pursue it. There is a comprehensive directory of four-year and junior colleges, showing you which schools offer athletic aid and approximate amounts, if available. The directory is accompanied by a sport-by-sport appendix to help identify the colleges that offer programs in your sport. This information will allow you to focus your energy on obtaining the athletic scholarship aid you deserve and it will maximize the probability of a winning effort.

The Game Plan

Perhaps the best way to go about formulating a strategy for winning an athletic scholarship is to first understand how the recruiters and coaches in search of athletic talent operate. When you have a line on their moves, you can pattern your offense accordingly.

For example, take a sports program at a Division I eastern university. Being with a state school, the coaches are always getting reports about local talent—from high school coaches, alumni, newspapers and that good old established standby, the grapevine.

The cycle begins in the spring when the coaches read through the recruiting services' scouting reports and files on young talent. In March or April, the school will send out questionnaires to potential prospects, asking them general questions about their physical attributes and athletic background. During the summer, the coaches will head for some sports camps, where they will have a chance to evaluate talent from all over. In addition to the camps, they will spend time sizing up players in summer league competitions, keeping notes on prospective talent.

By the end of the summer, the staff might have a list of 400 names to whom questionnaires were sent. Those players who did not respond will receive telephone calls to determine whether they might be interested in the school. In September the field will be narrowed down to include only those students who could possibly fit into the program and the coaches will arrange to start visiting them at their high schools or junior colleges.

When this list is complete, the coaches will begin their travels, which last until mid-October. They will visit with students and make presentations about their institution and its sports program. Generally, the students who receive visits are those the coaches believe they might be able to attract to the institution.

But once that visit is over, the student-athlete is not forgotten. Periodic mailings are sent out about the program and how the team is shaping up. During the last three weeks in December, the coaches are out on the road again, this time watching the talent in action. A transcript request form may be sent to a student-athlete's high school, so the coaches can decide whether it is feasible to continue with the recruitment process.

As the season progresses, the coaches will begin trying to determine who may give them a commitment. If the coaches are especially interested in certain players, they will try to get to all their games—even those 150 or 200 miles away. If they like what they see, they will try to assess what an athlete is thinking, perhaps by talking to friends or high school coaches. If the student-athlete is leaning in their direction, they will invite him or her to the school for a visit.

In February, they will have a better idea about a student-athlete's grades and how interested he or she really is in the school. The coach's office might now resemble a field general's headquarters, with a large board sitting in one corner listing the names of prospective student-athletes. Names are moved around or dropped off, depending on how the coaches assess each prospect.

The coaches will try to develop a rapport with the student-athlete and/or anyone who might be able to influence his or her decision. At the same time, they will be trying to establish exactly what their needs are and what sorts of players they would most like to have. As the school year draws to a close, the coaches will try to persuade the student-athletes they are interested in to sign letters of intent. Offers of financial aid are made at this time. The coaches, with an idea of what the team will look like the following season, then start the process all over, sending out questionnaires, reading scouting reports and adding new names to their lists. In other words, the recruiting process never ends.

Not every school works exactly this way, but it is typical of a big-time program. Coaches at smaller schools, which generally put less emphasis on sports, may visit fewer camps each summer, talk to fewer high school coaches about their talent, and watch fewer interscholastic games, but the methods are essentially the same. In the end, all roads lead in the same direction: Where possible, go out and see the talent in action.

At smaller schools, the recruiting budgets may not allow coaches to cover much territory. Nevertheless, these are the schools that provide the best scholarship opportunities for most students. So if you are interested in such a school, it is your job to make sure they know about you.

Collaborating with Your Coach

Do not rule yourself out of athletic scholarship aid. Talk with your coach about the matter. Ask for an honest assessment of your chances of obtaining athletic aid and ask how he or she can help you with the effort. Even if you do not like what you are hearing, hold any comments until the coach is finished speaking. Try to keep all discussions constructive by limiting discussion of past events and focusing on any areas in need of improvement. Before you leave, be sure to thank the coach for taking the time to talk with you.

The point cannot be overemphasized that a high school coach is crucial to the whole process of winning an athletic scholarship. Many times, college coaches will go directly to your high school coach for information about your ability and interest without your ever knowing about it. Such calls to your coach could come as a result of your initial contact, an alumni suggestion or a scouting report. If your coach is aware of your ambitions and interest in athletic scholarship aid, it will make matters easier for all concerned. Eventually, college coaches are going to get to your high school coach for information, so it is wise to work with that coach from the very beginning of your search.

Correspondence

It can be difficult for students to get athletic scholarships on their own. A coach who leads the way and makes contact can be an enormous asset. But coaches cannot do everything for you, and you are going to have to do your own investigation of where you might like to go and narrow down choices without much assistance from your coach. This is particularly true if you are investigating colleges outside your state or region.

Most college athletic departments have available general literature about their programs and obtaining it is often a good first step in the selection process. You should also check each college's website for more information. Schools make this information available to anyone who calls or writes, but you will want your initial contact to be more than a simple request for a brochure. For that first contact, a letter is usually better than a telephone call because what is said over the telephone may be forgotten, while a letter will probably go right into a permanent file. An initial letter to a college coach will tell a lot about you, so make certain you get off on the right foot.

A form letter will suffice if you have a general interest in the school (see Sample Letter #1), but if for some reason you are really enthusiastic about the institution, a personal letter explaining your interest is definitely more appropriate (see Sample Letter #2). Include in the letter if your parents or other relatives are alumni of the school or if you have friends who play sports there. The letter should be addressed to the appropriate coach; if you do not know the coach's name, you can contact the college for it or you can simply write to the athletic director.

It is a good idea to include a brief resume with your first letter. A one-page description of yourself will quickly give a coach an idea of whether you may be the sort of athlete the team needs. Make copies of your resume to send to all the schools you are investigating. But do not spread your focus too wide; a blanket mailing to every school you have heard of is of little value. The schools you should generally contact are the ones you are interested in attending and the ones that could be interested in you, given your athletic and academic credentials.

The resume should have all pertinent data, including your grade-point average, SAT scores, the sport(s) you play, awards and honors received, personal statistics, volunteer activities and other associations you have, along with some names, addresses and telephone numbers of a few athletic and personal references. Where appropriate, include your time for sprints and longer distances. A field hockey coach, for example, may be impressed with the way you handle a stick, but that coach may be even more impressed to learn how well you move—and how long you can continue moving.

The sample resume shown here does not have to be followed exactly, but yours should contain similar information. The idea behind a resume is to quickly give coaches an idea of who you are, what you have done and what your potential may be. If you play a sport such as tennis, by all means include your ranking. And if you have any press clippings, send copies along. Also, it is not a bad idea to include a copy of your upcoming game schedule, if available. A coach who is interested in your credentials will probably want to see you in action.

Neatly organize copies of all your correspondence. This will help greatly when you need to refer back to it. One way to do this is to punch holes in the copies and place them in a notebook with dividers for each school. Let your high school coach know which institutions you are contacting and who has responded. In many cases, it helps to run your correspondence past the coach or another guidance resource before mailing.

A word of caution: A number of athletic departments operate under the assumption that if they have not already heard of you, they are probably not interested. At such schools, a letter touting your abilities might be placed in the trash can. They may rely entirely on their paid recruiters to find talent. So do not be totally put off if you never hear back from a school you contact. You can never be certain about its needs and recruitment strategies, but there is never any harm in trying.

Obtaining athletic aid is much like a search for any other job. The superstars and well connected rarely have to look too hard . . . their main problem is choosing from among the offers. But, for most of us, it is hard work. The correspondence skills that have been described here are almost identical to those used when looking for employment, and the tactics you will learn from your efforts will provide valuable skills.

SAMPLE LETTER #1

Ralph Seidner
278 Perlov Street
Worcester, MA 01610
April 2, 20xx

Soccer Coach
University of Vermont
Patrick Gymnasium
Burlington, VT 05401

Dear Coach:

I am a junior at MacNeice High School, where I have played soccer for the last three years. I am in the process of investigating colleges and am interested in the University of Vermont. I am particularly interested in exploring the possibility of an athletic scholarship, as I believe I can be an asset to the team.

I have enclosed a brief resume outlining my accomplishments along with some newspaper clippings. I would appreciate it if you would provide me with information about your soccer program and scholarship opportunities. Thank you very much.

Sincerely,

Ralph Seidner

SAMPLE LETTER #2

Ralph Seidner
278 Perlov Street
Worcester, MA 01610
April 2, 20xx

Mr. Gary Prushansky
Soccer Coach
Gussie State College
San Diego, CA 92109

Dear Coach:

I am a junior at MacNeice High School, where I have played soccer for the last three years. As a freshman, I was the leading scorer on the junior varsity team with 11 goals and 21 assists. In my sophomore year, playing right wing for the varsity, I scored nine goals and had 24 assists, and was named Honorable Mention All-County. This past season, I led the league in scoring with 23 goals and was named third team All-State. Next year, I expect to do even better.

I am in the process of investigating colleges and am interested in Gussie State. Having grown up in the San Diego area, I am aware of the college's fine reputation. I am particularly interested in exploring the possibility of an athletic scholarship, as I believe I can be an asset to the Gussie State team.

I should add that I am quite familiar with the athletic program at Gussie State. My brother, Michael, graduated two years ago and was one of your top wrestlers.

I have enclosed a brief resume outlining my career to date, along with some newspaper clippings. I would appreciate it if you would provide me with information about the soccer program and the opportunities for athletic scholarship assistance. Thank you very much.

Sincerely,

Ralph Seidner

SAMPLE RESUME

RALPH SEIDNER
278 Perlov Street
Worcester, MA 01610
(617) 555-2345

ACADEMIC INFORMATION

MacNeice High School
Worcester, MA
Expected Graduation: June 20xx
PSAT scores: 594 (verbal) 636 (math)
GPA: 87
Expected field of study: Engineering
Student council treasurer, junior year.

PERSONAL STATISTICS

Date of birth: November 12, 19xx
Height: 5'9"
Weight: 164
40 yard time: 4.95
100 yard time: 10.9
Mile time: 5.12

ATHLETIC HISTORY

Soccer, freshman year: left wing, junior varsity; 11 goals, 21 assists.
Team finished second in league, 12-4.
Soccer, sophomore year: right wing, varsity; 9 goals, 24 assists. Team
finished first in league; named Honorable Mention All-County.

Track, sophomore year: quarter mile, best time 52.8.
All-American Soccer Camp, Sutton, N.H., summer of sophomore year.
Soccer, junior year: right wing, varsity; 23 goals, 19 assists. Team
made it to state quarter finals; named to third team All-State. Elect-
ed team captain for senior year.

REFERENCES

Charlie Russo, Varsity soccer coach, MacNeice High
Jerrold Schoenholtz, J.V. soccer coach, MacNeice High
Peter Goldwater, director, All-American Soccer Camp

Your Ticket to College Scholarship Awards

Getting seen in action by the college coaches and/or their recruiters will really enhance your chances of obtaining athletic scholarship assistance. Your letters will result in opportunities, and there are additional methods to gain exposure. College coaches rely heavily on films, which is another reason to work closely with your high school coach, who can see to it that a college receives any available footage of you in action.

Although not all sports are filmed, there are other opportunities for college coaches to get to see you play. One way is at a summer camp. Camps offer an excellent chance not only for you to be seen, but also to help improve your skills and to have fun. Just as there are scholarships available for college, athletic scholarship aid to summer camp is available. Recruiters also keep a close eye on summer leagues, so get involved with one of these, if possible. Your high school coach will be able to provide more information about camps and summer leagues.

Some schools, particularly junior and smaller four-year schools, allow walk-ins, where anyone can try out for the team. If the coach likes what he or she sees, you may end up with a scholarship, although chances are it will not be for the first year, after which time they are certain of your value to the team.

Be sure to thoroughly investigate other aid that an institution may offer. Virtually all institutions of higher education have very extensive need-based and merit-based aid programs. The cumulative value of non-athletic aid far exceeds the value of athletic aid.

Generally, steer clear of outside services that offer to match you with athletic scholarship aid for a fee. These services rarely do anything that you are not completely capable of doing yourself and some have been known to be unscrupulous. With the help of your high-school coaches and other resources, you can write the same letters, make the same contacts and get the same (or better) results without spending money that should be earmarked for college.

Key Points

1. Do not wait until your senior year to get the process going. As pointed out, the recruiting process is a long one. You should start pursuing athletic scholarship assistance at the beginning of your junior year or even by the middle of your sophomore year in high school. If you are already past that point, your effort will need to be more intense.

2. Work closely with your high school coach. He or she cannot completely read your intentions and interests. Respectfully seek their guidance and assistance, but do not rely on them to make decisions for you.

3. Be seen as often as possible. In most cases, the bottom line in obtaining athletic scholarship aid is being seen in action in your sport by college coaches and recruiters.

4. Explore all of your options. While this book focuses on athletic scholarship aid, there is an incredible level of nonathletic aid available as well.

Peptalk

The keys to winning anything are hard work and a good attitude. You are already ahead of the competition. By using this book, your search is on and it is up to you to win both the athletic and non-athletic college scholarship aid you need and deserve.

The work you put into the search in high school will probably take many, many hours over a long period of time. But all of those hours are nothing compared with the time you would have to work to earn the money at a job or when compared with the work needed to pay off college loans. When pursuing college scholarship aid, consider it among your most important jobs while in high school and make appropriate sacrifices so you have the time to find the financial assistance you need to *finish* college.

Don't get discouraged. Some doors will close but others will open. Be positive, active and upbeat. Every letter you write, every call you make, every good grade you get and every game you play are all steps toward your goal of a college education. Just take enough steps—you *will* reach that goal!

Understanding the State-by-State Listings

The directory is broken down by state and colleges are shown in alphabetical order within each state. The college name, address, telephone number and website address appear first in each record. Most of the telephone numbers will connect you to the Athletic Information Office, often to the individual listed as a contact. In other cases, they connect you with a main switchboard. The name given is the one provided by the college as a primary contact for student-athlete inquiries or the one that was on file from previous research. Some of the records do not have contact names, in which case contact the college and ask for the Athletic Information Office for further details. In any case, it is vital to verify the contact information before sending a letter, as the staffing situation at most colleges is subject to change.

The colleges were asked to provide approximate numbers of athletic scholarships awarded during the most recent year and the approximate dollar value of the aid. This information can be used to gauge the level of athletic aid awarded by a particular school. Many colleges chose to keep this information confidential; in those cases it is noted that unspecified athletic scholarship aid is available.

Some colleges provided notes or restrictions that may be applicable to their programs, which are included. Two-year colleges are specified; the rest are four-year institutions.

The athletic programs offered by the school come next. Programs in which athletic awards *are* available are listed for both men (M) and women (W). Men's and women's non-scholarship aid sports programs are also listed for each school, where applicable.

Again, it is important to confirm all information when making contact with the college. Every effort was made to ensure the accuracy of the information, however unintentional errors are still possible.

For additional information on specific colleges, check college websites or consult general guides to colleges.

STATE-BY-STATE LISTINGS

Alabama

ALABAMA A&M UNIVERSITY
P.O. Box 1597
Normal, AL 35762
(256) 851-5361
www.aamu.edu
Contact: Jim Martin
Unspecified athletic aid available
M: baseball, basketball, cross country,
football, golf, indoor track, soccer, tennis,
track&field
W: basketball, cross country, indoor
track, soccer, softball, track&field,
volleyball

ALABAMA STATE UNIVERSITY
915 S. Jackson Street
Montgomery, AL 36101-0271
(334) 229-4511 www.alasu.edu
Contact: Kevin Manns
Unspecified athletic aid available
M: baseball, basketball, cross country,
football, golf, indoor track, tennis,
track&field
W: basketball, bowling, cross country,
golf, indoor track, softball, tennis,
track&field, volleyball

ATHENS STATE COLLEGE
300 North Beaty Street
Athens, AL 35611-1902
Two-year college
(256) 233-8277 ext. 277
www.athens.edu
Contact: Barry DeVine
Unspecified athletic aid available
M: basketball
W: softball

AUBURN UNIVERSITY
P.O. Box 351
Auburn, AL 36831-0351
(334) 844-9800
www.auburn.edu
Contact: David Housel
Men's Aid (#/$): 158/$1,127,724
Women's Aid (#/$): 81/$605,178
M: baseball, basketball, cross country,
diving, football, golf, indoor track, swim-
ming, tennis, track&field
W: basketball, cross country, diving, golf,
gymnastics, indoor track, soccer, softball,
swimming, tennis, track&field, volleyball

AUBURN UNIVERSITY
(MONTGOMERY)
P.O. Box 244023
Montgomery, AL 36124-4023

(334) 244-3000
www.aum.edu
Contact: Michael Jones
Unspecified athletic aid available
M: baseball, basketball, soccer, tennis
W: basketball, soccer, tennis

BIRMINGHAM-SOUTHERN COLLEGE

Arkadelphia Road
Birmingham, AL 35254
(205) 226-4688
www.bsc.edu
Contact: Joe Dean
Men's Aid (#/$): 37/unspecified $
Women's Aid (#/$): 35/unspecified $
M: baseball, basketball, cross country, soccer, tennis
W: basketball, cross country, soccer, tennis, volleyball

CHATTAHOOCHEE VALLEY COMMUNITY COLLEGE

2602 College Drive
Phenix City, AL 36869
Two-year college
(334) 291-4900
www.cvcc.cc.al.vc
Contact: Adam Thomas
Unspecified athletic aid available
M: baseball, basketball
W: basketball, softball

ENTERPRISE STATE JUNIOR COLLEGE

P.O. Box 1300
Enterprise, AL 36331
Two-year college
(334) 393-3752
www.esjc.cc.al.us
Contact: Mike Pugh
Unspecified athletic aid available
M: baseball, basketball
W: basketball, softball

FAULKNER UNIVERSITY

5345 Atlantic Highway
Montgomery, AL 36109-3398
(334) 260-6200
www.faulkner.edu
Contact: Jim Sanderson
Unspecified athletic aid available
M: baseball, basketball
W: softball, volleyball

GADSDEN STATE COMMUNITY COLLEGE

P.O. Box 227
Gadsden, AL 35902-0227
Two-year college
(256) 549-8311
www.gadsdenst.cc.al.us
Contact: Riley Whitaker
Unspecified athletic aid available
M: baseball, basketball
W: basketball, softball

GEORGE C. WALLACE COMMUNITY COLLEGE

Route 6, Box 62
Dothan, AL 36303
Two-year college
(334) 983-3521 ext. 216
www.wallace.edu
Contact: Gene Dews
Unspecified athletic aid available
M: baseball, basketball, golf
W: basketball, softball

HUNTINGDON COLLEGE

1500 East Fairview Avenue
Montgomery, AL 36106-2148
(334) 833-4565
www.huntingdon.edu
Contact: Todd Schilperoort
Men's Aid (#/$): 6/unspecified $
Women's Aid (#/$): 10/unspecified $
M: baseball, basketball, golf, soccer, tennis
W: basketball, soccer, softball, tennis, volleyball

JACKSONVILLE STATE UNIVERSITY

800 Pelham Road
Jacksonville, AL 36265
(256) 782-5377
www.jsu.edu
Contact: Mike Galloway

Men's Aid (#/$): 98/unspecified $
Women's Aid (#/$): 42/unspecified $
M: baseball, basketball, cross country, football, golf, riflery, tennis
W: basketball, cross country, riflery, soccer, softball, tennis, volleyball

JEFFERSON DAVIS JUNIOR COLLEGE
P.O. Box 958
Brewton, AL 36427
Two-year college
(334) 809-1622
www.jeffdavis.cc.al.us
Contact: Karen Reynolds
Unspecified athletic aid available
M: baseball, basketball, cheerleading, tennis
W: basketball, cheerleading, softball, tennis, volleyball

JEFFERSON STATE COMMUNITY COLLEGE
2601 Carson Road
Birmingham, AL 35215
Two-year college
(205) 856-8523
www.jscc.cc.al.us
Contact: Ben Short
Unspecified athletic aid available
M: baseball, tennis
W: softball, tennis

JOHN C. CALHOUN COMMUNITY COLLEGE
Highway 31 North
P.O. Box 2216
Decatur, AL 35609-2216
Two-year college
(256) 306-2853
www.calhoun.cc.al.us
Contact: Mickey Sutton
Men's Aid (#/$): 41/$98,810
Women's Aid (#/$): 49/$118,090
M: baseball, basketball, cheerleading
W: basketball, cheerleading, softball

JUDSON COLLEGE
302 Bibb Street
Marion, AL 36756
(334) 683-5249
www.judson.edu
Contact: Michele Templin
Women's Aid (#/$): 16/$57,800
Restrictions and notes: Up to full tuition only, based on skills and academic qualifications.
W: basketball, golf, softball, tennis, volleyball

MARION MILITARY INSTITUTE
1101 Washington Street
Marion, AL 36756
Two-year college
(334) 683-2359
www.marion-institute.org
Contact: Tommy Murfee
Men's Non-aid: golf, riflery, soccer

MILES COLLEGE
P.O. Box 3800
Birmingham, AL 35208
(205) 929-1615
www.miles.edu
Contact: Augustus James
Unspecified athletic aid available
M: baseball, basketball, cross country, football, track&field
W: basketball, cross country, softball, track&field, volleyball

NORTHWEST SHOALS COMMUNITY COLLEGE
2080 College Road
Phil Campbell, AL 35581
Two-year college
(256) 331-6200
www.nwscc.cc.al.us
Contact: Bill Moss
Unspecified athletic aid available
M: baseball, basketball
W: basketball, softball

SAMFORD UNIVERSITY
800 Lakeshore Drive
Birmingham, AL 35229
(205) 726-2131
www.samford.edu
Contact: Bill Roller
Unspecified athletic aid available

M: baseball, basketball, cross country, football, golf, indoor track, tennis, track&field
W: basketball, cross country, golf, indoor track, softball, soccer, tennis, track&field, volleyball

SELMA UNIVERSITY
1501 Lapsley Street
Selma, AL 36701-5299
Two-year college
(334) 872-2533
Contact: Alvin Cleveland
Unspecified athletic aid available
M: basketball

SNEAD STATE COMMUNITY COLLEGE
P.O. Drawer D
Boaz, AL 35957
Two-year college
(256) 593-5120 ext. 264
www.snead.cc.al.us
Contact: David Wilson
Men's Aid (#/$): 45/$112,500
Women's Aid (#/$): 53/$132,000
Restrictions and notes: School also provides aid for their athletic manament/trainer program.
M: baseball, basketball, cheerleading
W: basketball, cheerleading, softball, tennis

SOUTHERN UNION STATE COMMUNITY COLLEGE
Robert Street
Wadley, AL 36276
Two-year college
(205) 395-5166
www.suscc.cc.al.us
Contact: Joe Jordan
Unspecified athletic aid available
M: baseball, basketball, cross country, volleyball
W: basketball, cross country, softball, volleyball

SPRING HILL COLLEGE
4000 Dauphin Street
Mobile, AL 36608

(334) 380-4461
www.shc.edu
Contact: Mark Priede
Men's Aid (#/$): 20/$420,000
Women's Aid (#/$): 20/$420,000
M: baseball, basketball, cross country, golf, soccer, tennis
W: basketball, cross country, golf, soccer, softball, tennis

TALLADEGA COLLEGE
627 West Battle Street
Talladega, AL 35160
(356) 362-0206
www.talladega.edu
Contact: Alfred Baker
Men's Aid (#/$): 20/unspecified $
Women's Aid (#/$): 20/unspecified $
M: baseball, basketball, cross country, golf
W: basketball, cross country, volleyball

TROY STATE UNIVERSITY
Athletic Department
Davis Field House
Troy, AL 36082
(334) 670-3480
www.troyst.edu
Contact: Scott Farmer
Unspecified athletic aid available
M: baseball, basketball, cross country, football, golf, tennis, track&field
W: basketball, cross country, indoor track, softball, tennis, track&field, volleyball

TUSKEGEE UNIVERSITY
321 James Center
Tuskegee, AL 36088
(334) 727-8150
www.tusk.edu
Contact: Arnold L. Houston
Unspecified athletic aid available
M: basketball, football. Men's Non-aid: cross country, tennis
W: basketball. Women's Non-aid: cross country, softball, tennis, volleyball

UNIVERSITY OF ALABAMA (BIRMINGHAM)
115 UAB Arena
Birmingham, AL 35294-1160
(205) 934-4011
www.uab.edu
Contact: Grant Shingleton
Unspecified athletic aid available
M: baseball, basketball, cross country, football, golf, soccer, tennis, track&field, volleyball
W: basketball, cross country, golf, soccer, softball, synchronized swimming, tennis, track&field, volleyball

UNIVERSITY OF ALABAMA (HUNTSVILLE)
205 Spragins Hall
Huntsville, AL 35899
(256) 890-6144
www.uah.edu
Contact: Julie Woltjen
Unspecified athletic aid available
M: baseball, basketball, cross country, golf, ice hockey, soccer, tennis
W: basketball, cross country, soccer, softball, tennis, volleyball

UNIVERSITY OF ALABAMA (TUSCALOOSA)
P.O. Box 870391
Tuscaloosa, AL 35487-0391
(205) 348-6084
www.ua.edu
Contact: Larry White
Unspecified athletic aid available
M: baseball, basketball, cross country, football, golf, indoor track, swimming-diving, tennis, track&field
W: basketball, cross country, golf, gymnastics, indoor track, soccer, softball, swimming-diving, tennis, track&field, volleyball

UNIVERSITY OF MOBILE
P.O. Box 13220
Mobile, AL 36663-0220
(334) 442-2279
www.umobile.edu

Contact: Craig Bogar
Unspecified athletic aid available
M: baseball, basketball, cross country, golf, indoor track, soccer
W: basketball, golf, indoor track, soccer, softball, track&field

UNIVERSITY OF MONTEVALLO
Station 6600
Montevallo, AL 35115-6000
(205) 665-6600
www.montevallo.edu
Contact: Ron Holsombeck
Unspecified athletic aid available
M: baseball, basketball, golf
W: basketball, volleyball

UNIVERSITY OF NORTH ALABAMA
Box 5038
Florence, AL 35632-0001
(256) 765-4397
www.una.edu
Contact: Dan Summy
Unspecified athletic aid available
M: baseball, basketball, cross country, football, golf, tennis
W: basketball, cross country, soccer, softball, tennis, volleyball

UNIVERSITY OF SOUTH ALABAMA
1107 HPELS Building
Mobile, AL 36688-0002
(334) 460-7121
www.southalabama.edu
Contact: Hal Williams
Unspecified athletic aid available
M: baseball, basketball, cross country, golf, indoor track, tennis, track&field
W: basketball, cross country, golf, indoor track, soccer, tennis, track&field, volleyball

UNIVERSITY OF WEST ALABAMA
UWA Stations
Livingston, AL 35470
(205) 652-3784
www.westal.edu
Contact: Dee Outlaw
Men's Aid (#/$): 60/$348,000

Women's Aid (#/$): 30/$172,000
M: baseball, basketball, cross country, football, rodeo
W: basketball, cross country, rodeo, softball, volleyball

WALLACE COMMUNITY COLLEGE SELMA
P.O. Box 1049
Selma, AL 36702-1049
Two-year college
(334) 876-9227
www.wccs.cc.al.us
Contact: Roland Maxwell/
Coach: Lothian Smallwood
Unspecified athletic aid available
M: baseball, basketball, cheerleading, tennis
W: cheerleading, softball, tennis

WALLACE STATE COMMUNITY COLLEGE
P.O. Box 2000
Hanceville, AL 35077-2000
Two-year college
(256) 352-8163
www.wallacestatehanceville.edu
Contact: Craig Derrick
Unspecified athletic aid available
M: baseball, basketball, golf, soccer, tennis, track&field
W: basketball, softball, tennis, track&field

Alaska

UNIVERSITY OF ALASKA
3211 Providence Drive
Anchorage, AK 99508
(907) 786-1230
www.uaa.alaska.edu
Contact: Tim McDiffett
Unspecified athletic aid available
M: alpine skiing, basketball, cross country, cross country skiing, ice hockey, swimming-diving

W: alpine skiing, basketball, cross country skiing, gymnastics, volleyball

UNIVERSITY OF ALASKA (FAIRBANKS)
101 Patty Center
Fairbanks, AK 99775-0240
(907) 474-6812
www.uaf.edu
Contact: Karen J. Jones
Unspecified athletic aid available
M: basketball, cross country, cross country skiing, ice hockey, riflery
W: basketball, cross country, cross country skiing, riflery, volleyball

UNIVERSITY OF ALASKA SOUTHEAST
11120 Glacier Highway
Juneau, AK 99801-8697
(907) 465-6457
www.jun.alaska.edu
Contact: Bruce Gifford
Unspecified athletic aid available
M: alpine skiing, basketball. Men's
Non-aid: riflery
W: alpine skiing, basketball. Women's
Non-aid: riflery

Arizona

ARIZONA STATE UNIVERSITY
ICA
First Floor
Tempe, AZ 85287-2505
(480) 965-6360
www.thesundevils.com
Contact: Dr. Kevin White
Unspecified athletic aid available
M: baseball, basketball, cross country, football, golf, indoor track, swimming-diving, tennis, track&field, wrestling
W: archery, badminton, basketball, cross country, golf, gymnastics, indoor track, soccer, softball, swimming-diving, tennis, track&field, volleyball

CENTRAL ARIZONA COLLEGE
8470 North Overfield Road
Coolidge, AZ 85228
Two-year college
(520) 426-4444
www.cac.cc.az.us
Contact: Gary Heintz
Unspecified athletic aid available
M: baseball, basketball, cross country, golf, rodeo, track&field
W: basketball, cross country, rodeo, softball, track&field

COCHISE COLLEGE
4190 West Highway 80
Douglas, AZ 85607-9724
Two-year college
(520) 364-0295
www.cochise.cc.az.us
Contact: Dr. James "Bo" Hall
Unspecified athletic aid available
M: baseball, basketball
W: basketball, soccer

DINÉ COLLEGE
Box 804
Tsaile, AZ 86556
Two-year college
(520) 724-6738
www.ncc.cc.nm.us
Contact: Mark Retaskin
Unspecified athletic aid available
M: archery, basketball, cross country, rodeo
W: archery, basketball, cross country, rodeo, volleyball

GLENDALE COMMUNITY COLLEGE
6000 West Olive Avenue
Glendale, AZ 85302
Two-year college
(623) 845-3000
www.gc.maricopa.edu
Contact: David Grant
Men's Aid (#/$): 95/unspecified $
Women's Aid (#/$): 65/unspecified $
M: archery, baseball, basketball, cross country, football, golf, soccer, tennis, track&field

W: archery, basketball, cross country, softball, tennis, track&field, volleyball

GRAND CANYON COLLEGE
3300 West Camelback
Phoenix, AZ 85017-1097
(602) 249-3300
www.grand-canyon.edu
Contact: Keith Baker
Unspecified athletic aid available
M: baseball, basketball, golf, soccer, tennis
W: basketball, soccer, tennis, volleyball

MESA COMMUNITY COLLEGE
1833 West Southern Avenue
Mesa, AZ 85202
Two-year college
(480) 461-7545
www.mc.maricopa.edu
Contact: Allen Benedict
Unspecified athletic aid available
Men's Non-aid: baseball, basketball, cross country, football, golf, soccer, tennis, track&field
W: basketball, golf, soccer, softball, tennis, volleyball. Women's Non-aid: cross country, track&field

NORTHERN ARIZONA UNIVERSITY
Box 15400
Flagstaff, AZ 86001
(520) 523-6330
www.nau.edu
Contact: David Woodburn
Unspecified athletic aid available
M: basketball, cross country, football, indoor track, swimming-diving, tennis, track&field
W: basketball, cross country, golf, indoor track, soccer, swimming-diving, tennis, track&field, volleyball

PHOENIX COLLEGE
1202 West Thomas Road
Phoenix, AZ 85013
Two-year college
(602) 264-2492
www.pc.maricopa.edu

Contact: JoAnn Dunlop
Unspecified athletic aid available
M: baseball, basketball, cross country, football, golf, soccer, track&field
W: basketball, cross country, golf, soccer, softball, track&field, volleyball

PIMA COMMUNITY COLLEGE (WEST CAMPUS)
2202 West Anklam Road
Tucson, AZ 85709-0001
Two-year college
(520) 206-6600
www.pima.edu
Contact: Mike Lopez
Unspecified athletic aid available
M: archery, baseball, basketball, cross country, golf, tennis, track&field, wrestling
W: archery, basketball, cross country, softball, tennis, track&field, volleyball

SCOTTSDALE COMMUNITY COLLEGE
9000 East Chaparral Road
Scottsdale, AZ 85256-2626
Two-year college
(480) 423-6000
www.sc.maricopa.edu
Contact: M – Art Becker, W – Dorcel Coco
Unspecified athletic aid available
M: baseball, basketball, football, golf, soccer, tennis, track&field
W: basketball, golf, soccer, softball, tennis, track&field, volleyball

UNIVERSITY OF ARIZONA
229 McKale Center
Tucson, AZ 85721
(520) 621-9874
www.arizcats.com
Contact: Lisa Watson
Men's Aid (#/$): 131/unspecified $
Women's Aid (#/$): 106/unspecified $
M: baseball, basketball, cross country, football, golf, swimming-diving, tennis, track&field
W: basketball, cross country, golf, gym-nastics, soccer, softball, swimming-diving, tennis, track&field, volleyball

YAVAPAI COLLEGE
1100 East Sheldon Street
Prescott, AZ 86301
Two-year college
(520) 445-7300
www.yavapai.cc.az.us
Contact: Jennifer Lerch
Unspecified athletic aid available
M: baseball, basketball, soccer
W: basketball, cross country, volleyball

Arkansas

ARKANSAS COLLEGE
2300 Highland Road
Batesville, AR 72501
(870) 698-4220
www.lyon.edu
Contact: Kevin Jenkins
Men's Aid (#/$): 12/$120,000
Women's Aid (#/$): 12/$120,000
M: baseball, basketball, cross country, golf, indoor track
W: basketball, cross country, golf, volleyball

ARKANSAS STATE UNIVERSITY
P.O. Box 1000
State University, AR 72467
(870) 972-3880
www.asuindians.com
Contact: Barry Dowd
Unspecified athletic aid available
M: baseball, basketball, cross country, football, golf, indoor track, track&field
W: basketball, cross country, golf, indoor track, tennis, track&field, volleyball

ARKANSAS TECH UNIVERSITY
Tucker Coliseum
Russellville, AR 72801
(501) 968-0645
www.atu.edu
Contact: Larry G. Smith

Men's Aid (#/$): 58/$348,000
Women's Aid (#/$): 24/$144,000
Restrictions and notes: In-state, 1 year
athletic aid only.
M: baseball, basketball, football, golf
W: basketball, cross country, tennis,
volleyball

CENTRAL BAPTIST COLLEGE
1501 College Avenue
Conway, AR 72035
(501) 329-6872
www.cbc.edu
Contact: William Kennedy
Men's Aid (#/$): 15/$26,117
Women's Aid (#/$): 1/$1,000
M: basketball
W: basketball

HARDING UNIVERSITY
900 East Center
Searcy, AR 72149
(501) 279-4760
www.harding.edu
Contact: Scott Goode
Unspecified athletic aid available
M: basketball, football. Men's Non-aid:
baseball, cross country, golf, indoor track,
soccer, tennis, track&field
W: basketball, volleyball. Women's Non-
aid: cross country, indoor track, soccer,
tennis, track&field

HENDERSON STATE UNIVERSITY
1100 Henderson Street
Arkadelphia, AR 71999
(870) 230-5000
www.hsu.edu
Contact: Steve Eddington
Men's Aid (#/$): 56/$336,000
Women's Aid (#/$): 32/$192,000
M: baseball, basketball, football, golf,
indoor track, swimming-diving, tennis
W: basketball, cross country, softball,
swimming-diving, tennis, volleyball

JOHN BROWN UNIVERSITY
2000 University Street
Siloam Springs, AR 72761

(501) 524-3131
www.jbu.edu
Contact: Donnie Bostwick
Unspecified athletic aid available
M: basketball, soccer, swimming,
tennis
W: basketball, swimming, tennis,
volleyball

NORTH ARKANSAS COLLEGE
1515 Pioneer Drive
Harrison, AR 72601
Two-year college
(870) 743-3000
www.northark.cc.ar.us
Contact: Jerry Thompson
Unspecified athletic aid available
M: basketball
W: basketball, softball

OUACHITA BAPTIST UNIVERSITY
410 Ouchita Street
Arkadelphia, AR 71998
(870) 245-5181
www.obu.edu
Contact: David Sharp
Unspecified athletic aid available
M: basketball. Men's Non-aid: baseball,
cross country, football, soccer, swimming, tennis
W: basketball, volleyball. Women's Non-
aid: cross country, soccer, swimming,
tennis

SOUTHERN ARKANSAS UNIVERSITY
100 East University
Magnolia, AR 71753-5000
(870) 235-4102
www.saumag.edu
Contact: Jay Adcox
Unspecified athletic aid available
M: basketball, football. Men's Non-aid:
baseball, cross country, golf, swimming,
track&field
W: basketball, softball, volleyball.
Women's Non-aid: cross country,
swimming, tennis, track&field

UNIVERSITY OF ARKANSAS (FAYETTEVILLE)
Broyles Athletics Complex
Fayetteville, AR 72701
(501) 575-2000
www.uark.edu
Contact: Rick Schaeffer
Unspecified athletic aid available
M: baseball, basketball, cross country, football, golf, indoor track, tennis, track&field
W: basketball, cross country, diving, golf, soccer, softball, swimming, tennis, track&field, volleyball

UNIVERSITY OF ARKANSAS (LITTLE ROCK)
2801 South University Avenue
Little Rock, AR 72204-1099
(501) 569-3449
www.ualr.edu
Contact: Mike Garitty
Unspecified athletic aid available
M: baseball, basketball, diving, golf, swimming, tennis
W: soccer, swimming, tennis, volleyball. Women's Non-aid: cross country

UNIVERSITY OF ARKANSAS (MONTICELLO)
UAM Box 3589
Monticello, AR 71655
(870) 460-1026
www.uamont.edu
Contact: James Brewer
Unspecified athletic aid available
M: baseball, basketball, football
W: basketball, softball

UNIVERSITY OF ARKANSAS (PINE BLUFF)
1200 North University
Pine Bluff, AR 71611
(870) 543-8684
www.uapb.edu
Contact: Carl Whimper
Unspecified athletic aid available
M: basketball, football. Men's Non-aid: golf, tennis, track&field

W: basketball, bowling, indoor track, softball, track&field, volleyball

UNIVERSITY OF CENTRAL ARKANSAS
201 Donaghey Avenue
Conway, AR 72035
(501) 450-5743
www.uca.edu
Contact: Steve East
Unspecified athletic aid available
M: basketball, football. Men's Non-aid: baseball, cross country, golf, soccer, tennis
W: basketball, volleyball. Women's Non-aid: cross country, soccer, softball, tennis

WESTARK COMMUNITY COLLEGE
5210 Grand Avenue
P.O. Box 3649
Fort Smith, AR 72913-3649
Two-year college
(501) 788-7000
www.westark.edu
Contact: Doc Sadler
Unspecified athletic aid available
M: baseball, basketball
W: basketball, volleyball

California

AZUSA PACIFIC UNIVERSITY
P.O. Box 7000
Azusa, CA 91702
(626) 812-3025
www.apu.edu
Contact: Gary Pine
Unspecified athletic aid available
M: baseball, basketball, cross country, football, soccer, tennis, track&field
W: basketball, cross country, soccer, softball, tennis, track&field, volleyball

BARSTOW COLLEGE
2700 Barstow Road
Barstow, CA 92311
Two-year college
(760) 252-2411
www.barstow.cc.ca.us
Contact: Ray Perea
Men's Non-aid: baseball, basketball,
cheerleading, tennis
Women's Non-aid: basketball, cheerleading, tennis, volleyball

BIOLA UNIVERSITY
13800 Biola Avenue
La Mirada, CA 90639
(562) 903-4889
www.biola.edu
Contact: Ken Carlson
Unspecified athletic aid available
M: baseball, basketball, cross country,
soccer, track&field
W: basketball, tennis, volleyball

BUTTE COLLEGE
3565 Butte Campus Drive
Oroville, CA 95265
Two-year college
(530) 895-2521
www.buttecollege.edu
Contact: Linda Bumgarner
Men's Non-aid: baseball, basketball,
cross country, football, golf, tennis,
track&field
Women's Non-aid: basketball, cross
country, soccer, softball, tennis,
track&field, volleyball

CABRILLO COLLEGE
6500 Soquel Drive
Aptos, CA 95003
Two-year college
(831) 479-6266
www.cabrillo.cc.ca.us
Contact: Dale Murray
Men's Non-aid: baseball, basketball,
cross country, football, golf, soccer,
swimming-diving, tennis, water polo
Women's Non-aid: basketball, cross

country, soccer, softball, swimming-
diving, tennis, volleyball

CALIFORNIA BAPTIST UNIVERSITY
8432 Magnolia Avenue
Riverside, CA 92504
(909) 343-4296
www.calbaptist.edu
Contact: Doug Huckaby
Unspecified athletic aid available
M: baseball, basketball, cross country,
golf, soccer, swimming-diving,
track&field, volleyball, water polo
W: basketball, cross country, soccer,
softball, swimming-diving, track&field,
volleyball, water polo

CALIFORNIA INSTITUTE OF TECHNOLOGY
1201 East California Boulevard
Pasadena, CA 91125
(626) 395-6811
www.caltech.edu
Contact: Wendell Jack
Men's Non-aid: baseball, basketball,
cross country, fencing, golf, soccer,
swimming-diving, tennis, track&field,
water polo
Women's Non-aid: basketball, cross
country, fencing, golf, swimming-diving,
tennis, track&field, volleyball, water polo

CALIFORNIA LUTHERAN UNIVERSITY
60 West Olsen Road
Thousand Oaks, CA 91360
(805) 493-3115
www.robles.callutheran.edu/scj/scj.html
Contact: Bruce Bryde
Men's Non-aid: baseball, basketball,
cross country, football, golf, soccer,
tennis, track&field
Women's Non-aid: basketball, cross
country, soccer, softball, tennis,
track&field, volleyball

CALIFORNIA MARITIME ACADEMY
200 Maritime Academy Drive
Vallejo, CA 94590

(707) 654-1050
www.csum.edu
Contact: Harry Diavatis
Men's Non-aid: basketball, crew, sailing, soccer, volleyball, water polo

CALIFORNIA POLYTECHNIC STATE UNIVERSITY
1 Grand Avenue
San Luis Obispo, CA 93407
(805) 756-2144
www.calpoly.edu
Contact: Mike La Plante
Unspecified athletic aid available
M: baseball, basketball, cross country, football, soccer, swimming, tennis, track&field, wrestling
W: basketball, cross country, soccer, softball, swimming, tennis, track&field, volleyball

CALIFORNIA STATE POLYTECHNIC UNIVERSITY
3801 West Temple Avenue
Pomona, CA 91768
(909) 869-2812
www.csupomona.edu/front
Contact: Steve Quintero
Men's Aid (#/$): 63/$101,569
Women's Aid (#/$): 61/$125,548
M: baseball, basketball, cross country, soccer, tennis, track&field
W: basketball, cross country, soccer, softball, tennis, track&field, volleyball

CALIFORNIA STATE UNIVERSITY (CHICO)
400 West First Street
Chico, CA 95929-0705
(916) 898-6451
www.csuchico.edu
Contact: Terrell Murphy
Men's Aid (#/$): 50/unspecified $
Women's Aid (#/$): 50/unspecified $
M: baseball, basketball, cross country, golf, soccer, track&field
W: basketball, cross country, soccer, softball, swimming-diving, tennis, track&field, volleyball

CALIFORNIA STATE UNIVERSITY (DOMINGUEZ HILLS)
1000 East Victoria Street
Carson, CA 90747-0005
(310) 243-3532
www.csudh.edu
Contact: Kevin Gilmore
Unspecified athletic aid available
M: baseball, basketball, golf, soccer
W: basketball, soccer, softball, volleyball

CALIFORNIA STATE UNIVERSITY (FRESNO)
5241 North Maple Avenue
Fresno, CA 93740-0064
(559) 278-6847
www.csufresno.edu
Contact: Dr. Al Bohl
Unspecified athletic aid available
M: baseball, basketball, cross country, football, golf, soccer, tennis, track&field, wrestling
W: basketball, cross country, equestrian, soccer, softball, swimming, tennis, track&field, volleyball

CALIFORNIA STATE UNIVERSITY (FULLERTON)
800 North State College Boulevard
Fullerton, CA 92634-9480
(714) 278-2011
www.fullerton.edu
Contact: John Easterbrook
Unspecified athletic aid available
M: baseball, basketball, cross country, fencing, soccer, track&field, wrestling
W: basketball, cross country, fencing, gymnastics, softball, tennis, track&field, volleyball

CALIFORNIA STATE UNIVERSITY (HAYWARD)
Athletic Department
Hayward, CA 94542-3062
(510) 885-3528
www.csuhayward.edu
Contact: Marty Valdez
Men's Non-aid: baseball, basketball, cross country, diving, football, soccer,

swimming, swimming-diving, tennis, track&field
Women's Non-aid: basketball, cross country, diving, soccer, softball, swimming, swimming-diving, tennis, track&field, volleyball

CALIFORNIA STATE UNIVERSITY (LONG BEACH)
1250 Bellflower Boulevard
Long Beach, CA 90840
(562) 985-7797
www.csulb.edu
Contact: Steve Janisch
Unspecified athletic aid available
M: baseball, basketball, golf, track&field, volleyball, water polo
W: basketball, cross country, golf, soccer, softball, tennis, track&field, volleyball, water polo

CALIFORNIA STATE UNIVERSITY (LOS ANGELES)
5151 State University Drive
Los Angeles, CA 90032-8240
(323) 343-3198
www.calstatela.edu
Contact: Lee DeLeon
Unspecified athletic aid available
M: baseball, basketball, cross country, soccer, tennis, track&field
W: basketball, cross country, soccer, tennis, track&field, volleyball

CALIFORNIA STATE UNIVERSITY (NORTHRIDGE)
18111 Nordhoff Street
Northridge, CA 91330
(818) 677-3208
www.csun.edu
Contact: Ryan Finney
Men's Aid (#/$): 68/$600,000
Women's Aid (#/$): 63/$500,000
M: baseball, basketball, football, golf, soccer, swimming-diving, track&field, volleyball
W: basketball, golf, softball, swimming-diving, tennis, track&field, volleyball

CALIFORNIA STATE UNIVERSITY (SACRAMENTO)
600 J Street
Sacramento, CA 95819-6073
(916) 278-6896
www.hornetsports.com
Contact: Ryan Bjork
Unspecified athletic aid available
M: baseball, basketball, cross country, football, golf, soccer, tennis, track&field
W: basketball, cross country, golf, gymnastics, rowing, soccer, softball, tennis, track&field, volleyball

CALIFORNIA STATE UNIVERSITY (SAN BERNARDINO)
5500 University Parkway
San Bernardino, CA 92407
(909) 880-5000
www.csush.edu
Contact: Nancy Simpson
Men's Aid (#/$): 39/unspecified $
Women's Aid (#/$): 66/unspecified $
M: baseball, basketball, golf, soccer
W: basketball, cross country, soccer, softball, tennis, volleyball, water polo

CALIFORNIA STATE UNIVERSITY (STANISLAUS)
801 West Monte Vista Avenue
Turlock, CA 95382
(209) 667-3566
www.csustan.edu
Contact: Kim Duyst
Men's Non-aid: baseball, basketball, cross country, golf, soccer, track&field
Women's Non-aid: basketball, cross country, indoor track, soccer, softball, track&field, volleyball

CALIFORNIA STATE UNIVERSITY AT BAKERSFIELD
9001 Stockdale Highway
Bakersfield, CA 93311-1099
(661) 664-3071
www.csubak.edu
Contact: Kevin Gilmore
Unspecified athletic aid available
M: basketball, golf, soccer, swimming-

diving, track&field, water polo, wrestling
W: cross country, soccer, softball,
swimming-diving, tennis, track&field,
volleyball

CERRITOS COLLEGE
11110 East Alondra Boulevard
Norwalk, CA 90650
Two-year college
(562) 860-2451
www.cerritos.edu
Contact: Patty Tugade
Men's Non-aid: baseball, basketball,
cross country, football, golf, soccer,
swimming-diving, tennis, track&field,
water polo, wrestling
Women's Non-aid: basketball, cross country, soccer, softball, swimming- diving,
tennis, track&field, volleyball, water polo

CHAFFEY COLLEGE
5885 Haven Avenue
Rancho Cucamonga, CA 91737
Two-year college
(909) 987-1737
www.chaffey.cc.ca.us
Contact: Robert Olivera
Men's Non-aid: baseball, basketball,
football, swimming-diving, water polo
Women's Non-aid: softball, swimming-
diving, volleyball

CHAPMAN UNIVERSITY
333 North Glassell
Orange, CA 92666
(714) 997-6900
www.chapman.edu
Contact: Doug Aiken
Men's Non-aid: baseball, basketball,
cross country, football, golf, soccer,
swimming, tennis, water polo
Women's Non-aid: basketball, cross
country, soccer, softball, swimming,
tennis, track&field, volleyball, water polo

CITY COLLEGE OF SAN FRANCISCO
50 Phelan Avenue
San Francisco, CA 94112

Two-year college
(415) 239-3412
www.ccsf.cc.ca.us
Contact: George Rush
Men's Non-aid: baseball, basketball,
cross country, football, soccer, tennis,
track&field
Women's Non-aid: badminton, basketball, cross country, tennis, track&field,
volleyball

COLLEGE OF NOTRE DAME
1500 Ralston Avenue
Belmont, CA 94002-1997
(650) 593-1001
www.cnd.edu
Contact: Virginia Babel
Men's Non-aid: basketball, cross country,
soccer, track&field
Women's Non-aid: basketball, cross
country, softball, track&field, volleyball

COLLEGE OF THE DESERT
43-500 Monterey Avenue
Palm Desert, CA 92260
Two-year college
(760) 773-2591
www.desert.cc.ca.us
Contact: John Marman
Men's Non-aid: baseball, basketball, cross
country, football, golf, soccer, tennis
Women's Non-aid: basketball, cross
country, soccer, softball, tennis, volleyball

COLLEGE OF THE REDWOODS
7351 Tompkins Hill Road
Eureka, CA 95501-9302
Two-year college
(707) 476-4212
www.redwood.cc.ca.us
Contact: Tom Giacomini
Men's Non-aid: baseball, basketball,
cross country, football, golf, track&field
Women's Non-aid: basketball, cross
country, softball, track&field, volleyball

COLLEGE OF THE SEQUOIAS
915 South Mooney Boulevard
Visalia, CA 93277

Two-year college
(559) 730-3911
www.sequoias.cc.ca.us
Contact: Al Branco
Men's Non-aid: baseball, basketball,
cross country, football, golf, swimming-
diving, tennis, track&field, water polo
Women's Non-aid: basketball, cross
country, softball, swimming-diving,
tennis, track&field, volleyball

COMPTON COMMUNITY COLLEGE
1111 East Artesia Boulevard
Compton, CA 90221
Two-year college
(310) 900-2942
www.compton.cc.ca.us
Contact: William Thomas
Men's Non-aid: baseball, basketball,
cross country, football, track&field
Women's Non-aid: basketball, cross
country, track&field

CONTRA COSTA COLLEGE
2600 Mission Bell Drive
San Pablo, CA 94806
Two-year college
(510) 235-7800
www.contracosta.cc.ca.us
Contact: Phil Clifton
Men's Non-aid: baseball, basketball,
cross country, football, tennis,
track&field
Women's Non-aid: basketball, tennis,
track&field

COSUMNES RIVER COLLEGE
8401 Center Parkway
Sacramento, CA 95823-5799
Two-year college
(916) 688-7261
wserver.crc.losrios.cc.ca.us
Contact: Travis Parker
Men's Non-aid: baseball, basketball,
soccer, tennis, track&field
Women's Non-aid: soccer, softball,
tennis, track&field, volleyball, water
polo

CUESTA COLLEGE
P.O. Box 8106
San Luis Obispo, CA 93403-8106
Two-year college
(805) 546-3211
www.cuesta.edu
Contact: Peter Schuler
Men's Non-aid: baseball, basketball,
cross country, swimming-diving,
track&field, water polo, wrestling
Women's Non-aid: basketball, cross
country, soccer, softball, swimming-
diving, tennis, track&field, volleyball,
water polo

DE ANZA COLLEGE
21250 Stevens Creek Boulevard
Cupertino, CA 95014
Two-year college
(408) 864-5678
www.deanza.fhda.edu
Contact: William Clinton
Men's Non-aid: football, soccer
Women's Non-aid: soccer

DIABLO VALLEY COMMUNITY COLLEGE
321 Golf Club Road
Pleasant Hill, CA 94523
Two-year college
(925) 685-1230
www.dvc.edu
Contact: Kenny Williams
Men's Non-aid: baseball, basketball,
cross country, diving, football, swimming, tennis, track&field, water polo,
wrestling
Women's Non-aid: basketball, cross
country, diving, soccer, softball, swimming, track&field, volleyball, water polo

DOMINICAN COLLEGE
50 Acacia Avenue
San Rafael, CA 94901-8008
(415) 485-3230
www.dominican.edu
Contact: Fred Lengyel
Men's Aid (#/$): 15/$50,825
Women's Aid (#/$): 20/$52,535

Restrictions and notes: Partial athletic scholarships available.
M: basketball, soccer, tennis
W: soccer, tennis, volleyball

EAST LOS ANGELES COLLEGE
1301 Avenida Cesar Chavez
Monterey Park, CA 91754
Two-year college
(323) 265-8950
www.elac.cc.ca.us
Contact: Jerry Heaps
Men's Non-aid: soccer
Women's Non-aid: soccer

EL CAMINO COLLEGE
16007 Crenshaw Boulevard
Torrance, CA 90506
Two-year college
(310) 532-3670
www.elcamino.cc.ca.us
Contact: Mary Ann Montomery
Men's Non-aid: baseball, basketball, cross country, football, golf, soccer, swimming-diving, tennis, track&field, volleyball, water polo
Women's Non-aid: basketball, cross country, soccer, softball, swimming-diving, tennis, track&field, volleyball

FOOTHILL COLLEGE
12345 El Monte Road
Los Altos Hills, CA 94022
Two-year college
(650) 949-7222
www.foothill.fhda.edu
Contact: Sue Gatlin
Men's Non-aid: basketball, football, golf, soccer, swimming-diving, tennis, track&field, water polo
Women's Non-aid: basketball, golf, soccer, softball, swimming-diving, track&field, volleyball, water polo

FRESNO CITY COLLEGE
1101 East University Avenue
Fresno, CA 93741
Two-year college
(559) 442-4600

www.fcc.cc.ca.us
Contact: M – Ron Scott, W – Susan Yates
Men's Non-aid: baseball, basketball, cross country, football, golf, soccer, tennis, track&field, wrestling
Women's Non-aid: badminton, basketball, cross country, golf, soccer, softball, tennis, track&field, volleyball

FRESNO PACIFIC UNIVERSITY
1717 South Chestnut Avenue
Fresno, CA 93702
(559) 453-2000
www.frescno.edu
Contact: Bruce Watts
Unspecified athletic aid available
M: basketball, cross country, indoor track, soccer, track&field
W: basketball, cross country, indoor track, track&field, volleyball

FULLERTON COLLEGE
321 East Chapman Avenue
Fullerton, CA 92634
Two-year college
(714) 992-7391
www.fullcoll.edu
Contact: Ken Hill
Men's Non-aid: baseball, basketball, cross country, football, golf, soccer, swimming-diving, tennis, track&field, water polo
Women's Non-aid: basketball, cross country, softball, swimming-diving, tennis, track&field, volleyball

GLENDALE COMMUNITY COLLEGE
1500 North Verdugo Road
Glendale, CA 91208
Two-year college
(818) 240-5163
www.glendale.cc.ca.us
Contact: Alex Leon
Men's Non-aid: baseball, basketball, cross country, football, soccer, tennis, track&field
Women's Non-aid: basketball, cross country, soccer, softball, tennis, track&field, volleyball

GOLDEN WEST COLLEGE
15744 Golden West Street
P.O. Box 2718
Huntington Beach, CA 92647-2748
Two-year college
(714) 892-7711
www.gwc.cccd.edu
Contact: Eric Maddy
Unspecified athletic aid available
M: baseball, basketball, cross country,
football, golf, soccer, swimming-diving,
tennis, track&field, water polo, wrestling
W: basketball, cross country, golf, soccer,
softball, swimming-diving, tennis,
track&field, volleyball, water polo

HUMBOLDT STATE UNIVERSITY
1 Harp Street
Arcata, CA 95521
(707) 826-3631
www.humbolt.edu
Contact: Dan Pambianco
Unspecified athletic aid available
M: basketball, cross country, football,
soccer, track&field
W: basketball, cross country, rowing,
soccer, softball, track&field, volleyball

LONG BEACH CITY COLLEGE
4901 East Carson Street
Long Beach, CA 90808
Two-year college
(562) 938-4237
www.lbcc.cc.ca.us
Contact: M – Chuck McFerrin, W –
Mickey Davis
Men's Non-aid: baseball, basketball,
cross country, football, golf, soccer,
swimming, tennis, track&field, volleyball,
water polo
Women's Non-aid: basketball, cross
country, golf, soccer, softball, swimming-
diving, tennis, track&field, volleyball,
water polo

LOS ANGELES PIERCE JUNIOR COLLEGE
6201 Winnetka Avenue
Woodland Hills, CA 91371
Two-year college
(818) 719-6421
www.lapc.cc.ca.us
Contact: Bob Lyons
Men's Non-aid: baseball, football, swimming-diving, tennis, volleyball, water polo
Women's Non-aid: basketball, softball,
swimming-diving, tennis

LOS ANGELES VALLEY COLLEGE
5800 Fulton Avenue
Van Nuys, CA 91401
Two-year college
(818) 781-1200 ext. 2508
www.lavc.cc.ca.us
Contact: Chuck Ferarro
Men's Non-aid: baseball, basketball,
cross country, football, swimming,
track&field, water polo
Women's Non-aid: basketball, cross
country, diving, softball, swimming,
track&field, water polo

LOS MEDANOS COLLEGE
2700 East Leland Road
Pittsburg, CA 94565
Two-year college
(510) 439-2181
www.losmedanos.net
Contact: Shirley Baskin
Men's Non-aid: baseball, basketball,
football, soccer
Women's Non-aid: basketball, softball

LOYOLA MARYMOUNT UNIVERSITY
7900 Loyola Boulevard
Los Angeles, CA 90045
(310) 338-2700
www.lmu.edu
Contact: Dan Smith
Unspecified athletic aid available
M: baseball, basketball, volleyball. Men's
Non-aid: crew, cross country, golf,
soccer, tennis, water polo
W: basketball, tennis, volleyball. Women's
Non-aid: crew, cross country, soccer,
softball, swimming, water polo

MARYMOUNT COLLEGE
30800 Palos Verdes Drive East
Rancho Palos Verdes, CA 90275-6299
Two-year college
(310) 377-5501
www.marymountpv.edu
Contact: Jim Masterson
Men's Non-aid: tennis
Women's Non-aid: tennis

MASTER'S COLLEGE
21726 West Placerita Canyon
Santa Clarita, CA 91321
(661) 259-3540
www.masters.edu
Contact: Jack Mutz
Unspecified athletic aid available
M: baseball, basketball, cross country,
golf, soccer
W: basketball, cross country, soccer,
softball, volleyball

MIRACOSTA COLLEGE
One Barnard Drive
Oceanside, CA 92056
Two-year college
(760) 795-6840
www.miracosta.cc.ca.us
Contact: Clete Adelman
Men's Non-aid: basketball, tennis
Women's Non-aid: cross country,
track&field

MODESTO JUNIOR COLLEGE
435 College Avenue
Modesto, CA 95350
Two-year college
(209) 575-6498
mjc.yosemite.cc.ca.us
Contact: Stan Hodges
Men's Non-aid: baseball, basketball,
cross country, football, golf, soccer,
swimming-diving, tennis, track&field,
water polo, wrestling
Women's Non-aid: basketball, cross
country, golf, soccer, softball, swimming-
diving, tennis, track&field, volleyball,
water polo

MOORPARK COLLEGE
7075 Campus Road
Moorpark, CA 93021
Two-year college
(805) 378-1457
www.moorpark.cc.ca.us
Contact: John Keever
Men's Non-aid: baseball, basketball,
cross country, football, soccer,
track&field, volleyball, wrestling
Women's Non-aid: basketball, cross
country, soccer, softball, tennis,
track&field, volleyball

MT. SAN ANTONIO COLLEGE
1100 North Grand Avenue
Walnut, CA 91789
Two-year college
(909) 594-5611
www.mtsac.edu
Contact: Brian Yokoyama
Men's Non-aid: baseball, basketball,
cross country, football, golf, soccer,
swimming-diving, tennis, track&field,
volleyball, water polo, wrestling
Women's Non-aid: basketball, cross
country, golf, soccer, softball, swimming-
diving, track&field, volleyball, water polo

OCCIDENTAL COLLEGE
1600 Campus Road
Los Angeles, CA 90041
(323) 259-2703
www.oxy.edu
Contact: Jim Kerman
Men's Non-aid: baseball, basketball,
cross country, football, golf, soccer,
swimming-diving, tennis, track&field,
water polo
Women's Non-aid: basketball, cross
country, soccer, swimming-diving, tennis,
track&field, volleyball

ORANGE COAST COLLEGE
2701 Fairview Road
Costa Mesa, CA 92628-0120
Two-year college
(714) 432-5175
www.occ.cccd.edu

Contact: Tyson Chaney
Men's Non-aid: baseball, basketball,
crew, cross country, football, golf, sailing,
soccer, swimming-diving, tennis,
track&field, volleyball, water polo
Women's Non-aid: basketball, crew, cross
country, golf, sailing, soccer, softball,
swimming-diving, tennis, track&field,
volleyball, water polo

OXNARD COLLEGE
4000 South Rose Avenue
Oxnard, CA 93033
Two-year college
(805) 986-5825
Contact: Jerry White
Men's Non-aid: baseball, basketball,
cross country, soccer
Women's Non-aid: basketball, cross
country, soccer

PALOMAR COLLEGE
1140 West Mission Road
San Marcos, CA 92069-1487
Two-year college
(760) 744-1150
www.palomar.edu
Contact: John Strey
Men's Non-aid: baseball, basketball,
football, golf, soccer, swimming-diving,
tennis, water polo, wrestling
Women's Non-aid: basketball, soccer,
softball, swimming-diving, tennis,
volleyball

PEPPERDINE UNIVERSITY
24255 Pacific Coast Highway
Malibu, CA 90263
(310) 456-4333
www.pepperdine.edu
Contact: Michael Zapolski
Men's Aid (#/$): 43/$1,366,000
Women's Aid (#/$): 51/$1,632,000
M: baseball, basketball, golf, tennis,
volleyball, water polo. Men's Non-aid:
cross country
W: basketball, golf, soccer, swimming,
tennis, volleyball. Women's Non-aid:
cross country

**POINT LOMA NAZARENE
COLLEGE**
3900 Lomaland Drive
San Diego, CA 92106
(619) 849-2200
www.ptloma.edu
Contact: Dan Van Ommen
Unspecified athletic aid available
M: baseball, basketball, cross country,
golf, soccer, tennis, track&field
W: basketball, cross country, tennis,
track&field

POMONA-PITZER COLLEGES
220 East 6th Street
Claremont, CA 91711
(714) 621-8119
www.physical-education.pomona.edu
Contact: Kirk Reynolds
Men's Non-aid: baseball, basketball,
cross country, football, golf, soccer,
swimming-diving, tennis, track&field,
water polo
Women's Non-aid: basketball, cross
country, soccer, softball, swimming-
diving, tennis, track&field, volleyball,
water polo

RANETTO SANTIAGO COLLEGE
17th&Bristol Street
Santa Ana, CA 92706
Two-year college
(714) 564-6475
Contact: Dave Ruite
Men's Non-aid: baseball, basketball,
cross country, football, golf, soccer,
swimming-diving, tennis, track&field,
water polo, wrestling
Women's Non-aid: basketball, cross
country, softball, swimming-diving,
tennis, track&field, volleyball

RIVERSIDE COMMUNITY COLLEGE
4800 Magnolia Avenue
Riverside, CA 92506-1299
Two-year college
(909) 222-8032
www.rccd.cc.ca.us
Contact: Robert Schmidt

Men's Non-aid: baseball, basketball, cross country, football, golf, swimming-diving, tennis, track&field, water polo
Women's Non-aid: basketball, cross country, softball, swimming-diving, tennis, track&field, water polo

SADDLEBACK COLLEGE
28000 Marguerite Parkway
Mission Viejo, CA 92692
Two-year college
(949) 582-4490
www.saddleback.cc.ca.us
Contact: Jerry Hannula
Men's Non-aid: baseball, basketball, cross country, football, golf, swimming-diving, tennis, track&field, water polo
Women's Non-aid: basketball, cross country, golf, softball, swimming-diving, tennis, track&field, volleyball, water polo

SAINT MARY'S COLLEGE OF CALIFORNIA
P.O. Box 5100
Moraga, CA 94575
(925) 631-4000
www.stmarys-ca.edu
Contact: Andy McDowell
Men's Aid ($): $800,000
Women's Aid ($): $700,000
M: baseball, basketball, cross country, football, golf, soccer, tennis. Men's Non-aid: crew, lacrosse, rugby
W: basketball, cross country, soccer, softball, tennis, volleyball. Women's Non-aid: crew, lacrosse

SAN BERNARDINO COMMUNITY COLLEGE
701 South Mt. Vernon Avenue
San Bernardino, CA 92410
Two-year college
(909) 888-6511 ext. 1470
www.sbccd.cc.ca.us
Contact: Atrina Sloan
Men's Non-aid: baseball, basketball, cross country, football, tennis, track&field, wrestling
Women's Non-aid: basketball, cross country, softball, tennis, track&field, volleyball

SAN DIEGO CITY COLLEGE
1313 12th Avenue
San Diego, CA 92101
Two-year college
(619) 230-2486
www.sdccd.cc.ca.us
Contact: Cassie Macias
Men's Non-aid: baseball, basketball, cross country, soccer, tennis
Women's Non-aid: badminton, cross country, soccer, softball, tennis, volleyball

SAN DIEGO MESA COLLEGE
7250 Mesa College Drive
San Diego, CA 92111
Two-year college
(858) 627-2767 ext. 4360
www.sdmesa.sdccd.cc.ca.us
Contact: Randy Behr
Men's Non-aid: badminton, baseball, basketball, cross country, football, soccer, swimming-diving, tennis, track&field, volleyball, water polo
Women's Non-aid: baseball, basketball, cross country, soccer, softball, swimming-diving, tennis, track&field, volleyball, water polo

SAN DIEGO STATE UNIVERSITY
San Diego, CA 92182
(619) 594-5547
www.sdsu.edu
Contact: John Rosenthal
Unspecified athletic aid available
M: baseball, basketball, football, golf, soccer, tennis, volleyball
W: basketball, crew, cross country, golf, soccer, softball, swimming, tennis, track&field, volleyball, water polo

SAN FRANCISCO STATE UNIVERSITY
1600 Holloway Avenue
San Francisco, CA 94132
(415) 338-2485
www.sfsu.edu

Contact: Kathleen Heitcman
Unspecified athletic aid available
M: baseball, basketball, cross country,
soccer, swimming, track&field, wrestling
W: basketball, cross country, soccer,
softball, swimming, tennis, track&field,
volleyball

SAN JOAQUIN DELTA COLLEGE
5151 Pacific Avenue
Stockton, CA 95207-6370
Two-year college
(209) 954-5151
www.sjdccd.cc.ca.us
Contact: Ernie Marcopulos
Men's Non-aid: baseball, basketball,
cross country, football, golf, soccer,
swimming, tennis, track&field, water
polo, wrestling
Women's Non-aid: basketball, cross
country, softball, swimming, tennis,
track&field, volleyball

SAN JOSE STATE UNIVERSITY
1 Washington Square
San Jose, CA 95192
(408) 924-1217
www.sjsu.edu
Contact: Lawrence Fan
Unspecified athletic aid available
Restrictions and notes: Meets NCAA
Division I Qualifications
M: baseball, basketball, cross country,
football, golf, soccer, tennis, track&field,
wrestling
W: basketball, golf, gymnastics, softball,
swimming, tennis, volleyball

**SANTA BARBARA CITY
COLLEGE**
721 Cliff Drive
Santa Barbara, CA 93109-2394
Two-year college
(805) 965-0581
www.sbcc.cc.ca.us
Contact: Jim Williams
Men's Non-aid: baseball, basketball,
cross country, football, golf, soccer,
tennis, track&field, volleyball

Women's Non-aid: basketball, cross
country, golf, soccer, tennis, track&field,
volleyball

SANTA CLARA UNIVERSITY
500 El Camino Real
Santa Clara, CA 95053
(408) 554-4661
www.santaclarabroncos.com
Contact: Jim Young
Men's Aid (#/$): 59.66/$907,884
Women's Aid (#/$): 37.50/$502,755
M: baseball, basketball, football, soccer.
Men's Non-aid: crew, cross country, golf,
tennis, water polo
W: basketball, soccer, volleyball. Women's
Non-aid: crew, cross country, golf, soft-
ball, tennis

SANTA MONICA COLLEGE
1900 Pico Boulevard
Santa Monica, CA 90405
Two-year college
(310) 434-4310
www.smc.edu
Contact: John Secia
Men's Non-aid: baseball, basketball,
cross country, football, soccer, swimming, tennis, track&field, volleyball,
water polo
Women's Non-aid: baseball, basketball,
cross country, softball, swimming, tennis,
track&field, volleyball

SANTA ROSA JUNIOR COLLEGE
1501 Mendocino Avenue
Santa Rosa, CA 95401
Two-year college
(707) 527-4237
www.santarosa.edu
Contact: Therese Jennings
Men's Non-aid: baseball, basketball,
cross country, football, golf, soccer,
swimming, tennis, track&field, water
polo, wrestling
Women's Non-aid: basketball, cross
country, soccer, softball, swimming,
tennis, track&field, volleyball, water
polo

SIERRA COLLEGE
5000 Rocklin Road
Rocklin, CA 95677
Two-year college
(916) 781-0583
www.sierra.cc.ca.us
Contact: Nancy Ackley
Men's Non-aid: alpine skiing, baseball, basketball, cross country, cross country skiing, football, golf, swimming-diving, tennis, water polo, wrestling
Women's Non-aid: alpine skiing, basketball, cross country, cross country skiing, golf, softball, swimming-diving, tennis, volleyball

SIMPSON COLLEGE
2211 Collegeview Drive
Redding, CA 96003
(530) 224-5606
www.simpsonca.edu
Contact: Chris Kinnier
Men's Non-aid: baseball, basketball, cross country, football, golf, indoor track, tennis, track&field, wrestling
Women's Non-aid: basketball, cross country, golf, indoor track, softball, tennis, track&field, volleyball

SKYLINE COLLEGE
3300 College Drive
San Bruno, CA 94066
Two-year college
(650) 738-4100
www.smcccd.cc.ca.us
Contact: Samuel Goldman
Men's Non-aid: baseball, basketball, cross country, soccer, track&field, wrestling
Women's Non-aid: cross country, softball, track&field, volleyball

SOLANO COMMUNITY COLLEGE
4000 Suisun Valley Road
Suisun City, CA 94585
Two-year college
(707) 864-7126
www.solano.cc.ca.us

Contact: Bob Myers
Men's Non-aid: baseball, basketball, football, swimming-diving, water polo
Women's Non-aid: basketball, softball, swimming-diving, volleyball

SOUTHERN CALIFORNIA COLLEGE
55 Fair Drive
Costa Mesa, CA 92626
(714) 556-3610
www.vanguard.edu
Contact: Bob Wilson
Unspecified athletic aid available
M: baseball, basketball, cross country, soccer, tennis
W: basketball, cross country, softball, tennis, volleyball

SOUTHWESTERN COLLEGE
900 Otay Lakes Road
Chula Vista, CA 91910
Two-year college
(619) 421-6700 ext. 6370
www.swc.cc.ca.us
Contact: Bob Mears
Men's Non-aid: baseball, basketball, football, soccer, track&field
Women's Non-aid: basketball, softball, tennis, track&field, volleyball

STANFORD UNIVERSITY
Sports Information Office
Stanford, CA 94305
(650) 723-4596
www.gostanford.com
Contact: Edward Leland
Men's Aid (#/$): 192/unspecified $
Women's Aid (#/$): 74/unspecified $
M: baseball, basketball, football, golf, gymnastics, soccer, swimming-diving, tennis, track&field, volleyball, water polo.
Men's Non-aid: crew, fencing, sailing, wrestling
W: basketball, golf, gymnastics, soccer, swimming-diving, tennis, track&field, volleyball. Women's Non-aid: crew, fencing, field hockey, sailing, softball

TAFT COLLEGE
29 Emmons Park Drive
Taft, CA 93268
Two-year college
(661) 763-4282
www.taft.cc.ca.us
Contact: Kanoe Bandy
Unspecified athletic aid available
Restrictions and notes: "Our financial aid package is considered one of the best in the state among community colleges and overall fees are among the lowest."
M: baseball, cross country, football, golf, track&field
W: cross country, softball, track&field, volleyball

UNIVERSI TY OF CALIFORNIA (BERKELEY)
210 Memorial Stadium
Berkeley, CA 94720
(510) 642-5363
www.calbears.com
Contact: Kevin Reneau
Unspecified athletic aid available
M: baseball, basketball, cross country, football, gymnastics, soccer, swimming-diving, tennis, track&field, water polo. Men's Non-aid: crew, golf, rugby
W: basketball, crew, cross country, diving, field hockey, golf, gymnastics, lacrosse, soccer, softball, swimming, tennis, track&field, volleyball. Women's Non-aid: water polo

UNIVERSITY OF CALIFORNIA (DAVIS)
116 A Street
Davis, CA 95616
(530) 752-3505
www.athletics.ucdavis.edu
Contact: Doug Dull
Unspecified athletic aid available
M: baseball, basketball, cross country, football, golf, soccer, swimming-diving, tennis, track&field, water polo, wrestling
W: basketball, cross country, gymnastics, lacrosse, rowing, soccer, softball, swimming-diving, tennis, track&field, volleyball, water polo

UNIVERSITY OF CALIFORNIA (IRVINE)
Crawford Hall
Irvine, CA 92717
(949) 824-5814
www.athletics.uci.edu
Contact: Bob Olson
Men's Aid (#/$): 107/$359,256
Women's Aid (#/$): 50/$169,252
M: basketball, soccer, swimming-diving, tennis, water polo. Men's Non-aid: crew, cross country, golf, sailing, track&field, volleyball
W: basketball, cross country, soccer, swimming-diving, tennis, track&field, volleyball. Women's Non-aid: crew, sailing

UNIVERSITY OF CALIFORNIA (RIVERSIDE)
900 University Avenue
Riverside, CA 92521
(909) 787-5438
www.ucr.edu
Contact: Tom Phillips
Unspecified athletic aid available
M: baseball, basketball, tennis, track&field. Men's Non-aid: cross country, swimming-diving, volleyball, water polo
W: basketball, softball, volleyball. Women's Non-aid: cross country, swimming-diving, tennis, track&field, water polo

UNIVERSITY OF CALIFORNIA (SAN DIEGO)
Intercollegiate Athletics ICA 0531
9500 Gilman Drive
La Jolla, CA 92093-0905
(619) 534-4211
www.athletics.ucsd.edu
Contact: Regena Sullivan
Men's Non-aid: baseball, basketball, crew, cross country, fencing, golf, soccer, swimming-diving, tennis, track&field, volleyball, water polo
Women's Non-aid: basketball, crew, cross country, fencing, soccer, softball,

swimming-diving, tennis, track&field, volleyball, water polo

UNIVERSITY OF CALIFORNIA (SANTA BARBARA)
Robertson Gym, 302 B
Santa Barbara, CA 93106
(805) 893-3428
www.ucsb.edu
Contact: Bill Mahoney
Men's Aid (#/$): 46/$408,782
Women's Aid (#/$): 43/$370,282
M: baseball, basketball, cross country, golf, gymnastics, soccer, swimming-diving, tennis, track&field, volleyball, water polo
W: basketball, cross country, gymnastics, soccer, softball, swimming-diving, tennis, track&field

UNIVERSITY OF CALIFORNIA (SANTA CRUZ)
1156 High Street
Santa Cruz, CA 95064
(831) 459-3362
www.ucsc.edu
Contact: Mark McJeski
Men's Non-aid: basketball, soccer, swimming-diving, tennis, volleyball, water polo
Women's Non-aid: basketball, soccer, swimming and diving, tennis, volleyball, water polo

UNIVERSITY OF CALIFORNIA (UCLA)
405 Hilgard Avenue
Morgan Center
Los Angeles, CA 90024
(310) 206-6831
www.ucla.edu
Contact: Marc Dellins
Men's Aid (#/$): 150/unspecified $
Women's Aid (#/$): 115/unspecified $
M: baseball, basketball, cross country, football, golf, soccer, tennis, track&field, volleyball, water polo
W: basketball, cross country, golf, gymnastics, soccer, softball, swimming-diving, tennis, track&field, volleyball, water polo

UNIVERSITY OF LA VERNE
1950 Third Street
La Verne, CA 91750
(909) 593-3511 ext. 4261
www.ulv.edu
Contact: Pam Maunakea
Men's Non-aid: baseball, basketball, cross country, football, golf, soccer, tennis, track&field, volleyball, wrestling
Women's Non-aid: basketball, cross country, softball, tennis, track&field, volleyball

UNIVERSITY OF REDLANDS
1200 East Colton Avenue
Redlands, CA 92373-0999
(909) 793-2121
www.newton.uor.edu
Contact: Ross French
Men's Non-aid: baseball, basketball, crew, cross country, football, golf, soccer, swimming, tennis, track&field, water polo
Women's Non-aid: baseball, basketball, crew, cross country, lacrosse, soccer, softball, swimming, tennis, track&field, volleyball

UNIVERSITY OF SAN DIEGO
Alcala Park
San Diego, CA 92110
(619) 260-4803
www.acusd.edu
Contact: Ted Gosen
Unspecified athletic aid available
M: baseball, basketball, cross country, golf, soccer, tennis. Men's Non-aid: crew, football
W: basketball, cross country, soccer, softball, swimming, tennis, volleyball. Women's Non-aid: crew

UNIVERSITY OF SAN FRANCISCO
2130 Fulton Street
San Francisco, CA 94117-1080
(415) 422-6161
www.usfca.edu
Contact: Peter H. Simon
Unspecified athletic aid available
M: baseball, basketball, golf, soccer,

tennis. Men's Non-aid: cross country, riflery
W: basketball, golf, soccer, tennis, volleyball. Women's Non-aid: cross country, riflery

UNIVERSITY OF SOUTHERN CALIFORNIA
University Park
Los Angeles, CA 90089-0601
(213) 740-8480
www.usc.edu
Contact: Tim Tessalone
Men's Aid (#/$): 150/$3,000,000
Women's Aid (#/$): 50/$1,000,000
M: baseball, basketball, diving, football, golf, swimming, tennis, track&field, volleyball, water polo
W: basketball, crew, cross country, golf, soccer, swimming-diving, tennis, track&field, volleyball, water polo

UNIVERSITY OF THE PACIFIC
3601 Pacific Avenue
Stockton, CA 95211
(209) 946-2479
www.uop.edu
Contact: Mike Millerick
Unspecified athletic aid available
M: baseball, basketball, golf, swimming, tennis, volleyball, water polo
W: basketball, cross country, field hockey, soccer, softball, swimming, tennis, volleyball, water polo

VENTURA COLLEGE
4667 Telegraph Road
Ventura, CA 93003
Two-year college
(805) 654-6348 ext. 1315
www.ventura.cc.ca.us
Contact: Don Adams
Men's Non-aid: baseball, basketball, cross country, football, golf, swimming, tennis, track&field, water polo
Women's Non-aid: basketball, cross country, gymnastics, softball, swimming, tennis, track&field, volleyball

WESTMONT COLLEGE
955 La Paz Road
Santa Barbara, CA 93108-1099
(805) 565-6000
www.westmont.edu
Contact: Jeff Raymond
Unspecified athletic aid available
M: baseball, basketball, cross country, soccer, tennis, track&field
W: basketball, cross country, soccer, tennis, track&field, volleyball

WHITTIER COLLEGE
13406 Philadelphia Street
P.O. Box 604
Whittier, CA 90608
(562) 907-4200
www.whittier.edu
Contact: Rock Carter
Men's Non-aid: baseball, basketball, cross country, diving, football, golf, lacrosse, soccer, swimming, swimming-diving, tennis, track&field, water polo
Women's Non-aid: basketball, cross country, diving, soccer, softball, swimming, swimming-diving, tennis, track&field, volleyball, water polo

YUBA COMMUNITY COLLEGE
2088 North Beale Road
Marysville, CA 95901
Two-year college
(530) 741-6779
www.yuba.cc.ca.us
Contact: Joe McCarron
Men's Non-aid: baseball, basketball, football, tennis, track&field
Women's Non-aid: softball, tennis, track&field, volleyball

Colorado

ADAMS STATE COLLEGE
Box B
Richardson Hall
Alamosa, CO 81102

(719) 587-7011
www.adams.edu
Contact: Larry Mortensen
Men's Aid (#/$): 50/unspecified $
Women's Aid (#/$): 50/unspecified $
M: basketball, cross country, football,
indoor track, track&field, wrestling.
Men's Non-aid: golf
W: basketball, cross country, indoor
track, softball, track&field, volleyball

COLORADO CHRISTIAN UNIVERSITY
180 South Garrison Street
Lakewood, CO 80226
(303) 202-0100
www.ccu.edu/home
Contact: Dave Foster
Unspecified athletic aid available
M: basketball, cross country, golf, soccer,
tennis
W: basketball, cross country, soccer,
tennis, volleyball

COLORADO COLLEGE
14 East Cache La Poudre
Colorado Springs, CO 80903
(719) 389-6755
www.coloradocollege.edu
Contact: Dave Moross
Men's Aid (#/$): 18/unspecified $
Women's Aid (#/$): 12/unspecified $
M: ice hockey. Men's Non-aid: basketball, cross country, football, indoor track,
lacrosse, soccer, swimming-diving, tennis,
track&field
W: soccer. Women's Non-aid: basketball,
cross country, indoor track, softball,
swimming-diving, tennis, track&field,
volleyball

COLORADO NORTHWESTERN COMMUNITY COLLEGE
500 Kennedy Drive
Rangely, CO 81648
Two-year college
(303) 675-2261
www.cncc.cc.co.us
Contact: Ron Hill

Unspecified athletic aid available
M: baseball, basketball
W: basketball, softball

COLORADO SCHOOL OF MINES
1500 Illinois Street
Golden, CO 80401-1877
(303) 273-3095
www.mines.edu
Contact: Jeff Duggan
Unspecified athletic aid available
M: baseball, basketball, cross country,
football, golf, indoor track, soccer, swimming-diving, tennis, track&field, wrestling
W: basketball, cross country, golf, indoor
track, softball, swimming-diving, tennis,
track&field, volleyball

COLORADO STATE UNIVERSITY
300 McGraw Center
Fort Collins, CO 80523
(970) 491-5067
www.colostate.edu
Contact: Marsha Smeltzer
Unspecified athletic aid available
M: basketball, cross country, football,
golf, indoor track, track&field
W: basketball, cross country, golf, indoor
track, softball, swimming-diving, tennis,
track&field, volleyball

FORT LEWIS COLLEGE
1000 Rim Drive
Durango, CO 81301-3999
(970) 247-7441
www.fortlewis.edu
Contact: Chris Aaland
Men's Aid (#/$): 85/$82,500
Women's Aid (#/$): 32/$43,000
M: basketball, cross country, football,
golf, soccer, wrestling
W: basketball, cross country, softball,
volleyball. Women's Non-aid: alpine
skiing

LAMAR COMMUNITY COLLEGE
2401 South Main Street
Lamar, CO 81052-3999
Two-year college

(719) 336-2248
www.lcc.cccoes.edu
Contact: Scott Crampton
Unspecified athletic aid available
M: baseball, basketball, golf
W: cross country, softball, volleyball

MESA STATE COLLEGE
P.O. Box 2647
Grand Junction, CO 81502
(970) 248-1143
www.mesa.colorado.edu
Contact: Tish Elliott
Unspecified athletic aid available
M: baseball, basketball, football, tennis,
wrestling
W: basketball, cross country, golf, soccer,
softball, tennis, volleyball

METROPOLITAN STATE
COLLEGE
P.O. Box 173362
Denver, CO 80227-3362
(303) 556-3431
www.mscd.edu
Contact: Steve Allen
Unspecified athletic aid available
M: baseball, basketball, soccer, swim-
ming, tennis
W: basketball, soccer, swimming, tennis,
volleyball

NORTHEASTERN JUNIOR
COLLEGE
100 College Drive
Sterling, CO 80751
Two-year college
(970) 522-6600
www.nejc.cc.co.us
Contact: Sheila Worley
Unspecified athletic aid available
M: baseball, basketball
W: basketball, soccer, softball, volleyball

OTERO JUNIOR COLLEGE
1802 Colorado Avenue
La Junta, CO 81050
Two-year college
(719) 384-6831

www.ojc.cccoes.edu
Contact: Brad Franz
Unspecified athletic aid available
M: baseball, basketball, golf
W: basketball, golf, softball, volleyball

REGIS UNIVERSITY
3333 Regis Boulevard
Denver, CO 80221-1099
(303) 458-4070
www.regis.edu
Contact: Mel Casper
Men's Aid (#/$): 20/unspecified $
Women's Aid (#/$): 20/unspecified $
M: baseball, basketball, golf, lacrosse,
soccer
W: basketball, lacrosse, soccer, softball,
tennis, volleyball

TRINIDAD STATE JUNIOR COLLEGE
600 Prospect Street
Trinidad, CO 81082
Two-year college
(719) 846-5510
www.tsjc.cccoes.edu
Contact: Jim Toupal
Unspecified athletic aid available
M: baseball, basketball, cross country, golf
W: golf, volleyball

UNIVERSITY OF COLORADO
AT BOULDER
Campus Box 357
Boulder, CO 80309
(303) 492-5626
www.colorado.edu
Contact: David Plati
Unspecified athletic aid available
M: alpine skiing, basketball, cross country, cross country skiing, football, golf,
indoor track, tennis, track&field
W: alpine skiing, basketball, cross
country, cross country skiing, golf,
indoor track, soccer, tennis, track&field

UNIVERSITY OF COLORADO
(COLORADO SPRINGS)
P.O. Box 7190
Colorado Springs, CO 80933

(719) 262-3003
www.uccs.edu
Contact: Jerry Cross
Men's Aid (#/$): 30/$27,492
Women's Aid (#/$): 34/$34,556
M: basketball, golf, soccer, tennis
W: basketball, softball, tennis, volleyball

UNIVERSITY OF DENVER
2201 East Asbury
Denver, CO 80208
(303) 871-3399
www.du.edu
Contact: Ron Grahame
Unspecified athletic aid available
M: basketball, cross country, golf, ice hockey, lacrosse, skiing, soccer, swimming-diving, tennis
W: basketball, cross country, golf, gymnastics, lacrosse, skiing, soccer, swimming-diving, tennis, volleyball

UNIVERSITY OF NORTHERN COLORADO
501 20th Street
Greeley, CO 80639
(970) 351-2534
www.uncbears.com
Contact: Jim Fallis
Men's Aid (#/$): 152/$416,958
Women's Aid (#/$): 98/$309,776
M: baseball, basketball, football, golf, tennis, track&field, wrestling
W: basketball, golf, soccer, softball, swimming-diving, tennis, track&field, volleyball

UNIVERSITY OF SOUTHERN COLORADO
2200 North Bonforte Boulevard
Pueblo, CO 81001
(719) 549-2753
www.uscolo.edu
Contact: Les Morken
Unspecified athletic aid available
M: baseball, basketball, golf, soccer, tennis, wrestling
W: basketball, soccer, softball, tennis, volleyball

WESTERN STATE COLLEGE
600 North Adams
Gunnison, CO 81231
(970) 943-2831
www.western.edu
Contact: Keith Hawkins
Unspecified athletic aid available
M: alpine skiing, basketball, cross country, cross country skiing, football, golf, track&field, wrestling
W: alpine skiing, basketball, cross country, cross country skiing, swimming-diving, track&field, volleyball

Connecticut

CENTRAL CONNECTICUT STATE UNIVERSITY
1615 Stanley Street
New Britain, CT 06050
(806) 832-3089
www.ccsustateu.edu
Contact: Brent Rutkowski
Unspecified athletic aid available
M: baseball, basketball, cross country, football, golf, indoor track, soccer, swimming-diving, tennis, track&field, wrestling
W: basketball, cross country, indoor track, softball, swimming-diving, tennis, track&field, volleyball

CONNECTICUT COLLEGE
270 Mohegan Avenue
New London, CT 06320
(860) 439-2501
www.conncoll.edu
Contact: Mike Salerno
Men's Non-aid: basketball, crew, cross country, ice hockey, lacrosse, sailing, squash, soccer, swimming, tennis, track&field
Women's Non-aid: basketball, crew, cross country, field hockey, ice hockey, lacrosse, sailing, soccer, swimming, tennis, track&field, volleyball

EASTERN CONNECTICUT STATE UNIVERSITY
83 Windham Street
Willimantic, CT 06226-2295
(860) 465-5172
www.ecsu.ctstateu.edu
Contact: Robert Molta
Men's Non-aid: baseball, basketball, cross country, lacrosse, soccer, track&field
Women's Non-aid: basketball, cross country, field hockey, lacrosse, soccer, softball, swimming, track&field, volleyball

FAIRFIELD UNIVERSITY
North Benson Road
Fairfield, CT 06430
(203) 254-4116
www.fairfield.edu/athletic/athletic.htm
Contact: Gail Wilson
Unspecified athletic aid available
M: baseball, basketball, lacrosse, soccer.
Men's Non-aid: alpine skiing, crew, cross country, golf, ice hockey, rugby, swimming-diving, tennis
W: basketball, crew, field hockey, lacrosse, soccer, softball, swimming-diving, tennis, volleyball. Women's Non-aid: alpine skiing, cross country, sailing

MANCHESTER COMMUNITY TECHNICAL COLLEGE
60 Bidwell Street
Manchester, CT 06040
Two-year college
(203) 646-6059
www.mctc.commnet.edu
Contact: Debbie Jezouit
Men's Non-aid: baseball, basketball, soccer
Women's Non-aid: soccer, softball

MITCHELL COLLEGE
437 Pequot Avenue
New London, CT 06320
Two-year college
(860) 701-5000
www.mitchell.edu
Contact: Doug Yarnall

Unspecified athletic aid available
M: baseball, basketball, cross country, lacrosse, soccer, tennis. Men's Non-aid: cheerleading, golf, sailing
W: basketball, cross country, soccer, softball, volleyball. Women's Non-aid: cheerleading, golf, sailing, tennis

QUINNIPIAC UNIVERSITY
New Road
Hamden, CT 06518
(203) 281-8625
www.quinnipiac.edu
Contact: Al Carbone
Unspecified athletic aid available
M: baseball, basketball, cross country, golf, ice hockey, lacrosse, soccer, tennis
W: basketball, cheerleading, cross country, field hockey, lacrosse, soccer, softball, tennis, volleyball

SACRED HEART UNIVERSITY
5151 Park Avenue
Fairfield, CT 06432-1000
(203) 371-7917
www.sacredheart.edu
Contact: Don Cook
Unspecified athletic aid available
M: baseball, basketball, bowling, crew, cross country, equestrian, fencing, golf, ice hockey, lacrosse, soccer, swimming, tennis, track&field, volleyball, wrestling
W: basketball, bowling, crew, cross country, equestrian, fencing, field hockey, golf, ice hockey, lacrosse, soccer, softball, swimming, tennis, track&field, volleyball

SOUTHERN CONNECTICUT STATE UNIVERSITY
501 Crescent Street
New Haven, CT 06515
(203) 392-6004
www.southernct.edu
Contact: Rick Leddy
Unspecified athletic aid available
M: basketball, gymnastics, soccer, softball, swimming-diving, volleyball

TEIKYO POST UNIVERSITY
800 Country Club Road
P.O. Box 2540
Waterbury, CT 06723
(203) 596-4531
www.teikyopost.edu
Contact: Claire Dwyer
Unspecified athletic aid available
M: baseball, basketball, equestrian, soccer
W: basketball, equestrian, soccer, softball

TRINITY COLLEGE
300 Summit Street
Hartford, CT 06106
(860) 297-2137
www.trincoll.edu
Contact: David Kingley
Men's Non-aid: baseball, crew, cross country, fencing, football, golf, ice hockey, indoor track, lacrosse, rugby, soccer, squash, swimming-diving, tennis, track&field, water polo, wrestling
Women's Non-aid: crew, cross country, fencing, field hockey, indoor track, lacrosse, rugby, soccer, softball, squash, swimming-diving, tennis, track&field, volleyball, water polo

UNIVERSITY OF BRIDGEPORT
126 Park Avenue
Bridgeport, CT 06601
(203) 576-4000 ext. 4726
www.bridgeport.edu
Contact: David Scrivines
Unspecified athletic aid available
M: basketball, soccer. Men's Non-aid: baseball, cross country, volleyball
W: basketball, cross country, gymnastics, softball. Women's Non-aid: soccer, volleyball

UNIVERSITY OF CONNECTICUT
U-78, 2111 Hillside Road
Storrs, CT 06269-3078
(860) 486-3531
www.uconn.edu
Contact: Tim Tolokan
Unspecified athletic aid available

M: baseball, basketball, cross country, football, golf, ice hockey, soccer, swimming-diving, tennis, track&field
W: basketball, cross country, field hockey, lacrosse, rowing, soccer, softball, swimming-diving, tennis, track&field, volleyball

UNIVERSITY OF HARTFORD
200 Bloomfield Avenue
West Hartford, CT 06117
(860) 768-4100
www.hartford.edu
Contact: James R. Keener, Jr.
Unspecified athletic aid available
M: baseball, basketball, cross country, golf, lacrosse, soccer, tennis, track&field
W: basketball, cross country, golf, soccer, softball, tennis, track&field, volleyball

UNIVERSITY OF NEW HAVEN
300 Orange Avenue
West Haven, CT 06516
(203) 932-7016
www.newhaven.edu
Contact: Deborah Chin
Unspecified athletic aid available
M: baseball, basketball, cross country, football, indoor track, soccer, track&field.
Men's Non-aid: lacrosse
W: basketball, cross country, indoor track, soccer, softball, tennis, track&field, volleyball

WESLEYAN UNIVERSITY
161 Cross Street
Freeman Athletic Center
Middletown, CT 06457
(860) 685-2000
www.wesleyan.edu
Contact: Janice DeFrance
Men's Non-aid: baseball, basketball, crew, cross country, football, golf, ice hockey, indoor track, lacrosse, soccer, squash, swimming, tennis, track&field, wrestling
Women's Non-aid: basketball, crew, cross country, field hockey, ice hockey, indoor track, lacrosse, soccer, softball, squash, swimming, tennis, track&field, volleyball

WESTERN CONNECTICUT STATE UNIVERSITY
181 White Street
Danbury, CT 06810
(203) 837-8200
www.wcsu.edu
Contact: Scott Ames
Men's Non-aid: baseball, basketball, football, soccer, tennis
Women's Non-aid: basketball, cross country, lacrosse, softball, swimming, tennis, volleyball

YALE UNIVERSITY
P.O. Box 208216
New Haven, CT 06520-8216
(203) 432-1456
www.yale.edu
Contact: Steve Conn
Men's Non-aid: baseball, basketball, crew, cross country, fencing, football, golf, ice hockey, lacrosse, soccer, squash, swimming-diving, tennis, track&field
Women's Non-aid: basketball, crew, cross country, fencing, field hockey, golf, gymnastics, ice hockey, lacrosse, soccer, softball, squash, swimming-diving, tennis, track&field, volleyball

Delaware

DELAWARE STATE UNIVERSITY
1200 North Dupont Highway
Dover, DE 19901
(302) 857-6030
www.dsc.edu
Contact: Bill Collick
Unspecified athletic aid available
M: baseball, basketball, cross country, football, indoor track, tennis, track&field, wrestling
W: basketball, bowling, cross country, indoor track, softball, tennis, track&field, volleyball

GOLDEY-BEACOM COLLEGE
4701 Limestone Road
Wilmington, DE 19808
(302) 998-8814
www.goldey.gbc.edu
Contact: Chris Morgan
Men's Aid (#/$): 20/unspecified $
Women's Aid (#/$): 20/unspecified $
M: basketball, soccer
W: basketball, soccer, softball, volleyball

UNIVERSITY OF DELAWARE
Bob Carpenter Center
Newark, DE 19716-2010
(302) 831-4006
www.udel.edu
Contact: Edgar Johnson
Unspecified athletic aid available
M: baseball, basketball, football, lacrosse, soccer. Men's Non-aid: cross country, golf, indoor track, swimming-diving, tennis, track&field
W: basketball, field hockey, lacrosse, soccer, softball, volleyball. Women's Non-aid: cross country, indoor track, rowing, swimming-diving, tennis, track&field

WESLEY COLLEGE
120 North State Street
Dover, DE 19901-3875
(302) 736-2400
www.wesley.edu
Contact: Bob Reed
Men's Non-aid: baseball, basketball, cross country, football, golf, lacrosse, soccer, tennis
Women's Non-aid: basketball, cheerleading, cross country, field hockey, lacrosse, soccer, softball, tennis

WILMINGTON COLLEGE
320 DuPont Highway
New Castle, DE 19720
(302) 328-9401
www.wilmcoll.edu
Contact: Tom Mason
Unspecified athletic aid available
M: baseball, basketball
W: basketball, softball, volleyball

District of Columbia

THE AMERICAN UNIVERSITY
4400 Massachusetts Avenue NW
Washington, DC 20016
(202) 885-3032
www.aueagles.com
Contact: Matt Winkler
Unspecified athletic aid available
M: basketball, cross country, golf, soccer, swimming-diving, tennis, track&field, wrestling
W: basketball, cross country, field hockey, lacrosse, swimming-diving, tennis, track&field, volleyball

CATHOLIC UNIVERSITY OF AMERICA
620 Michigan Avenue NE
Washington, DC 20064
(202) 319-5000
www.cua.edu.com
Contact: Robert Talbot
Men's Non-aid: baseball, basketball, cross country, football, lacrosse, soccer, swimming, tennis, track&field
Women's Non-aid: basketball, cross country, field hockey, lacrosse, softball, swimming, tennis, track&field, volleyball

GEORGE WASHINGTON UNIVERSITY
600 22nd Street NW
Washington, DC 20052
(202) 994-6650
www.gwu.edu
Contact: Jack Kuancz
Unspecified athletic aid available
M: baseball, basketball, crew, cross country, diving, golf, soccer, swimming, tennis, water polo
W: basketball, crew, cross country, diving, gymnastics, soccer, swimming, tennis, volleyball

GEORGETOWN UNIVERSITY
37th and O Street NW
Washington, DC 20057
(202) 687-2492
www.georgetown.edu
Contact: Bill Shapland
Unspecified athletic aid available
M: baseball, basketball, crew, football, golf, lacrosse, sailing, soccer, swimming-diving, tennis, track&field
W: basketball, crew, field hockey, lacrosse, sailing, soccer, swimming-diving, tennis, track&field, volleyball

HOWARD UNIVERSITY
2400 Sixth Street NW
Washington, DC 20059
(202) 806-7140
www.howard.edu
Contact: Debra Johnson
Unspecified athletic aid available
M: baseball, basketball, football, soccer, swimming, tennis, track&field, wrestling
W: basketball, bowling, lacrosse, soccer, swimming, tennis, track&field, volleyball

UNIVERSITY OF THE DISTRICT OF COLUMBIA
4200 Connecticut Avenue NW
Washington, DC 20008
(202) 274-5024
www.udc.edu
Contact: Jeanette Stephens
Unspecified athletic aid available
M: basketball, cross country, soccer, tennis
W: basketball, cross country, tennis, volleyball

Florida

BARRY UNIVERSITY
11300 Second Avenue NE
Miami Shores, FL 33161
(305) 899-3553
www.barry.edu
Contact: Fred Battenfield
Unspecified athletic aid available
M: baseball, basketball, golf, soccer, tennis

W: basketball, crew, golf, soccer, softball, tennis, volleyball

BETHUNE-COOKMAN COLLEGE
640 Second Avenue
Daytona Beach, FL 32015
(904) 255-1401 ext. 303
www.bethune.cookman.edu
Contact: Doris Godbey
Unspecified athletic aid available
M: baseball, basketball, cross country, football, golf, indoor track, tennis, track&field
W: basketball, cross country, golf, indoor track, softball, tennis, track&field, volleyball

BREVARD COMMUNITY COLLEGE
1519 Clearlake Road
Cocoa, FL 32922
Two-year college
(407) 632-1111
www.brevard.cc.fl.us
Contact: Don Smith
Unspecified athletic aid available
M: baseball, basketball, golf, swimming
W: basketball, softball, swimming, tennis, volleyball

BROWARD COMMUNITY COLLEGE
225 East Los Olas Boulevard
Ft. Lauderdale, FL 33314
Two-year college
(954) 475-6997
www.broward.cc.fl.us
Contact: Frank Message
Men's Aid (#/$): 70/$62,909
Women's Aid (#/$): 48/$43,401
M: baseball, basketball, golf. Men's Non-aid: bowling, racquetball, sailing, softball, swimming-diving, tennis, volleyball, weightlifting
W: baseball, basketball, golf. Women's Non-aid: bowling, racquetball, sailing, softball, swimming-diving, tennis, volleyball, weightlifting

CENTRAL FLORIDA COMMUNITY COLLEGE
3001 SW College Road
Ocala, FL 34474
Two-year college
(352) 854-2322 ext. 1325
www.cfcc.cc.fl.us
Contact: Bob Zelinski
Men's Aid (#/$): 30/unspecified $
Women's Aid (#/$): 38/unspecified $
M: baseball, basketball
W: basketball, softball, tennis

CHIPOLA JUNIOR COLLEGE
3094 Indian Circle
Marianna, FL 32446
Two-year college
(850) 718-2201
www.chipola.cc.fl.us
Contact: Dale O'Daniel
Unspecified athletic aid available
M: baseball, basketball
W: basketball, softball

DAYTONA BEACH COMMUNITY COLLEGE
P.O. Box 1111
Daytona Beach, FL 32015
Two-year college
(904) 255-8131 ext. 3302
www.dbcc.cc.fl.us
Contact: Thomas Schlageter
Men's Aid (#/$): 28/$100,000
Women's Aid (#/$): 44/$150,000
M: baseball, basketball
W: basketball, golf, softball

ECKERD COLLEGE
4200 54th Avenue S.
St. Petersburg, FL 33733
(727) 867-1166
www.eckerd.edu
Contact: Jim Harley
Unspecified athletic aid available
M: baseball, basketball, golf, soccer, tennis
W: basketball, cross country, soccer, softball, tennis, volleyball

EDWARD WATERS COLLEGE
1658 Kings Road
Jacksonville, FL 32209
(904) 366-2789
www.ewc.edu
Contact: James Day
Unspecified athletic aid available
M: baseball, basketball, cross country,
indoor track, track&field
W: basketball, cross country, indoor
track, softball, track&field

FLAGLER COLLEGE
King Street
St. Augustine, FL 32084
(904) 829-6481 ext. 225
www.flagler.edu
Contact: Bob Sterling
Unspecified athletic aid available
M: baseball, basketball, cross country,
golf, soccer, tennis
W: basketball, cross country, soccer,
tennis, volleyball

FLORIDA A&M UNIVERSITY
1500 Wahnihs Way
204 Gaither Gym
Tallahassee, FL 32307-3100
(850) 599-3868
www.famu.edu
Contact: Ken Riley
Unspecified athletic aid available
M: baseball, basketball, bowling, football,
golf, swimming, tennis, track&field
W: basketball, bowling, swimming,
tennis, track&field, volleyball

FLORIDA ATLANTIC UNIVERSITY
777 Glades Road
Boca Raton, FL 33431-0991
(561) 297-3000
www.fau.edu
Contact: Betty Surman
Unspecified athletic aid available
M: baseball, basketball, cross country,
football, golf, soccer, swimming-diving,
tennis
W: basketball, cross country, golf, soccer,
swimming-diving, tennis, volleyball

FLORIDA COLLEGE
119 Glen Arven Avenue
Temple Terrace, FL 33617-5578
Two-year college
(813) 899-6789
www.flcoll.edu
Contact: Kenny Moorer
Unspecified athletic aid available
M: baseball, basketball
W: volleyball

FLORIDA INSTITUTE OF TECHNOLOGY
Country Club Road
Melbourne, FL 32901
(407) 768-8000 ext. 8070
www.fit.edu
Contact: Lois Zabor
Unspecified athletic aid available
M: baseball, basketball, crew, soccer
W: basketball, crew, softball, volleyball

FLORIDA INTERNATIONAL UNIVERSITY
Athletic Department
Golden Panther Arena
University Park Campus
Miami, FL 33199
(305) 348-2843
www.fiu.edu
Contact: Paul Staffelbach
Unspecified athletic aid available
M: baseball, basketball, cross country,
soccer
W: basketball, cross country, golf, soccer,
tennis, volleyball

FLORIDA MEMORIAL COLLEGE
15800 NW 42nd Avenue
Miami, FL 33054
(305) 626-3165
www.fmc.edu
Contact: Bernard Johnson
Unspecified athletic aid available
M: baseball, basketball, cross country,
indoor track, track&field
W: basketball, cross country, indoor
track, track&field, volleyball

FLORIDA SOUTHERN COLLEGE
111 Lake Hollingsworth Drive
Lakeland, FL 33801-5698
(863) 680-4254
www.flsouthern.edu
Contact: Hal Smeltzly
Men's Aid (#/$): 30/$537,900
Women's Aid (#/$): 34/$609,620
M: baseball, basketball, cross country, golf, soccer, tennis
W: basketball, cross country, golf, soccer, softball, tennis, volleyball

FLORIDA STATE UNIVERSITY
P.O. Drawer 2195
Tallahassee, FL 32316
(850) 644-1402
www.seminoles.com
Contact: Rob Wilson
Unspecified athletic aid available
M: baseball, basketball, cross country, football, golf, swimming-diving, tennis, track&field
W: basketball, cross country, golf, swimming-diving, tennis, track&field, volleyball

GULF COAST COMMUNITY COLLEGE
5230 West Highway 98
Panama City, FL 32401
Two-year college
(800) 311-3685
www.gc.cc.fl.us
Contact: Gregg Wolfe
Unspecified athletic aid available
M: baseball, basketball
W: basketball, softball, volleyball

HILLSBOROUGH COMMUNITY COLLEGE
P.O. Box 30030
Tampa, FL 33630
Two-year college
(813) 253-7313
www.hcc.cc.fl.us
Contact: Vicki Schnurr
Unspecified athletic aid available
M: baseball, basketball
W: basketball, softball, tennis, volleyball

INDIAN RIVER COMMUNITY COLLEGE
3209 Virginia Avenue
Fort Pierce, FL 34981-5599
Two-year college
(561) 462-4772
www.ircc.cc.fl.us
Contact: Mike Easom
Unspecified athletic aid available
M: baseball, basketball, golf, swimming-diving, tennis
W: basketball, swimming-diving, tennis, volleyball

JACKSONVILLE UNIVERSITY
2800 University Boulevard North
Jacksonville, FL 32211
(904) 744-3950
www.ju.edu
Contact: Marsha Haskey
Unspecified athletic aid available
M: baseball, basketball, crew, cross country, golf, soccer, tennis
W: basketball, crew, cross country, golf, soccer, tennis, volleyball

LAKE-SUMTER COMMUNITY COLLEGE
9501 US Highway 441
Leesburg, FL 34788
Two-year college
(352) 787-3747
www.lscc.cc.fl.us
Contact: Michael Matulia
Unspecified athletic aid available
M: baseball
W: softball, volleyball

LYNN UNIVERSITY
3601 North Military Trail
Boca Raton, FL 33431
(561) 237-7278
www.lynn.edu
Contact: Doug Dodeck
Men's Aid (#/$): 53/$465,819
Women's Aid (#/$): 25/$197,870
M: baseball, golf, soccer, tennis
W: golf, soccer, tennis

MIAMI-DADE COMMUNITY COLLEGE NORTH
11380 Northwest 27th Avenue
Miami, FL 33167
Two-year college
(305) 237-0730
www.mdcc.edu
Contact: James Cox
Unspecified athletic aid available
M: baseball, basketball
W: basketball, softball, volleyball

MIAMI-DADE COMMUNITY COLLEGE SOUTH
11011 SW 104th Street
Miami, FL 33176
Two-year college
(305) 237-0730
www.mdcc.edu
Contact: James Cox
Unspecified athletic aid available
M: baseball, basketball
W: basketball, softball, volleyball

NORTH FLORIDA JUNIOR COLLEGE
1000 Turner Davis Drive
Madison, FL 32340
Two-year college
(850) 973-2288
www.nfcc.edu
Contact: Clyde Alexander
Men's Aid (#/$): 25/unspecified $
Women's Aid (#/$): 12/unspecified $
M: baseball
W: basketball, softball

NOVA SOUTHERN UNIVERSITY
3301 College Avenue
Fort Lauderdale, FL 33314
(954) 262-8261
www.nova.edu
Contact: Mike Laderman
Men's Aid (#/$): 76/$285,961
Women's Aid (#/$): 14/$38,900
M: baseball, basketball, cross country, golf, soccer
W: cross country, tennis, volleyball

OKALOOSA-WALTON COMMUNITY COLLEGE
100 College Boulevard
Niceville, FL 32578
Two-year college
(850) 729-5379
www.owcc.cc.fl.us
Contact: Mickey Englett
Men's Non-aid: tennis
Women's Non-aid: tennis

PALM BEACH ATLANTIC COLLEGE
P.O. Box 24708
West Palm Beach, FL 33416-4708
(561) 803-2533
www.pbac.edu
Contact: Lyle Wells
Men's Non-aid: baseball, basketball, soccer
Women's Non-aid: cheerleading, volleyball

PALM BEACH COMMUNITY COLLEGE
4200 Congress Avenue
Lake Worth, FL 33461
Two-year college
(561) 439-8067
www.pbcc.cc.fl.us
Contact: Hamid Faquir
Men's Aid (#/$): 35/unspecified $
Women's Aid (#/$): 38/unspecified $
M: baseball, basketball, tennis
W: basketball, softball, tennis

PENSACOLA JUNIOR COLLEGE
1000 College Boulevard
Pensacola, FL 32504
Two-year college
(850) 484-1314
www.pjc.cc.fl.us
Contact: Theresa Dillion
Unspecified athletic aid available
M: baseball, basketball
W: basketball, volleyball

POLK COMMUNITY COLLEGE
999 Avenue "H," NE
Winter Haven, FL 33881-4277

Two-year college
(863) 297-1000
www.polk.cc.fl.us
Contact: Bill Moore
Unspecified athletic aid available
M: baseball, basketball
W: basketball, volleyball

ROLLINS COLLEGE
1000 Holt Avenue-2730
Winter Park, FL 32789-4499
(407) 646-2661
www.rollins.edu
Contact: Dean Hylol
Unspecified athletic aid available
M: baseball, basketball, golf, soccer,
tennis. Men's Non-aid: cross country,
rowing, sailing, soccer, swimming, water
skiing
W: basketball, golf, tennis, volleyball.
Women's Non-aid: cross country, rowing,
sailing, soccer, softball, swimming, water
skiing

SAINT LEO UNIVERSITY
P.O. Box 2038
St. Leo, FL 33574
(352) 588-8506
www.saintleo.edu
Contact: Tom O'Brien
Unspecified athletic aid available
M: baseball, basketball, soccer, tennis.
Men's Non-aid: cross country
W: basketball, softball, tennis, volleyball.
Women's Non-aid: cheerleading, cross
country

SAINT THOMAS UNIVERSITY
16400 NW 32nd Avenue
Miami, FL 33054
(305) 628-6676
www.stu.edu
Contact: Laura Courtley
Men's Aid (#/$): 28/$178,000
Women's Aid (#/$): 17/$122,000
M: baseball, golf, soccer, tennis
W: soccer, softball, tennis, volleyball

SANTA FE COMMUNITY COLLEGE
3000 NW 83rd Street
Gainesville, FL 32606-6200
Two-year college
(352) 395-5616
www.santafe.cc.fl.us
Contact: Jim Keites
Men's Aid (#/$): 30/$48,000
Women's Aid (#/$): 30/$48,000
Restrictions and notes: Athletic aid
applies to tuition and books only.
M: baseball, basketball
W: basketball, softball

SEMINOLE COMMUNITY COLLEGE
100 Weldon Boulevard
Sanford, FL 32773-6199
Two-year college
(407) 328-2332
www.seminole.cc.fl.us
Contact: Courtney Miller
Unspecified athletic aid available
M: baseball, basketball, cross country,
tennis, track&field
W: basketball, softball, tennis, volleyball

SOUTH FLORIDA COMMUNITY COLLEGE
600 West College Drive
Avon Park, FL 33825-9356
Two-year college
(863) 453-6661 ext. 120
www.sfcc.cc.fl.us
Contact: Dr. Aubrey Gardner
Men's Aid (#/$): 12/$31,152
Women's Aid (#/$): 12/$31,152
M: basketball
W: volleyball

ST. JOHNS RIVER COMMUNITY COLLEGE
5001 St. Johns Avenue
Palatka, FL 32177
Two-year college
(904) 312-4200
www.sjcc.cc.fl.us
Contact: Joe Asher
Unspecified athletic aid available

M: baseball, basketball
W: softball

**ST. PETERSBURG JUNIOR
COLLEGE**
P.O. Box 13489
St. Petersburg, FL 33733
Two-year college
(727) 791-2662
www.spj.cc.fl.us
Contact: Dave Pano
Men's Aid (#/$): 30/unspecified $
Women's Aid (#/$): 42/unspecified $
M: baseball, basketball
W: basketball, softball, volleyball

STETSON UNIVERSITY
Campus Box 8359
Deland, FL 32720-3756
(904) 822-8100
www.stetson.edu
Contact: Jeff Altier
Men's Aid (#/$): 46/$1,399,632
Women's Aid (#/$): 53.4
M: baseball, basketball, cross country,
golf, soccer, tennis
W: basketball, cross country, golf, soccer,
softball, tennis, volleyball

**UNIVERSITY OF CENTRAL
FLORIDA**
P.O. Box 163555
Orlando, FL 32816-3555
(407) 823-2256
www.ucf.edu
Contact: Art Zeleznik
Unspecified athletic aid available
M: baseball, basketball, cross country,
football, golf, soccer, tennis
W: basketball, crew, cross country, golf,
soccer, tennis, track&field, volleyball

UNIVERSITY OF FLORIDA
P.O. Box 11485
Florida Field
Gainesville, FL 32611
(352) 375-4683 ext. 6123
www.ufl.edu
Contact: John Humenik

Unspecified athletic aid available
M: baseball, basketball, football, golf,
swimming-diving, tennis, track&field
W: basketball, cross country, golf,
gymnastics, swimming-diving, tennis,
track&field, volleyball

UNIVERSITY OF MIAMI
P.O. Box 248167
Coral Gables, FL 33124
(305) 284-3244
www.hurricanesports.com
Contact: Charles Campisi
Unspecified athletic aid available
M: baseball, basketball, cross country,
football, golf, swimming-diving, tennis
W: basketball, cross country, golf, soccer,
swimming-diving, tennis, track&field

UNIVERSITY OF NORTH FLORIDA
4567 St. Johns Bluff Road South
Jacksonville, FL 32224
(904) 620-2833
www.unf.edu
Contact: Sheri Hope
Unspecified athletic aid available
M: baseball, basketball, cross country,
golf, indoor track, tennis, track&field
W: basketball, cross country, indoor
track, softball, swimming, tennis,
track&field, volleyball

UNIVERSITY OF SOUTH FLORIDA
PED 214
Tampa, FL 33620
(813) 974-2125
www.gousfbulls.com
Contact: Paul Dodson
Unspecified athletic aid available
M: baseball, basketball, cross country,
football, golf, indoor track, soccer, tennis,
track&field
W: basketball, cross country, golf, indoor
track, soccer, softball, tennis, track&field,
volleyball

UNIVERSITY OF TAMPA
401 West Kennedy Boulevard
Tampa, FL 33606-1490

(813) 253-6241
www.utwed.utampa.edu
Contact: Matt Fairchild
Unspecified athletic aid available
M: baseball, basketball, golf, soccer, swimming, tennis. Men's Non-aid: crew, cross country
W: basketball, crew, softball, swimming, tennis, volleyball. Women's Non-aid: cross country

UNIVERSITY OF WEST FLORIDA
11000 University Parkway
Pensacola, FL 32514-5750
(850) 474-2400
www.uwf.edu
Contact: Dr. Ray Bennet
Unspecified athletic aid available
M: baseball, basketball, cross country, golf, soccer, tennis
W: basketball, cross country, soccer, softball, tennis, volleyball

WARNER SOUTHERN COLLEGE
5301 U.S. Highway 27 South
Lake Wales, FL 33853
(863) 638-2602
www.warner.edu
Contact: Kory Bays
Unspecified athletic aid available
M: baseball, basketball, golf, cross country, soccer, tennis (2001)
W: basketball, cross country, soccer, softball, tennis (2001), volleyball

WEBBER COLLEGE
P.O. Box 96
Babson Park, FL 33827-0096
(941) 638-1431
www.webber.edu
Contact: Nancy Nichols
Unspecified athletic aid available
Restrictions and notes: 200 athletes average $1,200 athletic aid each.
M: baseball, basketball, crew, cross country, golf, soccer, tennis
W: basketball, crew, cross country, golf, soccer, softball, tennis, volleyball

Georgia

AGNES SCOTT COLLEGE
141 East College Avenue
Decatur, GA 30030
(404) 471-6359
www.agnesscott.edu
Contact: Page Remillard
Women's Non-aid: basketball, cross country, soccer, swimming, tennis, volleyball

ALBANY STATE UNIVERSITY
504 College Drive
Albany, GA 31705
(912) 430-4673
www.asurams.edu
Contact: Edythe Bradley
Unspecified athletic aid available
M: baseball, basketball, cross country, football, track&field
W: basketball, cross country, track&field, volleyball. Women's Non-aid: tennis

ANDREW COLLEGE
413 College Street
Cuthbert, GA 31740-1395
Two-year college
(912) 732-2171
Contact: Ruth Eliason
Unspecified athletic aid available
M: baseball, cross country, soccer, tennis
W: cross country, soccer, tennis

ARMSTRONG ATLANTIC STATE UNIVERSITY
11935 Abercorn Extension
Savannah, GA 31419-1997
(912) 921-5854
www.armstrong.edu
Contact: Eddie Aenchbacher
Men's Aid (#/$): 17/$155,979
Women's Aid (#/$): 10/$92,400
M: baseball, basketball, cross country, tennis
W: basketball, cross country, softball, tennis, volleyball

AUGUSTA STATE UNIVERSITY
2500 Walton Way
Augusta, GA 30904
(706) 737-1431
www.aug.edu
Contact: Roxanne Padgett
Unspecified athletic aid available
M: baseball, basketball, cross country,
golf, soccer, tennis
W: basketball, cross country, softball,
tennis, volleyball

BERRY COLLEGE
P.O. Box 279
Mount Berry, GA 30149
(706) 236-2260
www.berry.edu
Contact: R.G. Smithson
Unspecified athletic aid available
M: baseball, basketball, cross country
golf, soccer, tennis
W: basketball, cross country, soccer,
tennis

BRENAU UNIVERSITY
1 Centennial Circle
Gainesville, GA 30501
(706) 534-6299
www.brenau.edu
Contact: Hal Henderson
Women's Aid (#/$): 8/$51,000
W: tennis

BREWTON PARKER COLLEGE
Vidalia Road
Highway 280
Mt. Vernon, GA 30445-0197
(912) 583-2241
www.bpc.edu
Contact: Steve Barker
Men's Aid (#/$): 26/$260,000
Women's Aid (#/$): 35/$360,000
M: baseball, basketball, soccer, tennis
W: basketball, soccer, softball, tennis

CLARK ATLANTA UNIVERSITY
Atlanta, GA 30314
(404) 880-8123
www.cau.edu

Contact: Richard Cosby
Unspecified athletic aid available
M: basketball, football, tennis,
track&field
W: basketball, cross country, tennis,
track&field, volleyball

COASTAL GEORGIA COMMUNITY COLLEGE
3700 Altama Avenue
Brunswick, GA 31520-3644
Two-year college
(912) 262-3299
www.peachnet.edu/inst/coastal.html
Contact: Gerald Cox
Unspecified athletic aid available
M: basketball
W: softball

COLUMBUS COLLEGE
13600 Algonquin Drive
Columbus, GA 31907-2079
(706) 568-2036
www.colstate.edu
Contact: Pam Kollerud
Unspecified athletic aid available
M: baseball, basketball, cross country,
golf, tennis
W: cross country, softball, tennis

COVENANT COLLEGE
14049 Scenic Highway
Lookout Mountain, GA 30750
(706) 820-1560
www.covenant.edu
Contact: Brian Crossman
Unspecified athletic aid available
M: basketball, soccer. Men's Non-aid:
cross country
W: basketball, soccer. Women's Non-aid:
cross country, volleyball

EMORY UNIVERSITY
Woodruff P.E. Center
Atlanta, GA 30322
(404) 727-6553
www.emory.edu
Contact: John Arenberg
Men's Non-aid: baseball, basketball,

cross country, golf, soccer, swimming-diving, tennis, track&field
Women's Non-aid: basketball, cross country, soccer, softball, swimming-diving, tennis, track&field, volleyball

FORT VALLEY STATE UNIVERSITY
1005 State College Drive
Fort Valley, GA 31030-3298
(912) 825-6208
www.fvsu.edu
Contact: Ed Wyche
Unspecified athletic aid available
M: basketball, cross country, football, tennis, track&field
W: basketball, cross country, softball, tennis, track&field, volleyball

GEORGIA COLLEGE STATE UNIVERSITY
Athletic Department
Milledgeville, GA 31061
(912) 455-1779
www.gac.peachnet.edu
Contact: Aurelia M. Dykes
Men's Aid (#/$): 21/$19,087
Women's Aid (#/$): 11/$12,722
M: baseball, basketball, golf, soccer, tennis
W: basketball, gymnastics, softball, tennis

GEORGIA INSTITUTE OF TECHNOLOGY
190 Third Street NW
Atlanta, GA 30332
(404) 894-4160
www.ramblingrock.com
Contact: Sandy Goldhahn
Unspecified athletic aid available
M: baseball, basketball, cross country, football, golf, indoor track, tennis, track&field
W: basketball, cross country, softball, tennis, track&field, volleyball

GEORGIA MILITARY COLLEGE
201 East Greene Street
Milledgeville, GA 31061
Two-year college

(912) 445-2690
www.gmc.cc.ga.us
Contact: Robert Nunn
Unspecified athletic aid available
M: football, tennis

GEORGIA SOUTHERN UNIVERSITY
Landrum Box 8085
Statesboro, GA 30460
(912) 681-5239
www.gasou.edu
Contact: Hank Schomber
Men's Aid (#/$): 94/$535,000
Women's Aid (#/$): 35/$200,000
M: baseball, basketball, football, golf, soccer, tennis
W: basketball, cross country, indoor track, softball, swimming-diving, tennis, track&field, volleyball

GEORGIA SOUTHWESTERN STATE UNIVERSITY
800 Wheatley Street
Americus, GA 31709
(912) 931-2222
www.gsw.edu
Contact: Dr. Steve Cobb
Unspecified athletic aid available
M: baseball, basketball, tennis
W: basketball, softball, tennis, volleyball

GEORGIA STATE UNIVERSITY
University Plaza
Atlanta, GA 30303-3083
(404) 651-3179
www.gsu.edu
Contact: Blaine Hughes
Unspecified athletic aid available
M: baseball, basketball, cross country, golf, soccer, tennis, wrestling
W: basketball, cross country, golf, soccer, softball, tennis, track&field, volleyball

KENNESAW STATE COLLEGE
P.O. Box 444
Marietta, GA 30061
(770) 423-6074
www.kennesaw.edu

Contact: Thomas I. Patterson
Unspecified athletic aid available
M: baseball, basketball, cross country,
golf, soccer. Men's Non-aid: track&field
W: basketball, cross country, softball.
Women's Non-aid: track&field

MERCER UNIVERSITY
1400 Coleman Avenue
Macon, GA 31207
(912) 301-4040
www.mercer.edu
Contact: Carol Farr
Unspecified athletic aid available
M: baseball, basketball, cross country,
golf, soccer, tennis
W: basketball, cheerleading, cross
country, golf, sailing, soccer, softball,
tennis, volleyball

MOREHOUSE COLLEGE
830 Westview Drive SW
Atlanta, GA 30314
(404) 681-2752
www.morehouse.edu
Contact: James Nix
Unspecified athletic aid available
M: baseball, basketball, cross country,
football, tennis, table tennis,
track&field

MORRIS BROWN COLLEGE
643 Martin Luther King Jr. Drive
Atlanta, GA 30314
(404) 220-3618
www.morrisbrown.edu
Contact: Gene Bright
Men's Aid (#/$): 44/$704,000
Women's Aid (#/$): 13/$208,000
M: basketball, football. Men's Non-aid:
baseball, cross country, tennis,
track&field
W: basketball, volleyball. Women's Non-
aid: cross country, tennis, track&field

NORTH GEORGIA COLLEGE &
STATE UNIVERSITY
Dahlonega, GA 30597
(706) 864-1627

www.ngc.peachnet.edu
Contact: Randy Dune
Unspecified athletic aid available
M: basketball, riflery, soccer, tennis.
Men's Non-aid: baseball, cross country
W: basketball, riflery, softball, tennis.
Women's Non-aid: soccer, cross
country

OGLETHORPE UNIVERSITY
4484 Peachtree Road NE
Atlanta, GA 30319
(404) 261-1441
www.oglethorpe.edu
Contact: Pat Elsey
Men's Non-aid: baseball, basketball,
cross country, golf, soccer, tennis,
track&field
Women's Non-aid: basketball, cross
country, golf, soccer, tennis, track&field,
volleyball

PAINE COLLEGE
1235 15th Street
Augusta, GA 30910-2799
(706) 821-8200
www.paine.edu
Contact: Robert G. Skinner
Unspecified athletic aid available
M: baseball, basketball, cross country,
track&field
W: basketball, cross country,
track&field, water polo. Women's Non-
aid: softball

PIEDMONT COLLEGE
Demorest, GA 30535
(706) 778-3000
www.piedmont.edu
Contact: Rene Van Winkle
Men's Non-aid: baseball, basketball,
cross country, soccer, tennis
Women's Non-aid: basketball, cross
country, soccer, softball, tennis,
volleyball

SAVANNAH STATE COLLEGE
P.O. Box 20427
Savannah, GA 31404

(912) 353-5181
www.savstate.edu
Contact: Jerome Fitch
Men's Aid (#/$): 54/unspecified $
Women's Aid (#/$): 20/unspecified $
M: baseball, basketball, football,
track&field
W: basketball, cross country, tennis,
volleyball

SHORTER COLLEGE
Rome, GA 30161-4298
(706) 291-2121
www.shorter.edu
Contact: Ricci Lattanzi
Men's Aid (#/$): 21/$178,200
Women's Aid (#/$): 12/$98,900
M: baseball, basketball, cross country,
golf, tennis
W: basketball, cross country, golf, tennis

SOUTHERN POLYTECHNIC STATE UNIVERSITY
1000 South Marietta Parkway
Marietta, GA 30060-2896
(770) 528-7290
www.spsu.edu
Contact: Karmika Triplett
Men's Aid (#/$): 34/$47,763
M: baseball, basketball, tennis

STATE UNIVERSITY OF WEST GEORGIA
1600 Maple Street
Carrollton, GA 30118
(770) 836-6542
www.westga.edu
Contact: Mitch Gray
Men's Aid (#/$): 61.2/$290,215
Women's Aid (#/$): 19.1/$90,661
M: baseball, basketball, cross country,
football, tennis
W: basketball, cross country, softball,
tennis, volleyball

TOCCOA FALLS COLLEGE
P.O. Box 800266
Toccoa Falls, GA 30598
(706) 886-6831

www.toccoafalls.edu
Contact: Lance Martin
Men's Non-aid: baseball, basketball, golf,
soccer
Women's Non-aid: basketball, soccer,
volleyball

TRUETT-MCCONNELL JUNIOR COLLEGE
100 Alumni Drive
Cleveland, GA 30528
Two-year college
(706) 865-2134 ext. 148
www.truett.cc.ga.us
Contact: Wayne Collett
Unspecified athletic aid available
M: baseball, basketball, cross country,
soccer
W: basketball, cross country, soccer

UNIVERSITY OF GEORGIA
Stegeman Coliseum
Athens, GA 30613
(706) 542-3579
www.uga.edu
Contact: Vince Dooley
Unspecified athletic aid available
Restrictions and notes: Athletic aid
limited to NCAA maximums
M: baseball, basketball, cross country,
football, golf, indoor track, swimming-
diving, tennis, track&field
W: cross country, golf, gymnastics,
indoor track, soccer, softball, swimming-diving, tennis, track&field, volleyball

VALDOSTA STATE UNIVERSITY
North Patterson Street
Valdosta, GA 31698
(912) 333-5903
www.valdosta.edu
Contact: Steve Roberts
Unspecified athletic aid available
M: baseball, basketball, cross country,
football, golf, tennis
W: basketball, cross country, softball,
tennis, volleyball

Hawaii

BRIGHAM YOUNG UNIVERSITY
55-222 Kulanui Street
Laie, HI 96762
(808) 293-3211
www.byuh.edu
Contact: Scott Lowe
Unspecified athletic aid available
M: basketball, cross country, soccer, tennis
W: cross country, softball, tennis, volleyball

CHAMINADE UNIVERSITY OF HONOLULU
3140 Waialae Avenue
Honolulu, HI 96816-1510
(808) 735-4790
www.chaminade.edu
Contact: Al Walker
Unspecified athletic aid available
M: basketball, cross country, tennis, water polo
W: cross country, softball, tennis, volleyball

HAWAII PACIFIC UNIVERSITY
1060 Bishop Street PH
Honolulu, HI 96813
(808) 544-0221
www.hpu.edu
Contact: Russ Dung
Unspecified athletic aid available
M: baseball, basketball, cross country, soccer, tennis
W: cross country, soccer, softball, tennis, volleyball

UNIVERSITY OF HAWAII (HILO)
200 W. Kawii Street
Hilo, HI 96720-4091
(808) 974-7520
www.uhh.hawaii.edu
Contact: Jean Coffman
Unspecified athletic aid available
M: baseball, basketball, cross country, golf, tennis
W: cross country, tennis, volleyball

UNIVERSITY OF HAWAII (MANOA)
2444 Dole Street
Honolulu, HI 96822-2370
(808) 956-8111
www.uhm.hawaii.edu
Contact: Hugh Yoshida
Unspecified athletic aid available
M: baseball, basketball, football, golf, swimming-diving, tennis, volleyball
W: basketball, cheerleading, cross country, golf, sailing, soccer, softball, swimming-diving, tennis, water polo, volleyball

Idaho

ALBERTSON COLLEGE OF IDAHO
2112 Cleveland Boulevard #39
Caldwell, ID 83605-4432
(208) 459-5681
www.acofi.edu
Contact: Todd Miles
Unspecified athletic aid available
M: alpine skiing, baseball, basketball, soccer
W: alpine skiing, basketball, soccer, volleyball

BOISE STATE UNIVERSITY
1910 University Drive
Boise, ID 83725
(208) 426-1515
www.broncosports.com
Contact: Max Corbet
Unspecified athletic aid available
M: basketball, cross country, football, golf, tennis, wrestling
W: basketball, cross country, golf, gymnastics, soccer, tennis, volleyball

COLLEGE OF SOUTHERN IDAHO
315 Falls Avenue
P.O. Box 1238
Twin Falls, ID 83303-1238
Two-year college
(208) 733-9554 ext. 2486

www.csi.cc.id.us
Contact: Jeff Duggan
Unspecified athletic aid available
M: baseball, basketball, cross country, rodeo
W: basketball, cross country, rodeo, volleyball

IDAHO STATE UNIVERSITY
P.O. Box 81241 SU
Pocatello, ID 83209
(208) 236-3651
www.isu.edu
Contact: Frank Mercogliano
Unspecified athletic aid available
M: basketball, cross country, football, golf, indoor track, track&field
W: basketball, soccer, track&field, volleyball

LEWIS CLARK STATE COLLEGE
6th Street and 8th Avenue
Lewiston, ID 83501
(208) 799-2273
www.lcsc.edu
Contact: Gary Picone
Unspecified athletic aid available
M: baseball, basketball, cross country, golf, rodeo, tennis
W: basketball, cross country, golf, rodeo, tennis, volleyball

NORTH IDAHO COLLEGE
1000 West Garden Avenue
Coeur d'Alene, ID 83814
Two-year college
(208) 769-3351
www.nidc.edu
Contact: Jim Headley
M: baseball, basketball, cross country, track&field, wrestling
W: basketball, cross country, soccer, softball, track&field, volleyball

NORTHWEST NAZARENE
UNIVERSITY
623 Holly Street
Nampa, ID 83686-5897
(877) 668-4968

www.nnc.edu
Contact: Rich Sanders
Men's Aid (#/$): 15/$120,000
Women's Aid (#/$): 15/$120,000
M: baseball, basketball, soccer, track&field
W: basketball, tennis, track&field, volleyball

RICKS COLLEGE
Hart 264
Rexburg, ID 83460-0900
Two-year college
(208) 356-2104
www.ricks.edu
Contact: Bryce Rydalch
Unspecified athletic aid available
M: baseball, basketball, cross country, football, indoor track, track&field, wrestling
W: basketball, cross country, indoor track, softball, track&field, volleyball

UNIVERSITY OF IDAHO
Kibbie Activity Center
Moscow, ID 83844-2302
(208) 885-0200
www.uidaho.edu
Contact: Maureen Taylor
Unspecified athletic aid available
M: basketball, cross country, football, golf, indoor track, tennis, track&field
W: basketball, cross country, golf, indoor track, soccer, tennis, track&field, volleyball

Illinois

AUGUSTANA COLLEGE
639 38th Street
Rock Island, IL 61201
(309) 794-7265
www.augustana.edu
Contact: David Wrath
Men's Non-aid: baseball, basketball, cross country, football, golf, soccer,

swimming-diving, tennis, track&field, wrestling
Women's Non-aid: basketball, cross country, golf, softball, swimming-diving, tennis, track&field, volleyball

AURORA UNIVERSITY
347 South Gladstone Avenue
Aurora, IL 60506
(603) 844-5533
www.aurora.edu
Contact: Dave Beyer
Men's Non-aid: baseball, basketball, football, golf, soccer, tennis
Women's Non-aid: basketball, golf, softball, tennis, volleyball

BELLEVILLE AREA COLLEGE
4950 Maryville Road
Granite City, IL 62040-2699
Two-year college
(618) 931-0600
www.bacnet.edu
Contact: Scott Wolf
Unspecified athletic aid available
M: baseball, basketball, soccer, tennis
W: basketball, softball, tennis, volleyball

BENEDICTINE UNIVERSITY
5700 College Road
Lisle, IL 60532
(630) 829-6150
www.ben.edu
Contact: John Stachniak
Men's Non-aid: baseball, basketball, cross country, football, golf, indoor track, soccer, swimming-diving, tennis, track&field
Women's Non-aid: basketball, cheerleading, cross country, dance, golf, indoor track, soccer, softball, swimming-diving, tennis, track&field, volleyball

BLACKBURN COLLEGE
700 College Avenue
Carlinville, IL 62626
(217) 854-3231
www.blackburn.edu
Contact: Cheryl Gardner

Men's Non-aid: baseball, basketball, cross country, football, golf, soccer
Women's Non-aid: basketball, cross country, soccer, volleyball

BLACK HAWK COLLEGE
6600 34th Avenue
Moline, IL 61265
Two-year college
(309) 796-1311
www.bhc.edu
Contact: Gary Huber
Unspecified athletic aid available
M: baseball, basketball, golf
W: basketball, softball, volleyball

BRADLEY UNIVERSITY
1501 West Bradley Avenue
Peoria, IL 61625
(309) 677-2670
www.bradley.edu
Contact: Mary Lou Jansen
Men's Aid (#/$): 44/$622,336
Women's Aid (#/$): 52/$608,192
M: baseball, basketball, cross country, golf, soccer, softball, swimming, tennis
W: basketball, cross country, golf, softball, swimming, tennis, volleyball

CHICAGO STATE UNIVERSITY
9501 South Martin Luther King Jr. Drive
Chicago, IL 60628
(773) 995-2217
www.csu.edu
Contact: Terrence Jackson
Unspecified athletic aid available
M: baseball, basketball, cross country, golf, indoor track, tennis, track&field
W: basketball, cross country, golf, indoor track, tennis, track&field, volleyball

COLLEGE OF ST. FRANCIS
500 Wilcox Street
Joliet, IL 60435
(815) 740-3842
www.stfrancis.edu
Contact: Dave Laketa
Unspecified athletic aid available

M: baseball, basketball, football, golf, soccer, tennis
W: basketball, cross country, golf, soccer, softball, tennis, track&field, volleyball

CONCORDIA UNIVERSITY
7400 Augusta Street
River Forest, IL 60305-1499
(708) 209-3116
www.curf.edu
Contact: Janet Fisher
Men's Non-aid: baseball, basketball, cross country, football, tennis, track&field
Women's Non-aid: basketball, softball, spirit squads, tennis, track&field, volleyball

DANVILLE AREA COMMUNITY COLLEGE
2000 East Main Street
Danville, IL 61832
Two-year college
(217) 443-3222
www.dacc.cc.il.us
Contact: John Spezia
Unspecified athletic aid available
M: baseball, basketball, cross country, golf, indoor track, soccer, track&field
W: basketball, cross country, indoor track, softball, track&field

DEPAUL UNIVERSITY
1 East Jackson
Chicago, IL 60604
(312) 362-8350
www.depaul.edu
Contact: John H. Schoultz
Unspecified athletic aid available
M: basketball, cross country, golf, indoor track, soccer, tennis, track&field
W: basketball, cross country, indoor track, soccer, softball, tennis, track&field, volleyball

DOMINICAN UNIVERSITY
7900 West Division Street
River Forest, IL 60305
(708) 524-6509
www.dom.edu
Contact: Ted Malek

Unspecified athletic aid available
M: baseball, basketball, cross country, golf, soccer, tennis, volleyball
W: basketball, cross country, golf, soccer, softball, tennis, volleyball

EASTERN ILLINOIS UNIVERSITY
Lantz Gym
Charleston, IL 61920
(217) 581-2319
www.eiu.edu
Contact: David Kidwell
Unspecified athletic aid available
M: baseball, basketball, cross country, football, indoor track, soccer, swimming-diving, tennis, track&field, wrestling
W: basketball, cross country, indoor track, softball, swimming-diving, tennis, track&field, volleyball

ELGIN COMMUNITY COLLEGE
1700 Spartan Drive
Elgin, IL 60123
Two-year college
(847) 214-7515
www.elgin.cc.il.us
Contact: Gayle Saunders
Men's Non-aid: baseball, basketball, golf, tennis
Women's Non-aid: basketball, golf, softball, tennis, volleyball

ELMHURST COLLEGE
190 Prospect Avenue
Elmhurst, IL 60126-3296
(630) 617-3075
www.elmhurst.edu
Contact: Chris Ragsdale
Men's Non-aid: baseball, basketball, cross country, football, golf, indoor track, tennis, track&field, wrestling
Women's Non-aid: basketball, cross country, indoor track, softball, tennis, track&field, volleyball

EUREKA COLLEGE
300 East College Street
Eureka, IL 61530
(309) 467-6310

www.@eureka.edu
Contact: Joe Barth
Men's Non-aid: basketball, football, golf, swimming-diving, tennis, track&field
Women's Non-aid: basketball, softball, swimming-diving, tennis, track&field, volleyball

GREENVILLE COLLEGE
315 East College Avenue
Greenville, IL 62246
(618) 664-1840
www.greenville.edu
Contact: Doug Faulkner
Men's Non-aid: baseball, basketball, cross country, golf, soccer, tennis, track&field
Women's Non-aid: basketball, cross country, softball, tennis, track&field, volleyball

ILLINOIS CENTRAL COLLEGE
One College Drive
East Peoria, IL 61635-0001
Two-year college
(309) 694-5330
www.icc.cc.il.us
Contact: Guy Goodmen
Men's Non-aid: baseball, basketball, golf
Women's Non-aid: basketball, softball, volleyball

ILLINOIS COLLEGE
1101 West College Avenue
Jacksonville, IL 62650
(217) 245-3048
www.ic.edu
Contact: James T. Murphy
Men's Non-aid: baseball, basketball, cross country, football, golf, indoor track, soccer, tennis, track&field, wrestling
Women's Non-aid: basketball, cross country, golf, indoor track, soccer, softball, tennis, track&field, volleyball

ILLINOIS INSTITUTE OF TECHNOLOGY
3040 South Wabash
Chicago, IL 60616

(312) 567-3298
www.iit.edu
Contact: Jim Darrah
Unspecified athletic aid available
M: baseball, basketball, cross country, swimming-diving
W: basketball, cross country, swimming-diving, volleyball

ILLINOIS STATE UNIVERSITY
123 Horton Field House
Normal, IL 61761-6901
(309) 438-3825
www.redbirds.org
Contact: Kenny Mossman
Unspecified athletic aid available
M: baseball, basketball, cross country, football, golf, indoor track, tennis, track&field
W: basketball, cross country, golf, gymnastics, indoor track, soccer, softball, swimming-diving, tennis, track&field, volleyball

ILLINOIS VALLEY COMMUNITY COLLEGE
2578 East 350th Road
Oglesby, IL 61348-1099
Two-year college
(815) 224-2720
www.ivcc.edu
Contact: Mike Riley
Unspecified athletic aid available
M: baseball, basketball, golf, tennis
W: basketball, softball, tennis, volleyball

ILLINOIS WESLEYAN UNIVERSITY
1312 N. Park Street
Bloomington, IL 61701-2900
(309) 556-1000
www.iwu.edu
Contact: Stew Salowitz
Men's Non-aid: baseball, basketball, cross country, football, golf, indoor track, soccer, swimming-diving, tennis, track&field
Women's Non-aid: basketball, cross country, indoor track, soccer, softball,

swimming-diving, tennis, track&field, volleyball

KANKAKEE COMMUNITY COLLEGE
Box 888
Kankakee, IL 60901
Two-year college
(815) 933-0234
www.kcc.cc.il.us
Contact: David Holstein
Unspecified athletic aid available
M: baseball, basketball
W: basketball, softball, volleyball

KASKASKIA COMMUNITY COLLEGE
27210 College Road
Centralia, IL 62801
Two-year college
(618) 545-3146
www.kc.cc.il.us
Contact: Jeff Carling
Men's Aid (#/$): 48/unspecified $
Women's Aid (#/$): 42/unspecified $
M: baseball, basketball, tennis
W: basketball, softball, volleyball

KISHWAUKEE COLLEGE
Malta Road
Malta, IL 60150-9699
Two-year college
(815) 825-2086
www.kish.cc.il.us
Contact: Jodi Lerd
Men's Aid (#/$): 28/unspecified $
Women's Aid (#/$): 25/unspecified $
M: baseball, basketball, golf, soccer
W: basketball, softball, tennis, volleyball

KNOX COLLEGE
South Street
Galesburg, IL 61401
(309) 341-7714
www.knox.edu
Contact: Bill Spilman
Men's Non-aid: baseball, basketball, cross country, football, golf, indoor track, soccer, swimming-diving, tennis, track&field, wrestling
Women's Non-aid: basketball, cross country, indoor track, soccer, softball, swimming-diving, tennis, track&field, volleyball

LAKE FOREST COLLEGE
555 North Sheridan Road
Lake Forest, IL 60045
(847) 735-5288
www.lfc.edu
Contact: Scott Rucker
Men's Non-aid: basketball, football, handball, ice hockey, lacrosse, soccer, swimming-diving, tennis
Women's Non-aid: basketball, handball, soccer, softball, swimming-diving, tennis, volleyball

LAKE LAND COLLEGE
5001 Lake Boulevard
Mattoon, IL 61938
Two-year college
(217) 234-5253
www.lakeland.cc.il.us
Contact: Pam Crimson
Men's Aid (#/$): 53/unspecified $
Women's Aid (#/$): 42/unspecified $
M: baseball, basketball, cross country, tennis
W: basketball, cross country, softball, volleyball

LEWIS AND CLARK COMMUNITY COLLEGE
5800 Godfrey Road
Godfrey, IL 62035
Two-year college
(618) 466-3411
www.lc.cc.il.us
Contact: George C. Terry
Unspecified athletic aid available
M: baseball, basketball, golf, soccer, tennis
W: basketball, soccer, softball, tennis, volleyball

LEWIS UNIVERSITY
Route 53
Romeoville, IL 60446

www.lewisu.edu
Contact: Paul Ruddy
Unspecified athletic aid available
M: baseball, basketball, cross country, golf, soccer, swimming, tennis, track&field, volleyball
W: basketball, cross country, golf, soccer, softball, swimming, tennis, track&field, volleyball

LINCOLN CHRISTIAN COLLEGE
100 Campus View Drive
Lincoln, IL 62656
(217) 732-3168
www.lccs.edu
Contact: Randy Kirk
Men's Non-aid: baseball, basketball, soccer
Women's Non-aid: basketball, volleyball

LINCOLN COLLEGE
300 Keokuk Street
Lincoln, IL 62656
Two-year college
(217) 732-3155
www.lincolncollege.com
Contact: Allen Pickering
Unspecified athletic aid available
M: baseball, basketball, golf, soccer, swimming-diving, wrestling
W: basketball, golf, softball, soccer, swimming-diving, volleyball

LINCOLN LAND COMMUNITY COLLEGE
Shepherd Road
Springfield, IL 62794-9256
Two-year college
(217) 786-2426
www.llcc.cc.il.us
Contact: Ron Riggle
Unspecified athletic aid available
M: baseball, basketball, soccer
W: basketball, softball, volleyball

LINCOLN TRAIL COLLEGE
11220 State Highway 1
Robinson, IL 62454
Two-year college

(618) 544-8657
www.iecc.cc.il.us
Contact: Tony Kestranck
Unspecified athletic aid available
M: baseball, basketball, golf, tennis
W: basketball, softball, tennis, volleyball

LOYOLA UNIVERSITY
6525 North Sheridan Road
Chicago, IL 60626
(773) 508-2560
www.loyolaramblers.com
Contact: Carolyn O'Connell
Unspecified athletic aid available
M: basketball, cross country, golf, indoor track, soccer, track&field, volleyball
W: basketball, cross country, golf, indoor track, soccer, softball, track&field, volleyball

MCHENRY COUNTY COLLEGE
8900 U.S. Highway 14
Crystal Lake, IL 60012-2761
Two-year college
(815) 455-8550
www.mchenry.cc.il.us
Contact: Wally Reynolds
Unspecified athletic aid available
Restrictions and notes: Athletic aid only for McHenry County H.S. or district residents.
M: baseball, basketball, soccer, tennis
W: basketball, softball, tennis, volleyball

MCKENDREE COLLEGE
701 College Road
Lebanon, IL 62254
(618) 537-6879
www.mckendree.edu
Contact: Scott Cummings
Unspecified athletic aid available
M: baseball, basketball, cross country, football, golf, soccer, tennis, track&field
W: basketball, cross country, golf, soccer, softball, tennis, track&field, volleyball

MILLIKIN UNIVERSITY
1184 West Main Street
Decatur, IL 62522

(217) 362-6429
www.millikin.edu
Contact: David Johnson
Men's Non-aid: baseball, basketball, cross country, football, golf, indoor track, soccer, swimming, tennis, track&field, wrestling
Women's Non-aid: basketball, cross country, golf, soccer, softball, swimming-diving, tennis, track&field, volleyball

MONMOUTH COLLEGE
700 East Broadway
Monmouth, IL 61462
(309) 457-2176
www.monm.edu
Contact: Dan Nolan
Men's Non-aid: baseball, basketball, cross country, football, golf, indoor track, soccer, track&field
Women's Non-aid: basketball, cross country, golf, indoor track, softball, track&field, volleyball

MOODY BIBLE INSTITUTE
820 North LaSalle Street
Chicago, IL 60610
(312) 329-4451
www.moody.edu
Contact: Sheldon Bassett
Men's Non-aid: basketball, soccer, volleyball
Women's Non-aid: basketball, volleyball

MORAINE VALLEY COMMUNITY COLLEGE
10900 South 88th Avenue
Palos Hills, IL 60465
Two-year college
(708) 974-5213
www.moraine.cc.il.us
Contact: Bill Finn
Men's Non-aid: baseball, basketball, soccer, tennis, volleyball
Women's Non-aid: basketball, soccer, softball, tennis, volleyball

MORTON COLLEGE
3801 South Central Avenue
Cicero, IL 60804

Two-year college
(708) 656-8000
www.morton.cc.il.edu
Contact: Robert Slivovsky
Unspecified athletic aid available
M: baseball, basketball, cross country, golf, soccer
W: basketball, cheerleading, cross country, softball, volleyball

NATIONAL-LOUIS UNIVERSITY
2840 Sheridan Road
Evanston, IL 60201
(847) 256-5156
www.nl.edu
Contact: Myra Minuskin
Unspecified athletic aid available
M: soccer
W: basketball, softball, volleyball

NORTH CENTRAL COLLEGE
30 N Brainard Street
P.O. Box 3063
Naperville, IL 60566-7063
(630) 637-5320
www.noctrl.edu
Contact: Tom Carlton
Men's Non-aid: baseball, basketball, cross country, football, golf, indoor track, soccer, swimming, tennis, track&field, wrestling
Women's Non-aid: basketball, cross country, indoor track, softball, swimming, tennis, track&field, volleyball

NORTHEASTERN ILLINOIS UNIVERSITY
5500 North St. Louis Avenue
Chicago, IL 60625-4699
(773) 583-4050
www.neiu.edu
Contact: Tom Lake
Unspecified athletic aid available
M: baseball, basketball, cross country, football, golf, tennis
W: basketball, cross country, softball, tennis, volleyball

NORTHERN ILLINOIS UNIVERSITY
112 Evans Field House
De Kalb, IL 60115
(815) 753-1706
www.niu.edu
Contact: Michael Korcek
Unspecified athletic aid available
M: baseball, basketball, football, golf, soccer, swimming-diving, tennis, wrestling
W: basketball, cross country, golf, gymnastics, soccer, softball, swimming-diving, tennis, volleyball

NORTHWESTERN UNIVERSITY
1501 Central Street
Evanston, IL 60201
(847) 491-3205
www.nusports.com
Contact:Tim Clodjeaux
Unspecified athletic aid available
M: baseball, basketball, cross country, football, golf, swimming-diving, tennis, track&field, wrestling. Men's Non-aid: fencing, indoor track, soccer
W: basketball, cross country, field hockey, softball, swimming-diving, tennis, track&field, volleyball. Women's Non-aid: fencing, indoor track, lacrosse

OAKTON COMMUNITY COLLEGE
1600 East Golf Road
Des Plaines, IL 60016
Two-year college
(847) 635-1753
www.oakton.edu
Contact: Cindy Doubek
Men's Non-aid: baseball, basketball, cross country, golf, indoor track, tennis, track&field, wrestling
Women's Non-aid: basketball, cross country, indoor track, softball, tennis, track&field, volleyball

OLIVET NAZARENE UNIVERSITY
P.O Box 592
Kankakee, IL 60901
(815) 939-5372
www.olivet.edu
Contact: Larry Watson
Unspecified athletic aid available
M: baseball, basketball, cross country, football, golf, soccer, tennis, track&field
W: basketball, cross country, soccer, softball, tennis, track&field, volleyball

OLNEY CENTRAL COLLEGE
35 Northwest Street
Olney, IL 62450
Two-year college
(618) 395-7777
www.iecc.cc.il.us
Contact: Dennis Conley
Unspecified athletic aid available
M: baseball, basketball, golf, tennis
W: basketball, softball, tennis, volleyball

PARKLAND COLLEGE
2400 West Bradley Avenue
Champaign, IL 61821
Two-year college
(217) 351-2226
www.parkland.cc.il.us
Contact: Jim Reed
Unspecified athletic aid available
M: baseball, basketball, cross country, golf, indoor track, softball, tennis, track&field, soccer. Men's Non-aid: cheerleading
W: basketball, cross country, indoor track, soccer, softball, tennis, track&field, volleyball. Women's Non-aid: cheerleading

PRINCIPIA COLLEGE
Elsah, IL 62028-9799
(618) 374-2131
www.prin.edu
Contact: Lee Suarez
Men's Non-aid: baseball, basketball, cross country, golf, football, soccer, swimming-diving, tennis, track&field
Women's Non-aid: basketball, cross country, golf, soccer, softball, swimming-diving, tennis, track&field, volleyball

QUINCY UNIVERSITY
530 North 18th Street
Quincy, IL 62301
(217) 228-5291
www.quincy.edu
Contact: Jim Naumovich
Unspecified athletic aid available
M: baseball, basketball, cross country,
football, golf, soccer, tennis
W: basketball, cross country, golf, soccer,
softball, tennis, volleyball

REND LAKE COLLEGE
Rural Route 1
Ina, IL 62846
Two-year college
(618) 437-5321
www.rlc.cc.il.us
Contact: Tim Willis
Men's Aid (#/$): 26/unspecified $
Women's Aid (#/$): 20/unspecified $
M: baseball, basketball, golf, tennis
W: basketball, golf, softball, tennis, volleyball

ROOSEVELT UNIVERSITY
430 South Michigan Avenue
Chicago, IL 60605
(312) 341-3500
www.roosevelt.edu
Contact: Ellen Mendorf
Unspecified athletic aid available
M: basketball, golf, soccer, tennis. Men's
Non-aid: badminton, bowling, cross
country, martial arts, swimming, tennis,
track&field, weightlifting
Women's Non-aid: badminton, bowling,
martial arts, swimming, tennis,
track&field, volleyball

SAINT XAVIER UNIVERSITY
3700 West 103rd Street
Chicago, IL 60655
(773) 298-3000
www.sxu.edu
Contact: Lynn O'Linski
Men's Aid (#/$): 60/$240,000
Women's Aid (#/$): 40/$160,000
M: baseball, basketball, soccer
W: softball, volleyball

SAUK VALLEY COLLEGE
173 Illinois Route 2
Dixon, IL 61021-9110
Two-year college
(815) 288-5511 ext. 234
www.svcc.cc.il.us
Contact: Ross Damhof
Unspecified athletic aid available
M: baseball, basketball, cross country,
golf
W: basketball, cross country, softball,
tennis, volleyball

SOUTHEASTERN ILLINOIS COLLEGE
3575 College Road
Harrisburg, IL 62946
Two-year college
(618) 252-6376
www.sic.cc.il.us
Contact: Britton Blair
Unspecified athletic aid available
M: baseball, basketball, golf
W: basketball, softball, volleyball

SOUTHERN ILLINOIS UNIVERSITY
SIU Arena/Lingle Hall
Carbondale, IL 62901
(618) 453-5463
www.siuc.edu
Contact: Nancy Bandy
Unspecified athletic aid available
M: baseball, basketball, cross country,
football, golf, indoor track, swimming-
diving, tennis, track&field
W: basketball, cross country, golf, indoor
track, softball, swimming-diving, tennis,
track&field, volleyball

SOUTHERN ILLINOIS UNIVERSITY (EDWARDSVILLE)
Box 1027
Edwardsville, IL 62026
(618) 650-3608
www.siue.edu
Contact: Eric Hess
Men's Aid (#/$): 74/$154,196
Women's Aid (#/$): 48/$77,799

M: baseball, basketball, cross country, golf, soccer, tennis, track&field, wrestling
W: basketball, cross country, soccer, softball, tennis, track&field

SPOON RIVER COLLEGE
23235 North County 22
Canton, IL 61520-9801
Two-year college
(309) 649-6303
www.spoonrivercollege.net
Contact: Patrick Ketcham
Unspecified athletic aid available
M: baseball, basketball, indoor track, track&field
W: basketball, indoor track, softball, track&field, volleyball

TRINITY CHRISTIAN COLLEGE
6601 West College Drive
Palos Heights, IL 60463
(800) 748-0085
www.trinity.edu
Contact: Steve Hilbelink
Men's Non-aid: baseball, basketball, soccer, track&field
Women's Non-aid: basketball, softball, track&field, volleyball

TRINITY COLLEGE OF ARTS & SCIENCES
2065 Halfday Road
Deerfield, IL 60015
(847) 317-7000
www.tiu.edu
Contact: John Damon
Men's Non-aid: baseball, basketball, soccer, swimming-diving, wrestling
Women's Non-aid: basketball, softball, swimming-diving, volleyball

TRITON COLLEGE
2000 North Fifth Avenue
River Grove, IL 60171
Two-year college
(708) 456-0300
www.triton.cc.il.us
Contact: Gary Stearns
M: baseball, basketball, soccer, swimming-diving, wrestling
W: basketball, softball, swimming-diving, volleyball

UNIVERSITY OF CHICAGO
5640 University Avenue
Chicago, IL 60637
(773) 702-7681
www.uchicago.edu
Contact: Tom Weingartner
Men's Non-aid: baseball, basketball, cross country, football, indoor track, swimming-diving, tennis, track&field, wrestling
Women's Non-aid: basketball, cross country, indoor track, softball, swimming-diving, tennis, track&field, volleyball

UNIVERSITY OF ILLINOIS (CHICAGO)
Chicago, IL 60612
(312) 996-5880
www.iuc.edu
Contact: Anne Schoenherr
Unspecified athletic aid available
M: basketball, cross country, fencing, football, golf, gymnastics, indoor track, swimming-diving, tennis, track&field, wrestling
W: basketball, cross country, golf, gymnastics, indoor track, swimming-diving, tennis, track&field, volleyball

UNIVERSITY OF ILLINOIS (URBANA-CHAMPAIGN)
1800 South First Street
115 Assembly Hall
Champaign, IL 61820
(217) 333-1390
www.fightingillini.com
Contact: Marsha Goldenstein
Unspecified athletic aid available
M: basketball, cross country, football, golf, gymnastics, indoor track, tennis, track&field, wrestling
W: basketball, cross country, golf, gymnastics, indoor track, soccer, softball, swimming-diving, tennis, track&field, volleyball

WABASH VALLEY COLLEGE
2200 College Drive
Mt. Carmel, IL 62863
Two-year college
(618) 262-8641
www.iecc.cc.il.us
Contact: Bill Hackler
Unspecified athletic aid available
M: baseball, basketball, golf, tennis
W: basketball, softball, tennis, volleyball

WAUBONSEE COMMUNITY COLLEGE
Route 47 at Harter Road
Sugar Grove, IL 60554-9799
Two-year college
(630) 466-7900 ext. 2527
www.wcc.cc.il.us
Contact: Dave Randall
Men's Non-aid: baseball, basketball, cross country, golf, soccer, tennis, wrestling
Women's Non-aid: basketball, softball, tennis, volleyball

WESTERN ILLINOIS UNIVERSITY
Western Hall 234
Macomb, IL 61455
(309) 298-1106
www.wiu.edu
Contact: Helen Smiley
Men's Aid (#/$): 100/$733,000
Women's Aid (#/$): 59/$420,000
Restrictions and notes: Aid numbers based on full equivalents.
M: baseball, basketball, cross country, football, golf, indoor track, soccer, swimming-diving, tennis, track&field
W: basketball, cross country, indoor track, soccer, softball, swimming-diving, tennis, track&field, volleyball

WHEATON COLLEGE
501 East College Avenue
Wheaton, IL 60187
(708) 752-5000
www.wheaton.edu
Contact: Steve Schwepker
Men's Non-aid: baseball, basketball,

cross country, football, golf, indoor track, soccer, swimming, tennis, track&field, wrestling
Women's Non-aid: basketball, cross country, indoor track, soccer, softball, swimming, tennis, track&field, volleyball

WILLIAM RAINEY HARPER COLLEGE
1200 West Algonquin Road
Palatine, IL 60067-7398
Two-year college
(847) 925-6466
www.harper.cc.il.us
Contact: Ron Lanham
Men's Non-aid: baseball, basketball, football, golf, soccer, swimming-diving, tennis, track&field, wrestling
Women's Non-aid: basketball, softball, swimming-diving, tennis, track&field, volleyball

Indiana

ANDERSON UNIVERSITY
1100 East Fifth Street
Anderson, IN 46012
(765) 641-4080
www.anderson.edu
Contact: Marcie Taylor
Men's Non-aid: baseball, basketball, cross country, football, golf, indoor track, soccer, tennis, track&field
Women's Non-aid: basketball, cross country, golf, indoor track, soccer, softball, tennis, track&field, volleyball

BALL STATE UNIVERSITY
HP 120
Muncie, IN 47306-0929
(765) 285-8242
www.bsu.edu
Contact: Joe Hernandez
Unspecified athletic aid available
M: baseball, basketball, cross country, football, golf, indoor track, swimming-

diving, tennis, track&field, volleyball. Men's Non-aid: ultimate frisbee W: basketball, cross country, field hockey, gymnastics, indoor track, softball, swimming-diving, tennis, track&field, volleyball. Women's Non-aid: lacrosse

BETHEL COLLEGE
1001 West McKinley Avenue
Mishawaka, IN 46545
(219) 257-3345
www.bethel.in.edu
Contact: Mike Lightfoot
Unspecified athletic aid available
M: baseball, basketball, cross country, golf, soccer, tennis
W: basketball, cross country, softball, tennis, volleyball

BUTLER UNIVERSITY
4600 Sunset Avenue
Indianapolis, IN 46208
(317) 940-9414
www.butlersports.com
Contact: Jim McGrath
Unspecified athletic aid available
M: baseball, basketball, cross country, football, golf, indoor track, lacrosse, soccer, swimming, tennis, track&field
W: basketball, cross country, golf, indoor track, soccer, softball, swimming, tennis, track&field, volleyball

DE PAUW UNIVERSITY
300 East Seminary Street
Greencastle, IN 46135
(765) 658-4630
www.depauw.edu
Contact: Bill Wagner
Men's Non-aid: baseball, basketball, cross country, football, golf, soccer, softball, swimming-diving, tennis, track&field, wrestling
Women's Non-aid: baseball, basketball, cross country, field hockey, golf, soccer, softball, swimming-diving, tennis, track&field, volleyball

EARLHAM COLLEGE
National Road West
Richmond, IN 47374
(765) 983-1414
www.earlham.edu
Contact: Joann Mikesell
Men's Non-aid: baseball, basketball, cross country, football, soccer, tennis, track&field
Women's Non-aid: basketball, cross country, field hockey, lacrosse, soccer, tennis, track&field, volleyball

GOSHEN COLLEGE
1700 S. Main Street
Goshen, IN 46526
(219) 535-7497
www.goshen.edu
Contact: Chris Chamberlin
Unspecified athletic aid available
M: baseball, basketball, cross country, golf, soccer, tennis, track&field
W: basketball, cross country, soccer, softball, tennis, track&field, volleyball

GRACE COLLEGE
200 Seminary Drive
Winona Lake, IN 46590
(219) 372-5100
www.grace.edu
Contact: Jason Knavel
Unspecified athletic aid available
M: baseball, basketball, cross country, golf, soccer, tennis, track&field
W: basketball, cross country, soccer, softball, tennis, track&field, volleyball

HANOVER COLLEGE
P.O. Box 108
Hanover, IN 47243-0108
(812) 866-7385
www.hanover.edu
Contact: Lynn Hall
Men's Non-aid: baseball, basketball, cross country, football, golf, soccer, tennis, track&field
Women's Non-aid: basketball, cross country, field hockey, golf, soccer, softball, tennis, track&field, volleyball

HUNTINGTON COLLEGE
2303 College Avenue
Huntington, IN 46750
(219) 356-4212
www.huntcol.edu
Contact: Carol Hill
Unspecified athletic aid available
M: baseball, basketball, cross country,
golf, soccer, tennis, track&field
W: basketball, cross country, soccer, softball, tennis, track&field, volleyball

INDIANA INSTITUTE OF TECHNOLOGY
1600 East Washington Boulevard
Fort Wayne, IN 46803
(219) 422-5561 ext. 2244
www.indtech.edu
Contact: Dan Kline
Unspecified athletic aid available
M: baseball, basketball, soccer
W: basketball, soccer, softball

INDIANA STATE UNIVERSITY
Room 118B
Indiana State Arena
Terre Haute, IN 47809
(812) 237-4161
www.isu.indstate.edu
Contact: Kent Johnson
Unspecified athletic aid available
M: baseball, basketball, cross country,
football, indoor track, tennis,
track&field
W: basketball, cross country, softball,
tennis, track&field, volleyball

INDIANA UNIVERSITY
17th and Fee Lane
Assembly Hall
Bloomington, IN 47405
(812) 855-1966
www.indiana.edu
Contact: Clarence Doninger
Unspecified athletic aid available
M: baseball, basketball, cross country,
football, golf, soccer, swimming-diving,
tennis, track&field, wrestling
W: basketball, crew, cross country, golf,
soccer, softball, swimming-diving, tennis,
track&field, volleyball

INDIANA UNIVERSITY (SOUTH BEND)
1700 Mighawaka Avenue
P.O. Box 7111
South Bend, IN 46634
(219) 237-4344
www.iusb.edu
Contact: Kevin MacDonald
Unspecified athletic aid available
M: basketball
W: basketball

INDIANA UNIVERSITY-PURDUE UNIVERSITY
901 West New York Street
Suite 105
Indianapolis, IN 46202-5193
(317) 274-4488
www.iupuijaguars.com
Contact: Michael Moore
Men's Aid (#/$): 30/$60,000
Women's Aid (#/$): 30/$60,000
M: baseball, basketball, cross country,
golf, soccer, swimming-diving, tennis
W: basketball, cross country, soccer, soft-
ball, swimming-diving, tennis

INDIANA UNIVERSITY-PURDUE UNIVERSITY (FORT WAYNE)
2101 Coliseum Boulevard East
Fort Wayne, IN 46805-1499
(219) 481-6645
www.infw.indiana.edu
Contact: Tim Heffron
Unspecified athletic aid available
M: baseball, basketball, cross country,
soccer, tennis, volleyball
W: basketball, cross country, soccer,
softball, tennis, volleyball

INDIANA UNIVERSITY SOUTHEAST
4201 Grantline Road
New Albany, IN 47150
(812) 941-2450

www.ius.indiana.edu
Contact: Ernest Neal
Unspecified athletic aid available
M: baseball, basketball, cross country,
tennis
W: basketball, cross country, softball,
tennis, volleyball

INDIANA WESLEYAN UNIVERSITY
4201 South Washington Street
Marion, IN 46953-4999
(765) 677-2318
www.indwes.edu
Contact: Linda Neill
Unspecified athletic aid available
M: baseball, basketball, cross country, golf,
indoor track, soccer, tennis, track&field
W: basketball, cheerleading, cross country, indoor track, soccer, softball, tennis,
track&field, volleyball

MANCHESTER COLLEGE
604 East College Avenue
North Manchester, IN 46962
(219) 982-5390
www.manchester.edu
Contact: Greg Miller
Men's Non-aid: baseball, basketball,
cross country, football, golf, indoor track,
soccer, tennis, track&field
Women's Non-aid: basketball, cross
country, indoor track, softball, tennis,
track&field, volleyball

MARIAN COLLEGE
3200 Cold Spring Road
Indianapolis, IN 46222-1997
(800) 722-7264
www.marian.edu
Contact: John E. Shelton
Men's Aid (#/$): 77/$113,391
Women's Aid (#/$):30/$74,978
M: baseball, basketball, cheerleading,
cross country, cycling, golf, soccer,
tennis, track&field
W: basketball, cheerleading, cross
country, cycling, soccer, softball, tennis,
track&field, volleyball

OAKLAND CITY UNIVERSITY
143 N. Lucretia Street
Oakland City, IN 47660-1099
(812) 749-1290
www.oak.edu
Contact: Mike Sandifar
Unspecified athletic aid available
M: baseball, basketball, cross country,
golf
W: basketball, cross country, golf, softball, volleyball

PURDUE UNIVERSITY
West Lafayette, IN 47907
(705) 494-3196
www.purduesports.com
Contact: Jim Vruggink
Men's Aid (#/$): 47/$323,292
Women's Aid (#/$): 28/$77,115
M: baseball, basketball, cross country,
football, golf, indoor track, swimming-
diving, tennis, track&field, wrestling
W: basketball, cross country, golf, indoor
track, soccer, softball, swimming-diving,
tennis, track&field, volleyball

PURDUE UNIVERSITY (CALUMET)
2200 169th Street
Hammond, IN 46323-2094
(219) 989-2540
www.calumet.purdue.edu
Contact: John Frind
Men's Aid (#/$): 20/$25,000
Women's Aid (#/$): 18/$35,000
M: basketball
W: basketball, volleyball

ROSE-HULMAN INSTITUTE OF TECHNOLOGY
5500 Wabash Avenue
Terre Haute, IN 47803
(812) 877-8418
www.rose-hulman.edu
Contact: Kevin Lanke
Men's Non-Aid: baseball, basketball,
cross country, football, golf, indoor track,
riflery, soccer, swimming-diving, tennis,
track&field, wrestling
Women's Non-aid: basketball, cross

country, indoor track, riflery, soccer, softball, swimming-diving, tennis, track&field, volleyball

SAINT FRANCIS COLLEGE
2701 Spring Street
Fort Wayne, IN 46808
(219) 434-7433
www.sfc.edu
Contact: Todd Oliver
Unspecified athletic aid available
M: baseball, basketball, cross country, football, golf, soccer, softball, tennis, track&field
W: basketball, cross country, soccer, softball, tennis, track&field, volleyball

SAINT JOSEPH'S COLLEGE
P.O. Box 875
Rensselaer, IN 47978
(219) 866-6000
www.saintjoe.edu
Contact: Bill Massoels
Unspecified athletic aid available
M: baseball, basketball, cross country, football, golf, soccer, tennis, track&field
W: basketball, cross country, soccer, softball, tennis, track&field, volleyball

SAINT MARY'S COLLEGE
Angela Athletic Facility
Notre Dame, IN 46556-5001
(219) 284-5548
www.saintmarys.edu
Contact: Lynn Kachmarik
Women's Non-aid: basketball, cross country, golf, soccer, softball, swimming-diving, tennis, track&field, volleyball

TRI-STATE UNIVERSITY
305 Hershey Hall
Angola, IN 46703-1764
(219) 665-4840
www.tristate.edu
Contact: Bob Muckian
Unspecified athletic aid available
M: baseball, basketball, cross country, football, golf, indoor track, soccer,

swimming, tennis, track&field, volleyball
W: basketball, cross country, golf, indoor track, soccer, softball, swimming, tennis, track&field, volleyball

UNIVERSITY OF EVANSVILLE
1800 Lincoln Avenue
Evansville, IN 47722
(812) 479-2285
www.evansville.edu
Contact: Bob Boxell
Unspecified athletic aid available
M: baseball, basketball, cross country, golf, soccer, swimming-diving, tennis
W: basketball, cross country, golf, soccer, softball, swimming-diving, tennis, volleyball

UNIVERSITY OF INDIANAPOLIS
1400 East Hanna Avenue
Indianapolis, IN 46227-3697
(317) 788-3494
www.uindy.edu
Contact: Joe Gentry
Unspecified athletic aid available
M: baseball, basketball, cross country, football, golf, soccer, swimming-diving, tennis, track&field, wrestling
W: basketball, cross country, golf, soccer, softball, swimming-diving, tennis, track&field, volleyball

UNIVERSITY OF NOTRE DAME
Joyce Center
Notre Dame, IN 46556
(219) 631-7516
www.und.com
Contact: John Heisler
Men's Aid (#/$): 154/$4,312,000
Women's Aid (#/$): 94.5/$2,646,000
M: baseball, basketball, cross country, fencing, football, golf, ice hockey, indoor track, soccer, swimming-diving, tennis, track&field
W: basketball, cross country, fencing, golf, indoor track, lacrosse, rowing, soccer, softball, swimming-diving, tennis, track&field, volleyball

UNIVERSITY OF SOUTHERN INDIANA
8600 University Boulevard
Evansville, IN 47712
(812) 464-1840
www.usi.edu
Contact: Steve Newton
Men's Aid (#/$): 16/$25,261
Women's Aid (#/$): 12/$11,775
M: baseball, basketball, cross country, golf, soccer, tennis
W: basketball, cross country, golf, soccer, softball, tennis, volleyball

VALPARAISO UNIVERSITY
Recreation Center
Valparaiso, IN 46383-6493
(219) 464-5000
www.valpo.edu
Contact: Bill Rogers
Unspecified athletic aid available
M: baseball, basketball, cross country, football, golf, soccer, swimming-diving, tennis, track&field, wrestling
W: basketball, cross country, soccer, softball, swimming-diving, tennis, track&field, volleyball

VINCENNES UNIVERSITY
1002 North First Street
Vincennes, IN 47591
Two-year college
(812) 888-4237
www.vinu.edu
Contact: Jerry Blomker
Unspecified athletic aid available
M: baseball, basketball, bowling, cross country, golf, indoor track, marathon, soccer, swimming-diving, tennis, track&field
W: basketball, bowling, cross country, indoor track, marathon, swimming-diving, track&field, volleyball

WABASH COLLEGE
P.O. Box 352
Crawfordsville, IN 47933-0352
(765) 361-6165
www.wabash.edu

Contact: Brent Harris
Men's Non-aid: baseball, basketball, cross country, football, golf, soccer, swimming-diving, tennis, track&field, wrestling

Iowa

BRIAR CLIFF COLLEGE
P.O. Box 2100
Sioux City, IA 51104-2100
(712) 279-1646
www.briar-cliff.edu
Contact: Jay Gunnels
Unspecified athletic aid available
M: baseball, basketball, cross country, golf, soccer, track&field, wrestling
W: basketball, cross country, golf, soccer, softball, track&field, volleyball

BUENA VISTA UNIVERSITY
610 West 4th Street
Storm Lake, IA 50588
(712) 749-2253
www.bvu.edu
Contact: Jan Thompson
Men's Non-aid: baseball, basketball, cross country, football, golf, swimming-diving, tennis, track&field, wrestling
Women's Non-aid: basketball, cross country, golf, softball, swimming-diving, tennis, track&field, volleyball

CENTRAL COLLEGE
812 University Avenue
Pella, IA 50219
(515) 628-5278
www.central.edu
Contact: Larry Happel
Men's Non-aid: baseball, basketball, cross country, football, golf, indoor track, soccer, tennis, track&field, wrestling
Women's Non-aid: basketball, cross country, golf, indoor track, soccer, softball, tennis, track&field, volleyball

CLINTON COMMUNITY COLLEGE
1000 Lincoln Boulevard
Clinton, IA 52732
Two-year college
(319) 244-7178
www.eiccd.cc.ia.us
Contact: Bob Walker
Men's Aid (#/$): 5/$4,000
Women's Aid (#/$): 4/$1,800
Restrictions and notes: Tuition awards
only.
M: basketball, cheerleading
W: volleyball, cheerleading

COE COLLEGE
1220 First Avenue NE
Cedar Rapids, IA 52402
(319) 399-8570
www.coe.edu
Contact: Michael Levin
Restrictions and notes: Wide variety of
non-athletic aid available.
Men's: Non-aid: baseball, basketball,
cross country, football, golf, indoor track,
soccer, swimming-diving, tennis,
track&field, wrestling
Women's Non-aid: basketball, cross
country, golf, indoor track, soccer, softball, swimming-diving, tennis, volleyball

CORNELL COLLEGE
600 First Street West
Mount Vernon, IA 52314
(319) 895-4000
www.cornell-iowa.edu
Contact: Stephen Miller
Men's Non-aid: baseball, basketball,
cross country, football, golf, indoor track,
soccer, tennis, track&field, wrestling
Women's Non-aid: basketball, cross
country, golf, indoor track, soccer, softball, tennis, track&field, volleyball

DES MOINES AREA COMMUNITY
COLLEGE
1125 Hancock Drive
Boone, IA 50036
Two-year college
(515) 432-7203

www.dmacc.cc.ia.us
Contact: Terry Jamieson
Men's Aid (#/$): 20/$10,000
Women's Aid (#/$): 20/$10,000
M: baseball, basketball
W: basketball, softball

DRAKE UNIVERSITY
2507 University Avenue
Des Moines, IA 50311-4505
(515) 271-2011
www.drake.edu
Contact: Mike Mahon
Men's Aid (#/$): 52/$814,004
Women's Aid (#/$): 51/$814,698
M: basketball, cross country, football,
golf, indoor track, soccer, tennis,
track&field
W: basketball, crew, cross country, indoor
track, softball, tennis, track&field,
volleyball

GRACELAND COLLEGE
700 College Avenue
Lamoni, IA 50140
(515) 784-5464
www.graceland.edu
Contact: Mike Cullina
Men's Aid (#/$): 216/$474,823
Women's Aid (#/$): 104/$171,217
M: baseball, basketball, cross country,
football, golf, soccer, tennis, track&field,
volleyball
W: basketball, cross country, soccer, softball, tennis, track&field, volleyball

GRAND VIEW COLLEGE
1200 Grand View Avenue
Des Moines, IA 50316
(515) 263-2897
www.gvc.edu
Contact: Lou Yacinich
Unspecified athletic aid available
M: baseball, basketball, soccer, tennis.
Men's Non-aid: cross country,
track&field
W: basketball, soccer, softball, tennis,
volleyball. Women's Non-aid: cross
country, track&field

GRINNELL COLLEGE
P.O. Box 805
Grinnell, IA 50112-0810
(515) 269-3832
www.grinnell.edu
Contact: Andy Hamilton
Men's Non-aid: baseball, basketball, cross country, football, golf, indoor track, soccer, swimming-diving, tennis, track&field
Women's Non-aid: basketball, cross country, golf, indoor track, soccer, softball, swimming-diving, tennis, track&field, volleyball

INDIAN HILLS COMMUNITY COLLEGE
721 North First Street
Centerville, IA 52544-1223
Two-year college
(515) 856-2143
www.ihcc.ccia.us
Contact: Dick Sharp
Unspecified athletic aid available
M: baseball, basketball, golf
W: softball, volleyball

IOWA STATE UNIVERSITY OF SCIENCE AND TECHNOLOGY
1802 South Fourth Street
Ames, IA 50010
(515) 294-3372
www.cyclones.com
Contact: Tom Krochell
Unspecified athletic aid available
M: baseball, basketball, cross country, football, golf, gymnastics, swimming, track&field, wrestling
W: basketball, cross country, golf, gymnastics, soccer, softball, tennis, track&field, volleyball

IOWA WESLEYAN COLLEGE
601 North Main Street
Mount Pleasant, IA 52641
(319) 385-6306
www.iwc.edu
Contact: Keith Kohorst
Unspecified athletic aid available

M: baseball, basketball, cross country, football, golf, indoor track, soccer, track&field. Men's Non-aid: swimming
W: basketball, cross country, golf, indoor track, soccer, softball, track&field, volleyball. Women's Non-aid: swimming

KIRKWOOD COMMUNITY COLLEGE
Box 2068
Cedar Rapids, IA 52406
Two-year college
(319) 398-4909
www.kirkwood.cc.ia.us
Contact: Dennis Usher
Unspecified athletic aid available
M: baseball, basketball, golf
W: basketball, softball, volleyball

LORAS COLLEGE
1450 Alta Vista
Dubuque, IA 52001
(319) 588-7407
www.loras.edu
Contact: Dave Beyer
Men's Non-aid: baseball, basketball, cross country, football, golf, soccer, swimming-diving, tennis, track&field, wrestling
Women's Non-aid: basketball, cross country, golf, indoor track, martial arts, softball, swimming-diving, tennis, track&field, volleyball

LUTHER COLLEGE
700 College Drive
Decorah, IA 52101
(319) 387-1586
www.luther.edu
Contact: Dave Blanchard
Men's Non-aid: baseball, basketball, cross country, football, golf, indoor track, soccer, swimming-diving, tennis, track&field, wrestling
Women's Non-aid: basketball, cross country, golf, indoor track, soccer, softball, swimming-diving, tennis, track&field, volleyball

MARYCREST INTERNATIONAL UNIVERSITY
1607 West 12th Street
Davenport, IA 52804-4906
(319) 326-9223
www.mcrest.edu
Contact: Dino Hayz
Unspecified athletic aid available
M: basketball, soccer, volleyball
W: basketball, soccer, softball

MORNINGSIDE COLLEGE
1501 Morningside Avenue
Sioux City, IA 51106
(712) 274-5127
www.morningside.edu
Contact: Dave Rebstock
Unspecified athletic aid available
M: baseball, basketball, cross country, football, track&field
W: basketball, cross country, soccer, softball, track&field, volleyball. Women's Non-aid: golf, tennis

MOUNT MERCY COLLEGE
1330 Elmhurst Drive
Cedar Rapids, IA 52402
(319) 363-1323
www.mtmercy.edu
Contact: John McCormick
Restrictions and notes: All aid is in the form of academic scholarships and grants for those who qualify.
Men's Non-aid: baseball, basketball, cross country, golf, soccer, track&field
Women's Non-aid: basketball, cross country, golf, soccer, softball, track&field, volleyball

NORTH IOWA AREA COMMUNITY COLLEGE
500 College Drive
Mason City, IA 50401-7299
Two-year college
(515) 422-4281
www.niacc.cc.ia.us
Contact: Jerry Dunbar
Unspecified athletic aid available
M: baseball, basketball, football, golf.

Men's Non-aid: cross country, skiing, volleyball, weightlifting
W: basketball, softball, volleyball.
Women's Non-aid: cross country skiing

NORTHWESTERN COLLEGE
101 Seventh Street SW
Orange City, IA 51041
(712) 737-7289
www.nwciowa.edu
Contact: Todd Barry
Unspecified athletic aid available
M: baseball, basketball, cross country, golf, football, indoor track, soccer, tennis, track&field, wrestling
W: basketball, cross country, golf, indoor track, soccer, softball, tennis, track&field, volleyball

SOUTHEASTERN COMMUNITY COLLEGE
1015 South Avenue
West Burlington, IA 52665
Two-year college
(319) 752-2731
www.secc.cc.ia.us
Contact: Steve Swanson
Unspecified athletic aid available
M: baseball, basketball
W: softball, volleyball

ST. AMBROSE UNIVERSITY
518 West Locust Street
Davenport, IA 52803
(319) 333-6229
www.sau.edu
Contact: Ray Shoulain
Unspecified athletic aid available
M: baseball, basketball, cross country, football, golf, soccer, tennis, track&field, volleyball
W: basketball, cheerleading, cross country, dance, golf, soccer, softball, tennis, track&field, volleyball

TEIKYO WESTMAR UNIVERSITY
1002 Third Avenue SE
Le Mars, IA 51031

(712) 546-2070
www.westmar.edu
Contact: Dennis J. Mertes
Men's Aid (#/$): 178/$339,186
Women's Aid (#/$): 64/$99,200
Restrictions and notes: In addition to
listed sports, this school offers women's
aid in Danceline.
M: baseball, basketball, football, golf,
indoor track, soccer, tennis, track&field,
wrestling
W: basketball, indoor track, soccer, soft-
ball, track&field, volleyball. Women's
Non-aid: golf

UNIVERSITY OF DUBUQUE
2000 University Avenue
Dubuque, IA 52001-5099
(800) 722-5583
www.dbq.edu
Contact: Dave Theilen
Men's Non-aid: baseball, basketball,
cross country, football, golf, tennis,
track&field, wrestling
Women's Non-aid: basketball, cross
country, golf, softball, tennis, track&field,
volleyball

UNIVERSITY OF IOWA
175 Carver-Hawkeye Arena
Iowa City, IA 52242-1020
(319) 335-9411
www.hawkeyesports.com
Contact: Phil Haddy
Unspecified athletic aid available
M: baseball, basketball, cross country,
football, golf, gymnastics, indoor track,
rowing, soccer, swimming-diving, tennis,
track&field, wrestling
W: basketball, cross country, field
hockey, golf, gymnastics, softball,
swimming- diving, tennis, track&field,
volleyball

UNIVERSITY OF NORTHERN IOWA
NW Upper UNI-Dome
Cedar Falls, IA 50614-0314
(319) 273-6354

www.uni.edu
Contact: Nancy Justis
Unspecified athletic aid available
M: baseball, basketball, cross country,
football, indoor track, track&field,
wrestling. Men's Non-aid: golf, swimming-diving, tennis
W: basketball, cross country, golf, indoor
track, softball, swimming-diving, tennis,
track&field, volleyball

UPPER IOWA UNIVERSITY
P.O. Box 1857
Fayette, IA 52142-1857
(319) 425-5700
www.uiu.edu
Contact: Sandy Miller
Men's Non-aid: baseball, basketball,
cross country, football, golf, tennis,
track&field, wrestling
Women's Non-aid: basketball, cross
country, golf, softball, tennis, track&field,
volleyball

WALDORF COLLEGE
106 South Sixth Street
Forest City, IA 50436
Two-year college
(515) 582-8182
www.waldorf.edu
Contact: Denny Gilbertson
Unspecified athletic aid available
M: baseball, basketball, football, golf,
soccer, wrestling
W: basketball, cheerleading, golf, soccer,
softball, volleyball

WARTBURG COLLEGE
222 Ninth Street NW
P.O. Box 1003
Waverly, IA 50677-0903
(319) 352-8277
www.wartburg.edu
Contact: Gary Grace
Men's Non-aid: baseball, basketball,
cross country, football, golf, indoor track,
soccer, tennis, track&field, wrestling
Women's Non-aid: basketball, cross

country, golf, indoor track, soccer, softball, tennis, track&field, volleyball

WILLIAM PENN COLLEGE
201 Trueblood Avenue
Oskaloosa, IA 52577
(515) 673-1001
www.wmpenn.edu
Contact: John Eberline
Men's Non-aid: baseball, basketball,
cross country, football, golf, indoor track,
tennis, track&field, wrestling
Women's Non-aid: basketball, cross
country, golf, indoor track, softball,
tennis, track&field, volleyball

Kansas

ALLEN COUNTY COLLEGE
1801 North Cottonwood
Iola, KS 66749
Two-year college
(316) 365-5116 ext. 206
www.allen.cc.ks.us
Contact: Kyle Malzahn
Unspecified athletic aid available
M: baseball, basketball, cross country,
golf, soccer, track&field
W: basketball, cross country, softball,
track&field, volleyball

BAKER UNIVERSITY
Eighth and Grove
P.O. Box 65
618 Eighth Street
Baldwin City, KS 66006-0065
(785) 594-8474
www.bakeru.edu
Contact: Dan Harris
Men's Aid (#/$): 77/unspecified $
Women's Aid (#/$): 22/unspecified $
M: baseball, basketball, cross country,
football, golf, indoor track, soccer, tennis,
track&field
W: basketball, cross country, indoor

track, soccer, softball, tennis, track&field,
volleyball

BARTON COUNTY COLLEGE
Route 3
Great Bend, KS 67530
Two-year college
(316) 792-9244
www.bart.an.cc.ks.us
Contact: Michael Doz
Men's Aid (#/$): 94/unspecified $
Women's Aid (#/$): 85/unspecified $
M: baseball, basketball, cross country,
golf, indoor track, track&field
W: basketball, cross country, indoor
track, softball, tennis, track&field, volley-
ball

BENEDICTINE COLLEGE
1020 North Second Street
Atchison, KS 66002
(913) 367-5340 ext. 2369
www.benedictine.edu
Contact: Jennifer Wright
Unspecified athletic aid available
M: baseball, basketball, football, golf,
indoor track, soccer, tennis, track&field
W: basketball, golf, indoor track, soccer,
softball, tennis, track&field, volleyball

BETHANY COLLEGE
425 North First Street
Lindsborg, KS 67456
(785) 227-3311 ext. 8184
www.bethanylb.edu
Contact: A. John Pearson
Men's Non-aid: baseball, basketball,
cross country, football, golf, soccer, softball, swimming-diving, tennis, track&field
Women's Non-aid: baseball, basketball,
cross country, field hockey, golf, softball,
swimming-diving, tennis, track&field,
volleyball

BETHEL COLLEGE
300 East 27th Street
North Newton, KS 67117-0531
(316) 283-2500

www.bethelks.edu
Contact: Diane Flickner
Unspecified athletic aid available
M: basketball, football, tennis,
track&field. Men's Non-aid: indoor track,
soccer
W: basketball, tennis, track&field, volley-
ball. Women's Non-aid: soccer

BUTLER COUNTY COMMUNITY COLLEGE
901 South Haverhill Road
El Dorado, KS 67042
Two-year college
(316) 322-3202
www.buccc.cc.ks.us
Contact: Kristin J. Blomquist
Men's Non-aid: baseball, basketball, golf,
racquetball, tennis
Women's Non-aid: softball, tennis, volleyball

CENTRAL CHRISTIAN COLLEGE
1200 South Main Street
McPherson, KS 67460
Two-year college
(316) 241-0723
www.centralchristian.edu
Contact: Gary Turner
Men's Non-aid: baseball, basketball,
cross country, golf, soccer
Women's Non-aid: basketball, cross
country, soccer, softball, tennis, volleyball

CLOUD COUNTY COMMUNITY COLLEGE
2221 Campus Drive
P.O. Box 1002
Concordia, KS 66901-1002
Two-year college
(785) 243-1435
www.cloudccc.cc.ks.us
Contact: Rod Stacken
Unspecified athletic aid available
M: baseball, basketball, cross country,
golf, indoor track, soccer, tennis,
track&field
W: basketball, cross country, indoor track,
softball, tennis, track&field, volleyball

COFFEYVILLE COMMUNITY COLLEGE
460 West 11th Street
Coffeyville, KS 67337
Two-year college
(316) 252-7095
www.ccc.cc.ks.us
Contact: Linda Moley
Unspecified athletic aid available
M: baseball, basketball, cross country,
football, golf, tennis, track&field
W: basketball, cross country, tennis,
track&field, volleyball

COLBY COMMUNITY COLLEGE
1255 South Range
Colby, KS 67701
Two-year college
(785) 462-3984
www.colby.cc.ks.us
Contact: Kurk Hunter
Unspecified athletic aid available
M: baseball, basketball, cross country,
indoor track, rodeo, track&field, wrestling
W: basketball, cross country, indoor
track, rodeo, softball, track&field, volleyball

COWLEY COUNTY COMMUNITY COLLEGE
P.O. Box 1147
Arkansas City, KS 67005-1147
Two-year college
(316) 441-5246
www.cowley.cc.ks.us
Contact: Tom Saia
Unspecified athletic aid available
M: baseball, basketball, golf, tennis
W: basketball, softball, tennis, volleyball

DODGE CITY COMMUNITY COLLEGE
2501 North 14th Avenue
Dodge City, KS 67801
Two-year college
(316) 227-9347
www.dccc.cc.ks.us
Contact: Casey Malek
Men's Aid (#/$): 163/unspecified $

Women's Aid (#/$): 84/unspecified $
M: baseball, basketball, cross country, football, golf, track&field
W: basketball, cross country, softball, track&field, volleyball

EMPORIA STATE UNIVERSITY
200 Commercial Street
Emporia, KS 66801-5087
(316) 341-5454
www.emporia.edu
Contact: Mason Logan
Unspecified athletic aid available
M: baseball, basketball, cross country, football, golf, indoor track, tennis, track&field
W: basketball, cross country, indoor track, softball, tennis, track&field, volleyball

FORT HAYS STATE UNIVERSITY
600 Park Street
Hays, KS 67601-4099
(785) 628-5903
www.fhsu.edu
Contact: Jack Kuestermeyer
Unspecified athletic aid available
M: baseball, basketball, cross country, football, golf, indoor track, tennis, track&field, wrestling
W: basketball, cross country, indoor track, softball, tennis, track&field, volleyball

FORT SCOTT COLLEGE
2108 South Horton
Fort Scott, KS 66701
Two-year college
(316) 223-2700
www.ftscott.cc.ks.us
Contact: Kevin Gundy
Unspecified athletic aid available
M: baseball, basketball, football, rodeo, track&field
W: basketball, rodeo, softball, volleyball

FRIENDS UNIVERSITY
2100 University
Wichita, KS 67213

(316) 295-5700
www.friends.edu
Contact: Anita K. Curry
Unspecified athletic aid available
M: baseball, basketball, football, soccer
W: basketball, softball, volleyball

GARDEN CITY COMMUNITY COLLEGE
801 Campus Drive
Garden City, KS 67846
Two-year college
(316) 276-9595
www.gccc.cc.ks.us
Contact: Dennis Perryman
M: baseball, basketball, cross country, football, indoor track, soccer, track&field, wrestling
W: basketball, cross country, indoor track, softball, track&field, volleyball

HASKELL INDIAN NATIONS UNIVERSITY
P.O. Box 461207
Lawrence, KS 66046
Two-year college
(785) 749-8459
www.haskell.edu
Contact: Phil Homeratha
Men's Non-aid: basketball, cross country, football, track&field
Women's Non-aid: basketball, cross country, golf, softball, track&field

HIGHLAND COMMUNITY COLLEGE
606 West Main Street
Highland, KS 66035
Two-year college
(785) 442-6000
www.highland.cc.ks.us
Contact: Tom Smith
Unspecified athletic aid available
M: baseball, basketball, cross country, football, indoor track, track&field
W: basketball, cross country, indoor track, softball, track&field, volleyball

HUTCHINSON COLLEGE
1300 North Plum
Hutchinson, KS 67501

Two-year college
(316) 665-3530
www.hutchcc.edu
Contact: Randy Stange
Unspecified athletic aid available
M: baseball, basketball, cross country,
football, golf, tennis, track&field
W: basketball, cross country, softball,
tennis, track&field, volleyball

JOHNSON COUNTY COMMUNITY COLLEGE

12345 College Boulevard
Overland Park, KS 66210
Two-year college
(913) 469-8500
www.jccc.net
Contact: Lori Mallory
Unspecified athletic aid available
M: baseball, basketball, cross country,
golf, indoor track, soccer, tennis,
track&field. Men's Non-aid: weightlifting
W: basketball, cross country, indoor
track, softball, tennis, track&field, volleyball

KANSAS CITY KANSAS COMMUNITY COLLEGE

7250 State Avenue
Kansas City, KS 66112
Two-year college
(913) 596-9656
www.kckcc.cc.ks.us
Contact: Alan Hoskins
Unspecified athletic aid available
M: baseball, basketball, cross country,
golf, soccer, track&field
W: basketball, cross country, soccer, soft-
ball, track&field, volleyball

KANSAS NEWMAN UNIVERSITY

3100 McCormick Avenue
Wichita, KS 67213
(316) 942-4291 ext. 118
www.ksnewman.edu
Contact: Diane Leary, CSJ
Unspecified athletic aid available
Restrictions and notes: 90% of all ath-
letes receive some assistance.

M: baseball, basketball, golf, soccer
W: basketball, golf, soccer, softball,
volleyball

KANSAS STATE UNIVERSITY

1800 College Avenue
Bramlage Coliseum
Manhattan, KS 66502-3355
(785) 532-6735
www.k-statesports.com
Contact: Kent Brown
Men's Aid (#/$): 194/$912,805
Women's Aid (#/$): 70/$347,298
M: baseball, basketball, football, golf,
indoor track, track&field
W: basketball, cross country, golf, indoor
track, tennis, track&field, volleyball

KANSAS WESLEYAN UNIVERSITY

100 East Claflin Avenue
Salina, KS 67401
(785) 827-5541
www.kwu.edu
Contact: Glenna Alexander
Unspecified athletic aid available
M: baseball, basketball, cross country,
football, indoor track, track&field
W: basketball, cross country, indoor
track, softball, track&field, volleyball

LABETTE COMMUNITY COLLEGE

200 South 14th Street
Parsons, KS 67357
Two-year college
(316) 421-0911
www.labette.cc.ks.us
Contact: Jody Thompson
Unspecified athletic aid available
M: baseball, basketball, wrestling
W: basketball, softball, tennis, volleyball

MCPHERSON COLLEGE

1600 East Euclid
P.O. Box 1402
McPherson, KS 67460
(316) 241-0731
www.mcpherson.edu
Contact: Glen E. Snell
Unspecified athletic aid available

M: basketball, cross country, football, golf, indoor track, tennis
W: basketball, cross country, golf, indoor track, tennis, volleyball

MIDAMERICA NAZARENE COLLEGE
2030 East College Way
Olathe, KS 66062-1899
(913) 791-3278
www.mnu.edu
Contact: Ron Hill
Men's Aid (#/$): 48/$47,500
Women's Aid (#/$): 8/$9,000
M: baseball, basketball, cross country, football, indoor track, track&field
W: basketball, cross country, indoor track, softball, track&field, volleyball

OTTAWA UNIVERSITY
1001 South Cedar Street
Ottawa, KS 66067-3399
(785) 242-5200
www.ott.edu
Contact: Andy Carrier
Unspecified athletic aid available
M: basketball, cross country, football, golf, soccer, tennis, track&field
W: basketball, cross country, golf, tennis, track&field, volleyball

PITTSBURG STATE UNIVERSITY
1701 South Broadway
Pittsburg, KS 66762
(316) 235-4067
www.pittstate.edu
Contact: Shannon Schmieg
Men's Aid (#/$): 68/$335,036
Women's Aid (#/$): 24/$118,248
M: baseball, basketball, cross country, football, golf, indoor track, track&field
W: basketball, cross country, indoor track, softball, track&field, volleyball

PRATT COMMUNITY COLLEGE
348 NE State Road 61
Pratt, KS 67124
Two-year college
(316) 672-5641

www.pcc.cc.ks.us
Contact: Jim Jackson
Unspecified athletic aid available
M: baseball, basketball, cheerleading, cross country, indoor track, rodeo, tennis, track&field
W: basketball, cheerleading, cross country, indoor track, rodeo, softball, tennis, track&field, volleyball

SAINT MARY COLLEGE
4100 South 4th Street
Leavenworth, KS 66048-5082
(913) 682-5151
www.smcks.edu
Contact: Tom Gioglio
Unspecified athletic aid available
M: baseball, basketball, football, golf, soccer, tennis
W: soccer, softball, volleyball

SEWARD COUNTY COMMUNITY COLLEGE
P.O. Box 1137
Liberal, KS 67905-1137
Two-year college
(316) 629-2615
www.sccc.cc.ks.us
Contact: Galen McSpadden
Unspecified athletic aid available
M: baseball, basketball, tennis
W: basketball, softball, tennis, volleyball

SOUTHWESTERN COLLEGE
100 College Street
Winfield, KS 67156
(316) 221-8327
www.sekans.edu
Contact: Bill Stevens
Unspecified athletic aid available
M: basketball, cross country, football, golf, indoor track, tennis, track&field
W: basketball, cross country, golf, indoor track, softball, tennis, track&field, volleyball

STERLING COLLEGE
Broadway and Cleveland
Sterling, KS 67579

(316) 278-4277
www.sterling.edu
Contact: Lonnie Kruse
Unspecified athletic aid available
M: baseball, basketball, cross country,
football, soccer, tennis, track&field
W: basketball, cross country, soccer,
softball, tennis, track&field, volleyball

TABOR COLLEGE
400 South Jefferson
Hillsboro, KS 67063
(316) 947-3121
www.tabor.edu
Contact: Don Brubacher
Unspecified athletic aid available
M: baseball, basketball, cross country,
football, golf, soccer, tennis,
track&field
W: basketball, cross country, softball,
tennis, track&field, volleyball

UNIVERSITY OF KANSAS
104 Allen Fieldhouse
Lawrence, KS 66045-8881
(785) 864-3470
www.jayhawks.org
Contact: Paul Buskirk
Unspecified athletic aid available
M: baseball, basketball, cross country,
football, golf, indoor track, swimming-
diving, tennis, track&field
W: basketball, cross country, golf,
indoor track, rowing, soccer, softball,
swimming-diving, tennis, track&field,
volleyball

WASHBURN UNIVERSITY
1700 SW College
Topeka, KS 66621
(785) 295-6334
(785) 231-1010 ext. 1791
www.washburn.edu
Contact: Gene Cassell
Men's Aid (#/$): 26/$53,551
Women's Aid (#/$): 11/$22,950
M: baseball, basketball, football, golf,
tennis
W: basketball, softball, tennis, volleyball

WICHITA STATE UNIVERSITY
1845 Fairmont
Wichita, KS 67260
(316) 978-3265
www.wichita.edu
Contact: Larry Rankin
Men's Aid (#/$): 48/$330,000
Women's Aid (#/$): 57/$356,000
M: baseball, basketball, cross country,
golf, indoor track, tennis, track&field
W: basketball, cross country, golf, indoor
track, softball, tennis, track&field,
volleyball

Kentucky

ALICE LLOYD COLLEGE
100 Purpose Road
Pippa Passes, KY 41844-9988
(606) 368-2101 ext. 4801
www.alicelloyd.edu
Contact: Nancy Melton
Unspecified athletic aid available
M: baseball, basketball. Men's Non-aid:
tennis
W: basketball. Women's Non-aid: softball

ASBURY COLLEGE
North Lexington Avenue
Wilmore, KY 40390-1148
(606) 858-3511 ext. 2470
www.asbury.edu
Contact: David Boillie
Restrictions and notes: No athletic scholarships. Full program of need and merit-
based aid.
Men's Non-aid: baseball, basketball,
cross country, soccer, swimming, tennis
Women's Non-aid: basketball, cross
country, softball, swimming, tennis,
volleyball

BELLARMINE COLLEGE
Newburg Road
Louisville, KY 40205-0671
(502) 452-8380

www.bellarmine.edu
Contact: David O'Toole
Unspecified athletic aid available
Restrictions and notes: Men's basketball,
10 full grants. Women's basketball, 10.
Partial tuition grants available in all other
sports.
M: baseball, basketball, cross country,
golf, soccer, tennis, track&field
W: basketball, cross country, field hockey,
golf, soccer, softball, tennis, track&field,
volleyball

BRESCIA UNIVERSITY
717 Frederica Street
Owensboro, KY 42303
(502) 685-3131
www.brescia.edu
Contact: John Reiley
Unspecified athletic aid available
M: baseball, basketball, golf, soccer
W: basketball, golf, softball, tennis, volleyball

CAMPBELLSVILLE UNIVERSITY
1 University Drive
Campbellsville, KY 42718-1657
(502) 789-5009
www.campbellsvil.edu
Contact: Matt Jenkins
Unspecified athletic aid available
M: baseball, basketball, cross country,
football, golf, soccer, swimming, tennis
W: basketball, cheerleading, cross country, soccer, softball, swimming, tennis,
volleyball

CUMBERLAND COLLEGE
7526 College Station Drive
Williamsburg, KY 40769
(606) 539-4389
www.cumber.edu
Contact: Floyd Stroud
Unspecified athletic aid available
M: baseball, basketball, cheerleading,
cross country, football, golf, judo, soccer,
swimming, tennis, track&field, wrestling
W: basketball, cheerleading, cross country, golf, judo, soccer, softball, swimming,
tennis, track&field, volleyball

EASTERN KENTUCKY UNIVERSITY
Lancaster Avenue
Richmond, KY 40475
(606) 622-2120
www.eku.edu
Contact: Jeff Long
Unspecified athletic aid available
M: baseball, basketball, cross country,
football, golf, indoor track, tennis,
track&field
W: basketball, cross country, golf, indoor
track, softball, tennis, track&field,
volleyball

GEORGETOWN COLLEGE
400 East College Street
Georgetown, KY 40324-1696
(502) 863-7972
www.gtc.georgetown.ky.us
Contact: Jason Falls
Men's Aid (#/$): 137/$406,804
Women's Aid (#/$): 27/$56,753
M: baseball, basketball, cross country,
football, golf, soccer, tennis
W: basketball, cross country, golf, soccer,
softball, tennis, volleyball

KENTUCKY CHRISTIAN COLLEGE
100 Academic Parkway
Grayson, KY 41143-1199
(606) 474-3215
www.kcc.edu
Contact: Bruce W. Dixon
Men's Non-aid: baseball, basketball,
cross country, soccer, tennis
Women's Non-aid: basketball, cross
country, tennis, volleyball

KENTUCKY STATE UNIVERSITY
400 East Main Street
Frankfort, KY 40601
(502) 227-6509
www.kysu.edu
Contact: Ron Braden
Unspecified athletic aid available
M: baseball, basketball, cross country,
football, golf, indoor track, tennis,
track&field

W: basketball, cross country, indoor track, softball, tennis, track&field, volleyball

KENTUCKY WESLEYAN COLLEGE
3000 Frederica Street
Owensboro, KY 42301-1039
(502) 683-4795
www.kwc.edu
Contact: Roy Pickerill
Unspecified athletic aid available
M: baseball, basketball, golf, soccer, tennis. Men's Non-aid: football
W: basketball, soccer, softball, tennis, volleyball

LEES JUNIOR COLLEGE
601 Jefferson
Jackson, KY 41339
Two-year college
(606) 666-7521
www.leecc.uky.edu
Contact: Kevin Keathley
Unspecified athletic aid available
M: basketball
W: softball

MOREHEAD STATE UNIVERSITY
UPO 1023
Morehead, KY 40351
(606) 783-2500
www.morehead-st.edu
Contact: Randy Stacy
Unspecified athletic aid available
M: baseball, basketball, cross country, golf, riflery, tennis, track&field
W: basketball, cross country, soccer, softball, tennis, track&field, volleyball

MURRAY STATE UNIVERSITY
Stewart Stadium
Room 217
Murray, KY 42071
(502) 762-4271
www.murraystate.edu
Contact: Chris Pope
Unspecified athletic aid available
M: baseball, basketball, cross country,

football, golf, indoor track, riflery, tennis, track&field
W: basketball, cross country, indoor track, riflery, tennis, track&field, volleyball

NORTHERN KENTUCKY UNIVERSITY
250 Albright Health Center
Nunn Drive
Higland Heights, KY 41076
(606) 572-5470
www.nku.edu
Contact: Don Owen
Unspecified athletic aid available
M: baseball, basketball, cross country, golf, soccer, tennis
W: basketball, cross country, golf, soccer, softball, tennis, volleyball

PADUCAH COMMUNITY COLLEGE
4810 Alben Barkley Drive
P.O. Box 7380
Paducah, KY 42002-7380
Two-year college
(270) 554-9200
www.pccky.edu
Contact: Tony McClure
Unspecified athletic aid available
M: baseball, basketball, golf, tennis
W: basketball, softball, tennis

PIKEVILLE COLLEGE
Sycamore Street
Pikeville, KY 41501
(606) 432-9382
www.pc.edu
Contact: Zelena O'Sullivan
Men's Aid (#/$>): 55/unspecified $
Women's Aid (#/$): 66/unspecified $
M: baseball, basketball, cross country, golf, tennis
W: basketball, cross country, golf, softball, tennis, volleyball

ST. CATHERINE COLLEGE
Bardstown Road
Springfield, KY 40061
Two-year college

(606) 336-5082
www.sccky.edu
Contact: Jeff Britt
Unspecified athletic aid available
M: baseball, basketball, golf, soccer
W: basketball, golf, soccer, softball

THOMAS MORE COLLEGE
333 Thomas More Parkway
Crestview Hills, KY 41017
(606) 344-3673
www.thomasmore.edu
Contact: James Neyhouse
Men's Non-aid: baseball, basketball, football, soccer, tennis
Women's Non-aid: basketball, soccer, softball, tennis, volleyball

TRANSYLVANIA UNIVERSITY
300 North Broadway
Lexington, KY 40508-1797
(606) 233-8202
www.transy.edu
Contact: Carol Jones
Men's Non-aid: baseball, basketball, cross country, golf, soccer, swimming, tennis
Women's Non-aid: basketball, cross country, field hockey, golf, soccer, softball, swimming, tennis

UNION COLLEGE
310 College Street
Barbourville, KY 40906
(606) 546-4151
www.unionky.edu
Contact: Jay Stancil
Unspecified athletic aid available
M: baseball, basketball, cross country, football, golf, soccer, swimming-diving
W: basketball, cross country, golf, soccer, softball, swimming-diving, volleyball

UNIVERSITY OF KENTUCKY
Memorial Coliseum
Room 23
Lexington, KY 40506-0019
(606) 257-8604
www.uky.edu

Contact: Sandra Bell
Men's Aid (#/$): 1355/$1,533,000
Women's Aid (#/$): 89/$,119,000
M: baseball, basketball, cross country, diving, football, golf, indoor track, riflery, soccer, swimming-diving, tennis, track&field
W: basketball, cross country, golf, gymnastics, indoor track, riflery, soccer, softball, swimming-diving, tennis, track&field, volleyball

UNIVERSITY OF LOUISVILLE
Floyd and Brandeis Street
Louisville, KY 40292
(502) 852-6581
www.uoflsports.com
Contact: Kenny Klein
Men's Aid (#/$): 231/$1,232,332
Women's Aid (#/$): 95/$449,050
M: baseball, basketball, cross country, diving, football, golf, indoor track, soccer, swimming, tennis, track&field
W: basketball, cross country, diving, field hockey, indoor track, soccer, swimming, tennis, track&field, volleyball

WESTERN KENTUCKY UNIVERSITY
Wetherby Administration Building
Bowling Green, KY 42101
(502) 745-4295
www.wku.edu
Contact: Paul Just
Unspecified athletic aid available
M: baseball, basketball, cross country, football, golf, indoor track, soccer, swimming-diving, tennis, track&field
W: basketball, cross country, golf, indoor track, swimming-diving, tennis, track&field, volleyball

Louisiana

CENTENARY COLLEGE
P.O. Box 41188
Shreveport, LA 71134-1188

(318) 869-5098
www.centenary.edu
Contact: Terry Ennis
Men's Aid (#/$): 37/$596,450
Women's Aid (#/$): 31/$491,564
M: baseball, basketball, cross country,
golf, riflery, soccer, tennis
W: basketball, cross country, gymnastics,
riflery, soccer, softball, tennis, volleyball

DELGADO COMMUNITY COLLEGE
615 City Park Avenue
New Orleans, LA 70119
Two-year college
(504) 483-4454
www.dcc.edu
Contact: Tim Galliano
Unspecified athletic aid available
M: baseball, basketball
W: basketball

DILLARD UNIVERSITY
2601 Gentilly Boulevard
New Orleans, LA 70122
(504) 283-8822
www.dillard.edu
Contact: Mary Horne
Unspecified athletic aid available
M: basketball
W: basketball

GRAMBLING STATE UNIVERSITY
P.O. Box N
Grambling, LA 71245
(318) 274-6199
www.gram.edu
Contact: Stanley O. Lewis
Men's Aid (#/$): 118/unspecified $
Women's Aid (#/$): 46/unspecified $
M: baseball, basketball, cross country,
football, golf, soccer, tennis
W: basketball, bowling, cross country, golf,
indoor track, softball, tennis, volleyball

LOUISIANA COLLEGE
1140 College Drive
Pineville, LA 71360
(318) 487-7275
www.lacollege.edu

Contact: Rae Champagne
Men's Aid (#/$): 12/$96,000
Women's Aid (#/$): 10/$80,000
M: baseball, basketball, cross country,
football, soccer
W: basketball, cross country, soccer, soft-
ball, tennis

LOUISIANA STATE UNIVERSITY (BATON ROUGE)
P.O. Box 25095
Baton Rouge, LA 70803
(225) 388-8226
www.sports.lsu.edu
Contact: Herb Vincent
Men's Aid (#/$): 73/$299,154
Women's Aid (#/$): 34/$159,444
M: baseball, basketball, cross country,
diving, football, golf, indoor track, swim-
ming, tennis, track&field
W: basketball, cross country, diving, golf,
gymnastics, indoor track, soccer, softball,
swimming, tennis, track&field, volleyball

LOUISIANA STATE UNIVERSITY (EUNICE)
P.O. Box 1129
Eunice, LA 70535
Two-year college
(318) 550-1394
www.lsue.edu
Contact: Kathy Barlow
Unspecified athletic aid available
M: baseball
W: basketball

LOUISIANA TECH UNIVERSITY
P.O. Box 3178
Tech Station
Ruston, LA 71272
(318) 257-036
www.latechsports.com
Contact: Jim Cakes
Unspecified athletic aid available
M: baseball, basketball, cross country,
football, golf, indoor track, track&field.
Men's Non-aid: power lifting, racquet-
ball, soccer
W: basketball, cross country, indoor

track, softball, tennis, track&field, volley-ball. Women's Non-aid: power lifting, racquetball, soccer

MCNEESE STATE UNIVERSITY
P.O. Box 92735
Lake Charles, LA 70609-2735
(318) 475-5200
www.mcneest.edu
Contact: Ron Everhart
Unspecified athletic aid available
M: baseball, basketball, cross country, football, golf, track&field
W: basketball, cross country, golf, soccer, softball, tennis, track&field, volleyball

NICHOLLS STATE UNIVERSITY
P.O. Box 2032
Thibodaux, LA 70310
(504) 448-4794
www.nich.edu
Contact: Stan Williamson
Unspecified athletic aid available
M: baseball, basketball, cross country, football, golf, track&field
W: basketball, cross country, soccer, soft-ball, tennis, track&field, volleyball

NORTHEAST LOUISIANA UNIVERSITY
100 Stadium Drive
Monroe, LA 71209
(318) 342-5368
www.ulm.edu
Contact: Diane Stark
Men's Aid (#/$): 130/$642,000
Women's Aid (#/$): 50/$232,000
M: baseball, basketball, cross country, football, golf, indoor track, softball, swimming, tennis, track&field
W: basketball, cross country, indoor track, soccer, softball, swimming, track&field, volleyball

NORTHWESTERN STATE UNIVERSITY OF LOUISIANA
Athletic Department
Athletic Fieldhouse
Natchitoches, LA 71497

(318) 357-4272
www.nsula.edu
Contact: Charlie Vienne
Men's Aid (#/$): 134/$800,000
Women's Aid (#/$): 81/$800,000
M: baseball, basketball, football, track&field
W: basketball, soccer, softball, tennis, track&field, volleyball

SOUTHEASTERN LOUISIANA UNIVERSITY
Box 880
Hammond, LA 70402
(504) 549-2253
www.selu.edu
Contact: Dick Sharp
Unspecified athletic aid available
M: baseball, basketball, cross country, golf, indoor track, tennis, track&field
W: basketball, cross country, indoor track, soccer, softball, tennis, track&field, volleyball

SOUTHERN UNIVERSITY AND A&M COLLEGE
Baton Rouge, LA 70813
(225) 771-4500
www.subr.edu
Contact: Cynthia Taiver
Unspecified athletic aid available
M: baseball, basketball, cross country, foot-ball, golf, indoor track, tennis, track&field
W: basketball, cross country, indoor track, track&field, volleyball. Women's Non-aid: tennis

TULANE UNIVERSITY
James W. Wilson Jr. Center
Benweiner Drive
New Orleans, LA 70118
(504) 865-5506 ext. 2
www.tulanegreenwave.com
Contact: Richard Page
Unspecified athletic aid available
M: baseball, cross country, football, golf, swimming, tennis, track&field
W: basketball, cross country, swimming, tennis, track&field, volleyball

UNIVERSITY OF LOUISIANA AT LAFAYETTE

201 Reinhardt Drive
Lafayette, LA 70504
(318) 482-5393
www.ragincajuns.com
Contact: Nelson Schexnayder
Men's Aid (#/$): 133/unspecified $
Women's Aid (#/$): 50/unspecified $
M: baseball, basketball, cross country, football, golf, indoor track, tennis, track&field
W: basketball, cross country, indoor track, softball, tennis, track&field, volleyball

UNIVERSITY OF NEW ORLEANS

Lakefront Arena
New Orleans, LA 70148-1613
(504) 280-6000
www.uno.edu
Contact: Ed Cassiere
Men's Aid (#/$): 33.2/$188,481
Women's Aid (#/$): 18.2/$121,737
M: baseball, basketball, cross country, golf, indoor track, swimming-diving, track&field
W: basketball, cross country, indoor track, swimming-diving, tennis, track&field, volleyball

XAVIER UNIVERSITY OF LOUISIANA

7325 Palmetto Street
New Orleans, LA 70125
(504) 486-7411
www.xula.edu
Contact: Todd Keller
Men's Aid (#/$): 15/$100,000
Women's Aid (#/$): 15/$100,000
M: basketball
W: basketball

Maine

BATES COLLEGE

News Bureau
Lewiston, ME 04240
(207) 786-6330
www.bates.edu
Contact: Adam Levin
Men's Non-aid: alpine skiing, baseball, basketball, cross country, cross country skiing, football, golf, indoor track, lacrosse, rowing, soccer, squash, swimming-diving, tennis, track&field
Women's Non-aid: alpine skiing, basketball, cross country, cross country skiing, field hockey, golf, indoor track, lacrosse, rowing, soccer, softball, squash, swimming-diving, tennis, track&field, volleyball

BOWDOIN COLLEGE

Public Relations Office
Brunswick, ME 04011
(207) 725-3326
www.bowdoin.edu
Contact: Jeffrey Ward
Restrictions and notes: No athletic scholarships available.
Men's Non-aid: alpine skiing, baseball, basketball, cross country, cross country skiing, football, golf, ice hockey, indoor track, lacrosse, sailing, soccer, squash, swimming-diving, tennis, track&field
Women's Non-aid: alpine skiing, basketball, cross country, cross country skiing, field hockey, golf, ice hockey, indoor track, lacrosse, sailing, soccer, squash, softball, swimming-diving, tennis, track&field, volleyball

HUSSON COLLEGE

One College Circle
Bangor, ME 04401-2999
(207) 941-7129
www.husson.edu
Contact: Julie Green
Men's Non-aid: baseball, basketball, golf, soccer
Women's Non-aid: basketball, softball, volleyball

THOMAS COLLEGE

180 West River Road
Waterville, ME 04901-5097

(207) 873-0771 ext. 404
www.thomas.edu
Contact: Chris Young
Men's Non-aid: baseball, basketball, golf, soccer, softball, tennis
Women's Non-aid: baseball, basketball, golf, soccer, softball, tennis

UNITY COLLEGE
HC 78, Box 1
Unity, ME 04988
(207) 948-3131
www.unity.edu
Contact: Gary Zane
Men's Non-aid: baseball, basketball, cross country, lacrosse, soccer
Women's Non-aid: basketball, cross country, soccer, softball, volleyball

UNIVERSITY OF MAINE
186 Memorial Gym
Orono, ME 04469
(207) 581-1052
www.umaine.edu
Contact: Suzanne Tyler
Unspecified athletic aid available
M: baseball, basketball, cross country, diving, football, ice hockey, soccer, swimming, track&field
W: basketball, cross country, diving, field hockey, ice hockey swimming, track&field, volleyball

UNIVERSITY OF MAINE (FORT KENT)
Pleasant Street
Fort Kent, ME 04743
(888) 879-8635
www.umtk.maine.edu
Contact: James J. Grandmaison
Men's Non-aid: basketball
Women's Non-aid: basketball, soccer, volleyball

UNIVERSITY OF MAINE (MACHIAS)
9 O'Brien Avenue
Machias, ME 04654-1397
(207) 255-1290

www.umm.maine.edu
Contact: Richard Ward
Men's Non-aid: basketball, soccer
Women's Non-aid: basketball, soccer, volleyball

UNIVERSITY OF MAINE (PRESQUE ISLE)
181 Main Street
Presque Isle, ME 04769-2888
(207) 768-9400
www.umpi.maine.edu
Contact: Barbara J. Bridges
Men's Aid (#/$): 3/$5,289
Women's Aid (#/$): 4/$4,519
Restrictions and notes: Tuition waivers also available to qualified student-athletes.
M: baseball, basketball, cross country, soccer
W: basketball, cross country, soccer, softball

UNIVERSITY OF NEW ENGLAND
11 Hills Beach Road
Biddeford, ME 04005
(207) 283-0171 ext. 2429
www.une.edu
Contact: Curt Smyth
Unspecified athletic aid available
M: basketball, cross country, golf, lacrosse, soccer
W: basketball, cross country, lacrosse, soccer, softball, volleyball

Maryland

BALTIMORE CITY COMMUNITY COLLEGE
2901 Liberty Heights Avenue
Baltimore, MD 21215
Two-year college
(410) 462-8320
www.bccc.state.md.us
Contact: Elliott Oppenheim
Unspecified athletic aid available

M: baseball, basketball, cross country, indoor track, track&field
W: basketball, cross country, indoor track, track&field

BOWIE STATE UNIVERSITY
Bowie, MD 20715
(301) 464-6683
www.bowiestate.edu
Contact: David Thomas
Men's Aid (#/$): 40/$135,629
Women's Aid (#/$): 40/$135,629
M: baseball, basketball, cross country, football, indoor track, track&field
W: basketball, cross country, indoor track, softball, track&field, volleyball

CATONSVILLE COMMUNITY COLLEGE
800 South Rolling Road
Baltimore, MD 21228
Two-year college
(410) 455-4197
www.ccbc.cc.md.us
Contact: Gary Keedy
Unspecified athletic aid available
M: baseball, basketball, lacrosse, soccer
W: basketball, lacrosse, soccer, softball, volleyball. Women's Non-aid: tennis

CECIL COMMUNITY COLLEGE
1000 North East Road
North East, MD 21901
Two-year college
(410) 287-6060
www.cecil.cc.md.us
Contact: Karen Weaver
Unspecified athletic aid available
M: baseball, basketball, soccer
W: basketball, softball, tennis, volleyball

CHARLES COUNTY COMMUNITY COLLEGE
P.O. Box 910
La Plata, MD 20646-0910
Two-year college
(301) 934-2251 ext. 7727
www.charles.cc.md.us
Contact: Trevor Carpenter

Unspecified athletic aid available
M: basketball, soccer, tennis
W: softball, volleyball

COLLEGE OF NOTRE DAME OF MARYLAND
701 North Charles Street
Baltimore, MD 21210
(410) 532-3588
www.ndm.edu
Contact: Margie Tversky
Women's Non-aid: basketball, cross country, field hockey, lacrosse, soccer, softball, swimming, tennis, volleyball

COLUMBIA UNION COLLEGE
Takoma Park, MD 20912
(301) 891-4195
www.cuc.edu
Contact: Laura Maxson
Unspecified athletic aid available
M: baseball, basketball, cross country, soccer, track&field
W: basketball, cross country, soccer, softball, tennis, track&field, volleyball

COPPIN STATE COLLEGE
2500 W. North Avenue
Baltimore, MD 21216
(410) 383-5400
www.coppin.umd.edu
Contact: Michael Preston
Unspecified athletic aid available
M: basketball, indoor track, track&field, wrestling. Men's Non-aid: baseball, cross country, soccer, tennis
W: basketball, indoor track, track&field. Women's Non-aid: cross country, tennis, volleyball

DUNDALK COMMUNITY COLLEGE
7200 Sollers Point Road
Baltimore, MD 21222
Two-year college
(410) 285-9849
www.ccbc.cc.md.us
Contact: Kody Syzmanski
Unspecified athletic aid available

M: baseball, basketball, soccer
W: soccer, softball

ESSEX COMMUNITY COLLEGE
7201 Rossville Boulevard
Baltimore, MD 21237
Two-year college
(410) 780-6479
www.essex.cc.md.us
Contact: Tim Puls
Unspecified athletic aid available
M: baseball, basketball, bowling, cross country, golf, indoor track, lacrosse, softball, tennis, track&field
W: basketball, bowling, cross country, field hockey, lacrosse, tennis, track&field, volleyball

FREDERICK COMMUNITY COLLEGE
7932 Opossumtown Pike
Frederick, MD 21702
Two-year college
(301) 846-2501
http://209.36.53.58
Contact: Tom Jandovitz
Men's Non-aid: baseball, basketball, golf, soccer
Women's Non-aid: basketball, golf

GARRETT COMMUNITY COLLEGE
P.O. Box 151
687 Mosser Road
McHenry, MD 21541
Two-year college
(301) 387-3052
www.garrett.gcc.cc.md.us
Contact: Ann Wellham
Unspecified athletic aid available
M: baseball, basketball
W: basketball, volleyball. Women's Non-aid: softball

GOUCHER COLLEGE
1021 Dulaney Valley Road
Baltimore, MD 21204
(410) 337-6383
www.goucher.edu
Contact: Ian Frink

Men's Non-aid: basketball, cross country, equestrian, lacrosse, soccer, swimming, tennis, track&field
Women's Non-aid: basketball, cross country, equestrian, field hockey, lacrosse, soccer, swimming, tennis, track&field, volleyball

HAGERSTOWN JUNIOR COLLEGE
11400 Robinwood Drive
Hagerstown MD 21742-6590
Two-year college
(301) 790-2800 ext. 367
www.hcc.cc.md.us
Contact: Brian Beck
Unspecified athletic aid available
M: baseball, basketball, cross country, indoor track, soccer, track&field
W: basketball, cross country, indoor track, softball, track&field, volleyball

HARFORD COMMUNITY COLLEGE
401 Thomas Run Road
Bel Air, MD 21015
Two-year college
(410) 836-4226
www.harford.cc.md.us
Contact: Allison Geczy
Unspecified athletic aid available
M: baseball, basketball, lacrosse, soccer. Men's Non-aid: tennis
W: basketball, field hockey, lacrosse, softball. Women's Non-aid: tennis

HOOD COLLEGE
401 Rosemont Avenue
Frederick, MD 21701-8575
(301) 696-3836
www.hood.edu
Contact: Eric Dennis
Women's Non-aid: basketball, field hockey, lacrosse, soccer, swimming, tennis, volleyball

JOHNS HOPKINS UNIVERSITY
Charles and 34th Streets
Baltimore, MD 21218
(410) 516-7490
www.jhu.edu

Contact: Faith Sheer
Unspecified athletic aid available
Restrictions and notes: Athletic aid only
in men's lacrosse.
M: lacrosse. Men's Non-aid: baseball,
basketball, crew, cross country, indoor
track, fencing, soccer, swimming-diving,
tennis, track&field, water polo, wrestling
W: lacrosse. Women's Non-aid: basketball, crew, cross country, fencing, field
hockey, indoor track, soccer, squash,
swimming-diving, tennis, track&field,
volleyball

LOYOLA COLLEGE
4501 North Charles Street
Baltimore, MD 21210
(410) 617-2777
www.loyola.edu
Contact: David Rosenfield
Men's Aid (#/$): 12/$70,500
Women's Aid (#/$): 18/$111,180
M: basketball, crew, cross country,
diving, golf, lacrosse, soccer, swimming,
tennis
W: basketball, crew, cross country,
diving, lacrosse, soccer, swimming,
tennis, volleyball

MONTGOMERY COLLEGE
7600 Takoma Avenue
Takoma Park, MD 20912
Two-year college
(301) 650-1447
www.mc.cc.md.us
Contact: Al Murray
Men's Non-aid: basketball, diving,
soccer, swimming, tennis
Women's Non-aid: diving, swimming,
tennis, volleyball

MORGAN STATE UNIVERSITY
1700 East Cold Spring Lane
Baltimore, MD 21251
(443) 885-3881
www.morgan.edu
Contact: Joe McIver
Unspecified athletic aid available
M: baseball, basketball, cross country,

football, indoor track, tennis, track&field
W: basketball, bowling, cross country,
indoor track, softball, tennis, track&field,
volleyball

MOUNT ST. MARY'S COLLEGE
Route 15
Emmitsburg, MD 21727
(301) 447-5384
www.mountathletics.com
Contact: Eric Klober
Men's Aid (#/$): 27/$602,100
Women's Aid (#/$): 22.5/$369,562
M: baseball, basketball, cross country,
golf, indoor track, lacrosse, soccer, tennis,
track&field
W: basketball, cross country, golf, indoor
track, lacrosse, soccer, softball, tennis,
track&field

PRINCE GEORGE'S COMMUNITY COLLEGE
301 Largo Road
Largo, MD 20774
Two-year college
(301) 322-0518
pgweb.pg.cc.md.us
Contact: Ronald Mann
Unspecified athletic aid available
M: baseball, basketball, bowling, soccer.
Men's Non-aid: golf, tennis
W: basketball, bowling, softball, volley-
ball. Women's Non-aid: tennis

TOWSON STATE UNIVERSITY
8000 York Road
Towson, MD 21252-0001
(410) 830-2232
www.towson.edu
Contact: Peter Schlehr
Unspecified athletic aid available
M: baseball, basketball, football, lacrosse,
soccer, swimming, tennis. Men's Non-
aid: cross country, golf, indoor track,
track&field
W: basketball, field hockey, soccer, gymnastics, lacrosse, softball, tennis, volleyball. Women's Non-aid: cross country,
indoor track, swimming, track&field

UNIVERSITY OF MARYLAND
College Park, MD 20742
(301) 314-7064
www.umterps.com
Contact: Dave Haglund
Men's Aid (#/$): 193.5/$1,682,369
Women's Aid (#/$): 107/$702,999
Restrictions and notes: Partials to fulls
available in various sports.
M: baseball, basketball, cross country,
football, golf, indoor track, lacrosse, soccer, swimming-diving, tennis, track&field,
wrestling
W: basketball, cross country, field hockey,
gymnastics, indoor track, lacrosse, soccer,
swimming-diving, tennis, volleyball

UNIVERSITY OF MARYLAND
(BALTIMORE COUNTY)
1000 Hilltop Circle
Baltimore, MD 21250
(410) 455-2012
www.umbc.edu
Contact: Kathy Zerrlaot
Men's Aid (#/$): 90/$350,000
Women's Aid (#/$): 90/$350,000
M: baseball, basketball, cross country,
golf, indoor track, lacrosse, soccer,
swimming-diving, tennis, track&field
W: basketball, cross country, golf, indoor
track, lacrosse, soccer, softball, swimming-
diving, tennis, track&field, volleyball

UNIVERSITY OF MARYLAND
(EASTERN SHORE)
Backbone Road
Princess Anne, MD 21853
(410) 651-6499
www.umes.umd.edu
Contact: Romanda Noble
Unspecified athletic aid available
M: baseball, basketball, cross country,
golf, indoor track, tennis, track&field
W: basketball, cross country, golf, indoor
track, tennis, track&field, volleyball

WASHINGTON COLLEGE
Washington Avenue
Chestertown, MD 21620
(410) 778-7238
www.washcoll.edu
Contact: Ann Schlottman
Men's Non-aid: basketball, rowing, sailing, soccer, swimming
Women's Non-aid: basketball, field hockey, rowing, sailing, soccer, swimming,
volleyball

WESTERN MARYLAND COLLEGE
2 College Hill
Westminster, MD 21157-4390
(410) 857-2291
www.wmdc.edu
Contact: Elliot Tannenbaum
Men's Non-aid: baseball, basketball,
cross country, football, golf, lacrosse,
soccer, swimming, tennis, track&field,
wrestling
Women's Non-aid: basketball, cross
country, field hockey, lacrosse, soccer,
softball, swimming, tennis, track&field,
volleyball

Massachusetts

AMERICAN INTERNATIONAL
COLLEGE
1000 State Street
Springfield, MA 01109-3189
(413) 747-6201
www.aic.edu
Contact: Frank Polera
Unspecified athletic aid available
M: baseball, basketball, football, ice
hockey. Men's Non-aid: golf, soccer,
tennis
W: basketball, softball, volleyball.
Women's Non-aid: soccer, tennis

AMHERST COLLEGE
P.O. Box 5000
Amherst, MA 01002-5000
(413) 542-2321
www.amherstcollege.edu
Contact: Peter Gooding

Men's Non-aid: baseball, basketball, cross country, football, golf, ice hockey, indoor track, lacrosse, soccer, squash, swimming-diving, tennis, track&field
Women's Non-aid: basketball, cross country, field hockey, golf, indoor track, lacrosse, soccer, squash, swimming-diving, tennis, track&field, volleyball

ASSUMPTION COLLEGE
500 Salisbury Street
Worcester, MA 01609
(508) 767-7416
www.assumption.edu
Contact: Rita Castagna
Men's Aid (#/$): 12/unspecified $
Women's Aid (#/$): 12/unspecified $
M: baseball, basketball, crew, cross country, football, ice hockey, lacrosse, soccer, tennis
W: basketball, crew, cross country, field hockey, lacrosse, soccer, softball, tennis, volleyball

ATLANTIC UNION COLLEGE
338 Main Street
South Lancaster, MA 01561-1000
(978) 368-2143
www.atlanticuc.edu
Contact: Lance Harris
Unspecified athletic aid available
M: basketball, soccer
W: volleyball

BABSON COLLEGE
Athletic Department
Babson Park, MA 02457-0310
(781) 239-4553
www.babson.edu
Contact: Chris Buck
Men's Non-aid: baseball, basketball, cross country, diving, golf, ice hockey, lacrosse, soccer, swimming, tennis
Women's Non-aid: basketball, cross country, diving, field hockey, lacrosse, soccer, softball, swimming, tennis, volleyball

BECKER COLLEGE
3 Paxton Street
Leicester, MA 01524

Two-year college
(508) 892-9471
www.beckercollege.edu
Contact: Gene Allex
Men's Non-aid: baseball, basketball, cross country, golf, soccer, tennis
Women's Non-aid: basketball, cross country, equestrian, field hockey, soccer, softball, volleyball

BENTLEY COLLEGE
175 Forest Street
Waltham, MA 02154-4705
(781) 891-2334
www.bentley.edu
Contact: Dick Lipe
Unspecified athletic aid available
M: basketball. Men's Non-aid: baseball, cross country, ice hockey, indoor track, lacrosse, soccer, swimming, tennis, track&field
W: basketball. Women's Non-aid: cross country, field hockey, indoor track, lacrosse, softball, swimming, tennis, track&field, volleyball

BOSTON COLLEGE
321 Conte Forum
Chestnut Hill, MA 02167
(617) 552-8570
www.dceagles.com
Contact: Allison Wallace
Unspecified athletic aid available
M: baseball, basketball, cross country, football, ice hockey, soccer, track&field. Men's Non-aid: alpine skiing, fencing, golf, ice hockey, lacrosse, sailing, swimming-diving, tennis, water polo, wrestling.
W: basketball, cross country, field hockey, golf, ice hockey, indoor track, lacrosse, soccer, softball, swimming-diving, tennis, track&field, volleyball. Women's Non-aid: alpine skiing, fencing, sailing

BOSTON UNIVERSITY
285 Babcock Street
Boston, MA 02215
(617) 353-2872

www.gobu.com
Contact: Ed Carpenter
Men's Aid (#/$): 302/$3,200,280
Women's Aid (#/$): 129/$1,310,452
M: basketball, crew, cross country,
diving, ice hockey, indoor track, soccer,
swimming, track&field, wrestling. Men's
Non-aid: golf, tennis
W: basketball, crew, cross country, diving,
field hockey, indoor track, lacrosse,
soccer, softball, swimming, tennis,
track&field. Women's Non-aid: golf

BRANDEIS UNIVERSITY
415 South Street
Waltham, MA 02454-9110
(781) 736-3631
www.brandeis.edu
Contact: Jack Molloy
Men's Non-aid: baseball, basketball, cross
country, fencing, indoor track, sailing, soccer, swimming-diving, tennis, track&field
Women's Non-aid: basketball, cross
country, fencing, indoor track, sailing,
soccer, softball, swimming-diving, tennis,
track&field

BRIDGEWATER STATE COLLEGE
Bridgewater, MA 02325
(508) 531-1352
www.bridgew.edu
Contact: John Harper
Men's Non-aid: baseball, basketball,
cross country, football, soccer, swimming, tennis, track&field, wrestling
Women's Non-aid: basketball, cross
country, field hockey, lacrosse, soccer,
swimming, tennis, track&field, volleyball

BUNKER HILL COMMUNITY COLLEGE
250 New Rutherford Avenue
Boston, MA 02129-2991
Two-year college
(617) 228-2422
www.bhcc.state.ma.us
Contact: Peter Siatta
Men's Non-aid: baseball, basketball,
soccer, softball

Women's Non-aid: baseball, basketball,
soccer, softball

CLARK UNIVERSITY
950 Main Street
Kneller Athletic Center
Worcester, MA 01610
(508) 793-7164
www.clarku.edu
Contact: Roxanne Ball
Men's Non-aid: baseball, basketball,
crew, cross country, lacrosse, soccer,
swimming-diving, tennis
Women's Non-aid: basketball, crew,
cross country, field hockey, soccer, softball, swimming-diving, tennis, volleyball

CURRY COLLEGE
1071 Blue Hill Avenue
Milton, MA 02186
(617) 333-2216
www.curry.edu
Contact: Teresa Hood
Men's Non-aid: baseball, basketball, football, ice hockey, lacrosse, soccer, tennis
Women's Non-aid: basketball, cross
country, lacrosse, soccer, softball, tennis

DEAN JUNIOR COLLEGE
99 Main Street
Franklin, MA 02038-1994
Two-year college
(508) 541-1552
www.dean.edu
Contact: Mary Anne Dean
Men's Non-aid: baseball, basketball, football, lacrosse, soccer, tennis
Women's Non-aid: basketball, soccer,
softball, volleyball

EASTERN NAZARENE COLLEGE
23 East Elm Avenue
Quincy, MA 02170
(617) 773-6350
www.enc.edu
Contact: Dr. Nancy Detwiler
Men's Non-aid: baseball, basketball,
cross country, soccer, tennis

Women's Non-aid: basketball, cross country, soccer, softball, tennis, volleyball

EMERSON COLLEGE
100 Beacon Street
Boston, MA 02116-1596
(617) 824-8690
www.emerson.edu
Contact: James Peckham
Men's Non-aid: baseball, basketball, golf, ice hockey, soccer, wrestling
Women's Non-aid: basketball, softball, tennis, volleyball

FITCHBURG STATE COLLEGE
160 Pearl Street
Fitchburg, MA 01420
(978) 665-3343
www.fsc.edu
Contact: Jonathan Harper
Men's Non-aid: baseball, basketball, cross country, football, ice hockey, soccer, track&field
Women's Non-aid: basketball, cross country, field hockey, softball, track&field, volleyball

GORDON COLLEGE
255 Grapevine Road
Wenham, MA 01984
(978) 927-2306 ext. 4335
www.gordonc.edu
Contact: Mark Sylvestor
Men's Non-aid: baseball, basketball, cross country, soccer, tennis
Women's Non-aid: basketball, cross country, field hockey, soccer, softball, tennis, volleyball

GREENFIELD COMMUNITY COLLEGE
One College Drive
Greenfield, MA 01301-9739
Two-year college
(413) 775-1000
www.gcc.mass.edu
Contact: John H. Palmer
Men's Non-aid: baseball, basketball, cross country, golf, soccer, volleyball

Women's Non-aid: basketball, cross country, golf, soccer, softball, volleyball

HARVARD UNIVERSITY
Murr Center
65 North Harvard Street
Boston, MA 02103
(617) 495-4848
www.fasharvard.edu
Contact: William J. Cleary
Men's Non-aid: alpine skiing, baseball, basketball, crew, cross country, cross country skiing, fencing, football, golf, ice hockey, lacrosse, sailing, soccer, squash, swimming-diving, tennis, track&field, volleyball, water polo, wrestling
Women's Non-aid: alpine skiing, basketball, crew, cross country, cross country skiing, fencing, field hockey, golf, ice hockey, lacrosse, sailing, soccer, softball, squash, swimming-diving, tennis, track&field, volleyball, water polo

COLLEGE OF THE HOLY CROSS
1 College Street
Worcester, MA 01610-2393
(508) 793-2571
www.holycross.edu
Contact: Frank Mastrandia
Unspecified athletic aid available
M: baseball, basketball, football, golf, ice hockey, indoor track, lacrosse, rowing, soccer, swimming-diving, tennis, track&field
W: basketball, crew, field hockey, ice hockey, indoor track, lacrosse, rowing, soccer, softball, swimming-diving, tennis, track&field, volleyball

MASSACHUSETTS BAY COMMUNITY COLLEGE
47 Flagg Drive
Framingham, MA 01701
Two-year college
(508) 875-5300
www.mbcc.mass.edu
Contact: Alan Harrison
Men's Non-aid: baseball, basketball, soccer

Women's Non-aid: basketball, soccer, softball

MASSACHUSETTS COLLEGE OF LIBERAL ARTS
375 Church Street
North Adams, MA 01247
(413) 662-5411 ext. 357
www.mcla.mass.edu
Contact: Tim Kelly
Unspecified athletic aid available
M: alpine skiing, baseball, basketball, cross country, ice hockey, soccer, softball, tennis
W: alpine skiing, baseball, basketball, cross country, soccer, softball, tennis, volleyball

MASSACHUSETTS INSTITUTE OF TECHNOLOGY
P.O. Box 397404
Cambridge, MA 02139-4307
(617) 253-7946
www.mit.edu
Contact: Roger F. Crosley
Men's Non-aid: alpine skiing, baseball, basketball, cross country, cross country skiing, fencing, football, golf, gymnastics, heavyweight crew, ice hockey, indoor track, lacrosse, lightweight crew, riflery, sailing, soccer, squash, swimming-diving, tennis, track&field, volleyball, water polo, wrestling
Women's Non-aid: alpine skiing, basketball, crew, cross country, cross country skiing, fencing, field hockey, gymnastics, ice hockey, indoor track, lacrosse, riflery, sailing, soccer, softball, swimming-diving, tennis, track&field, volleyball

MASSASOIT COMMUNITY COLLEGE
1 Massasoit Boulevard
Brockton, MA 02302
Two-year college
(508) 588-9100 ext. 1431
www.massasoit.mass.edu
Contact: Bruce Langlan
Unspecified athletic aid available

M: baseball, basketball, soccer
W: soccer, softball

MERRIMACK COLLEGE
315 Turnpike Street
North Andover, MA 01845
(978) 837-5341
www.merrimack.edu
Contact: Robert DeGregorio
Men's Aid (#/$): 10/$150,000
Women's Aid (#/$): 5/$75,000
M: baseball, ice hockey, soccer. Men's Non-aid: cross country, golf, lacrosse, tennis
W: basketball, soccer, softball. Women's Non-aid: cross country, field hockey, tennis, volleyball

MOUNT HOLYOKE COLLEGE
Kendall Hall
South Hadley, MA 01075
(413) 538-2472
www.mtholyoke.edu
Contact: Carol Anne Beach
Women's Non-aid: basketball, crew, cross country, equestrian, field hockey, golf, indoor track, lacrosse, soccer, softball, squash, swimming-diving, tennis, track&field, volleyball

MOUNT WACHUSETT COMMUNITY COLLEGE
444 Green Street
Gardner, MA 01440
Two-year college
(978) 632-6600
www.mwcc.mass.edu
Contact: Dr. Richard G. Rollins
Men's Non-aid: baseball, basketball, cross country, tennis
Women's Non-aid: basketball, cross country, softball, tennis

NICHOLS COLLEGE
Dudley Hill
Dudley, MA 01570
(508) 943-1560
www.nichols.edu
Contact: Mike Serijan

Men's Non-aid: baseball, basketball, football, golf, ice hockey, lacrosse, soccer, tennis
Women's Non-aid: basketball, field hockey, lacrosse, soccer, softball, tennis

NORTHEASTERN UNIVERSITY
360 Huntington Avenue
Boston, MA 02115
(617) 373-2691
www.gonv.com
Contact: Jack Grinold
Men's Aid (#/$): 31/$317,130
Women's Aid (#/$): 22/$225,060
No sports information provided

QUINSIGAMOND COLLEGE
670 West Boylston Street
Worcester, MA 01606
Two-year college
(508) 853-2300
www.qccmass.edu
Contact: Barry Glinski
Men's Non-aid: baseball, basketball, golf
Women's Non-aid: basketball, golf, softball

REGIS COLLEGE
235 Wellesley Street
Weston, MA 02493-1571
(781) 768-7141
www.regiscollege.edu
Contact: Dr. Judy Burling
Women's Non-aid: basketball, cross country, soccer, softball, swimming-diving, tennis, volleyball

SALEM STATE COLLEGE
352 Lafayette Street
Salem, MA 01970
(978) 542-6549
www.salem.mass.edu
Contact: Thomas Roundy
Men's Non-aid: baseball, basketball, cross country, golf, ice hockey, sailing, soccer, swimming, tennis, track&field
Women's Non-aid: basketball, cross country, field hockey, gymnastics, sailing, soccer, softball, swimming, tennis, track&field, volleyball

SMITH COLLEGE
Ainsworth Gym
Northampton, MA 01063
(413) 585-2701
www.smith.edu
Contact: Lynn Oberbillig
Women's Non-aid: alpine skiing, baseball, crew, cross country, equestrian, field hockey, indoor track, lacrosse, soccer, softball, squash, swimming-diving, tennis, track&field, volleyball

SPRINGFIELD COLLEGE
263 Alden Street
Springfield, MA 01109
(413) 748-3341
www.spfldcol.edu
Contact: Ken Cerino
Men's Non-aid: baseball, basketball, cross country, football, gymnastics, indoor track, lacrosse, soccer, swimming-diving, tennis, track&field, volleyball, wrestling
Women's Non-aid: basketball, cross country, field hockey, gymnastics, indoor track, lacrosse, soccer, softball, swimming-diving, tennis, track&field, volleyball

SPRINGFIELD TECHNICAL COMMUNITY COLLEGE
1 Armory Square
Springfield, MA 01105
Two-year college
(413) 781-7822
www.stcc.mass.edu
Contact: J. Vincent Grassetti
Men's Non-aid: baseball, basketball, soccer
Women's Non-aid: basketball, soccer, softball

STONEHILL COLLEGE
320 Washington Street
North Easton, MA 02357
(508) 565-1000
www.stonehill.edu
Contact: Eileen O'Leary
Men's Aid (#/$): 12/$200,700

Women's Aid (#/$): 12/$200,700
M: basketball. Men's Non-aid: baseball, cross country, equestrian, football, ice hockey, indoor track, sailing, soccer, tennis, track&field
W: basketball. Women's Non-aid: cross country, equestrian, indoor track, sailing, soccer, softball, tennis, track&field, volleyball

SUFFOLK UNIVERSITY
8 Ashburton Place
Boston, MA 02108
(617) 573-8379
www.suffolk.edu
Contact: Jim Nelson
Men's Non-aid: baseball, basketball, cross country, golf, ice hockey, soccer, tennis
Women's Non-aid: basketball, cross country, softball, tennis, volleyball

TUFTS UNIVERSITY
Cousens Gym
College Avenue
Medford, MA 02155
(617) 628-5000
www.tufts.edu
Contact: Ann Marie Rowe
Men's Non-aid: baseball, basketball, crew, cross country, football, golf, ice hockey, indoor track, lacrosse, soccer, squash, swimming-diving, tennis, track&field
Women's Non-aid: basketball, crew, cross country, fencing, field hockey, indoor track, lacrosse, sailing, soccer, softball, squash, swimming-diving, tennis, track&field, volleyball

UNIVERSITY OF MASSACHUSETTS (AMHERST)
205 Boyden Building
Amherst, MA 01003
(413) 545-2691
www.umass.edu
Contact: Al Rufe
Unspecified athletic aid available
M: alpine skiing, baseball, basketball,

cross country, football, gymnastics, ice hockey, indoor track, lacrosse, soccer, swimming-diving, tennis, track&field, water polo
W: alpine skiing, basketball, crew, cross country, field hockey, gymnastics, indoor track, lacrosse, soccer, softball, swimming-diving, tennis, track&field, volleyball, water polo

UNIVERSITY OF MASSACHUSETTS (BOSTON)
Harbor Campus
Boston, MA 02125-3393
(617) 287-7815
www.umb.edu
Contact: Chuck Sullivan
Men's Non-aid: baseball, basketball, cross country, football, ice hockey, indoor track, lacrosse, soccer, tennis, track&field, wrestling
Women's Non-aid: basketball, cross country, indoor track, soccer, softball, tennis, track&field, volleyball

UNIVERSITY OF MASSACHUSETTS (DARTMOUTH)
285 Old Westport Road
North Dartmouth, MA 02747-2300
(508) 999-8727
www.umassd.edu
Contact: William Gathright
Men's Non-aid: baseball, basketball, cross country, fencing, golf, ice hockey, indoor track, soccer, swimming-diving, tennis, track&field
Women's Non-aid: basketball, cross country, fencing, field hockey, indoor track, softball, swimming-diving, tennis, track&field, volleyball

UNIVERSITY OF MASSACHUSETTS (LOWELL)
One University Avenue
Lowell, MA 01854
(978) 934-2310
www.uml.edu
Contact: B.L. Elfring
Men's Aid (#/$): 92/$492,432

Women's Aid (#/$): 48/$207,687
Restrictions and notes: All athletic aid
restricted to Massachusetts residents
except hockey and basketball.
M: baseball, basketball, cross country,
golf, ice hockey, indoor track, soccer,
swimming-diving, tennis, track&field,
wrestling. Men's Non-aid: crew, football
W: basketball, cross country, field hockey,
indoor track, softball, tennis, track&field,
volleyball. Women's Non-aid: crew

WELLESLEY COLLEGE
106 Central Street
Wellesley, MA 02181
(781) 283-1000
www.wellesley.edu
Contact: Glenna Fortier
Women's Non-aid: basketball, crew, cross
country, fencing, field hockey, lacrosse,
soccer, squash, swimming-diving, tennis,
volleyball

WESTERN NEW ENGLAND COLLEGE
1215 Wilbraham Road
Springfield, MA 01119
(413) 782-1227
www.wnec.edu
Contact: Gene Gumbs
Men's Non-aid: baseball, basketball,
bowling, football, golf, ice hockey,
lacrosse, soccer, tennis, volleyball,
wrestling
Women's Non-aid: basketball, bowling,
field hockey, lacrosse, soccer, softball,
tennis, volleyball

WESTFIELD STATE COLLEGE
Western Avenue
Westfield, MA 01086
(413) 568-3311
www.wsc.mass.edu
Contact: Mickey Curtis
Men's Non-aid: baseball, basketball,
cross country, football, indoor track,
soccer, track&field
Women's Non-aid: basketball, cross
country, field hockey, indoor track,

soccer, softball, swimming-diving,
track&field, volleyball

WILLIAMS COLLEGE
P.O. Box 676
Williamstown, MA 01267
(413) 597-4982
www.williams.edu
Contact: Dick Quinn
Men's Non-aid: baseball, basketball,
crew, cross country, cross country skiing,
football, golf, ice hockey, indoor track,
lacrosse, soccer, squash, swimming-
diving, tennis, track&field, volleyball,
wrestling
Women's Non-aid: basketball, crew, cross
country, cross country skiing, ice hockey,
indoor track, lacrosse, soccer, softball,
squash, swimming-diving, tennis,
track&field, volleyball

WORCESTER STATE COLLEGE
486 Chandler Street
Worcester, MA 01602-2597
(508) 929-8128
www.worc.mass.edu
Contact: Bruce Baker
Unspecified athletic aid available
M: baseball, basketball, cross country,
football, golf, ice hockey, indoor track,
tennis, track&field
Women's Non-aid: baseball, basketball,
cross country, field hockey, indoor track,
softball, tennis, track&field, volleyball

Michigan

ADRIAN COLLEGE
110 South Madison Street
Adrian, MI 49221
(517) 265-5161
www.adrian.edu
Contact: Darcy Gifford
Men's Non-aid: baseball, basketball,
cross country, football, golf, soccer,

tennis, track&field
Women's Non-aid: basketball, cross country, golf, soccer, softball, tennis, track&field, volleyball

ALBION COLLEGE
611 East Porter
Albion, MI 49224
(517) 629-0434
www.albion.edu
Contact: J. Robin Hartman
Men's Non-aid: baseball, basketball, cross country, football, golf, soccer, swimming-diving, tennis, track&field
Women's Non-aid: basketball, cross country, golf, soccer, softball, swimming-diving, tennis, track&field, volleyball

ALMA COLLEGE
614 West Superior Street
Alma, MI 48801-1599
(517) 463-7114
www.alma.edu
Contact: Eric Sieger
Men's Non-aid: baseball, basketball, cross country, football, golf, soccer, swimming-diving, tennis, track&field
Women's Non-aid: basketball, cross country, golf, soccer, softball, swimming-diving, tennis, track&field, volleyball

AQUINAS COLLEGE
1607 Robinson Road
Grand Rapids, MI 49506
(616) 459-8281 ext. 3120
www.aquinas.edu
Contact: Jan Bennett
Unspecified athletic aid available
M: baseball, basketball, cross country, golf, indoor track, soccer, tennis, track&field
W: basketball, cheerleading, cross country, dance, golf, indoor track, soccer, softball, tennis, track&field, volleyball

CALVIN COLLEGE
3201 Burton SE
Grand Rapids, MI 49546
(616) 957-6475
www.calvin.edu
Contact: Phil de Haan
Men's Non-aid: baseball, basketball, cross country, diving, golf, soccer, swimming, tennis, track&field
Women's Non-aid: basketball, cross country, diving, golf, soccer, softball, swimming, tennis, track&field, volleyball

CENTRAL MICHIGAN UNIVERSITY
108 West Hall
Mount Pleasant, MI 48859
(517) 774-3277
www.cmich.edu
Contact: Fred Stabley, Jr.
Men's Aid (#/$): 127/unspecified $
Women's Aid (#/$): 895/unspecified $
M: baseball, basketball, cross country, football, indoor track, track&field, wrestling
W: basketball, cross country, field hockey, gymnastics, indoor track, soccer, softball, track&field, volleyball

CONCORDIA COLLEGE
4090 Geddes Road
Ann Arbor, MI 48105
(734) 995-7344
www.ccad.edu
Contact: Chip Wildy
Men's Aid (#/$): 27/$32,000
Women's Aid (#/$): 30/$33,800
M: baseball, basketball, cross country, soccer, track&field
W: basketball, cross country, soccer, softball, track&field, volleyball

DELTA COLLEGE
University Center, MI 48710
Two-year college
(517) 686-9025
www.delta.edu
Contact: Chuck Lord
Unspecified athletic aid available
M: basketball, soccer. Men's Non-aid: golf, tennis
W: basketball, softball, volleyball

DETROIT COLLEGE OF BUSINESS
4801 Oakman Boulevard
Dearborn, MI 48126
(313) 581-4400
www.dcb.edu
Contact: Kevin Brazell
Men's Aid (#/$): 16/$77,760
M: golf, soccer

EASTERN MICHIGAN UNIVERSITY
200 Bowen Fieldhouse
Ypsilanti, MI 48197
(734) 487-5279
www.emich.edu
Contact: Lee Reed
Unspecified athletic aid available
M: baseball, basketball, cross country, football, golf, indoor track, soccer, swimming-diving, tennis, track&field, wrestling
W: basketball, cross country, golf, gymnastics, indoor track, soccer, softball, swimming-diving, tennis, track&field, volleyball

FERRIS STATE COLLEGE
901 South State Street
110 West Building
Big Rapids, MI 49307
(231) 591-2863
www.ferris.edu
Contact: Tom Kirinovic
Unspecified athletic aid available
M: basketball, cross country, football, golf, ice hockey, indoor track, tennis, track&field
W: basketball, cross country, golf, indoor track, soccer, softball, tennis, track&field, volleyball

GLEN OAKS COMMUNITY COLLEGE
62249 Shimmel Road
Centreville, MI 49032
Two-year college
(616) 467-9945
www.glenoaks.cc.mi.us
Contact: Kathy Patrick
Men's Aid (#/$): 22/unspecified $

Women's Aid (#/$): 36/unspecified $
M: baseball, basketball, golf
W: basketball, golf, softball, tennis, volleyball

GRAND RAPIDS BAPTIST SEMINARY OF CORNERSTONE UNIVERSITY
1001 East Beltline Avenue NE
Grand Rapids, MI 49525
(616) 949-5300
www.cornerstone.edu.lgrbsnsf
Contact: John F. VerBerkmoes
Men's Aid (#/$): 17/$18,888
Women's Aid (#/$): 6/$10,550
M: basketball, cross country, golf, soccer, tennis, track&field
W: basketball, cheerleading, cross country, soccer, softball, track&field, volleyball

GRAND RAPIDS COMMUNITY COLLEGE
143 Bostwick Avenue NE
Grand Rapids, MI 49503
Two-year college
(616) 234-4261
www.grcc.mi.us
Contact: Rick Vanderveen
Unspecified athletic aid available
M: baseball, basketball, cross country, football, swimming-diving, tennis, wrestling
W: basketball, cross country, softball, swimming-diving, tennis, volleyball

GRAND VALLEY STATE COLLEGE
1 Campus Drive
Allendale, MI 49401
(616) 895-3275
www.gvsu.edu
Contact: Tim Selgo
Unspecified athletic aid available
M: baseball, basketball, cross country, football, indoor track, swimming-diving, track&field
W: basketball, cross country, indoor track, softball, swimming-diving, track&field, volleyball

HENRY FORD COMMUNITY COLLEGE
5101 Evergreen Road
Dearborn, MI 48128
Two-year college
(313) 845-9647
www.henryford.cc.mi.us
Contact: Nancy Bryden
Men's Aid (#/$): 32/unspecified $
Women's Aid (#/$): 37/unspecified $
M: basketball
W: basketball, volleyball

HIGHLAND PARK COMMUNITY COLLEGE
Glendale at Third Avenue
Highland Park, MI 48203
Two-year college
(313) 252-2093
Contact: Glen Donahue
Unspecified athletic aid available
M: baseball, basketball, tennis
W: basketball, cross country

HILLSDALE COLLEGE
201 Oak Street
Hillsdale, MI 49242
(517) 437-7364
www.hillsdale.edu
Contact: Mike Kovalchik
Men's Aid (#/$): 23/$114,096
Women's Aid (#/$): 23/$114,096
M: baseball, basketball, cross country, football, indoor track, soccer, track&field. Men's Non-aid: tennis
W: basketball, cross country, indoor track, soccer, softball, swimming, track&field, volleyball. Women's Non-aid: tennis

HOPE COLLEGE
137 East 12th Street
Holland, MI 49423
(616) 395-7860
www.hope.edu
Contact: Tom Renner
Men's Non-aid: baseball, basketball, cross country, football, golf, soccer, swimming-diving, tennis, track&field, water polo

Women's Non-aid: basketball, cross country, field hockey, softball, swimming-diving, tennis, track&field, volleyball

KALAMAZOO COLLEGE
1200 Academy Street
Kalamazoo, MI 49007
(616) 337-7287
www.kzoo.edu
Contact: Steve Wideen
Men's Non-aid: baseball, basketball, cross country, football, golf, soccer, swimming-diving, tennis
Women's Non-aid: basketball, cross country, soccer, softball, swimming-diving, tennis, volleyball

KALAMAZOO VALLEY COMMUNITY COLLEGE
6767 West "O" Avenue
Kalamazoo, MI 49003-4070
Two-year college
(616) 372-5395
www.kvcc.edu
Contact: Dick Shilts
Unspecified athletic aid available
M: baseball, basketball, golf, tennis
W: basketball, golf, softball, tennis, volleyball

LAKE MICHIGAN COLLEGE
2755 East Napier Avenue
Benton Harbor, MI 49022
Two-year college
(616) 927-8165
www./mc.cc.mi.us
Contact: Kathy Leitke
Men's Aid (#/$): 24/unspecified $
Women's Aid (#/$): 26/unspecified $
M: baseball, basketball, golf
W: basketball, softball, volleyball

LAKE SUPERIOR STATE UNIVERSITY
Norris Center
Sault Sainte Marie, MI 49783
(906) 635-2601
www.lssu.edu
Contact: Bill Crawford

Men's Aid (#/$): 37/$406,445
Women's Aid (#/$): 31/$340,573
M: basketball, cross country, golf, ice hockey, indoor track, tennis, track&field
W: basketball, cross country, indoor track, softball, tennis, track&field, volleyball

LANSING COMMUNITY COLLEGE
P.O. Box 40010
Lansing, MI 48901-7210
Two-year college
(517) 483-1624
www.lansing.cc.mi.us
Contact: Richard Mull
Unspecified athletic aid available
M: baseball, basketball, cross country, golf
W: basketball, cross country, golf, softball, volleyball

MACOMB COMMUNITY COLLEGE
14500 East 12 Mile Road
Warren, MI 48093-3896
Two-year college
(810) 445-7346
www.macomb.cc.mi.us
Contact: Nancy Kosinski
Unspecified athletic aid available
M: baseball, basketball, cross country, golf, indoor track, soccer, tennis, track&field
W: cross country, indoor track, softball, tennis, track&field, volleyball

MADONNA UNIVERSITY
36600 Schoolcraft Road
Livonia, MI 48150-1173
(734) 432-5604
www.munet.edu
Contact: Bryan Rizzo
Unspecified athletic aid available
M: baseball, basketball, golf
W: basketball, softball, volleyball

ROCHESTER COLLEGE
800 West Avon Road
Rochester Hills, MI 48307
Two-year college
(248) 218-2135

www.rc.edu
Contact: Garth Pleasant
Unspecified athletic aid available
M: baseball, basketball, cross country, soccer, track&field
W: basketball, cross country, softball, track&field, volleyball

MICHIGAN STATE UNIVERSITY
223 Jenison Field House
East Lansing, MI 48824
(517) 432-5510
www.msuspartans.com
Contact: Charles Wilson
Unspecified athletic aid available
M: baseball, basketball, cross country, football, golf, gymnastics, ice hockey, lacrosse, soccer, swimming-diving, tennis, track&field, wrestling. Men's Non-aid: fencing
W: basketball, cross country, field hockey, golf, gymnastics, soccer, softball, swimming-diving, tennis, track&field, volleyball

MICHIGAN TECHNOLOGICAL UNIVERSITY
1400 Townsend Drive
Athletic Department
Houghton, MI 49931-1295
(906) 487-2990
www.mtu.edu
Contact: Suzanne Sanregret
Men's Aid (#/$): 47/unspecified $
Women's Aid (#/$): 17/unspecified $
M: basketball, football, ice hockey. Men's Non-aid: cross country, cross country skiing, tennis, track&field
W: basketball, tennis, volleyball. Women's Non-aid: cross country, cross country skiing, track&field

MOTT COMMUNITY COLLEGE
1401 East Court Street BFH
Flint, MI 48503
Two-year college
(810) 762-0417
www.mcc.edu
Contact: Richard Zanetta

Unspecified athletic aid available
M: baseball, basketball, cross country, golf
W: basketball, softball, volleyball

MUSKEGON COMMUNITY COLLEGE
221 South Quarterline Road
Muskegon, MI 49442
Two-year college
(231) 777-0381
www.muskegon.cc.mi.us
Contact: Gene Gifford
Unspecified athletic aid available
M: baseball, basketball, golf, wrestling
W: basketball, golf, softball, volleyball

NORTHERN MICHIGAN UNIVERSITY
607 Cohodas Building
Marquette, MI 49855
(906) 227-1012
www.nmu.edu
Contact: Jim Pinar
Men's Aid (#/$): 69.9/$530,482
Women's Aid (#/$): 31.6/$228,599
M: basketball, cross country, cross country skiing, football, ice hockey, golf
W: alpine skiing, basketball, cross country, cross country skiing, swimming-diving, volleyball, tennis

NORTHWOOD INSTITUTE
3225 Cook Road
Midland, MI 48640
(517) 837-4239
www.northwood.edu
Contact: Dave Marsh
Unspecified athletic aid available
M: baseball, basketball, cross country, football, golf, indoor track, lacrosse, tennis, track&field
W: basketball, cross country, indoor track, soccer, softball, track&field, volleyball

OAKLAND COMMUNITY COLLEGE
Auburn Hills Campus
2900 Featherstone Road
Auburn Hills, MI 48326-2845
Two-year college
www.occ.cc.mi.us
Contact: Prentice Ryan
Unspecified athletic aid available
M: basketball, cross country, golf, tennis
W: basketball, cross country, softball, tennis, volleyball

OAKLAND UNIVERSITY
Lepley Sports Center
Rochester, MI 48309-4401
(248) 370-4008
www.oakland.edu
Contact: Amy Stabley Hirshman
Men's Aid (#/$): 10/$25,909
Women's Aid (#/$): 8/$29,153
M: basketball, cross country, diving, golf, soccer, swimming, tennis
W: basketball, diving, swimming, tennis, volleyball

OLIVET COLLEGE
News and Information Department
Olivet, MI 49076
(616) 749-7672
www.olivetnet.edu
Contact: Charlie Wilson
Men's Non-aid: baseball, basketball, cross country, football, golf, soccer, swimming-diving, track&field, wrestling
Women's Non-aid: basketball, golf, soccer, softball, swimming-diving, tennis, track&field, volleyball

SAGINAW VALLEY STATE UNIVERSITY
2250 Pierce Road
University Center, MI 48710
(517) 791-7306
www.svsu.edu
Contact: Dick Thompson
Unspecified athletic aid available
M: baseball, basketball, bowling, cross country, football, golf, indoor track, soccer, track&field
W: basketball, cross country, indoor track, soccer, softball, tennis, track&field, volleyball

SAINT MARY'S COLLEGE
3535 Indian Trail
Orchard Lake, MI 48324
(248) 682-1885
www.stmarys-orchardlake.edu
Contact: Darrell Brockway
Women's Non-aid: basketball, fencing, soccer, softball, swimming-diving, tennis, track&field, volleyball

SCHOOLCRAFT COLLEGE
18600 Haggerty Road
Livonia, MI 48152
Two-year college
(734) 462-4400
www.lv.schoolcraft.cc.mi.us
Contact: Ed Kavanaugh
Men's Aid (#/$): 28/$18,500
Women's Aid (#/$): 29/$18,500
M: basketball, golf, soccer
W: basketball, cross country, soccer, volleyball

SIENA HEIGHTS UNIVERSITY
1247 East Siena Heights Drive
Adrian, MI 49221
(517) 263-0731
www.sienahts.edu
Contact: Scott McClure
Men's Aid (#/$): 160/$175,893
Women's Aid (#/$): 113/$127,895
M: baseball, basketball, cross country, golf, soccer, tennis, track&field
W: basketball, cross country, soccer, softball, tennis, track&field, volleyball

SPRING ARBOR COLLEGE
College Street
Spring Arbor, MI 49283
(517) 750-1200
www.arbor.edu
Contact: Hank Burbridge
Unspecified athletic aid available
M: baseball, basketball, cross country, golf, indoor track, soccer, tennis, track&field
W: basketball, cross country, indoor track, soccer, softball, tennis, track&field, volleyball

UNIVERSITY OF DETROIT MERCY
4001 West McNichols Road
P.O. Box 19900
Detroit, MI 48219-0900
(313) 933-1745
www.udmercy.edu
Contact: Mark Engel
Unspecified athletic aid available
M: baseball, basketball, cross country, fencing, golf, indoor track, soccer, tennis, track&field
W: basketball, cross country, equestrian, indoor track, soccer, softball, tennis, track&field

UNIVERSITY OF MICHIGAN
1000 South State Street
Ann Arbor, MI 48109-2201
(734) 647-1194
www.mgoblue.com
Contact: Leigh Evilisizer
Men's Aid (#/$): 189.8/$3,301,000
Women's Aid (#/$): 102.4/$1,645,000
M: baseball, basketball, cross country, football, golf, gymnastics, ice hockey, indoor track, rowing, swimming-diving, tennis, track&field, wrestling
W: basketball, cross country, field hockey, golf, gymnastics, indoor track, rowing, softball, swimming-diving, track&field, tennis

WAYNE STATE UNIVERSITY
101 Matthaei Building
Detroit, MI 48202-3489
(313) 577-7542
www.wayne.edu
Contact: Lisa McCoy
Unspecified athletic aid available
M: baseball, basketball, cross country, fencing, football, golf, swimming-diving, tennis
W: basketball, fencing, softball, swimming-diving, tennis, volleyball

WESTERN MICHIGAN UNIVERSITY
102 West Hall
Kalamazoo, MI 49008
(616) 387-8620

www.wmubroncos.com
Contact: Kathy B. Beauregard
Men's Aid (#/$):152/unspecified $
Women's Aid (#/$): 66/unspecified $
M: baseball, basketball, cross country, football, gymnastics, ice hockey, indoor track, soccer, tennis, track&field
W: basketball, cross country, gymnastics, indoor track, softball, tennis, track&field, volleyball

Minnesota

ANOKA-RAMSEY COLLEGE
11200 Mississippi Boulevard NW
Coon Rapids, MN 55433
Two-year college
(612) 422-3526
www.ar.cc.mn.us
Contact: Paul Fessler
Men's Non-aid: baseball, basketball, football, wrestling
Women's Non-aid: basketball, softball, volleyball

AUGSBURG COLLEGE
2211 Riverside Avenue
Minneapolis, MN 55454
(612) 330-1677
www.augsburg.edu
Contact: Don Stoner
Men's Non-aid: baseball, basketball, cross country, football, ice hockey, indoor track, soccer, track&field, wrestling
Women's Non-aid: basketball, cross country, indoor track, soccer, softball, track&field

BEMIDJI STATE UNIVERSITY
1500 Birchmont Drive NE
Bemidji, MN 56601-2699
(218) 755-2940
www.bemidjisus.edu
Contact: Ronald Christian
Unspecified athletic aid available
M: basketball, football, golf, ice hockey, indoor track, track&field

W: basketball, cross country, golf, ice hockey, indoor track, soccer, softball, tennis, track&field, volleyball

BETHANY LUTHERAN COLLEGE
700 Luther Drive
Mankato, MN 56001-6163
Two-year college
(507) 344-7000
www.blc.edu
Contact: Lyle Jones
Men's Aid (#/$): 60/$72,000
Women's Aid (#/$): 60/$72,000
M: baseball, basketball, soccer
W: basketball, softball, volleyball

BETHEL COLLEGE
3900 Bethel Drive
St. Paul, MN 55112
(651) 638-6394
www.bethel.edu
Contact: Greg Peterson
Men's Non-aid: baseball, basketball, cross country, football, golf, ice hockey, indoor track, soccer, tennis, track&field
Women's Non-aid: basketball, cross country, indoor track, soccer, softball, tennis, track&field, volleyball

CARLETON COLLEGE
100 South College Street
Northfield, MN 55057-4016
(507) 646-4185
www.carleton.edu
Contact: Rob Lewis
Men's Non-aid: alpine skiing, baseball, basketball, cross country, cross country skiing, football, golf, indoor track, soccer, swimming-diving, tennis, track&field, volleyball, wrestling
Women's Non-aid: alpine skiing, basketball, cross country, cross country skiing, golf, indoor track, soccer, swimming-diving, tennis, track&field, volleyball

CENTRAL LAKES COLLEGE
College Drive
Brainerd, MN 56401
Two-year college

(218) 855-8196
www.clc.cc.mn.us
Contact: John De Breeze
Men's Non-aid: baseball, basketball, football, tennis
Women's Non-aid: basketball, softball, tennis, volleyball

COLLEGE OF SAINT BENEDICT
37 South College Avenue
St. Joseph, MN 56374-2099
(320) 363-5073
www.csbsju.edu
Contact: Mike Durbin
Women's Non-aid: basketball, cross country, diving, soccer, softball, swimming, tennis, volleyball

COLLEGE OF ST. SCHOLASTICA
Duluth, MN 55811
(218) 723-6397
www.ess.edu
Contact: Jim Datka
Men's Non-aid: baseball, basketball, cross country, ice hockey, soccer, tennis
Women's Non-aid: basketball, cross country, soccer, softball, tennis, volleyball

CONCORDIA COLLEGE
901 South 8th Street
Moorhead, MN 56562
(218) 299-3194
www.cord.edu
Contact: Jerry Pyle
M: baseball, basketball, cross country, football, golf, ice hockey, soccer, tennis, track&field, wrestling
W: basketball, cross country, golf, ice hockey, soccer, softball, swimming, tennis, track&field, volleyball

CONCORDIA UNIVERSITY
275 Syndicate Street North
St. Paul, MN 55104
(651) 641-8278
www.csp.edu
Contact: Dan O'Brien

Men's Non-aid: badminton, baseball, basketball, bowling, football, golf, soccer, tennis, track&field, wrestling
Women's Non-aid: basketball, softball, tennis, track&field, volleyball

FERGUS FALLS COMMUNITY COLLEGE
1414 College Way
Fergus Falls, MN 56537
Two-year college
(218) 739-7538
www.ff.cc.mu.us
Contact: Dave Retzlaff
Men's Non-aid: baseball, basketball, football, golf
Women's Non-aid: basketball, golf, softball, volleyball

GUSTAVUS ADOLPHUS COLLEGE
800 College Avenue
St. Peter, MN 56082
(507) 933-7647
www.gustavus.edu
Contact: Tim Kennedy
Men's Non-aid: baseball, basketball, cross country, football, golf, ice hockey, indoor track, nordic skiing, soccer, swimming-diving, tennis, track&field
Women's Non-aid: basketball, cross country, golf, gymnastics, ice hockey, indoor track, nordic skiing, soccer, softball, swimming-diving, tennis, track&field, volleyball

HAMLINE UNIVERSITY
1536 Hewitt Avenue
St. Paul, MN 55104-1284
(651) 523-2280
www.hamline.edu
Contact: Richard Manderfeld
Men's Non-aid: baseball, basketball, cross country, diving, football, golf, ice hockey, indoor track, soccer, softball, swimming-diving, track&field, wrestling
Women's Non-aid: basketball, cross country, diving, gymnastics, indoor track, softball, swimming-diving, track&field, volleyball

HIBBING COMMUNITY COLLEGE
1515 East 25th Street
Hibbing, MN 55746
Two-year college
(218) 262-6749
www.hcc.mnscu.edu
Contact: Anna Van Tassel
Men's Non-aid: baseball, basketball, football, ice hockey
Women's Non-aid: basketball, softball, volleyball

INVER HILLS COMMUNITY COLLEGE
2500 80th Street East
Inver Grove Heights, MN 55076-3224
Two-year college
(651) 450-6676
www.ih.cc.mn.us
Contact: Tom Johnson
Men's Non-aid: baseball, basketball, football, golf, track&field
Women's Non-aid: basketball, softball, track&field, volleyball

MACALESTER COLLEGE
1600 Grand Avenue
St. Paul, MN 55105-1899
(651) 696-6533
www.macalstr.edu
Contact: Andy Johnson
Men's Non-aid: baseball, basketball, cross country, football, golf, indoor track, nordic skiing, soccer, swimming-diving, tennis, track&field
Women's Non-aid: basketball, cross country, golf, indoor track, nordic skiing, soccer, softball, swimming-diving, tennis, track&field, volleyball

MANKATO STATE UNIVERSITY
Box 28, MSU
Mankato, MN 56001
(507) 389-3625
www.mankato.msus.edu
Contact: Paul Allan
Unspecified athletic aid available
M: baseball, basketball, cross country, football, golf, ice hockey, indoor track, swimming-diving, tennis, track&field, wrestling
W: basketball, cross country, golf, indoor track, softball, swimming-diving, tennis, track&field, volleyball

MINNEAPOLIS COMMUNITY & TECHNICAL COLLEGE
1501 Hennepin Avenue S.
Minneapolis, MN 55403
Two-year college
(612) 341-7070
www.mctc.mnsc.edu
Contact: Jay Pivec
Men's Non-aid: basketball, golf
Women's Non-aid: golf, volleyball

MOORHEAD STATE UNIVERSITY
Moorhead, MN 56563
(218) 236-2113
www.moorhead.msus.edu
Contact: Larry Scott
Unspecified athletic aid available
M: basketball, cross country, football, track&field, wrestling
W: basketball, cross country, golf, soccer, softball, swimming, tennis, track&field, volleyball

NORTH HENNEPIN COMMUNITY COLLEGE
7411 85th Avenue North
Brooklyn Park, MN 55445-2299
Two-year college
(612) 424-0796
www.nh.cc.mn.us
Contact: Julie Zieminski
Men's Non-aid: baseball, football, golf, tennis
Women's Non-aid: golf, softball, tennis, volleyball

NORTHLAND COMMUNITY & TECHNICAL COLLEGE
1101 Highway One East
Thief River Falls, MN 56701
Two-year college
(218) 681-0725

www.northland.cc.mn.us
Contact: Rick Nelson
Men's Non-aid: basketball, football, golf
Women's Non-aid: basketball, volleyball

NORTHWESTERN COLLEGE
3003 Snelling Avenue North
St. Paul, MN 55113-1598
(651) 631-5219
www.nwc.edu
Contact: Richard Blatchley
Men's Non-aid: baseball, basketball, cross country, football, golf, soccer, softball, tennis, track&field, wrestling
Women's Non-aid: baseball, basketball, softball, track&field, volleyball

RAINY RIVER COMMUNITY COLLEGE
Highway 71
International Falls, MN 56649-2187
Two-year college
(218) 285-7722
www.rr.cc.mns.cu.edu
Contact: Dave Horner
Men's Non-aid: basketball, ice hockey
Women's Non-aid: basketball, volleyball

RIVERLAND COMMUNITY COLLEGE
1900 8th Avenue NW
Austin, MN 55912-1470
Two-year college
(507) 433-0543
www.riverland.cc.mn.us
Contact: David Lillemon
Men's Non-aid: baseball, basketball, golf, soccer, tennis
Women's Non-aid: basketball, golf, soccer, softball, tennis, volleyball

ROCHESTER COMMUNITY & TECHNICAL COLLEGE
851 30th Avenue SE
Rochester, MN 55904
Two-year college
(507) 285-7219
www.roch.edu
Contact: Ann Green

Men's Non-aid: baseball, basketball, football, golf, wrestling
Women's Non-aid: basketball, golf, soccer, softball, volleyball

SAINT JOHN'S UNIVERSITY
Wimmer Hall 208
Collegeville, MN 56321
(320) 363-2595
www.csbsju.edu
Contact: Michael Hemmesch
Men's Non-aid: baseball, basketball, cross country, diving, football, golf, ice hockey, indoor track, soccer, swimming, tennis, track&field, wrestling

SAINT OLAF COLLEGE
1520 St. Olaf Avenue
Northfield, MN 55057-1098
(507) 646-3834
www.stolaf.edu
Contact: Scott King
Men's Non-aid: alpine skiing, baseball, basketball, cross country, cross country skiing, football, golf, ice hockey, indoor track, soccer, swimming-diving, tennis, track&field, wrestling
Women's Non-aid: alpine skiing, basketball, cross country, cross country skiing, golf, indoor track, soccer, softball, swimming-diving, tennis, track&field, volleyball

ST. CLOUD STATE UNIVERSITY
720 Fourth Avenue South
St. Cloud, MN 56301-4498
(320) 255-2141
www.stcloudstate.edu
Contact: Anne Abicht
Unspecified athletic aid available
M: baseball, basketball, cross country, football, golf, ice hockey, indoor track, swimming-diving, tennis, track&field, wrestling
W: basketball, indoor track, softball, swimming-diving, tennis, track&field, volleyball. Women's Non-aid: cross country, golf.

SOUTHWEST STATE UNIVERSITY
1501 State Street
Marshall, MN 56258
(507) 537-7177
www.southwest.msus.edu
Contact: Kelly Loft
Unspecified athletic aid available
M: baseball, basketball, football, wrestling
W: basketball, golf, soccer, softball,
tennis, volleyball

UNIVERSITY OF MINNESOTA
(Duluth)
10 University Drive, c/o Athletics
Duluth, MN 55812-2496
(218) 726-8720
www.d.umn.edu
Contact: Bill Haller
Unspecified athletic aid available
M: baseball, basketball, cross country,
football, ice hockey, indoor track, tennis,
track&field, wrestling
W: basketball, cross country, indoor
track, softball, tennis, track&field,
volleyball

UNIVERSITY OF MINNESOTA
(Morris)
600 East 4th Street
Morris, MN 56267
(320) 589-2111
www.mrs.umn.edu
Contact: Judy Riley
Men's Non-aid: baseball, basketball,
cross country, football, golf, tennis,
track&field, wrestling
Women's Non-aid: basketball, golf, softball, tennis, track&field, volleyball

UNIVERSITY OF MINNESOTA
(Twin Cities)
516 15th Avenue SE
Minneapolis, MN 55455
(612) 625-4090
www.gophersports.com
Contact: M – Marc Ryan, W – Becky
Bohm
Unspecified athletic aid available
M: baseball, basketball, cross country,
football, golf, gymnastics, ice hockey,
indoor track, swimming-diving, tennis,
track&field, wrestling
W: basketball, crew, cross country, golf,
gymnastics, ice hockey, indoor track,
soccer, softball, swimming-diving, tennis,
track&field, volleyball

UNIVERSITY OF ST. THOMAS
Mail #5003
2115 Summit Avenue
St. Paul, MN 55105
(651) 962-5903
www.stthomas.edu
Contact: Gene McGiven
Men's Non-aid: baseball, basketball,
cross country, football, golf, ice hockey,
indoor track, soccer, swimming-diving,
tennis, track&field, wrestling
Women's Non-aid: basketball, cross
country, golf, ice hockey, indoor track,
soccer, softball, swimming-diving, tennis,
track&field, volleyball

WINONA STATE UNIVERSITY
P.O. Box 5838
Winona, MN 55987-5838
(507) 457-5576
www.winona.msus.edu
Contact: Michael Herzberg
Unspecified athletic aid available
M: baseball, basketball, football, golf,
tennis
W: basketball, cross country, golf, gym-
nastics, indoor track, soccer, softball,
tennis, track&field, volleyball

WORTHINGTON COMMUNITY COLLEGE
1450 College Way
Worthington, MN 56187
Two-year college
(507) 372-2904
www.wr.cc.mn.us
Contact: Arlo Mogck
Unspecified athletic aid available
Restrictions and notes: Athletic aid
provides free books for all men and
women student-athletes.

M: basketball, football, wrestling
W: basketball, volleyball

Mississippi

ALCORN STATE UNIVERSITY
P.O. Box 510-ASU
Lorman, MS 39096
(601) 877-6500
www.alcorn.edu
Contact: Lloyd Hill
Unspecified athletic aid available
M: baseball, basketball, cross country,
football, golf, indoor track, track&field
W: basketball, cross country, tennis,
track&field, volleyball

BELHAVEN COLLEGE
1500 Peachtree Street
Jackson, MS 39202
(601) 968-5986
www.belhaven.edu
Contact: Dr. Joseph Cole
Unspecified athletic aid available
M: baseball, basketball, cross country,
golf, soccer, softball, tennis
W: basketball. Women's Non-aid: baseball, cross country, soccer, softball,
tennis, volleyball

BLUE MOUNTAIN COLLEGE
Box 336
Blue Mountain, MS 38610
(601) 685-4771
www.baptistschools.org
Contact: Johnnie Armstrong
Women's Aid (#/$): 17/unspecified $
W: basketball, tennis

COAHOMA COMMUNITY COLLEGE
3240 Friars Point Road
Clarksdale, MS 38614-9799
Two-year college
(601) 627-2571
www.ccc.cc.ms.us
Contact: John Mayo

Unspecified athletic aid available
M: basketball, football. Men's Non-aid:
baseball, golf, track&field
W: basketball. Women's Non-aid: softball

COPIAH-LINCOLN COMMUNITY COLLEGE
P.O. Box 649
Wesson, MS 39191
Two-year college
(601) 643-8381
www.colin.cc.ms.us
Contact: Gwyn Young
Unspecified athletic aid available
M: baseball, basketball, football, soccer,
tennis
W: basketball, soccer, softball, tennis

DELTA STATE UNIVERSITY
P.O. Box D-3
Cleveland, MS 38733
(601) 846-4677
www.deltast.edu
Contact: Fred Sington
Unspecified athletic aid available
M: baseball, basketball, football, golf,
swimming-diving, tennis
W: basketball, cross country, softball,
swimming-diving, tennis

HINDS COMMUNITY COLLEGE
P.O. Box 1286
Raymond, MS 39154
Two-year college
(601) 857-3362
www.hinds.cc.ms.us
Contact: Dot Murphy
Unspecified athletic aid available
M: basketball, football. Men's Non-aid:
baseball, golf, synchronized swimming,
track&field
W: basketball. Women's Non-aid: softball,
synchronized swimming

HINDS COMMUNITY COLLEGE
Utica Campus
Utica, MS 39175
Two-year college
(601) 885-6062

www.hinds.cc.ms.us
Contact: Earl Joe Nelson
Unspecified athletic aid available
M: basketball
W: basketball

HOLMES JUNIOR COLLEGE
P.O. Box 369
Goodman, MS 39079
Two-year college
(601) 472-2312
www.holmes.cc.ms.us
Contact: James G. Williams
Unspecified athletic aid available
M: baseball, basketball, football, golf,
soccer, tennis, track&field
W: basketball, soccer, tennis, track&field

ITAWAMBA COMMUNITY COLLEGE
602 West Hill Street
Fulton, MS 38843
Two-year college
(662) 862-8000
www.icc.cc.ms.us
Contact: Donna Thomas
Men's Aid (#/$): 53/unspecified $
Women's Aid (#/$): 10/unspecified $
M: baseball, basketball, cross country,
football, golf, soccer, tennis
W: basketball, cross country, golf, soccer,
softball, tennis

JACKSON STATE UNIVERSITY
P.O. Box 17490
Jackson, MS 39217-0390
(601) 968-2273
www.jsu.edu
Contact: Sam Jefferson
Unspecified athletic aid available
M: baseball, basketball, cross country,
football, golf, indoor track, tennis,
track&field
W: basketball, cross country, indoor track,
softball, tennis, track&field, volleyball

JONES COUNTY JUNIOR COLLEGE
900 South Court Street
Ellisville, MS 39437

Two-year college
(601) 477-4032
www.jcjc.cc.ms.us
Contact: George Harrison
Unspecified athletic aid available
M: baseball, basketball, football, golf,
soccer, tennis, track&field
W: basketball, soccer, softball, tennis

MARY HOLMES COLLEGE
P.O. Drawer 1257
Highway 50 West
West Point, MS 39773-1257
Two-year college
(662) 494-6820
www.maryholmes.edu
Contact: Joe N. Nimock
Unspecified athletic aid available
M: baseball, basketball. Men's Non-aid:
cross country
W: baseball, basketball. Women's Non-
aid: cross country, softball

MISSISSIPPI COLLEGE
Box 4009
Clinton, MS 39058
(601) 925-3255
www.mc.edu
Contact: Dr. Terry McMillan
Unspecified athletic aid available
M: baseball, basketball, cross country,
football, golf, tennis, track&field
W: basketball, softball, tennis,
volleyball

MISSISSIPPI DELTA COMMUNITY COLLEGE
P.O. Box 668
Moorhead, MS 38761
Two-year college
(601) 246-6472
www.mdcc.cc.ms.us.
Contact: Buddy Walden
Men's Aid (#/$): 94/$84,600
Women's Aid (#/$): 15/$13,500
M: baseball, basketball, football. Men's
Non-aid: track&field
W: basketball, softball. Women's Non-aid:
tennis

MISSISSIPPI GULF COAST COMMUNITY COLLEGE

P.O. Box 64
Perkinston, MS 39573
Two-year college
(601) 928-6224
www.mgccc.cc.ms.us
Contact: Chris Calcote
Unspecified athletic aid available
M: baseball, basketball, football, golf, soccer, tennis, track&field
W: basketball, soccer, softball, tennis

MISSISSIPPI STATE UNIVERSITY

P.O. Box 5325
Mississippi State, MS 39762
(601) 325-2808
www.msstate.edu
Contact: Larry Templeton
Unspecified athletic aid available
M: baseball, basketball, football, golf, indoor track, soccer, tennis, track&field. Men's Non-aid: bowling, fencing, martial arts, power lifting, riflery, rodeo, rugby, water skiing, weightlifting
W: basketball, golf, indoor track, soccer, softball, tennis, track&field, volleyball. Women's Non-aid: bowling, martial arts, power lifting, riflery, rodeo, water skiing, weightlifting

MISSISSIPPI UNIVERSITY FOR WOMEN

Box 1636
Columbus, MS 39701
(601) 329-7119
www.muw.edu
Contact: Bobby Galinsky
Unspecified athletic aid available
W: basketball, softball, tennis, volleyball

MISSISSIPPI VALLEY STATE UNIVERSITY

P.O. Box 743
Itta Bena, MS 38941
(662) 254-3550
www.musu.edu

Contact: Chuck Prophet
Unspecified athletic aid available
M: baseball, basketball, cross country, football, golf, indoor track, tennis, track&field. Men's Non-aid: diving, gymnastics, martial arts, power lifting, swimming, volleyball
W: basketball, cross country, golf, indoor track, tennis, track&field, volleyball. Women's Non-aid: diving, softball

NORTHEAST MISSISSIPPI COMMUNITY COLLEGE

101 Cunningham Boulevard
Booneville, MS 38829
Two-year college
(601) 728-7751
www.necc.cc.ms.us
Contact: David Carnell
Unspecified athletic aid available
M: basketball, football, tennis. Men's Non-aid: baseball, golf
W: basketball, softball, tennis

NORTHWEST MISSISSIPPI COMMUNITY COLLEGE

P.O. Box 7039
Senatobia, MS 38668
Two-year college
(662) 562-3276
www.nwcc.cc.ms.us
Contact: Mr. Brett Brown
Unspecified athletic aid available
M: baseball, basketball, football, golf, rodeo, tennis
W: basketball, rodeo, softball, tennis

RUST COLLEGE

150 Rust Avenue
Holly Springs, MS 38635
(601) 252-8000
www.rustcollege.edu
Contact: Paula Clark
Unspecified athletic aid available
M: baseball, basketball, cross country, tennis, track&field
W: basketball, cross country, tennis, track&field

TOUGALOO COLLEGE
500 W. Countyline Road
Tougaloo, MS 39174
(601) 978-1198
www.tougaloo.edu
Contact: James Turner
Men's Aid (#/$): 14/$32,745
Women's Aid (#/$): 12/$26,210
M: basketball, track&field
W: basketball, track&field

UNIVERSITY OF MISSISSIPPI
P.O. Box 217
Oxford, MS 38677
(601) 232-7522
www.olemisssports.com
Contact: Langston Rogers
Unspecified athletic aid available
M: baseball, basketball, cross country,
football, golf, indoor track, tennis,
track&field
W: basketball, cross country, golf, rifle,
soccer, tennis, track&field, volleyball

**UNIVERSITY OF SOUTHERN
MISSISSIPPI**
Box 5161
Hattiesburg, MS 39406-5161
(601) 266-4503
www.usmathletics.edu
Contact: M.R. Napier
Men's Aid (#/$): 159/$1,005,774
Women's Aid (#/$): 91/$519,817
M: baseball, basketball, cross country,
football, golf, indoor track, tennis,
track&field
W: basketball, cross country, golf, indoor
track, soccer, softball, tennis, track&field,
volleyball

Missouri

AVILA COLLEGE
11901 Wornall Road
Kansas City, MO 64145-1698
(816) 942-8400 ext. 223

www.avila.edu
Contact: Michael Kosier
Unspecified athletic aid available
M: baseball, basketball, football, soccer
W: basketball, soccer, softball, volleyball

BAPTIST BIBLE COLLEGE
628 East Kearney
Springfield, MO 65803
(417) 268-6000
www.seebbc.edu
Contact: Dick Bemarkt
Men's Non-aid: basketball
Women's Non-aid: volleyball

CENTRAL METHODIST COLLEGE
411 Central Methodist Square
Fayette, MO 65248
(660) 248-3391
www.cmc.edu
Contact: Debbie Thompson
Aid (#/$): 335/$425,138 (M&W)
M: baseball, basketball, cross country,
football, golf, soccer, tennis, track&field,
volleyball
W: basketball, cross country, golf, soccer,
softball, tennis, track&field, volleyball

**CENTRAL MISSOURI STATE
UNIVERSITY**
Room 203, Multipurpose Building
Warrensburg, MO 64093
(660) 543-4312
www.cmsu.edu
Contact: Cindy Parks
Men's Aid (#/$): 68/unspecified $
Women's Aid (#/$): 31/unspecified $
M: baseball, basketball, cross country,
football, golf, indoor track, track&field,
wrestling
W: basketball, cross country, indoor
track, soccer, softball, track&field,
volleyball

COLLEGE OF THE OZARKS
Point Lookout, MO 65726
(417) 334-6411 ext. 4393
www.cofo.edu
Contact: Al Waller

Men's Aid (#/$): 24/$38,400
Women's Aid (#/$): 24/$38,400
Restrictions and notes: All students must participate in a work program of 15 hours per week plus 2-40 hour work weeks during vacation.
M: baseball, basketball
W: basketball. Women's Non-aid: volleyball

COLUMBIA COLLEGE OF MISSOURI
1001 Rogers Street
Columbia, MO 65216
(573) 875-7419
www.ccis.edu
Contact: Jason Becking
Men's Aid (#/$): 44/$195,341
Women's Aid (#/$): 32/$148,162
M: basketball, soccer. Men's Non-aid: golf
W: softball, volleyball

CONCORDIA SEMINARY
801 DeMun Avenue
St. Louis, MO 63105
(314) 505-7000
www.cs.edu
Contact: Mark Shaltanis
Men's Non-aid: bowling, tennis
Women's Non-aid: bowling, tennis

CROWDER COLLEGE
601 Laclede
Neosho, MO 64850
Two-year college
(417) 451-3223
www.crowder.cc.mo.us
Contact: Gary Roark
Men's Aid (#/$): 10/unspecified $
Women's Aid (#/$): 10/unspecified $
M: baseball
W: basketball, softball

CULVER-STOCKTON COLLEGE
1 College Hill
Canton, MO 63435
(217) 231-6530
www.culver.edu
Contact: Amy Looten

Unspecified athletic aid available
M: baseball, basketball, football, golf, tennis
W: basketball, golf, softball, tennis, volleyball

DRURY COLLEGE
900 North Benton Avenue
Springfield, MO 65802
(417) 873-7222
www.drury.edu
Contact: Dan Cashel
Men's Aid (#/$): 30/$41,900
Women's Aid (#/$): 27/$36,200
Restrictions and notes: Full grants only in basketball.
M: basketball, golf, soccer, swimming-diving, tennis. Men's Non-aid: volleyball

EAST CENTRAL COLLEGE
P.O. Box 529
Union, MO 63084
Two-year college
(314) 583-5193
www.ecc.cc.mu.us
Contact: Ruth Dace
Unspecified athletic aid available
M: baseball, basketball, soccer
W: basketball, softball, volleyball

EVANGEL COLLEGE
1111 N. Glenstone
Springfield, MO 65802
(417) 865-2811 ext. 7282
www.evangel.edu
Contact: Faye Liddle
Unspecified athletic aid available
M: baseball, basketball, football
W: basketball, tennis, volleyball

HANNIBAL-LAGRANGE COLLEGE
2800 Palmyra Road
Hannibal, MO 63401
(573) 221-3111 ext. 312
www.hlg.edu
Contact: Scott Ashton
Unspecified athletic aid available
M: baseball, basketball, golf
W: softball, volleyball

HARRIS-STOWE STATE COLLEGE
3026 LaClede Avenue
St. Louis, MO 63103
(314) 340-3366
www.hssc.edu
Contact: Lee O'Donnell
Men's Aid (#/$): 18/$25,272
Women's Aid (#/$): 18/$25,272
M: baseball, basketball, soccer
W: basketball, track&field, volleyball

JEFFERSON COLLEGE
1000 Viking Drive
Hillsboro, MO 63050
Two-year college
(314) 789-3951 ext. 380
www.jeffco.edu
Contact: Harold R. Oetting
Unspecified athletic aid available
M: baseball, tennis
W: basketball, volleyball

KEMPER MILITARY SCHOOL AND COLLEGE
701 Third Street
Boonville, MO 65233
Two-year college
(660) 882-5623
www.kemper.org
Contact: Alan Foster
Men's Aid (#/$): 10/unspecified $
M: basketball

LINCOLN UNIVERSITY
820 Chestnut Street
Jefferson City, MO 65101
(573) 681-5343
www.lincolnu.edu
Contact: Wald Klein
Men's Non-aid: baseball, basketball, cross country, golf, indoor track, soccer, tennis, track&field
Women's Non-aid: basketball, softball, tennis, track&field, volleyball

LINDENWOOD COLLEGE
209 South Kingshighway
St. Charles, MO 63301
(636) 916-1935
www.lindenwood.edu
Contact: Pam Jones Williams
Unspecified athletic aid available
M: basketball, soccer
W: basketball, soccer. Women's Non-aid: softball

MARYVILLE UNIVERSITY OF SAINT LOUIS
13550 Conway Road
St. Louis, MO 63141
(314) 529-9483
www.maryvillest.edu
Contact: David Pierce
Men's Non-aid: baseball, basketball, cross country, soccer, tennis, track&field
Women's Non-aid: basketball, cross country, soccer, softball, tennis, track&field, volleyball

MINERAL AREA COLLEGE
P.O. Box 1000
Park Hills, MO 63601
Two-year college
(573) 431-4593
www.mac.cc.mo.us
Contact: Bob Sechrest
Unspecified athletic aid available
M: baseball, basketball
W: basketball, volleyball

MISSOURI BAPTIST COLLEGE
12542 Conway Road
St. Louis, MO 63141
(314) 434-1115
www.mobap.edu
Contact: Andy Carter
Unspecified athletic aid available
M: baseball, basketball, soccer. Men's Non-aid: golf
W: basketball, soccer, softball, volleyball

MISSOURI SOUTHERN STATE COLLEGE
3950 Newman Road
Joplin, MO 64801-1595
(417) 625-9399
www.mssc.edu
Contact: Jim Frazier

Unspecified athletic aid available
M: baseball, basketball, cross country, football, golf, indoor track, soccer, track&field
W: basketball, cheerleading, cross country, indoor track, softball, tennis, track&field, volleyball

MISSOURI VALLEY COLLEGE
500 East College
Marshall, MO 65340
(660) 831-4219
www.moval.edu
Contact: Gayle Carter
Unspecified athletic aid available
M: baseball, basketball, cross country, football, golf, indoor track, soccer, track&field
W: basketball, cross country, golf, indoor track, soccer, softball, track&field, volleyball

MISSOURI WESTERN STATE COLLEGE
4525 Downs Drive
St. Joseph, MO 64507
(816) 271-4481
www.mwsc.edu
Contact: Ed Harris
Unspecified athletic aid available
Restrictions and notes: Most athletic aid is partial scholarships.
M: baseball, basketball, football, golf
W: basketball, softball, tennis, volleyball

NORTH CENTRAL MISSOURI COLLEGE
Main Street
Trenton, MO 64683
Two-year college
(660) 359-3948
www.ncmc.cc.mo.us
Contact: Robert Shields
Unspecified athletic aid available
M: baseball, softball
W: soccer

NORTHEAST MISSOURI STATE UNIVERSITY
112 McClain Hall
Kirksville, MO 63501

(660) 785-4276
www.nemostate.edu
Contact: Melissa Ware
Unspecified athletic aid available
M: baseball, basketball, cross country, football, golf, soccer, tennis, track&field.
Men's Non-aid: swimming-diving
W: basketball, cross country, golf, softball, swimming-diving, tennis, track&field, volleyball. Women's Non-aid: soccer

NORTHWEST MISSOURI STATE UNIVERSITY
800 University Drive
Maryville, MO 64468
(660) 562-1713
www.nwmissouri.edu
Contact: James Redd
Men's Aid (#/$): 65.5/unspecified $
Women's Aid (#/$): 46.5/unspecified $
M: baseball, basketball, cross country, football, indoor track, tennis, track&field
W: basketball, cross country, indoor track, soccer, softball, tennis, track&field, volleyball

PARK COLLEGE
8700 River Park Drive, Box 44
Parkville, MO 64152
(816) 741-2000 ext. 6492
www.park.edu
Contact: Claude English
Unspecified athletic aid available
M: basketball, cross country, equestrian, soccer, track&field, volleyball
W: basketball, cross country, equestrian, soccer, track&field, volleyball

PENN VALLEY COMMUNITY COLLEGE
3201 Southwest Trafficway
Kansas City, MO 64111
Two-year college
(816) 759-4000
www.kcmetro.cc.mo.us
Contact: Fred Pohlman
Men's Aid (#/$): 16/$20,000
M: basketball, golf
W: volleyball

ROCKHURST UNIVERSITY
1100 Rockhurst Road
Kansas City, MO 64110
(816) 501-4000
www.rockhurst.edu
Contact: Sid Bordman
Unspecified athletic aid available
M: basketball, soccer. Men's Non-aid:
cross country
W: basketball, volleyball. Women's Non-
aid: cross country

SAINT LOUIS UNIVERSITY
221 North Grand Boulevard
St. Louis, MO 63103
(314) 977-2524
www.slu.edu
Contact: Doug McIlhagga
Men's Aid (#/$): 20/$169,600
Women's Aid (#/$): 10/$84,800
M: baseball, basketball, soccer,
swimming-diving, tennis. Men's Non-aid:
cross country, golf, riflery
W: basketball, field hockey, softball,
swimming-diving, tennis, volleyball

SOUTHEAST MISSOURI STATE UNIVERSITY
1 University Plaza
Houck Fieldhouse MSO200
Cape Girardeau, MO 63701
(573) 651-2294
www.semo.edu
Contact: Ron Hines
Unspecified athletic aid available
M: baseball, basketball, cross country,
football, indoor track, soccer, track&field
W: basketball, cross country, gymnastics,
indoor track, softball, track&field,
volleyball

SOUTHWEST BAPTIST UNIVERSITY
1600 University Avenue
Bolivar, MO 65613
(417) 326-1799
www.sbuniv.edu
Contact: Steve Schwepker
Unspecified athletic aid available

M: baseball, basketball, cross country,
football, golf, soccer, tennis
W: basketball, cross country, soccer, softball, tennis, volleyball

SOUTHWEST MISSOURI STATE UNIVERSITY
901 South National
Springfield, MO 65804
(417) 836-5402
www.sports.smsu.edu
Contact: Mark Stillwell
Unspecified athletic aid available
M: baseball, basketball, cross country,
football, golf, indoor track, soccer,
swimming-diving, tennis, track&field
W: basketball, cross country, field hockey,
golf, indoor track, soccer, softball,
swimming, tennis, track&field, volleyball

ST. LOUIS COMMUNITY COLLEGE—FLORISSANT VALLEY
3400 Pershall Road
St. Louis, MO 63135-1499
Two-year college
(314) 595-4275
www.stlcc.cc.mo.us/fv
Contact: Diana Crowell
M: baseball, basketball, soccer, wrestling
W: softball, volleyball

ST. LOUIS COMMUNITY COLLEGE—FOREST PARK
5600 Oakland Avenue
St. Louis, MO 63110-1393
Two-year college
(314) 644-9100
www.stlcc.cc.mo.us/ff
Contact: Russ Dippold
Unspecified athletic aid available
M: baseball, basketball, soccer, wrestling
W: basketball, softball, volleyball

STATE FAIR COMMUNITY COLLEGE
1900 Clarendon Road
Sedalia, MO 65301
Two-year college
(660) 826-9635
www.sfcc.cc.mo.us

Contact: Bill Barton
Unspecified athletic aid available
M: baseball, basketball, golf
W: basketball, soccer

THREE RIVERS COMMUNITY COLLEGE
Three Rivers Boulevard
Poplar Bluff, MO 63901
Two-year college
(573) 840-9611
www.trcc.cc.mo.us
Contact: Gene Bess
Unspecified athletic aid available
M: baseball, basketball, golf
W: basketball, volleyball

UNIVERSITY OF MISSOURI
8001 Natural Bridge Road
St. Louis, MO 63121
(314) 516-5660
www.umsl.edu
Contact: Michael Deford
Unspecified athletic aid available
M: baseball, basketball, cross country,
football, golf, indoor track, swimming-
diving, track&field, wrestling
W: cross country, golf, gymnastics,
indoor track, softball, swimming-diving,
track&field, volleyball

UNIVERSITY OF MISSOURI (COLUMBIA)
330 Hearnes Center
600 Stadium Boulevard
Columbia, MO 65211
(573) 882-0712
www.mutigers.com
Contact: Bob Brendel
Men's Aid (#/$): 217/$1,062,863
Women's Aid (#/$): 117/$498,103
M: basketball, crew, cross country, football, golf, indoor track, swimming-diving,
track&field, wrestling. Men's Non-aid:
tennis
W: basketball, cross country, golf, gymnastics, indoor track, softball, swimming-
diving, track&field, volleyball. Women's
Non-aid: tennis

UNIVERSITY OF MISSOURI (KANSAS CITY)
5100 Rockhill Road
Kansas City, MO 64110
(816) 235-1036
www.umkc.edu
Contact: Barney Turk
Unspecified athletic aid available
M: basketball. Men's Non-aid: golf,
tennis
W: basketball. Women's Non-aid: golf,
tennis

UNIVERSITY OF MISSOURI (ROLLA)
Multipurpose Building
Rolla, MO 65401
(314) 341-4175
www.umr.edu
Contact: John Kean
Unspecified athletic aid available
M: baseball, basketball, cross country,
football, golf, soccer, swimming
W: basketball, cross country, soccer,
softball

WASHINGTON UNIVERSITY
One Brooklings Drive
St. Louis, MO 63130-4890
(314) 935-5077
www.bearsports.wust.edu
Contact: Kevin Berkowitz
Men's Non-aid: baseball, basketball,
cross country, football, soccer,
swimming-diving, tennis, track&field
Women's Non-aid: basketball, cross
country, softball, swimming-diving,
tennis, track&field, volleyball

WEBSTER UNIVERSITY
470 East Lockwood Avenue
St. Louis, MO 63119-9986
(314) 968-6984
www.webster.edu
Contact: Bob Delaney
Men's Non-aid: baseball, basketball,
soccer, tennis
Women's Non-aid: basketball, cross
country, tennis, volleyball

WENTWORTH MILITARY ACADEMY AND COLLEGE
1800 Washington Avenue
Lexington, MO 64067
Two-year college
(660) 259-2221
www.uma1880.org
Contact: Bob Florence
Unspecified athletic aid available
M: basketball

WILLIAM JEWELL COLLEGE
500 College Hill
Liberty, MO 64068
(816) 781-7700 ext. 5146
www.jewel.edu
Contact: Sue Armstrong
Unspecified athletic aid available
M: baseball, basketball, cross country, football, golf, indoor track, soccer, tennis, track&field
W: basketball, cross country, golf, indoor track, soccer, softball, tennis, track&field, volleyball

WILLIAM WOODS UNIVERSITY
200 West 12th Street
Fulton, MO 65251-1098
(573) 592-1129
www.umwoods.edu
Contact: Venita Mitchell
Unspecified athletic aid available
Restrictions and notes: William Woods is an all-women's college that provides full and partial tuition scholarships.
W: basketball, soccer, softball, swimming-diving, tennis, volleyball

Montana

CARROLL COLLEGE
North Benton Avenue
Helena, MT 59625
(406) 447-5411
www.carroll.edu
Contact: Peggy Stebbins
Unspecified athletic aid available
M: basketball, football
W: basketball, volleyball

DAWSON COMMUNITY COLLEGE
P.O. Box 421
Glendive, MT 59330
Two-year college
(406) 365-3396
www.dawson.cc.mt.us
Contact: Joyce Ayre
Men's Aid (#/$): 15/unspecified $
Women's Aid (#/$): 15/unspecified $
M: basketball, rodeo. Men's Non-aid: baseball
W: basketball, rodeo. Women's Non-aid: softball

EASTERN MONTANA COLLEGE
1500 North 30th
Billings, MT 59101-0298
(406) 657-2369
Contact: Heather Taylor
Unspecified athletic aid available
M: basketball, golf, gymnastics, tennis, volleyball
W: basketball, golf, tennis, volleyball

MILES COMMUNITY COLLEGE
2715 Dickinson Street
Miles City, MT 59301
Two-year college
(406) 234-3031
www.mcc.cc.mt.us
Contact: Dan Connors
Unspecified athletic aid available
M: basketball, rodeo
W: basketball, rodeo

MONTANA COLLEGE OF MINERAL SCIENCE AND TECHNOLOGY
1300 West Park Street
Butte, MT 59701
(406) 496-4292
www.mtec.edu
Contact: Bob Green
Unspecified athletic aid available
M: basketball, football, golf
W: basketball, golf, volleyball

MONTANA STATE UNIVERSITY
416 Culbertson Hall
Bozeman, MT 59717
(406) 994-5133
www.msu.bobcats.com
Contact: Bill Lamberty
Unspecified athletic aid available
M: basketball, cross country, football, indoor track, tennis, track&field
W: alpine skiing, basketball, cross country, cross country skiing, golf, indoor track, tennis, track&field, volleyball

NORTHERN MONTANA COLLEGE
P.O. Box 7751
Havre, MT 59501
(406) 265-3761
www.msun.edu
Contact: Ted Spatkowski
Unspecified athletic aid available
M: basketball, football, rodeo, wrestling
W: basketball, golf, rodeo, soccer, volleyball

ROCKY MOUNTAIN COLLEGE
1511 Poly Drive
Billings, MT 59102-1796
(406) 657-1124
www.rocky.edu
Contact: Terry Corey
Unspecified athletic aid available
M: basketball, football, golf, skiing
W: basketball, golf, skiing, soccer, volleyball

UNIVERSITY OF MONTANA
Adams Field House
Missoula, MT 59812
(406) 243-5404
www.umt.edu
Contact: Patty Dwight
Men's Aid (#/$): 110/$900,000
Women's Aid (#/$): 91/$700,000
M: basketball, cross country, football, rodeo, tennis, track&field
W: basketball, cross country, golf, indoor track, soccer, tennis, track&field, volleyball

WESTERN MONTANA COLLEGE
Campus Box 74
Dillon, MT 59725
(406) 683-7201
www.wmc.edu
Contact: Wally Feldt
Unspecified athletic aid available
M: basketball, football, golf, rodeo
W: basketball, golf, rodeo, volleyball

Nebraska

BELLEVUE UNIVERSITY
Galvin Road and Harvell Drive
Bellevue, NE 68005
(402) 293-3781
www.bellevue.edu
Contact: Jenny Cook
Unspecified athletic aid available
M: baseball, basketball, softball
W: baseball, softball, volleyball

CENTRAL COMMUNITY COLLEGE
P.O. Box 1027
Columbus, NE 68601
Two-year college
(402) 564-7132
www.megavision.net
Contact: Jack Gutierrez
Unspecified athletic aid available
M: basketball, soccer
W: basketball, volleyball

CHADRON STATE COLLEGE
1000 Main Street
Chadron, NE 69337
(308) 432-6263
www.csc.edu
Contact: Con Marshall
Men's Aid (#/$): 70/unspecified $
Women's Aid (#/$): 40/unspecified $
M: basketball, football, indoor track, rodeo, track&field, wrestling
W: basketball, golf, indoor track, track&field, volleyball

COLLEGE OF ST. MARY
1901 South 72nd Street
Omaha, NE 68124
(402) 399-2451
www.csm.edu
Contact: Ron Romine
Women's Aid (#/$): 37/unspecified $
W: softball, tennis, volleyball

CONCORDIA UNIVERSITY
800 N. Columbia Avenue
Seward, NE 68434
(402) 643-7270
www.ccsw.edu
Contact: Judy J. Williams
Unspecified athletic aid available
M: baseball, basketball, cross country,
football, golf, indoor track, soccer,
swimming-diving, tennis, track&field
W: basketball, cross country, golf, indoor
track, soccer, softball, swimming-diving,
tennis, track&field, volleyball

CREIGHTON UNIVERSITY
24th and California
Vinardi Athletic Center
Omaha, NE 68178
(402) 280-2488
www.creighton.edu
Contact: Kyran Anderson
Unspecified athletic aid available
M: baseball, basketball. Men's Non-aid:
cross country, golf, swimming, tennis
W: basketball, softball. Women's Non-aid:
cross country, golf, swimming, tennis

DANA COLLEGE
2848 College Drive
Blair, NE 68008-1099
(402) 426-7293
www.dana.edu
Contact: Jim Krause
Men's Aid (#/$): 125/$282,725
Women's Aid (#/$): 58/$132,430
M: baseball, basketball, cross country,
football, track&field, wrestling
W: basketball, cross country, soccer, soft-
ball, track&field, volleyball

DOANE COLLEGE
1014 Boswell Avenue
Crete, NE 68333
(402) 826-8248
www.doane.edu
Contact: Tami Capek
Unspecified athletic aid available
M: basketball, cross country, football,
indoor track, soccer, track&field. Men's
Non-aid: golf, tennis
W: basketball, cross country, indoor
track, soccer, softball, track&field, volleyball. Women's Non-aid: golf, tennis

HASTINGS COLLEGE
800 North Turner
Hastings, NE 68901
(402) 463-2402
www.hastings.edu
Contact: Bob Boerigter
Men's Aid (#/$): 275/unspecified $
Women's Aid (#/$): 150/unspecified $
M: baseball, basketball, cross country,
football, golf, indoor track, soccer, tennis,
track&field
W: basketball, cross country, golf, indoor
track, soccer, softball, tennis, track&field,
volleyball

MCCOOK COMMUNITY COLLEGE
1205 East Third
McCook, NE 69001
Two-year college
(308) 345-6303
mcc.mccook.cc.ne.us
Contact: Robert Christie
Unspecified athletic aid available
M: basketball, golf
W: basketball, volleyball

MIDLAND LUTHERAN COLLEGE
900 North Clarkson
Fremont, NE 68025
(402) 721-5480
www.mlc.edu
Contact: Keith Kramme
Unspecified athletic aid available
Restrictions and notes: All athletic aid
based on need.

M: baseball, basketball, cross country, football, golf, indoor track, tennis, track&field
W: basketball, cross country, golf, indoor track, soccer, softball, tennis, track&field, volleyball

MID-PLAINS JUNIOR COLLEGE
601 State Farm Road
North Platte, NE 69101
Two-year college
(308) 532-8980
www.geocities.com
Contact: Kevin O'Connor
Men's Aid (#/$): 15/unspecified $
Women's Aid (#/$): 30/unspecified $
M: basketball
W: basketball, volleyball

NEBRASKA WESLEYAN UNIVERSITY
5000 St. Paul Avenue
Lincoln, NE 68504-2796
(402) 465-2151
www.nebrwesleyan.edu
Contact: Kevin Wickham
Men's Non-aid: baseball, basketball, cross country, football, golf, tennis, track&field
Women's Non-aid: basketball, cross country, golf, softball, tennis, track&field, volleyball

PERU STATE COLLEGE
RR 1, Box 10
Peru, NE 68421
(402) 872-2350
pscosf.peru.edu
Contact: Vince Henzel
Unspecified athletic aid available
M: baseball, basketball, football
W: basketball, softball, volleyball

SOUTHEAST COMMUNITY COLLEGE
4771 W. Scott Road
Beatrice, NE 68310-7042
Two-year college
(402) 228-3468 ext. 232
www.college.sccm.cc.ne.us
Contact: Dan Johnson

Unspecified athletic aid available
M: basketball, golf
W: basketball, softball, volleyball

UNIVERSITY OF NEBRASKA (KEARNEY)
102 Health & Sports Center
Kearney, NE 68849
(308) 865-8334
www.unk.edu
Contact: Peter Yazvac
Unspecified athletic aid available
M: baseball, basketball, cheerleading, cross country, football, golf, tennis, track&field, wrestling
W: basketball, cheerleading, cross country, diving, softball, swimming, tennis, track&field, volleyball

UNIVERSITY OF NEBRASKA (LINCOLN)
116 South Stadium
Lincoln, NE 68588-0123
(402) 472-5959
www.huskerwebcast.com
Contact: Don Bryant
Unspecified athletic aid available
M: baseball, basketball, cross country, football, golf, gymnastics, indoor track, swimming-diving, tennis, track&field, wrestling
W: basketball, cross country, golf, gymnastics, indoor track, soccer, softball, swimming-diving, tennis, track&field, volleyball

UNIVERSITY OF NEBRASKA (OMAHA)
6001 Dodge Street
Omaha, NE 68182
(402) 554-3387
www.unomaha.edu
Contact: Gary Anderson
Unspecified athletic aid available
M: baseball, basketball, cross country, football, golf, indoor track, tennis, track&field, wrestling
W: swimming-diving, tennis, track&field, volleyball

WAYNE STATE COLLEGE
1111 North Main Street
Wayne, NE 68787
(402) 375-7326
www.wsc.edu
Contact: Greg McDermott
Unspecified athletic aid available
M: baseball, basketball, cross country,
football, golf, indoor track, track&field
W: basketball, cross country, golf, indoor
track, soccer, softball, track&field, volleyball

**WESTERN NEBRASKA
COMMUNITY COLLEGE**
1601 E. 27th Street
Scottsbluff, NE 69361
Two-year college
(308) 635-3606 ext. 6026
www.wncc.cc.ne.us
Contact: John Perry
Unspecified athletic aid available
M: basketball, golf
W: basketball, volleyball

Nevada

SIERRA NEVADA COLLEGE
P.O. Box 4269
Incline Village, NV 89450
(775) 831-1314
www.sierranevada.edu
Contact: Chris Hendrickson
Men's Non-aid: alpine skiing, equestrian,
snowboarding, soccer
Women's Non-aid: alpine skiing,
equestrian, snowboarding, soccer

UNIVERSITY OF NEVADA
4505 Maryland Parkway
Las Vegas, NV 89154
(702) 895-3995
www.unlvrebels.com
Contact: Jim Gemma
Unspecified athletic aid available
M: baseball, basketball, cross country,
football, golf, soccer, swimming-diving,
tennis

W: cross country, indoor track, softball,
swimming-diving, tennis, track&field

UNIVERSITY OF NEVADA (RENO)
Mall Stop 232
Reno, NV 89557
(775) 784-1110
www.nevadawolfpack.com
Contact: Paul Stuart
Men's Aid (#/$): 113.7/$1,036,276
Women's Aid (#/$): 52.3/$451,000
M: baseball, basketball, cross country,
football, golf, tennis, track&field
W: basketball, cross country, swimming,
tennis, track&field, volleyball

New Hampshire

COLBY-SAWYER COLLEGE
100 Main Street
New London, NH 03257
(603) 526-2010 ext. 414
www.colby.sawyer.edu
Contact: Deb McGrath
Men's Non-aid: alpine skiing, baseball,
basketball, equestrian, soccer, tennis,
track&field
Women's Non-aid: alpine skiing, basketball, equestrian, lacrosse, soccer, tennis,
track&field, volleyball

DARTMOUTH COLLEGE
110 Alumni Gym
Hanover, NH 03755
(603) 646-2468
www.dartmouth.edu
Contact: Kathy Slattery
Men's Non-aid: alpine skiing, baseball,
basketball, crew, cross country, cross
country skiing, diving, equestrian, football, golf, ice hockey, indoor track,
lacrosse, sailing, soccer, squash, swimming, tennis, track&field
Women's Non-aid: alpine skiing, basketball, crew, cross country, cross country
skiing, diving, equestrian, field hockey,

golf, ice hockey, indoor track, lacrosse, sailing, soccer, squash, swimming, tennis, track&field

FRANKLIN PIERCE COLLEGE
College Road, P.O. Box 60
Rindge, NH 03461
(603) 899-4180
www.fpc.edu
Contact: Susan Howard
Unspecified athletic aid available
M: baseball, basketball, soccer, tennis.
Men's Non-aid: alpine skiing, cross country, golf, sailing
W: basketball, soccer, softball. Women's Non-aid: alpine skiing, sailing, tennis

HESSER COLLEGE
3 Sundial Avenue
Manchester, NH 03103
Two-year college
(603) 668-6660
www.hesser.com
Contact: Gary LeSuer
Men's Non-aid: basketball, soccer
Women's Non-aid: softball, volleyball

KEENE STATE COLLEGE
229 Main Street
Keene, NH 03431
(603) 358-2280
www.keene.edu
Contact: Stuart Kaufman
Men's Non-aid: baseball, basketball, cross country, diving, indoor track, lacrosse, soccer, swimming, track&field
Women's Non-aid: basketball, cross country, diving, field hockey, indoor track, lacrosse, soccer, softball, swimming, track&field, volleyball

NEW HAMPSHIRE COLLEGE
2500 North River Road
Manchester, NH 03104-1045
(603) 645-9626
www.nhc.edu
Contact: Tom McDermott
Unspecified athletic aid available
M: baseball, basketball, soccer, tennis.

Men's Non-aid: ice hockey, lacrosse
W: basketball, soccer, softball, tennis, volleyball

PLYMOUTH STATE COLLEGE
Holderness Road
Plymouth, NH 03264
(603) 535-2477
www.plymouth.edu
Contact: Kent Cherrington
Men's Non-aid: alpine skiing, baseball, basketball, football, ice hockey, lacrosse, soccer, tennis, wrestling
Women's Non-aid: alpine skiing, basketball, field hockey, lacrosse, soccer, softball, swimming-diving, tennis, volleyball

SAINT ANSELM COLLEGE
100 St. Anselm Drive
Manchester, NH 03102-1310
(603) 641-7810
www.anselm.edu
Contact: Ken Belbin
Men's Aid (#/$): 5/unspecified $
Women's Aid (#/$): 5/unspecified $
M: alpine skiing, basketball, ice hockey.
Men's Non-aid: baseball, cross country, football, golf, lacrosse, soccer, tennis
W: basketball. Women's Non-aid: alpine skiing, cross country, golf, lacrosse, soccer, softball, tennis

UNIVERSITY OF NEW HAMPSHIRE
224 Field House
Durham, NH 03824
(603) 862-2013
www.unh.edu
Contact: Judy Rae
Unspecified athletic aid available
M: basketball, football, ice hockey. Men's Non-aid: alpine skiing, baseball, cross country, cross country skiing, golf, indoor track, lacrosse, soccer, swimming-diving, tennis, track&field, wrestling
W: basketball, field hockey, gymnastics, ice hockey, soccer. Women's Non-aid: alpine skiing, cross country, cross country skiing, indoor track, lacrosse, swimming-diving, tennis, track&field

New Jersey

ATLANTIC COMMUNITY COLLEGE
5100 Black Horse Pike
Mays Landing, NJ 08330
Two-year college
(609) 343-5087
www.atlantic.edu
Contact: Carmen Royal
Men's Non-aid: archery, baseball, basketball, cross country, golf, soccer, tennis
Women's Non-aid: archery, basketball, cross country, golf, squash, tennis

BERGEN COMMUNITY COLLEGE
Paramus Road
Paramus, NJ 07652-1595
Two-year college
(201) 447-7183
www.bergen.cc.nj.us
Contact: Bernie Fuersich
Unspecified athletic aid available
M: cross country, track&field. Men's Non-aid: baseball, basketball, golf, soccer, wrestling
W: cross country, track&field. Women's Non-aid: basketball, softball, volleyball

BLOOMFIELD COLLEGE
Franklin Street
Bloomfield, NJ 07003
(973) 748-9000
www.bloomfield.edu
Contact: Al Restaino
Men's Aid (#/$): 6/$60,000
Women's Aid (#/$): 4/$60,000
M: baseball, basketball, soccer. Men's Non-aid: lacrosse
W: basketball, softball. Women's Non-aid: volleyball

CALDWELL COLLEGE
9 Ryerson Avenue
Caldwell, NJ 07006
(973) 618-3567
www.caldwell.edu
Contact: Mike Lamberti
Unspecified athletic aid available

M: basketball
W: basketball, volleyball

CENTENARY COLLEGE
400 Jefferson Street
Hackettstown, NJ 07840
(908) 852-1400 ext. 2297
www.centenarycollege.edu
Contact: Diane Finnan
Unspecified athletic aid available
M: basketball, cross country, equestrian, golf, lacrosse, soccer, wrestling
W: basketball, cross country, equestrian, golf, lacrosse, soccer, softball, volleyball

THE COLLEGE OF NEW JERSEY
P.O. Box 7718
Going, NJ 08628-7718
(609) 771-2517
www.tcnj.edu
Contact: Ann Bready
Men's Non-aid: baseball, basketball, cross country, football, golf, soccer, swimming-diving, tennis, track&field, wrestling
Women's Non-aid: basketball, cross country, field hockey, indoor track, lacrosse, soccer, softball, swimming-diving, tennis, track&field

DREW UNIVERSITY
36 Madison Avenue
Madison, NJ 07940-4015
(973) 408-3574
www.drew.edu
Contact: Jennifer Brauner
Men's Non-aid: baseball, basketball, cross country, equestrian, fencing, lacrosse, soccer, tennis
Women's Non-aid: basketball, cross country, equestrian, fencing, field hockey, lacrosse, tennis

FAIRLEIGH DICKINSON UNIVERSITY (FLORHAM-MADISON)
285 Madison Avenue
Madison, NJ 07940
(973) 433-8500

www.fdu.edu
Contact: Tom Bonerbo
Men's Non-aid: baseball, basketball, football, golf, lacrosse, soccer, tennis
Women's Non-aid: basketball, field hockey, softball, tennis, volleyball

FAIRLEIGH DICKINSON UNIVERSITY (TEANECK-HACKENSACK)
1000 River Road
Teaneck, NJ 07666
(201) 692-2000
www.fdu.edu
Contact: Bob Roghwell
Unspecified athletic aid available
M: baseball, basketball, cross country, golf, indoor track, lacrosse, soccer, tennis, track&field
W: basketball, cross country, fencing, indoor track, softball, tennis, track&field.
Women's Non-aid: equestrian

GEORGIAN COURT COLLEGE
900 Lakewood Avenue
Lakewood, NJ 08701-2697
(732) 364-2200 ext. 683
www.georgian.edu
Contact: Anita Caswell
Women's Aid (#/$): 35/$70,000
W: basketball, cross country, martial arts, softball, volleyball

GLOUCESTER COUNTY COLLEGE
1400 Tanyard Road
Sewell, NJ 08080
Two-year college
(609) 468-5000
www.gccnj.edu
Contact: Ron Case
Men's Non-aid: baseball, basketball, cross country, soccer, tennis, track&field, wrestling
Women's Non-aid: basketball, cross country, soccer, softball, tennis, track&field

KEAN UNIVERSITY
1000 Morris Avenue
Union, NJ 07083

(908) 527-2436
www.kean.edu
Contact: Adam Fenton
Men's Non-aid: baseball, basketball, football, golf, ice hockey, lacrosse, soccer, tennis, wrestling
Women's Non-aid: basketball, field hockey, soccer, softball, swimming-diving, tennis, volleyball

MERCER COUNTY COMMUNITY COLLEGE
P.O. Box B
Trenton, NJ 08690
Two-year college
(609) 586-4800
www.mccc.edu
Contact: John Simone
Unspecified athletic aid available
M: baseball, basketball, indoor track, soccer, tennis, track&field
W: basketball, indoor track, soccer, softball, track&field

MIDDLESEX COUNTY COLLEGE
2600 Woodbridge Avenue
Edison, NJ 08818
Two-year college
(732) 906-2558
www.middlesex.cc.njus
Contact: Robert Zifchak
Unspecified athletic aid available
Restrictions and notes: Athletic aid restricted to Middlesex County residents with H.S. GPA of 2.0 or better.
M: track&field. Men's Non-aid: baseball, basketball, cross country, golf, soccer, tennis, wrestling
W: softball. Women's Non-aid: basketball, cross country, soccer, tennis, track&field

MONMOUTH UNIVERSITY
Cedar Avenue
West Long Branch, NJ 07764-1898
(732) 571-3415
www.monmouth.edu
Contact: Mike Scala
Unspecified athletic aid available

M: baseball, basketball, cross country, diving, football, soccer, swimming, tennis, track&field
W: basketball, diving, soccer, softball, swimming

MONTCLAIR STATE UNIVERSITY
1 Normal Avenue
Upper Montclair, NJ 07043
(973) 655-5249
www.montclair.edu
Contact: Al Langer
Men's Non-aid: baseball, basketball, cross country, football, golf, indoor track, lacrosse, soccer, swimming-diving, tennis, track&field, water polo, wrestling
Women's Non-aid: basketball, cross country, field hockey, gymnastics, indoor track, softball, swimming-diving, tennis, track&field

NEW JERSEY INSTITUTE OF TECHNOLOGY
323 King Boulevard
Newark, NJ 07102
(973) 596-5727
www.njit.edu
Contact: James Catalano
Men's Non-aid: baseball, basketball, bowling, ice hockey, riflery, soccer, tennis, volleyball
Women's Non-aid: softball, tennis

OCEAN COUNTY COLLEGE
College Drive
P.O. Box 2001
Toms River, NJ 08754-2001
Two-year college
(732) 255-0400 ext. 2118
www.ocean.cc.nj.us
Contact: John Stauff
Men's Non-aid: baseball, basketball, cross country, golf, ice hockey, soccer, swimming-diving, tennis, track&field
Women's Non-aid: basketball, cross country, field hockey, golf, softball, swimming-diving, tennis, track&field

PASSAIC COUNTY COMMUNITY COLLEGE
One College Boulevard
Paterson, NJ 07505
Two-year college
(973) 684-6868
www.pccc.cc.nj.us
Contact: Nate Malachi
Men's Non-aid: basketball, cross country skiing, soccer
Women's Non-aid: basketball, cross country skiing

PRINCETON UNIVERSITY
P.O. Box 71
Room 9, Jadwin Gym
Princeton, NJ 08544-0071
(609) 258-3568
www.princeton.edu
Contact: Nancy Dunigan
Men's Non-aid: baseball, basketball, crew, cross country, fencing, football, golf, ice hockey, lacrosse, soccer, squash, swimming-diving, tennis, track&field, wrestling
Women's Non-aid: baseball, basketball, crew, cross country, field hockey, ice hockey, lacrosse, soccer, squash, swimming-diving, tennis, track&field, volleyball

RAMAPO COLLEGE OF NEW JERSEY
505 Ramapo Valley Road
Mahwah, NJ 07430-1630
(201) 684-7091
www.ramapo.edu
Contact: Eugene Marshall
Men's Non-aid: baseball, basketball, cross country, football, golf, soccer, tennis, track&field, volleyball
Women's Non-aid: basketball, cross country, softball, tennis, track&field, volleyball

RIDER COLLEGE
2083 Lawrenceville Road
Lawrenceville, NJ 08648-3099
(609) 896-5138

www.rider.edu
Contact: Bud Focht
Unspecified athletic aid available
M: baseball, basketball, cross country, golf, indoor track, soccer, swimming-diving, tennis, track&field, wrestling
W: basketball, cross country, diving, field hockey, indoor track, soccer, softball, swimming, tennis, track&field, volleyball

ROWAN UNIVERSITY
201 Millica Hill Road
Glassboro, NJ 08028-1701
(856) 256-4252
www.rowan.edu
Contact: Sheila Stevenson
Men's Non-aid: baseball, basketball, football, soccer, swimming-diving, tennis, track&field
Women's Non-aid: basketball, cross country, field hockey, lacrosse, softball, swimming-diving, tennis, track&field

RUTGERS, CAMDEN COLLEGE OF ARTS AND SCIENCES
Third and Linden Streets
Camden, NJ 08102
(609) 225-6193
www.camden.rutgers.edu
Contact: Diana Compo
Men's Non-aid: baseball, basketball, cross country, golf, soccer, track&field
Women's Non-aid: basketball, cheerleading, cross country, soccer, softball, track&field

RUTGERS, COLLEGE AVENUE CAMPUS
Lewis Brown Athletic Center
83 Rockefeller Road
Piscataway, NJ 08854
(732) 445-7842
www.athletics.rutgers.edu
Contact: Terry Beachem
Unspecified athletic aid available
M: baseball, basketball, crew, cross country, diving, fencing, football, golf, lacrosse, soccer, swimming, tennis, track&field, wrestling
W: crew, diving, fencing, field hockey, golf, gymnastics, lacrosse, soccer, swimming, tennis, track&field, volleyball

RUTGERS, NEWARK COLLEGE OF ARTS AND SCIENCES
University Heights
Newark, NJ 08903
(973) 353-5474
rutgers-newark.rutgers.edu
Contact: Howard Pachasa
Unspecified athletic aid available
M: volleyball. Men's Non-aid: baseball, basketball, fencing, wrestling
Women's Non-aid: basketball, fencing, golf, softball

SAINT PETER'S COLLEGE
2641 Kennedy Boulevard
Jersey City, NJ 07306
(201) 915-9101
www.spc.edu
Contact: Tim Camp
Men's Aid (#/$): 43/unspecified $
Women's Aid (#/$): 46/unspecified $
M: baseball, basketball, cross country, golf, indoor track, soccer, swimming-diving, tennis, track&field. Men's Non-aid: bowling, football
W: basketball, cross country, indoor track, soccer, softball, swimming-diving, tennis, track&field, volleyball. Women's Non-aid: bowling

SETON HALL UNIVERSITY
400 South Orange Avenue
South Orange, NJ 07079
(973) 761-9493
www.shu.edu
Contact: Jeffrey Fogelson
Unspecified athletic aid available
M: baseball, basketball, cross country, golf, indoor track, soccer, swimming-diving, tennis, track&field, wrestling
W: basketball, cross country, indoor track, soccer, softball, swimming-diving, tennis, track&field, volleyball

STEVENS INSTITUTE OF TECHNOLOGY
Castle Point Station
Hoboken, NJ 07030
(201) 216-5078
www.stevens-tech.edu
Contact: Russell Rogers
Men's Non-aid: baseball, basketball, cross country, fencing, lacrosse, soccer, squash, tennis, volleyball, wrestling
Women's Non-aid: cross country, fencing, tennis, volleyball

UNION COUNTY COLLEGE
1033 Springfield Avenue
Cranford, NJ 07016
Two-year college
(908) 709-7093
www.ucc.edu
Contact: Joseph Placa
Women's Aid (#/$): 8/unspecified $
Men's Non-aid: baseball, basketball, golf, soccer
W: basketball. Women's Non-aid: softball

WILLIAM PATTERSON UNIVERSITY
300 Pompton Road
Wayne, NJ 07470
(973) 720-2705
www.wilpaterson.edu
Contact: Joe Martinelli
Men's Non-aid: baseball, basketball, bowling, cross country, fencing, football, golf, ice hockey, indoor track, soccer, swimming-diving, track&field
Women's Non-aid: basketball, bowling, cross country, fencing, field hockey, indoor track, softball, swimming-diving, tennis, track&field, volleyball

New Mexico

COLLEGE OF THE SOUTHWEST
6610 Lovington Highway
Hobbs, NM 88240
(505) 392-6561

Contact: Diane Lloyd
Unspecified athletic aid available
M: baseball, soccer
W: soccer

EASTERN NEW MEXICO UNIVERSITY
Station 17
Portales, NM 88130
(505) 562-4309
www.enmu.edu
Contact: Robert McKinney
Unspecified athletic aid available
M: baseball, basketball, cross country, football, rodeo
W: basketball, cross country, rodeo, softball, tennis, volleyball

NEW MEXICO HIGHLANDS UNIVERSITY
P.O. Box 9000
Las Vegas, NM 87701
(505) 454-3393
www.nmhu.edu
Contact: Dave Kavanaugh
Men's Aid (#/$): 44/unspecified $
Women's Aid (#/$): 20/unspecified $
M: baseball, basketball, cross country, football
W: basketball, cross country, softball, volleyball

NEW MEXICO JUNIOR COLLEGE
5317 Lovington Highway
Hobbs, NM 88240
Two-year college
(505) 392-4510
www.nmjc.cc.nm.us
Contact: Richard Morris
Unspecified athletic aid available
M: baseball, basketball, golf, rodeo
W: basketball, rodeo

NEW MEXICO STATE UNIVERSITY
Box 3001, Department 5100
Los Cruces, NM 88003
(505) 646-1208
www.nmsu.edu
Contact: Flora Franco

Unspecified athletic aid available
M: baseball, basketball, cross country, diving, football, golf, swimming, tennis, track&field
W: basketball, cross country, diving, golf, softball, swimming, tennis, track&field, volleyball

UNIVERSITY OF NEW MEXICO
Mesa Vista North
Albuquerque, NM 87131
(505) 277-6479
www.unm.edu
Contact: Janice Ruggiero
Unspecified athletic aid available
Women's Aid (#/$): 100/$530,455
M: alpine skiing, baseball, basketball, cross country, football, golf, gymnastics, soccer, swimming, tennis, track&field, wrestling
W: alpine skiing, basketball, cross country, golf, softball, swimming, tennis, track&field, volleyball

WESTERN NEW MEXICO UNIVERSITY
Box 680
Silver City, NM 88061
(505) 538-6173
www.wnmu.edu
Contact: Charles P. Kelly
Unspecified athletic aid available
M: baseball, basketball, football, track&field
W: basketball, softball, track&field, volleyball

New York

ADELPHI UNIVERSITY
South Avenue
Woodruff Hall
Garden City, NY 11530
(516) 877-4236
www.adelphi.edu
Contact: Dan Booth
Unspecified athletic aid available

M: baseball, basketball, cross country, golf, lacrosse, soccer, swimming, tennis
W: basketball, cross country, soccer, softball, swimming, tennis, volleyball

ADIRONDACK COMMUNITY COLLEGE
640 Bay Road
Queensbury, NY 12804
Two-year college
(518) 743-2264
www.sunyacc.edu
Contact: Robert L. Harris
Men's Non-aid: alpine skiing, basketball, bowling, golf, soccer, tennis
Women's Non-aid: alpine skiing, basketball, bowling, soccer, softball, tennis, volleyball

ALFRED UNIVERSITY
1 Saxon Drive
Alfred, NY 14802
(607) 871-2904
www.alfred.edu
Contact: Mark Whitehouse
Men's Non-aid: alpine skiing, basketball, cross country, equestrian, football, golf, indoor track, lacrosse, soccer, swimming-diving, tennis, track&field
Women's Non-aid: alpine skiing, basketball, cross country, equestrian, indoor track, lacrosse, soccer, softball, swimming-diving, tennis, track&field, volleyball

BARD COLLEGE
Stevenson Gymnasium
Annandale-on-Hudson, NY 12504
(914) 758-7530
www.bard.edu
Contact: Scott Swere
Men's Non-aid: basketball, cross country, soccer, tennis, volleyball
Women's Non-aid: basketball, cross country, softball, tennis, volleyball

BINGHAMTON UNIVERSITY (STATE UNIVERSITY OF NEW YORK)
P.O. Box 6000
Binghamton, NY 13902-6000

(607) 777-4257
www.binghamton.edu
Contact: Dr. Joel Thirer
Men's Non-aid: baseball, basketball, golf,
soccer, swimming-diving, tennis,
track&field, wrestling
Women's Non-aid: basketball, cross
country, soccer, softball, swimming-
diving, tennis, track&field, volleyball

BOROUGH OF MANHATTAN COMMUNITY COLLEGE (CITY UNIVERSITY OF NEW YORK)
199 Chambers Street
New York, NY 10007
Two-year college
(212) 346-8279
www.bmcc.cuny.edu
Contact: Steve Kelly
Men's Non-aid: baseball, basketball,
soccer

BRONX COMMUNITY COLLEGE
West 181 Street & University Avenue
Bronx, NY 10453
Two-year college
(718) 289-5268
www.bcc.cuny.edu
Contact: Michael Steuerman
Men's Non-aid: baseball, basketball,
cross country, indoor track, soccer,
track&field
Women's Non-aid: basketball, cross
country, indoor track, softball,
track&field, volleyball

BROOKLYN COLLEGE — CITY UNIVERSITY OF NEW YORK
2900 Bedford Avenue
Brooklyn, NY 11210
(718) 951-5366
www.brooklyn.cuny.edu
Contact: Yakik Rumley
Men's Non-aid: basketball, cross country,
soccer, tennis, track&field, volleyball
Women's Non-aid: basketball, cross
country, soccer, softball, swimming,
tennis, track&field

BROOME COMMUNITY COLLEGE
P.O. Box 1017
Binghamton, NY 13902
Two-year college
(607) 778-5003
www.sunybroome.edu
Contact: Dan Minch
Men's Non-aid: baseball, basketball,
cross country, golf, ice hockey, lacrosse,
soccer, tennis
Women's Non-aid: basketball, cross
country, soccer, softball, volleyball

BUFFALO STATE COLLEGE
1300 Elmwood Avenue
Buffalo, NY 14222
(716) 878-6030
www.buffalostate.edu
Contact: Paul Martello
Men's Non-aid: basketball, cross country,
football, ice hockey, indoor track, soccer,
swimming-diving, track&field
Women's Non-aid: basketball, cross
country, ice hockey, indoor track, soccer,
softball, swimming-diving, tennis,
track&field, volleyball

CANISIUS COLLEGE
2001 Main Street
Buffalo, NY 14208
(716) 888-2977
www.canisius.edu
Contact: John Maddock
Men's Aid (#/$): 95/$547,131
Women's Aid (#/$): 104/$591,176
M: baseball, basketball, cross country,
golf, ice hockey, indoor track, lacrosse,
riflery, soccer, tennis, track&field. Men's
Non-aid: football
W: basketball, cross country, indoor
track, riflery, soccer, swimming, synchronized swimming, tennis, track&field,
volleyball

CAYUGA COMMUNITY COLLEGE
197 Franklin Street
Auburn, NY 13021
Two-year college
(315) 255-1743

www.cayuga-cc.edu
Contact: Ed Wagner
Men's Non-aid: basketball, cross country, football, golf, indoor track, martial arts, power lifting, racquetball, tennis, track&field
Women's Non-aid: basketball, cross country, indoor track, racquetball, softball, tennis, track&field, volleyball

CITY COLLEGE OF NEW YORK
138th Street and Convent Avenue
New York, NY 10031
(212) 650-8228
www.ccny.cuny.edu
Contact: Rob Coleman
Men's Non-aid: basketball, indoor track, lacrosse, soccer, tennis, track&field, volleyball
Women's Non-aid: basketball, fencing, indoor track, soccer, tennis, track&field, volleyball

CLARKSON UNIVERSITY
Alumni Gym
Potsdam, NY 13699-5830
(315) 268-6673
www.clarkson.edu
Contact: Gary Mikel
Men's Aid (#/$): 18/$387,000
Restrictions and notes: All athletic aid for Division I ice hockey
M: ice hockey. Men's Non-aid: alpine skiing, baseball, basketball, cross country, golf, lacrosse, nordic skiing, soccer, swimming-diving, tennis
Women's Non-aid: alpine skiing, basketball, cross country, golf, lacrosse, nordic skiing, soccer, swimming-diving, tennis, volleyball

CLINTON COMMUNITY COLLEGE
136 Clinton Point Drive
Plattsburgh, NY 12901
Two-year college
(518) 562-4170
www.northnet.org/clintoncc
Contact: Todd Roenbeck
Unspecified athletic aid available

M: baseball, basketball, soccer
W: basketball, soccer, softball

COLGATE UNIVERSITY
13 Oak Drive
Hamilton, NY 13346
(315) 228-7616
www.colgate.edu
Contact: Bob Cornell
Restrictions and notes: All aid awarded on the basis of need
Men's Non-aid: basketball, crew, cross country, diving, football, golf, ice hockey, indoor track, lacrosse, soccer, swimming, tennis, track&field
Women's Non-aid: basketball, crew, cross country, diving, field hockey, ice hockey, indoor track, lacrosse, soccer, softball, swimming, tennis, track&field, volleyball

COLLEGE OF NEW ROCHELLE
29 Castle Place
New Rochelle, NY 10805
(914) 654-5225
www.cnr.edu
Contact: Dr. Ronald Pollack
Women's Non-aid: basketball, cross country, softball, swimming, tennis, volleyball

COLLEGE OF SAINT ROSE
432 Western Avenue
Albany, NY 12203
(518) 458-5491
www.strose.edu
Contact: Cathy Haker
Unspecified athletic aid available
M: baseball, basketball, cross country, soccer, swimming
W: cross country, soccer, softball, swimming-diving, volleyball

COLUMBIA-GREENE COMMUNITY COLLEGE
4400 Route 23
Hudson, NY 12534
Two-year college
(518) 828-4181
www.sunycgcc.edu

Contact: David Heath
Men's Non-aid: baseball, basketball, golf, soccer
Women's Non-aid: basketball, soccer, softball

COLUMBIA UNIVERSITY
3030 Broadway
New York, NY 10027
(212) 854-2544
www.columbia.edu
Contact: Jacqueline Blackett
Men's Non-aid: baseball, basketball, crew, cross country, fencing, football, golf, indoor track, soccer, swimming-diving, tennis, track&field, wrestling
Women's Non-aid: archery, basketball, crew, cross country, fencing, field hockey, indoor track, lacrosse, soccer, softball, swimming-diving, tennis, track&field, volleyball

CONCORDIA COLLEGE
171 White Plains Road
Bronxville, NY 10708
(914) 337-9300 ext. 2447
www.concordia-ny.edu
Contact: Ivan Marquez
Unspecified athletic aid available
M: baseball, basketball, soccer, tennis, volleyball
W: basketball, soccer, softball, tennis, volleyball

CORNELL UNIVERSITY
Teagle Hall
Ithaca, NY 14853-6501
(607) 255-3752
www.cornell.edu
Contact: Patrick Gillespie
Men's Non-aid: baseball, basketball, cross country, football, golf, heavyweight crew, ice hockey, indoor track, lacrosse, lightweight crew, polo, soccer, sprint football, squash, swimming-diving, tennis, wrestling
Women's Non-aid: basketball, crew, cross country, equestrian, fencing, field hockey, gymnastics, ice hockey, indoor track,

lacrosse, polo, soccer, softball, swimming-diving, tennis, track&field, volleyball

DAEMEN COLLEGE
4380 Main Street
Amherst, NY 14226
(716) 839-3600
www.daemen.edu
Contact: Don Silveri
Men's Aid (#/$): 8/$73,498
Women's Aid (#/$): 3/$26,905
M: basketball
W: basketball

DELHI COLLEGE OF TECHNOLOGY (STATE UNIVERSITY OF NEW YORK)
Main Street
Delhi, NY 13753
Two-year college
(607) 746-4522
www.delhi.edu
Contact: Joel Smith
Men's Non-aid: basketball, cross country, golf, indoor track, lacrosse, soccer, swimming-diving, tennis, track&field
Women's Non-aid: basketball, cross country, indoor track, soccer, softball, swimming-diving, tennis, track&field, volleyball

DOMINICAN COLLEGE
470 Western Highway
Orangeburg, NY 10962
(914) 398-3008
www.dc.edu
Contact: Joe Clinton
Men's Aid (#/$): 20/$300,000
Women's Aid (#/$): 20/$300,000
M: baseball, basketball, golf, soccer
W: basketball, soccer, softball, volleyball

DOWLING COLLEGE
Idlehour Boulevard
Oakdale, NY 11769
(631) 244-3019
www.dowling.edu
Contact: Joanne Desantis
Unspecified athletic aid available

M: baseball, basketball, golf, lacrosse, soccer, tennis. Men's Non-aid: crew
W: basketball, crew, golf, softball, tennis, volleyball

DUTCHESS COMMUNITY COLLEGE
53 Pendell Road
Poughkeepsie, NY 12601-1595
Two-year college
(914) 431-8468
www.sunydutchess.edu
Contact: Bill Holland
Men's Non-aid: baseball, basketball, bowling, golf, soccer, tennis
Women's Non-aid: softball, tennis, volleyball

D'YOUVILLE COLLEGE
320 Porter Avenue
Buffalo, NY 14201
(716) 881-3200
www.dyc.edu
Contact: Brian Miller
Unspecified athletic aid available
M: basketball
W: basketball, volleyball

ELMIRA COLLEGE
1 Park Place
Elmira, NY 14901
(607) 735-1730
www.elmira.edu
Contact: Pat Thompson
Men's Non-aid: basketball, golf, ice hockey, lacrosse, soccer, tennis
Women's Non-aid: basketball, cheerleading, field hockey, lacrosse, soccer, softball, tennis, volleyball

FASHION INSTITUTE OF TECHNOLOGY
227 West 27th Street
New York, NY 10001-5992
Two-year college
(212) 217-7999
www.fitnyc.suny.edu
Contact: Nancy Yeldin
Men's Non-aid: alpine skiing, basketball, bowling, tennis

Women's Non-aid: alpine skiing, bowling, tennis, volleyball

FINGER LAKES COMMUNITY COLLEGE
4355 Lakeshore Drive
Canandaigua, NY 14424-0359
Two-year college
(716) 394-3522
www.fingerlakes.edu
Contact: Putt Moore
Men's Non-aid: baseball, basketball, cross country, lacrosse, soccer, timbersports
Women's Non-aid: basketball, cross country, lacrosse, soccer, timbersports

FORDHAM UNIVERSITY
441 East Fordham Road
Bronx, NY 10458
(718) 817-4300
www.fordham.edu
Contact: Jack Hayes
Unspecified athletic aid available
M: baseball, basketball, cross country, football, golf, indoor track, soccer, swimming-diving, tennis, track&field, water polo. Men's Non-aid: crew, ice hockey, lacrosse, volleyball, wrestling
W: baseball, basketball, cross country, indoor track, softball, swimming-diving, tennis, track&field, volleyball. Women's Non-aid: crew, soccer

FULTON-MONTGOMERY COMMUNITY COLLEGE
2805 State Highway 67
Johnstown, NY 12095-3790
Two-year college
(518) 762-4651 ext. 2100
www.fmcc.suny.edu
Contact: Dan Jarvis
Men's Non-aid: baseball, basketball, soccer
Women's Non-aid: basketball, soccer, softball, volleyball

GENESEE COMMUNITY COLLEGE
1 College Road
Batavia, NY 14020
Two-year college

(716) 343-0055 ext. 6246
www.sunygenesee.cc.ny.us
Contact: Len Nardone
Men's Aid (#/$): 7/$10,000
Women's Aid (#/$): 21/$25,700
M: basketball. Men's Non-aid: baseball,
cross country, soccer, swimming,
volleyball
W: basketball, soccer, volleyball.
Women's Non-aid: cross country, soft-
ball, swimming

HAMILTON COLLEGE
198 College Hill Road
Clinton, NY 13323
(315) 859-4685
www.hamilton.edu
Contact: Stephen Jaynes
Men's Non-aid: baseball, basketball,
cross country, football, golf, ice hockey,
indoor track, lacrosse, soccer, squash,
swimming-diving, tennis, track&field
Women's Non-aid: basketball, cross
country, field hockey, golf, ice hockey,
indoor track, lacrosse, soccer, softball,
squash, swimming-diving, tennis,
track&field, volleyball

HARTWICK COLLEGE
Binder Physical Education Center
Oneonta, NY 13820-4020
(607) 431-4703
www.hartwick.edu
Contact: Bill Sodoma
Unspecified athletic aid available
M: soccer. Men's Non-aid: baseball, basketball, cross country, golf, indoor track,
lacrosse, swimming-diving, tennis,
track&field
W: water polo. Women's Non-aid: basketball, cross country, equestrian, field
hockey, golf, indoor track, lacrosse,
soccer, softball, swimming-diving, tennis,
track&field

HERKIMER COUNTY
COMMUNITY COLLEGE
Reservoir Road
Herkimer, NY 13350

Two-year college
(315) 866-0300 ext. 255
www.hccc.ntcnet.com
Contact: Troy Tucker
Men's Non-aid: baseball, basketball,
bowling, cross country, golf, lacrosse,
soccer, swimming, tennis, track&field
Women's Non-aid: basketball, bowling,
cross country, field hockey, golf, soccer,
softball, swimming, tennis, track&field,
volleyball

HILBERT COLLEGE
5200 South Park Avenue
Hamburg, NY 14075-1597
Two-year college
(716) 649-7900 ext. 254
www.hilbert.edu
Contact: Wayne Porterfield
Unspecified athletic aid available
M: baseball, basketball, soccer
W: basketball, soccer, softball, volleyball

HOFSTRA UNIVERSITY
1000 Hempstead Turnpike
Hempstead, NY 11549
(516) 463-6764
www.hofstra.edu
Contact: Jim Sheehan
Men's Aid (#/$): 38/unspecified $
Women's Aid (#/$): 30/unspecified $
M: baseball, basketball, cross country,
football, golf, lacrosse, soccer, tennis,
wrestling
W: basketball, cross country, field hockey,
lacrosse, soccer, softball, tennis, volleyball

HOUGHTON COLLEGE
One Willard Avenue
Houghton, NY 14744
(716) 567-9559
www.houghton.edu
Contact: Jason Mucher
Unspecified athletic aid available
M: basketball, cross country, soccer,
track&field
W: basketball, cheerleading, cross coun-
try, field hockey, soccer, track&field,
volleyball

HUDSON VALLEY COMMUNITY COLLEGE
80 Vandenburgh Avenue
Troy, NY 12180
Two-year college
(518) 629-7328
www.hvcc.edu
Contact: Andrew Marrochello
Men's Non-aid: baseball, basketball, bowling, football, ice hockey, lacrosse, soccer
Women's Non-aid: basketball, bowling, cross country, soccer, softball, tennis, volleyball

HUNTER COLLEGE OF THE CITY UNIVERSITY OF NEW YORK
695 Park Avenue
New York, NY 10021
(212) 772-4783
www.hunter.cuny.edu
Contact: Damion Jones
Men's Non-aid: basketball, cheerleading, cross country, fencing, soccer, tennis, track&field, volleyball, wrestling
Women's Non-aid: basketball, cheerleading, cross country, fencing, softball, swimming, tennis, track&field, volleyball

IONA COLLEGE
715 North Avenue
New Rochelle, NY 10801-1890
(914) 633-2334
www.iona.edu
Contact: David Cagianello
Unspecified athletic aid available
M: baseball, basketball, cross country, diving, golf, ice hockey, indoor track, soccer, swimming, tennis, track&field.
Men's Non-aid: crew, football
W: basketball, cross country, indoor track, soccer, softball, swimming-diving, tennis, track&field, volleyball. Women's Non-aid: crew

ITHACA COLLEGE
953 Danby Road
Ithaca, NY 14850
(607) 274-3397

www.ithaca.edu
Contact: Mike Warwick
Men's Non-aid: baseball, basketball, crew, cross country, football, indoor track, lacrosse, soccer, swimming-diving, tennis, track&field, wrestling
Women's Non-aid: basketball, crew, cross country, field hockey, gymnastics, indoor track, lacrosse, soccer, softball, swimming-diving, tennis, track&field, volleyball

JEFFERSON COMMUNITY COLLEGE
Coffeen Street
Watertown, NY 13601
Two-year college
(315) 786-2248
www.sunyjefferson.edu
Contact: Tom Baker
Unspecified athletic aid available
M: lacrosse, soccer. Men's Non-aid: baseball, basketball, golf
W: soccer, softball, volleyball. Women's Non-aid: basketball, cheerleading, golf

LE MOYNE COLLEGE
Springfield Road
Syracuse, NY 13214
(315) 445-4450
www.lemoyne.edu
Contact: Dick Rockwell
Men's Aid (#/$): 13/$54,430
Women's Aid (#/$): 8/$15,700
M: baseball, basketball, cross country, golf, soccer, tennis. Men's Non-aid: lacrosse
W: basketball, cross country, soccer, softball, tennis, volleyball

LONG ISLAND UNIVERSITY (BROOKLYN CAMPUS)
1 University Plaza
Brooklyn, NY 11201-8423
(718) 488-1011
www.brooklyn.liunet.edu
Contact: Rose Iannicelli
Unspecified athletic aid available
M: baseball, basketball, cross country, golf, gymnastics, indoor track, soccer,

tennis, track&field
W: basketball, cross country, gymnastics, indoor track, softball, tennis, track&field

LONG ISLAND UNIVERSITY (C.W. POST CAMPUS)
720 Northern Boulevard
Brookville, NY 11548-1300
(516) 299-4156
www.cwpost.liunet.edu
Contact: Brad Sullivan
Unspecified athletic aid available
M: baseball, basketball, lacrosse, soccer, track&field. Men's Non-aid: football
W: basketball, cross country, field hockey, lacrosse, softball, tennis, track&field, volleyball

LONG ISLAND UNIVERSITY (SOUTHAMPTON COLLEGE)
239 Montauk Highway
Southampton, NY 11968-4198
(631) 287-8360
www.southampton.liunet.edu
Contact: Susan M. Taylor
Men's Aid (#/$): 41/$221,355
Women's Aid (#/$): 42/$155,736
M: basketball, soccer, volleyball. Men's Non-aid: lacrosse
W: basketball, soccer, softball, volleyball

MANHATTAN COLLEGE
Manhattan College Parkway
Riverdale, NY 10471
(718) 862-7228
www.manhattan.edu
Contact: Bob Byrnes
Unspecified athletic aid available
M: baseball, basketball, cross country, golf, indoor track and field, lacrosse, soccer, tennis. Men's Non-aid: crew
W: basketball, cross country, indoor track, lacrosse, soccer, softball, tennis, track&field, volleyball. Women's Non-aid: crew, swimming

MANHATTANVILLE COLLEGE
2900 Purchase Street
Purchase, NY 10577

(914) 323-5280
www.mville.edu
Contact: Mark Meachem
Men's Non-aid: baseball, basketball, lacrosse, rugby, soccer, tennis
Women's Non-aid: basketball, diving, field hockey, soccer, softball, swimming-diving, tennis, volleyball

MARIST COLLEGE
290 North Road
Poughkeepsie, NY 12601-1387
(914) 575-3000 ext. 2463
www.marist.edu
Contact: Chandra Bierwirth
Men's Aid (#/$): 36/$846,000
Women's Aid (#/$): 42/$987,000
M: baseball, basketball, cross country, indoor track, lacrosse, soccer, swimming-diving, tennis, track&field. Men's Non-aid: crew, football
W: basketball, cross country, indoor track, lacrosse, soccer, softball, swimming-diving, tennis, track&field, volleyball, water polo. Women's Non-aid: crew

MERCY COLLEGE
555 Broadway
Dobbs Ferry, NY 10522-1189
(914) 693-7281
www.mercynet.edu
Contact: Steve Balsan
Unspecified athletic aid available
M: baseball, basketball, cross country, golf, soccer, tennis
W: basketball, cross country, golf, soccer, softball, volleyball

MOHAWK VALLEY COMMUNITY COLLEGE
1101 Sherman Drive
Utica, NY 13501
Two-year college
(315) 792-5570
www.mvcc.edu
Contact: Gary Broadhurst
Men's Non-aid: baseball, basketball, bowling, cross country, golf, ice hockey,

indoor track, lacrosse, soccer, tennis, track&field
Women's Non-aid: basketball, bowling, cross country, indoor track, soccer, softball, tennis, track&field, volleyball

MOLLOY COLLEGE
1000 Hempstead Avenue
Rockville Centre, NY 11571-5002
(516) 256-2207
www.molloy.edu
Contact: Bob Houlihan
Unspecified athletic aid available
M: baseball, basketball, cross country, lacrosse, soccer
W: basketball, cross country, equestrian, soccer, softball, tennis, volleyball

NASSAU COMMUNITY COLLEGE
One Education Drive
Garden City, NY 11530
Two-year college
(516) 572-7522
www.sunynassau.edu
Contact: Michael Pelliccia
Men's Non-aid: baseball, basketball, bowling, cross country, football, golf, indoor track, lacrosse, soccer, tennis, track&field, wrestling
Women's Non-aid: basketball, bowling, cross country, indoor track, soccer, softball, tennis, track&field, volleyball

NAZARETH COLLEGE
4245 East Avenue
Rochester, NY 14618
(716) 389-2452
www.naz.edu
Contact: Joe Seil
Men's Non-aid: basketball, golf, lacrosse, soccer, swimming-diving, tennis
Women's Non-aid: basketball, golf, soccer, swimming-diving, tennis, volleyball

NEW YORK INSTITUTE OF TECHNOLOGY
P.O. Box 8000
Old Westbury, NY 11568-8000

(516) 686-7626
www.nyit.edu
Contact: Clyde Doughty
Unspecified athletic aid available
M: baseball, basketball, indoor track, soccer, softball, track&field, volleyball

NEW YORK UNIVERSITY
Coles Sports Center
181 Mercer Street
New York, NY 10012
(212) 998-2031
www.nyu.edu
Contact: Jeff Bernstein
Men's Non-aid: basketball, cross country, fencing, golf, indoor track, soccer, swimming-diving, tennis, track&field, volleyball, wrestling
Women's Non-aid: basketball, cross country, fencing, indoor track, soccer, swimming-diving, tennis, track&field, volleyball

NIAGARA COUNTY COMMUNITY COLLEGE
3111 Saunders Settlement Road
Sanborn, NY 14132
Two-year college
(716) 731-3271 ext. 519
www.sunyniagara.cc.ny.us
Contact: Lee Wallace
Men's Non-aid: baseball, basketball, soccer, wrestling
Women's Non-aid: basketball, soccer, softball, volleyball

NIAGARA UNIVERSITY
Niagara University, NY 14109-2011
(716) 286-8600
www.niagara.edu
Contact: Mike Hermann
Unspecified athletic aid available
M: baseball, basketball, cross country, golf, ice hockey, soccer, swimming-diving, tennis
W: basketball, cross country, ice hockey, lacrosse, soccer, softball, swimming-diving, tennis, volleyball

NORTH COUNTRY COMMUNITY COLLEGE

20 Winona Avenue
P.O. Box 89
Saranac Lake, NY 12983-0089
Two-year college
(518) 891-2920
www.nccc.edu
Contact: Frank Burns
Unspecified athletic aid available
Men's Non-aid: basketball, ice hockey, lacrosse, soccer
Women's Non-aid: basketball, ice hockey, soccer, softball

NYACK COLLEGE

1 South Boulevard
Nyack, NY 10960-3698
(914) 358-1710 ext. 151
www.nyackcollege.edu
Contact: Kyle Jarrett
Men's Aid (#/$): 12/$22,975
Women's Aid (#/$): 12/$18,901
M: baseball, basketball, cross country, golf, soccer
W: basketball, softball, volleyball

ORANGE COUNTY COMMUNITY COLLEGE

115 South Street
Middletown, NY 10940
Two-year college
(914) 341-4215
www.orange.cc.ny.us
Contact: Sue Deer
Men's Non-aid: baseball, basketball, golf, soccer, tennis
Women's Non-aid: basketball, soccer, softball, tennis, volleyball

OSWEGO STATE UNIVERSITY (STATE UNIVERSITY OF NEW YORK)

Laker Hall
Oswego, NY 13126-3599
(315) 341-2378
www.oswego.edu
Contact: Dr. Sandra L. Moore
Men's Non-aid: baseball, basketball, cross country, golf, ice hockey, lacrosse, soccer, swimming-diving, tennis, track&field, wrestling
Women's Non-aid: basketball, cross country, field hockey, soccer, softball, swimming-diving, tennis, track&field, volleyball

PACE UNIVERSITY

861 Bedford Road
Pleasantville, NY 10570
(914) 773-3888
www.pace.edu
Contact: Brian Mundy
Unspecified athletic aid available
Restrictions and notes: All Pace University branch campuses administrated in Pleasantville.
M: baseball, basketball, cross country, indoor track, track&field. Men's Non-aid: bowling, football, ice hockey, lacrosse, tennis, volleyball
W: basketball, cross country, indoor track, softball, tennis, track&field, volleyball. Women's Non-aid: bowling

PLATTSBURGH STATE UNIVERSITY (STATE UNIVERSITY OF NEW YORK)

101 Broad Street
Plattsburgh, NY 12901
(518) 564-4148
www.plattsburgh.edu
Contact: Brian Micheels
Men's Non-aid: basketball, cross country, ice hockey, indoor track, soccer, swimming-diving, tennis, track&field
Women's Non-aid: basketball, cross country, indoor track, soccer, swimming-diving, tennis, track&field, volleyball

POLYTECHNIC UNIVERSITY (BROOKLYN CAMPUS)

6 MetroTech Center
Brooklyn, NY 11201
(718) 637-5900
www.poly.edu
Contact: Maureen Braziel
Men's Non-aid: baseball, basketball,

cross country, judo, soccer, tennis
Women's Non-aid: judo, volleyball

PURCHASE COLLEGE (STATE UNIVERSITY OF NEW YORK)
735 Anderson Hill Road
Purchase, NY 10577-1400
(914) 251-6357
www.purchase.edu
Contact: Ernie Palmieri
Men's Non-aid: basketball, cross country, soccer
Women's Non-aid: basketball, cross country, volleyball

QUEENSBOROUGH COMMUNITY COLLEGE
222-05 56th Avenue
Bayside, NY 11364
Two-year college
(718) 631-6322
www.qcc.cuny.edu
Contact: Maria Macarle
Men's Non-aid: baseball, basketball, cross country, soccer, tennis, track&field
Women's Non-aid: basketball, cross country, soccer, softball, tennis, track&field, volleyball

QUEENS COLLEGE (CITY UNIVERSITY OF NEW YORK)
65-30 Kissena Boulevard
Flushing, NY 11367
(718) 997-2758
www.qc.edu
Contact: Neal Kaufer
Unspecified athletic aid available
M: baseball, basketball, cross country, diving, indoor track, soccer, swimming, tennis, track&field, water polo. Men's Non-aid: bowling, golf, lacrosse, volleyball
W: basketball, cross country, diving, indoor track, softball, swimming, tennis, track&field, volleyball

RENSSELAER POLYTECHNIC INSTITUTE
110 Eighth Street
Troy, NY 12180-3590

(518) 276-2137
www.rpi.edu
Contact: Kevin Beattie
Unspecified athletic aid available
M: ice hockey. Men's Non-aid: baseball, basketball, cross country, football, golf, indoor track, lacrosse, soccer, swimming-diving, tennis, track&field
Women's Non-aid: basketball, cross country, field hockey, soccer, softball, swimming-diving, tennis

ROBERTS WESLEYAN COLLEGE
2301 Westside Drive
Rochester, NY 14624-1997
(716) 594-6357
www.roberts.edu
Contact: Chris Williams
Unspecified athletic aid available
M: basketball, cross country, indoor track, soccer, track&field. Men's Non-aid: baseball, tennis
W: basketball, cross country, indoor track, soccer, softball, track&field, volleyball. Women's Non-aid: tennis

ROCHESTER INSTITUTE OF TECHNOLOGY
51 Lomb Memorial Drive
Rochester, NY 14623
(716) 475-6154
www.rit.edu
Contact: Chuck Mitrano
Men's Non-aid: baseball, basketball, cross country, ice hockey, indoor track, lacrosse, soccer, swimming-diving, tennis, track&field, wrestling
Women's Non-aid: cross country, ice hockey, soccer, softball, swimming-diving, tennis, track&field, volleyball

ROCKLAND COMMUNITY COLLEGE
145 College Road
Suffern, NY 10901
Two-year college
(914) 574-4451
www.sunyrockland.edu
Contact: Dan Keeley

Unspecified athletic aid available
M: baseball, basketball, golf, soccer, tennis
W: basketball, softball, tennis, volleyball

SAGE JUNIOR COLLEGE OF ALBANY
140 New Scotland Avenue
Albany, NY 12208
Two-year college
(518) 292-1967
www.sage.edu
Contact: Louisa Fumo
Unspecified athletic aid available
M: basketball
W: basketball, volleyball

ST. BONAVENTURE UNIVERSITY
Box G
St. Bonaventure, NY 14778
(716) 375-2282
www.sbu.edu
Contact: Jim Engelhardt
Men's Aid (#/$): 17/$422,140
Women's Aid (#/$): 12/$88,213
M: baseball, basketball, diving, soccer, swimming, swimming-diving, tennis. Men's Non-aid: cross country, golf, lacrosse
W: basketball, diving, softball, swimming, swimming-diving, tennis, volleyball. Women's Non-aid: cross country, golf, soccer

ST. FRANCIS COLLEGE
180 Remsen Street
Brooklyn Heights, NY 11201
(718) 489-5490
www.stfranciscollege.edu
Contact: Jim Hoffman
Men's Aid (#/$): 40/$600,000
Women's Aid (#/$): 40/$600,000
M: baseball, basketball, cross country, indoor track, soccer, swimming-diving, tennis, track&field, water polo
W: basketball, cross country, indoor track, softball, swimming-diving, tennis, track&field, volleyball, water polo

ST. JOHN FISHER COLLEGE
3690 East Avenue
Rochester, NY 14618
(716) 385-8421
www.sjfc.edu
Contact: Norm Kieffer
Men's Non-aid: baseball, basketball, cross country, football, golf, soccer, tennis
Women's Non-aid: basketball, cheerleading, cross country, lacrosse, soccer, softball, tennis, volleyball

ST. JOHN'S UNIVERSITY
8000 Utopia Parkway
Jamaica, NY 11439
(718) 990-6150
www.stjohns.edu
Contact: Dominic Scianna
Men's Aid (#/$): 54/$371,771
Women's Aid (#/$): 20/$107,591
M: baseball, basketball, bowling, cross country, fencing, golf, indoor track, lacrosse, soccer, swimming-diving, tennis, track&field. Men's Non-aid: crew, equestrian, football, ice hockey
W: basketball, bowling, cross country, fencing, golf, softball, swimming-diving, synchronized swimming, tennis, track&field. Women's Non-aid: football

ST. LAWRENCE UNIVERSITY
23 Ramoda Drive
Canton, NY 13617
(315) 229-5011
www.stlawu.edu
Contact: Wally Johnson
Men's Non-aid: alpine skiing, baseball, basketball, cross country skiing, equestrian, football, ice hockey, indoor track, lacrosse, soccer, swimming-diving, tennis, track&field, wrestling
Women's Non-aid: alpine skiing, basketball, cross country, cross country skiing, equestrian, field hockey, ice hockey, indoor track, lacrosse, soccer, swimming-diving, tennis, track&field, volleyball

ST. THOMAS AQUINAS COLLEGE
125 Route 340
Sparkill, NY 10976
(914) 398-4058
www.stac.edu
Contact: Barbara Vano
Men's Aid (#/$): 5/$72,000
Women's Aid (#/$): 5/$72,000
Restrictions and notes: Athletic aid for tuition only.
M: baseball, basketball, cross country, golf, soccer
W: basketball, cross country, soccer, softball, volleyball

SIENA COLLEGE
515 Loudon Road
Loudonville, NY 12211-1462
(518) 783-2411
www.siena.edu
Contact: Jason Rich
Men's Aid (#/$): 34/$714,000
Women's Aid (#/$): 54/$1,134,000
M: baseball, basketball, cross country, golf, lacrosse, soccer, tennis
Men's Non-aid: football
W: basketball, cross country, field hockey, soccer, softball, swimming-diving, tennis, volleyball

SKIDMORE COLLEGE
815 North Broadway
Saratoga Springs, NY 12866
(518) 580-5364
www.skidmore.edu
Contact: Bill Jones
Men's Non-aid: alpine skiing, baseball, basketball, crew, equestrian, golf, ice hockey, lacrosse, polo, soccer, tennis
Women's Non-aid: alpine skiing, basketball, crew, equestrian, field hockey, ice hockey, lacrosse, polo, soccer, swimming-diving, tennis, volleyball

STATE UNIVERSITY OF NEW YORK COLLEGE AT BROCKPORT
350 New Campus Drive
Brockport, NY 14420-2989
(716) 395-2218
www.brockport.edu
Contact: Mike Andriatch
Men's Non-aid: baseball, basketball, cross country, football, ice hockey, indoor track, soccer, swimming-diving, track&field, wrestling
Women's Non-aid: basketball, cross country, field hockey, golf, gymnastics, indoor track, soccer, softball, swimming-diving, tennis, track&field, volleyball

STATE UNIVERSITY OF NEW YORK COLLEGE AT CORTLAND
P.O. Box 2000
Cortland, NY 13045-0900
(607) 753-5673
www.cortland.edu
Contact: Fran Elia
Men's Non-aid: baseball, basketball, cross country, football, ice hockey, indoor track, lacrosse, soccer, swimming-diving, track&field, wrestling
Women's Non-aid: basketball, cross country, field hockey, gymnastics, ice hockey, indoor track, lacrosse, soccer, softball, swimming-diving, tennis, track&field, volleyball

STATE UNIVERSITY OF NEW YORK COLLEGE AT FREDONIA
Dods Hall
Fredonia, NY 14063
(716) 673-3100
www.fredonia.edu
Contact: Donna Valone
Men's Non-aid: baseball, basketball, cross country, ice hockey, indoor track, soccer, tennis, track&field
Women's Non-aid: basketball, cross country, indoor track, lacrosse, soccer, softball, tennis, track&field, volleyball

STATE UNIVERSITY OF NEW YORK COLLEGE AT GENESEO
1 College Circle
Geneseo, NY 14454
(716) 245-5211
www.geneseo.edu
Contact: Fred Bright

Men's Non-aid: basketball, cross country, ice hockey, indoor track, lacrosse, soccer, swimming-diving, track&field
Women's Non-aid: basketball, cross country, field hockey, indoor track, lacrosse, soccer, softball, swimming-diving, tennis, track&field, volleyball

STATE UNIVERSITY OF NEW YORK COLLEGE AT NEW PALTZ
75 South Manheim Boulevard
New Paltz, NY 12561
(914) 257-3927
www.newpaltz.edu
Contact: Dave Hines
Men's Non-aid: baseball, basketball, cross country, golf, indoor track, soccer, swimming-diving, tennis, track&field, volleyball
Women's Non-aid: basketball, cross country, field hockey, indoor track, lacrosse, soccer, softball, swimming-diving, tennis, track&field, volleyball

STATE UNIVERSITY OF NEW YORK COLLEGE AT POTSDAM
Maxcy Hall
44 Pierrepont Street
Potsdam, NY 13676
(315) 267-2315
www.potsdam.edu
Contact: Tony Difabio
Men's Non-aid: basketball, equestrian, ice hockey, lacrosse, soccer, swimming-diving
Women's Non-aid: basketball, equestrian, lacrosse, soccer, softball, swimming-diving, tennis, volleyball

STATE UNIVERSITY OF NEW YORK INSTITUTE OF TECHNOLOGY AT UTICA/ROME
P.O. Box 3050
Utica, NY 13504-3050
(315) 792-7520
www.sunyit.edu
Contact: Kevin Grimmer
Men's Non-aid: baseball, basketball, golf, soccer

Women's Non-aid: basketball, soccer, softball, volleyball

STATE UNIVERSITY OF NEW YORK MARITIME COLLEGE
6 Pennyfield Avenue
Throgs Neck, NY 10465
(718) 409-7220
www.sunymaritime.edu
Contact: Kathy Hewitt
Men's Non-aid: baseball, basketball, crew, cross country, football, golf, ice hockey, lacrosse, riflery, rugby, sailing, soccer, swimming, tennis, volleyball
Women's Non-aid: basketball, crew, softball, tennis, volleyball

SUFFOLK COUNTY COMMUNITY COLLEGE
533 College Road
Selden, NY 11784
Two-year college
(631) 451-4881
www.sunysuffolk.edu
Contact: Arthur Del Ducka
Men's Non-aid: baseball, basketball, cross country, golf, soccer, tennis
Women's Non-aid: basketball, softball, tennis, volleyball

SYRACUSE UNIVERSITY
Manley Field House
Syracuse, NY 13244-5020
(315) 443-2608
www.suathletics.com
Contact: Sue Edson
Unspecified athletic aid available
M: basketball, crew, cross country, football, indoor track, lacrosse, soccer, swimming-diving, track&field, wrestling
W: basketball, crew, cross country, field hockey, indoor track, lacrosse, soccer, softball, swimming-diving, tennis, track&field, volleyball

UNION COLLEGE
17 South Lane
Schenectady, NY 12308
(518) 388-6170

www.union.edu
Contact: George Cuttita
Men's Non-aid: baseball, basketball, crew, cross country, football, ice hockey, indoor track, lacrosse, soccer, swimming-diving, tennis, track&field
Women's Non-aid: basketball, crew, cross country, field hockey, ice hockey, indoor track, lacrosse, soccer, softball, swimming-diving, tennis, track&field, volleyball

UNIVERSITY AT ALBANY (STATE UNIVERSITY OF NEW YORK)
1400 Washington Avenue
Albany, NY 12222
(518) 442-3072
www.albany.edu
Contact: Brian De Pasquale
Men's Non-aid: baseball, basketball, cross country, football, indoor track, lacrosse, soccer, tennis, track&field
Women's Non-aid: basketball, cross country, field hockey, golf, lacrosse, indoor track, soccer, softball, tennis, track&field, volleyball

UNIVERSITY AT BUFFALO (STATE UNIVERSITY OF NEW YORK)
175 Alumni Arena, North Campus
Buffalo, NY 14260
(716) 645-6761
www.buffalo.edu
Contact: Paul Vecchio
Men's Non-aid: baseball, basketball, cross country, football, golf, ice hockey, indoor track, soccer, swimming-diving, tennis, track&field, wrestling
Women's Non-aid: basketball, cross country, field hockey, indoor track, soccer, softball, swimming-diving, tennis, track&field, volleyball

UNIVERSITY AT STONY BROOK (STATE UNIVERSITY OF NEW YORK)
Sports Complex
Stony Brook, NY 11794-3500

(631) 632-6312
www.goseawolves.org
Contact: Robert Emmerich, Jr.
M: baseball, basketball, cross country, indoor track, lacrosse, soccer, swimming-diving, tennis, track&field. Men's Non-aid: football
W: basketball, cross country, golf, indoor track, soccer, softball, swimming-diving, tennis, track&field, volleyball

VASSAR COLLEGE
124 Raymond Avenue
Poughkeepsie, NY 12604
(914) 437-7469
www.vassar.edu
Contact: Tony Brown
Men's Non-aid: baseball, basketball, cross country, fencing, lacrosse, rowing, soccer, squash, swimming-diving, tennis, volleyball
Women's Non-aid: basketball, cross country, fencing, field hockey, lacrosse, rowing, soccer, squash, swimming-diving, tennis, volleyball

WAGNER COLLEGE
1 Campus Road
Staten Island, NY 10301
(718) 390-3227
www.wagner.edu
Contact: Bob Balut
Unspecified athletic aid available
M: baseball, basketball, cross country, golf, indoor track, tennis, track&field, wrestling
W: basketball, cross country, indoor track, softball, tennis, track&field, volleyball

YESHIVA UNIVERSITY
500 West 185th Street
New York, NY 10033-3201
(212) 960-5211
www.yu.edu
Contact: Richard Zerneck
Men's Non-aid: basketball, cross country, fencing, golf, tennis, volleyball, wrestling
Women's Non-aid: basketball, fencing, tennis

YORK COLLEGE (CUNY)
94-20 Guy R. Brewer Boulevard
Jamaica, NY 11451
(718) 262-5100
www.york.cuny.edu
Contact: George Paz
Men's Non-aid: basketball, cross country,
indoor track, soccer, tennis, track&field,
volleyball
Women's Non-aid: basketball, cheerleading, cross country, indoor track,
track&field, volleyball

North Carolina

**APPALACHIAN STATE
UNIVERSITY**
P.O. Box 32023
Broome Kirk Gymnasium
Boone, NC 28608
(828) 262-2018
www.goasu.com
Contact: Mike Waddell
Men's Aid (#/$): 166/$657,624
Women's Aid (#/$): 73/$179,916
M: baseball, basketball, cross country,
football, golf, indoor track, soccer, tennis,
track&field, wrestling
W: basketball, cross country, field hockey,
golf, indoor track, tennis, track&field,
volleyball

BARBER-SCOTIA COLLEGE
145 Cabarrus Avenue
Concord, NC 28025
(828) 789-2997
www.barber-scotia.edu
Contact: Dr. William Madrey
Unspecified athletic aid available
Restrictions and notes: Partial aid, based
on need
M: basketball, cross country, tennis,
track&field. Men's Non-aid: indoor track
W: basketball, cross country, softball,
tennis, track&field, volleyball. Women's
Non-aid: indoor track

BARTON COLLEGE
Athletic Office
P.O. Box 5000
Wilson, NC 27893
(252) 399-6517
www.barton.edu
Contact: Gary W. Hall
Men's Aid (#/$): 18.5/unspecified $
Women's Aid (#/$): 18.5/unspecified $
M: baseball, basketball, cross country,
golf, soccer, tennis
W: basketball, cross country, soccer,
softball, tennis, volleyball

BELMONT ABBEY COLLEGE
Mount Holly Road
Belmont, NC 28012
(704) 825-6718
www.bac.edu
Contact: Ann Stevens
Unspecified athletic aid available
M: baseball, basketball, golf, soccer,
tennis. Men's Non-aid: cross country
W: basketball, cross country, tennis,
volleyball

**BLANTON JUNIOR
COLLEGE**
126 College Street
Asheville, NC 28801
Two-year college
(828) 252-7346
Contact: Doug Allen
Unspecified athletic aid available
M: basketball, cross country

BREVARD COLLEGE
400 North Broad Street
Brevard, NC 28712
Two-year college
(828) 884-8300
www.brevard.edu
Contact: Norm Witek
Unspecified athletic aid available
M: basketball, cross country, indoor
track, soccer, tennis, track&field
W: basketball, cross country, indoor
track, soccer, tennis, track&field

CAMPBELL UNIVERSITY
P.O. Box 10
Buies Creek, NC 27506
(910) 893-1331
www.campbell.edu
Contact: Stan Cole
Men's Aid (#/$): 50/unspecified $
Women's Aid (#/$): 45/unspecified $
M: baseball, basketball, cross country,
golf, soccer, tennis, track&field, wrestling
W: basketball, cross country, golf, soccer,
softball, tennis, track&field, volleyball

CATAWBA COLLEGE
2300 West Innes Street
Salisbury, NC 28144
(704) 637-4720
www.catawba.edu
Contact: Dennis Davidson
Unspecified athletic aid available
M: baseball, basketball, cross country,
football, golf, lacrosse, soccer, tennis
W: basketball, cross country, field hockey,
golf, soccer, softball, tennis, volleyball

CHOWAN COLLEGE
200 Jones Drive
Murfreesboro, NC 27855
Two-year college
(252) 398-6500
www.chowan.edu
Contact: Bill Stiles
Unspecified athletic aid available
M: baseball, basketball, football, golf,
tennis. Men's Non-aid: soccer
W: basketball, soccer, softball, tennis,
volleyball

COASTAL CAROLINA COMMUNITY COLLEGE
444 Western Boulevard
Jacksonville, NC 28540
Two-year college
(910) 938-6250
www.coastal.cc.nc.us
Contact: C. Ronald Cox
Unspecified athletic aid available
M: golf, softball, tennis
W: softball, tennis

DAVIDSON COLLEGE
P.O. Box 1750
Davidson, NC 28036
(704) 892-2395
www.davidson.edu
Contact: John Anderson
Unspecified athletic aid available
M: baseball, basketball, cross country,
diving, golf, soccer, swimming, tennis,
track&field. Men's Non-aid: football
W: basketball, cross country, field hockey,
lacrosse, soccer, swimming-diving, tennis,
track&field, volleyball

DUKE UNIVERSITY
115 Cameron Indoor Stadium
Durham, NC 27706
(919) 684-2633
www.goduke.com
Contact: Mike Cragg
Unspecified athletic aid available
M: baseball, basketball, football, golf,
lacrosse, soccer, tennis, wrestling. Men's
Non-aid: cross country, fencing, indoor
track, swimming-diving, track&field
W: basketball, cross country, field hockey,
golf, indoor track, tennis, track&field,
volleyball. Women's Non-aid: fencing,
rowing, swimming-diving

EAST CAROLINA UNIVERSITY
Sports Medicine Building
Greenville, NC 27858-4353
(252) 328-6131
www.ecupirates.com
Contact: Charles Bloom
Unspecified athletic aid available
M: baseball, basketball, cross country,
football, golf, indoor track, soccer,
swimming-diving, tennis, track&field
W: basketball, cross country, indoor
track, softball, swimming-diving, tennis,
track&field, volleyball

ELIZABETH CITY STATE UNIVERSITY
1704 Weeksville Road
Campus Box 900
Elizabeth City, NC 27909

(252) 335-3588
www.ecsu.edu
Contact: Glen Mason
Men's Aid (#/$): 52/$239,000
Women's Aid (#/$): 12/$39,000
M: basketball, football. Men's Non-aid:
baseball, cross country, track&field
W: basketball. Women's Non-aid: cross
country, softball, track&field

ELON COLLEGE
Campus Box 2500
Elon College, NC 27244-2010
(336) 584-2420
www.elon.edu
Contact: David Hibbard
Unspecified athletic aid available
Restrictions and notes: 61.5 equivalent
grants for 12 sports (men and women).
M: baseball, basketball, football, golf,
soccer, tennis, track&field
W: basketball, soccer, softball, tennis,
volleyball

FAYETTEVILLE STATE
UNIVERSITY
1200 Murchison Road
Fayetteville, NC 28301-4298
(919) 486-1325
www.uncfsu.edu
Contact: June Donarumo
Unspecified athletic aid available
M: basketball, cross country, football,
golf
W: basketball, cross country, golf,
softball, volleyball

GARDNER-WEBB UNIVERSITY
P.O. Box 804
Boiling Springs, NC 28017
(704) 434-2361
www.gardner-webb.edu
Contact: Chuck Birch
Unspecified athletic aid available
M: baseball, basketball, football, golf,
tennis. Men's Non-aid: cross country,
track&field
W: basketball, tennis, volleyball. Women's
Non-aid: softball

GREENSBORO COLLEGE
815 West Market Street
Greensboro, NC 27401-1875
(336) 272-7102
www.gborocollege.edu
Contact: Katharine Bonisolli
Men's Non-aid: basketball, golf, soccer,
tennis
Women's Non-aid: basketball, softball,
tennis, volleyball

HIGH POINT UNIVERSITY
University Station
Montlieu Avenue
High Point, NC 27262-3598
(919) 841-4605
www.highpoint.edu
Contact: Jamie Joss
Men's Aid (#/$): 21.5/$232,200
Women's Aid (#/$): 13/$140,400
M: baseball, basketball, cross country,
golf, soccer, tennis, track&field
W: basketball, cross country, soccer,
tennis, volleyball. Women's Non-aid:
field hockey

JOHNSON C. SMITH UNIVERSITY
100 Beatties Ford Road
Charlotte, NC 28216
(704) 378-1035
www.jcsu.edu
Contact: Carolyn B. Smith
Unspecified athletic aid available
M: basketball, cross country, football,
golf, indoor track, tennis, track&field
W: basketball, cross country, indoor
track, track&field. Women's Non-aid:
softball

LEES-MCRAE COLLEGE
P.O. Box 128
Banner Elk, NC 28604-0128
(828) 898-8725
www.lmc.edu
Contact: Craig McPhail
Men's Aid (#/$): 27.5/$253,960
Women's Aid (#/$): 9.75/$90,055
M: alpine skiing, basketball, football,
soccer, tennis

W: alpine skiing, basketball, soccer, tennis, volleyball

LENOIR COMMUNITY COLLEGE
P.O. Box 188
Kinston, NC 28501
Two-year college
(252) 527-6223
www.lenoir.cc.nc.us
Contact: Glen Hartsdale
Unspecified athletic aid available
M: baseball, basketball, golf

LENOIR-RHYNE COLLEGE
LRC Box 7356
Hickory, NC 28603
(828) 328-7174
www.lrc.edu
Contact: Joe Smith
Unspecified athletic aid available
M: baseball, basketball, cross country, football, golf, soccer
W: basketball, cross country, golf, soccer, softball, volleyball

LIVINGSTONE COLLEGE
701 West Monroe Street
Salisbury, NC 28144
(828) 638-5500
www.livingstone.edu
Contact: Annie L. Pruitt
Unspecified athletic aid available
M: basketball, football, golf, tennis, wrestling. Men's Non-aid: track&field
W: basketball, tennis. Women's Non-aid: track&field

LOUISBURG COLLEGE
Louisburg, NC 27549
Two-year college
(919) 496-2521
www.louisburg.edu
Contact: Ross Frasier
Unspecified athletic aid available
M: basketball. Men's Non-aid: baseball, golf
W: basketball, volleyball

MARS HILL COLLEGE
Main Street
Mars Hill, NC 28754
(828) 689-1373
www.mhc.edu
Contact: Rick Baker
Unspecified athletic aid available
M: baseball, basketball, cross country, football, golf, soccer, tennis
W: basketball, cross country, soccer, softball, tennis, volleyball

MITCHELL COMMUNITY COLLEGE
West Broad Street
Statesville, NC 28677
Two-year college
(704) 878-3200
www.mitchell.cc.nc.us
Contact: Bill Moose
Unspecified athletic aid available
M: basketball, golf, tennis

MONTREAT-ANDERSON COLLEGE
P.O. Box 1267
Montreat, NC 28757
(828) 669-8011
www.montreat.edu
Contact: John Sullivan
Unspecified athletic aid available
M: baseball, basketball, cross country, golf, soccer, tennis
W: basketball, cross country, soccer, softball, tennis, volleyball

MOUNT OLIVE COLLEGE
634 Henderson Street
Mount Olive, NC 28365
(919) 658-5050
www.mountolive.edu
Contact: Benny Benton
Men's Aid (#/$): 17.5/$168,875
Women's Aid (#/$): 11/$106,150
M: baseball, basketball, golf, soccer, tennis
W: basketball, softball, tennis, volleyball

NORTH CAROLINA A & T STATE UNIVERSITY
1601 East Market Street
Greensboro, NC 27411

(336) 334-7141
www.ncat.edu
Contact: Donal Ware
Unspecified athletic aid available
M: baseball, basketball, cross country, football, indoor track, tennis, track&field, wrestling
W: basketball, indoor track, softball, tennis, track&field, volleyball

NORTH CAROLINA CENTRAL UNIVERSITY
1801 Fayetteville
Durham, NC 27707
(919) 530-7054
www.nccu.edu
Contact: Lola T. McKnight
Unspecified athletic aid available
M: basketball, cross country, football, indoor track, tennis, track&field
W: basketball, indoor track, softball, tennis, track&field, volleyball. Women's Non-aid: cross country

NORTH CAROLINA STATE UNIVERSITY
Box 8105
Reynolds Coliseum, Room 113
Raleigh, NC 27695-8501
(919) 515-2102
www.ncsu.edu
Contact: Mark Bockelman
Men's Aid (#/$): 53/$246,823
Women's Aid (#/$): 22/$140,553
M: baseball, basketball, cross country, football, golf, gymnastics, riflery, soccer, swimming-diving, tennis, track&field, wrestling. Men's Non-aid: fencing
W: basketball, cross country, golf, gymnastics, riflery, soccer, swimming-diving, tennis, track&field, volleyball. Women's Non-aid: fencing

NORTH CAROLINA WESLEYAN COLLEGE
3400 North Wesleyan Boulevard
Rocky Mount, NC 27804
(252) 985-5214
www.ncwc.edu

Contact: Renny Taylor
Men's Non-aid: baseball, basketball, soccer, tennis
Women's Non-aid: basketball, soccer, squash, volleyball

PFEIFFER UNIVERSITY
P.O. Box 960
Misenheimer, NC 28109
(704) 463-7343
www.pfeiffer.edu
Contact: Ruby B. Mason
Unspecified athletic aid available
M: baseball, basketball, cross country, golf, soccer, tennis, wrestling. Men's Non-aid: lacrosse
W: basketball, diving, field hockey, softball, swimming, swimming-diving, tennis, volleyball

QUEENS COLLEGE
1900 Selwyn Avenue
Charlotte, NC 28274
(704) 337-2225
www.queens.edu
Contact: Tony Carter
Men's Aid (#/$): 16/$230,400
Women's Aid (#/$): 16/$230,400
M: basketball, golf, soccer, tennis
W: basketball, soccer, tennis, volleyball

SAINT ANDREWS PRESBYTERIAN COLLEGE
1700 Dogwood Mile
Laurinburg, NC 28352-5589
(910) 277-5426
www.sape.edu
Contact: Bobby Simmons
Men's Non-aid: baseball, basketball, cross country, equestrian, golf, soccer, softball, tennis, track&field
Women's Non-aid: baseball, basketball, cross country, equestrian, softball, tennis, track&field, volleyball

SAINT AUGUSTINE'S COLLEGE
1315 Oakwood Avenue
Raleigh, NC 27610-2298
(919) 516-4000

www.st-aug.edu
Contact: Sherri Avent
Men's Aid (#/$): 85/$313,188
Women's Aid (#/$): 79/$282,364
M: baseball, basketball, golf, soccer, tennis, track&field
W: basketball, softball, track&field, volleyball

SOUTHEASTERN COMMUNITY COLLEGE
P.O. Box 151
4564 Chadbourn Highway
Whiteville, NC 28472
Two-year college
(910) 642-7141
www.southeastern.cc.nc.us
Contact: Robert Brooks
Men's Aid (#/$): 10/$5,000
Women's Aid (#/$): 5/$2,940
M: baseball
W: softball

UNIVERSITY OF NORTH CAROLINA (ASHEVILLE)
One University Heights
Asheville, NC 28804
(828) 251-6926
www.unca.edu
Contact: Tom Hunnicut
Men's Aid (#/$): 8/$25,673
Women's Aid (#/$): 7/$7,832
M: baseball, basketball, cross country, football, golf, indoor track, lacrosse, soccer, swimming-diving, tennis, track&field, wrestling. Men's Non-aid: fencing
W: basketball, cross country, field hockey, golf, gymnastics, lacrosse, soccer, softball, swimming-diving, tennis, track&field, volleyball. Women's Non-aid: fencing

UNIVERSITY OF NORTH CAROLINA (CHAPEL HILL)
P.O. Box 2126
Chapel Hill, NC 27514
(919) 962-7851
www.unc.edu

Contact: Lisa Deibler
Unspecified athletic aid available
M: baseball, basketball, cross country, football, golf, indoor track, lacrosse, soccer, swimming-diving, tennis, track&field, wrestling. Men's Non-aid: fencing
W: basketball, cross country, field hockey, golf, gymnastics, indoor track, lacrosse, soccer, softball, swimming-diving, tennis, track&field, volleyball. Women's Non-aid: fencing, rowing

UNIVERSITY OF NORTH CAROLINA (CHARLOTTE)
9201 University City Boulevard
Charlotte, NC 28223
(704) 547-4937
www.uncc.edu
Contact: Thomas Whitestone
Unspecified athletic aid available
M: baseball, basketball, cross country, golf, soccer, tennis, track&field
W: basketball, cross country, soccer, softball, tennis, track&field, volleyball

UNIVERSITY OF NORTH CAROLINA (GREENSBORO)
HHP Building
Greensboro, NC 27412-5001
(336) 334-5000
www.uncgsfartans.com
Contact: Ty Buckner
Men's Aid (#/$): 19/$49,741
Women's Aid (#/$): 14/$38,675
M: basketball, golf, soccer, tennis
W: basketball, softball, tennis, volleyball

UNIVERSITY OF NORTH CAROLINA (PEMBROKE)
P.O. Box 1510
1 University Drive
Pembroke, NC 28372-1510
(910) 521-6370
www.uncp.edu
Contact: Matthew Sullivan
Men's Aid (#/$): 27/$94,500
Women's Aid (#/$): 22/$77,000

M: baseball, basketball, cross country, golf, soccer, track&field, wrestling
W: basketball, cross country, softball, volleyball

UNIVERSITY OF NORTH CAROLINA (WILMINGTON)
601 S. College Road
Wilmington, NC 28403-3297
(910) 962-3236
www.uncwil.edu
Contact: Joe Browning
Men's Aid (#/$): 22/$41,601
Women's Aid (#/$): 24/$49,106
M: baseball, basketball, cross country, golf, soccer, swimming-diving, tennis, track&field
W: basketball, cross country, golf, softball, swimming-diving, tennis, track&field, volleyball

WAKE FOREST UNIVERSITY
P.O. Box 7426
Winston-Salem, NC 27109
(336) 758-5640
www.wakeforestsports.com
Contact: Jennifer Hoover
Men's Aid (#/$): 51/$534,000
Women's Aid (#/$): 16/$119,000
M: baseball, basketball, cross country, football, golf, indoor track, soccer, tennis
W: basketball, cross country, field hockey, golf, indoor track, tennis

WARREN WILSON COLLEGE
P.O. Box 9000
Asheville, NC 28815
(828) 298-3325
www.warren-wilson.edu
Contact: Robert Somerville
Men's Non-aid: baseball, basketball, cross country, soccer, swimming
Women's Non-aid: basketball, cross country, soccer, softball, swimming

WESTERN CAROLINA UNIVERSITY
2517 Ramsey Center
Cullowhee, NC 28723
(704) 227-7171
www.wcu.edu
Contact: Steve White
Unspecified athletic aid available
M: baseball, basketball, football, golf, indoor track, tennis, track&field
W: basketball, cross country, indoor track, tennis, track&field, volleyball

WILKES COMMUNITY COLLEGE
1328 Collegiate Drive
Wilkesboro, NC 28697
Two-year college
(336) 838-6100
www.wilkes.cc.nc.us
Contact: Kathron Richards
Aid (#/$): 12/$37,400 (M&W)
M: wrestling. Men's Non-aid: baseball, basketball, cross country, football, golf, soccer, tennis
W: basketball, field hockey, softball, tennis, volleyball

WINGATE UNIVERSITY
Campus Box 3051
Wingate, NC 28174
(704) 233-8186
www.wingate.edu
Contact: David Sherwood
Unspecified athletic aid available
M: baseball, basketball, football, golf, soccer, tennis
W: basketball, softball, tennis, volleyball

WINSTON-SALEM STATE UNIVERSITY
601 Martin Luther King Jr. Drive
Winston-Salem, NC 27110
(336) 750-2000
www.wssu.edu
Contact: Joseph V. Valls
Unspecified athletic aid available
M: basketball, cross country, football, tennis, track&field, wrestling. Men's Non-aid: golf, indoor track, swimming
W: basketball, cross country, softball, tennis, track&field, volleyball. Women's Non-aid: indoor track, swimming

North Dakota

BISMARCK STATE COLLEGE
1500 Edwards Avenue
Bismarck, ND 58506-5587
Two-year college
(701) 224-5480
www.bsc.nodak.edu
Contact: Buster Gillis
Unspecified athletic aid available
M: baseball, basketball, golf
W: basketball, golf, volleyball

DICKINSON STATE UNIVERSITY
291 Campus Drive
Dickinson, ND 58601-4896
(701) 483-2181
www.dsu.nodak.edu
Contact: LaVern Jessen
Unspecified athletic aid available
M: baseball, basketball, cross country,
football, golf, indoor track, rodeo, tennis,
track&field, wrestling
W: basketball, cross country, indoor
track, rodeo, tennis, track&field,
volleyball

JAMESTOWN COLLEGE
Box 6040
Jamestown, ND 58401
(701) 252-3467
www.jc.edu
Contact: Bud Etzold
Unspecified athletic aid available
M: baseball, basketball, cross country,
football, golf, indoor track, track&field,
wrestling
W: basketball, cross country, golf, indoor
track, soccer, softball, track&field,
volleyball

LAKE REGION STATE COLLEGE
1801 North College Drive
Devils Lake, ND 58301-1598
Two-year college
(701) 662-1600
www.lrsc.nodak.edu
Contact: Doug Darling

Unspecified athletic aid available
M: basketball
W: basketball, volleyball

MAYVILLE STATE COLLEGE
330 Third Street NE
Mayville, ND 58257-1299
(701) 786-4834
www.masu.nodak.edu
Contact: Stan Rettew
Unspecified athletic aid available
M: baseball, basketball, football
W: basketball, softball, volleyball

MINOT STATE UNIVERSITY
500 University Avenue West
Minot, ND 58707-0001
(701) 858-3000
www.misu.nodak.edu
Contact: Fran Hommel
Men's Aid (#/$): 80/$50,000
Women's Aid (#/$): 45/$40,000
Restrictions and notes: Tuition and fee
athletic award limits are applicable.
M: basketball, cross country, football,
indoor track, track&field. Men's Non-aid:
golf, tennis
W: basketball, cross country, indoor
track, tennis, track&field, volleyball.
Women's Non-aid: football

MINOT STATE UNIVERSITY (BOTTINEAU)
105 Simrall Boulevard
Bottineau, ND 58318-1198
Two-year college
(701) 228-2277
www.misu-b.nodak.edu
Contact: Craig Gerwin
Men's Aid (#/$): 42/unspecified $
Women's Aid (#/$): 22/unspecified $
M: baseball, basketball, ice hockey
W: basketball, volleyball

NORTH DAKOTA STATE COLLEGE OF SCIENCE
800 6th Street N
Wahpeton, ND 58076-0002
Two-year college

(701) 671-2281
www.ndscs.nodak.edu
Contact: Blayne Helgeson
Unspecified athletic aid available
M: basketball, football, indoor track,
track&field. Men's Non-aid: cross
country, golf, tennis
W: basketball, indoor track, track&field,
volleyball. Women's Non-aid: cross
country, golf, tennis

NORTH DAKOTA STATE UNIVERSITY

P.O. Box 5167
Fargo, ND 58105-5167
(701) 231-8331
www.gobison.com
Contact: George A. Ellis
Unspecified athletic aid available
M: baseball, basketball, cross country,
football, indoor track, track&field,
wrestling. Men's Non-aid: golf
W: basketball, cross country, indoor
track, track&field, volleyball. Women's
Non-aid: softball

UNIVERSITY OF MARY

7500 University Drive
Bismarck, ND 58504
(701) 255-7500
Contact: Louise Wetzel
Unspecified athletic aid available
M: basketball, cross country, football,
indoor track, tennis, track&field,
wrestling
W: basketball, cross country, indoor
track, softball, tennis, track&field,
volleyball

UNIVERSITY OF NORTH DAKOTA

University Station
Grand Forks, ND 58202-8193
(701) 777-2234
www.und.edu
Contact: Pete Oliszozak
Unspecified athletic aid available
M: baseball, basketball, cross country,
football, ice hockey, indoor track,
swimming-diving, track&field, wrestling.

Men's Non-aid: golf
W: basketball, cross country, indoor
track, softball, swimming-diving,
track&field, volleyball

VALLEY CITY STATE UNIVERSITY

101 College Street SW
Valley City, ND 58072-4098
(701) 845-7412
www.vcsu.nodak.edu
Contact: Betty Kuss Schumacher
Unspecified athletic aid available
M: baseball, basketball, cross country,
football, golf, tennis, track&field
W: basketball, cross country, softball,
tennis, track&field, volleyball

Ohio

ASHLAND COLLEGE

Athletic Department
Ashland, OH 44805
(419) 289-5442
www.ashland.edu
Contact: Al King
Men's Aid (#/$): 71/unspecified $
Women's Aid (#/$): 34/unspecified $
M: baseball, basketball, cross country,
football, indoor track, soccer, swimming-
diving, track&field, wrestling. Men's
Non-aid: golf, tennis
W: basketball, cross country, indoor
track, softball, swimming-diving,
track&field, volleyball. Women's Non-aid:
tennis

BLUFFTON COLLEGE

280 West College Avenue
Bluffton, OH 45817
(419) 358-3241
www.bluffton.edu
Contact: Tim Stried
Men's Non-aid: baseball, basketball,
cross country, football, golf, soccer,
tennis, track&field
Women's Non-aid: basketball, cross

country, soccer, softball, tennis, track&field, volleyball

BOWLING GREEN STATE UNIVERSITY
Athletic Department
Stadium East
Bowling Green, OH 43403
(419) 372-7076
www.bgsu.edu
Contact: Steve Barr
Unspecified athletic aid available
M: baseball, basketball, cross country, football, golf, ice hockey, soccer, swimming-diving, tennis, track&field
W: basketball, cross country, golf, gymnastics, softball, swimming-diving, tennis, track&field, volleyball

CAPITAL UNIVERSITY
2199 East Main Street
Columbus, OH 43209-2394
(614) 236-6174
www.capital.edu
Contact: Chris Rollman
Men's Non-aid: baseball, basketball, football, golf, soccer, tennis, wrestling
Women's Non-aid: basketball, softball, tennis, volleyball

CASE WESTERN RESERVE UNIVERSITY
10900 Euclid Avenue
Emerson PE Center
Cleveland, OH 44106-7223
(216) 368-6517
www.cwru.edu
Contact: Creg Jantz
Men's Non-aid: baseball, basketball, cross country, fencing, football, golf, indoor track, soccer, swimming-diving, tennis, track&field, wrestling
Women's Non-aid: basketball, cross country, fencing, indoor track, soccer, softball, swimming-diving, tennis, track&field, volleyball

CEDARVILLE COLLEGE
P.O. Box 601
Cedarville, OH 45314

(937) 766-7766
www.cedarville.edu
Contact: Mark Womack
Men's Aid (#/$): 11.6/$110,000
Women's Aid (#/$): 2.1/$22,000
M: baseball, basketball, cross country, golf, indoor track, soccer, tennis, track&field
W: basketball, cross country, indoor track, softball, tennis, track&field, volleyball

CINCINNATI STATE TECHNICAL & COMMUNITY COLLEGE
3520 Central Parkway
Cincinnati, OH 45223
Two-year college
(513) 569-1500
www.cinstate.cc.oh.us
Contact: Michelle Imhoff
Unspecified athletic aid available
M: basketball

CLARK STATE COMMUNITY COLLEGE
570 East Leffels Lane
Springfield, OH 45501
Two-year college
(937) 328-6027
www.clark.cc.oh.us
Contact: Lynn M. Rector
Men's Aid (#/$): 15/$9,500
Women's Aid (#/$): 20/$12,000
M: basketball, golf
W: basketball, volleyball

CLEVELAND STATE UNIVERSITY
East 18th and Prospect Avenue
Cleveland, OH 44115
(216) 687-4818
www.csuohio.edu
Contact: Paulet Welch
Unspecified athletic aid available
M: baseball, basketball, diving, fencing, golf, indoor track, soccer, swimming, swimming-diving, tennis, track&field, wrestling. Men's Non-aid: bowling, martial arts, sailing, water polo
W: basketball, cross country, diving,

fencing, golf, indoor track, softball, swimming, swimming-diving, tennis, track&field, volleyball. Women's Non-aid: martial arts, sailing

COLLEGE OF MOUNT ST. JOSEPH
5701 Delhi Road
Mount St. Joseph, OH 45051
(513) 244-4311
www.msj.edu
Contact: Steve Radcliffe
Unspecified athletic aid available
M: baseball, basketball, football, tennis, wrestling
W: basketball, cross country, soccer, softball, tennis, volleyball

THE COLLEGE OF WOOSTER
Office of News Service
Wooster, OH 44691
(330) 263-2000
www.wooster.edu
Contact: John P. Finn
Men's Non-aid: baseball, basketball, cross country, diving, football, golf, indoor track, lacrosse, soccer, swimming, tennis, track&field
Women's Non-aid: basketball, cross country, diving, field hockey, indoor track, lacrosse, soccer, swimming, tennis, track&field, volleyball

COLUMBUS STATE COMMUNITY COLLEGE
500 East Spring Street
Columbus, OH 43215
Two-year college
(614) 227-2637
www.cscc.edu
Contact: Tom Habegger
Men's Non-aid: baseball, basketball, cross country, golf, soccer
Women's Non-aid: cross country, equestrian, golf, softball, volleyball

CUYAHOGA COMMUNITY COLLEGE (EASTERN CAMPUS)
4250 Richmond Road
Highland Hills Village, OH 44122

Two-year college
(216) 987-2075
www.tri-c.cc.oh.us
Contact: Jan Schmidt
Unspecified athletic aid available
M: basketball, golf
W: basketball, volleyball

CUYAHOGA COMMUNITY COLLEGE (METROPOLITAN CAMPUS)
2900 Community College Avenue
Cleveland, OH 44115
Two-year college
(216) 987-4180
www.tri-c.cc.oh.us
Contact: Dan O'Connor
Unspecified athletic aid available
M: basketball, soccer, track&field, wrestling
W: basketball, soccer, softball, track&field, volleyball

CUYAHOGA COMMUNITY COLLEGE (WESTERN CAMPUS)
11000 Pleasant Valley Road
Parma, OH 44130
Two-year college
(216) 987-5134
www.tri-c.cc.oh.us
Contact: Dolores A. Sistrunk
Unspecified athletic aid available
M: baseball, track&field
W: softball, track&field

DEFIANCE COLLEGE
701 North Clinton Street
Defiance, OH 43512
(419) 783-2346
www.defiance.edu
Contact: Cindy Elliott
Men's Non-aid: baseball, basketball, cheerleading, cross country, golf, soccer, tennis, track&field
Women's Non-aid: basketball, cheerleading, cross country, softball, track&field, volleyball

DENISON UNIVERSITY
Granville, OH 43023
(740) 587-6242

www.denison.edu
Contact: Marilyn Gilbert
Men's Non-aid: baseball, basketball,
cross country, diving, football, golf,
indoor track, lacrosse, soccer, swimming,
tennis, track&field
Women's Non-aid: basketball, cross
country, diving, field hockey, indoor
track, lacrosse, soccer, softball,
swimming, tennis, track&field

HEIDELBERG COLLEGE
310 Market Street
Tiffin, OH 44883
(419) 448-2140
www.heidelberg.edu
Contact: Toby Voice
Men's Non-aid: baseball, basketball,
cross country, football, golf, indoor track,
soccer, tennis, track&field, wrestling
Women's Non-aid: basketball, cheerleading, cross country, golf, indoor track,
soccer, softball, tennis, track&field,
volleyball

HIRAM COLLEGE
P.O. Box 67
Hiram, OH 44234
(330) 569-3211
www.hiram.edu
Contact: Tim Bryan
Men's Non-aid: baseball, basketball,
cross country, diving, football, golf,
indoor track, soccer, swimming, tennis,
track&field
Women's Non-aid: basketball, cross
country, diving, indoor track, soccer,
softball, swimming, tennis, track&field,
volleyball

JOHN CARROLL UNIVERSITY
20700 North Park Boulevard
University Heights, OH 44118
(216) 397-4676
www.jcu.edu
Contact: Christopher Wenzler
Men's Non-aid: baseball, basketball,
cross country, football, golf, indoor track,
soccer, swimming-diving, tennis,

track&field, wrestling
Women's Non-aid: basketball, cross
country, indoor track, softball, swimming-diving, tennis, track&field,
volleyball

KENT STATE UNIVERSITY
(ASHTABULA)
3325 West 13th Street
Ashtabula, OH 44004
Two-year college
(440) 964-3322
www.ashtabula.kent.edu
Contact: Robert M. Dulak
Unspecified athletic aid available
M: baseball, basketball, cross country,
football, golf, gymnastics, ice hockey,
swimming, swimming-diving, track&field,
wrestling
W: basketball, cross country, field hockey,
gymnastics, softball, swimming,
swimming-diving, track&field, volleyball

KENT STATE UNIVERSITY
(EAST LIVERPOOL)
400 East 4th Street
East Liverpool, OH 43920
Two-year college
(330) 385-6348
www.kenteliv.kent.edu
Contact: Darwin Smith
Men's Non-aid: baseball, basketball, golf,
tennis
Women's Non-aid: basketball, tennis,
volleyball

KENT STATE UNIVERSITY (KENT)
106 Memorial Athletic and
Convocation Center
Kent, OH 44242-0001
(330) 672-2110
www.kent.edu
Contact: Will Roleson
Men's Aid (#/$): 161/unspecified $
Women's Aid (#/$): 68/unspecified $
M: baseball, basketball, cross country,
football, golf, gymnastics, ice hockey,
indoor track, track&field, wrestling
W: basketball, cross country, field hockey,

gymnastics, indoor track, softball, track&field, volleyball

KENT STATE UNIVERSITY (TRUMBULL)
4314 Mahoning Avenue NW
Warren, OH 44483
Two-year college
(330) 847-0571
www.trumbull.kent.edu
Contact: William Sandora
Unspecified athletic aid available
M: baseball, basketball, cross country, football, golf, gymnastics, ice hockey, swimming-diving, track&field, wrestling
W: basketball, cross country, field hockey, gymnastics, softball, swimming-diving, track&field, volleyball

KENT STATE UNIVERSITY (TUSCARAWAS)
University Drive NE
New Philadelphia, OH 44663
Two-year college
(330) 339-3391
www.tusc.kent.edu
Contact: Doyle W. Bolyard
Unspecified athletic aid available
M: baseball, basketball, cross country, football, golf, gymnastics, ice hockey, swimming-diving, track&field, wrestling
W: basketball, cross country, field hockey, gymnastics, softball, swimming-diving, track&field, volleyball

KENYON COLLEGE
Gambier, OH 43022-9623
(740) 427-5000
www.kenyon.edu
Contact: Jenny Bruening
Men's Non-aid: baseball, basketball, cross country, diving, football, golf, indoor track, lacrosse, soccer, swimming, tennis, track&field
Women's Non-aid: basketball, cross country, diving, field hockey, indoor track, lacrosse, soccer, softball, swimming, tennis, track&field, volleyball

LAKE ERIE COLLEGE
391 Washington Street
Painesville, OH 44077
(440) 352-3361
www.lakeerie.edu
Contact: David Poorman
Unspecified athletic aid available
M: basketball
W: basketball, softball, volleyball

MALONE COLLEGE
515 25th Street NW
Canton, OH 44709
(330) 471-8100
www.malone.edu
Contact: Mark W. Bankert
Men's Aid (#/$): 110/$82,500
Women's Aid (#/$): 60/$45,000
M: baseball, basketball, cross country, golf, indoor track, soccer, tennis, track&field
W: basketball, cross country, indoor track, softball, tennis, track&field, volleyball

MARIETTA COLLEGE
Box C96
Marietta, OH 45750
(740) 376-4891
www.marietta.edu
Contact: Brian Deitz
Men's Non-aid: baseball, basketball, crew, cross country, football, golf, indoor track, lacrosse, soccer, tennis, track&field
Women's Non-aid: basketball, crew, cross country, field hockey, softball, tennis, track&field, volleyball

MIAMI UNIVERSITY
210 Millett Hall
Oxford, OH 45056
(513) 529-4327
www.muohio.edu
Contact: Ken Peters
Men's Aid (#/$): 156/unspecified $
Women's Aid (#/$): 68/unspecified $
M: baseball, basketball, cross country, football, golf, ice hockey, swimming-diving, track&field

W: basketball, cross country, field hockey, soccer, softball, swimming-diving, tennis, track&field, volleyball

MOUNT UNION COLLEGE
1972 Clark Avenue
Alliance, OH 44601
(330) 821-5320
www.muc.edu
Contact: Michael De Matteis
Men's Non-aid: baseball, basketball, cross country, football, golf, lacrosse, soccer, softball, swimming-diving, tennis, track&field, wrestling
Women's Non-aid: baseball, cross country, softball, swimming-diving, tennis, track&field, volleyball

MOUNT VERNON NAZARENE COLLEGE
800 Martinsburg Road
Mount Vernon, OH 43050
(740) 397-1244
www.mvnc.edu
Contact: Paul Furey
Unspecified athletic aid available
M: baseball, basketball, soccer, tennis
W: basketball, softball, volleyball

MUSKINGUM COLLEGE
Public Relations Office
New Concord, OH 43762
(740) 826-8022
www.musking.edu
Contact: Bobby Lee
Men's Non-aid: baseball, basketball, cross country, football, golf, indoor track, soccer, tennis, track&field, wrestling
Women's Non-aid: basketball, cheer-leading, cross country, indoor track, soccer, softball, tennis, track&field, volleyball

NOTRE DAME COLLEGE OF OHIO
454 College Road
South Euclid, OH 44121
(216) 381-1680
www.ndc.edu
Contact: Susan Hlavacek

Unspecified athletic aid available
W: basketball, cross country, soccer, softball, tennis, volleyball

OBERLIN COLLEGE
200 Woodland Avenue
Oberlin, OH 44074
(440) 775-8503
www.oberlin.edu
Contact: Jeff Miller
Men's Non-aid: baseball, basketball, cross country, football, indoor track, lacrosse, soccer, swimming-diving, tennis, track&field
Women's Non-aid: basketball, cross country, field hockey, indoor track, lacrosse, soccer, softball, swimming-diving, tennis, track&field, volleyball

OHIO DOMINICAN COLLEGE
1216 Sunbury Road
Columbus, OH 43219
(614) 253-2741
www.odc.edu
Contact: Cynthia A. Diller
Unspecified athletic aid available
M: baseball, basketball, soccer
W: basketball, softball, volleyball

OHIO NORTHERN UNIVERSITY
525 South Main Street
Ada, OH 45810
(419) 772-2046
www.onu.edu
Contact: Tim Glon
Men's Non-aid: baseball, basketball, cross country, football, golf, indoor track, soccer, swimming-diving, tennis, track&field, wrestling
Women's Non-aid: basketball, cross country, golf, indoor track, soccer, softball, swimming-diving, tennis, track&field, volleyball

OHIO STATE UNIVERSITY
410 Woody Hayes Drive
124 St. John Arena
Columbus, OH 43210
(614) 292-6861

www.ohiostatebuckeyes.com
Contact: Gerry Emig
Unspecified athletic aid available
M: baseball, basketball, cross country,
football, golf, gymnastics, ice hockey,
indoor track, soccer, swimming-diving,
tennis, track&field, volleyball, wrestling.
Men's Non-aid: fencing, lacrosse, riflery
W: basketball, cross country, fencing,
field hockey, golf, gymnastics, indoor
track, softball, swimming-diving, synchronized swimming, tennis, track&field,
volleyball. Women's Non-aid: riflery

OHIO UNIVERSITY
105 Convocation Center
Athens, OH 45701
(740) 593-1298
www.ohiou.edu
Contact: Trina Jones
Unspecified athletic aid available
M: baseball, basketball, cross country,
football, golf, indoor track, swimming-
diving, tennis, track&field, wrestling
W: basketball, cross country, field hockey,
indoor track, softball, swimming-diving,
tennis, track&field, volleyball

OHIO WESLEYAN UNIVERSITY
Mowry Center
Delaware, OH 43015
(740) 368-3340
www.owu.edu
Contact: Mark Beckenbach
Men's Non-aid: baseball, basketball,
cross country, football, golf, lacrosse,
soccer, softball, swimming-diving, tennis,
track&field
Women's Non-aid: basketball, cross
country, field hockey, lacrosse,
swimming-diving, tennis, track&field,
volleyball

OTTERBEIN COLLEGE
Rike Center
Westerville, OH 43081-2006
(614) 823-3518
www.otterbein.edu
Contact: Ed Syguda

Men's Non-aid: baseball, basketball,
cross country, equestrian, football, golf,
indoor track, soccer, tennis, track&field
Women's Non-aid: basketball, cross
country, equestrian, indoor track, soccer,
softball, tennis, track&field, volleyball

SHAWNEE STATE UNIVERSITY
940 Second Street
Portsmouth, OH 45662
Two-year college
(740) 354-3205
www.shawnee.edu
Contact: Jared Shoemaker
Unspecified athletic aid available
M: baseball, basketball, cross country,
golf, soccer
W: basketball, cross country, soccer, soft-
ball, tennis, volleyball

SINCLAIR COMMUNITY COLLEGE
444 West Third Street
Dayton, OH 45402
Two-year college
(937) 226-2730
www.sinclair.edu
Contact: Donald Cundiff
Unspecified athletic aid available
M: baseball, basketball, golf, tennis
W: basketball, tennis, volleyball

TIFFIN UNIVERSITY
155 Miami Street
Tiffin, OH 44883
(419) 447-6444
www.tiffin.edu
Contact: Ron Shoemaker
Men's Aid (#/$): 92/$171,000
Women's Aid: (#/$): 36/$45,000
Men's Non-aid: baseball, basketball,
cross country, soccer
Women's Non-aid: basketball, cross
country, volleyball

UNIVERSITY OF AKRON
302 E. Buchtel Mall
Akron, OH 44325-5201
(330) 972-7468
www.gozips.com

Contact: Jeff Brewer
Unspecified athletic aid available
M: baseball, basketball, cross country,
football, golf, soccer, tennis, track&field.
Men's Non-aid: riflery
W: basketball, cross country, softball,
tennis, track&field, volleyball

UNIVERSITY OF CINCINNATI
309 Laurence Hall
Cincinnati, OH 45221-0021
(513) 556-5191
www.ucbearcats.com
Contact: Tom Hathaway
Unspecified athletic aid available
M: baseball, basketball, cross country,
football, golf, soccer, swimming-diving,
track&field
W: basketball, cross country, golf, rowing,
soccer, swimming-diving, tennis, volleyball

UNIVERSITY OF DAYTON
300 College Park
Dayton, OH 45469-1679
(937) 229-4460
www.daytonflyers.com
Contact: Doug Hauschild
Men's Aid (#/$): 27/$378,000
Women's Aid (#/$): 24/$336,000
M: baseball, basketball, soccer. Men's
Non-aid: cross country, football, golf,
tennis, water polo, wrestling
W: basketball, soccer, volleyball. Women's
Non-aid: cross country, golf, softball,
tennis

UNIVERSITY OF FINDLAY
1000 North Main Street
Findlay, OH 45840
(419) 424-4727
www.findlay.edu
Contact: David Faiella
Unspecified athletic aid available
M: baseball, basketball, cross country,
diving, football, golf, indoor track, soccer,
swimming, tennis, track&field, wrestling
W: basketball, cross country, diving,
indoor track, soccer, softball, swimming,
tennis, track&field, volleyball

UNIVERSITY OF RIO GRANDE
218 North Atwood Street
Rio Grande, OH 45674-3131
(740) 245-7213
www.urgrgcc.edu
Contact: Mark Williams
Unspecified athletic aid available
M: baseball, basketball, cheerleading,
cross country, soccer, track&field
W: basketball, cheerleading, softball,
track&field, volleyball

UNIVERSITY OF TOLEDO
2801 West Bancroft Street
Toledo, OH 43606-3390
(419) 530-3979
www.utrockets.com
Contact: Paul Helgren
Unspecified athletic aid available
M: baseball, basketball, cross country,
football, golf, indoor track, swimming-
diving, tennis, track&field, wrestling
W: basketball, cross country, field hockey,
indoor track, softball, tennis, track&field,
volleyball

URBANA UNIVERSITY
579 College Way
Urbana, OH 43078
(513) 652-1301
www.urbana.edu
Contact: Ron Bolender
Unspecified athletic aid available
M: baseball, basketball, cheerleading,
cross country, golf, indoor track,
track&field
W: basketball, cheerleading, cross
country, golf, indoor track, softball,
track&field

WALSH UNIVERSITY
2020 Easton Street NW
N. Canton, OH 44720
(330) 490-7017
www.walsh.edu
Contact: Jim Clark
Unspecified athletic aid available
M: baseball, basketball, cross country,
golf, soccer, tennis, track&field

W: basketball, cross country, softball, tennis, track&field, volleyball. Women's Non-aid: synchronized swimming

WILBERFORCE UNIVERSITY
1055 North Bickett Road
Wilberforce, OH 45384
(937) 708-5536
www.wilberforce.edu
Contact: Johnny Cunningham
Unspecified athletic aid available
M: baseball, basketball, football, indoor track, volleyball. Men's Non-aid: track&field

WILMINGTON COLLEGE
Pyle Center, Box 1265
Wilmington, OH 45177
(937) 382-6661 ext. 347
www.wilmington.edu
Contact: Marty Fuller
Men's Non-aid: baseball, basketball, cross country, football, golf, soccer, tennis, track&field, wrestling
Women's Non-aid: basketball, cross country, soccer, softball, tennis, track&field, volleyball

WRIGHT STATE UNIVERSITY
Nutter Center
Dayton, OH 45435
(937) 873-2771
www.wright.edu
Contact: Peggy Wynkoop
Unspecified athletic aid available
M: baseball, basketball, cross country, golf, soccer, swimming-diving, tennis
W: basketball, cross country, soccer, softball, swimming-diving, tennis, volleyball

XAVIER UNIVERSITY
3800 Victory Parkway
Cincinnati, OH 45207
(513) 745-3416
www.xu.edu
Contact: Tom Eiser
Unspecified athletic aid available
M: baseball, basketball, cross country, golf, riflery, soccer, swimming, tennis

W: basketball, cross country, golf, riflery, soccer, swimming, tennis, volleyball

YOUNGSTOWN STATE UNIVERSITY
1 University Plaza
Youngstown, OH 44555-0001
(330) 742-3192
www.ysu.edu
Contact: Rocco Gasparro
Men's Non-aid: baseball, basketball, cross country, diving, football, golf, soccer, swimming, tennis, track&field
Women's Non-aid: basketball, cross country, diving, softball, swimming, tennis, track&field, volleyball

Oklahoma

BACONE JUNIOR COLLEGE
2299 Old Bacone Road
Muskogee, OK 74403-1597
Two-year college
(918) 683-4581
Contact: Carl Scott
Unspecified athletic aid available
M: baseball, basketball. Men's Non-aid: cross country, track&field
W: basketball, softball. Women's Non-aid: cross country, track&field

BARTLESVILLE WESLEYAN COLLEGE
2201 Silver Lake Road
Bartlesville, OK 74006
(580) 335-6219
www.bwc.edu
Contact: Steve Douting
Unspecified athletic aid available
M: basketball, soccer
W: basketball

CAMERON UNIVERSITY
2800 Gore Boulevard
Lawton, OK 73505
(580) 581-2303
www.cameron.edu

Contact: Steve Douting
Unspecified athletic aid available
M: baseball, basketball, football, golf
W: basketball, softball, tennis, volleyball

CARL ALBERT STATE COLLEGE
1507 South McKenna
Poteau, OK 74953-5208
Two-year college
(918) 647-1200
www.casc.cc.ok.us
Contact: Bill San Millan
Unspecified athletic aid available
M: baseball, basketball
W: basketball

CONNORS STATE COLLEGE
1000 College Road
Warner, OK 74469
Two-year college
(918) 463-2931
www.connors.cc.ok.us
Contact: Manny Medwell
Unspecified athletic aid available
M: baseball, basketball, tennis
W: basketball, softball, tennis

EAST CENTRAL UNIVERSITY
East 14th Street
Ada, OK 74820-6899
(580) 332-8000 ext. 310
www.ecok.edu
Contact: Dr. Tim Green
Unspecified athletic aid available
M: basketball, football. Men's Non-aid:
baseball, golf, tennis, track&field
W: basketball, tennis

EASTERN OKLAHOMA STATE COLLEGE
Wilburton, OK 74578
Two-year college
(918) 465-2361 ext. 277
www.eosc.cc.ok.us
Contact: Anna Vee Hill
Unspecified athletic aid available
M: baseball, basketball, cross country,
indoor track, rodeo, track&field. Men's
Non-aid: gymnastics, swimming, tennis

W: basketball, cross country, indoor
track, track&field. Women's Non-aid:
gymnastics, swimming, tennis

LANGSTON UNIVERSITY
P.O. Box 175
Langston, OK 73050
(405) 466-3243
www.lunet.edu
Contact: James W. Hillard, Jr.
Unspecified athletic aid available
M: basketball, football, track&field
W: basketball, cross country, track&field

NORTHEASTERN STATE UNIVERSITY
600 North Grand Avenue
Tahlequah, OK 74464-2399
(918) 456-5511
www.nsuok.edu
Contact: Scott Pettus
Men's Aid: (#/$): 50/unspecified $
Women's Aid: (#/$): 27/unspecified $
M: baseball, basketball, football, golf,
soccer, tennis
W: basketball, golf, soccer, softball, tennis

NORTHWESTERN OKLAHOMA STATE UNIVERSITY
709 Oklahoma Boulevard
Alva, OK 73717
(580) 327-1700
www.nwalva.edu
Contact: Justin Tinder
Unspecified athletic aid available
M: baseball, basketball, football, rodeo.
Men's Non-aid: golf, power lifting,
tennis
W: basketball. Women's Non-aid: golf,
tennis

OKLAHOMA BAPTIST UNIVERSITY
500 West University
Shawnee, OK 74804
(405) 275-2850
www.okbu.edu
Contact: Marty O'Gwynn
Unspecified athletic aid available

M: baseball, basketball, cross country,
tennis, track&field
W: basketball, softball

OKLAHOMA CHRISTIAN UNIVERSITY
2501 East Memorial Road, Box 11000
Oklahoma City, OK 73136
(405) 425-5000
www.oc.edu
Contact: Larry Hollingsworth
Men's Aid (#/$): 40/#308,500
Women's Aid (#/$): 12.5/$94,675
M: baseball, basketball, cross country,
indoor track, soccer, tennis, track&field
W: basketball, cross country, indoor
track, track&field

OKLAHOMA CITY UNIVERSITY
2501 North Blackwelder
Oklahoma City, OK 73106
(405) 521-5211
www.okcu.edu
Contact: Rosa Linda
M: baseball, basketball, golf, soccer,
tennis
W: basketball, softball, tennis

OKLAHOMA PANHANDLE STATE UNIVERSITY
P.O. Box 430
Goodwell, OK 73939
(580) 349-2611
www.opsu.edu
Contact: M. C. Rider
Unspecified athletic aid available
M: basketball, cross country, football,
track&field
W: basketball, cheerleading, cross
country, track&field

OKLAHOMA STATE UNIVERSITY
424 Squires Street
Suite 200
Stillwater, OK 74075
(405) 707-7800
www.osu.okc.edu
Contact: Terry Don Phillips
Unspecified athletic aid available

M: baseball, basketball, cross country,
football, golf, indoor track, tennis,
track&field, wrestling
W: basketball, cross country, golf, indoor
track, softball, tennis, track&field

ORAL ROBERTS UNIVERSITY
7777 South Lewis Avenue
Tulsa, OK 74171
(918) 495-7102
www.oru.edu
Contact: Scott Williams
Men's Aid (#/$): 55/unspecified $
Women's Aid (#/$): 68/unspecified $
M: baseball, basketball, cross country,
golf, indoor track, soccer, tennis
W: basketball, cross country, golf, indoor
track, soccer, tennis, volleyball

PHILLIPS UNIVERSITY
100 South University Avenue
Enid, OK 73701
(580) 237-4433
www.phillips.edu
Contact: Shawn Martin
Unspecified athletic aid available
M: baseball, basketball, soccer, tennis
W: basketball

ROSE STATE COLLEGE
6420 SE 15th Street
Midwest City, OK 73110
Two-year college
(405) 733-7350
www.rose.cc.ok.us
Contact: Les Berryhill
Unspecified athletic aid available
M: baseball, basketball. Men's Non-aid:
gymnastics, swimming-diving, tennis,
weightlifting
W: basketball. Women's Non-aid:
gymnastics, swimming-diving, tennis,
weightlifting

SEMINOLE STATE COLLEGE
P.O. Box 351
Seminole, OK 74868
Two-year college
(405) 382-9950

www.ssc.cc.ok.us
Contact: Tracy Lucas
Unspecified athletic aid available
M: baseball, basketball
W: basketball

SOUTHEASTERN OKLAHOMA STATE UNIVERSITY
P.O. Box 4225
Durant, OK 74701
(580) 924-0121
www.sosu.edu
Contact: Sherry Foster
Unspecified athletic aid available
M: baseball, basketball, football, golf, tennis, track&field, volleyball
W: basketball, golf, tennis, track&field, volleyball

SOUTHERN NAZARENE UNIVERSITY
6729 NW 39th Expressway
Bethany, OK 73008
(405) 789-6400
www.snu.edu
Contact: Diana Lee
Unspecified athletic aid available
M: basketball, soccer
W: basketball, volleyball

SOUTHWESTERN OKLAHOMA STATE UNIVERSITY
100 Campus Drive
Weatherford, OK 73096
(580) 772-6611
www.swosu.edu
Contact: Cecil Perkins
Men's Aid (#/$): 41/$199,920
Women's Aid (#/$): 23/$109,480
M: baseball, basketball, football, golf, rodeo, soccer
W: basketball, cross country, golf, rodeo, soccer, softball

ST. GREGORY'S UNIVERSITY
1900 West MacArthur Drive
Shawnee, OK 74804
Two-year college
(405) 878-5444

www.sgc.edu
Contact: Alan Wilson
Unspecified athletic aid available
M: basketball. Men's Non-aid: fencing, golf, tennis
W: basketball. Women's Non-aid: fencing, tennis

UNIVERSITY OF CENTRAL OKLAHOMA
100 North University Drive
Edmond, OK 73034
(405) 974-2000 ext. 2142
www.ucok.edu
Contact: John "Skip" Wagnon
Unspecified athletic aid available
M: baseball, basketball, cross country, football, golf, indoor track, tennis, track&field, wrestling
W: basketball, cross country, indoor track, softball, tennis, track&field, volleyball

UNIVERSITY OF OKLAHOMA
180 W. Brooks
Memorial Stadium Room 235
Norman, OK 73019
(405) 325-8228
www.ou.edu
Contact: Mike Prusiruski
Unspecified athletic aid available
M: baseball, basketball, cross country, football, golf, gymnastics, indoor track, tennis, track&field, wrestling
W: basketball, cross country, golf, gymnastics, indoor track, soccer, softball, tennis, track&field, volleyball

UNIVERSITY OF TULSA
600 South College Avenue
Tulsa, OK 74104
(918) 631-2383
www.utulsa.edu
Contact: Michael Stevens
Unspecified athletic aid available
M: basketball, cross country, football, golf, indoor track, soccer, tennis, track&field
W: cross country, golf, indoor track,

soccer, softball, tennis, track&field, volleyball

Oregon

BLUE MOUNTAIN COLLEGE
2411 NW Carden Avenue
Pendleton, OR 97801
Two-year college
(541) 276-1260
www.bmcc.cc.or.us
Contact: Larry Bartee
Unspecified athletic aid available
M: basketball, tennis, track&field. Men's Non-aid: baseball
W: basketball, tennis, track&field, volleyball

CHEMEKETA COMMUNITY COLLEGE
4000 Lancaster Drive
Salem, OR 97303
Two-year college
(503) 399-5081
www.chemek.cc.or.us
Contact: Ward Paldanius
Unspecified athletic aid available
M: basketball, track&field
W: basketball, track&field, volleyball

CLACKAMAS COMMUNITY COLLEGE
19600 South Molalla Avenue
Oregon City, OR 97045
Two-year college
(503) 657-6958 ext. 2435
www.clackamas.cc.or.us
Contact: Mike Hodges
Unspecified athletic aid available
M: baseball, basketball, cross country, track&field, wrestling
W: basketball, cross country, softball, track&field, volleyball

COLUMBIA CHRISTIAN COLLEGE
Portland, OR 97220
(503) 257-1209

Contact: Terry Fields
Unspecified athletic aid available
M: basketball. Men's Non-aid: soccer
W: volleyball. Women's Non-aid: basketball

EASTERN OREGON UNIVERSITY
1 University Boulevard
La Grande, OR 97850-2899
(541) 962-3672
www.eou.edu
Contact: Bob Evans
Men's Non-aid: alpine skiing, baseball, basketball, cross country, cross country skiing, football, softball
Women's Non-aid: alpine skiing, basketball, cross country, cross country skiing, volleyball

GEORGE FOX UNIVERSITY
414 North Meridian Street
Newberg, OR 97132
(503) 538-8383
www.georgefox.edu
Contact: Bryon Shenk
Men's Non-aid: baseball, basketball, cross country, soccer, tennis, track&field
Women's Non-aid: basketball, cross country, soccer, softball, tennis, track&field, volleyball

LANE COMMUNITY COLLEGE
4000 East 30th Avenue
Eugene, OR 97405
Two-year college
(541) 747-4501
www.lanecc.edu
Contact: Sue Thompson
Unspecified athletic aid available
M: basketball, track&field
W: basketball, track&field

LEWIS AND CLARK COLLEGE
615 SW Palatine Hill Road
Portland, OR 97219
(503) 768-7067
www.lcark.edu
Contact: Steve Wallo
Men's Non-aid: baseball, basketball,

crew, cross country, football, golf, swimming-diving, tennis, track&field
Women's Non-aid: basketball, crew, cross country, softball, swimming-diving, tennis, track&field, volleyball

LINFIELD COLLEGE
900 Southeast Baker Street
McMinnville, OR 97128-8947
(503) 434-2200
www.linfield.edu
Contact: Kelly Bird
Men's Non-aid: baseball, basketball, cross country, football, golf, soccer, swimming, tennis, track&field, wrestling
Women's Non-aid: basketball, cross country, soccer, softball, swimming, tennis, track&field, volleyball

MULTNOMAH BIBLE COLLEGE
8435 Glisan NE
Portland, OR 97220
Two-year college
(503) 255-0332
www.multnomah.edu
Contact: Chris Reese
Men's Non-aid: basketball
Women's Non-aid: basketball, volleyball

OREGON INSTITUTE OF TECHNOLOGY
3201 Campus Drive
Klamath Falls, OR 97601-8801
(541) 885-1000
www.oit.osshe.edu
Contact: John C. Huntley
Men's Non-aid: baseball, basketball, football, wrestling
Women's Non-aid: basketball, softball, volleyball

OREGON STATE UNIVERSITY
103 Gill Coliseum
Corvallis, OR 97331
(541) 737-1000
www.orst.edu
Contact: Hal Cowan
Unspecified athletic aid available

M: baseball, basketball, cross country, football, golf, softball, track&field, wrestling. Men's Non-aid: crew
W: baseball, basketball, cross country, golf, gymnastics, softball, swimming-diving, track&field, volleyball. Women's Non-aid: crew, tennis

PACIFIC UNIVERSITY
2043 College Way
Forest Grove, OR 97116
(503) 357-6151
www.pacific.edu
Contact: Ken Schumann
Men's Non-aid: baseball, basketball, cross country, golf, handball, soccer, tennis, track&field, wrestling
Women's Non-aid: basketball, cross country, golf, handball, soccer, softball, tennis, track&field, volleyball

PORTLAND STATE UNIVERSITY
P.O. Box 751
Portland, OR 97207
(503) 725-2525
www.pdx.edu
Contact: Jim Sarah
Men's Aid (#/$): 106/$371,716
Women's Aid (#/$): 38/$128,844
M: baseball, cross country, football, golf, track&field, wrestling
W: basketball, cross country, softball, tennis, track&field, volleyball

SOUTHERN OREGON UNIVERSITY
1250 Siskiyou Boulevard
Ashland, OR 97520
(541) 552-7672
www.sou.edu
Contact: Al Blaszak
Men's Non-aid: basketball, cross country, football, indoor track, soccer, swimming, tennis, track&field, water polo, wrestling
Women's Non-aid: basketball, cross country, indoor track, soccer, swimming, tennis, track&field, volleyball, water polo

SOUTHWESTERN OREGON COMMUNITY COLLEGE
1988 Newmark Avenue
Coos Bay, OR 97420-2912
Two-year college
(800) 962-2838
www.southwestern.cc.or.us
Contact: John Speasl
Unspecified athletic aid available
M: basketball, track&field, wrestling
W: basketball, volleyball

UMPQUA COLLEGE
P.O. Box 967
Roseburg, OR 97470
Two-year college
(541) 440-4600
www.umpqua.cc.or.us
Contact: Cy Perkins
Unspecified athletic aid available
M: basketball, cross country, track&field
W: basketball, cross country, track&field, volleyball

UNIVERSITY OF OREGON
Casanova Center
Eugene, OR 97403
(541) 346-3111
www.uoregon.edu
Contact: Steve Hellyer
Unspecified athletic aid available
M: basketball, cross country, football, golf, tennis, track&field, wrestling
W: basketball, cross country, golf, softball, tennis, track&field, volleyball

UNIVERSITY OF PORTLAND
5000 North Willamette Boulevard
Portland, OR 97203-5798
(503) 943-7911
www.uofport.edu
Contact: Steve Walker
Unspecified athletic aid available
M: baseball, basketball, cross country, golf, soccer, tennis, track&field
W: basketball, cross country, soccer, tennis, track&field, volleyball

WARNER PACIFIC COLLEGE
2219 SE 68th Street
Portland, OR 97215
(503) 775-4366
www.warnerpacific.edu
Contact: John Eakman
Unspecified athletic aid available
M: basketball, soccer
W: basketball, volleyball. Women's Non-aid: softball

WESTERN OREGON UNIVERSITY
AD 308
Monmouth, OR 97361-1394
(503) 838-8281
www.wosc.osshe.edu
Contact: Jeanette Kruljac
Men's Non-aid: baseball, basketball, cross country, football, indoor track, track&field
Women's Non-aid: basketball, cross country, indoor track, softball, track&field, volleyball

WILLAMETTE UNIVERSITY
900 State Street
Salem, OR 97301
(503) 370-6110
www.willamette.edu
Contact: Cliff Voliva
Men's Non-aid: baseball, basketball, cross country, football, golf, indoor track, lacrosse, soccer, swimming-diving, tennis, track&field, weightlifting
Women's Non-aid: basketball, cross country, indoor track, softball, swimming-diving, tennis, track&field, volleyball

Pennsylvania

ALBRIGHT COLLEGE
13th and Bern Streets
P.O. Box 15234
Reading, PA 19612-5234
(610) 921-7833

www.alb.edu
Contact: Sally Stetler
Men's Non-aid: baseball, basketball, cross country, football, golf, soccer, swimming, tennis, track&field, wrestling
Women's Non-aid: badminton, basketball, cross country, field hockey, soccer, softball, swimming, tennis, track&field, volleyball

ALLEGHENY COLLEGE
520 N. Main Street
Meadville, PA 16335
(814) 332-3351
www.alleg.edu
Contact: Jeff Schaefer
Men's Non-aid: baseball, basketball, cross country, football, golf, indoor track, soccer, swimming-diving, tennis, track&field
Women's Non-aid: basketball, cross country, indoor track, lacrosse, soccer, softball, swimming-diving, tennis, track&field, volleyball

ALLENTOWN COLLEGE OF SAINT FRANCIS DE SALES
2755 Station Avenue
Center Valley, PA 18034-9568
(610) 282-1100 ext. 1228
www.allencol.edu
Contact: Tim Brooks
Men's Non-aid: baseball, basketball, cross country, golf, indoor track, lacrosse, soccer, tennis, track&field
Women's Non-aid: basketball, cross country, soccer, softball, tennis, track, track&field, volleyball

ALVERNIA COLLEGE
400 Saint Bernardine Street
Reading, PA 19607
(610) 796-8315
www.alvernia.edu
Contact: Vali G. Heist
Unspecified athletic aid available
M: baseball, basketball, cross country.
Men's Non-aid: golf, lacrosse, soccer, tennis, volleyball

W: volleyball. Women's Non-aid: basketball, cross country, field hockey, lacrosse, softball, tennis

BLOOMSBURG UNIVERSITY
400 East Second Street
Bloomsburg, PA 17815-1301
(570) 389-4413
www.bloomu.edu
Contact: Tom McGuire
Men's Aid (#/$): 24/$193,434
Women's Aid (#/$): 22/$172,186
M: baseball, basketball, football, swimming-diving, tennis, wrestling. Men's Non-aid: cross country, soccer, track&field
W: basketball, field hockey, lacrosse, soccer, softball, swimming-diving, tennis.
Women's Non-aid: cross country, track&field

BRYN MAWR COLLEGE
101 North Merion Avenue
Bryn Mawr, PA 19010-2899
(610) 526-7308
www.brynmawr.edu
Contact: Marc Chalufour
Women's Non-aid: badminton, basketball, cross country, field hockey, lacrosse, soccer, swimming, tennis, track&field, volleyball

BUCKNELL UNIVERSITY
Athletic Communications
Davis Gym
Lewisburg, PA 17837
(570) 577-1227
www.bucknell.edu
Contact: Todd Newcomb
Restrictions and notes: All aid is need based and is granted through the Financial Aid Office.
Men's Non-aid: baseball, basketball, crew, cross country, football, golf, indoor track, lacrosse, soccer, swimming, tennis, track&field, water polo, wrestling
Women's Non-aid: basketball, crew, cross country, field hockey, golf, indoor track, lacrosse, soccer, softball, swimming, tennis, track&field, volleyball, water polo

BUCKS COUNTY COMMUNITY COLLEGE
434 Swamp Road
Newtown, PA 18940
Two-year college
(215) 968-8000
www.bucks.edu
Contact: Louis Pacchioli
Men's Non-aid: baseball, basketball, cross country, equestrian, golf, soccer, tennis
Women's Non-aid: basketball, cross country, equestrian, golf, soccer, softball, tennis

BUTLER COUNTY COMMUNITY COLLEGE
P.O. Box 1203
Butler, PA 16003-1203
Two-year college
(724) 287-8711 ext. 249
www.bc3.cc.pa.us
Contact: Rob Snyder
Men's Non-aid: baseball, basketball, golf, racquetball, tennis
Women's Non-aid: softball, tennis, volleyball

CABRINI COLLEGE
610 King of Prussia Road
Radnor, PA 19087-3698
(610) 902-8254
www.cabrini.edu
Contact: Bob MacCartney
Men's Non-aid: basketball, cross country, golf, lacrosse, soccer, tennis, track&field
Women's Non-aid: basketball, cross country, field hockey, lacrosse, softball, tennis, track&field, volleyball

CALIFORNIA UNIVERSITY OF PENNSYLVANIA
250 University Avenue
California, PA 15419-1394
(724) 938-4552
www.cup.edu
Contact: Dave Smith
Men's Aid (#/$): 40/$200,000
Women's Aid (#/$): 30/$145,000
M: baseball, basketball, cross country, football, soccer, track&field
W: basketball, cross country, soccer, softball, tennis, track&field, volleyball

CARLOW COLLEGE
3333 Fifth Avenue
Pittsburgh, PA 15213
(412) 578-8826
www.carlow.edu
Contact: George Sliman
Women's Aid (#/$): 60/$150,000
W: basketball, soccer, softball, tennis, volleyball. Women's Non-aid: crew

CARNEGIE MELLON UNIVERSITY
5000 Forbes Avenue
Pittsburgh, PA 15213
(412) 268-2211
www.cmu.edu
Contact: Lou Noce
Men's Non-aid: basketball, cross country, football, indoor track, soccer, swimming, tennis, track&field
Women's Non-aid: basketball, cross country, indoor track, soccer, swimming, tennis, track&field, volleyball

CHEYNEY UNIVERSITY OF PENNSYLVANIA
Cheyney and Creek Roads
Cheyney, PA 19319
(610) 399-2287
www.cheyney.edu
Contact: Harold Johnson
Men's Non-aid: basketball, football, tennis, track&field, wrestling
Women's Non-aid: basketball, bowling, tennis, track&field, volleyball

CLARION UNIVERSITY
Alumni House
Clarion, PA 16214
(814) 226-2334
www.clarion.edu
Contact: Rich Herman
Unspecified athletic aid available
M: baseball, basketball, cross country, football, golf, swimming-diving, track&field, wrestling

W: basketball, cross country, softball, swimming-diving, tennis, track&field, volleyball

COMMUNITY COLLEGE OF ALLEGHENY COUNTY (ALLEGHENY CAMPUS)
808 Ridge Avenue
Pittsburgh, PA 15212-6097
Two-year college
(412) 237-2533
www.ccac.edu
Contact: Ken Hoeltje
Men's Aid (#/$): 5/$6,000
Women's Aid (#/$): 5/$6,000
M: basketball. Men's Non-aid: baseball
W: basketball. Women's Non-aid: softball

COMMUNITY COLLEGE OF ALLEGHENY COUNTY (SOUTH CAMPUS)
1750 Clairton Road
West Mifflin, PA 15122
Two-year college
(412) 469-6245
www.ccac.edu
Contact: Lee Frank
Men's Aid (#/$): 5/$16,000
Women's Aid (#/$): 5/$16,000
M: baseball, basketball. Men's Non-aid: bowling, golf
W: softball, volleyball. Women's Non-aid: bowling, golf, tennis

COMMUNITY COLLEGE OF PHILADELPHIA
1700 Spring Garden Street
Philadelphia, PA 19130-3991
Two-year college
(215) 751-8964
www.ccp.cc.pa.us
Contact: James Burton
Men's Non-aid: basketball, cross country, soccer, softball, tennis
Women's Non-aid: basketball, cross country, softball, tennis, volleyball

DELAWARE COUNTY COMMUNITY COLLEGE
Route 252 & Media Line Road
Media, PA 19063
Two-year college
(610) 359-5047
www.dccc.edu
Contact: Cheryl Massaro
Men's Non-aid: baseball, basketball, cross country, softball, tennis
Women's Non-aid: cross country, softball

DELAWARE VALLEY COLLEGE
700 East Butler Avenue
Doylestown, PA 18901-2697
(215) 489-2937
www.devalcol.edu
Contact: Matt Levy
Men's Non-aid: baseball, basketball, cross country, football, golf, soccer, track&field, wrestling
Women's Non-aid: basketball, cross country, field hockey, soccer, softball, track&field, volleyball

DICKINSON COLLEGE
P.O. Box 1773
College and Louther Streets
Carlisle, PA 17013-2896
(717) 245-1652
www.dickinson.edu
Contact: Charlie McGuire
Men's Non-aid: baseball, basketball, cross country, football, golf, indoor track, lacrosse, soccer, swimming, tennis, track&field
Women's Non-aid: basketball, cross country, field hockey, golf, indoor track, lacrosse, soccer, softball, swimming, tennis, track&field, volleyball

DREXEL UNIVERSITY
3141 Chestnut Street
Philadelphia, PA 19104
(215) 895-1570
www.drexel.edu
Contact: Christopher Beckett
Unspecified athletic aid available
M: baseball, basketball, cross country,

diving, indoor track, lacrosse, soccer, swimming, swimming-diving, track&field, wrestling. Men's Non-aid: crew, golf, tennis
W: basketball, diving, field hockey, lacrosse, softball, swimming, swimming-diving, volleyball. Women's Non-aid: crew, tennis

DUQUESNE UNIVERSITY
600 Forbes Avenue
Pittsburgh, PA 15282
(412) 396-6565
www.duq.edu
Contact: Dave Soba
Men's Aid (#/$): 47/$878,900
Women's Aid (#/$): 70/$1,309,000
M: baseball, basketball, cross country, golf, riflery, soccer, swimming-diving, tennis, wrestling. Men's Non-aid: football
W: basketball, cross country, crew, lacrosse, riflery, soccer, swimming-diving, tennis, track&field, volleyball

EASTERN COLLEGE
1300 Eagle Road
St. Davids, PA 19087
(610) 341-1784
www.eastern.edu
Contact: Mark Birtwistle
Men's Non-aid: baseball, basketball, cross country, soccer, tennis
Women's Non-aid: basketball, cross country, field hockey, lacrosse, soccer, softball, tennis, volleyball

EAST STROUDSBURG UNIVERSITY
Koehler Fieldhouse
200 Prospect Street
East Stroudsburg, PA 18310-2999
(570) 422-3312
www.esu.edu
Contact: Peter Nevins
Unspecified athletic aid available
M: basketball, football, soccer, wrestling. Men's Non-aid: baseball, cross country, indoor track, tennis, track&field, volleyball
W: basketball, field hockey, softball

Women's Non-aid: cross country, indoor track, lacrosse, swimming-diving, tennis, track&field, volleyball

EDINBORO UNIVERSITY OF PENNSYLVANIA
RT 6N
Edinboro, PA 16444
(814) 732-2000
www.edinboro.edu
Contact: Todd B. Jay
Men's Aid (#/$): 34/$65,733
Women's Aid (#/$): 30/$17,836
M: basketball, cross country, football, wrestling. Men's Non-aid: baseball, soccer, swimming-diving, tennis, track&field, volleyball
W: basketball, cross country. Women's Non-aid: softball, swimming-diving, tennis, track&field

ELIZABETHTOWN COLLEGE
One Alpha Drive
Elizabethtown, PA 17022-2298
(717) 361-1311
www.etown.edu
Contact: Ian Showalter
Men's Non-aid: baseball, basketball, cross country, golf, soccer, swimming-diving, tennis, track&field, wrestling
Women's Non-aid: basketball, cross country, field hockey, soccer, softball, swimming-diving, tennis, track&field, volleyball

FRANKLIN & MARSHALL COLLEGE
P.O. Box 3003
Lancaster, PA 17604-3003
(717) 291-3838
www.fandm.edu
Contact: Tom Byrnes
Men's Non-aid: baseball, basketball, cross country, football, golf, indoor track, lacrosse, soccer, squash, swimming, tennis, track&field, wrestling
Women's Non-aid: basketball, cross country, field hockey, golf, indoor track, lacrosse, soccer, softball, squash, swimming, tennis, track&field, volleyball

GANNON UNIVERSITY
109 University Square
Erie, PA 16541-0001
(814) 871-7418
www.gannon.edu
Contact: Dan Teliski
Unspecified athletic aid available
M: baseball, basketball, cross country,
football, golf, swimming-diving, tennis,
wrestling. Men's Non-aid: football
W: basketball, cross country, softball,
swimming-diving, tennis, volleyball

GENEVA COLLEGE
3200 College Avenue
Beaver Falls, PA 15010
(724) 847-6886
www.geneva.edu
Contact: Van Zanick
Unspecified athletic aid available
M: baseball, basketball. Men's Non-aid:
cheerleading, cross country, football,
indoor track, soccer, tennis, track&field
W: basketball, volleyball. Women's Non-
aid: cheerleading, cross country, indoor
track, soccer, softball, tennis, track&field,
volleyball

GETTYSBURG COLLEGE
North Washington Street
Gettysburg, PA 17325
(717) 337-6000
www.gettysburg.edu
Contact: Matt Daskivich
Restrictions and notes: Financial aid
strictly based on need.
Men's Non-aid: baseball, basketball,
cross country, football, golf, indoor track,
lacrosse, soccer, swimming, tennis,
track&field, wrestling
Women's Non-aid: basketball, cross
country, field hockey, golf, indoor track,
lacrosse, soccer, softball, swimming,
tennis, track&field

GROVE CITY COLLEGE
100 Campus Drive
Grove City, PA 16127-2104
(724) 458-3365

www.gcc.edu
Contact: Joe Klimchak
Men's Non-aid: baseball, basketball, cross
country, football, golf, soccer, swimming-
diving, tennis, track&field, water polo
Women's Non-aid: basketball, cross
country, golf, soccer, softball, swimming-
diving, tennis, track&field, volleyball,
water polo

HAVERFORD COLLEGE
370 Lancaster Avenue
Haverford, PA 19041-1392
(610) 896-1042
www.haverford.edu
Contact: John Douglas
Men's Non-aid: baseball, basketball,
cricket, cross country, fencing, indoor
track, lacrosse, soccer, squash, tennis,
track&field
Women's Non-aid: basketball, cross
country, fencing, field hockey, indoor
track, lacrosse, soccer, softball, squash,
tennis, track&field, volleyball

HOLY FAMILY COLLEGE
Grant and Frankford Avenues
Philadelphia, PA 19114-2094
(215) 632-8284
www.hfc.edu
Contact: Sandra Michael
Unspecified athletic aid available
M: basketball, golf, soccer
W: basketball, cross country, soccer,
softball

INDIANA UNIVERSITY OF PENNSYLVANIA
107 Memorial Field House
Indiana, PA 15705-0001
(724) 357-2747
www.iup.edu
Contact: Mike Hoffman
Unspecified athletic aid available
M: baseball, basketball, cross country,
football, golf, swimming, track&field
W: basketball, cross country, field hockey,
lacrosse, soccer, softball, swimming,
tennis, track&field, volleyball

JUNIATA COLLEGE
1700 Moore Street
Huntingdon, PA 16652-2119
(814) 641-3134
www.juniata.edu
Contact: Bob Parker
Men's Non-aid: baseball, basketball, football, soccer, track&field, volleyball
Women's Non-aid: basketball, cross country, field hockey, soccer, softball, swimming, tennis, track&field, volleyball

KEYSTONE COLLEGE
One College Green
La Plume, PA 18440-0200
(570) 945-5144
www.keystone.edu
Contact: Terry Wise
Men's Non-aid: baseball, basketball, soccer, tennis
Women's Non-aid: basketball, field hockey, softball

KING'S COLLEGE
133 North River Street
Wilkes-Barre, PA 18711
(570) 208-5855
www.kings.edu
Contact: Bob Ziadie
Men's Non-aid: baseball, basketball, cross country, football, golf, lacrosse, riflery, soccer, swimming-diving, tennis, wrestling
Women's Non-aid: basketball, cross country, field hockey, lacrosse, riflery, soccer, softball, swimming-diving, tennis, volleyball

KUTZTOWN UNIVERSITY OF PENNSYLVANIA
Keystone Hill
Kutztown, PA 19530
(610) 683-4182
www.kutztown.edu
Contact: Josh Leiboff
Men's Aid (#/$): 18/$151,000
Women's Aid (#/$): 13/$113,000

M: baseball, basketball, cross country, football, indoor track, soccer, swimming-diving, tennis, track&field, wrestling
W: basketball, cross country, field hockey, indoor track, soccer, softball, swimming-diving, tennis, track&field, volleyball

LACKAWANNA JUNIOR COLLEGE
501 Vine Street
Scranton, PA 18509
Two-year college
(570) 961-0700
members.aol.com/grifflew/ljc
Contact: Tim Dempsey
Unspecified athletic aid available
Restrictions and notes: Scholarships only cover tuition and fees.
M: baseball, basketball, golf
W: basketball, cheerleading, softball, volleyball

LAFAYETTE COLLEGE
108 Watson Hall
Easton, PA 18042
(610) 330-5122
www.lafayette.edu
Contact: Scott Morse
Men's Non-aid: baseball, basketball, crew, cross country, fencing, football, golf, indoor track, lacrosse, power lifting, rugby, soccer, swimming-diving, tennis, track&field, weightlifting, wrestling
Women's Non-aid: basketball, cross country, fencing, field hockey, indoor track, lacrosse, softball, swimming-diving, tennis, track&field, volleyball

LA ROCHE COLLEGE
9000 Babcock Boulevard
Pittsburgh, PA 15237
(412) 536-1004
www.laroche.edu
Contact: Scott Lang
Men's Non-aid: baseball, basketball, cross country, golf, soccer
Women's Non-aid: basketball, cross country, soccer, softball, tennis, volleyball

LA SALLE UNIVERSITY
1900 West Olney Avenue
Philadelphia, PA 19141
(215) 951-1513
www.lasalle.edu
Contact: Kevin Currie
Unspecified athletic aid available
M: baseball, basketball, cross country, golf, indoor track, soccer, swimming-diving, tennis, track&field. Men's Non-aid: crew, football
W: basketball, cross country, field hockey, indoor track, lacrosse, soccer, softball, swimming-diving, tennis, track&field, volleyball. Women's Non-aid: crew

LEBANON VALLEY COLLEGE
101 North College Avenue
Annville, PA 17003
(717) 867-6033
www.lvc.edu
Contact: Jim Miller
Men's Non-aid: baseball, basketball, cross country, football, golf, ice hockey, soccer, swimming, tennis, track&field, wrestling
Women's Non-aid: basketball, cheerleading, cross country, field hockey, soccer, softball, swimming, tennis, track&field, volleyball

LEHIGH CARBON COMMUNITY COLLEGE
4525 Education Park Drive
Schnecksville, PA 18078-2598
Two-year college
(610) 799-1155
www.lccc.edu
Contact: Douglas Stewart
Men's Non-aid: basketball, golf
Women's Non-aid: golf, volleyball

LEHIGH UNIVERSITY
641 Taylor Street
Bethlehem, PA 18015
(610) 758-3158
www.lehigh.edu
Contact: Chris Blake
Unspecified athletic aid available

M: basketball, wrestling. Men's Non-aid: baseball, cross country, football, golf, indoor track, lacrosse, soccer, swimming-diving, tennis, track&field
W: basketball. Women's Non-aid: cross country, field hockey, lacrosse, soccer, softball, swimming-diving, tennis, volleyball

LOCK HAVEN UNIVERSITY OF PENNSYLVANIA
125 Akeley Hall
Lock Haven, PA 17745
(570) 893-2350
www.lhup.edu
Contact: Danielle Barney
Unspecified athletic aid available
M: basketball, football, soccer, wrestling
W: basketball, field hockey

LYCOMING COLLEGE
700 College Place
Williamsport, PA 17701
(570) 321-4260
www.lycoming.edu
Contact: Frank Grandi
Men's Non-aid: basketball, cross country, football, golf, lacrosse, soccer, swimming-diving, tennis, track&field, wrestling
Women's Non-aid: basketball, cross country, field hockey, lacrosse, soccer, softball, swimming-diving, tennis, track&field, volleyball

MANSFIELD UNIVERSITY
Beecher House
Mansfield, PA 16933
(570) 662-4845
www.mnsfld.edu
Contact: Steve McCloskey
Unspecified athletic aid available
M: baseball, basketball, cross country, football, indoor track, track&field
W: basketball, cross country, field hockey, indoor track, softball, swimming, track&field

MARYWOOD UNIVERSITY
2300 Adams Avenue
Scranton, PA 18509

(570) 961-4724 ext. 2348
www.marywood.edu
Contact: Will Donohue
Men's Non-aid: baseball, basketball,
cross country, soccer, tennis
Women's Non-aid: basketball, cross
country, field hockey, soccer, softball,
tennis, volleyball

MERCYHURST COLLEGE
501 East 38th Street
Erie, PA 16546
(814) 824-2226
www.mercy.edu
Contact: Pete Russo
Unspecified athletic aid available
M: baseball, basketball, crew, cross
country, golf, soccer, tennis. Men's
Non-aid: football, ice hockey
W: basketball, crew, cross country,
soccer, softball, tennis, volleyball

MESSIAH COLLEGE
Grantham, PA 17027
(717) 796-5359
www.messiah.edu
Contact: Becky Craig
Men's Non-aid: baseball, basketball,
cross country, golf, indoor track,
lacrosse, soccer, tennis, track&field,
wrestling
Women's Non-aid: basketball, cross
country, field hockey, indoor track,
lacrosse, soccer, softball, tennis,
track&field, volleyball

MILLERSVILLE UNIVERSITY
P.O. Box 1002
Millersville, PA 17551-0302
(717) 872-3100
www.millersu.edu
Contact: Greg Wright
Unspecified athletic aid available
M: baseball, basketball, cross country,
football, golf, soccer, tennis, track&field,
wrestling
W: basketball, cross country, field hockey,
lacrosse, softball, swimming-diving,
tennis, track&field, volleyball

MORAVIAN COLLEGE
1200 Main Street
Bethlehem, PA 18018
(610) 861-1320
www.moravian.edu
Contact: Jim Walker
Men's Non-aid: baseball, basketball,
cross country, equestrian, football, golf,
ice hockey, indoor track, soccer, tennis,
track&field, wrestling
Women's Non-aid: basketball, cross
country, equestrian, field hockey, indoor
track, tennis, volleyball

MOUNT ALOYSIUS COLLEGE
7373 Admiral Peary Highway
Cresson, PA 16630
Two-year college
(814) 886-4131
www.mtaloy.edu
Contact: Dr. Judith Newton
Unspecified athletic aid available
M: basketball
W: basketball

MUHLENBERG COLLEGE
2400 Chew Street
Allentown, PA 18104-5586
(484) 664-3232
www.muhlberg.edu
Contact: Mike Falk
Men's Non-aid: baseball, basketball,
cross country, football, golf, indoor track,
soccer, tennis, track&field, wrestling
Women's Non-aid: basketball, cross
country, field hockey, golf, indoor track,
lacrosse, soccer, softball, tennis,
track&field, volleyball

PENN STATE ABINGTON
COLLEGE
1600 Woodland Road
Abington, PA 19001-3900
Two-year college
(215) 881-7442
www.abington.psu.edu
Contact: Robert Berton
Men's Non-aid: baseball, basketball, golf,
soccer, tennis, volleyball

Women's Non-aid: basketball, softball, tennis, volleyball

PENN STATE BEHREND COLLEGE
5091 Station Road
Erie, PA 16563-0107
(814) 898-6322
www.pserie.psu.edu
Contact: Paul Benim
Men's Non-aid: baseball, basketball, cross country, golf, soccer, tennis, track&field, volleyball
Women's Non-aid: basketball, cross country, softball, tennis, track&field, volleyball

PENN STATE BERKS-LEHIGH VALLEY COLLEGE
P.O. Box 7009
Tulpehocken Road
Reading, PA 19610-6009
Two-year college
www.bklv.psu.edu
Contact: William Sutherland
Men's Non-aid: baseball, basketball, cheerleading, cross country, soccer, tennis
Women's Non-aid: basketball, cheerleading, cross country, softball, tennis, volleyball

THE PENNSYLVANIA STATE UNIVERSITY
101 Bryce Jordan Center
University Park, PA 16802
(814) 865-1757
www.psu.edu
Contact: L. Budd Thalman
Unspecified athletic aid available
M: baseball, basketball, cross country, fencing, football, golf, gymnastics, indoor track, lacrosse, soccer, swimming-diving, tennis, track&field, volleyball, wrestling
W: basketball, cross country, fencing, field hockey, golf, gymnastics, indoor track, lacrosse, soccer, softball, swimming-diving, tennis, track&field, volleyball

PHILADELPHIA UNIVERSITY
School House Lane and Henry Avenue
Philadelphia, PA 19144-5497
(215) 951-2852
www.philau.edu
Contact: Tony Berich
Unspecified athletic aid available
M: baseball, basketball, soccer, tennis
W: basketball, field hockey, lacrosse, soccer, softball, tennis, volleyball

POINT PARK COLLEGE
201 Wood Street
Pittsburgh, PA 15222-1984
(412) 391-4100
www.ppc.edu
Contact: Mark Cohen
Unspecified athletic aid available
M: baseball, basketball, soccer
W: basketball, softball

ROBERT MORRIS COLLEGE
881 Narrows Run Road
Moon Township, PA 15108-1189
(412) 262-8314
www.robert-morris.edu
Contact: Marty Galosi
Unspecified athletic aid available
M: basketball, cross country, football, golf, indoor track, soccer, tennis, track&field
W: basketball, crew, cross country, indoor track, soccer, softball, tennis, track&field, volleyball

SAINT FRANCIS COLLEGE
Maurice Stokes Building
Loretto, PA 15940
(814) 472-3128
www.sfcpa.edu
Contact: Pat Farabaugh
Men's Aid (#/$): 28/unspecified $
Women's Aid (#/$): 28/unspecified $
M: basketball, cross country, golf, indoor track, soccer, tennis, track&field, volleyball. Men's Non-aid: football
W: basketball, cross country, golf, indoor track, soccer, softball, tennis, track&field, volleyball

SAINT JOSEPH'S UNIVERSITY
5600 City Avenue
Philadelphia, PA 19131
(610) 660-1704
www.sjuhawks.com
Contact: Ken Krsolovic
Unspecified athletic aid available
M: baseball, basketball, crew, cross country, golf, indoor track, lacrosse, soccer, tennis, track&field
W: basketball, crew, cross country, field hockey, indoor track, lacrosse, softball, tennis, track&field

SAINT VINCENT COLLEGE
300 Fraser Purchase Road
Latrobe, PA 15650-2690
(724) 532-6600
www.stvincent.edu
Contact: Kristen M. Zawacki
Men's Aid ($): $22,250
Women's Aid ($): $22,250
M: baseball, basketball, cross country, lacrosse, soccer, tennis
W: basketball, cross country, softball, volleyball

SETON HILL COLLEGE
Seton Hill Drive
Greensburg, PA 15601
(724) 838-4259
www.setonhill.edu
Contact: John Fogle
Women's Aid (#/$): 21/$294,000
W: basketball, cross country, golf, soccer, softball, tennis, volleyball. Women's Non-aid: equestrian

SHIPPENSBURG UNIVERSITY OF PENNSYLVANIA
1871 Old Main Drive
Shippensburg, PA 17257
(717) 477-1201
www.ship.edu
Contact: John Alosi
Unspecified athletic aid available
M: baseball, basketball, cross country, football, indoor track, soccer, swimming, track&field, wrestling

W: basketball, cross country, field hockey, indoor track, lacrosse, soccer, softball, swimming, tennis, track&field, volleyball

SLIPPERY ROCK UNIVERSITY OF PENNSYLVANIA
103 Morrow Field House
Slippery Rock, PA 16057-1324
(724) 738-2777
www.sru.edu
Contact: John Stroh
Unspecified athletic aid available
M: baseball, basketball, cross country, football, golf, judo, soccer, swimming-diving, track&field, wrestling. Men's Non-aid: water polo
W: basketball, cross country, field hockey, soccer, softball, swimming-diving, tennis, track&field, volleyball, water polo. Women's Non-aid: judo

SWARTHMORE COLLEGE
500 College Avenue
Swarthmore, PA 19081-1397
(610) 328-8206
www.swarthmore.edu
Contact: Mark Duzenski
Men's Non-aid: baseball, basketball, cross country, football, golf, indoor track, lacrosse, soccer, swimming, tennis, track&field, wrestling
Women's Non-aid: badminton, basketball, cross country, field hockey, indoor track, lacrosse, soccer, softball, swimming, tennis, track&field, volleyball

TEMPLE UNIVERSITY
1700 North Broad Street
Philadelphia, PA 19122
(215) 204-4824
www.owlsports.com
Contact: Brian Kirschner
Unspecified athletic aid available
M: baseball, basketball, crew, football, golf, gymnastics, soccer, tennis, track&field
W: basketball, crew, fencing, field hockey, gymnastics, lacrosse, soccer, softball, tennis, track&field, volleyball

UNIVERSITY OF PENNSYLVANIA
Weightman Hall
235 South 33rd Street
Philadelphia, PA 19104
(215) 898-6128
www.pennathletics.com
Contact: Gail Stasulli
Men's Non-aid: baseball, basketball, crew, cross country, fencing, football, indoor track, lacrosse, soccer, squash, swimming-diving, tennis, track&field, wrestling
Women's Non-aid: basketball, crew, cross country, fencing, field hockey, gymnastics, indoor track, lacrosse, squash, softball, swimming-diving, tennis, track&field, volleyball

UNIVERSITY OF PITTSBURGH
P.O. Box 7436
Pittsburgh, PA 15213-0436
(412) 648-8240
www.pittsburghpanthers.com
Contact: E.J. Borghetti
Unspecified athletic aid available
M: baseball, basketball, cross country, football, indoor track, soccer, swimming-diving, track&field, wrestling
W: basketball, cross country, gymnastics, indoor track, soccer, softball, swimming-diving, tennis, track&field, volleyball

UNIVERSITY OF PITTSBURGH (BRADFORD)
300 Campus Drive
Bradford, PA 16701
(814) 362-5086
www.upb.pitt.edu
Contact: Fred Wallace
Men's Aid (#/$): 10/unspecified $
Women's Aid (#/$): 10/unspecified $
M: basketball. Men's Non-aid: cross country, soccer
W: basketball. Women's Non-aid: cross country, volleyball

UNIVERSITY OF PITTSBURGH (JOHNSTOWN)
450 School House Road
Johnstown, PA 15904

(814) 269-2031
www.pitt.edu/~upjweb
Contact: Chris Caputo
Unspecified athletic aid available
M: baseball, basketball, wrestling. Men's Non-aid: soccer
W: basketball, cross country, indoor track, track&field, volleyball. Women's Non-aid: cheerleading

UNIVERSITY OF SCRANTON
John Long Center
Scranton, PA 18510-4650
(570) 941-7571
www.uofs.edu
Contact: Kevin Southard
Men's Non-aid: baseball, basketball, cross country, golf, ice hockey, lacrosse, soccer, swimming, tennis, wrestling
Women's Non-aid: basketball, cross country, field hockey, lacrosse, soccer, softball, swimming, tennis, volleyball

UNIVERSITY OF THE SCIENCES IN PHILADELPHIA
600 South 43rd Street
Philadelphia, PA 19104-4495
(215) 895-3133
www.usip.edu
Contact: Bob Heller
Unspecified athletic aid available
Athletic programs not specified

URSINUS COLLEGE
P.O. Box 1000
Collegeville, PA 19426-1000
(610) 409-3606
www.ursinus.edu
Contact: Bill Akin
Men's Non-aid: baseball, basketball, cross country, football, golf, indoor track, soccer, swimming, tennis, track&field, wrestling
Women's Non-aid: basketball, cross country, field hockey, gymnastics, indoor track, lacrosse, softball, swimming, tennis, track&field, volleyball

VALLEY FORGE CHRISTIAN COLLEGE
1401 Charlestown Road
Phoenixville, PA 19460
(610) 935-0450
www.vfcc.edu
Contact: Dan Boothman
Men's Non-aid: baseball, basketball, soccer
Women's Non-aid: basketball, volleyball

VILLANOVA UNIVERSITY
800 Lancaster Avenue
Villanova, PA 19085-1674
(610) 519-4120
www.villanova.com
Contact: Dean Kenefick
Unspecified athletic aid available
M: baseball, basketball, cross country, football, soccer, swimming-diving. Men's Non-aid: golf, lacrosse, tennis
W: basketball, cross country, field hockey, soccer, softball, swimming-diving, volleyball. Women's Non-aid: crew, lacrosse, tennis, water polo

WASHINGTON AND JEFFERSON COLLEGE
50 South Lincoln Street
Washington, PA 15301
(724) 223-6079
www.washjeff.edu
Contact: Susan Isola
Men's Non-aid: baseball, basketball, cross country, football, golf, soccer, swimming-diving, tennis, track&field, wrestling, water polo
Women's Non-aid: basketball, cross country, soccer, softball, swimming-diving, tennis, volleyball, water polo

WEST CHESTER UNIVERSITY OF PENNSYLVANIA
Sturzebecker Health Sciences Center
West Chester, PA 19383
(610) 436-3316
www.wcupa.edu
Contact: Tom DiCamillo
Unspecified athletic aid available
M: baseball, basketball, cross country, football, golf, indoor track, lacrosse, soccer, swimming-diving, tennis, track&field
W: basketball, cross country, field hockey, gymnastics, indoor track, lacrosse, soccer, softball, swimming-diving, tennis, track&field, volleyball

WESTMINSTER COLLEGE
Market Street
New Wilmington, PA 16172-0001
(724) 946-6357
www.westminster.edu
Contact: Joe Onderko
Men's Non-aid: baseball, basketball, cross country, football, golf, soccer, swimming, tennis, track&field
Women's Non-aid: basketball, cross country, soccer, softball, swimming, tennis, volleyball

WILKES UNIVERSITY
P.O. Box 111
Wilkes-Barre, PA 18766
(570) 408-5000
www.wilkes.edu
Contact: Tom McGuire
Men's Non-aid: baseball, basketball, cross country, football, golf, soccer, tennis, wrestling
Women's Non-aid: basketball, cross country, field hockey, soccer, softball, tennis

WILLIAMSON FREE SCHOOL OF MECHANICAL TRADES
106 South New Middletown Road
Media, PA 19063
Two-year college
(610) 566-1776 ext. 237
www.williamsonschool.org
Contact: Tony Wolski
Unspecified athletic aid available
M: baseball, basketball, cross country, football, soccer, wrestling

WILSON COLLEGE
Phil Avenue
Chambersburg, PA 17201

(717) 262-2012
www.wilson.edu
Contact: Lori Frey
Women's Non-aid: equestrian, field
hockey, softball, tennis, volleyball

**YORK COLLEGE OF
PENNSYLVANIA**
Country Club Road
York, PA 17405-7199
(717) 815-1394
www.ycp.edu
Contact: Scott Guise
Men's Non-aid: baseball, basketball,
diving, golf, soccer, swimming,
swimming-diving, tennis, track&field,
wrestling
Women's Non-aid: basketball, diving,
field hockey, softball, swimming,
swimming-diving, tennis, volleyball

Puerto Rico

BAYAMON CENTRAL UNIVERSITY
P.O. Box 1725
Bayamon, PR 00960
(787) 786-3030 ext. 263
Contact: Henry Mirand Vasquez
Men's Aid (#/$): 124/$45,000
Women's Aid (#/$): 70/$25,000
M: basketball, track&field, volleyball.
Men's Non-aid: bowling, power lifting,
weightlifting
W: basketball, track&field, volleyball.
Women's Non-aid: bowling, power
lifting, weightlifting

**PONTIFICAL CATHOLIC
UNIVERSITY OF PUERTO RICO**
2250 Las Americas Avenue
Suite 625
Ponce, PR 00717-0777
(787) 841-2000
www.pcupr.edu
Contact: Carlos Mario
Unspecified athletic aid available

M: basketball, cross country, martial arts,
softball, swimming, tennis, track&field,
volleyball, weightlifting, wrestling
W: basketball, cross country, martial arts,
softball, swimming, tennis, track&field,
volleyball

**UNIVERSITY OF PUERTO RICO
(BAYAMON)**
Bayamon University College
Bayamon, PR 00959
(787) 786-2412
www.cutb.upr.clu.edu
Contact: Luis Roberto Reeves Garcia
Unspecified athletic aid available
M: baseball, basketball, cross country,
judo, ping-pong, swimming, tennis,
track&field, volleyball, weightlifting,
wrestling
W: basketball, cheerleading, cross
country, judo, ping-pong, swimming,
tennis, track&field, volleyball, weightlifting

**UNIVERSITY OF PUERTO RICO
(CAYEY)**
Cayey University College
Cayey, PR 00736-5000
(787) 738-2161
www.cuc.upr.clu.edu
Contact: Josefina Hernandez
Men's Non-aid: basketball, cross country,
soccer, softball, swimming, tennis,
track&field, volleyball, water polo,
weightlifting, wrestling
Women's Non-aid: basketball, cross
country, tennis, track&field, volleyball

**UNIVERSITY OF PUERTO RICO
(PONCE)**
Ponce, PR 00732
(787) 844-8181
Contact: Carmelo Vega Montes
Men's Aid (#/$): 49/$22,560
Women's Aid (#/$): 30/$13,620
M: basketball, cross country, tennis,
track&field, volleyball, weightlifting
W: basketball, cross country, tennis,
track&field, volleyball, weightlifting

Rhode Island

BROWN UNIVERSITY
Box 1932
Providence, RI 02912
(401) 863-1000
www.brownbears.com
Contact: Christopher Humm
Men's Non-aid: baseball, basketball, crew, cross country, football, golf, ice hockey, indoor track, lacrosse, soccer, swimming-diving, tennis, track&field, water polo, wrestling
Women's Non-aid: basketball, crew, cross country, field hockey, golf, gymnastics, ice hockey, indoor track, lacrosse, soccer, softball, squash, swimming-diving, tennis, track&field, volleyball, water polo

BRYANT COLLEGE
450 Douglas Pike
Smithfield, RI 02917
(401) 232-6070
www.bryant.edu
Contact: John Rupert
Men's Aid (#/$): 10/$233,000
Women's Aid (#/$): 10/$233,000
M: basketball. Men's Non-aid: baseball, cross country, football, golf, lacrosse, soccer, tennis, track&field
W: basketball. Women's Non-aid: cross country, field hockey, golf, soccer, softball, tennis, track&field, volleyball

COMMUNITY COLLEGE OF RHODE ISLAND
1762 Louisquisset Pike
Lincoln, RI 02865-4585
Two-year college
(401) 333-7313
www.ccri.cc.ri.us
Contact: Israel Siperstein
Men's Non-aid: baseball, basketball, cross country, golf, ice hockey, soccer, tennis, weightlifting
Women's Non-aid: basketball, cross country, softball, tennis, volleyball, weightlifting

PROVIDENCE COLLEGE
River Avenue
Providence, RI 02918
(401) 865-2272
www.providence.edu
Contact: Gregg Burke
Unspecified athletic aid available
M: baseball, basketball, cross country, ice hockey, soccer, softball, swimming-diving, tennis, track&field. Men's Non-aid: golf, lacrosse
W: baseball, basketball, cross country, field hockey, lacrosse, soccer, softball, swimming-diving, tennis, track&field, volleyball. Women's Non-aid: ice hockey

RHODE ISLAND COLLEGE
600 Mount Pleasant Avenue
Providence, RI 02908
(401) 456-8516
www.ric.edu
Contact: Scott Gibbons
Men's Non-aid: baseball, basketball, cross country, golf, indoor track, soccer, tennis, track&field, wrestling
Women's Non-aid: basketball, cross country, gymnastics, indoor track, lacrosse, softball, tennis, track&field, volleyball

SALVE REGINA COLLEGE
100 Ochre Point Avenue
Newport, RI 02840
(401) 847-6650
www.salve.edu
Contact: Joyce M. Yarrow
Men's Non-aid: baseball, basketball, cross country, golf, indoor track, soccer, tennis, track&field
Women's Non-aid: basketball, cross country, golf, indoor track, soccer, softball, tennis, track&field

UNIVERSITY OF RHODE ISLAND
207 Keaney Gymnasium
Kinston, RI 02881
(401) 874-1000
www.uri.edu
Contact: Ron Petro

Unspecified athletic aid available
M: baseball, basketball, field hockey, football, gymnastics, indoor track, soccer, softball, swimming-diving, track&field, volleyball. Men's Non-aid: crew, cross country, golf, ice hockey, lacrosse, rugby, sailing, tennis, water polo, wrestling
W: basketball, cross country, field hockey, gymnastics, indoor track, soccer, softball, swimming-diving, track&field, volleyball. Women's Non-aid: sailing, tennis

South Carolina

ALLEN UNIVERSITY
1530 Harden Street
Columbia, SC 29204
(803) 254-4165
www.scicu.org/allen
Contact: W.M. Jefferson
Unspecified athletic aid available
M: baseball, basketball
W: basketball

ANDERSON COLLEGE
316 Boulevard
Anderson, SC 29621
(765) 641-4080
www.anderson.edu
Contact: James L. Owens
Men's Non-aid: baseball, basketball, cross country, golf, indoor track, soccer, tennis, track&field, wrestling
Women's Non-aid: basketball, soccer, softball, tennis, volleyball

BENEDICT COLLEGE
Harden Street
Columbia, SC 29204
(803) 253-5105
www.scicu.org/benedict
Contact: Willie Washington
Unspecified athletic aid available
M: baseball, basketball, cross country, indoor track, tennis, track&field
W: basketball, softball, tennis, track&field, volleyball

CHARLESTON SOUTHERN UNIVERSITY
P.O. Box 10087
Charleston, SC 29411
(843) 863-7050
www.csuniv.edu
Contact: Ellen C. Green
Unspecified athletic aid available
M: baseball, basketball, cross country, golf, indoor track, soccer, tennis, track&field
W: basketball, cross country, indoor track, softball, tennis, track&field, volleyball

THE CITADEL
171 Moultrie Street
Charleston, SC 29409
(843) 953-5000
www.citadel.edu
Contact: Josh Baker
Unspecified athletic aid available
M: baseball, basketball, cross country, football, golf, riflery, soccer, tennis, track&field, wrestling

CLAFLIN COLLEGE
700 College Avenue
Orangeburg, SC 29115
(843) 534-2710
www.scicu.org/claflin
Contact: Yvonne C. Claflin
Unspecified athletic aid available
M: basketball, track&field
W: basketball, squash, track&field

CLEMSON UNIVERSITY
P.O. Box 632
Clemson, SC 29633
(803) 656-2114
www.clemsontigers.com
Contact: Bobby Robinson
Men's Aid (#/$): 11/unspecified $
Women's Aid (#/$): 7/unspecified $
M: baseball, basketball, cross country, football, golf, indoor track, soccer, swimming-diving, tennis, track&field, wrestling
W: cross country, indoor track, swimming-diving, tennis, track&field, volleyball

COASTAL CAROLINA COLLEGE

P.O. Box 261954
Conway, SC 29528
(803) 349-2822
www.coastal.edu
Contact: Jeff Dannelly
Unspecified athletic aid available
M: baseball, basketball, cross country, golf, soccer, tennis, track&field
W: basketball, cross country, golf, indoor track, soccer, softball, tennis, track&field, volleyball

COKER COLLEGE

300E College Avenue
Hartsville, SC 29550
(843) 383-8073
www.coker.edu
Contact: Cale Bigbee
Men's Aid (#/$): 13.5/$256,500
Women's Aid (#/$): 13.5/$256,500
M: baseball, basketball, cross country, golf, soccer, tennis
W: basketball, cross country, soccer, softball, tennis, volleyball

COLLEGE OF CHARLESTON

66 George Street
Charleston, SC 29424
(843) 792-5465
www.cofc.edu
Contact: Tony Ciuffo
Unspecified athletic aid available
M: baseball, basketball, cross country, golf, soccer, swimming-diving, tennis.
Men's Non-aid: equestrian, sailing
W: basketball, cross country, golf, softball, swimming-diving, tennis, volleyball.
Women's Non-aid: equestrian, sailing

COLUMBIA COLLEGE

1301 Columbia College Drive
Columbia, SC 29203
(803) 786-3644
www.colacoll.edu
Contact: Anita Kaminer
Women's Aid (#/$): 22/$29,150
W: tennis, volleyball

CONVERSE COLLEGE

580 East Main Street
Spartanburg, SC 29301-0006
(864) 596-9040
www.converse.edu
Contact: Patricia Chandler
Unspecified athletic aid available
W: basketball, tennis, volleyball. Women's Non-aid: equestrian

ERSKINE COLLEGE

Due West, SC 29639
(864) 379-2131
www.erskine.edu
Contact: Dot Carter
Unspecified athletic aid available
M: baseball, basketball, cross country, golf, soccer, tennis
W: basketball, soccer, softball, tennis, volleyball

FRANCIS MARION UNIVERSITY

P.O. Box 100547
Florence, SC 29501-0547
(843) 661-1222
www.fmarion.edu
Contact: Michael G. Hawkins
Men's Aid (#/$): 25/$217,160
Women's Aid (#/$): 25/$217,160
M: baseball, basketball, cross country, golf, soccer, tennis, track&field
W: basketball, cross country, soccer, softball, tennis, track&field, volleyball

FURMAN UNIVERSITY

Poinsett Highway
Greenville, SC 29613
(864) 294-2000
www.furman.edu
Contact: Hunter Reid
Unspecified athletic aid available
M: baseball, basketball, cross country, football, golf, soccer, swimming-diving, tennis, track&field. Men's Non-aid: wrestling
W: basketball, golf, softball, swimming-diving, tennis, volleyball. Women's Non-aid: cross country

LANDER COLLEGE
P.O. Box 6005
Greenwood, SC 29649
(888) 452-6337
www.lander.edu
Contact: Bob Stoner
Unspecified athletic aid available
M: basketball, cross country, soccer, tennis
W: basketball, cross country, softball, tennis

LIMESTONE COLLEGE
1115 College Drive
Gaffney, SC 29340
(800)-795-1151
www.limestone.edu
Contact: Dennis Bloomer
Unspecified athletic aid available
M: baseball, basketball, golf, lacrosse, soccer, tennis
W: basketball, lacrosse, soccer, softball, tennis, volleyball

NEWBERRY COLLEGE
2100 College Street
Newberry, SC 29108
(800) 845-4955
www.newberry.com
Contact: Patrick Stewart
Unspecified athletic aid available
M: baseball, basketball, football, golf, tennis
W: basketball, softball, tennis, volleyball

NORTH GREENVILLE COLLEGE
P.O. Box 1892
Tigerville, SC 29688
Two-year college
(803) 895-1410
www.ngc.edu
Contact: Jan McDonald
Unspecified athletic aid available
M: baseball, basketball, cheerleading, football, golf, soccer, tennis
W: basketball, cheerleading, softball, soccer, tennis, volleyball

PRESBYTERIAN COLLEGE
503 South Broad Street
Clinton, SC 29325
(843) 833-2820
www.presby.edu
Contact: David Hibbard
Unspecified athletic aid available
M: baseball, basketball, football, golf, soccer, tennis, track&field
W: basketball, soccer, tennis, volleyball

SOUTH CAROLINA STATE COLLEGE
300 College Street NE
Orangeburg, SC 29117-0001
(803) 536-7060
www.scsu.edu
Contact: William P. Hamilton
Men's Aid (#/$): 107/$555,758
Women's Aid (#/$): 39/$202,566
M: basketball, cross country, football, golf, indoor track, tennis, track&field. Men's Non-aid: baseball
W: basketball, bowling, cross country, golf, indoor track, soccer, softball, tennis, track&field, volleyball

SOUTHERN WESLEYAN UNIVERSITY
907 Wesleyan Drive
Central, SC 29630
(864) 639-2453
www.swu.edu
Contact: D.W. Hamilton
Unspecified athletic aid available
M: baseball, basketball, golf, soccer
W: basketball, softball, volleyball

SPARTANBURG METHODIST
1200 Textile Road
Spartanburg, SC 29301-0009
Two-year college
(864) 587-4213
www.smcsc.edu
Contact: Kevin Good
Unspecified athletic aid available
M: baseball, basketball, cross country, golf, soccer
W: basketball, cross country, soccer, softball, tennis, volleyball

UNIVERSITY OF SOUTH CAROLINA

Coastal Carolina College
Myrtle Beach, SC 29578
(843) 347-3161
www.sc.edu
Contact: Charlotte Jones
Unspecified athletic aid available
M: baseball, basketball, cross country, golf, soccer, tennis, track&field
W: basketball, cross country, diving, golf, indoor track, soccer, softball, tennis, track&field, volleyball

UNIVERSITY OF SOUTH CAROLINA

Rosewood Drive
Columbia, SC 29208
(803) 777-5204
www.sc.edu
Contact: Kerry Tharp
Unspecified athletic aid available
M: baseball, basketball, cross country, football, golf, soccer, swimming-diving, tennis, track&field
W: basketball, golf, soccer, soccer, softball, swimming-diving, tennis, volleyball

UNIVERSITY OF SOUTH CAROLINA (AIKEN)

171 University Parkway
Aiken, SC 29801
(803) 648-6851
www.usca.sc.edu
Contact: A. Glenn Shumpert
Men's Aid (#/$): 25/unspecified $
Women's Aid (#/$): 25/unspecified $
M: baseball, basketball, cross country, golf, soccer, tennis
W: basketball, cross country, soccer, softball, volleyball

UNIVERSITY OF SOUTH CAROLINA (SPARTANBURG)

800 University Way
Spartanburg, SC 29303-9982
(864) 503-5000
www.uscs.edu
Contact: Michael F. MacEachern

Men's Aid (#/$): 23/unspecified $
Women's Aid (#/$): 15/unspecified $
M: baseball, basketball, cross country, soccer, tennis
W: basketball, soccer, softball, tennis, volleyball

WINTHROP UNIVERSITY

Department of Athletics
Eden Terrace
Rock Hill, SC 29733
(803) 323-2129 ext. 6226
www.winthrop.edu
Contact: Tom Hickman
Men's Aid (#/$): 39/$246,948
Women's Aid (#/$): 26/$164,632
M: baseball, basketball, cross country, golf, soccer, tennis, track&field
W: basketball, cross country, golf, soccer, softball, tennis, track&field, volleyball

WOFFORD COLLEGE

429 North Church Street
Spartanburg, SC 29303-3663
(864) 597-4000
www.wofford.edu
Contact: Mark Cohen
Men's Aid (#/$): 54.5/unspecified $
Women's Aid (#/$): 50/unspecified $
M: baseball, basketball, cross country, football, golf, soccer, tennis
W: basketball, cross country, soccer, tennis, volleyball

South Dakota

AUGUSTANA COLLEGE

2001 South Summit Avenue
Sioux Falls, SD 57197
(605) 336-5216
www.augie.edu
Contact: Brenda Mortha
Unspecified athletic aid available
M: baseball, basketball, cross country, football, indoor track, track&field, wrestling. Men's Non-aid: golf, tennis

W: basketball, cross country, indoor track, soccer, softball, track&field, volleyball
Women's Non-aid: golf

BLACK HILLS STATE UNIVERSITY
Box 9512
Spearfish, SD 57799-9512
(605) 642-6445
www.bhsu.edu
Contact: John R. Buxton
Unspecified athletic aid available
M: basketball, cross country, football, indoor track, track&field
W: basketball, cross country, track&field, volleyball

DAKOTA STATE UNIVERSITY
820 North Washington Avenue
Madison, SD 57042-1799
(605) 256-5152
www.dsu.edu
Contact: Judy Dittman
Unspecified athletic aid available
M: basketball, cross country, football, indoor track, track&field. Men's Non-aid: baseball
W: basketball, cross country, indoor track, track&field, volleyball. Women's Non-aid: softball

DAKOTA WESLEYAN UNIVERSITY
1200 West University Avenue
Mitchell, SD 57301
(605) 995-2654
www.dwu.edu
Contact: Wilma Hjellum
Unspecified athletic aid available
M: baseball, basketball, cross country, football, golf, rodeo, track&field, wrestling
W: basketball, cross country, golf, softball, track&field, volleyball

HURON UNIVERSITY
9th and Ohio
Huron, SD 57350
(605) 352-8721
www.huron.edu

Contact: Darnley Hendley
Unspecified athletic aid available
M: basketball, cross country, football, golf, wrestling
W: basketball, cross country, golf, volleyball

MOUNT MARTY COLLEGE
1105 West 8th Street
Yankton, SD 57078
(605) 668-1529
www.mtmc.edu
Contact: Chuck Iverson
Men's Aid (#/$): 9/$130,000
Women's Aid (#/$): 9/$130,000
M: baseball, basketball, cross country, golf, soccer, track&field
W: basketball, cross country, golf, softball, track&field, volleyball

NORTHERN STATE UNIVERSITY
1200 South Jay
Aberdeen, SD 57401
(800) 678-5300
www.northern.edu
Contact: Deb Smith
Unspecified athletic aid available
M: basketball, cross country, football, wrestling. Men's Non-aid: baseball, golf, tennis
W: basketball, cross country, golf, softball, tennis, volleyball

SIOUX FALLS COLLEGE
1101 West 22nd Street
Sioux Falls, SD 57105
(605) 331-6791
www.usiouxfalls.edu
Contact: Tim Hyatt
Unspecified athletic aid available
M: baseball, basketball, cross country, football, soccer, tennis, track&field
W: basketball, cross country, soccer, softball, tennis, track&field, volleyball

SOUTH DAKOTA SCHOOL OF MINES AND TECHNOLOGY
501 East Saint Joseph
Rapid City, SD 57701

(605) 394-2351
www.sdsmt.edu
Contact: Laurie Hoffman
Men's Aid (#/$): 58/unspecified $
Women's Aid (#/$): 32/unspecified $
M: basketball, cross country, football, tennis, track&field
W: basketball, cross country, track&field, volleyball

SOUTH DAKOTA STATE UNIVERSITY
Box 2820
Brookings, SD 57007-1497
(605) 688-4623
www.sdstate.edu
Contact: Ron Lenz
Unspecified athletic aid available
M: baseball, basketball, cross country, football, indoor track, swimming, track&field, wrestling
W: basketball, cross country, golf, indoor track, softball, swimming, track&field, volleyball

UNIVERSITY OF SOUTH DAKOTA
414 East Clark Street
Vermillion, SD 57069
(605) 677-5309
www.usd.edu
Contact: Kelly Higgins
Unspecified athletic aid available
Restrictions and notes: Aid figures based on full tuition equivalents.
M: baseball, basketball, cross country, football, indoor track, swimming-diving, tennis, track&field
W: basketball, cross country, indoor track, soccer, softball, swimming-diving, tennis, track&field, volleyball

Tennessee

AQUINAS COLLEGE
4210 Harding Road
Nashville, TN 37205
Two-year college
(615) 297-7653

www.aquinas.tn.edu
Contact: Charles Anderson
Unspecified athletic aid available
M: baseball, basketball

AUSTIN PEAY STATE UNIVERSITY
P.O. Box 4515
Clarksville, TN 37044
(931) 648-7561
www.apsu.edu
Contact: Brad Kirtley
Unspecified athletic aid available
M: baseball, basketball, cross country, football, golf, tennis, track&field
W: basketball, cross country, indoor track, softball, tennis, track&field, volleyball

BELMONT COLLEGE
Belmont Boulevard
Nashville, TN 37203
(615) 460-5662
www.belmont.edu
Contact: Casey Alexander
Men's Aid (#/$): 25/$250,000
Women's Aid (#/$): 20/$200,000
M: baseball, basketball, cross country, soccer, tennis, track&field. Men's Non-aid: golf
W: basketball, cross country, softball, tennis, track&field, volleyball. Women's Non-aid: golf

CARSON-NEWMAN COLLEGE
Campus Box 2009
Jefferson City, TN 37760
(423) 475-9061
www.cn.edu
Contact: Steve Cotton
Unspecified athletic aid available
M: baseball, basketball, cross country, football, golf, soccer, tennis, track&field, wrestling
W: basketball, cross country, soccer, softball, tennis, track&field, volleyball

CHRISTIAN BROTHERS COLLEGE
650 East Parkway Street
Memphis, TN 38104

(901) 321-3205
www.cbu.edu
Contact: Sandi Mayo
Unspecified athletic aid available
M: baseball, basketball, soccer
W: basketball, soccer, softball, tennis, volleyball

CLEVELAND STATE COMMUNITY COLLEGE

P.O. Box 3570
3535 Adkisson Drive West
Cleveland, TN 37320-3570
Two-year college
(423) 472-7141
www.clscc.cc.ts.us
Contact: Jim Cigliano
Unspecified athletic aid available
M: baseball, basketball
W: basketball

DYERSBURG STATE COMMUNITY COLLEGE

150 Lake Road
Dyersburg, TN 38024
Two-year college
(901) 286-3200
www.dscc.cc.tn.us
Contact: Barry Young
Unspecified athletic aid available
M: baseball, basketball. Men's Non-aid: basketball

EAST TENNESSEE STATE UNIVERSITY

P.O. Box 21730A
Johnson City, TN 37614
(423) 439-4317
www.etsu.edu
Contact: John Cathey
Unspecified athletic aid available
M: baseball, basketball, cross country, football, golf, indoor track, tennis, track&field
W: basketball, cross country, indoor track, tennis, track&field

FISK UNIVERSITY

17th Avenue North
Nashville, TN 37203

(615) 329-8735
www.fisk.edu
Contact: Annette Miller
Men's Non-aid: basketball, cross country, soccer, track&field
Women's Non-aid: basketball, cross country, track&field, volleyball

FREED-HARDEMAN COLLEGE

158 East Main
Henderson, TN 38340
(800) 630-3480
www.fhu.edu
Contact: Mike McCutchen
Unspecified athletic aid available
M: baseball, basketball, golf, tennis
W: basketball, softball, tennis, volleyball

HIWASSEE COLLEGE

Hiwassee Road
Madisonville, TN 37354
Two-year college
(800) 356-2187
www.hiwassee.edu
Contact: Eugene Kiger
Men's Aid (#/$): 11/$75,000
Women's Aid (#/$): 11/$75,000
M: baseball, basketball
W: basketball, softball

JACKSON STATE COMMUNITY COLLEGE

2046 North Parkway
Jackson, TN 38301
Two-year college
(901) 424-3520
www.jscc.cc.tn.us
Contact: Jack Martin
Unspecified athletic aid available
M: baseball, basketball
W: basketball

KING COLLEGE

1350 King College Road
Bristol, TN 37620-2699
(423) 968-1187
www.king.edu
Contact: Mildred B. Greeson
Unspecified athletic aid available

M: baseball, basketball, cross country, golf, soccer, tennis
W: basketball, cross country, soccer, softball, tennis, volleyball

LAMBUTH UNIVERSITY
705 Lambuth Boulevard
Jackson, TN 38301
(800) 919-8326
www.lambuth.edu
Contact: Will Atkinson
Men's Aid (#/$): 39/unspecified $
Women's Aid (#/$): 36/unspecified $
M: badminton, baseball, football, sailing, tennis. Men's Non-aid: field hockey
W: basketball, soccer, softball, tennis, volleyball

LEE UNIVERSITY
Ocoee Street
Cleveland, TN 37311
(423) 614-8000
www.leeuniversity.edu
Contact: Michael Ellis
Unspecified athletic aid available
M: basketball, golf, soccer, tennis
W: basketball, soccer, softball, tennis, volleyball

LEMOYNE-OWEN COLLEGE
807 Walker Avenue
Memphis, TN 38126
(901) 774-9090
www.lemoyne-owen.edu
Contact: Eddie Cook
Men's Non-aid: baseball, basketball, track&field
Women's Non-aid: basketball

LINCOLN MEMORIAL UNIVERSITY
Cumberland Gap Parkway
Harrogate, TN 37752
(800) 325-0900
www.lmunet.edu
Contact: Tom Amis
Unspecified athletic aid available
M: baseball, basketball, cross country, golf, soccer, tennis

W: basketball, cross country, soccer, softball, tennis, volleyball

MARYVILLE COLLEGE
502 E. Lamar Alexander Parkway
Maryville, TN 37804
(800) 597-2687
www.maryvillecollege.edu
Contact: Wes Moore
Men's Non-aid: baseball, basketball, football, soccer, tennis
Women's Non-aid: basketball, softball, tennis, volleyball

MIDDLE TENNESSEE STATE UNIVERSITY
MTSU Box 20
Murfreesboro, TN 37132
(615) 898-2450
www.mtsu.edu
Contact: Ed Given
Unspecified athletic aid available
M: baseball, basketball, cross country, football, golf, indoor track, tennis, track&field
W: basketball, cross country, indoor track, softball, tennis, track&field, volleyball

MILLIGAN COLLEGE
P.O. Box 101
Milligan College, TN 37682
(423) 929-0116
www.milligan.edu
Contact: Paul Bader
Unspecified athletic aid available
M: baseball, basketball, tennis
W: basketball, softball, tennis, volleyball

MOTLOW STATE COMMUNITY COLLEGE
P.O. Box 88100
Ledford Mill Road
Tullahoma, TN 37388-8100
Two-year college
(931) 393-1500
www.mscc.cc.tn.us
Contact: Charles Coffey
Unspecified athletic aid available

M: baseball, basketball
W: basketball

ROANE STATE COMMUNITY COLLEGE
Patton Lane
Harriman, TN 37748
Two-year college
(423) 882-4550
www.rscc.cc.tn.us
Contact: Randy Nesbit
Unspecified athletic aid available
M: baseball, basketball
W: basketball, softball

SHELBY STATE COMMUNITY COLLEGE
P.O. Box 40568
Memphis, TN 38174-0568
Two-year college
(901) 333-5143
www.sscc.cc.tn.us
Contact: Verde Sails
Unspecified athletic aid available
M: baseball, basketball, golf
W: basketball

TEMPLE BAPTIST SEMINARY
1815 Union Avenue
Chattanooga, TN 37404
(931) 493-4100
www.templebaptistseminary.edu
Contact: Randy Stem
Unspecified athletic aid available
M: baseball, basketball, soccer. Men's Non-aid: bowling
W: basketball, volleyball. Women's Non-aid: softball

TENNESSEE STATE UNIVERSITY
3500 John A. Merritt Boulevard
Nashville, TN 37209
(615) 963-5000
www.tnstate.edu
Contact: Homer R. Wheaton
Unspecified athletic aid available
M: baseball, basketball, football, indoor track, swimming, track&field

W: basketball, indoor track, softball, track&field

TENNESSEE TECHNOLOGICAL UNIVERSITY
P.O. Box 5006
Cookeville, TN 38505
(615) 372-3888
www.tntech.edu
Contact: Rob Schabert
Unspecified athletic aid available
M: baseball, basketball, cross country, football, golf, indoor track, tennis
W: basketball, cross country, golf, indoor track, softball, tennis, volleyball

TENNESSEE WESLEYAN COLLEGE
255 Hiwassee College Drive
Madisonville, TN 37354
(931) 745-7504
www.tnwc.edu
Contact: Wayne Norfleet
Unspecified athletic aid available
M: baseball, basketball, soccer. Men's Non-aid: football, golf, tennis
W: basketball, tennis. Women's Non-aid: soccer, softball

TREVECCA NAZARENE COLLEGE
333 Murfreesboro Road
Nashville, TN 37203
(615) 248-1271
www.trevecca.edu
Contact: Alan Smith
Unspecified athletic aid available
M: baseball, basketball, golf, soccer
W: basketball, golf, soccer, softball, volleyball

TUSCULUM COLLEGE
60 Shiloh Road
Greeneville, TN 37743
(423) 636-7300
www.tusculum.edu
Contact: Diane L. Keasling
Unspecified athletic aid available

M: baseball, basketball, golf, soccer, tennis
W: basketball, softball, tennis, volleyball

UNION UNIVERSITY
1050 Union University Drive
Jackson, TN 38305
(901) 668-1818 ext. 5325
www.uu.edu
Contact: Don Morris
Unspecified athletic aid available
M: baseball, basketball, golf, soccer, tennis
W: basketball, cross country, softball, tennis, volleyball

UNIVERSITY OF MEMPHIS
205 Athletic Office Building
Memphis, TN 38152
(901) 678-2337
www.memphis.edu
Contact: Martha Woods
Unspecified athletic aid available
M: baseball, basketball, cross country, football, golf, indoor track, soccer, tennis, track&field
W: basketball, cross country, golf, indoor track, soccer, softball, tennis, volleyball

UNIVERSITY OF TENNESSEE
615 McCallie Avenue
Chattanooga, TN 37402-2598
(423) 755-4662
www.utc.edu
Contact: Neil Magnussen
Unspecified athletic aid available
M: baseball, basketball, cross country, football, golf, indoor track, soccer, swimming-diving, tennis, track&field
W: basketball, cross country, indoor track, soccer, swimming-diving, tennis, track&field, volleyball

UNIVERSITY OF TENNESSEE (KNOXVILLE)
1720 Volunteer Boulevard
Knoxville, TN 37996

(423) 974-1000
www.utk.edu
Contact: Bud Ford
Unspecified athletic aid available
M: baseball, basketball, cross country, football, golf, indoor track, swimming-diving, tennis, track&field. Men's Non-aid: crew, ice hockey, soccer
W: basketball, cross country, golf, indoor track, soccer, swimming-diving, tennis, track&field, volleyball

UNIVERSITY OF TENNESSEE (MARTIN)
304 Administration
Martin, TN 38238-5070
(901) 587-7630 ext. 7632
www.utm.edu
Contact: Lee Wilmot
Unspecified athletic aid available
M: baseball, basketball, cross country, football, golf, riflery, tennis, track&field
W: basketball, cross country, riflery, softball, tennis, track&field, volleyball

VANDERBILT UNIVERSITY
2601 Jess Neely Drive
Nashville, TN 37203
(615) 322-4121
www.vanderbilt.edu
Contact: Lew Harris
Unspecified athletic aid available
M: baseball, basketball, cross country, football, golf, soccer, tennis
W: basketball, cross country, golf, indoor track, soccer, tennis, track&field

WALTERS STATE COMMUNITY COLLEGE
500 South Davy Crockett Parkway
Morristown, TN 37813
Two-year college
(423) 585-2600
www.wscc.cc.tn.us
Contact: Bill Brittain

Unspecified athletic aid available
M: baseball, basketball, tennis
W: basketball

Texas

ABILENE CHRISTIAN UNIVERSITY
P.O. Box 7795
Abilene, TX 79699
(915) 674-2693
www.acu.edu
Contact: Garner Roberts
Unspecified athletic aid available
M: basketball, cross country, football,
golf, tennis, track&field
W: basketball, cross country, indoor
track, tennis, track&field, volleyball

ANGELINA COLLEGE
P.O. Box 1768
Lufkin, TX 75902-1768
Two-year college
(409) 633-5282
www.angelina.cc.tx.us
Contact: Guy Davis
Unspecified athletic aid available
M: baseball, basketball
W: basketball

ANGELO STATE UNIVERSITY
P.O. Box 10889
ASU Station
San Angelo, TX 76909
(915) 942-2091
www.angelo.edu
Contact: M.L. Hinkle
Unspecified athletic aid available
M: basketball, cross country, football,
track&field
W: basketball, cross country, soccer,
tennis, track&field, volleyball

AUSTIN COLLEGE
900 N. Grand Avenue
Sherman, TX 75090
(254) 813-2318

www.austin.edu
Contact: Charlene Rowland
Men's Non-aid: baseball, basketball,
diving, football, golf, rodeo, soccer,
softball, tennis, track&field, water polo
Women's Non-aid: basketball, diving,
martial arts, rodeo, soccer, softball,
tennis, volleyball

BAYLOR UNIVERSITY
3031 Dutton Avenue
Waco, TX 76711
(817) 755-1234
www.baylor.edu
Contact: Maxey Parrish
Unspecified athletic aid available
M: baseball, basketball, cross country,
football, golf, indoor track, tennis,
track&field
W: basketball, cross country, indoor track,
softball, tennis, track&field, volleyball

CONCORDIA UNIVERSITY
Interstate 35 North
Austin, TX 78705
(512) 486-1162
www.concordia.edu
Contact: Linda Loury
Men's Aid ($): $75,000
Women's Aid ($): $75,000
M: baseball, basketball, tennis. Men's
Non-aid: golf
W: basketball, tennis, volleyball. Women's
Non-aid: golf

DALLAS BAPTIST UNIVERSITY
7777 West Kiest
Dallas, TX 75211
(214) 333-5340
www.abu.edu
Contact: Wayne Poage
Men's Aid (#/$): 12/$150,000
Women's Aid (#/$): 7/$35,000
M: baseball. Men's Non-aid: golf, soccer
W: volleyball

EAST TEXAS BAPTIST UNIVERSITY
1209 North Grove
Marshall, TX 75670

(903) 935-7963 ext. 374
www.etbu.edu
Contact: Kent Reeves
Men's Non-aid: baseball, basketball, football, golf, soccer
Women's Non-aid: basketball, soccer, softball, volleyball

EASTFIELD COLLEGE
3737 Motley Drive
Mesquite, TX 75150
Two-year college
(972) 860-7100
www.efc.dcccd.edu
Contact: Bob Flickner
Men's Non-aid: baseball, basketball, golf, softball, tennis
Women's Non-aid: softball, tennis, volleyball

FRANK PHILLIPS COLLEGE
Box 5118
Borger, TX 79007-5118
Two-year college
(806) 274-5311
www.fpc.cc.tx.us
Contact: John Green
Unspecified athletic aid available
M: baseball, basketball, horse judging, livestock judging, rodeo
W: basketball, horse judging, livestock judging, rodeo, volleyball

GRAYSON COUNTY COLLEGE
6101 Grayson Drive
Denison, TX 75020
Two-year college
(903) 465-6030
www.grayson.edu
Contact: Roy Jackson
Unspecified athletic aid available
M: baseball, basketball
W: basketball, softball

HARDIN-SIMMONS UNIVERSITY
Drawer H, HSU
Abilene, TX 79698
(915) 670-1273
www.hsutx.edu

Contact: John Niece
Unspecified athletic aid available
M: baseball, basketball, golf, riflery, soccer, tennis
W: cross country, golf, riflery, soccer, tennis, volleyball

HOUSTON BAPTIST UNIVERSITY
7502 Fondern Road
Houston, TX 77074
(713) 774-7661
www.hbu.edu
Contact: Ken Rogers
Unspecified athletic aid available
M: basketball, cross country, golf, gymnastics, indoor track, soccer, tennis, track&field
W: cross country, gymnastics, indoor track, soccer, track&field, volleyball

HOWARD PAYNE UNIVERSITY
1000 Fisk
Brownwood, TX 76801
(404) 679-4501
www.hputx.edu
Contact: Mike Blackwell
Unspecified athletic aid available
M: basketball, cross country, football, golf, indoor track
W: basketball, tennis, volleyball. Women's Non-aid: cross country

HUSTON-TILLOTSON COLLEGE
900 Chicon Street
Austin, TX 78702
(512) 505-3000
www.htc.edu
Contact: Jackie Wilson
Unspecified athletic aid available
M: baseball, basketball, golf, tennis
W: basketball, tennis, volleyball

JACKSONVILLE COLLEGE
105 B.J. Albritton Drive
Jacksonville, TX 75766
Two-year college
(903) 586-2518
www.rsts.net/colleges/texas/jackson/htm
Contact: Patrick Smith

Unspecified athletic aid available
M: basketball, golf
W: volleyball

KILGORE COLLEGE
1100 Broadway
Kilgore, TX 75662
Two-year college
(903) 983-8181
www.kilgore.cc.tx.us
Contact: Archie Whitfield
Men's Aid (#/$): 50/unspecified $
Women's Aid (#/$): 20/unspecified $
M: basketball, football
W: basketball

LAMAR UNIVERSITY
Box 10066 LU Station
Beaumont, TX 77710
(409) 880-8329
www.athletics.lamar.edu
Contact: Daucy Crizer
Unspecified athletic aid available
M: baseball, basketball, cross country,
golf, indoor track, tennis, track&field
W: basketball, cross country, golf, indoor
track, tennis, track&field, volleyball

LEE COLLEGE
P.O. Box 818
Baytown, TX 77522-0818
Two-year college
(713) 425-6487
www.lee.edu
Contact: Brenda Gentry
Unspecified athletic aid available
M: baseball, basketball
W: volleyball

LETOURNEAU COLLEGE
P.O. Box 7001
Longview, TX 75607
(903) 233-3472
www.letu.edu
Contact: Linda Fitzugh
Men's Non-aid: baseball, basketball,
cross country, golf, soccer, tennis
Women's Non-aid: basketball, cross country,
golf, soccer, softball, tennis, volleyball

LUBBOCK CHRISTIAN COLLEGE
5601 West 19th Street
Lubbock, TX 79407
(806) 792-3221
www.lcu.edu
Contact: Marcus Wilson
Unspecified athletic aid available
M: baseball, basketball, cross country,
indoor track, soccer, track&field
W: basketball, cross country, indoor
track, soccer, track&field, volleyball

MCLENNAN COMMUNITY COLLEGE
1400 College Drive
Waco, TX 76708
Two-year college
(254) 299-8622
www.mcc.cc.tx.us
Contact: Wendell Hudson
Unspecified athletic aid available
M: baseball, basketball, golf
W: basketball, golf, softball, tennis

MIDLAND COLLEGE
3600 North Garfield
Midland, TX 79705-6399
Two-year college
(915) 685-4581
www.midland.cc.tx.us
Contact: Joe Williams
Unspecified athletic aid available
M: basketball, golf
W: basketball, golf, softball

MIDWESTERN STATE UNIVERSITY
3400 Taft
Wichita Falls, TX 76308
(940) 397-4000
www.mwsu.edu
Contact: Harve Allen
Unspecified athletic aid available
M: basketball, field hockey, golf, soccer,
tennis, track&field
W: basketball, tennis, track&field, volleyball

NAVARRO COLLEGE
3200 West 7th Avenue
Corsicana, TX 75110

Two-year college
(903) 874-6508
www.nav.cc.tx.us
Contact: Roark Montgomery
Unspecified athletic aid available
M: baseball, basketball, football
W: softball, volleyball

NORTH CENTRAL TEXAS COLLEGE
1525 W. California Street
Gainesville, TX 76240-4699
Two-year college
(940) 668-7731
www.nctc.cc.tx.us
Contact: Kevin Darwin
Unspecified athletic aid available
M: baseball, rodeo
W: tennis, rodeo, softball, volleyball

NORTHWOOD UNIVERSITY
(TEXAS CAMPUS)
1114 West Farm Market Road
Cedar Hill, TX 75104
(972) 291-1541
www.northwood.edu
Contact: Al Williams
Unspecified athletic aid available
M: baseball, cross country, golf, indoor
track, soccer, track&field
W: cross country, golf, indoor track,
soccer, softball, track&field

ODESSA COLLEGE
201 West University
Odessa, TX 79764
Two-year college
(915) 335-6567
www.odessa.edu
Contact: Jim Carlson
Unspecified athletic aid available
M: baseball, basketball, golf, rodeo
W: basketball, cross country, indoor
track, rodeo, track&field

PANOLA COLLEGE
1109 West Panola Street
Carthage, TX 75633
Two-year college
(903) 693-2062

www.panola.cc.tx.us
Contact: Brenda Allums
Unspecified athletic aid available
M: baseball, basketball
W: basketball, volleyball

PARIS JUNIOR COLLEGE
2400 Clarksville Street
Paris, TX 75460
Two-year college
(903) 785-7661
www.paris.cc.tx.us
Contact: Don C. Wilhelm
Men's Aid (#/$): 48/unspecified $
Women's Aid (#/$): 16/unspecified $
M: baseball, basketball, golf, softball
W: basketball, softball

PRAIRIE VIEW A&M UNIVERSITY
Prairie View, TX 77446-2610
(409) 857-3311
www.pvamu.edu
Contact: A.D. James, Jr.
Unspecified athletic aid available
M: baseball, basketball, cross country,
football, golf, track&field. Men's Non-
aid: indoor track, tennis
W: basketball, cross country, track&field.
Women's Non-aid: indoor track, tennis,
volleyball

RICE UNIVERSITY
P.O. Box 1892
Houston, TX 77251-1892
(713) 527-4034
www.rice.edu
Contact: Bill Cousins
Unspecified athletic aid available
M: baseball, basketball, cross country,
football, golf, indoor track, tennis,
track&field. Men's Non-aid: swimming-
diving
W: basketball, cross country, indoor
track, swimming, tennis, track&field,
volleyball

SAINT EDWARD'S UNIVERSITY
3001 South Congress Avenue
Austin, TX 78704

(512) 448-8525
www.stewards.edu
Contact: Doris F. Constantine
Unspecified athletic aid available
M: baseball, basketball, golf, soccer, tennis
W: basketball, soccer, softball, tennis, volleyball

SAINT MARY'S UNIVERSITY
One Camino Santa Maria
San Antonio, TX 78228-8503
(210) 436-3126
www.stmarytx.edu
Contact: David R. Krause
Unspecified athletic aid available
M: baseball, basketball. Men's Non-aid: golf, soccer, tennis
W: basketball, softball, tennis, volley-ball

SAM HOUSTON STATE UNIVERSITY
1700 Sam Houston Avenue
Huntsville, TX 77340
(409) 294-1725
www.shsu.edu
Contact: John Lumie
Unspecified athletic aid available
M: baseball, basketball, cross country, football, golf, rodeo, soccer, tennis, track&field
W: basketball, golf, rodeo, softball, tennis, track&field, volleyball

SCHREINER COLLEGE
2100 Memorial Boulevard
Kerrville, TX 78028
(830) 896-5411
www.schreiner.edu
Contact: Jeff R. Scofield
Unspecified athletic aid available
M: baseball, basketball, cross country, soccer, tennis
W: basketball, cross country, soccer, tennis, volleyball

SOUTH PLAINS COLLEGE
1400 College Avenue
Levelland, TX 79336

Two-year college
(806) 894-9611
www.spc.cc.tx.us
Contact: Stephen John
Unspecified athletic aid available
M: basketball, cross country, golf, indoor track, tennis, track&field
W: basketball, tennis

SOUTHERN METHODIST UNIVERSITY
P.O. Box 750216
Dallas, TX 75275
(214) 768-2864
www.smu.edu
Contact: Ed Wisneski
Unspecified athletic aid available
M: basketball, cross country, football, golf, indoor track, soccer, swimming-diving, tennis, track&field
W: basketball, golf, swimming-diving, tennis. Women's Non-aid: cross country, indoor track, soccer, track&field

SOUTHWESTERN UNIVERSITY
P.O. Box 6273, SU Station
Georgetown, TX 78626
(512) 863-1381
www.southwestern.edu
Contact: Carla Lowryine
Men's Non-aid: baseball, basketball, cross country, golf, tennis
Women's Non-aid: basketball, cross country, golf, tennis, volleyball

SOUTHWEST TEXAS STATE UNIVERSITY
601 University
San Marcos, TX 78666-4616
(512) 245-2111
www.swt.edu
Contact: Tony Brubaker
Unspecified athletic aid available
M: baseball, basketball, cross country, football, golf, tennis, track&field
W: basketball, cross country, softball, tennis, track&field, volleyball

STEPHEN F. AUSTIN STATE UNIVERSITY
P.O. Box 13010, SFA Station
Nacogdoches, TX 75962-3010
(409) 486-2011
www.sfasu.edu
Contact: Greg Fort
Unspecified athletic aid available
M: baseball, basketball, cross country, football, golf, indoor track, track&field
W: basketball, cross country, indoor track, softball, track&field, volleyball

ST. PHILIP'S COLLEGE
1801 Martin Luther King Drive
San Antonio, TX 78203
Two-year college
(210) 531-3200
www.accd.edu
Contact: Jim Dalglish
Unspecified athletic aid available
M: basketball
W: volleyball

SUL ROSS STATE UNIVERSITY
Box C-112 Alpine
Alpine, TX 79832
(915) 837-8226
www.sulross.edu
Contact: Steve Lang
Unspecified athletic aid available
M: rodeo. Men's Non-aid: baseball, basketball, football, golf, tennis, track&field
W: rodeo. Women's Non-aid: basketball, golf, softball, tennis, track&field, volleyball

TARLETON STATE UNIVERSITY
P.O. Box 0720
Tarleton Station, TX 76402
(254) 968-9077
www.tarleton.edu
Contact: Reed Richmond
Men's Non-aid: baseball, basketball, cross country, football, indoor track, rodeo, track&field
Women's Non-aid: basketball, cross country, indoor track, rodeo, softball, tennis, track&field, volleyball

TEMPLE COLLEGE
2600 South First Street
Temple, TX 76504-7435
Two-year college
(254) 298-8282
www.templejc.edu
Contact: Danny Joe Scott
Men's Aid (#/$): 22/unspecified $
Women's Aid (#/$): 22/unspecified $
M: baseball, basketball, golf, tennis
W: basketball, softball, tennis

TEXARKANA COLLEGE
2500 North Robinson Road
Texarkana, TX 75599
Two-year college
(903) 838-4541
www.tc.cc.tx.us
Contact: Debbie Doffer
Men's Aid (#/$): 16/unspecified $
Women's Aid (#/$): 16/unspecified $
M: baseball
W: softball

TEXAS A&M COMMERCE
P.O. Box 3011
Commerce, TX 75429
(903) 886-5131
www.tamu.-commerce.edu
Contact: Bill Powers
Unspecified athletic aid available
M: basketball, cross country, football, golf, track&field
W: basketball, cross country, golf, soccer, track&field, volleyball

TEXAS A&M UNIVERSITY (KINGSVILLE)
MSC 114
Kingsville, TX 78363
(361) 593-2111
www.tamuk.edu
Contact: Fred Nuesch
Unspecified athletic aid available
M: baseball, basketball, cross country, football, golf, indoor track, swimming-diving, tennis, track&field. Men's Non-aid: riflery
W: basketball, cross country, golf, indoor track, softball, swimming-diving, tennis,

track&field, volleyball. Women's Non-aid: riflery, soccer

TEXAS A&M UNIVERSITY
P.O. Box 30017
College Station, TX 77842-3017
(409) 845-8757
www.agsieathletics.com
Contact: Don Oberhellman
Men's Aid (#/$): 140.2/unspecified $
Women's Aid (#/$): 102/unspecified $
M: baseball, basketball, cross country, football, golf, indoor track, swimming-diving, tennis, track&field
W: archery, basketball, cross country, equestrian, golf, indoor track, soccer, softball, swimming-diving, tennis, track&field, volleyball

TEXAS CHRISTIAN UNIVERSITY
2900 University Drive
Fort Worth, TX 76129
(817) 857-6899
www.pcu.edu
Contact: Kevin Price
Unspecified athletic aid available
M: baseball, basketball, cross country, football, golf, swimming-diving, tennis, track&field. Men's Non-aid: soccer
W: basketball, cross country, golf, soccer, swimming-diving, tennis, track&field, volleyball. Women's Non-aid: riflery

TEXAS LUTHERAN COLLEGE
1000 West Court Street
Seguin, TX 78155
(830) 372-6877
www.txlutheran.edu
Contact: Tim Clark
Unspecified athletic aid available
M: baseball, basketball, football, golf, soccer, tennis
W: basketball, cross country, golf, soccer, softball, tennis, track&field, volleyball

TEXAS SOUTHERN UNIVERSITY
3100 Cleburne Avenue
Houston, TX 77004
(713) 213-7270

www.tsu.edu
Contact: Bob Moreland
Unspecified athletic aid available
M: baseball, basketball, football, indoor track, soccer, track&field, volleyball
W: basketball

TEXAS TECH UNIVERSITY
P.O. Box 4199
Lubbock, TX 79409
(806) 742-2011
www.texastech.edu
Contact: Joe Hornaday
Unspecified athletic aid available
M: baseball, basketball, cross country, football, golf, indoor track, tennis, track&field. Men's Non-aid: gymnastics, lacrosse, rodeo, soccer
W: basketball, cross country, golf, indoor track, tennis, track&field, volleyball. Women's Non-aid: gymnastics, rodeo

TEXAS WESLEYAN UNIVERSITY
Roller Sleyan Street
Fort Worth, TX 76105-1536
(817) 531-4444
www.txwesleyan.edu
Contact: Dr. Skip Applin
Unspecified athletic aid available
M: baseball, basketball, golf, soccer, tennis
W: basketball, soccer, softball, tennis, volleyball

TEXAS WOMAN'S UNIVERSITY
P.O. Box 425349
Denton, TX 76204-5349
(940) 898-2373
www.twu.edu
Contact: Judy Southard
Women's Aid (#/$): unspecified#/$175,000
W: basketball, gymnastics, softball, tennis, volleyball

TRINITY UNIVERSITY
715 Stadium Drive
San Antonio, TX 78212

(210) 999-8447
www.trinity.edu
Contact: Granger Huntress
Unspecified athletic aid available
M: tennis. Men's Non-aid: baseball,
basketball, cross country, football, golf,
riflery, soccer, swimming-diving,
track&field
W: tennis. Women's Non-aid: basketball, cross country, riflery, soccer, softball, swimming-diving, track&field,
volleyball

TYLER JUNIOR COLLEGE
P.O. Box 9020
Tyler, TX 75711
Two-year college
(903) 510-2458
www.tyler.cc.tx.us
Contact: Dr. Tim Drain
Unspecified athletic aid available
M: baseball, basketball, golf, football,
soccer, tennis
W: basketball, golf, tennis, volleyball

UNIVERSITY OF DALLAS
1845 East Northgate Drive
Irving, TX 75062
(972) 721-5000
www.udallas.edu
Contact: Patty Danko
Men's Non-aid: baseball, basketball,
cross country, golf, soccer, tennis,
track&field
Women's Non-aid: basketball, cross
country, soccer, track&field, volleyball

UNIVERSITY OF HOUSTON
4800 Talhoun Road
Houston, TX 77004-5121
(713) 743-9370
www.uh.edu
Contact: Ted Gladchuk
Unspecified athletic aid available
M: baseball, basketball, cross country,
football, golf, indoor track, track&field
W: basketball, cross country, indoor
track, soccer, swimming-diving, tennis,
track&field, volleyball

UNIVERSITY OF INCARNATE WORD
4301 Broadway
San Antonio, TX 78209
(512) 829-3828
www.uiw.edu
Contact: Charles Olmstead
M: baseball, basketball, cross country,
golf, soccer, tennis
W: basketball, cross country, soccer,
softball, tennis, volleyball

UNIVERSITY OF MARY HARDIN-BAYLOR
UMHB Station 900 College
Belton, TX 76513
(800) 727-8642
www.umhb.edu
Contact: James Cohagan
Men's Aid (#/$): 20/unspecified $
Women's Aid (#/$): 20/unspecified $
M: baseball, basketball, golf, soccer,
tennis
W: basketball, softball, tennis, volleyball

UNIVERSITY OF NORTH TEXAS
P.O. Box 13917
Denton, TX 76203-3917
(940) 565-2000
www.unt.edu
Contact: Brian Briscoe
Unspecified athletic aid available
M: basketball, cross country, football,
golf, indoor track, track&field
W: basketball, cross country, golf, indoor
track, soccer, swimming-diving, tennis,
track&field, volleyball

UNIVERSITY OF TEXAS (ARLINGTON)
701 South Medderman Drive
Arlington, TX 76019
(817) 272-2222
www.uta.edu
Contact: Steve Weller
Unspecified athletic aid available
M: baseball, basketball, cross country,
golf, indoor track, tennis, track&field.
Men's Non-aid: riflery

W: basketball, indoor track, softball, tennis, track&field, volleyball. Women's Non-aid: riflery

UNIVERSITY OF TEXAS (AUSTIN)
P.O. Box 7399
Austin, TX 78713
(512) 471-7437
www.texassports.edu
Contact: Bill Little
Unspecified athletic aid available
M: baseball, basketball, cross country, football, golf, indoor track, swimming-diving, tennis, track&field
W: basketball, cross country, diving, golf, rowing, soccer, softball, swimming, tennis, track&field, volleyball

THE UNIVERSITY OF TEXAS AT BROWNSVILLE AND TEXAS SOUTHMOST COLLEGE
80 Fort Brown
Brownsville, TX 78520
Two-year college
(956) 544-8200
www.utb.edu
Contact: Daniel Ramirez
Unspecified athletic aid available
M: baseball
W: volleyball

UNIVERSITY OF TEXAS (EL PASO)
500 West University
El Paso, TX 79968
(915) 747-5347
www.utep.edu
Contact: Eddie Mullens
Unspecified athletic aid available
M: basketball, cross country, football, golf, indoor track, track&field
W: basketball, cross country, golf, indoor track, riflery, soccer, tennis, track&field, volleyball

UNIVERSITY OF TEXAS (PAN AMERICAN)
1201 West University Drive
Edinburg, TX 78539-2999
(956) 381-2011

www.panam.edu
Contact: Arnold Trejo
Unspecified athletic aid available
M: baseball, basketball, cross country, golf, indoor track, soccer, tennis, track&field
W: basketball, cross country, indoor track, tennis, track&field, volleyball

UNIVERSITY OF TEXAS (SAN ANTONIO)
6900 North Loop 1604 West
San Antonio, TX 78249-0619
(210) 458-4569
www.utsa.edu
Contact: Craig Merrimen
Men's Aid (#/$): 28/$51,904
Women's Aid (#/$): 25/$46,853
M: baseball, basketball, cross country, golf, indoor track, riflery, soccer, tennis, track&field. Men's Non-aid: volleyball
W: basketball, cross country, indoor track, riflery, softball, tennis, track&field, volleyball

WAYLAND BAPTIST UNIVERSITY
Campus Box 321
1900 West 7th Street
Plainview, TX 79072
(806) 296-5521
www.wbu.edu
Contact: Renee Jeffries
Unspecified athletic aid available
M: basketball, cross country, indoor track, track&field
W: basketball, cross country, indoor track, track&field

WEST TEXAS STATE UNIVERSITY
P.O. Box 939
Canyon, TX 79016-0001
(806) 651-2687
www.wtamu.edu
Contact: Bill Kauffman
Unspecified athletic aid available
M: baseball, basketball, cross country, football, golf, riflery, soccer, tennis
W: basketball, cross country, equestrian, golf, riflery, soccer, tennis, volleyball

WESTERN TEXAS COLLEGE
6200 College Avenue
Snyder, TX 79549
Two-year college
(888) 468-6982
www.wtc.cc.tx.us
Contact: Milton Ham
Unspecified athletic aid available
M: basketball, golf, rodeo
W: basketball, rodeo

WHARTON COUNTY JUNIOR COLLEGE
911 Boling Highway
Wharton, TX 77488
Two-year college
(409) 532-4560
198.64.57.10/wharton/wcjchome.htm
Contact: Gene Bahnsen
Unspecified athletic aid available
M: rodeo, tennis
W: rodeo, tennis, volleyball

Utah

BRIGHAM YOUNG UNIVERSITY
228 SFIT
Provo, UT 84602
(801) 378-4909
www.byu.edu
Contact: M - Pat Conroy
W - Karen Marshall
Unspecified athletic aid available
M: baseball, basketball, cross country, diving, football, golf, indoor track, soccer, swimming, tennis, track&field, volleyball
W: basketball, cross country, diving, golf, gymnastics, indoor track, soccer, softball, swimming, tennis, track&field, volleyball

DIXIE COLLEGE
225 South 700 East
St. George, UT 84770
Two-year college
(435) 652-7525
www.dixie.edu

Contact: Jason Glover
Unspecified athletic aid available
M: baseball, basketball, football, tennis
W: basketball, softball, volleyball

SNOW COLLEGE
150 College Avenue
Ephraim, UT 84627
Two-year college
(801) 283-4021
www.snow.edu
Contact: Bob Trythall
Unspecified athletic aid available
M: baseball, basketball, football. Men's Non-aid: alpine skiing, archery, badminton, bowling, cross country skiing, equestrian, golf, power lifting, racquetball, soccer, swimming, tennis, volleyball, weightlifting
W: basketball, softball, volleyball. Women's Non-aid: alpine skiing, archery, badminton, bowling, cross country skiing, equestrian, golf, power lifting, racquetball, soccer, swimming, tennis, weightlifting

SOUTHERN UTAH UNIVERSITY
351 West Center Street
Cedar City, UT 84720
(801) 586-7752
www.suu.edu
Contact: Neil Gardner
Unspecified athletic aid available
M: baseball, basketball, cross country, football, golf, track&field
W: basketball, cross country, gymnastics, softball, track&field, volleyball

UNIVERSITY OF UTAH
Huntsman Center
Salt Lake City, UT 84112
(801) 581-3507
www.utah.edu
Contact: Amy Hachet
Unspecified athletic aid available
M: alpine skiing, baseball, basketball, cross country, cross country skiing, football, golf, indoor track, swimming-diving, tennis, track&field

W: alpine skiing, basketball, cross country, cross country skiing, gymnastics, indoor track, softball, swimming-diving, tennis, track&field, volleyball

UTAH STATE UNIVERSITY
Athletics Spectrum Annex, VMC 7400
Logan, UT 84322
(435) 797-1361
www.usu.edu
Contact: Mike Strawes
Unspecified athletic aid available
M: baseball, basketball, cross country, football, golf, indoor track, tennis, track&field, wrestling. Men's Non-aid: rodeo, rugby
W: basketball, cross country, gymnastics, indoor track, softball, volleyball

WEBER STATE COLLEGE
3750 Harrison Boulevard
Ogden, UT 84408-2702
(801) 626-6010
www.weber.edu
Contact: Brad Larsen
Unspecified athletic aid available
M: basketball, cross country, football, golf, tennis, track&field. Men's Non-aid: rodeo
W: basketball, cross country, golf, soccer, tennis, track&field, volleyball. Women's Non-aid: rodeo

Vermont

CASTLETON STATE COLLEGE
Box 227
Castleton, VT 05735
(802) 468-1468
www.csc.usc.edu
Contact: Tim Barrett
Men's Non-aid: alpine skiing, baseball, basketball, cross country, cross country skiing, lacrosse, soccer, tennis
Women's Non-aid: alpine skiing, basketball, cross country, cross country skiing,

field hockey, lacrosse, soccer, softball, tennis

CHAMPLAIN COLLEGE
P.O. Box 670
Burlington, VT 05402
Two-year college
(802) 860-2792
www.champlain.edu
Contact: Susan Rand
Unspecified athletic aid available
M: basketball, soccer
W: soccer

GREEN MOUNTAIN COLLEGE
College Street
Poultney, VT 05764
(802) 287-9313 ext. 210
www.greenmtn.edu
Contact: Richard Hendrickson
Unspecified athletic aid available
M: basketball, golf, lacrosse, skiing, soccer, tennis
W: basketball, golf, skiing, soccer, softball, tennis, volleyball

JOHNSON STATE COLLEGE
College Road
Johnson, VT 05656
(802) 635-2356
www.jscbsc.edu
Contact: Patrick Green
Men's Non-aid: basketball, cross country, lacrosse, soccer, tennis
Women's Non-aid: basketball, cross country, soccer, softball, tennis

LYNDON STATE COLLEGE
1001 College Road
P.O. Box 919
Lyndonville, VT 05851
(802) 626-6200
ww.lsc.usc.edu
Contact: Skip Pound
Men's Non-aid: baseball, basketball, cross country, soccer, tennis
Women's Non-aid: basketball, cheerleading, cross country, soccer, softball, tennis

MIDDLEBURY COLLEGE
Memorial Fieldhouse
Middlebury, VT 05753
(802) 443-5000
www.middlebury.edu
Contact: Thomas Lawson
Unspecified athletic aid available
M: alpine skiing, cross country, ice hockey. Men's Non-aid: baseball, basketball, cross country, football, golf, lacrosse, soccer, swimming-diving, tennis, track&field
W: alpine skiing, cross country skiing, ice hockey. Women's Non-aid: basketball, cross country, field hockey, lacrosse, soccer, squash, swimming-diving, tennis, track&field

NORWICH UNIVERSITY
158 Harmon Drive
Northfield, VT 05663-2232
(802) 485-2230
www.norwich.edu
Contact: Anthony Mariano
Men's Non-aid: baseball, basketball, cross country, cross country skiing, football, golf, ice hockey, indoor track, lacrosse, riflery, rugby, sailing, soccer, swimming-diving, track&field, wrestling
Women's Non-aid: basketball, cross country, cross country skiing, golf, indoor track, riflery, rugby, sailing, soccer, softball, swimming-diving, track&field

SAINT MICHAEL'S COLLEGE
Winooski Park
Colchester, VT 05439
(802) 654-2000
www.smcvt.edu
Contact: Christopher Kenney
Unspecified athletic aid available
M: basketball. Men's Non-aid: alpine skiing, cross country, cross country skiing, golf, ice hockey, lacrosse, soccer, swimming-diving, tennis
W: basketball. Women's Non-aid: alpine skiing, cross country, cross country skiing, field hockey, golf, lacrosse, soccer, swimming-diving, tennis, volleyball

UNIVERSITY OF VERMONT
86 South Williams Street
Burlington, VT 05405
(802) 656-3480
www.uvm.edu
Contact: Bruce Bosley
Unspecified athletic aid available
M: alpine skiing, basketball, cross country skiing, ice hockey, soccer. Men's Non-aid: baseball, cross country, golf, gymnastics, indoor track, lacrosse, swimming-diving, tennis, track&field
W: alpine skiing, basketball, cross country, cross country skiing, soccer. Women's Non-aid: field hockey, gymnastics, indoor track, lacrosse, softball, swimming-diving, tennis, track&field, volleyball

Virginia

APPRENTICE SCHOOL
4101 Washington Avenue
Newport News, VA 23607
(757) 380-3809
www.apprenticeschool.com
Contact: Horace Underwood
Men's Non-aid: baseball, basketball, cross country, football, golf, soccer, tennis, track&field, wrestling
Women's Non-aid: softball, track&field, volleyball

AVERETT COLLEGE
420 West Main Street
Danville, VA 24541
(804) 791-5700
www.averett.edu
Contact: Linda W. Shields
Men's Non-aid: basketball, golf, soccer, tennis
Women's Non-aid: basketball, softball, tennis, volleyball

BLUEFIELD COLLEGE
3000 College Drive
Bluefield, VA 24605

(540) 326-3682
www.bluefield.edu
Contact: Nina Wilburn
Unspecified athletic aid available
M: baseball, basketball, golf. Men's
Non-aid: bowling
W: basketball

BRIDGEWATER COLLEGE
402 East College Street
Bridgewater, VA 22812
(540) 828-5360
www.bridgewater.edu
Contact: Scott Garbarino
Men's Non-aid: baseball, basketball,
cross country, football, golf, indoor track,
soccer, tennis, track&field
Women's Non-aid: basketball, cheerleading, cross country, field hockey,
indoor track, lacrosse, softball, tennis,
track&field

CHRISTOPHER NEWPORT
UNIVERSITY
1 University Place
Newport News, VA 23606
(757) 594-7100
www.cnu.edu
Contact: Wayne Block
Men's Non-aid: baseball, basketball,
cross country, golf, indoor track, sailing,
soccer, tennis, track&field
Women's Non-aid: basketball, cross
country, indoor track, sailing, softball,
tennis, track&field, volleyball

COLLEGE OF WILLIAM
AND MARY
P.O. Box 8795
Williamsburg, VA 23187
(757) 221-3480
www.um.edu
Contact: Jean Elliot
Unspecified athletic aid available
M: baseball, basketball, cross country,
football, gymnastics, indoor track, soc-
cer, tennis, track&field, wrestling. Men's
Non-aid: fencing, golf, swimming-
diving

W: basketball, cross country, field hockey,
gymnastics, indoor track, lacrosse, soccer,
tennis, track&field, volleyball. Women's
Non-aid: golf, swimming-diving

EASTERN MENNONITE
UNIVERSITY
1200 Park Road
Harrisonburg, VA 22802-2462
(540) 432-4000
www.emu.edu
Contact: David Schrock
Men's Non-aid: baseball, basketball,
cross country, soccer, track&field
Women's Non-aid: basketball, cross
country, field hockey, softball,
track&field, volleyball

EMORY AND HENRY COLLEGE
P.O. Box 947
Emory, VA 24327
(540) 944-4121
www.ehc.edu
Contact: Nathan Graybeal
Men's Non-aid: baseball, basketball,
football, tennis, track&field
Women's Non-aid: basketball, tennis,
track&field, volleyball

FERRUM COLLEGE
Public Relations
Ferrum, VA 24088
(703) 365-4306
www.ferrum.edu
Contact: Gary Holden
Men's Non-aid: baseball, basketball,
equestrian, football, golf, soccer, tennis
Women's Non-aid: basketball, equestrian,
golf, soccer, softball, tennis, volleyball

GEORGE MASON UNIVERSITY
4400 University Drive
Fairfax, VA 22030-4444
(703) 993-3269
www.gmu.edu
Contact: Jim Engelhard
Unspecified athletic aid available
M: baseball, basketball, cross country,
golf, indoor track, soccer, swimming-

diving, tennis, track&field, volleyball,
wrestling
W: basketball, cross country, indoor
track, soccer, softball, swimming-diving,
tennis, track&field, volleyball

HAMPDEN-SYDNEY COLLEGE
P.O. Box 698
Hampden-Sydney, VA 23943
(804) 223-6156
www.hsc.edu
Contact: Dan McCormick
Men's Non-aid: baseball, basketball,
cross country, football, golf, lacrosse,
soccer, tennis

HAMPTON UNIVERSITY
Office of Sports Information
Hampton, VA 23668
(757) 727-5757
www.hamptonu.edu
Contact: LeCounte Conaway
Unspecified athletic aid available
M: basketball, football, indoor track,
tennis, track&field. Men's Non-aid: cross
country, golf, wrestling
W: basketball, indoor track, track&field.
Women's Non-aid: baseball, cross
country, volleyball

JAMES MADISON
UNIVERSITY
800 S. Main Street
Harrisonburg, VA 22807
(540) 568-6211
www.jmu.edu
Contact: Gary Michael
Unspecified athletic aid available
M: baseball, basketball, cross country,
football, golf, gymnastics, indoor track,
soccer, swimming-diving, tennis,
track&field, wrestling. Men's Non-aid:
archery
W: basketball, cross country, field hockey, golf, gymnastics, indoor track,
lacrosse, swimming-diving, tennis,
track&field, volleyball. Women's Non-aid:
archery, fencing

LIBERTY UNIVERSITY
1971 University Boulevard
Lynchburg, VA 24502
(804) 582-2292
www.liberty.edu
Contact: Mike Montoro
Unspecified athletic aid available
M: baseball, basketball, cheerleading,
cross country, football, golf, indoor track,
soccer, tennis, track&field
W: basketball, cheerleading, cross
country, indoor track, soccer, softball,
track&field, volleyball

LONGWOOD COLLEGE
201 High Street
Farmville, VA 23909
(804) 395-2097
www.lwc.edu
Contact: Greg Pouty
Men's Aid: (#/$): 18/$133,000
Women's Aid: (#/$): 18/$133,000
M: baseball, basketball, golf, soccer,
tennis, wrestling
W: basketball, field hockey, golf, lacrosse,
soccer, softball, tennis

LYNCHBURG COLLEGE
1501 Lakeside Drive
Lynchburg, VA 24501
(804) 544-8100
www.lynchburg.edu
Contact: Lee Ashby
Men's Non-aid: baseball, basketball,
cross country, equestrian, golf, indoor
track, lacrosse, soccer, tennis, track&field,
water polo
Women's Non-aid: basketball, cross
country, equestrian, field hockey, indoor
track, lacrosse, softball, tennis,
track&field, volleyball

MARY BALDWIN COLLEGE
Director of Athletics
Staunton, VA 24401
(800) 468-2262
www.mbc.edu
Contact: Mary Ann Kasselmann
Women's Non-aid: basketball, field

hockey, swimming-diving, tennis, volleyball

MARYMOUNT UNIVERSITY
2807 North Glebe Road
Arlington, VA 22207-4299
(703) 522-5600
www.marymount.edu
Contact: Webb Hatch
Men's Non-aid: basketball, golf, lacrosse, soccer, swimming, tennis
Women's Non-aid: basketball, soccer, swimming, tennis, volleyball

MARY WASHINGTON COLLEGE
1301 College Avenue
Fredericksburg, VA 22401-5358
(540) 654-1000
www.mwc.edu
Contact: Vince Benigni
Men's Non-aid: baseball, basketball, cross country, equestrian, indoor track, softball, soccer, swimming, tennis, track&field
Women's Non-aid: basketball, cross country, equestrian, field hockey, indoor track, lacrosse, soccer, softball, swimming, tennis, track&field, volleyball

NORFOLK STATE UNIVERSITY
2401 Corprew Avenue
Norfolk, VA 23504
(757) 623-8152
www.nsu.edu
Contact: Kenny Snelling
Unspecified athletic aid available
M: baseball, basketball, cross country, football, indoor track, track&field, wrestling
W: basketball, cross country, indoor track, softball, track&field

OLD DOMINION UNIVERSITY
Athletic Administration
Building 136
Norfolk, VA 23529-0201
(757) 683-3372
www.odusports.com
Contact: Carol Hudson, Jr.

Unspecified athletic aid available
M: baseball, basketball, golf, soccer, swimming, tennis, wrestling. Men's Non-aid: sailing
W: basketball, cross country, field hockey, lacrosse, swimming, tennis. Women's Non-aid: sailing

RADFORD UNIVERSITY
East Norwood Street
Radford, VA 24142
(540) 831-5228
www.runet.edu
Contact: Greig Denny
Unspecified athletic aid available
M: baseball, basketball, cross country, golf, gymnastics, lacrosse, soccer, tennis
W: basketball, cross country, field hockey, gymnastics, soccer, tennis, volleyball

RANDOLPH-MACON COLLEGE
P.O. Box 5005
Ashland, VA 23005-5505
(804) 798-8372
www.rmc.edu
Contact: Gregg Waters
Men's Non-aid:baseball, basketball, football, golf, lacrosse, soccer, swimming, tennis
Women's Non-aid: basketball, field hockey, lacrosse, soccer, softball, swimming, tennis, volleyball

ROANOKE COLLEGE
221 College Lane
Salem, VA 24153-3794
(540) 375-2500
www.roanoke.edu
Contact: Howard Wimmer
Men's Non-aid: basketball, cross country, golf, lacrosse, soccer, tennis, track&field
Women's Non-aid: basketball, cross country, field hockey, lacrosse, swimming-diving, tennis, volleyball

SAINT PAUL'S COLLEGE
406 Windsor Avenue
Lawrenceville, VA 23868
(540) 848-2001

www.utoledo.edu
Contact: Monique Jones
Unspecified athletic aid available
M: basketball, cross country, football, track&field. Men's Non-aid: badminton, indoor track
W: basketball, softball, track&field, volleyball

SWEET BRIAR COLLEGE
P.O. Box F
Sweet Briar, VA 24595
(804) 381-6336
www.sbc.edu
Contact: Bonnie Kestner
Restrictions and notes: No athletic aid but college policy guarantees 100% of need-based aid.
Women's Non-aid: basketball, diving, equestrian, field hockey, lacrosse, soccer, swimming-diving, tennis, volleyball

UNIVERSITY OF RICHMOND
Robins Center College
Richmond, VA 23173
(804) 289-8371
www.urich.edu
Contact: Barry Barnum
Aid (#/$): 52/$547,042 (M&W)
M: baseball, basketball, field hockey, football, golf, soccer, tennis. Men's Non-aid: cross country, indoor track, swimming-diving, track&field, water polo
W: basketball, field hockey, lacrosse, tennis. Women's Non-aid: cross country, indoor track, swimming-diving, synchronized swimming, track&field

UNIVERSITY OF VIRGINIA
P.O. Box 3785
Charlottesville, VA 22903
(804) 982-5230
www.virginia.edu
Contact: Keith Vanderbeek
Men's Aid (#/$): 163/$2,600,000
Women's Aid (#/$): 120/$2,200,000
M: baseball, basketball, cross country, football, golf, indoor track, lacrosse, soccer, swimming-diving, tennis, track&field, wrestling
W: basketball, cross country, field hockey, indoor track, lacrosse, rowing, soccer, softball, swimming-diving, tennis, track&field, volleyball

THE UNIVERSITY OF VIRGINIA'S COLLEGE AT WISE
1 College Avenue
Wise, VA 24293
(800) 468-3412
www.wise.virginia.edu
Contact: Russell B. Necessary
Unspecified athletic aid available
M: baseball, basketball, cross country, football, golf, tennis
W: basketball, cross country, softball, tennis

VIRGINIA COMMONWEALTH UNIVERSITY
821 W. Franklin Street
Richmond, VA 23284-2003
(804) 828-0100
www.vcu.edu
Contact: Mark Halstead
Unspecified athletic aid available
M: baseball, basketball, cross country, golf, indoor track, soccer, tennis, track&field
W: basketball, cross country, field hockey, indoor track, tennis, track&field, volleyball

VIRGINIA INTERMONT COLLEGE
1013 Moore Street
Bristol, VA 24201
(540) 669-6101
www.vic.edu
Contact: Cathy Ramsey
Men's Aid (#/$): 46/$200,000
Women's Aid (#/$): 30/$100,000
M: baseball, basketball, tennis
W: basketball, tennis

VIRGINIA MILITARY INSTITUTE
303 Letcher Avenue
Lexington, VA 24450

(540) 464-7253
www.vmi.edu
Contact: Mike Strickler
Unspecified athletic aid available
M: baseball, basketball, cross country,
football, golf, indoor track, lacrosse,
riflery, soccer, swimming, tennis,
track&field, wrestling

**VIRGINIA POLYTECHNIC
INSTITUTE & STATE
UNIVERSITY**
Jamerson Athletic Center
Blacksburg, VA 24061-0502
(540) 231-6726
www.hokiesport.com
Contact: Dave Smith
Unspecified athletic aid available
M: baseball, basketball, cross country,
football, indoor track, soccer, track&field,
wrestling
W: basketball, cross country, indoor
track, soccer, track&field, volleyball

VIRGINIA STATE UNIVERSITY
P.O. Box 9058
Petersburg, VA 23806-9058
(804) 524-5028
www.vsu.edu
Contact: Gregory Goings
Unspecified athletic aid available
M: baseball, basketball, football, golf,
indoor track, tennis
W: basketball, indoor track, softball,
tennis, track&field, volleyball

VIRGINIA UNION UNIVERSITY
1500 North Lombardy Street
Richmond, VA 23220
(804) 257-5882
www.vu.edu
Contact: Phenie D. Golatt
Men's Aid (#/$): 52/unspecified $
Women's Aid (#/$): 25/unspecified $
M: basketball, cross country, football,
golf, tennis, track&field
W: basketball, cross country, softball,
track&field, volleyball

VIRGINIA WESLEYAN COLLEGE
1584 Wesleyan Drive
Norfolk, VA 23502
(757) 455-3200
www.vwu.edu
Contact: Steve Stocks
Men's Non-aid: baseball, basketball, golf,
soccer, tennis
Women's Non-aid: basketball, soccer,
softball, tennis

Washington

BELLEVUE COMMUNITY COLLEGE
3000 Landersholm Circle SE
Bellevue, WA 98007-6484
Two-year college
(425) 641-2391
www.bcc.ctc.edu
Contact: Rick Turner
Unspecified athletic aid available
M: baseball, basketball, cross country,
soccer
W: cross country, soccer, softball, tennis,
volleyball

BIG BEND COMMUNITY COLLEGE
7662 Chanute Street
Moses Lake, WA 98837
Two-year college
(509) 762-5351 ext. 227
www.bbcc.ctc.edu
Contact: Mary Anne Allard
Unspecified athletic aid available
M: baseball, basketball
W: basketball, volleyball

**CENTRAL WASHINGTON
UNIVERSITY**
400 E. 8th Avenue
Ellensburg, WA 98926
(509) 963-1485
www.cwu.edu
Contact: Bob Guptill
Men's Non-aid: baseball, basketball,
cross country, football, golf, swimming-

diving, tennis, track&field, wrestling
Women's Non-aid: basketball, cross
country, swimming-diving, tennis,
track&field, volleyball

CLARK COLLEGE
1800 East McLoughlin Boulevard
Vancouver, WA 98663
Two-year college
(360) 792-2000
www.clark.edu
Contact: Roger D. Daniels
Unspecified athletic aid available
M: baseball, basketball, golf
W: basketball, tennis, volleyball

COLUMBIA BASIN COLLEGE
2600 North 20th Avenue
Pasco, WA 99301
Two-year college
(509) 547-0511 ext. 2239
www.cbc2.org
Contact: Dave Dunterman
Men's Aid (#/$): 36/$23,472
Women's Aid (#/$): 21/$12,639
M: baseball, basketball, golf, tennis
W: basketball, golf, tennis, volleyball

EASTERN WASHINGTON
UNIVERSITY
M566
5268 Fifth Street
Cheney, WA 99004-2499
(509) 359-6334
www.ewu.edu
Contact: David Cook
Unspecified athletic aid available
M: basketball, cross country, football,
golf, indoor track, tennis, track&field
W: basketball, cross country, golf, indoor
track, soccer, tennis, track&field,
volleyball

EDMONDS COMMUNITY COLLEGE
20000 68th Avenue West
Lynnwood, WA 98036-5999
Two-year college
(425) 640-1507
www.edcc.edu

Contact: Mark B. Honey
Unspecified athletic aid available
M: baseball, basketball, golf, soccer
W: basketball, golf, softball, volleyball

EVERETT COMMUNITY COLLEGE
801 Wetmore Avenue
Everett, WA 98201
Two-year college
(425) 388-9328
www.evcc.ctc.edu
Contact: Larry Walker
Unspecified athletic aid available
M: basketball, cross country, golf, indoor
track, soccer, tennis, track&field
W: basketball, cross country, golf, indoor
track, tennis, track&field, volleyball

EVERGREEN STATE COLLEGE
2700 Evergreen Parkway NW
CRC 210
Olympia, WA 98505
(360) 866-6000 ext. 6530
www.evergreen.edu
Contact: Rick Harden
Unspecified athletic aid available
M: basketball, soccer, swimming, tennis
W: basketball, soccer, swimming, tennis

GONZAGA UNIVERSITY
East 502 Boone Avenue
Spokane, WA 99258
(509) 328-4220
www.gonzaga.edu
Contact: Melissa Freigang
Men's Aid (#/$): 34/unspecified $
Women's Aid (#/$): 36/unspecified $
M: baseball, basketball, soccer, tennis.
Men's Non-aid: crew, cross country, golf,
indoor track, track&field
W: basketball, soccer, tennis, volleyball.
Women's Non-aid: crew, cross country,
golf, track&field

GRAYS HARBOR COLLEGE
1620 Edward P. Smith Drive
Aberdeen, WA 98520
Two-year college
(360) 538-4207

ghc.library.ctc.edu
Contact: Diane Smith
Unspecified athletic aid available
M: baseball, basketball, golf, soccer
W: basketball, golf, soccer, softball,
volleyball

GREEN RIVER COMMUNITY COLLEGE
12401 320th Street
Auburn, WA 98092-3699
Two-year college
(253) 833-9111
Contact: Gary Hayes
Unspecified athletic aid available
M: baseball, basketball, golf, soccer, tennis
W: basketball, golf, soccer, softball,
tennis, volleyball

LOWER COLUMBIA COLLEGE
P.O. Box 3010
Longview, WA 98632
Two-year college
(360) 577-2311
www.lfc.ctc.edu
Contact: Gary Earnest
Unspecified athletic aid available
M: baseball, basketball, cross country,
golf, soccer, wrestling
W: baseball, basketball, cross country,
golf, softball, volleyball

OLYMPIC COLLEGE
1600 Chester Avenue
Bremerton, WA 98337-1699
Two-year college
(360) 475-7458
www.oc.cfc.edu
Contact: Barry Janusch
Men's Aid (#/$): 51/unspecified $
Women's Aid (#/$): 51/unspecified $
M: baseball, basketball
W: basketball, softball, volleyball

PACIFIC LUTHERAN UNIVERSITY
Tacoma, WA 98447
(253) 535-7356
www.plu.edu
Contact: Nick Dawson

Men's Aid (#/$): 291/$394,000
Women's Aid (#/$): 125/$253,000
M: baseball, basketball, crew, cross
country, football, golf, soccer, swimming,
tennis, track&field, wrestling
W: basketball, crew, cross country,
soccer, softball, swimming, tennis,
track&field, volleyball

PIERCE COLLEGE
9401 Far West Drive SW
Tacoma, WA 98498
Two-year college
(253) 964-6614
www.pierce.ctc.edu
Contact: Duncan Stevenson
Unspecified athletic aid available
M: baseball, basketball, soccer
W: basketball, softball, volleyball

SAINT MARTIN'S COLLEGE
5300 Pacific Avenue SE
Lacey, WA 98503-1297
(360) 491-4700
www.stmartin.edu
Contact: Marianna Deeken
Unspecified athletic aid available
M: basketball, golf
W: basketball, golf, volleyball

SEATTLE PACIFIC UNIVERSITY
3307 Third Avenue West
Seattle, WA 98119
(206) 281-2772
www.spu.edu
Contact: Frank MacDonald
Men's Aid (#/$): 14.25/unspecified $
Women's Aid (#/$): 20.8/unspecified $
M: basketball, cross country, soccer,
track&field. Men's Non-aid: crew
W: basketball, cross country, gymnastics,
track&field, volleyball. Women's Non-aid:
crew

SEATTLE UNIVERSITY
900 Broadway
Seattle, WA 98122-4340
(206) 296-5915
www.seattleu.edu

Contact: Jason Lichtenberger
Men's Aid (#/$): $100,000
Women's Aid (#/$): $100,000
M: alpine skiing, basketball, cross country, soccer, tennis
W: alpine skiing, basketball, cross country, soccer, tennis

SHORELINE COMMUNITY COLLEGE
16101 Greenwood Avenue North
Seattle, WA 98133
Two-year college
(206) 546-4745
www.shore.ctc.edu
Contact: Ken Burren
Unspecified athletic aid available
M: baseball, basketball, soccer, tennis
W: basketball, soccer, softball, tennis, volleyball

SKAGIT VALLEY COLLEGE
2405 E. College Way
Mount Vernon, WA 98273-5899
Two-year college
(360) 416-7000
www.svc.ctc.edu
Contact: Tomi Clarke
Unspecified athletic aid available
M: baseball, basketball, cross country, soccer, tennis
W: basketball, cross country, softball, tennis, volleyball

SPOKANE COMMUNITY COLLEGE
1810 North Greene Street
Spokane, WA 99217
Two-year college
(509) 533-7231
www.scc.spokane.cc.wa.us
Contact: Michael R. Pidding
Unspecified athletic aid available
M: baseball, basketball, cross country, football, golf, soccer, tennis, track&field
W: basketball, cross country, golf, soccer, softball, tennis, track&field, volleyball

UNIVERSITY OF PUGET SOUND
1500 North Warner
Tacoma, WA 98416
(253) 756-3141
www.ups.edu
Contact: Robin Hamilton
Men's Non-aid: alpine skiing, baseball, basketball, cross country, football, golf, soccer, swimming, tennis, track&field
Women's Non-aid: alpine skiing, basketball, crew, cross country, golf, lacrosse, soccer, softball, swimming, tennis, track&field, volleyball

UNIVERSITY OF WASHINGTON
202 Graves Building
Seattle, WA 98195
(206) 543-2230
www.washington.edu
Contact: Jim Daves
Unspecified athletic aid available
M: baseball, basketball, cross country, crew, football, golf, indoor track, soccer, swimming-diving, tennis, track&field
W: basketball, cross country, golf, gymnastics, indoor track, softball, swimming-diving, tennis, track&field, volleyball

WALLA WALLA COMMUNITY COLLEGE
500 Tausick Way
Walla Walla, WA 99362
Two-year college
(509) 527-4306
www.wallawalla.cc
Contact: Jeff Reinland
Unspecified athletic aid available
M: baseball, basketball, football, golf, rodeo, soccer, tennis
W: basketball, cross country, golf, rodeo, soccer, softball, tennis, volleyball

WASHINGTON STATE UNIVERSITY
M-8 Bohler Gym
Pullman, WA 99164-1040
(509) 335-3581
www.wsu.edu
Contact: Wendy Peterson
Men's Aid (#/$): 142/$1,250,556
Women's Aid (#/$): 112/$723,943
M: baseball, basketball, cross country, football, golf, tennis, track&field

W: basketball, crew, cross country, golf, soccer, swimming, tennis, volleyball

**WESTERN WASHINGTON
UNIVERSITY**
516 High Street
Bellingham, WA 98225
(360) 650-3109
www.wwuvikings.com
Contact: Paul Madison
Unspecified athletic aid available
M: basketball, crew, cross country, football, golf, indoor track, soccer, track&field, volleyball
W: basketball, cheerleading, crew, cross country, golf, indoor track, soccer, softball, track&field, volleyball

WHITMAN COLLEGE
345 Boyer Ave
Walla Walla, WA 99362-2083
(509) 527-5414
www.whitman.edu
Contact: Scott Shields
Men's Non-aid: alpine skiing, baseball, basketball, cross country, cross country skiing, golf, soccer, swimming-diving, tennis, track&field
Women's Non-aid: alpine skiing, basketball, cross country, cross country skiing, soccer, swimming-diving, tennis, track&field, volleyball

WHITWORTH COLLEGE
300 West Hawthorne Road
Spokane, WA 99251
(509) 717-1000
www.whitworth.edu
Contact: Paul J. Merkel
Unspecified athletic aid available
M: baseball, basketball, cross country, football, soccer, swimming, tennis, track&field
W: bowling, cross country, soccer, swimming, tennis, track&field, volleyball

YAKIMA VALLEY COLLEGE
P.O. Box 22520
Yakima, WA 98907-2520

Two-year college
(509) 574-4600
www.yucc.cc.wa.us
Contact: Jerry Ward
Unspecified athletic aid available
M: baseball, basketball, football, tennis
W: basketball, softball, tennis, volleyball

West Virginia

ALDERSON-BROADDUS COLLEGE
500 College Hill
Philippi, WV 26416
(304) 457-1700
www.ab.edu
Contact: Allen Wethers
Men's Aid (#/$): 17/$316,880
Women's Aid (#/$): 17/$316,880
Restrictions and notes: All recipients must apply for all federal and state funds first.
M: baseball, basketball, cross country, soccer
W: basketball, cross country, softball, volleyball

BETHANY COLLEGE
Athletic Department
Bethany, WV 26032
(304) 829-7231
www.bethany.wv.edu
Contact: Brian Rose
Men's Non-aid: baseball, basketball, cross country, football, golf, soccer, swimming-diving, tennis, track&field
Women's Non-aid: basketball, cross country, field hockey, golf, softball, swimming-diving, tennis, track&field, volleyball

BLUEFIELD STATE COLLEGE
219 Rock Street
Bluefield, WV 24701
(304) 327-4022
www.bluefield.wv.net.edu

Contact: Tom Ilse
M: baseball, basketball, cross country, golf, tennis
W: basketball, cheerleading, cross country, softball, tennis

CONCORD COLLEGE
P.O. Box 1000
Campus Box 77
Athens, WV 24712
(304) 384-5358
www.concord.edu
Contact: Ron Macosko
Unspecified athletic aid available
M: baseball, basketball, cross country, football, golf, soccer, tennis, track&field
W: basketball, cross country, soccer, softball, tennis, track&field, volleyball

DAVIS & ELKINS COLLEGE
100 Campus Drive
Elkins, WV 26241
(800) 624-3157
www.dne.edu
Contact: Will Shaw
Unspecified athletic aid available
M: baseball, basketball, cross country, golf, soccer, tennis
W: basketball, cross country, field hockey, softball, tennis

FAIRMONT STATE COLLEGE
1201 Locust Avenue
Fairmont, WV 26554
(800) 641-5678
www.fscwv.edu
Contact: Dave Cooper
Unspecified athletic aid available
M: basketball, football, swimming-diving
W: basketball, swimming-diving

GLENVILLE STATE COLLEGE
200 High Street
Glenville, WV 26351
(304) 462-4102
www.glenville.wvndt.edu
Contact: Steve Harlod
Men's Aid (#/$): 5/$12,430
Women's Aid (#/$): 3/$2,970

M: basketball, cross country, football, golf, track&field
W: basketball, cross country, track&field, volleyball

MARSHALL UNIVERSITY
P.O. Box 1360
Huntington, WV 25715
(304) 696-5275
www.herdzone.com
Contact: Ricky Hazel
Unspecified athletic aid available
M: baseball, basketball, cross country, football, golf, indoor track, soccer, track&field
W: basketball, cross country, indoor track, tennis, track&field, volleyball

OHIO VALLEY COLLEGE
College Parkway
Parkersburg, WV 26101
Two-year college
(800) 678-6780
www.ovc.edu
Contact: Lori McKain
Unspecified athletic aid available
M: baseball, basketball
W: basketball, cheerleading, cross country, softball, volleyball

SALEM-TEIKYO UNIVERSITY
223 West Main Street
Salem, WV 26426
(304) 782-5286
www.salem-teikyo.wvnet.edu
Contact: Don Bordner
Unspecified athletic aid available
M: baseball, basketball, golf, soccer, swimming, tennis, water polo
W: basketball, cheerleading, softball, swimming, tennis, volleyball

SHEPHERD COLLEGE
Butcher Center
Shepherdstown, WV 25443-1569
(304) 876-2511
www.shepherd.wvnet.edu
Contact: Chip Ransom
Unspecified athletic aid available

M: basketball, football. Men's Non-aid: baseball, cross country, golf, soccer, tennis W: basketball, volleyball. Women's Non-aid: cross country, soccer, softball, tennis

UNIVERSITY OF CHARLESTON
2300 MacCorkle Avenue SE
Charleston, WV 25304
(304) 357-4750
Contact: Jeff Jost
Unspecified athletic aid available
M: baseball, basketball, crew, golf, soccer, swimming, tennis
W: basketball, crew, soccer, softball, swimming, tennis, volleyball

WEST LIBERTY STATE COLLEGE
West Liberty, WV 26074
(304) 336-8212
www.wlsc.wvnet.edu
Contact: James Watson
Unspecified athletic aid available
M: baseball, basketball, football, tennis. Men's Non-aid: cross country, golf, track&field, wrestling
W: baseball, basketball, cross country, soccer, softball, track&field, volleyball

WEST VIRGINIA UNIVERSITY INSTITUTE OF TECHNOLOGY
Athletic Department
405 Fayette Pike
Montgomery, WV 25136-2436
(304) 442-3121
www.wvit.wvnet.edu
Contact: CJ Lanham
Unspecified athletic aid available
M: basketball, football, tennis, golf
W: softball, tennis, volleyball

WEST VIRGINIA STATE COLLEGE
P.O. Box 1000
Institute, WV 25112
(304) 766-4122
www.wvsc.edu

Contact: Sean McAndrews
Unspecified athletic aid available
M: basketball, football. Men's Non-aid: baseball, tennis, track&field
W: basketball. Women's Non-aid: tennis, track&field

WEST VIRGINIA UNIVERSITY
P.O. Box 877
Morgantown, WV 26506-0877
(304) 293-2821
www.msnsportsnet.com
Contact: Ed Pastilong
Unspecified athletic aid available
M: baseball, basketball, cross country, football, indoor track, riflery, soccer, swimming-diving, tennis, track&field, wrestling
W: basketball, cross country, gymnastics, indoor track, riflery, soccer, swimming-diving, tennis, track&field, volleyball

WEST VIRGINIA WESLEYAN COLLEGE
Buckhannon, WV 26201-2998
(304) 473-8102
www.wvwc.edu
Contact: John Scott
Unspecified athletic aid available
M: basketball, soccer. Men's Non-aid: baseball, cross country, football, golf, swimming, tennis, track&field
W: basketball, tennis. Women's Non-aid: cross country, softball, swimming, track&field, volleyball

WHEELING JESUIT UNIVERSITY
316 Washington Avenue
Wheeling, WV 26003
(304) 243-2304
www.wju.edu
Contact: Karen McKay
Men's Aid (#/$): 36/$147,865
Women's Aid (#/$): 50/$109,842
M: basketball, cross country, golf, soccer
W: basketball, cross country, golf, soccer, volleyball

Wisconsin

BELOIT COLLEGE
700 College Street
Beloit, WI 53511
(608) 363-2229
www.beloit.edu
Contact: Ed DeGeorge
Men's Non-aid: baseball, basketball,
cross country, football, golf, indoor track,
soccer, swimming-diving, tennis,
track&field
Women's Non-aid: basketball, cross
country, indoor track, soccer, softball,
swimming-diving, tennis, track&field,
volleyball

CARDINAL STRITCH UNIVERSITY
6801 North Yates Road
Milwaukee, WI 53217-3985
(414) 352-5400
www.stritch.edu
Contact: Denny Fox
Unspecified athletic aid available
M: baseball, basketball, cheerleading,
cross country, soccer, volleyball
W: basketball, cheerleading, cross
country, soccer, softball, volleyball

CARROLL COLLEGE
100 North East Avenue
Waukesha, WI 53186
(800) 227-7655
www.cc.edu
Contact: Jane A. Lemke
Men's Non-aid: baseball, basketball,
cross country, football, golf, indoor track,
soccer, swimming, tennis, track&field,
wrestling
Women's Non-aid: basketball, cross
country, golf, indoor track, soccer, swimming, tennis, track&field, volleyball

CARTHAGE COLLEGE
2001 Alford Park Drive
Kenosha, WI 53140-1994
(262) 551-5740
www.carthage.edu

Contact: Steve Marovich
Men's Non-aid: baseball, basketball,
cross country, football, golf, indoor track,
swimming, tennis, track&field
Women's Non-aid: basketball, cross
country, indoor track, softball, swimming, tennis, track&field, volleyball

**CONCORDIA UNIVERSITY
WISCONSIN**
12800 North Lakeshore Drive
Mequon, WI 53092
(414) 243-5700
www.cuw.edu
Contact: Ken Witte
Unspecified athletic aid available
M: baseball, basketball, football. Men's
Non-aid: golf, soccer, tennis,
track&field
W: basketball, softball. Women's Non-aid:
golf, cross country, soccer, tennis,
track&field, volleyball

EDGEWOOD COLLEGE
Edgewood College Drive
Madison, WI 53711
(608) 663-4861
www.edgewood.edu
Contact: Dave Smith
Men's Non-aid: baseball, basketball, golf,
soccer, tennis
Women's Non-aid: basketball, golf, soft-
ball, tennis, volleyball

LAWRENCE UNIVERSITY
P.O. Box 599
Appleton, WI 54912
(920) 832-7000
www.lawrence.edu
Contact: Rick Peterson
Men's Non-aid: baseball, basketball,
cross country, fencing, football, golf,
ice hockey, indoor track, soccer, swimming-diving, tennis, track&field,
wrestling
Women's Non-aid: basketball, cross
country, fencing, indoor track, soccer,
softball, swimming-diving, tennis,
track&field, volleyball

MADISON AREA TECHNICAL COLLEGE
3550 Anderson Street
Madison, WI 53704
Two-year college
(608) 246-6098
www.madison.tec.wi.us
Contact: Peter Olson
Unspecified athletic aid available
M: baseball. Men's Non-aid: basketball, bowling, cross country, golf, soccer, tennis, track&field, wrestling
W: basketball, softball, volleyball. Women's Non-aid: bowling, cross country, golf, tennis, track&field, volleyball

MARIAN COLLEGE
45 South National Avenue
Fond du Lac, WI 54935
(920) 923-7625
www.mariancoll.edu
Contact: Brian Gillogly
Men's Non-aid: baseball, basketball, cross country, golf, soccer, tennis
Women's Non-aid: basketball, cross country, soccer, softball, tennis, volleyball

MARQUETTE UNIVERSITY
P.O. Box 1881
Milwaukee, WI 53201-1881
(414) 288-7302
www.mu.edu
Contact: Kathleen Hohl
Men's Aid (#/$): 33/$445,000
Women's Aid (#/$): 23/$306,000
M: basketball, cross country, golf, indoor track, soccer, tennis, track&field, wrestling
W: basketball, cross country, indoor track, soccer, tennis, track&field, volleyball

MILWAUKEE AREA TECHNICAL COLLEGE
700 West State Street
Milwaukee, WI 53233
Two-year college
(414) 297-6600
www.milwaukee.tec.wi.us
Contact: Mike Basile

Unspecified athletic aid available
M: baseball, basketball, cross country, indoor track, soccer, track&field
W: basketball, cross country, indoor track, track&field

NORTHLAND COLLEGE
1411 Ellis Avenue
Ashland, WI 54806-3999
(715) 682-1243
www.northland.edu
Contact: Steve Walmer
Unspecified athletic aid available
M: basketball, soccer
W: basketball, volleyball

RIPON COLLEGE
300 Seward Street
P.O. Box 248
Ripon, WI 54971
(920) 748-8101
www.ripon.edu
Contact: Michelle Krajnik
Men's Non-aid: baseball, basketball, cross country, football, golf, indoor track, soccer, swimming-diving, tennis, track&field
Women's Non-aid: basketball, cross country, indoor track, soccer, softball, swimming-diving, tennis, track&field, volleyball

SAINT NORBERT COLLEGE
100 Grant Street
De Pere, WI 54115
(920) 337-3181
www.snc.edu
Contact: Larry Van Alstine
Men's Non-aid: baseball, basketball, cross country, football, golf, indoor track, soccer, tennis, track&field
Women's Non-aid: basketball, cross country, golf, indoor track, soccer, softball, tennis, track&field, volleyball

UNIVERSITY OF WISCONSIN (EAU CLAIRE)
P.O. Box 4004
Eau Claire, WI 54702-4004

(715) 836-4184
www.uwec.edu
Contact: Tim Petermann
Men's Non-aid: baseball, basketball, cross country, football, golf, ice hockey, indoor track, swimming-diving, tennis, track&field, wrestling
Women's Non-aid: basketball, cross country, gymnastics, indoor track, soccer, softball, swimming-diving, tennis, track&field, volleyball

UNIVERSITY OF WISCONSIN (GREEN BAY)

2420 Nicolet Drive
Green Bay, WI 54311-7001
(920) 465-2145
www.uwgb.edu
Contact: Terry Powers
Unspecified athletic aid available
M: basketball, soccer. Men's Non-aid: cross country, cross country skiing, golf, sailing, swimming-diving, tennis
W: basketball. Women's Non-aid: cross country, cross country skiing, golf, sailing, softball, swimming-diving, tennis, volleyball

UNIVERSITY OF WISCONSIN (LA CROSSE)

1725 State Street
La Crosse, WI 54601
(608) 785-8604
www.uwlax.edu
Contact: Al C. Stadthaus
Men's Non-aid: baseball, basketball, bowling, cross country, football, golf, gymnastics, ice hockey, indoor track, rugby, swimming-diving, tennis, track&field, wrestling
Women's Non-aid: basketball, bowling, cross country, gymnastics, indoor track, softball, swimming-diving, tennis, track&field, volleyball

UNIVERSITY OF WISCONSIN (MADISON)

1440 Monroe Street
Madison, WI 53706

(608) 263-5502
www.wisc.edu
Contact: Pat Richter
Unspecified athletic aid available
M: basketball, cross country, football, golf, ice hockey, indoor track, soccer, swimming-diving, tennis, track&field, wrestling. Men's Non-aid: crew
W: basketball, crew, cross country, golf, ice hockey, indoor track, soccer, softball, swimming-diving, tennis, track&field, volleyball

UNIVERSITY OF WISCONSIN (MILWAUKEE)

North Building P.O. Box 413
Milwaukee, WI 53201
(414) 229-4593
www.uwmpanthers.com
Contact: Traci Huntemann-Peteriatt
Men's Aid (#/$): 94/$374,255
Women's Aid (#/$): 94/$315,552
M: baseball, basketball, cross country, indoor track, soccer, swimming-diving, track&field
W: basketball, cross country, indoor track, soccer, swimming-diving, tennis, track&field, volleyball

UNIVERSITY OF WISCONSIN (OSHKOSH)

108 Kolf Sports Center
Oshkosh, WI 54901
(920) 424-0365
www.uwosh.edu
Contact: Kennan Timm
Men's Non-aid: baseball, basketball, cross country, football, golf, gymnastics, indoor track, soccer, swimming-diving, tennis, track&field, wrestling
Women's Non-aid: basketball, cross country, gymnastics, indoor track, softball, swimming-diving, tennis, track&field, volleyball

UNIVERSITY OF WISCONSIN (PLATTEVILLE)

One University Plaza
Platteville, WI 53818-3099

(608) 342-1574
www.uwplatt.edu
Contact: Paul Erickson
Men's Non-aid: baseball, basketball,
cross country, football, golf, indoor track,
soccer, tennis, track&field, wrestling
Women's Non-aid: basketball, cross
country, indoor track, softball, tennis,
track&field, volleyball

UNIVERSITY OF WISCONSIN (RIVER FALLS)
410 South Third Street
River Falls, WI 54022-5001
(715) 425-3846
www.uwrf.edu
Contact: Jim Thies
Men's Non-aid: baseball, basketball,
cross country, football, golf, ice hockey,
indoor track, swimming-diving, tennis,
track&field, wrestling
Women's Non-aid: basketball, cross
country, gymnastics, indoor track, softball, swimming-diving, tennis,
track&field, volleyball

UNIVERSITY OF WISCONSIN (STEVENS POINT)
106 Student Service Building
Stevens Point, WI 54481
(715) 346-0123
www.uwsp.edu
Contact: Phillip C. George
Men's Non-aid: baseball, basketball,
cross country, diving, football, golf, ice
hockey, indoor track, swimming, tennis,
track&field, wrestling
Women's Non-aid: basketball, cross
country, diving, indoor track, soccer, softball, swimming, tennis, track&field,
volleyball

UNIVERSITY OF WISCONSIN (STOUT)
1401 Third Street
Johnson Field House
Menomonie, WI 54751
(715) 232-1363

www.uwstout.edu
Contact: Steve Terry
Men's Non-aid: baseball, basketball,
cross country, football, indoor track,
track&field
Women's Non-aid: basketball, cross
country, gymnastics, indoor track, soccer,
tennis, track&field, volleyball

UNIVERSITY OF WISCONSIN (SUPERIOR)
P.O. Box 2000
Belknap & Catlin
Superior, WI 54880-4500
(715) 394-8371
www.uwsuper.edu
Contact: Tracy Majeske
Men's Non-aid: baseball, basketball,
cross country, football, golf, ice hockey,
indoor track, track&field, wrestling
Women's Non-aid: baseball, basketball,
cross country, gymnastics, ice hockey,
indoor track, track&field, volleyball

VITERBO COLLEGE
815 South 9th Street
La Crosse, WI 54601
(608) 796-3000
Contact: Terry Norman
Men's Non-aid: baseball, basketball,
soccer
Women's Non-aid: basketball, softball,
volleyball

Wyoming

CENTRAL WYOMING COLLEGE
2660 Peck Avenue
Riverton, WY 82501
Two-year college
(307) 855-2000
www.cwc.whecn.edu
Contact: Carolyne Perry
Unspecified athletic aid available
M: basketball, rodeo
W: basketball, rodeo, volleyball

EASTERN WYOMING COLLEGE
3200 West C Street
Torrington, WY 82240
Two-year college
(307) 532-8200
www.ewc.whecn.edu
Contact: Holly Sims
Men's Aid (#/$): 12/unspecified $
Women's Aid (#/$): 12/unspecified $
M: basketball, cheerleading, golf, rodeo
W: cheerleading, rodeo, volleyball

LARAMIE COUNTY COMMUNITY COLLEGE
1400 East College Drive
Cheyenne, WY 82007
Two-year college
(307) 778-5222
www.lc.whecn.edu
Contact: Woody Halverson
Men's Non-aid: rodeo
Women's Non-aid: rodeo

NORTHWEST COLLEGE
Athletics
231 West 6th Street
Powell, WY 82435-1895
Two-year college
(307) 754-6000
www.nwc.whecn.edu
Contact: Ken Rochlitz
Unspecified athletic aid available
M: basketball, wrestling
W: basketball, volleyball

SHERIDAN COLLEGE
Athletic Department
Box 1500
Sheridan, WY 82801

Two-year college
(307) 674-6446 ext. 6251
www.sc.whecn.edu
Contact: Mark Englert
Men's Aid (#/$): 12/$43,000
Women's Aid (#/$): 14/$42,000
M: basketball
W: basketball, volleyball

UNIVERSITY OF WYOMING
P.O. Box 3414
Laramie, WY 8207-3414
(307) 766-2256
www.wyomingathletics.edu
Contact: Kevin M. McKinney
Unspecified athletic aid available
M: basketball, cross country, football, golf, indoor track, swimming-diving, track&field, wrestling
W: basketball, cross country, golf, indoor track, tennis, swimming-diving, track&field, soccer, volleyball

WESTERN WYOMING COMMUNITY COLLEGE
2500 College Drive
P.O. Box 428
Rock Springs, WY 82902-0428
Two-year college
(307) 382-1651
www.wwcc.cc.wy.us
Contact: Dick Flores
Unspecified athletic aid available
M: basketball, tennis. Men's Non-aid: alpine skiing, bowling
W: basketball, tennis, volleyball. Women's Non-aid: alpine skiing, bowling

SPORT-BY-SPORT APPENDIX

Understanding the Appendix

The Appendix is an alphabetical list of sports programs and the colleges that offer each program. The state code for each college is also shown. (M) indicates that the program is only offered to men. (W) means it is offered to women, and (MW) indicates the program is offered to both men and women.

Keep in mind that this list mixes both scholarship and non-scholarship programs together. Thus, it is important to use the directory listings to determine which kind of scholarship is offered.

Sports Programs Listed

The following programs are included in the Appendix:
Alpine Skiing, 213; Archery, 213; Badminton, 213; Baseball, 213; Basketball, 223; Bowling, 236; Cheerleading, 237; Crew, 237; Cricket, 238; Cross Country, 238; Cross Country Skiing, 247; Cycling, 247; Dance, 247; Diving, 247; Equestrian, 247; Fencing, 248; Field Hockey, 248; Football, 250; Golf, 255; Gymnastics, 263; Handball, 264; Heavyweight Crew, 264; Horse Judging, 264; Ice Hockey, 265; Indoor Track, 266; Judo, 270; Lacrosse, 270; Lightweight Crew, 271; Livestock Judging, 271; Marathon, 271; Martial Arts, 271; Nordic Skiing, 272; Ping Pong, 272; Pistol, 272; Polo, 272; Power Lifting, 272; Racquetball, 272; Riflery, 272; Rodeo, 272; Rowing, 273; Rugby, 273; Sailing, 273; Skiing, 273; Snowboarding, 273; Soccer, 273; Softball, 282; Spirit Squads, 291; Sprint Football, 291; Squash, 291; Swimming, 291; Swimming-Diving, 292; Synchronized Swimming, 295; Table Tennis, 295; Tennis, 295; Timber Sports, 304; Track&Field, 294; Volleyball, 312; Water Polo, 322; Water Skiing, 323; Weightlifting, 323; and Wrestling, 323.

State Abbreviations

Alabama	AL	Montana	MT
Alaska	AK	Nebraska	NE
Arizona	AZ	Nevada	NV
Arkansas	AR	New Hampshire	NH
California	CA	New Jersey	NJ
Colorado	CO	New Mexico	NM
Connecticut	CT	New York	NY
Delaware	DE	North Carolina	NC
District of Columbia	DC	North Dakota	ND
Florida	FL	Ohio	OH
Georgia	GA	Oklahoma	OK
Hawaii	HI	Oregon	OR
Idaho	ID	Pennsylvania	PA
Illinois	IL	Puerto Rico	PR
Indiana	IN	Rhode Island	RI
Iowa	IA	South Carolina	SC
Kansas	KS	South Dakota	SD
Kentucky	KY	Tennessee	TN
Louisiana	LA	Texas	TX
Maine	ME	Utah	UT
Maryland	MD	Vermont	VT
Massachusetts	MA	Virginia	VA
Michigan	MI	Washington	WA
Minnesota	MN	West Virginia	WV
Mississippi	MS	Wisconsin	WI
Missouri	MO	Wyoming	WY

Alpine Skiing

Adirondack College, NY (MW)
Albertson College of Idaho, ID (MW)
Alfred University, NY (MW)
Bates College, ME (MW)
Boston College, MA (MW)
Bowdoin College, ME (MW)
Carleton College, MN (MW)
Castleton State College, VT (MW)
Clarkson University, NY (MW)
Colby-Sawyer College, NH (MW)
Dartmouth College, NH (MW)
Eastern Oregon State College, OR (MW)
Fairfield University, CT (MW)
Fashion Institute of Technology, NY (MW)
Fort Lewis College, CO (W)
Franklin Pierce College, NH (MW)
Harvard University, MA (MW)
Lees-McRae College, NC (MW)
Massachusetts College of Liberal Arts, MA (MW)
Massachusetts Institute of Technology, MA (MW)
Middlebury College, VT (MW)
Montana State University, MT (W)
Northern Michigan University, MI (W)
Plymouth State College, NH (MW)
Saint Anselm College, NH (MW)
Saint Lawrence University, NY (MW)
Saint Michael's College, VT (MW)
Saint Olaf College, MN (MW)
Seattle University, WA (MW)
Sierra College, CA (MW)
Sierra Nevada College, NV (MW)
Skidmore College, NY (MW)
Smith College, MA (W)
Snow College, UT (MW)
University of Alaska, AK (MW)
University of Alaska Southeast, AK (MW)
University of Colorado, CO (MW)
University of Massachusetts (Amherst), MA (MW)
University of New Hampshire, NH (MW)
University of New Mexico, NM (MW)
University of Puget Sound, WA (MW)
University of Utah, UT (MW)
University of Vermont, VT (MW)
Western State College, CO (MW)
Western Wyoming Community College, WY (MW)
Whitman College, WA (MW)

Archery

Atlantic Community College, NJ (MW)
Columbia University, NY (W)
Diné College, AZ (MW)
Glendale Community College, AZ (MW)
James Madison University, VA (MW)
Pima Community College (West Campus), AZ (MW)
Snow College, UT (MW)
Texas A&M University, TX (W)

Badminton

Albright College, PA (W)
Bryn Mawr College, PA (W)
City College of San Francisco, CA (W)
Concordia University, MN (M)
Fresno City College, CA (W)
Lambuth University, TN (M)
Roosevelt University, IL (MW)
Saint Paul's College, VA (M)
San Diego City College, CA (W)
San Diego Mesa College, CA (M)
Snow College, UT (MW)
Swarthmore College, PA (W)

Baseball

Adelphi University, NY (M)
Adrian College, MI (M)
Alabama A&M University, AL (M)
Alabama State University, AL (M)
Albany State University, GA (M)
Albertson College, ID (M)
Albion College, MI (M)
Albright College, PA (M)
Alcorn State University, MS (M)
Alderson-Broaddus College, WV (M)
Alice Lloyd College, KY (M)
Allegheny College, PA (M)
Allen County College, KS (M)
Allentown College, PA (M)
Allen University, SC (M)
Alma College, MI (M)
Alvernia College, PA (M)
American International College, MA (M)
Amherst College, MA (M)
Anderson College, SC (M)
Anderson University, IN (M)
Andrew College, GA (M)
Angelina College, TX (M)
Anoka-Ramsey College, MN (M)
Appalachian State University, NC (M)
Apprentice School, VA (M)
Aquinas College, MI (M)
Aquinas Junior College, TN (M)
Arizona State University, AZ (M)
Arkansas College, AR (M)
Arkansas State University, AR (M)
Arkansas Tech University, AR (M)
Armstrong Atlantic State University, GA (M)
Asbury College, KY (M)
Ashland College, OH (M)
Assumption College, MA (M)
Atlantic Community College, NJ (M)
Auburn University, AL (M)
Auburn University (Montgomery), AL (M)
Augsburg College, MN (M)
Augusta State University, GA (M)
Augustana College, IL (M)
Augustana College, SD (M)
Aurora University, IL (M)
Austin College, TX (M)
Austin Community College, MN (M)
Austin Peay State University, TN (M)
Avila College, MO (M)
Azusa Pacific University, CA (M)
Babson College, MA (M)
Bacone Junior College, OK (M)
Baker University, KS (M)
Ball State University, IN (M)
Baltimore City Community College, MD (M)
Barry University, FL (M)
Barstow College, CA (M)
Barton College, NC (M)
Barton County College, KS (M)
Bates College, ME (M)
Baylor University, TX (M)
Becker College, MA (M)
Belhaven College, MS (M)
Bellarmine College, KY (M)
Belleville Area College, IL (M)

Bellevue College, NE (M)
Bellevue Community College, WA (M)
Belmont Abbey College, NC (M)
Belmont College, TN (M)
Beloit College, WI (M)
Benedict College, SC (M)
Benedictine College, KS (M)
Benedictine University, IL (M)
Bentley College, MA (M)
Bergen Community College, NJ (M)
Berry College, GA (M)
Bethany College, KS (M)
Bethany College, WV (M)
Bethany Lutheran College, MN (M)
Bethel College, IN (M)
Bethel College, MN (M)
Bethune-Cookman College, FL (M)
Big Bend Community College, WA (M)
Biola University, CA (M)
Binghamton University (SUNY), NY (M)
Birmingham-Southern College, AL (M)
Bismarck State College, ND (M)
Blackburn College, IL (M)
Black Hawk College, IL (M)
Bloomfield College, NJ (M)
Bloomsburg University, PA (M)
Bluefield College, VA (M)
Bluefield State College, WV (M)
Blue Mountain College, OR (M)
Bluffton College, OH (M)
Borough of Manhattan Community College (CUNY), NY (M)
Boston College, MA (M)
Bowdoin College, ME (M)
Bowie State University, MD (M)
Bowling Green State University, OH (M)
Bradley University, IL (M)
Brainerd Community College, MN (M)
Brandeis University, MA (M)
Brescia University, KY (M)
Brevard Community College, FL (M)
Brewton Parker College, GA (M)
Briar Cliff College, IA (M)
Bridgewater College, VA (M)
Bridgewater State College, MA (M)
Brigham Young University, UT (M)
Bronx Community College, NY (M)

Broome Community College, NY (M)
Broward Community College, FL (M)
Brown University, RI (M)
Bryant College, RI (M)
Bucknell University, PA (M)
Bucks County Community College, PA (M)
Buena Vista University, IA (M)
Bunker Hill Community College, MA (M)
Butler County Community College, KS (M)
Butler County Community College, PA (M)
Butler University, IN (M)
Butte College, CA (M)
Cabrillo College, CA (M)
California Baptist University, CA (M)
California Institute of Technology, CA (M)
California Lutheran University, CA (M)
California Polytechnic State University, CA (M)
California State Polytechnic University, CA (M)
California State University (Chico), CA (M)
California State University (Dominguez Hills), CA (M)
California State University (Fresno), CA (M)
California State University (Fullerton), CA (M)
California State University (Hayward), CA (M)
California State University (Long Beach), CA (M)
California State University (Los Angeles), CA (M)
California State University (Northridge), CA (M)
California State University (Sacramento), CA (M)
California State University (San Bernardino), CA (M)
California State University (Stanislaus), CA (M)
California University, PA (M)
Calvin College, MI (M)
Cameron University, OK (M)
Campbellsville University, KY (M)
Campbell University, NC (M)
Canisius College, NY (M)
Capital University, OH (M)
Cardinal Stritch College, WI (M)

Carl Albert Junior College, OK (M)
Carleton College, MN (M)
Carroll College, WI (M)
Carson-Newman College, TN (M)
Carthage College, WI (M)
Case Western Reserve University, OH (M)
Castleton State College, VT (M)
Catawba College, NC (M)
Catholic University of America, DC (M)
Catonsville Community College, MD (M)
Cecil Community College, MD (M)
Cedarville College, OH (M)
Centenary College, LA (M)
Central Arizona College, AZ (M)
Central College, IA (M)
Central Christian College, KS (M)
Central Connecticut State University, CT (M)
Central Florida Community College, FL (M)
Central Lakes College, MN (M)
Central Methodist College, MO (M)
Central Michigan University, MI (M)
Central Missouri State University, MO (M)
Central Washington University, WA (M)
Central Wesleyan College, SC (M)
Cerritos College, CA (M)
Chaffey College, CA (M)
Chapman University, CA (M)
Charleston Southern University, SC (M)
Chattahoochee Valley Community College, AL (M)
Chicago State University, IL (M)
Chipola Junior College, FL (M)
Chowan College, NC (M)
Christian Brothers College, TN (M)
Christopher Newport College, VA (M)
Citadel, SC (M)
City College of San Francisco, CA (M)
Clackamas Community College, OR (M)
Clarion University, PA (M)
Clark College, WA (M)
Clarkson University, NY (M)
Clark University, MA (M)

Clemson University, SC (M)
Cleveland State Community College, TN (M)
Cleveland State University, OH (M)
Clinton Community College, NY (M)
Cloud County Community College, KS (M)
Coahoma Junior College, MS (M)
Coastal Carolina College, SC (M)
Cochise College, AZ (M)
Coe College, IA (M)
Coffeyville Community College, KS (M)
Coker College, SC (M)
Colby Community College, KS (M)
Colby-Sawyer College, NH (M)
College of Allegheny County, PA (M)
College of Charleston, SC (M)
College of Mount St. Joseph, OH (M)
The College of New Jersey, NJ (M)
College of Southern Idaho, ID (M)
College of St. Francis, IL (M)
College of St. Rose, NY (M)
College of St. Scholastica, MN (M)
College of William and Mary, VA (M)
College of the Desert, CA (M)
College of the Holy Cross, MA (M)
College of the Ozarks, MO (M)
College of the Redwoods, CA (M)
College of the Sequoias, CA (M)
College of Wooster, OH (M)
Colorado Northwestern Community College, CO (M)
Colorado School of Mines, CO (M)
Columbia Basin Community College, WA (M)
Columbia-Greene Community College, NY (M)
Columbia Union College, MD (M)
Columbia University, NY (M)
Columbus College, GA (M)
Columbus State Community College, OH (M)
Community College of Rhode Island, RI (M)
Compton Community College, CA (M)

Concord College, WV (M)
Concordia College, MI (M)
Concordia College (Moorhead), MN (M)
Concordia College (St. Paul), MN (M)
Concordia College, NY (M)
Concordia Lutheran College, TX (M)
Concordia University, NE (M)
Concordia University, IL (M)
Concordia University Wisconsin, WI (M)
Connors State College, OK (M)
Contra Costa College, CA (M)
Copiah-Lincoln Community College, MS (M)
Coppin State College, MD (M)
Cornell College, IA (M)
Cornell University, NY (M)
Cosumnes River College, CA (M)
Cowley County Community College, KS (M)
Creighton University, NE (M)
Crowder College, MO (M)
Cuesta College, CA (M)
Culver-Stockton College, MO (M)
Cumberland College, KY (M)
Curry College, MA (M)
Cuyahoga Community College, OH (M)
Dakota State University, SD (M)
Dakota Wesleyan University, SD (M)
Dallas Baptist University, TX (M)
Dana College, NE (M)
Danville Area Community College, IL (M)
Dartmouth College, NH (M)
Davidson College, NC (M)
Davis&Elkins College, WV (M)
Dawson Community College, MT (M)
Daytona Beach Community College, FL (M)
Dean Junior College, MA (M)
Defiance College, OH (M)
Delaware County Community College, PA (M)
Delaware State University, DE (M)
Delaware Valley College, PA (M)
Delgado Community College, LA (M)
Delta State University, MS (M)
Denison University, OH (M)
De Pauw University, IN (M)

Des Moines Area Community College, IA (M)
Diablo Valley Community College, CA (M)
Dickinson College, PA (M)
Dickinson State University, ND (M)
Dixie College, UT (M)
Doane College, NE (M)
Dodge City Community College, KS (M)
Dominican College of Blauvelt, NY (M)
Dominican University, IL (M)
Dowling College, NY (M)
Drew University, NJ (M)
Drexel University, PA (M)
Duke University, NC (M)
Dundalk Community College, MD (M)
Duquesne University, PA (M)
Dutchess Junior College, NY (M)
Dyersburg State Community College, TN (M)
Earlham College, IN (M)
East Carolina University, NC (M)
East Central College, MO (M)
East Central University, OK (M)
Eastern College, PA (M)
Eastern Connecticut State University, CT (M)
Eastern Illinois University, IL (M)
Eastern Kentucky University, KY (M)
Eastern Mennonite College, VA (M)
Eastern Michigan University, MI (M)
Eastern Nazarene College, MA (M)
Eastern New Mexico University, NM (M)
Eastern Oklahoma State College, OR (M)
Eastern Oregon State College, OR (M)
Eastfield College, TX (M)
East Stroudsburg University, PA (M)
East Tennessee State University, TN (M)
East Texas Baptist University, TX (M)
Eckerd College, FL (M)
Edgewood College, WI (M)
Edinboro University of Pennsylvania, PA (M)
Edmonds Community College, WA (M)

Edward Waters College, FL (M)
El Camino College, CA (M)
Elgin Community College, IL (M)
Elizabeth City State University, NC (M)
Elizabethtown College, PA (M)
Elmhurst College, IL (M)
Elon College, NC (M)
Emerson College, MA (M)
Emory and Henry College, VA (M)
Emory University, GA (M)
Emporia State University, KS (M)
Enterprise State Junior College, AL (M)
Erskine College, SC (M)
Essex Community College, MD (M)
Evangel College, MO (M)
Fairfield University, CT (M)
Fairleigh Dickinson University (Madison), NJ (M)
Farleigh Dickinson University (Teaneck), NJ (M)
Faulkner University, AL (M)
Fergus Falls Community College, MN (M)
Ferrum College, VA (M)
Finger Lakes Community College, NY (M)
Fitchburg State College, MA (M)
Flagler College, FL (M)
Florida A&M University, FL (M)
Florida Atlantic University, FL (M)
Florida College, FL (M)
Florida Institute of Technology, FL (M)
Florida International University, FL (M)
Florida Memorial College, FL (M)
Florida Southern College, FL (M)
Florida State University, FL (M)
Fordham University, NY (M)
Fort Hays State University, KS (M)
Fort Scott College, KS (M)
Francis Marion University, SC (M)
Franklin&Marshall College, PA (M)
Franklin Pierce College, NH (M)
Frank Phillips College, TX (M)
Frederick Community College, MD (M)
Freed-Hardeman College, TN (M)
Fresno City College, CA (M)

Friends University, KS (M)
Fullerton College, CA (M)
Fulton-Montgomery Community College, NY (M)
Furman University, SC (M)
Gadsden State Community College, AL (M)
Gannon College, PA (M)
Garden City Community College, KS (M)
Gardner-Webb College, NC (M)
Garrett Community College, MD (M)
Genesee Community College, NY (M)
Geneva College, PA (M)
George C. Wallace Community College, AL (M)
George Fox College, OR (M)
George Mason University, VA (M)
Georgetown College, KY (M)
Georgetown University, DC (M)
George Washington University, DC (M)
Georgia College State University, GA (M)
Georgia Institute of Technology, GA (M)
Georgia Southern University, GA (M)
Georgia Southwestern State University, GA (M)
Georgia State University, GA (M)
Gettysburg College, PA (M)
Glendale Community College, AZ (M)
Glendale Community College, CA (M)
Glen Oaks Community College, MI (M)
Gloucester County College, NJ (M)
Golden West College, (CA)
Gonzaga University, WA (M)
Gordon College, MA (M)
Goshen College, IN (M)
Grace College, IN (M)
Graceland College, IA (M)
Grambling State University, LA (M)
Grand Canyon College, AZ (M)
Grand Rapids Community College, MI (M)
Grand Valley State College, MI (M)
Grand View College, IA (M)
Grays Harbor College, WA (M)
Grayson County College, TX (M)

Greenfield Community College, MA (M)
Green River Community College, WA (M)
Greenville College, IL (M)
Grinnel College, IA (M)
Grove City College, PA (M)
Gulf Coast Community College, FL (M)
Gustavus Adolphus College, MN (M)
Hagerstown Junior College, MD (M)
Hamilton College, NY (M)
Hamline University, MN (M)
Hampden-Sydney College, VA (M)
Hannibal-Lagrange College, MO (M)
Hanover College, IN (M)
Harding University, AR (M)
Hardin-Simmons University, TX (M)
Harford Community College, MD (M)
Harris-Stowe State College, MO (M)
Hartwick College, NY (M)
Harvard University, MA (M)
Hastings College, NE (M)
Haverford College, PA (M)
Hawaii Pacific University, HI (M)
Heidelberg College, OH (M)
Henderson State University, AR (M)
Herkimer County Community College, NY (M)
Hibbing Community College, MN (M)
Highland Community College, KS (M)
Highland Park Community College, MI (M)
High Point University, NC (M)
Hilbert College, NY (M)
Hillsborough Community College, FL (M)
Hillsdale College, MI (M)
Hinds Community College (Raymund), MS (M)
Hiram College, OH (M)
Hiwassee College, TN (M)
Hofstra University, NY (M)
Holmes Junior College, MS (M)
Hope College, MI (M)
Howard University, DC (M)
Hudson Valley Community College, NY (MW)
Huntingdon College, AL (M)
Huntington College, IN (M)

Husson College, ME (M)
Huston-Tillotson College, TX (M)
Hutchinson College, KS (M)
Illinois Central College, IL (M)
Illinois College, IL (M)
Illinois Institute of Technology, IL (M)
Illinois State University, IL (M)
Illinois Valley Community College, IL (M)
Illinois Wesleyan University, IL (M)
Indiana Institute of Technology, IN (M)
Indiana State University, IN (M)
Indiana University, IN (M)
Indiana University of Pennsylvania, PA (M)
Indiana University-Purdue University, IN (M)
Indiana University-Purdue University (Fort Wayne), IN (M)
Indiana University Southeast, IN (M)
Indiana Wesleyan University, IN (M)
Indian Hills Community College, IA (M)
Indian River Community College, FL (M)
Inver Hills Community College, MN (M)
Iona College, NY (M)
Iowa State University of Science and Technology, IA (M)
Iowa Wesleyan College, IA (M)
Itawamba Community College, MS (M)
Ithaca College, NY (M)
Jackson State Community College, TN (M)
Jackson State University, MS (M)
Jacksonville State University, AL (M)
Jacksonville University, FL (M)
James Madison University, VA (M)
Jamestown College, ND (M)
Jefferson College, MO (M)
Jefferson Community College, NY (M)
Jefferson Davis Junior College, AL (M)
Jefferson State Community College, AL (M)
John Carroll University, OH (M)
John C. Calhoun Community College, AL (M)

Johns Hopkins University, MD (M)
Johnson County Community College, KS (M)
Jones County Junior College, MS (M)
Juniata College, PA (M)
Kalamazoo College, MI (M)
Kalamazoo Valley Community College, MI (M)
Kankakee Community College, IL (M)
Kansas City Kansas Community College, KS (M)
Kansas Newman University, KS (M)
Kansas State University, KS (M)
Kansas Wesleyan College, KS (M)
Kaskaskia Community College, IL (M)
Kean University, NJ (M)
Keene State College, NH (M)
Kennesaw State College, GA (M)
Kent State University (Kent), OH (M)
Kent State University (New Philadelphia), OH (M)
Kent State University (Warren), OH (M)
Kent State University (Ashtabula), OH (M)
Kent State University (East Liverpool), OH (M)
Kentucky Christian College, KY (M)
Kentucky State University, KY (M)
Kentucky Wesleyan College, KY (M)
Kenyon College, OH (M)
Keystone Junior College, PA (M)
King College, TN (M)
King's College, PA (M)
Kirkwood Community College, IA (M)
Kishwaukee College, IL (M)
Knox College, IL (M)
Kutztown University, PA (M)
Labette Community College, KS (M)
Lackawanna Junior College, PA (M)
Lafayette College, PA (M)
Lake Land College, IL (M)
Lake Michigan College, MI (M)
Lake-Sumter Community College, FL (M)
Lamar Community College, CO (M)

Lamar University, TX (M)
Lambuth University, TN (M)
Lansing Community College, MI (M)
La Roche College, PA (M)
La Salle University, PA (M)
Lawrence University, WI (M)
Lebanon Valley College, PA (M)
Lee College, TX (M)
Lehigh University, PA (M)
Le Moyne College, NY (M)
LeMoyne-Owen College, TN (M)
Lenoir Community College, NC (M)
Lenoir-Rhyne College, NC (M)
LeTourneau College, TX (M)
Lewis and Clark College, OR (M)
Lewis and Clark Community College, IL (M)
Lewis Clark State College, ID (M)
Lewis University, IL (M)
Liberty University, VA (M)
Limestone College, SC (M)
Lincoln Christian College, IL (M)
Lincoln College, IL (M)
Lincoln Land Community College, IL (M)
Lincoln Memorial University, TN (M)
Lincoln Trail College, IL (M)
Lincoln University, MO (M)
Linfield College, OR (M)
Long Beach City College, CA (M)
Long Island University (Brooklyn), NY (M)
Long Island University (C.W. Post Campus), NY (M)
Longwood College, VA (M)
Loras College, IA (M)
Los Angeles Pierce Junior College, CA (M)
Los Angeles Valley College, CA (M)
Los Medanos College, CA (M)
Louisburg College, NC (M)
Louisiana State University (Baton Rouge), LA (M)
Louisiana State University (Eunice), LA (M)
Louisiana Tech University, LA (M)
Lower Columbia College, WA (M)
Loyola Marymount University, CA (M)
Lubbock Christian College, TX (M)

Luther College, IA (M)
Lynchburg College, VA (M)
Lyndon State College, VT (M)
Lynn University, FL (M)
Macalester College, MN (M)
Macomb Community College,
MI (M)
Madison Area Technical College,
MI (M)
Madonna University, MI (M)
Malone College, OH (M)
Manchester College, IN (M)
Manchester Community Techni-
cal College, CT (M)
Manhattan College, NY (M)
Manhattanville College, NY (M)
Mankato State University, MN
(M)
Mansfield University, PA (M)
Maple Woods Community Col-
lege, MO (M)
Marian College, IN (M)
Marian College, WI (M)
Marietta College, OH (M)
Marist College, NY (M)
Marshall University, WV (M)
Mars Hill College, NC (M)
Mary Holmes College, MS (
M)
Maryville College, TN (M)
Maryville University, MO (M)
Mary Washington College, VA
(M)
Marywood University, PA (M)
Massachusetts Bay Community
College, MA (M)
Massachusetts College of Liberal
Arts, MA (M)
Massachusetts Institute of Tech-
nology, MA (M)
Massasoit Community College,
MA (M)
Master's College, CA (M)
Mayville State College, ND (M)
McHenry County College, IL
(M)
McKendree College, IL (M)
McLennan Community College,
TX (M)
McNeese State University, LA
(M)
Mercer County Community Col-
lege, NJ (M)
Mercer University, GA (M)
Mercy College, NY (M)
Mercyhurst College, PA (M)
Merrimack College, MA (M)
Mesa Community College, AZ
(M)
Mesa State College, CO (M)
Messiah College, PA (M)

Metropolitan State College, CO
(M)
Miami-Dade Community Col-
lege (North), FL (M)
Miami-Dade Community Col-
lege (South Campus), FL (M)
Miami University, OH (M)
Michigan State University, MI
(M)
Mid-America Nazarene College,
KS (M)
Middlebury College, VT (M)
Middlesex County College, NJ
(M)
Middle Tennessee State Univer-
sity, TN (M)
Midland Lutheran College, NE
(M)
Miles College, AL (M)
Millersville University, PA (M)
Milligan College, TN (M)
Millikin University, IL (M)
Milwaukee Area Technology Col-
lege, WI (M)
Mineral Area College, MO (M)
Minot State University (Bot-
tineau), ND (M)
Mississippi College, MS (M)
Mississippi Delta Junior College,
MS (M)
Mississippi Gulf Coast Junior
College, MS (M)
Mississippi State University, MS
(M)
Mississippi Valley State Univer-
sity, MS (M)
Missouri Baptist College, MO
(M)
Missouri Southern State College,
MO (M)
Missouri Valley College, MO (M)
Missouri Western State College,
MO (M)
Mitchell College, CT (M)
Modesto Junior College, CA (M)
Mohawk Valley Community Col-
lege, NY (M)
Molloy College, NY (M)
Monmouth College, IL (M)
Monmouth College, NJ (M)
Montclair State College, NJ (M)
Montreat-Anderson College, NC
(M)
Moorpark College, CA (M)
Moraine Valley Community Col-
lege, IL (M)
Moravian College, PA (M)
Morehead State University, KY
(M)
Morgan State University, MD
(M)

Morningside College, IA (M)
Morris Brown College, GA (M)
Morton College, IL (M)
Motlow State Community Col-
lege, TN (M)
Mott Community College, MI
(M)
Mount Marty College, SD (M)
Mount Mercy College, IA (M)
Mount Olive College, NC (M)
Mount St. Mary College, MD
(M)
Mount Union College, OH (M)
Mount Vernon Nazarene College,
OH (M)
Mt. San Antonio College, CA
(M)
Mt. Wachusett Community Col-
lege, MA (M)
Muhlenberg College, PA (M)
Murray State University, KY
(M)
Muskegon Community College,
MI (M)
Muskingum College, OH (M)
Nassau Community College, NY
(M)
Navarro College, TX (M)
Nebraska Wesleyan University,
NE (M)
Newberry College, SC (M)
New Hampshire College, NH
(M)
New Jersey Institute of Technol-
ogy, NJ (M)
New Mexico Highlands Univer-
sity, NM (M)
New Mexico Junior College, NM
(M)
New Mexico State University,
NM (M)
New York Institute of Technol-
ogy, NY (M)
Niagara County Community
College, NY (M)
Niagara University, NY (M)
Nicholls State University, LA
(M)
Nichols College, MA (M)
Norfolk State University, VA (M)
North Carolina A and T State
University, NC (M)
North Carolina State University,
NC (M)
North Carolina Wesleyan Col-
lege, NC (M)
North Central College, IL (M)
North Central Missouri College,
MO (M)
North Central Texas College, TX
(M)

North Dakota State University, ND (M)
North Georgia College & State University, GA (M)
Northeastern Illinois University, IL (M)
Northeastern Junior College, CO (M)
Northeastern State University, OK (M)
Northeast Louisiana University, LA (M)
Northeast Mississippi Community College, MS (M)
Northeast Missouri State University, MO (M)
Northern Illinois University, IL (M)
Northern Kentucky University, KY (M)
Northern State University, SD (M)
North Florida Junior College, FL (M)
North Greenville College, SC (M)
North Hennepin Community College, MN (M)
North Idaho College, ID (M)
North Iowa Area Community College, IA (M)
Northwest Shoals Community College, AL (M)
Northwestern College, IA (M)
Northwestern College, MN (M)
Northwestern Oklahoma State University, OK (M)
Northwestern State University of Louisiana, LA (M)
Northwestern University, IL (M)
Northwest Mississippi Community College, MS (M)
Northwest Missouri State University, MO (M)
Northwest Nazarene University, ID (M)
Northwood Institute, MI (M)
Northwood Institute (Texas Campus), TX (M)
Norwich University, VT (M)
Nova Southern University, FL (M)
Nyack College, NY (M)
Oakland City University, IN (M)
Oakton Community College, IL (M)
Oberlin College, OH (M)
Occidental College, CA (M)
Ocean County College, NJ (M)
Odessa College, TX (M)
Oglethorpe University, GA (M)

Ohio Dominican College, OH (M)
Ohio Northern University, OH (M)
Ohio State University, OH (M)
Ohio University, OH (M)
Ohio Valley College, WV (M)
Ohio Wesleyan University, OH (M)
Oklahoma Baptist University, OK (M)
Oklahoma Christian University of Science&Art, OK (M)
Oklahoma City University, OK (M)
Oklahoma State University, OK (M)
Old Dominion University, VA (M)
Olivet College, MI (M)
Olivet Nazarene University, IL (M)
Olney Central College, IL (M)
Olympic College, WA (M)
Oral Roberts University, OK (M)
Orange Coast College, CA (M)
Orange County Community College, NY (M)
Oregon Institute of Technology, OR (M)
Oregon State University, OR (M)
Oswego State University (SUNY), NY (M)
Otero Junior College, CO (M)
Otterbein College, OH (M)
Ouachita Baptist University, AR (M)
Oxnard College, CA (M)
Pace University, NY (M)
Pacific Lutheran University, WA (M)
Pacific University, OR (M)
Paducah Community College, CA (M)
Paine College, GA (M)
Palm Beach Atlantic College, FL (M)
Palm Beach Community College, FL (M)
Palomar College, CA (M)
Pan American University, TX (M)
Panola Junior College, TX (M)
Paris Junior College, TX (M)
Parkland College, IL (M)
Penn State Abington College, PA (M)
Pennsylvania State University, PA (M)
Penn State Behrend College, PA (M)

Penn State Berks-Lehigh Valley College, PA (M)
Pensacola Junior College, FL (M)
Pepperdine University, CA (M)
Peru State College, NE (M)
Pfeiffer College, NC (M)
Philadelphia University, PA (M)
Phillips University, OK (M)
Phoenix College, AZ (M)
Piedmont College, GA (M)
Pierce College, WA (M)
Pikeville College, KY (M)
Pima Community College (West Campus), AZ (M)
Pittsburg State University, KS (M)
Plymouth State College, NH (M)
Point Loma Nazarene College, CA (M)
Point Park College, PA (M)
Polk Community College, FL (M)
Polytechnic University (Brooklyn Campus), NY (M)
Pomona-Pitzer Colleges, CA (M)
Portland State University, OR (M)
Prairie View A&M University, TX (M)
Pratt Community College, KS (M)
Presbyterian College, SC (M)
Prince George's Community College, MD (M)
Princeton University, NJ (M)
Principia College, IL (M)
Providence College, RI (M)
Purdue University, IN (M)
Queens College, NY (M)
Queensborough Community College, NY (M)
Quincy University, IL (M)
Quinnipiac University, CT (M)
Quinsigamond College, MA (M)
Radford University, VA (M)
Ramapo College, NJ (M)
Randolph-Macon College, VA (M)
Ranetto Santiago College, CA (M)
Regis University, CO (M)
Rend Lake, IL (M)
Rensselaer Polytechnic Institute, NY (M)
Rhode Island College, RI (M)
Rice University, TX (M)
Ricks College, ID (M)
Rider College, NJ (M)
Ripon College, WI (M)

Riverland Community College, MN (M)
Riverside Community College, CA (M)
Roane State Community College, TN (M)
Roberts Wesleyan College, NY (M)
Rochester College, MI (M)
Rochester Community College, MN (M)
Rochester Institute of Technology, NY (M)
Rockland Community College, NY (M)
Rollins College, FL (M)
Rose-Hulman Institute of Technology, IN (M)
Rose State Junior College, OK (M)
Rowan University, NJ (M)
Rust College, MS (M)
Rutgers, Newark College of Arts and Sciences, NJ (M)
Sacred Heart University, CT (M)
Saddleback College, CA (M)
Saginaw Valley State University, MI (M)
Saint Ambrose University, IA (M)
Saint Andrews Presbyterian College, NC (M)
Saint Anselm College, NH (M)
Saint Augustine's College, NC (M)
Saint Bonaventure University, NY (M)
Saint Cloud State University, MN (M)
Saint Edward's University, TX (M)
Saint Francis College, IN (M)
Saint Francis College, NY (M)
Saint John Fisher College, NY (M)
Saint John's University, MN (M)
Saint John's University, NY (M)
Saint Joseph's College, IN (M)
Saint Joseph's University, PA (M)
Saint Lawrence University, NY (M)
Saint Leo University, FL (M)
Saint Louis University, MO (M)
Saint Mary College, KS (M)
Saint Mary's College of California, CA (M)
Saint Mary's University, TX (M)
Saint Norbert College, WI (M)
Saint Olaf College, MN (M)
Saint Peter's College, NJ (M)

Saint Thomas Aquinas College, NY (M)
Saint Thomas University, FL (M)
Saint Vincent College, PA (M)
Saint Xavier University, IL (M)
Salem State College, MA (M)
Salem-Teikyo University, WV (M)
Salve Regina College, RI (M)
Samford University, AL (M)
Sam Houston State University, TX (M)
San Bernardino Community College, CA (M)
San Diego City College, CA (M)
San Diego Mesa College, CA (M)
San Diego State University, CA (M)
San Francisco State University, CA (M)
San Joaquin Delta College, CA (M)
San Jose State University, CA (M)
Santa Barbara City College, CA (M)
Santa Clara University, CA (M)
Santa Fe Community College, FL (M)
Santa Monica College, CA (M)
Santa Rosa Junior College, CA (M)
Sauk Valley College, IL (M)
Savannah State College, GA (M)
Schreiner College, TX (M)
Scottsdale Community College, AZ (M)
Seminole Community College, FL (M)
Seminole Junior College, OK (M)
Seton Hall University, NJ (M)
Seward County Community College, KS (M)
Shawnee State University, OH (M)
Shelby State University College, TN (M)
Shepherd College, WV (M)
Shippensburg University of Pennsylvania, PA (M)
Shoreline Community College, WA (M)
Shorter College, GA (M)
Siena College, NY (M)
Siena Heights College, MI (M)
Sierra College, CA (M)
Simpson College, CA (M)

Sinclair Community College, OH (M)
Sioux Falls College, SD (M)
Skagit Valley College, WA (M)
Skidmore College, NY (M)
Skyline College, CA (M)
Slippery Rock University of Pennsylvania, PA (M)
Snead State Community College, AL (M)
Snow College, UT (M)
Solano Community College, CA (M)
South Carolina State College, SC (M)
South Dakota State University, SD (M)
Southeastern Community College, IA (M)
Southeastern Community College, NC (M)
Southeastern Illinois College, IL (M)
Southeastern Louisiana University, LA (M)
Southeastern Oklahoma State University, OK (M)
Southeastern Missouri State University, MO (M)
Southern Arkansas University, AR (M)
Southern California College, CA (M)
Southern Polytechnic State University, GA (M)
Southern Illinois University, IL (M)
Southern Illinois University (Edwardsville), IL (M)
Southern Union State Community College, AL (M)
Southern University and A&M College, LA (M)
Southern Utah University, UT (M)
Southern Wesleyan University, SC (M)
Southwest, NM (M)
Southwest Baptist University, MO (M)
Southwestern College, CA (M)
Southwestern Oklahoma State University, OK (M)
Southwestern University, TX (M)
Southwest Missouri State University, MO (M)
Southwest State University, MN (M)
Southwest Texas State University, TX (M)

Spartanburg Methodist, SC (M)
Spokane Community College, WA (M)
Spoon River College, IL (M)
Spring Arbor College, MI (M)
Springfield College, MA (M)
Springfield Technical Community College, MA (M)
Spring Hill College, AL (M)
Stanford University, CA (M)
State Fair Community College, MO (M)
State University of New York College (Brockport), NY (M)
State University of New York College (Cortland), NY (M)
State University of New York College (Fredonia), NY (M)
State University of New York College (New Paltz), NY (M)
State University of New York Institute of Technology at Utica/Rome, NY (M)
State University of New York Maritime College, NY (M)
State University of West Georgia, GA (M)
Stephen F. Austin State University, TX (M)
Sterling College, KS (M)
Stetson University, FL (M)
Stevens Institute of Technology, NJ (M)
St. Catherine College, KY (M)
St. Johns River Community College, FL (M)
St. Louis Community College (Florissant Valley), MO (M)
St. Mary of the Plains College, KS (M)
Stonehill College, MA (M)
St. Petersburg Junior College, FL (M)
Suffolk County Community College, NY (M)
Suffolk University, MA (M)
Sul Ross State University, TX (M)
Swarthmore College, PA (M)
Tabor College, KS (M)
Taft College, CA (M)
Talledaga College, AL (M)
Tarleton State University, TX (M)
Teikyo Post University, CT (M)
Teikyo Westmar University, IA (M)
Temple Baptist Seminary, TN (M)
Temple College, TX (M)
Temple University, PA (M)

Tennessee State University, TN (M)
Tennessee Technological University, TN (M)
Tennessee Wesleyan College, TN (M)
Texarkana College, TX (M)
Texas A&I University, TX (M)
Texas A&M University, TX (M)
Texas Christian University, TX (M)
Texas Lutheran College, TX (M)
Texas Southern University, TX (M)
Texas Tech University, TX (M)
Texas Wesleyan College, TX (M)
Thomas College, ME (M)
Thomas More College, KY (M)
Three Rivers Community College, MO (M)
Tiffin University, OH (M)
Toccoa Falls College, GA (M)
Towson State University, MD (M)
Transylvania University, KY (M)
Trevecca Nazarene College, TN (M)
Trinidad State Junior College, CO (M)
Trinity Christian College, IL (M)
Trinity College, CT (M)
Trinity College, IL (M)
Trinity University, TX (M)
Tri-State University, IN (M)
Triton College, IL (M)
Troy State University, AL (M)
Truett-McConnell Junior College, GA (M)
Tufts University, MA (M)
Tulane University, LA (M)
Tusculum College, TN (M)
Tyler Junior College, TX (M)
Union College, KY (M)
Union College, NY (M)
Union County College, NJ (M)
Union University, TN (M)
Unity College, ME (M)
University of Akron, OH (M)
University of Alabama (Birmingham), AL (M)
University of Alabama (Huntsville), AL (M)
University of Alabama (Tuscaloosa), AL (M)
University at Albany (SUNY), NY (M)
University of Arizona, AZ (M)
University of Arkansas (Fayetteville), AR (M)
University of Arkansas (Little Rock), AR (M)

University of Arkansas (Monticello), AR (M)
University of Bridgeport, CT (M)
University at Buffalo (SUNY), NY (M)
University of California (Berkeley), CA (M)
University of California (Davis), CA (M)
University of California (Riverside), CA (M)
University of California (San Diego), CA (M)
University of California (Santa Barbara), CA (M)
University of California (UCLA), CA (M)
University of Central Arkansas, AR (M)
University of Central Florida, FL (M)
University of Central Oklahoma, OK (M)
University of Charleston, WV (M)
University of Chicago, IL (M)
University of Cincinnati, OH (M)
University of Connecticut, CT (M)
University of Dallas, TX (M)
University of Dayton, OH (M)
University of Delaware, DE (M)
University of Detroit Mercy, MI (M)
University of Dubuque, IA (M)
University of Evansville, IN (M)
University of Findlay, OH (M)
University of Florida, FL (M)
University of Georgia, GA (M)
University of Hartford, CT (M)
University of Hawaii (Hilo), HI (M)
University of Hawaii (Manoa), HI (M)
University of Houston, TX (M)
University of Incarnate Word, TX (M)
University of Indianapolis, IN (M)
University of Iowa, IA (M)
University of Kansas, KS (M)
University of Kentucky, KY (M)
University of La Verne, CA (M)
University of Louisiana at Lafeyette, LA (M)
University of Louisville, KY (M)
University of Maine, ME (M)
University of Maine (Presque Isle), ME (M)

University of Mary Hardin-Baylor, TX (M)
University of Maryland, MD (M)
University of Maryland (Baltimore County), MD (M)
University of Maryland (Eastern Shore), MD (M)
University of Massachusetts (Amherst), MA (M)
University of Massachusetts (Boston), MA (M)
University of Massachusetts (Dartmouth), MA (M)
University of Massachusetts (Lowell), MA (M)
University of Memphis, TN (M)
University of Miami, FL (M)
University of Michigan, MI (M)
University of Minnesota (Duluth), MN (M)
University of Minnesota (Minneapolis), MN (M)
University of Minnesota (Morris), MN (M)
University of Mississippi, MS (M)
University of Missouri, MO (M)
University of Missouri (Rolla), MO (M)
University of Mobile, AL (M)
University of Montevallo, AL (M)
University of Nebraska, NE (M)
University of Nebraska (Kearney), NE (M)
University of Nebraska (Lincoln), NE (M)
University of Nevada, NV (M)
University of Nevada (Reno), NV (M)
University of New Hampshire, NH (M)
University of New Haven, CT (M)
University of New Mexico, NM (M)
University of New Orleans, LA (M)
University of North Alabama, AL (M)
University of North Carolina (Asheville), NC (M)
University of North Carolina (Chapel Hill), NC (M)
University of North Carolina (Charlotte), NC (M)
University of North Carolina (Pembroke), NC (M)
University of North Carolina (Wilmington), NC (M)

University of North Dakota, ND (M)
University of North Florida, FL (M)
University of Northern Colorado, CO (M)
University of Northern Iowa, IA (M)
University of Notre Dame, IN (M)
University of Oklahoma, OK (M)
University of Pennsylvania, PA (M)
University of Pittsburgh, PA (M)
University of Pittsburgh (Johnstown), PA (M)
University of Portland, OR (M)
University of Puerto Rico (Bayamon), PR (M)
University of Puget Sound, WA (M)
University of Redlands, CA (M)
University of Rhode Island, RI (M)
University of Richmond, VA (M)
University of Rio Grande, OH (M)
University of San Diego, CA (M)
University of San Francisco, CA (M)
University of Scranton, PA (M)
University of South Alabama, AL (M)
University of South Carolina (Columbia), SC (M)
University of South Carolina (Myrtle Beach), SC (M)
University of South Carolina (Aiken), SC (M)
University of South Carolina (Spartanburg), SC (M)
University of South Dakota, SD (M)
University of Southern California, CA (M)
University of Southern Colorado, CO (M)
University of Southern Indiana, IN (M)
University of Southern Mississippi, MS (M)
University of South Florida, FL (M)
University of St. Thomas, MN (M)
University at Stony Brook (SUNY), NY (M)
University of Tampa, FL (M)
University of Tennessee, TN (M)
University of Tennessee (Knoxville), TN (M)

University of Tennessee (Martin), TN (M)
University of Texas (Arlington), TX (M)
University of Texas (Austin), TX (M)
The University of Texas at Brownsville and Texas Southmost College, TX (M)
University of Texas (Pan American), TX (M)
University of Texas (San Antonio), TX (M)
University of the Pacific, CA (M)
University of Toledo, OH (M)
University of Utah, UT (M)
University of Vermont, VT (M)
University of Virginia, VA (M)
The University of Virginia's College at Wise, VA (M)
University of Washington, WA (M)
University of West Alabama, AL (M)
University of West Florida, FL (M)
University of Wisconsin (Eau Claire), WI (M)
University of Wisconsin (La Crosse), WI (M)
University of Wisconsin (Milwaukee), WI (M)
University of Wisconsin (Oshkosh), WI (M)
University of Wisconsin (Platteville), WI (M)
University of Wisconsin (River Falls), WI (M)
University of Wisconsin (Stevens Point), WI (M)
University of Wisconsin (Stout), WI (M)
University of Wisconsin (Superior), WI (M)
Upper Iowa University, IA (M)
Urbana University, OH (M)
Ursinus College, PA (M)
U.S. International University, CA (M)
Utah State University, UT (M)
Valdosta State University, GA (M)
Valley City State University, ND (M)
Valley Forge Christian College, PA (M)
Valparaiso University, IN (M)
Vanderbilt University, TN (M)
Vassar College, NY (M)
Ventura College, CA (M)
Villanova University, PA (M)

Vincennes University, IN (M)
Virginia Commonwealth University, VA (M)
Virginia Intermont College, VA (M)
Virginia Military Institute, VA (M)
Virginia Polytechnic Institute & State University, VA (M)
Virginia State University, VA (M)
Virginia Wesleyan College, VA (M)
Viterbo College, WI (M)
Wabash College, IN (M)
Wabash Valley College, IL (M)
Wagner College, NY (M)
Wake Forest University, NC (M)
Waldorf College, IA (M)
Wallace Community College (Selma), AL (M)
Wallace State Community College, AL (M)
Walla Walla Community College, WA (M)
Walsh College, OH (M)
Walters State Community College, TN (M)
Warner Southern College, FL (M)
Warren Wilson College, NC (M)
Wartburg College, IA (M)
Washburn University, KS (M)
Washington and Jefferson College, PA (M)
Washington State University, WA (M)
Washington University, MO (M)
Waubonsee College, IL (M)
Wayne State College, NE (M)
Wayne State University, MI (M)
Webber College, FL (M)
Webster University, MO (M)
Wesleyan University, CT (M)
Wesley College, DE (M)
Westark Community College, AR (M)
West Chester University, PA (M)
Western Carolina University, NC (M)
Western Connecticut State University, CT (M)
Western Illinois University, IL (M)
Western Kentucky University, KY (M)
Western Maryland College, MD (M)
Western Michigan University, MI (M)
Western New England College, MA (M)

Western New Mexico University, NM (M)
Western Oregon State College, OR (M)
Westfield State College, MA (M)
West Liberty State College, WV (M)
Westminster College, PA (M)
Westmont College, CA (M)
West Texas State University, TX (M)
West Virginia State College, WV (M)
West Virginia University, WV (M)
West Virginia Wesleyan College, WV (M)
Wheaton College, IL (M)
Whitman College, WA (M)
Whittier College, CA (M)
Whitworth College, WA (M)
Wichita State University, KS (M)
Wilberforce University, OH (M)
Wilkes College, NC (M)
Wilkes University, PA (M)
Willamette University, OR (M)
William Jewell College, MO (M)
William Patterson College, NJ (M)
William Penn College, IA (M)
William Rainey Harper College, IL (M)
Williams College, MA (M)
Williamson Trade School, PA (M)
Wilmington College, DE (M)
Wilmington College, OH (M)
Wingate College, NC (M)
Winona State University, MN (M)
Winthrop University, SC (M)
Wofford College, SC (M)
Worcester State College, MA (M)
Wright State University, OH (M)
Xavier University, OH (M)
Yakima Valley College, WA (M)
Yale University, CT (M)
Yavapai College, AZ (M)
York College of Pennsylvania, PA (M)
Youngstown State University, OH (M)
Yuba Community College, CA (M)

Basketball

Abilene Christian University, TX (MW)
Adams State College, CO (MW)
Adelphi University, NY (MW)

Adirondack College, NY (MW)
Adrian College, MI (MW)
Agnes Scott College, GA (W)
Alabama A&M University, AL (MW)
Alabama State University, AL (MW)
Albany State University, GA (MW)
Albertson College of Idaho, ID (MW)
Albion College, MI (MW)
Albright College, PA (MW)
Alcorn State University, MS (MW)
Alderson-Broaddus College, WV (MW)
Alfred University, NY (MW)
Alice Lloyd College, KY (MW)
Allegheny College, PA (MW)
Allen County College, KS (MW)
Allentown College, PA (MW)
Allen University, SC (MW)
Alma College, MI (MW)
Alvernia College, PA (MW)
American International College, MA (MW)
American University, DC (MW)
Amherst College, MA (MW)
Anderson College, SC (MW)
Anderson University, IN (MW)
Angelina College, TX (MW)
Angelo State University, TX (MW)
Anoka-Ramsey College, MN (MW)
Appalachian State University, NC (MW)
Apprentice School, VA (MW)
Aquinas College, MI (MW)
Aquinas Junior College, TN (M)
Arizona State University, AZ (MW)
Arkansas College, AR (MW)
Arkansas State University, AR (MW)
Arkansas Tech University, AR (MW)
Armstrong Atlantic State University, GA (MW)
Asbury College, KY (MW)
Ashland College, OH (MW)
Assumption College, MA (MW)
Athens State College, AL (M)
Atlantic Community College, NJ (MW)
Atlantic Union College, MA (M)
Auburn University, AL (MW)
Auburn University (Montgomery), AL (MW)
Augsburg College, MN (MW)

Augusta State University, GA
(MW)
Augustana College, IL (MW)
Augustana College, SD (MW)
Aurora University, IL (MW)
Austin College, TX (MW)
Austin Community College, MN
(MW)
Austin Peay State University, TN
(MW)
Averett College, VA (MW)
Avila College, MO (MW)
Azusa Pacific University, CA
(MW)
Babson College, MA (MW)
Bacone Junior College, OK
(MW)
Baker University, KS (MW)
Ball State University, IN (MW)
Baltimore City Community Col-
lege, MD (MW)
Baptist Bible College, MO (M)
Barber-Scotia College, NC
(MW)
Bard College, NY (MW)
Barry University, FL (MW)
Barstow College, CA (MW)
Bartlesville Wesleyan, OK (MW)
Barton College, NC (MW)
Barton County College, KS
(MW)
Bates College, ME (MW)
Bayamon Central University, PR
(MW)
Baylor University, TX (MW)
Becker College, MA (MW)
Belhaven College, MS (MW)
Bellarmine College, KY (MW)
Belleville Area College, IL (MW)
Bellevue College, NE (M)
Bellevue Community College,
WA (M)
Belmont Abbey College, NC
(MW)
Belmont College, TN (MW)
Beloit College, WI (MW)
Bemidji State University, MN
(MW)
Benedict College, SC (MW)
Benedictine College, KS (MW)
Benedictine University, IL (MW)
Bentley College, MA (MW)
Bergen Community College, NJ
(MW)
Berry College, GA (MW)
Bethany College, KS (MW)
Bethany College, WV (MW)
Bethany Lutheran College, MN
(MW)
Bethel College, IN (MW)
Bethel College, KS (MW)

Bethel College, MN (MW)
Bethune-Cookman College, FL
(MW)
Big Bend Community College,
WA (MW)
Binghamton University (SUNY),
NY (MW)
Biola University, CA (MW)
Birmingham-Southern College,
AL (MW)
Bismarck State College, ND
(MW)
Blackburn College, IL (MW)
Black Hawk College (Moline), IL
(MW)
Black Hills State University, SD
(MW)
Blanton Junior College, NC (M)
Bloomfield College, NJ (MW)
Bloomsburg University, PA
(MW)
Bluefield College, VA (MW)
Bluefield State College, WV
(MW)
Blue Mountain College, MS (W)
Blue Mountain College, OR
(MW)
Bluffton College, OH (MW)
Boise State University, ID (MW)
Borough of Manhattan Commu-
nity College (CUNY), NY
(M)
Boston College, MA (MW)
Boston University, MA (MW)
Bowdoin College, ME (MW)
Bowie State University, MD
(MW)
Bowling Green State University,
OH (MW)
Bradley University, IL (MW)
Brainerd Community College,
MN (MW)
Brandeis University, MA (MW)
Brescia University, KY (MW)
Brevard Community College, FL
(MW)
Brevard College, NC (MW)
Brewton Parker College, GA
(MW)
Briar Cliff College, IA (MW)
Bridgewater College, VA (MW)
Bridgewater State College, MA
(MW)
Brigham Young University, HI
(M)
Brigham Young University, UT
(MW)
Bronx Community College, NY
(MW)
Brooklyn College (CUNY), NY
(MW)

Broome Community College,
NY (MW)
Broward Community College,
FL (MW)
Brown University, RI (MW)
Bryant College, RI (MW)
Bryn Mawr College, PA (W)
Bucknell University, PA (MW)
Bucks County Community Col-
lege, PA (MW)
Buena Vista University, IA (MW)
Buffalo State College, NY (MW)
Bunker Hill Community College,
MA (MW)
Butler County Community Col-
lege, KS (M)
Butler County Community Col-
lege, PA (M)
Butler University, IN (MW)
Butte College, CA (MW)
Cabrillo College, CA (MW)
Cabrini College, PA (MW)
Caldwell College, NJ (MW)
California Baptist University, CA
(MW)
California Institute of Technol-
ogy, CA (MW)
California Lutheran University,
CA (MW)
California Maritime Academy,
CA (M)
California Polytechnic State Uni-
versity, CA (MW)
California State Polytechnic Uni-
versity, CA (MW)
California State University at
Bakersfield, CA (M)
California State University
(Chico), CA (MW)
California State University
(Dominguez Hills), CA (MW)
California State University
(Fresno), CA (MW)
California State University
(Fullerton), CA (MW)
California State University (Hay-
ward), CA (MW)
California State University (Long
Beach), CA (MW)
California State University (Los
Angeles), CA (MW)
California State University
(Northridge), CA (MW)
California State University
(Sacramento), CA (MW)
California State University (San
Bernardino), CA (MW)
California State University
(Stanislaus), CA (MW)
California University, PA (MW)
Calvin College, MI (MW)

Cameron University, OK (MW)
Campbellsville University, KY (MW)
Campbell University, NC (MW)
Canisius College, NY (MW)
Capital University, OH (MW)
Cardinal Stritch College, WI (MW)
Carl Albert Junior College, OK (MW)
Carleton College, MN (MW)
Carlow College, PA (W)
Carnegie-Mellon University, PA (MW)
Carroll College, MT (MW)
Carroll College, WI (MW)
Carson-Newman College, TN (MW)
Carthage College, WI (MW)
Case Western Reserve University, OH (MW)
Castleton State College, VT (MW)
Catawba College, NC (MW)
Catholic University of America, DC (MW)
Catonsville Community College, MD (MW)
Cayuga County Community College, NY (MW)
Cecil Community College, MD (MW)
Cedarville College, OH (MW)
Centenary College, LA (MW)
Centenary College, NJ (MW)
Central Arizona College, AZ (MW)
Central Baptist College, AR (MW)
Central College, IA (MW)
Central Christian College, KS (MW)
Central Community College, NE (MW)
Central Connecticut State University, CT (MW)
Central Florida Community College, FL (MW)
Central Lakes College, MN (MW)
Central Methodist College, MO (MW)
Central Michigan University, MI (MW)
Central Missouri State University, MO (MW)
Central Washington University, WA (MW)
Central Wesleyan College, SC (MW)

Central Wyoming College, WY (MW)
Cerritos College, CA (MW)
Chadron State College, NE (MW)
Chaffey College, CA (M)
Chaminade University of Honolulu, HI (M)
Champlain College, VT (M)
Chapman University, CA (MW)
Charles County Community College, MD (M)
Charleston Southern University, SC (MW)
Chattahoochee Valley Community College, AL (MW)
Chemeketa Community College, OR (MW)
Cheyney University of Pennsylvania, PA (MW)
Chicago State University, IL (MW)
Chipola Junior College, FL (MW)
Chowan College, NC (MW)
Christian Brothers College, TN (MW)
Christopher Newport College, VA (MW)
Cincinnati Technical College, OH (M)
Citadel, SC (M)
City College of New York, NY (MW)
City College of San Francisco, CA (MW)
Clackamas Community College, OR (MW)
Claflin College, SC (MW)
Clarion University, PA (MW)
Clark Atlanta University, GA (MW)
Clark College, WA (MW)
Clarkson University, NY (MW)
Clark State College, OH (MW)
Clark University, MA (MW)
Clemson University, SC (M)
Cleveland State Community College, TN (MW)
Cleveland State University, OH (MW)
Clinton Community College, IA (M)
Clinton Community College, NY (MW)
Cloud County Community College, KS (MW)
Coahoma Junior College, MS (MW)
Coastal Carolina College, SC (MW)

Coastal Georgia Community College, GA (M)
Cochise College, AZ (MW)
Coe College, IA (MW)
Coffeyville Community College, KS (MW)
Coker College, SC (MW)
Colby Community College, KS (MW)
Colby-Sawyer College, NH (MW)
Colgate University, NY (MW)
College of Allegheny County, PA (M)
College of Charleston, SC (MW)
College of Charleston, SC (MW)
College of Mount St. Joseph, OH (MW)
The College of New Jersey, NJ (MW)
College of New Rochelle, NY (W)
College of Notre Dame, CA (MW)
College of Notre Dame of Maryland, MD (W)
College of Saint Mary, NE (W)
College of Southern Idaho, ID (MW)
College of St. Benedict, MN (W)
College of St. Francis, IL (MW)
College of St. Rose, NY (M)
College of St. Scholastica, MN (MW)
College of the Desert, CA (MW)
College of the Holy Cross, MA (MW)
College of the Ozarks, MO (MW)
College of the Redwoods, CA (MW)
College of the Sequoias, CA (MW)
College of William and Mary, VA (MW)
College of Wooster, OH (MW)
Colorado Christian University, CO (MW)
Colorado College, CO (MW)
Colorado Northwestern Community College, CO (MW)
Colorado School of Mines, CO (MW)
Colorado State University, CO (MW)
Columbia Basin Community College, WA (MW)
Columbia Christian College, OR (MW)
Columbia College, MO (M)

Columbia-Greene Community College, NY (MW)
Columbia Union College, MD (MW)
Columbia University, NY (MW)
Columbus College, GA (M)
Columbus State Community College, OH (M)
Community College of Allegheny County (Allegheny Campus), PA (MW)
Community College of Philadelphia, PA (MW)
Community College of Rhode Island, RI (MW)
Compton Community College, CA (MW)
Concord College, WV (MW)
Concordia University, MI (MW)
Concordia College (Moorhead), MN (MW)
Concordia College (St. Paul), MN (MW)
Concordia College, NY (MW)
Concordia Lutheran College, TX (MW)
Concordia University, NE (MW)
Concordia University, IL (MW)
Concordia University Wisconsin, WI (MW)
Connecticut College, CT (MW)
Connors State College, OK (MW)
Contra Costa College, CA (MW)
Converse College, SC (W)
Copiah-Lincoln Community College, MS (MW)
Coppin State College, MD (MW)
Cornell College, IA (MW)
Cornell University, NY (MW)
Consumnes River College, CA (M)
Covenant College, GA (MW)
Cowley County Community College, KS (MW)
Creighton University, NE (MW)
Crowder College, MO (W)
Cuesta College, CA (MW)
Culver-Stockton College, MO (MW)
Cumberland College, KY (MW)
Curry College, MA (MW)
Cuyahoga Community College (Cleveland), OH (MW)
Cuyahoga Community College (Highland Hills Village), OH (MW)
Daemen College, NY (MW)
Dakota State University, SD (MW)

Dakota Wesleyan University, SD (MW)
Dana College, NE (MW)
Danville Area Community College, IL (MW)
Dartmouth College, NH (MW)
Davidson College, NC (MW)
Davis & Elkins College, WV (MW)
Dawson Community College, MT (MW)
Daytona Beach Community College, FL (MW)
Dean Junior College, MA (MW)
Defiance College, OH (MW)
Delaware County Community College, PA (M)
Delaware State University, DE (MW)
Delaware Valley College, PA (MW)
Delgado Community College, LA (MW)
Delhi College of Technology (SUNY), NY (MW)
Delta College, MI (MW)
Delta State University, MS (MW)
Denison University, OH (MW)
DePaul University, IL (MW)
De Pauw University, IN (MW)
Des Moines Area Community College, IA (MW)
Diablo Valley Community College, CA (MW)
Dickinson College, PA (MW)
Dickinson State University, ND (MW)
Dillard University, LA (MW)
Diné College, AZ (MW)
Dixie College, UT (MW)
Doane College, NE (MW)
Dodge City Community College, KS (MW)
Dominican College, CA (M)
Dominican College of Blauvelt, NY (MW)
Dominican University, IL (MW)
Dowling College, NY (MW)
Drake University, IA (MW)
Drew University, NJ (MW)
Drexel University, PA (MW)
Drury College, MO (M)
Duke University, NC (MW)
Dundalk Community College, MD (M)
Duquesne University, PA (MW)
Dutchess Community College, NY (M)
Dyersburg State Community College, TN (M)

D'Youville College, NY (MW)
Earlham College, IN (MW)
East Carolina University, NC (MW)
East Central College, MO (MW)
East Central University, OK (MW)
Eastern College, PA (MW)
Eastern Connecticut State University, CT (MW)
Eastern Illinois University, IL (MW)
Eastern Kentucky University, KY (MW)
Eastern Mennonite College, VA (MW)
Eastern Michigan University, MI (MW)
Eastern Montana College, MT (MW)
Eastern Nazarene College, MA (MW)
Eastern New Mexico University, NM (MW)
Eastern Oklahoma State College, OK (MW)
Eastern Oregon State College, OR (MW)
Eastern Washington University, WA (MW)
Eastern Wyoming College, WY (M)
Eastfield College, TX (M)
East Stroudsburg University, PA (MW)
East Tennessee State University, TN (MW)
East Texas Baptist University, TX (MW)
Eckerd College, FL (MW)
Edgewood College, WI (MW)
Edinboro University of Pennsylvania, PA (MW)
Edmonds Community College, WA (MW)
Edward Waters College, FL (MW)
El Camino College, CA (MW)
Elgin Community College, IL (MW)
Elizabeth City State University, NC (MW)
Elizabethtown College, PA (MW)
Elmhurst College, IL (MW)
Elmira College, NY (MW)
Elon College, NC (MW)
Emerson College, MA (MW)
Emory and Henry College, VA (MW)
Emory University, GA (MW)

Emporia State University, KS (MW)

Enterprise State Junior College, AL (MW)

Erskine College, SC (MW)

Essex Community College, MD (MW)

Eureka College, IL (MW)

Evangel College, MO (MW)

Everett Community College, WA (MW)

Evergreen State College, WA (MW)

Fairfield University, CT (MW)

Fairleigh Dickinson University (Madison), NJ (MW)

Fairleigh Dickinson University (Teaneck), NJ (MW)

Fairmont State College, WV (MW)

Fashion Institute of Technology, NY (M)

Faulkner University, AL (M)

Fayetteville State University, NC (MW)

Fergus Falls Community College, MN (MW)

Ferris State College, MI (MW)

Ferrum College, VA (MW)

Finger Lakes Community College, NY (MW)

Fisk University, TN (MW)

Fitchburg State College, MA (MW)

Flagler College, FL (MW)

Florida A&M University, FL (MW)

Florida Atlantic University, FL (MW)

Florida College, FL (M)

Florida Institute of Technology, FL (MW)

Florida International University, FL (MW)

Florida Memorial College, FL (MW)

Florida Southern College, FL (MW)

Florida State University, FL (MW)

Foothill College, CA (MW)

Fordham University, NY (MW)

Fort Hays State University, KS (MW)

Fort Lewis College, CO (MW)

Fort Scott College, KS (MW)

Fort Valley State University, GA (MW)

Francis Marion University, SC (MW)

Franklin & Marshall College, PA (MW)

Franklin Pierce College, NH (MW)

Frank Phillips College, TX (MW)

Frederick Community College, MD (MW)

Freed-Hardeman College, TN (MW)

Fresno City College, CA (MW)

Fresno Pacific University, CA (MW)

Friends University, KS (MW)

Fullerton College, CA (MW)

Fulton-Montgomery Community College, NY (MW)

Furman University, SC (MW)

Gadsden State Community College, AL (MW)

Gannon College, PA (MW)

Garden City Community College, KS (MW)

Gardner-Webb College, NC (MW)

Garrett Community College, MD (MW)

Genesee Community College, NY (MW)

Geneva College, PA (MW)

George C. Wallace Community College, AL (MW)

George Fox College, OR (MW)

George Mason University, VA (MW)

Georgetown College, KY (MW)

Georgetown University, DC (MW)

George Washington University, DC (MW)

Georgia College State University, GA (MW)

Georgia Institute of Technology, GA (MW)

Georgian Court College, NJ (W)

Georgia Southern University, GA (MW)

Georgia Southwestern State University, GA (MW)

Georgia State University, GA (MW)

Gettysburg College, PA (MW)

Glendale Community College, AZ (MW)

Glendale Community College, CA (MW)

Glen Oaks Community College, MI (MW)

Glenville State College, WV (MW)

Gloucester County College, NJ (MW)

Golden West College, CA (MW)

Goldey-Beacom College, DE (MW)

Gonzaga University, WA (MW)

Gordon College, MA (MW)

Goshen College, IN (MW)

Goucher College, MD (MW)

Grace College, IN (MW)

Graceland College, IA (MW)

Grambling State University, LA (MW)

Grand Canyon College, AZ (MW)

Grand Rapids Baptist Seminary of Cornerstone University, MI (MW)

Grand Rapids Community College, MI (MW)

Grand Valley State College, MI (MW)

Grand View College, IA (MW)

Grays Harbor College, WA (MW)

Grayson County College, TX (MW)

Greenfield Community College, MA (MW)

Green Mountain College, VT (MW)

Green River Community College, WA (MW)

Greensboro College, NC (MW)

Greenville College, IL (MW)

Grinnell College, IA (MW)

Grove City College, PA (MW)

Gulf Coast Community College, FL (MW)

Gustavus Adolphus College, MN (MW)

Hagerstown Junior College, MD (MW)

Hamilton College, NY (MW)

Hamline University, MN (MW)

Hampden-Sydney College, VA (M)

Hampton University, VA (MW)

Hannibal-Lagrange College, MO (M)

Hanover College, IN (MW)

Harding University, AR (MW)

Hardin-Simmons University, TX (M)

Harford Community College, MD (MW)

Harris-Stowe State College, MO (MW)

Hartwick College, NY (MW)

Harvard University, MA (MW)

Haskell Indian Nations University, KS (MW)
Hastings College, NE (MW)
Haverford College, PA (MW)
Hawaii Pacific University, HI (M)
Heidelberg College, OH (MW)
Henderson State University, AR (MW)
Henry Ford Community College, MI (MW)
Herkimer County Community College, NY (MW)
Hesser College, NH (M)
Hibbing Community College, MN (MW)
Highland Community College, KS (MW)
Highland Park Community College, MI (MW)
High Point University, NC (MW)
Hilbert College, NY (MW)
Hillsborough Community College, FL (MW)
Hillsdale College, MI (MW)
Hinds Community College (Raymond), MS (MW)
Hinds Community College (Utica), MS (MW)
Hiram College, OH (MW)
Hiwassee College, TN (MW)
Hofstra University, NY (MW)
Holmes Junior College, MS (MW)
Holy Family College, PA (MW)
Hood College, MD (W)
Hope College, MI (MW)
Houghton College, NY (MW)
Houston Baptist University, TX (M)
Howard Payne University, TX (MW)
Howard University, DC (MW)
Hudson Valley Community College, NY (M)
Humboldt State University, CA (MW)
Hunter College of the City University of New York, NY (MW)
Huntingdon College, AL (MW)
Huntington College, IN (MW)
Huron University, SD (MW)
Husson College, ME (MW)
Huston-Tillotson College, TX (MW)
Hutchinson College, KS (MW)
Idaho State University, ID (MW)
Illinois Central College, IL (MW)
Illinois College, IL (MW)

Illinois Institute of Technology, IL (MW)
Illinois State University, IL (MW)
Illinois Valley Community College, IL (MW)
Illinois Wesleyan University, IL (MW)
Indiana Institute of Technology, IN (MW)
Indiana State University, IN (MW)
Indiana University, IN (MW)
Indiana University of Pennsylvania, PA (MW)
Indiana University-Purdue University, IN (MW)
Indiana University-Purdue University (Fort Wayne), IN (MW)
Indiana University (South Bend), IN (MW)
Indiana University Southeast, IN (MW)
Indiana Wesleyan University, IN (MW)
Indian Hills Community College, IA (M)
Indian River Community College, FL (MW)
Inver Hills Community College, MN (MW)
Iona College, NY (MW)
Iowa State University of Science and Technology, IA (MW)
Iowa Wesleyan College, IA (MW)
Itawamba Community College, MS (MW)
Ithaca College, NY (MW)
Jackson State Community College, TN (MW)
Jackson State University, MS (MW)
Jacksonville College, TX (M)
Jacksonville State University, AL (MW)
Jacksonville University, FL (MW)
James Madison University, VA (MW)
Jamestown College, ND (MW)
Jefferson College, MO (W)
Jefferson Community College, NY (MW)
Jefferson Davis Junior College, AL (MW)
John Brown University, AR (MW)
John Carroll University, OH (MW)
John C. Calhoun Community College, AL (MW)

Johns Hopkins University, MD (MW)
Johnson County Community College, KS (MW)
Johnson C. Smith University, NC (MW)
Johnson State College, VT (MW)
Jones County Junior College, MS (MW)
Judson College, AL (W)
Junianta College, PA (MW)
Kalamazoo College, MI (MW)
Kalamazoo Valley Community College, MI (MW)
Kankakee Community College, IL (MW)
Kansas City Kansas Community College, KS (MW)
Kansas Newman University, KS (MW)
Kansas State University, KS (MW)
Kansas Wesleyan College, KS (MW)
Kaskaskia Community College, IL (MW)
Kean University, NJ (MW)
Keene State College, NH (MW)
Kemper Military School and College, MO (M)
Kennesaw State College, GA (MW)
Kent State University (Ashtabula), OH (MW)
Kent State University (East Liverpool), OH (MW)
Kent State University (Kent), OH (MW)
Kent State University (New Philadelphia), OH (MW)
Kent State University (Warren), OH (MW)
Kentucky Christian College, KY (MW)
Kentucky State University, KY (MW)
Kentucky Wesleyan College, KY (MW)
Kenyon College, OH (MW)
Keystone Junior College, PA (MW)
Kilgore College, TX (MW)
King College, TN (MW)
King's College, PA (MW)
Kirkwood Community College, IA (MW)
Kishwaukee College, IL (MW)
Knox College, IL (MW)
Kutztown University, PA (MW)
Labette Community College, KS (MW)

Lackawanna Junior College, PA (MW)
Lafayette College, PA (MW)
Lake Erie College, OH (MW)
Lake Forest College, IL (MW)
Lake Land College, IL (MW)
Lake Michigan College, MI (MW)
Lake Region State College, ND (MW)
Lake Superior State University, MI (MW)
Lamar Community College, CO (M)
Lamar University, TX (MW)
Lambuth University, TN (W)
Lander College, SC (MW)
Lane Community College, OR (MW)
Langston University, OK (MW)
Lansing Community College, MI (MW)
La Roche College, PA (MW)
La Salle University, PA (MW)
Lawrence University, WI (MW)
Lebanon Valley College, PA (MW)
Lee College, TN (MW)
Lee College, TX (M)
Lees Junior College, KY (M)
Lees-McRae College, NC (MW)
Lehigh County Community College, PA (M)
Lehigh University, PA (MW)
Le Moyne College, NY (MW)
LeMoyne-Owen College, TN (MW)
Lenoir Community College, NC (M)
Lenoir-Rhyne College, NC (MW)
LeTourneau College, TX (MW)
Lewis and Clark College, OR (MW)
Lewis and Clark Community College, IL (MW)
Lewis/Clark State College, ID (MW)
Lewis University, IL (MW)
Liberty University, VA (MW)
Limestone College, SC (MW)
Lincoln Christian College, IL (MW)
Lincoln College, IL (MW)
Lincoln Land Community College, IL (MW)
Lincoln Memorial University, TN (MW)
Lincoln Trail College, IL (MW)
Lincoln University, MO (MW)
Lindenwood College, MO (MW)

Linfield College, OR (MW)
Livingstone College, NC (MW)
Lock Haven University of Pennsylvania, PA (MW)
Long Beach City College, CA (MW)
Long Island University (Brooklyn), NY (MW)
Long Island University (C.W. Post Campus), NY (MW)
Long Island University (Southampton Campus), NY (MW)
Longwood College, VA (MW)
Loras College, IA (MW)
Los Angeles Pierce Junior College, CA (W)
Los Angeles Valley College, CA (MW)
Los Medanos College, CA (MW)
Louisburg College, NC (MW)
Louisiana College, LA (MW)
Louisiana State University (Baton Rouge), LA (MW)
Louisiana State University (Eunice), LA (W)
Louisiana Tech University, LA (MW)
Lower Columbia College, WA (MW)
Loyola College, MD (MW)
Loyola Marymount University, CA (MW)
Loyola University, IL (MW)
Lubbock Christian College, TX (MW)
Luther College, IA (MW)
Lycoming College, PA (MW)
Lynchburg College, VA (MW)
Lyndon State College, VT (MW)
Macalester College, MN (MW)
Macomb Community College, MI (M)
Madison Area Technical College, WI (MW)
Madonna University, MI (MW)
Malone College, OH (MW)
Manchester College, IN (MW)
Manchester Community Technical College, CT (M)
Manhattan College, NY (MW)
Manhattanville College, NY (MW)
Mankato State University, MN (MW)
Mansfield University, PA (MW)
Marian College, IN (MW)
Marian College, WI (MW)
Marietta College, OH (MW)
Marist College, NY (MW)
Marquette University, WI (MW)
Marshall University, WV (MW)

Mars Hill College, NC (MW)
Mary Baldwin College, VA (W)
Marycrest College, IA (MW)
Marycrest International University, IA (MW)
Mary Holmes College, MS (MW)
Marymount University, VA (MW)
Maryville College, TN (MW)
Maryville University, MO (MW)
Mary Washington College, VA (MW)
Marywood College, PA (MW)
Massachusetts Bay Community College, MA (MW)
Massachusetts College of Liberal Arts, MA (MW)
Massachusetts Institute of Technology, MA (MW)
Massasoit Community College, MA (M)
Master's College, CA (MW)
Mayville State College, ND (MW)
McCook Community College, NE (MW)
McHenry County College, IL (MW)
McKendree College, IL (MW)
McLennan Community College, TX (MW)
McNeese State University, LA (MW)
McPherson College, KS (MW)
Mercer County Community College, NJ (MW)
Mercer University, GA (MW)
Mercy College, NY (MW)
Mercyhurst College, PA (MW)
Merrimack College, MA (W)
Mesa Community College, AZ (MW)
Mesa State College, CO (MW)
Messiah College, PA (MW)
Metropolitan State College, CO (MW)
Miami-Dade Community College (North), FL (MW)
Miami-Dade Community College (South), FL (MW)
Miami University, OH (MW)
Michigan State University, MI (MW)
Michigan Technological University, MI (MW)
Mid-America Nazarene College, KS (MW)
Middle Tennessee State University, TN (MW)
Middlebury College, VT (MW)

Middlesex County College, NJ
(MW)
Midland College, TX (MW)
Midland Lutheran College, NE
(MW)
Mid-Plains Community College,
NE (MW)
Midwestern State University, TX
(MW)
Miles College, AL (MW)
Miles Community College, MT
(MW)
Millersville University, PA (MW)
Milligan College, TN (MW)
Millikin University, IL (MW)
Milwaukee Area Technology Col-
lege, WI (MW)
Mineral Area College, MO (MW)
Minneapolis Community &
Technical College, MN (M)
Minot State University, ND
(MW)
Minot State University (Bot-
tineau), ND (MW)
MiraCosta College, CA (M)
Mississippi College, MS (MW)
Mississippi Delta Junior College,
MS (MW)
Mississippi Gulf Coast Junior
College, MS (MW)
Mississippi State University, MS
(MW)
Mississippi University for
Women, MS (W)
Mississippi Valley State Univer-
sity, MS (MW)
Missouri Baptist College, MO
(MW)
Missouri Southern State College,
MO (MW)
Missouri Valley College, MO
(MW)
Missouri Western State College,
MO (MW)
Mitchell College, CT (MW)
Mitchell Community College,
NC (M)
Modesto Junior College, CA
(MW)
Mohawk Valley Community Col-
lege, NY (MW)
Molloy College, NY (MW)
Monmouth College, IL (MW)
Monmouth College, NJ (MW)
Montana College of Mineral Sci-
ence and Technology, MT
(MW)
Montana State University, MT
(MW)
Montclair State College, NJ
(MW)

Montgomery College, MD (M)
Montreat-Anderson College, NC
(MW)
Moody Bible Institute, IL
(MW)
Moorhead State University, MN
(MW)
Moorpark College, CA (MW)
Moraine Valley Community Col-
lege, IL (MW)
Moravian College, PA (MW)
Morehead State University, KY
(MW)
Morehouse College, GA (M)
Morgan State University, MD
(MW)
Morningside College, IA (MW)
Morris Brown College, GA
(MW)
Morton College, IL (MW)
Motlow State Community Col-
lege, TN (MW)
Mott Community College, MI
(MW)
Mount Holyoke College, MA
(W)
Mount Marty College, SD
(MW)
Mount Mercy College, IA (MW)
Mount Olive College, NC (MW)
Mount St. Mary College, MD
(MW)
Mount Union College, OH (M)
Mount Vernon Nazarene College,
OH (MW)
Mt. Aloysius College, PA (MW)
Mt. San Antonio College, CA
(MW)
Mt. Wachusett Community Col-
lege, MA (MW)
Muhlenberg College, PA (MW)
Multnomah Bible College, OR
(MW)
Murray State University, KY
(MW)
Muskegon Community College,
MI (MW)
Muskingum College, OH (MW)
Nassau Community College, NY
(MW)
National-Louis University, IL
(W)
Navarro College, TX (M)
Nazareth College, NY (MW)
Nebraska Wesleyan University,
NE (MW)
Newberry College, SC (MW)
New Hampshire College, NH
(MW)
New Jersey Institute of Technol-
ogy, NJ (M)

New Mexico Highlands Univer-
sity, NM (MW)
New Mexico Junior College, NM
(MW)
New Mexico State University,
NM (MW)
New York Institute of Technol-
ogy, NY (M)
New York University, NY (MW)
Niagara County Community
College, NY (MW)
Niagara University, NY (MW)
Nicholls State University, LA
(MW)
Nichols College, MA (MW)
Norfolk State University, VA
(MW)
North Arkansas College, AR
(MW)
North Carolina A & T State Uni-
versity, NC (MW)
North Carolina Central Univer-
sity, NC (MW)
North Carolina State University,
NC (MW)
North Carolina Wesleyan Col-
lege, NC (MW)
North Central College, IL (MW)
North Country Community Col-
lege, NY (MW)
North Dakota State, ND (MW)
North Dakota State University,
ND (MW)
Northeastern Illinois University,
IL (MW)
Northeastern Junior College, CO
(MW)
Northeastern State University,
OK (MW)
Northeast Louisiana University,
LA (MW)
Northeast Mississippi Commu-
nity College, MS (MW)
Northeast Missouri State Univer-
sity, MO (MW)
Northern Arizona University, AZ
(MW)
Northern Illinois University, IL
(MW)
Northern Kentucky University,
KY (MW)
Northern Michigan University,
MI (MW)
Northern Montana College, MT
(MW)
Northern State University, SD
(MW)
North Florida Junior College, FL
(W)
North Georgia College & State
University, GA (MW)

North Greenville College, SC (MW)
North Idaho College, ID (MW)
North Iowa Area Community College, IA (MW)
Northland College, WI (MW)
Northland Community College, MN (MW)
Northwest Shoals Community College, AL (MW)
Northwest College, WY (MW)
Northwestern College, IA (MW)
Northwestern College, MN (MW)
Northwestern Oklahoma State University, OK (MW)
Northwestern State University of Louisiana, LA (MW)
Northwestern University, IL (MW)
Northwest Mississippi Community College, MS (MW)
Northwest Missouri State University, MO (MW)
Northwest Nazarene University, ID (MW)
Northwood Institute, MI (MW)
Norwich University, VT (MW)
Notre Dame College of Ohio, OH (W)
Nova Southern University, FL (M)
Nyack College, NY (MW)
Oakland City University, IN (MW)
Oakland Community College, MI (MW)
Oakland University, MI (MW)
Oakton Community College, IL (MW)
Oberlin College, OH (MW)
Occidental College, CA (MW)
Ocean County College, NJ (MW)
Odessa College, TX (MW)
Oglethorpe University, GA (MW)
Ohio Dominican College, OH (MW)
Ohio Northern University, OH (MW)
Ohio State University, OH (MW)
Ohio University, OH (MW)
Ohio Valley College, WV (MW)
Ohio Wesleyan University, OH (MW)
Oklahoma Baptist University, OK (MW)
Oklahoma Christian University of Science & Art, OK (MW)

Oklahoma City University, OK (MW)
Oklahoma Panhandle State University, OK (MW)
Oklahoma State University, OK (MW)
Old Dominion University, VA (MW)
Olivet College, MI (MW)
Olivet Nazarene University, IL (MW)
Olney Central College, IL (MW)
Olympic College, WA (MW)
Oral Roberts University, OK (MW)
Orange Coast College, CA (MW)
Orange County Community College, NY (MW)
Oregon Institute of Technology, OR (MW)
Oregon State University, OR (MW)
Oswego State University (SUNY), NY (MW)
Otero Junior College, CO (MW)
Ottawa University, KS (MW)
Otterbein College, OH (MW)
Ouachita Baptist University, AR (MW)
Oxnard College, CA (MW)
Pace University, NY (MW)
Pacific Lutheran University, WA (MW)
Pacific University, OR (MW)
Paducah Community College, CA (MW)
Paine College, GA (MW)
Palm Beach Atlantic College, FL (M)
Palm Beach Community College, FL (MW)
Palomar College, CA (MW)
Panola Junior College, TX (MW)
Paris Junior College, TX (MW)
Park College, MO (MW)
Parkland College, IL (MW)
Passaic County Community College, NJ (MW)
Penn State Abington College, PA (MW)
Penn State Berk-Leigh Valley College, PA (MW)
Pennsylvania State University, PA (MW)
Penn State (Behrend College), PA (MW)
Penn Valley Community College, MO (M)
Pensacola Junior College, FL (MW)

Pepperdine University, CA (MW)
Peru State College, NE (MW)
Pfeiffer College, NC (MW)
Philadelphia University, PA (MW)
Phillips University, OK (MW)
Phoenix College, AZ (MW)
Piedmont College, GA (MW)
Pierce College, WA (MW)
Pikeville College, KY (MW)
Pima Community College (West Campus), AZ (MW)
Pittsburg State University, KS (MW)
Plattsburgh State University (SUNY), NY (MW)
Plymouth State College, NH (MW)
Point Loma Nazarene College, CA (MW)
Point Park College, PA (MW)
Polk Community College, FL (MW)
Polytechnic University (Brooklyn Campus), NY (M)
Pomona-Pitzer Colleges, CA (MW)
Pontifical Catholic University of Puerto Rico, PR (MW)
Portland State University, OR (W)
Prairie View A&M University, TX (MW)
Pratt Community College, KS (MW)
Presbyterian College, SC (MW)
Prince George's Community College, MD (MW)
Princeton University, NJ (MW)
Principia College, IL (MW)
Providence College, RI (MW)
Purchase College (SUNY), NY (MW)
Purdue University, IN (MW)
Purdue University (Calumet), IN (MW)
Queensborough Community College, NY (MW)
Queens College, NY (MW)
Queens College, NC (MW)
Quincy University, IL (MW)
Quinnipiac University, CT (MW)
Quinsigamond College, MA (MW)
Radford University, VA (MW)
Rainy River Community College, MN (MW)
Ramapo College, NJ (MW)
Randolph-Macon College, VA (MW)

Ranetto Santiago College, CA (MW)
Regis College, MA (W)
Regis University, CO (MW)
Rend Lake, IL (MW)
Rensselaer Polytechnic Institute, NY (MW)
Rhode Island College, RI (MW)
Rice University, TX (MW)
Ricks College, ID (MW)
Rider College, NJ (MW)
Ripon College, WI (MW)
Riverland Community College, MN (MW)
Riverside Community College, CA (MW)
Roane State Community College, TN (MW)
Roanoke College, VA (MW)
Robert Morris College, PA (MW)
Roberts Wesleyan College, NY (MW)
Rochester College, MI (MW)
Rochester Community College, MN (MW)
Rochester Institute of Technology, NY (M)
Rockhurst College, MO (MW)
Rockland Community College, NY (MW)
Rocky Mountain College, MT (MW)
Rollins College, FL (MW)
Roosevelt University, IL (M)
Rose-Hulman Institute of Technology, IN (MW)
Rose State Junior College, OK (MW)
Rowan University, NJ (MW)
Rust College, MS (MW)
Rutgers, Newark College of Arts and Sciences, NJ (MW)
Sacred Heart University, CT (MW)
Saddleback College, CA (MW)
Sage Junior College of Albany, NY (MW)
Saginaw Valley State University, MI (MW)
Saint Ambrose University, IA (MW)
Saint Andrews Presbyterian College, NC (MW)
Saint Anselm College, NH (MW)
Saint Augustine's College, NC (MW)
Saint Bonaventure University, NY (MW)
Saint Cloud State University, MN (MW)

Saint Edward's University, TX (MW)
Saint Francis College, IN (MW)
Saint Francis College, NY (MW)
Saint Francis College, PA (MW)
Saint John Fisher College, NY (MW)
Saint John's University, MN (M)
Saint John's University, NY (MW)
Saint Joseph's College, IN (MW)
Saint Joseph's University, PA (MW)
Saint Lawrence University, NY (MW)
Saint Leo University, FL (MW)
Saint Louis University, MO (MW)
Saint Martin's College, WA (MW)
Saint Mary College, KS (M)
Saint Mary's College, IN (W)
Saint Mary's College, MI (W)
Saint Mary's College of California, CA (MW)
Saint Mary's University, TX (MW)
Saint Michael's College, VT (MW)
Saint Norbert College, WI (MW)
Saint Olaf College, MN (MW)
Saint Paul's College, VA (MW)
Saint Peter's College, NJ (MW)
Saint Thomas Aquinas College, NY (MW)
Saint Vincent College, PA (MW)
Saint Xavier University, IL (M)
Salem State College, MA (MW)
Salem-Teikyo University, WV (MW)
Salve Regina College, RI (MW)
Samford University, AL (MW)
Sam Houston State University, TX (MW)
San Bernardino Community College, CA (MW)
San Diego City College, CA (M)
San Diego Mesa College, CA (MW)
San Diego State University, CA (MW)
San Francisco State University, CA (MW)
San Joaquin Delta College, CA (MW)
San Jose State University, CA (MW)
Santa Barbara City College, CA (MW)
Santa Clara University, CA (MW)

Santa Fe Community College, FL (MW)
Santa Monica College, CA (MW)
Santa Rosa Junior College, CA (MW)
Sauk Valley College, IL (MW)
Savannah State College, GA (MW)
Schoolcraft College, MI (MW)
Schreiner College, TX (MW)
Scottsdale Community College, AZ (MW)
Seattle Pacific University, WA (MW)
Seattle University, WA (MW)
Selma University, AL (M)
Seminole Community College, FL (MW)
Seminole Junior College, OK (MW)
Seton Hall University, NJ (MW)
Seton Hill College, PA (W)
Seward County Community College, KS (MW)
Shawnee State College, OH (MW)
Shelby State Community College, TN (MW)
Sheldon Jackson College, AK (MW)
Shepherd College, WV (MW)
Sheridan College, WY (MW)
Shippensburg University of Pennsylvania, PA (MW)
Shoreline Community College, WA (MW)
Shorter College, GA (MW)
Siena College, NY (MW)
Siena Heights College, MI (MW)
Sierra College, CA (MW)
Simpson College, CA (MW)
Sinclair Community College, OH (MW)
Sioux Falls College, SD (MW)
Skagit Valley College, WA (MW)
Skidmore College, NY (MW)
Skyline College, CA (MW)
Slippery Rock University of Pennsylvania, PA (MW)
Snead State Community College, AL (MW)
Snow College, UT (MW)
Solano Community College, CA (MW)
South Carolina State College, SC (MW)
South Dakota School of Mines and Technology, SD (MW)
South Dakota State University, SD (MW)

Southeast Community College, NE (MW)

Southeastern Community College, IA (M)

Southeastern Illinois College, IL (MW)

Southeastern Louisiana University, LA (MW)

Southeastern Oklahoma State University, OK (MW)

Southeast Missouri State University, MO (MW)

Southern Arkansas University, AR (MW)

Southern California College, CA (MW)

Southern Connecticut State University, CT (MW)

Southern Illinois University, IL (MW)

Southern Illinois University (Edwardsville), IL (MW)

Southern Methodist University, TX (MW)

Southern Nazarene University, OK (MW)

Southern Oregon State College, OR (MW)

Southern Polytechnic State University, GA (M)

Southern Union State Community College, AL (MW)

Southern University and A&M College, LA (MW)

Southern Utah University, UT (MW)

Southern Wesleyan University, SC (MW)

South Florida Community College, FL (M)

South Plains Community College, TX (MW)

Southwest Baptist University, MO (MW)

Southwestern College, CA (MW)

Southwestern College, KS (MW)

Southwestern Oklahoma State University, OK (MW)

Southwestern Oregon Community College, OR (MW)

Southwestern University, TX (MW)

Southwest Missouri State University, MO (MW)

Southwest State University, MN (MW)

Southwest Texas State University, TX (MW)

Spartanburg Methodist, SC (MW)

Spokane Community College, WA (MW)

Spoon River College, IL (MW)

Spring Arbor College, MI (MW)

Springfield College, MA (MW)

Springfield Technical Community College, MA (MW)

Spring Hill College, AL (MW)

Stanford University, CA (MW)

State Fair Community College, MO (MW)

State University of New York College (Brockport), NY (MW)

State University of New York College (Cortland), NY (MW)

State University of New York College (Fredonia), NY (MW)

State University of New York College (Geneseo), NY (MW)

State University of New York College (New Paltz), NY (MW)

State University of New York College (Potsdam), NY (MW)

State University of New York Institute of Technology at Utica/Rome, NY (MW)

State University of New York Maritime College, NY (MW)

State University of West Georgia, GA (MW)

St. Catherine College, KY (MW)

Stephen F. Austin State University, TX (MW)

Sterling College, KS (MW)

Stetson University, FL (MW)

Stevens Institute of Technology, NJ (M)

St. Gregory's College, OK (MW)

St. Johns River Community College, FL (M)

St. Louis Community College (Florissant Valley), MO (M)

St. Louis Community College (Forest Park), MO (M)

St. Mary of the Plains College, KS (MW)

Stonehill College, MA (MW)

St. Petersburg Junior College, FL (MW)

St. Philip's College, TX (M)

Suffolk County Community College, NY (MW)

Suffolk University, MA (MW)

Sul Ross State University, TX (MW)

Swarthmore College, PA (MW)

Sweet Briar College, VA (W)

Syracuse University, NY (MW)

Tabor College, KS (MW)

Talledaga College, AL (MW)

Tarleton State University, TX (MW)

Teikyo Post University, CT (MW)

Teikyo Westmar University, IA (MW)

Temple Baptist Seminary, TN (MW)

Temple Junior College, TX (MW)

Temple University, PA (MW)

Tennessee State University, TN (MW)

Tennessee Technological University, TN (MW)

Tennessee Wesleyan College, TN (MW)

Texas A&I University, TX (MW)

Texas A&M Commerce, TX (MW)

Texas A&M University, TX (MW)

Texas Christian University, TX (MW)

Texas Lutheran College, TX (MW)

Texas Southern University, TX (MW)

Texas Tech University, TX (MW)

Texas Wesleyan College, TX (MW)

Texas Woman's University, TX (W)

Thomas College, ME (MW)

Thomas More College, KY (MW)

Three Rivers Community College, MO (MW)

Tiffin University, OH (MW)

Toccoa Falls College, GA (MW)

Tougaloo College, MS (MW)

Towson State University, MD (MW)

Transylvania University, KY (MW)

Trevecca Nazarene College, TN (MW)

Trinidad State Junior College, CO (M)

Trinity Christian College, IL (MW)

Trinity College of Arts & Sciences, IL (MW)

Trinity University, TX (MW)

Tri-State University, IN (MW)

Triton College, IL (MW)

Troy State University, AL (MW)

Truett-McConnell Junior College, GA (MW)

Tufts University, MA (MW)

Tulane University, LA (W)
Tusculum College, TN (MW)
Tuskegee University, AL (MW)
Tyler Junior College, TX (MW)
Umpqua College, OR (MW)
Union College, KY (MW)
Union College, NY (MW)
Union County College, NJ (MW)
Union University, TN (MW)
Unity College, ME (MW)
University of Akron, OH (MW)
University of Alabama (Birmingham), AL (MW)
University of Alabama (Huntsville), AL (MW)
University of Alabama (Tuscaloosa), AL (MW)
University of Alaska, AK (MW)
University of Alaska (Fairbanks), AK (MW)
University of Alaska Southeast, AK (MW)
University at Albany (SUNY), NY (MW)
University of Arizona, AZ (MW)
University of Arkansas (Fayetteville), AR (MW)
University of Arkansas (Little Rock), AR (M)
University of Arkansas (Monticello), AR (MW)
University of Arkansas (Pine Bluff), AR (MW)
University of Bridgeport, CT (MW)
University at Buffalo (SUNY), NY (MW)
University of California (Berkeley), CA (MW)
University of California (Davis), CA (MW)
University of California (Irvine), CA (MW)
University of California (Riverside), CA (MW)
University of California (San Diego), CA (MW)
University of California (Santa Barbara), CA (MW)
University of California (Santa Cruz), CA (MW)
University of California (UCLA), CA (MW)
University of Central Arkansas, AR (MW)
University of Central Florida, FL (MW)
University of Central Oklahoma, OK (MW)

University of Charleston, WV (MW)
University of Chicago, IL (MW)
University of Cincinnati, OH (MW)
University of Colorado, CO (MW)
University of Colorado (Colorado Springs), CO (MW)
University of Connecticut, CT (MW)
University of Dallas, TX (MW)
University of Dayton, OH (MW)
University of Delaware, DE (MW)
University of Denver, CO (MW)
University of Detroit Mercy, MI (MW)
University of Dubuque, IA (MW)
University of Evansville, IN (MW)
University of Findlay, OH (MW)
University of Florida, FL (MW)
University of Georgia, GA (M)
University of Guam, PA (MW)
University of Hartford, CT (MW)
University of Hawaii (Hilo), HI (M)
University of Hawaii (Manoa), HI (MW)
University of Houston, TX (MW)
University of Idaho, ID (MW)
University of Illinois (Chicago), IL (MW)
University of Illinois (Urbana-Champaign), IL (MW)
University of Incarnate Word, TX (MW)
University of Indianapolis, IN (MW)
University of Iowa, IA (MW)
University of Kansas, KS (MW)
University of Kentucky, KY (MW)
University of La Verne, CA (MW)
University of Louisiana at Lafayette, LA (MW)
University of Louisville, KY (MW)
University of Maine, ME (MW)
University of Maine (Fort Kent), ME (MW)
University of Maine (Machias), ME (MW)
University of Maine (Presque Isle), ME (MW)
University of Mary, ND (MW)
University of Mary Hardin-Baylor, TX (MW)

University of Maryland, MD (MW)
University of Maryland (Baltimore County), MD (MW)
University of Maryland (Eastern Shore), MD (MW)
University of Massachusetts (Amherst), MA (MW)
University of Massachusetts (Boston), MA (MW)
University of Massachusetts (Dartmouth), MA (MW)
University of Massachusetts (Lowell), MA (MW)
University of Memphis, TN (MW)
University of Miami, FL (MW)
University of Michigan, MI (MW)
University of Minnesota (Duluth), MN (MW)
University of Minnesota (Minneapolis), MN (MW)
University of Minnesota (Morris), MN (MW)
University of Mississippi, MS (MW)
University of Missouri, MO (M)
University of Missouri (Columbia), MO (MW)
University of Missouri (Kansas City), MO (MW)
University of Missouri (Rolla), MO (MW)
University of Mobile, AL (MW)
University of Montana, MT (MW)
University of Montevallo, AL (MW)
University of Nebraska, NE (M)
University of Nebraska (Kearney), NE (MW)
University of Nebraska (Lincoln), NE (MW)
University of Nevada, NV (M)
University of Nevada (Reno), NV (MW)
University of New England, ME (MW)
University of New Hampshire, NH (MW)
University of New Haven, CT (MW)
University of New Mexico, NM (MW)
University of New Orleans, LA (MW)
University of North Alabama, AL (MW)
University of North Carolina (Asheville), NC (MW)

University of North Carolina (Chapel Hill), NC (MW)
University of North Carolina (Charlotte), NC (MW)
University of North Carolina (Greensboro), NC (MW)
University of North Carolina (Pembroke), NC (MW)
University of North Carolina (Wilmington), NC (MW)
University of North Dakota, ND (MW)
University of North Florida, FL (MW)
University of Northern Colorado, CO (MW)
University of Northern Iowa, IA (MW)
University of North Texas, TX (MW)
University of Notre Dame, IN (MW)
University of Oklahoma, OK (MW)
University of Oregon, OR (MW)
University of Pennsylvania, PA (MW)
University of Pittsburgh, PA (MW)
University of Pittsburgh (Bradford), PA (MW)
University of Pittsburgh (Johnstown), PA (MW)
University of Portland, OR (MW)
University of Puerto Rico, PR (MW)
University of Puerto Rico (Bayamon), PR (MW)
University of Puerto Rico (Ponce), PR (MW)
University of Puget Sound, WA (MW)
University of Redlands, CA (MW)
University of Rhode Island, RI (MW)
University of Richmond, VA (MW)
University of Rio Grande, OH (MW)
University of San Diego, CA (MW)
University of San Francisco, CA (MW)
University of Scranton, PA (MW)
University of South Alabama, AL (MW)
University of South Carolina (Aiken), SC (MW)

University of South Carolina (Columbia), SC (MW)
University of South Carolina (Myrtle Beach), SC (MW)
University of South Carolina (Spartanburg), SC (MW)
University of South Dakota, SD (MW)
University of Southern California, CA (MW)
University of Southern Colorado, CO (MW)
University of Southern Indiana, IN (MW)
University of Southern Mississippi, MS (MW)
University of South Florida, FL (MW)
University of St. Thomas, MN (MW)
University at Stony Brook (SUNY), NY (MW)
University of Tampa, FL (MW)
University of Tennessee, TN (MW)
University of Tennessee (Knoxville), TN (MW)
University of Tennessee (Martin), TN (MW)
University of Texas (Arlington), TX (MW)
University of Texas (Austin), TX (MW)
University of Texas (El Paso), TX (MW)
University of Texas (Pan American), TX (MW)
University of Texas (San Antonio), TX (MW)
University of the District of Columbia, DC (MW)
University of the Pacific, CA (MW)
University of Toledo, OH (MW)
University of Tulsa, OK (M)
University of Utah, UT (MW)
University of Vermont, VT (MW)
University of Virginia, VA (MW)
The University of Virginia's College at Wise, VA (MW)
University of Washington, WA (MW)
University of West Alabama, AL (MW)
University of West Florida, FL (MW)
University of Wisconsin (Eau Claire), WI (MW)
University of Wisconsin (Green Bay), WI (MW)

University of Wisconsin (La Crosse), WI (MW)
University of Wisconsin (Madison), WI (MW)
University of Wisconsin (Milwaukee), WI (MW)
University of Wisconsin (Oshkosh), WI (MW)
University of Wisconsin (Platteville), WI (MW)
University of Wisconsin (River Falls), WI (MW)
University of Wisconsin (Stevens Point), WI (MW)
University of Wisconsin (Stout), WI (MW)
University of Wisconsin (Superior), WI (MW)
University of Wyoming, WY (MW)
Upper Iowa University, IA (MW)
Urbana University, OH (MW)
Ursinus College, PA (MW)
U.S. International University, CA (MW)
Utah State University, UT (MW)
Valdosta State University, GA (MW)
Valley City State University, ND (MW)
Valley Forge Christian College, PA (MW)
Valparaiso University, IN (MW)
Vanderbilt University, TN (MW)
Vassar College, NY (MW)
Ventura College, CA (MW)
Villanova University, PA (MW)
Vincennes University, IN (MW)
Virginia Commonwealth University, VA (MW)
Virginia Intermont College, VA (MW)
Virginia Military Institute, VA (M)
Virginia Polytechnic Institute & State University, VA (MW)
Virginia State University, VA (MW)
Virginia Union University, VA (MW)
Virginia Wesleyan College, VA (MW)
Viterbo College, WI (MW)
Wabash College, IN (M)
Wabash Valley College, IL (MW)
Wagner College, NY (MW)
Wake Forest University, NC (MW)
Waldorf College, IA (MW)
Wallace Community College (Selma), AL (M)

Wallace State Community College, AL (MW)
Walla Walla Community College, WA (MW)
Walsh College, OH (MW)
Walters State Community College, TN (MW)
Warner Pacific College, OR (MW)
Warner Southern College, FL (MW)
Warren Wilson College, NC (MW)
Wartburg College, IA (MW)
Washburn University, KS (MW)
Washington and Jefferson College, PA (MW)
Washington College, MD (MW)
Washington State University, WA (MW)
Washington University, MO (MW)
Waubonsee College, IL (MW)
Wayland Baptist University, TX (MW)
Wayne State College, NE (MW)
Wayne State University, MI (MW)
Webber College, FL (MW)
Weber State College, UT (MW)
Webster University, MO (MW)
Wellesley College, MA (MW)
Wentworth Military Academy and Junior College, MO (M)
Wesleyan University, CT (MW)
Wesley College, DE (MW)
Westark Community College, AR (MW)
West Chester University, PA (MW)
Western Carolina University, NC (MW)
Western Connecticut State University, CT (MW)
Western Illinois University, IL (MW)
Western Kentucky University, KY (MW)
Western Maryland College, MD (MW)
Western Michigan University, MI (MW)
Western Montana College, MT (MW)
Western Nebraska Community College, NE (MW)
Western New England College, MA (MW)
Western New Mexico University, NM (MW)
Western Oregon State College, OR (MW)

Western State College, CO (MW)
Western Texas College, TX (MW)
Western Washington University, WA (MW)
Western Wyoming Community College, WY (MW)
Westfield State College, MA (MW)
West Liberty State College, WV (MW)
Westminster College, PA (MW)
Westmont College, CA (MW)
West Texas State University, TX (MW)
West Virginia Institute of Technology, WV (M)
West Virginia State College, WV (MW)
West Virginia University, WV (MW)
West Virginia Wesleyan College, WV (MW)
Wheaton College, IL (MW)
Wheeling Jesuit College, WV (MW)
Whitman College, WA (MW)
Whittier College, CA (MW)
Whitworth College, WA (M)
Wichita State University, KS (MW)
Wilberforce University, OH (M)
Wilkes College, NC (MW)
Wilkes University, PA (MW)
Willamette University, OR (MW)
William Jewell College, MO (MW)
William Patterson College, NJ (MW)
William Penn College, IA (MW)
William Rainey Harper College, IL (MW)
Williams College, MA (MW)
Williamson Trade School, PA (M)
William Woods College, MO (W)
Wilmington College, DE (MW)
Wilmington College, OH (MW)
Wingate College, NC (MW)
Winona State University, MN (MW)
Winston-Salem State University, NC (MW)
Winthrop University, SC (MW)
Wofford College, SC (MW)
Worcester State College, MA (MW)
Worthington Community College, MN (MW)

Wright State University, OH (MW)
Xavier University, OH (MW)
Xavier University of Louisiana, LA (MW)
Yakima Valley College, WA (MW)
Yale University, CT (MW)
Yavapai College, AZ (MW)
Yeshiva University, NY (MW)
York College (CUNY), NY (MW)
York College of Pennsylvania, PA (MW)
Youngstown State University, OH (MW)
Yuba Community College, CA (M)

Bowling

Adirondack College, NY (MW)
Alabama State University, AL (W)
Bayamon Central University, PR (MW)
Bluefield College, VA (M)
Broward Community College, FL (MW)
Cheyney University of Pennsylvania, PA (W)
Cleveland State University, OH (M)
College of Allegheny County, PA (MW)
Concordia University, MN (M)
Concordia Seminary, MO (MW)
Delaware State University, DE (W)
Dutchess Community College, NY (M)
Essex Community College, MD (MW)
Fashion Institute of Technology, NY (MW)
Florida A&M University, FL (MW)
Grambling State University, LA (W)
Herkimer County Community College, NY (MW)
Howard University, DC (W)
Hudson Valley Community College, NY (MW)
Madison Area Technical College, WI (MW)
Maple Woods Community College, MO (M)
Mississippi State University, MS (MW)
Mohawk Valley Community College, NY (MW)

Morgan State University, MD (W)
Nassau Community College, NY (MW)
New Jersey Institute of Technology, NJ (M)
Pace University, NY (MW)
Prince George's Community College, MD (MW)
Queens College, NY (M)
Roosevelt University, IL (MW)
Sacred Heart University, CT (MW)
Saginaw Valley State University, MI (M)
Saint John's University, NY (MW)
Saint Peter's College, NJ (MW)
Snow College, UT (MW)
South Carolina State College, SC (W)
Temple Baptist Seminary, TN (M)
University of Arkansas (Pine Bluff), AR (W)
University of Wisconsin (La Crosse), WI (MW)
Vincennes University, IN (MW)
Western New England College, MA (MW)
Western Wyoming Community College, WY (MW)
Whitworth College, WA (W)
William Patterson College, NJ (MW)

Cheerleading

Aquinas College, MI (W)
Barstow College, CA (MW)
Benedictine University, IL (W)
Bluefield State College, WV (W)
Bridgewater College, VA (W)
Campbellsville University, KY (W)
Cardinal Stritch College, WI (MW)
Clinton Community College, IA (MW)
Cumberland College, KY (MW)
Defiance College, OH (MW)
Eastern Wyoming College, WY (MW)
Elmira College, NY (W)
Geneva College, PA (MW)
Grand Rapids Baptist Seminary of Cornerstone University, MI (W)
Heidelberg College, OH (W)
Houghton College, NY (W)
Hunter College of the City University of New York, NY (MW)

Indiana Wesleyan University, IN (W)
Jefferson Community College, NY (W)
Jefferson Davis Junior College, AL (MW)
John C. Calhoun Community College, AL (MW)
Lackawanna Junior College, PA (W)
Lebanon Valley College, PA (W)
Liberty University, VA (MW)
Lyndon State College, VT (W)
Marian College, IN (MW)
Mercer University, GA (W)
Missouri Southern State College, MO (W)
Mitchell College, CT (MW)
Morton College, IL (W)
Muskingum College, OH (W)
Northeastern State University, OK (MW)
North Greenville College, SC (MW)
Ohio Valley College, WV (W)
Oklahoma Panhandle State University, OK (W)
Palm Beach Atlantic College, FL (W)
Parkland College, IL (MW)
Penn State Berks-Lehigh Valley College, PA (MW)
Pratt Community College, KS (MW)
Quinnipiac University, CT (W)
Saint Ambrose University, IA (W)
Saint Leo University, FL (W)
Salem-Teikyo University, WV (W)
Snead State Community College, AL (MW)
St. John Fisher College, NY (W)
University of Hawaii (Manoa), HI (W)
University of Nebraska (Kearney), NE (MW)
University of Pittsburgh (Johnstown), PA (W)
University of Puerto Rico (Bayamon), PR (W)
University of Rio Grande, OH (MW)
Urbana University, OH (MW)
Waldorf College, IA (W)
Wallace Community College (Selma), AL (MW)
Wesley College, DE (W)
Western Washington University, WA (W)
York College (CUNY), NY (W)

Crew

Assumption College, MA (MW)
Barry University, FL (W)
Boston University, MA (MW)
Brown University, RI (MW)
Bucknell University, PA (MW)
California Maritime Academy, CA (M)
Carlow College, PA (W)
Clark University, MA (MW)
Colgate University, NY (MW)
Columbia University, NY (MW)
Connecticut College, CT (MW)
Cornell University, NY (W)
Dartmouth College, NH (MW)
Dowling College, NY (MW)
Drake University, IA (W)
Drexel University, PA (MW)
Duquesne University, PA (W)
Fairfield University, CT (MW)
Florida Institute of Technology, FL (MW)
Fordham University, NY (MW)
George Washington University, DC (MW)
Georgetown University, DC (MW)
Gonzaga University, WA (MW)
Harvard University, MA (MW)
Indiana University, IN (W)
Iona College, NY (MW)
Ithaca College, NY (MW)
Jacksonville University, FL (MW)
Johns Hopkins University, MD (MW)
Lafayette College, PA (MW)
La Salle University, PA (MW)
Lewis and Clark College, OR (MW)
Loyola College, MD (MW)
Loyola Marymount University, CA (MW)
Manhattan College, NY (MW)
Marietta College, OH (MW)
Marist College, NY (MW)
Massachusetts Institute of Technology, MA (W)
Mercyhurst College, PA (MW)
Mount Holyoke College, MA (W)
Orange Coast College, CA (MW)
Oregon State University, OR (MW)
Pacific Lutheran University, WA (MW)
Princeton University, NJ (MW)
Robert Morris College, PA (W)
Sacred Heart University, CT (MW)

Saint John's University, NY (M)
Saint Joseph's University, PA (MW)
Saint Mary's College of California, CA (MW)
San Diego State University, CA (W)
Santa Clara University, CA (MW)
Seattle Pacific University, WA (MW)
Skidmore College, NY (MW)
Smith College, MA (W)
Stanford University, CA (MW)
State University of New York Maritime College, NY (MW)
Syracuse University, NY (MW)
Temple University, PA (MW)
Trinity College, CT (MW)
Tufts University, MA (MW)
Union College, NY (MW)
University of California (Berkeley), CA (MW)
University of California (Irvine), CA (MW)
University of California (San Diego), CA (MW)
University of Central Florida, FL (W)
University of Charleston, WV (MW)
University of Massachusetts (Amherst), MA (W)
University of Massachusetts (Lowell), MA (MW)
University of Minnesota, MN (W)
University of Missouri (Columbia), MO (W)
University of Pennsylvania, PA (MW)
University of Puget Sound, WA (MW)
University of Redlands, CA (MW)
University of Rhode Island, RI (M)
University of San Diego, CA (MW)
University of Southern California, CA (W)
University of Tampa, FL (MW)
University of Tennessee (Knoxville), TN (M)
University of Washington, WA (M)
University of Wisconsin (Madison), WI (MW)
Villanova University, PA (W)
Washington State University, WA (W)
Webber College, FL (MW)
Wellesley College, MA (W)
Wesleyan University, CT (MW)
Western Washington University, WA (MW)
Williams College, MA (MW)
Yale University, CT (MW)

Cricket

Haverford College, PA (M)

Cross Country

Abilene Christian University, TX (MW)
Adams State College, CO (MW)
Adelphi University, NY (MW)
Adrian College, MI (MW)
Agnes Scott College, GA (W)
Alabama A&M University, AL (MW)
Alabama State University, AL (MW)
Albany State University, GA (MW)
Albion College, MI (MW)
Albright College, PA (MW)
Alcorn State University, MS (MW)
Alderson-Broaddus College, WV (MW)
Alfred University, NY (MW)
Allegheny College, PA (MW)
Allen County College, KS (MW)
Allentown College, PA (MW)
Alma College, MI (MW)
Alvernia College, PA (MW)
American University, DC (MW)
Amherst College, MA (MW)
Anderson College, SC (MW)
Anderson University, IN (MW)
Andrew College, GA (MW)
Angelo State University, TX (MW)
Appalachian State University, NC (MW)
Apprentice School, VA (M)
Aquinas College, MI (MW)
Arizona State University, AZ (MW)
Arkansas College, AR (MW)
Arkansas State University, AR (MW)
Arkansas Tech University, AR (W)
Armstrong Atlantic State University, GA (MW)
Asbury College, KY (MW)
Ashland College, OH (MW)
Assumption College, MA (MW)
Atlantic Community College, NJ (MW)
Auburn University, AL (MW)
Augsburg College, MN (MW)
Augusta State University, GA (MW)
Augustana College, IL (MW)
Augustana College, SD (MW)
Austin Peay State University, TN (MW)
Azusa Pacific University, CA (MW)
Babson College, MA (MW)
Bacone Junior College, OK (MW)
Baker University, KS (MW)
Ball State University, IN (MW)
Balmont Abbey College, NC (MW)
Baltimore City Community College, MD (MW)
Barber-Scotia College, NC (MW)
Bard College, NY (MW)
Barton College, NC (MW)
Barton County College, KS (MW)
Bates College, ME (MW)
Baylor University, TX (MW)
Becker College, MA (MW)
Beloit College, WI (MW)
Bellarmine College, KY (MW)
Belhaven College, MS (MW)
Bellevue Community College, WA (MW)
Belmont College, TN (MW)
Bemidji State University, MN (W)
Benedict College, SC (M)
Benedictine University, IL (MW)
Bentley College, MA (MW)
Bergen Community College, NJ (MW)
Berry College, GA (MW)
Bethany College, KS (MW)
Bethany College, WV (MW)
Bethel College, IN (MW)
Bethel College, MN (MW)
Bethune-Cookman College, FL (MW)
Binghamton University (SUNY), NY (W)
Biola University, CA (M)
Birmingham-Southern College, AL (MW)
Blackburn College, IL (MW)
Black Hills State University, SD (MW)
Blanton Junior College, NC (M)

Bloomsburg University, PA (MW)
Bluefield State College, WV (MW)
Bluffton College, OH (MW)
Boise State University, ID (MW)
Boston College, MA (MW)
Boston University, MA (MW)
Bowdoin College, ME (MW)
Bowie State University, MD (MW)
Bowling Green State University, OH (MW)
Bradley University, IL (MW)
Brandeis University, MA (MW)
Brevard College, NC (MW)
Briar Cliff College, IA (MW)
Bridgewater College, VA (MW)
Bridgewater State College, MA (MW)
Brigham Young University, HI (MW)
Brigham Young University, UT (MW)
Bronx Community College, NY (MW)
Brooklyn College (CUNY), NY (MW)
Broome Community College, NY (MW)
Brown University, RI (MW)
Bryant College, RI (MW)
Bryn Mawr College, PA (W)
Bucknell University, PA (MW)
Bucks County Community College, PA (MW)
Buena Vista University, IA (MW)
Buffalo State College, NY (MW)
Butler University, IN (MW)
Butte College, CA (MW)
Cabrillo College, CA (MW)
Cabrini College, PA (MW)
California Baptist University, CA (MW)
California Institute of Technology, CA (MW)
California Lutheran University, CA (MW)
California Polytechnic State University, CA (MW)
California State Polytechnic University, CA (MW)
California State University at Bakersfield, CA (W)
California State University (Chico), CA (MW)
California State University (Fresno), CA (MW)
California State University (Fullerton), CA (MW)

California State University (Hayward), CA (MW)
California State University (Long Beach), CA (MW)
California State University (Los Angeles), CA (MW)
California State University (Sacramento), CA (MW)
California State University (San Bernardino), CA (W)
California State University (Stanislaus), CA (MW)
California University, PA (MW)
Calvin College, MI (MW)
Campbellsville University, KY (MW)
Campbell University, NC (MW)
Canisius College, NY (MW)
Cardinal Stritch University, WI (MW)
Carleton College, MN (MW)
Carnegie-Mellon University, PA (MW)
Carroll College, WI (MW)
Carson-Newman College, TN (MW)
Carthage College, WI (MW)
Case Western Reserve University, OH (MW)
Castleton State College, VT (MW)
Catawba College, NC (MW)
Catholic University of America, DC (MW)
Cayuga County Community College, NY (MW)
Cedarville College, OH (MW)
Centenary College, LA (MW)
Centenary College, NJ (MW)
Central Arizona College, AZ (MW)
Central College, IA (MW)
Central Christian College, KS (MW)
Central Connecticut State University, CT (MW)
Central Methodist College, MO (MW)
Central Michigan University, MI (MW)
Central Missouri State University, MO (MW)
Central Washington University, WA (MW)
Cerritos College, CA (MW)
Chaminade University of Honolulu, HI (MW)
Chapman University, CA (MW)
Charleston Southern University, SC (MW)
Chicago State University, IL (MW)

Christopher Newport College, VA (MW)
Citadel, SC (M)
City College of San Francisco, CA (MW)
Clackamas Community College, OR (MW)
Clarion University, PA (MW)
Clark Atlanta University, GA (W)
Clarkson University, NY (MW)
Clark University, MA (MW)
Clemson University, SC (MW)
Cleveland State University, OH (W)
Cloud County Community College, KS (MW)
Coastal Carolina College, SC (MW)
Coe College, IA (MW)
Coffeyville Community College, KS (MW)
Coker College, SC (MW)
Colby Community College, KS (MW)
Colgate University, NY (MW)
College of Charleston, SC (MW)
College of Mount St. Joseph, OH (W)
The College of New Jersey, NJ (MW)
College of New Rochelle, NY (W)
College of Notre Dame, CA (MW)
College of Notre Dame of Maryland, MD (W)
College of Southern Idaho, ID (MW)
College of St. Benedict, MN (W)
College of St. Francis, IL (W)
College of St. Rose, NY (MW)
College of St. Scholastica, MN (MW)
College of the Desert, CA (MW)
College of the Redwoods, CA (MW)
College of the Sequoias, CA (MW)
College of William and Mary, VA (MW)
College of Wooster, OH (MW)
Colorado Christian University, CO (MW)
Colorado College, CO (MW)
Colorado School of Mines, CO (MW)
Colorado State University, CO (MW)
Columbia Union College, MD (MW)

Columbia University, NY (MW)
Columbus College, GA (MW)
Columbus State Community College, OH (MW)
Community College of Philadelphia, PA (MW)
Community College of Rhode Island, RI (MW)
Compton Community College, CA (MW)
Concord College, WV (MW)
Concordia College, MI (MW)
Concordia College, MN (MW)
Concordia University, NE (MW)
Concordia University, IL (M)
Concordia University Wisconsin, WI (W)
Connecticut College, CT (MW)
Contra Costa College, CA (M)
Coppin State College, MD (MW)
Cornell College, IA (MW)
Cornell University, NY (MW)
Covenant College, GA (MW)
Creighton University, NE (MW)
Cuesta College, CA (MW)
Cumberland College, KY (MW)
Curry College, MA (W)
Dakota State University, SD (MW)
Dakota Wesleyan University, SD (MW)
Dana College, NE (MW)
Danville Area Community College, IL (MW)
Dartmouth College, NH (MW)
Davidson College, NC (MW)
Davis & Elkins College, WV (MW)
Defiance College, OH (MW)
Delaware County Community College, PA (MW)
Delaware State University, DE (MW)
Delaware Valley College, PA (MW)
Delhi College of Technology (SUNY), NY (MW)
Delta State University, MS (W)
Denison University, OH (MW)
DePaul University, IL (MW)
De Pauw University, IN (MW)
Diablo Valley Community College, CA (MW)
Dickinson College, PA (MW)
Dickinson State University, ND (MW)
Diné College, AZ (MW)
Doane College, NE (MW)
Dodge City Community College, KS (MW)

Dominican University, IL (MW)
Drake University, IA (MW)
Drew University, NJ (MW)
Drexel University, PA (M)
Duke University, NC (MW)
Duquesne University, PA (MW)
Earlham College, IN (MW)
East Carolina University, NC (MW)
Eastern College, PA (MW)
Eastern Connecticut State University, CT (MW)
Eastern Illinois University, IL (MW)
Eastern Kentucky University, KY (MW)
Eastern Mennonite College, VA (MW)
Eastern Michigan University, MI (MW)
Eastern Nazarene College, MA (MW)
Eastern New Mexico University, NM (MW)
Eastern Oklahoma College, OK (MW)
Eastern Oregon State College, OR (MW)
Eastern Washington University, WA (MW)
East Stroudsburg University, PA (MW)
East Texas State University, TX (MW)
Eckerd College, FL (W)
Edinboro University of Pennsylvania, PA (MW)
Edward Waters College, FL (MW)
El Camino College, CA (MW)
Elizabeth City State University, NC (MW)
Elizabethtown College, PA (MW)
Elmhurst College, IL (MW)
Emory University, GA (MW)
Emporia State University, KS (MW)
Erskine College, SC (M)
Essex Community College, MD (MW)
Everett Community College, WA (MW)
Fairfield University, CT (MW)
Fairleigh Dickinson University, NJ (MW)
Fayetteville State University, NC (MW)
Ferris State College, MI (MW)
Finger Lakes Community College, NY (MW)

Fisk University, TN (MW)
Fitchburg State College, MA (MW)
Flagler College, FL (MW)
Florida Atlantic University, FL (MW)
Florida International University, FL (MW)
Florida Memorial College, FL (MW)
Florida Southern College, FL (MW)
Florida State University, FL (MW)
Fordham University, NY (MW)
Fort Hays State University, KS (MW)
Fort Lewis College, CO (MW)
Fort Valley State University, GA (MW)
Francis Marion University, SC (MW)
Franklin & Marshall College, PA (MW)
Franklin Pierce College, NH (M)
Fresno City College, CA (MW)
Fresno Pacific University, CA (MW)
Fullerton College, CA (MW)
Furman University, SC (MW)
Gannon College, PA (MW)
Garden City Community College, KS (MW)
Gardner-Webb College, NC (M)
Genesee Community College, NY (MW)
Geneva College, PA (MW)
George Fox College, OR (MW)
George-Mason University, VA (MW)
Georgetown College, KY (MW)
George Washington University, DC (MW)
Georgia Institute of Technology, GA (MW)
Georgia Southern University, GA (W)
Georgia State University, GA (MW)
Georgian Court College, NJ (W)
Gettysburg College, PA (MW)
Glendale Community College, AZ (MW)
Glendale Community College, CA (MW)
Glenville State College, WV (MW)
Gloucester County College, NJ (MW)
Golden West College, CA (MW)
Gonzaga University, WA (MW)

Gordon College, MA (MW)
Goshen College, IN (MW)
Goucher College, MD (MW)
Grace College, IN (MW)
Graceland College, IA (MW)
Grambling State University, LA (MW)
Grand Rapids Baptist Seminary of Cornerstone University, MI (MW)
Grand Rapids Community College, MI (MW)
Grand Valley State College, MI (MW)
Grand View College, IA (MW)
Greenfield Community College, MA (MW)
Greenville College, IL (MW)
Grinnell College, IA (MW)
Grove City College, PA (MW)
Gustavus Adolphus College, MN (MW)
Hagerstown Junior College, MD (MW)
Hamilton College, NY (MW)
Hamline University, MN (MW)
Hampden-Sydney College, VA (M)
Hampton University, VA (MW)
Hanover College, IN (MW)
Harding University, AR (MW)
Hardin-Simmons University, TX (W)
Hartwick College, NY (MW)
Harvard University, MA (MW)
Haskell Indian Nations University, KS (MW)
Hastings College, NE (MW)
Haverford College, PA (MW)
Hawaii Pacific University, HI (MW)
Heidelberg College, OH (MW)
Henderson State University, AR (W)
Herkimer County Community College, NY (MW)
Highland Community College, KS (MW)
Highland Park Community College, MI (W)
High Point University, NC (MW)
Hillsdale College, MI (MW)
Hiram College, OH (MW)
Hofstra University, NY (MW)
Holy Family College, PA (M)
Hope College, MI (MW)
Houghton College, NY (MW)
Houston Baptist University, TX (MW)

Howard Payne University, TX (MW)
Hudson Valley Community College, NY (W)
Humboldt State University, CA (MW)
Hunter College of the City University of New York, NY (MW)
Huntington College, IN (MW)
Huron University, SD (MW)
Hutchinson College, KS (MW)
Idaho State University, ID (MW)
Illinois College, IL (MW)
Illinois Institute of Technology, IL (MW)
Illinois State University, IL (MW)
Illinois Wesleyan University, IL (MW)
Indiana State University, IN (MW)
Indiana University, IN (MW)
Indiana University of Pennsylvania, PA (MW)
Indiana University-Purdue University, IN (MW)
Indiana University-Purdue University (Fort Wayne), IN (MW)
Indiana University Southeast, IN (MW)
Indiana Wesleyan University, IN (MW)
Iona College, NY (MW)
Iowa State University of Science and Technology, IA (MW)
Iowa Wesleyan College, IA (MW)
Itawamba Community College, MS (MW)
Ithaca College, NY (MW)
Jackson State University, MS (MW)
Jacksonville State University, AL (MW)
Jacksonville University, FL (M)
James Madison University, VA (MW)
Jamestown College, ND (MW)
John Carroll University, OH (MW)
Johns Hopkins University, MD (MW)
Johnson County Community College, KS (MW)
Johnson C. Smith University, NC (MW)
Johnson State College, VT (MW)
Juniata College, PA (W)
Kalamazoo College, MI (MW)
Kansas City Kansas Community College, KS (MW)
Kansas State University, KS (W)

Kansas Wesleyan College, KS (MW)
Kennesaw State College, GA (MW)
Keene State College, NH (MW)
Kent State University (Ashtabula), OH (MW)
Kent State University (Kent), OH (MW)
Kent State University (New Philadelphia), OH (MW)
Kent State University (Warren), OH, (MW)
Kentucky Christian College, KY (MW)
Kentucky State University, KY (MW)
Kenyon College, OH (MW)
King College, TN (MW)
King's College, PA (MW)
Knox College, IL (MW)
Kutztown University, PA (MW)
Lafayette College, PA (MW)
Lake Land College, IL (MW)
Lake Superior State University, MI (MW)
Lamar Community College, CO (W)
Lamar University, TX (MW)
Lander College, SC (MW)
Langston University, OK (W)
Lansing Community College, MI (MW)
La Roche College, PA (MW)
La Salle University, PA (MW)
Lawrence University, WI (MW)
Lebanon Valley College, PA (MW)
Lehigh University, PA (MW)
Le Moyne College, NY (MW)
Lenoir-Rhyne College, NC (MW)
LeTourneau College, TX (MW)
Lewis and Clark College, OR (MW)
Lewis Clark State College, ID (MW)
Lewis University, IL (MW)
Liberty University, VA (MW)
Lincoln Memorial University, TN (MW)
Lincoln University, MO (M)
Linfield College, OR (MW)
Long Beach City College, CA (MW)
Long Island University (Brooklyn), NY (MW)
Long Island University (C.W. Post), NY (W)
Loras College, IA (MW)
Los Angeles Valley College, CA (MW)

Louisiana College, LA (MW)
Louisiana State University (Baton Rouge), LA (MW)
Louisiana Tech University, LA (MW)
Lower Columbia College, WA (MW)
Loyola College, MD (MW)
Loyola Marymount University, CA (MW)
Loyola University, IL (MW)
Lubbock Christian College, TX (MW)
Luther College, IA (MW)
Lycoming College, PA (MW)
Lynchburg College, VA (MW)
Lyndon State College, VT (MW)
Macalester College, MN (MW)
Macomb Community College, MI (MW)
Madison Area Technical College, WI (MW)
Malone College, OH (MW)
Manchester College, IN (MW)
Manhattan College, NY (MW)
Mankato State University, MN (MW)
Mansfield University, PA (MW)
Marian College, IN (MW)
Marian College, WI (MW)
Marietta College, OH (MW)
Marist College, NY (MW)
Marquette University, WI (MW)
Marshall University, WV (MW)
Mars Hill College, NC (MW)
Mary Holmes College, MS (MW)
Maryville University, MO (MW)
Mary Washington College, VA (MW)
Marywood University, PA (MW)
Massachusetts College of Liberal Arts, MA (MW)
Massachusetts Institute of Technology, MA (MW)
Master's College, CA (MW)
McKendree College, IL (MW)
McNeese State University, LA (MW)
McPherson College, KS (MW)
Mercer University, GA (MW)
Mercy College, NY (MW)
Mercyhurst College, PA (MW)
Merrimack College, MA (MW)
Mesa Community College, AZ (MW)
Mesa State College, CO (W)
Messiah College, PA (MW)
Miami University, OH (MW)
Michigan State University, MI (MW)

Michigan Technological University, MI (MW)
Mid-America Nazarene College, KS (MW)
Middlebury College, VT (MW)
Middlesex County College, NJ (MW)
Middle Tennessee State University, TN (MW)
Midland Lutheran College, NE (MW)
Miles College, AL (MW)
Millersville University, PA (MW)
Millikin University, IL (MW)
Milwaukee Area Technology College, WI (MW)
Minot State, ND (MW)
MiraCosta College, CA (W)
Mississippi College, MS (M)
Mississippi Valley State University, MS (MW)
Missouri Southern State College, MO (MW)
Missouri Valley College, MO (MW)
Mitchell College, CT (MW)
Modesto Junior College, CA (MW)
Mohawk Valley Community College, NY (MW)
Molloy College, NY (MW)
Monmouth College, IL (MW)
Monmouth College, NJ (M)
Montana State University, MT (MW)
Montclair State College, NJ (MW)
Montreat-Anderson College, NC (MW)
Moorhead State University, MN (MW)
Moorpark College, CA (MW)
Moravian College, PA (MW)
Morehead State University, KY (MW)
Morehouse College, GA (M)
Morgan State University, MD (MW)
Morningside College, IA (MW)
Morris Brown College, GA (MW)
Morton College, IL (MW)
Mott Community College, MI (M)
Mount Holyoke College, MA (W)
Mount Marty College, SD (MW)
Mount Mercy College, IA (MW)
Mount St. Mary College, MD (MW)

Mount Union College, OH (MW)
Mt. San Antonio College, CA (MW)
Mt. Wachusett Community College, MA (MW)
Muhlenberg College, PA (MW)
Murray State University, KY (MW)
Muskingum College, OH (MW)
Nassau Community College, NY (MW)
Nebraska Wesleyan University, NE (MW)
New Mexico Highlands University, NM (MW)
New Mexico State University, NM (MW)
New York University, NY (MW)
Niagara University, NY (MW)
Nicholls State University, LA (MW)
Norfolk State University, VA (MW)
North Carolina A&T State University, NC (M)
North Carolina Central University, NC (MW)
North Carolina State University, NC (MW)
North Central College, IL (MW)
North Dakota State, ND (MW)
North Dakota State University, ND (MW)
North Georgia College&State University, GA (MW)
Northeastern Illinois University, IL (MW)
Northeast Louisiana University, LA (MW)
Northeast Missouri State University, MO (MW)
Northern Arizona University, AZ (MW)
Northern Illinois University, IL (W)
Northern Kentucky University, KY (MW)
Northern Michigan University, MI (MW)
Northern State University, SD (MW)
North Idaho College, ID (MW)
Northwestern College, IA (MW)
Northwestern College, MN (M)
Northwestern University, IL (MW)
Northwest Missouri State University, MO (MW)
Northwood Institute, MI (MW)
Northwood University (Texas Campus), TX (MW)

Norwich University, VT (MW)
Notre Dame College of Ohio, OH (W)
Nova Southern University, FL (MW)
Nyack College, NY (MW)
Oakland City University, IN (MW)
Oakland Community College, MI (MW)
Oakland University, MI (M)
Oakton Community College, IL (MW)
Oberlin College, OH (MW)
Occidental College, CA (MW)
Ocean County College, NJ (MW)
Odessa College, TX (W)
Oglethorpe University, GA (MW)
Ohio Northern University, OH (MW)
Ohio State University, OH (MW)
Ohio University, OH (MW)
Ohio Valley College, WV (W)
Ohio Wesleyan University, OH (MW)
Oklahoma Baptist University, OK (M)
Oklahoma Christian University of Science & Art, OK (MW)
Oklahoma Panhandle State University, OK (MW)
Oklahoma State University, OK (MW)
Old Dominion University, VA (W)
Olivet College, MI (M)
Olivet Nazarene University, IL (MW)
Oral Roberts University, OK (MW)
Orange Coast College, CA (MW)
Oregon State University, OR (MW)
Oswego State University (SUNY), NY (MW)
Ottawa University, KS (MW)
Otterbein College, OH (MW)
Ouachita Baptist University, AR (MW)
Oxnard College, CA (MW)
Pace University, NY (MW)
Pace University (White Plains Campus), NY (MW)
Pacific Lutheran University, WA (MW)
Pacific University, OR (MW)
Paine College, GA (MW)

Park College, MO (MW)
Parkland College, IL (MW)
Penn State Berks-Lehigh Valley College, PA (MW)
Penn State Behrend College, PA (MW)
Pennsylvania State University, PA (MW)
Pepperdine University, CA (MW)
Pfeiffer College, NC (M)
Phoenix College, AZ (MW)
Piedmont College, GA (MW)
Pikeville College, KY (MW)
Pima Community College (West Campus), AZ (MW)
Pittsburg State University, KS (MW)
Plattsburgh State University (SUNY), NY (MW)
Point Loma Nazarene College, CA (MW)
Polytechnic University (Brooklyn Campus), NY (M)
Pomona-Pitzer Colleges, CA (MW)
Pontifical Catholic University of Puerto Rico, PR (MW)
Portland State University, OR (MW)
Prairie View A&M University, TX (MW)
Pratt Community College, KS (MW)
Princeton University, NJ (MW)
Principia College, IL (MW)
Providence College, RI (MW)
Purchase College (SUNY), NY (MW)
Purdue University, IN (MW)
Queensborough Community College, NY (MW)
Queens College, NY (MW)
Quincy University, IL (MW)
Quinnipiac University, CT (MW)
Radford University, VA (MW)
Ramapo College, NJ (MW)
Ranetto Santiago College, CA (MW)
Regis College, MA (W)
Rensselaer Polytechnic Institute, NY (MW)
Rhode Island College, RI (MW)
Rice University, TX (MW)
Ricks College, ID (MW)
Rider College, NJ (MW)
Ripon College, WI (MW)
Riverside Community College, CA (MW)
Roanoke College, VA (MW)

Robert Morris College, PA (MW)
Roberts Wesleyan College, NY (MW)
Rochester College, MI (MW)
Rochester Institute of Technology, NY (MW)
Rockhurst College, MO (MW)
Rollins College, FL (MW)
Roosevelt University, IL (M)
Rose-Hulman Institute of Technology, IN (MW)
Rowan University, NJ (W)
Rust College, MS (MW)
Rutgers, Camden College of Arts and Sciences, NJ (MW)
Sacred Heart University, CT (MW)
Saddleback College, CA (MW)
Saginaw Valley State University, MI (MW)
Saint Ambrose University, IA (MW)
Saint Andrews Presbyterian College, NC (MW)
Saint Anselm College, NH (MW)
Saint Bonaventure University, NY (MW)
Saint Cloud State University, MN (MW)
Saint Francis College, IN (MW)
Saint Francis College, NY (MW)
Saint Francis College, PA (MW)
Saint John Fisher College, NY (MW)
Saint John's University, MN (M)
Saint John's University, NY (MW)
Saint Joseph's College, IN (MW)
Saint Joseph's University, PA (MW)
Saint Lawrence University, NY (MW)
Saint Leo University, FL (MW)
Saint Louis University, MO (M)
Saint Mary's College, IN (MW)
Saint Mary's College of California, CA (MW)
Saint Michael's College, VT (MW)
Saint Norbert College, WI (MW)
Saint Olaf College, MN (MW)
Saint Paul's College, VA (M)
Saint Peter's College, NJ (MW)
Saint Thomas Aquinas College, NY (MW)
Saint Vincent College, PA (MW)
Salem State College, MA (MW)
Salve Regina College, RI (MW)
Samford University, AL (M)

San Bernardino Community College, CA (MW)
San Diego City College, CA (MW)
San Diego Mesa College, CA (MW)
San Diego State University, CA (W)
San Francisco State University, CA (MW)
San Joaquin Delta College, CA (MW)
San Jose State University, CA (M)
Santa Barbara City College, CA (MW)
Santa Clara University, CA (MW)
Santa Monica College, CA (MW)
Santa Rosa Junior College, CA (MW)
Sauk Valley College, IL (MW)
Savannah State College, GA (W)
Schoolcraft College, MI (W)
Schreiner College, TX (MW)
Seattle Pacific University, WA (MW)
Seattle University, WA (MW)
Seminole Community College, FL (M)
Seton Hall University, NJ (MW)
Seton Hill College, PA (W)
Shawnee State University, OH (MW)
Shepherd College, WV (MW)
Shippensburg University of Pennsylvania, PA (MW)
Shorter College, GA (MW)
Siena College, NY (MW)
Siena Heights College, MI (MW)
Sierra College, CA (MW)
Simpson College, CA (MW)
Sioux Falls College, SD (MW)
Skagit Valley College, WA (MW)
Skyline College, CA (MW)
Slippery Rock University of Pennsylvania, PA (MW)
Smith College, MA (W)
South Carolina State College, SC (MW)
South Dakota School of Mines and Technology, SD (MW)
South Dakota State University, SD (MW)
Southeast Missouri State University, MO (MW)
Southeastern Louisiana University, LA (MW)
Southern Arkansas University, AR (MW)

Southern California College, CA (MW)
Southern Illinois University, IL (MW)
Southern Illinois University (Edwardsville), IL (MW)
Southern Methodist University, TX (MW)
Southern Oregon State College, OR (MW)
Southern Union State Community College, AL (MW)
Southern University and A&M College, LA (MW)
Southern Utah University, UT (MW)
South Plains Community College, TX (M)
Southwest Baptist University, MO (MW)
Southwestern College, KS (MW)
Southwestern Oklahoma State University, OK (W)
Southwestern University, TX (MW)
Southwest Missouri State University, MO (MW)
Southwest Texas State University, TX (MW)
Spartanburg Methodist, SC (MW)
Spokane Community College, WA (MW)
Spring Arbor College, MI (MW)
Spring Hill College, AL (MW)
Springfield College, MA (MW)
State University of New York College (Brockport), NY (MW)
State University of New York College (Cortland), NY (MW)
State University of New York College (Fredonia), NY (MW)
State University of New York College (Geneseo), NY (MW)
State University of New York College (New Paltz), NY (MW)
State University of New York Maritime College, NY (M)
State University of West Georgia, GA (MW)
Stephen F. Austin State University, TX (MW)
Sterling College, KS (MW)
Stetson University, FL (MW)
Stevens Institute of Technology, NJ (MW)
Stonehill College, MA (MW)
Suffolk County Community College, NY (M)

Suffolk University, MA (MW)
Swarthmore College, PA (MW)
Syracuse University, NY (MW)
Tabor College, KS (MW)
Taft College, CA (MW)
Talledaga College, AL (MW)
Tarleton State University, TX (MW)
Tennessee Technological University, TN (MW)
Texas A&I University, TX (MW)
Texas A&M Commerce, TX (MW)
Texas A&M University, TX (MW)
Texas Christian University, TX (MW)
Texas Lutheran College, TX (W)
Texas Tech University, TX (MW)
Tiffin University, OH (MW)
Towson State University, MD (MW)
Transylvania University, KY (MW)
Trinidad State Junior College, CO (W)
Trinity College, CT (MW)
Trinity University, TX (MW)
Tri-State University, IN (MW)
Troy State University, AL (MW)
Truett-McConnell Junior College, GA (MW)
Tufts University, MA (MW)
Tulane University, LA (MW)
Tuskegee University, AL (MW)
Umpqua College, OR (MW)
Union College, KY (MW)
Union College, NY (MW)
Union University, TN (W)
Unity College, ME (MW)
University of Akron, OH (MW)
University of Alabama (Birmingham), AL (MW)
University of Alabama (Huntsville), AL (MW)
University of Alabama (Tuscaloosa), AL (MW)
University of Alaska, AK (M)
University of Alaska (Fairbanks), AK (MW)
University at Albany (SUNY), NY (MW)
University of Arizona, AZ (MW)
University of Arkansas (Fayetteville), AR (MW)
University of Arkansas (Little Rock), AR (W)
University of Bridgeport, CT (MW)
University at Buffalo (SUNY), NY (MW)

University of California (Berkeley), CA (MW)
University of California (Davis), CA (MW)
University of California (Irvine), CA (MW)
University of California (Riverside), CA (MW)
University of California (San Diego), CA (MW)
University of California (Santa Barbara), CA (MW)
University of California (UCLA), CA (MW)
University of Central Arkansas, AR (MW)
University of Central Florida, FL (MW)
University of Central Oklahoma, OK (MW)
University of Chicago, IL (MW)
University of Cincinnati, OH (MW)
University of Colorado, CO (MW)
University of Connecticut, CT (MW)
University of Dallas, TX (MW)
University of Dayton, OH (MW)
University of Delaware, DE (MW)
University of Denver, CO (MW)
University of Detroit Mercy, MI (MW)
University of Dubuque, IA (MW)
University of Evansville, IN (MW)
University of Findlay, OH (MW)
University of Florida, FL (W)
University of Georgia, GA (MW)
University of Hartford, CT (MW)
University of Hawaii (Hilo), HI (MW)
University of Hawaii (Manoa), HI (W)
University of Houston, TX (MW)
University of Idaho, ID (MW)
University of Illinois (Chicago), IL (MW)
University of Illinois (Urbana-Champaign), IL (MW)
University of Incarnate Word, TX (MW)
University of Indianapolis, IN (MW)
University of Iowa, IA (MW)
University of Kansas, KS (MW)
University of Kentucky, KY (MW)

University of La Verne, CA (MW)
University of Louisiana at Lafayette, LA (MW)
University of Louisville, KY (MW)
University of Maine, ME (MW)
University of Maine (Presque Isle), ME (MW)
University of Mary, ND (MW)
University of Maryland, MD (MW)
University of Maryland (Baltimore County), MD (MW)
University of Maryland (Eastern Shore), MD (MW)
University of Massachusetts (Amherst), MA (MW)
University of Massachusetts (Boston), MA (MW)
University of Massachusetts (Dartmouth), MA (MW)
University of Massachusetts (Lowell), MA (MW)
University of Memphis, TN (MW)
University of Miami, FL (MW)
University of Michigan, MI (MW)
University of Minnesota (Duluth), MN (MW)
University of Minnesota (Minneapolis), MN (MW)
University of Minnesota (Morris), MN (M)
University of Mississippi, MS (MW)
University of Missouri, MO (MW)
University of Missouri (Columbia), MO (MW)
University of Missouri (Rolla), MO (MW)
University of Mobile, AL (M)
University of Montana, MT (MW)
University of Nebraska, NE (M)
University of Nebraska (Kearney), NE (MW)
University of Nebraska (Lincoln), NE (MW)
University of Nevada, NV (MW)
University of Nevada (Reno), NV (MW)
University of New England, ME (MW)
University of New Hampshire, NH (MW)
University of New Haven, CT (MW)
University of New Mexico, NM (MW)

University of New Orleans, LA (MW)
University of North Alabama, AL (MW)
University of North Carolina (Asheville), NC (MW)
University of North Carolina (Chapel Hill), NC (MW)
University of North Carolina (Charlotte), NC (MW)
University of North Carolina (Pembroke), NC (MW)
University of North Carolina (Wilmington), NC (MW)
University of North Dakota, ND (MW)
University of Northern Iowa, IA (MW)
University of North Florida, FL (MW)
University of North Texas, TX (MW)
University of Notre Dame, IN (MW)
University of Oklahoma, OK (MW)
University of Oregon, OR (MW)
University of Pennsylvania, PA (MW)
University of Pittsburgh, PA (W)
University of Pittsburgh (Bradford), PA (MW)
University of Pittsburgh (Johnstown), PA (MW)
University of Portland, OR (MW)
University of Puerto Rico, PR (MW)
University of Puerto Rico (Bayamon), PR (MW)
University of Puerto Rico (Ponce), PR (MW)
University of Puget Sound, WA (MW)
University of Redlands, CA (MW)
University of Rhode Island, RI (MW)
University of Richmond, VA (MW)
University of Rio Grande, OH (M)
University of San Diego, CA (MW)
University of San Francisco, CA (MW)
University of Scranton, PA (MW)
University of South Alabama, AL (MW)

University of South Carolina, SC (MW)
University of South Carolina (Aiken), SC (MW)
University of South Carolina (Spartanburg), SC (M)
University of South Dakota, SD (MW)
University of Southern California, CA (W)
University of Southern Indiana, IN (MW)
University of Southern Mississippi, MS (MW)
University of South Florida, FL (MW)
University of St. Thomas, MN (MW)
University at Stony Brook (SUNY), NY (MW)
University of Tampa, FL (MW)
University of Tennessee, TN (MW)
University of Tennessee (Knoxville), TN (MW)
University of Tennessee (Martin), TN (MW)
University of Texas (Arlington), TX (M)
University of Texas (Austin), TX (MW)
University of Texas (El Paso), TX (MW)
University of Texas (Pan American), TX (MW)
University of Texas (San Antonio), TX (MW)
University of the District of Columbia, DC (MW)
University of the Pacific, CA (W)
University of Toledo, OH (MW)
University of Tulsa, OK (MW)
University of Utah, UT (MW)
University of Vermont, VT (MW)
University of Virginia, VA (MW)
The University of Virginia's College at Wise, VA (MW)
University of Washington, WA (MW)
University of West Alabama, AL (MW)
University of West Florida, FL (MW)
University of Wisconsin (Eau Claire), WI (MW)
University of Wisconsin (Green Bay), WI (MW)
University of Wisconsin (La Crosse), WI (MW)
University of Wisconsin (Madison), WI (MW)

University of Wisconsin (Milwaukee), WI (MW)
University of Wisconsin (Oshkosh), WI (MW)
University of Wisconsin (Platteville), WI (MW)
University of Wisconsin (River Falls), WI (MW)
University of Wisconsin (Stevens Point), WI (MW)
University of Wisconsin (Stout), WI (MW)
University of Wisconsin (Superior), WI (MW)
University of Wyoming, WY (MW)
Upper Iowa University, IA (MW)
Urbana University, OH (MW)
Ursinus College, PA (MW)
U.S. International University, CA (MW)
Utah State University, UT (MW)
Valdosta State University, GA (MW)
Valley City State University, ND (MW)
Valparaiso University, IN (MW)
Vanderbilt University, TN (MW)
Vassar College, NY (MW)
Ventura College, CA (MW)
Villanova University, PA (MW)
Vincennes University, IN (MW)
Virginia Commonwealth University, VA (MW)
Virginia Military Institute, VA (M)
Virginia Polytechnic Institute & State University, VA (MW)
Virginia Union University, VA (MW)
Wabash College, IN (M)
Wagner College, NY (MW)
Wake Forest University, NC (MW)
Walla Walla Community College, WA (W)
Walsh College, OH (MW)
Warner Southern College, FL (MW)
Warren Wilson College, NC (MW)
Wartburg College, IA (MW)
Washington and Jefferson College, PA (MW)
Washington State University, WA (MW)
Washington University, MO (MW)
Waubonsee College, IL (M)
Wayland Baptist University, TX (MW)

Wayne State College, NE (MW)
Wayne State University, MI (M)
Webber College, FL (MW)
Weber State College, UT (MW)
Webster University, MO (W)
Wellesley College, MA (W)
Wesley College, DE (MW)
Wesleyan University, CT (MW)
West Chester University, PA (MW)
Western Carolina University, NC (W)
Western Connecticut State University, CT (W)
Western Illinois University, IL (MW)
Western Kentucky University, KY (MW)
Western Maryland College, MD (MW)
Western Michigan University, MI (MW)
Western Oregon State College, OR (MW)
Western State College, CO (MW)
Western Washington University, WA (MW)
Westfield State College, MA (MW)
West Liberty State College, WV (MW)
Westminster College, PA (MW)
Westmont College, CA (MW)
West Texas State University, TX (MW)
West Virginia University, WV (MW)
West Virginia Wesleyan College, WV (MW)
Wheaton College, IL (MW)
Wheeling Jesuit College, WV (MW)
Whitman College, WA (MW)
Whittier College, CA (MW)
Whitworth College, WA (MW)
Wichita State University, KS (MW)
Wilkes College, NC (M)
Wilkes University, PA (MW)
Willamette University, OR (MW)
William Jewell College, MO (MW)
William Patterson College, NJ (MW)
William Penn College, IA (MW)
Williams College, MA (MW)
Williamson Trade School, PA (M)
Wilmington College, OH (MW)
Winona State University, MN (W)

Winston-Salem State University, NC (MW)
Winthrop University, SC (MW)
Wofford College, SC (MW)
Worcester State College, MA (MW)
Wright State University, OH (MW)
Xavier University, OH (MW)
Yale University, CT (MW)
Yavapai College, AZ (W)
Yeshiva University, NY (M)
York College (CUNY), NY (MW)
Youngstown State University, OH (MW)

Cross Country Skiing

Bates College, ME (MW)
Bowdoin College, ME (MW)
Carleton College, MN (MW)
Castleton State College, VT (MW)
Dartmouth College, NH (MW)
Eastern Oregon State College, OR (MW)
Harvard University, MA (MW)
Massachusetts Institute of Technology, MA (MW)
Michigan Technological University, MI (MW)
Middlebury College, VT (MW)
Montana State University, MT (W)
Northern Michigan University, MI (MW)
North Iowa Area Community College, IA (MW)
Norwich University, VT (MW)
Passaic County Community College, NJ (MW)
Saint Lawrence University, NY (MW)
Saint Michael's College, VT (MW)
Saint Olaf College, MN (MW)
Samford University, AL (W)
Sierra College, CA (MW)
Snow College, UT (MW)
University of Alaska, AK (MW)
University of Alaska (Fairbanks), AK (MW)
University of Colorado, CO (MW)
University of New Hampshire, NH (MW)
University of Utah, UT (MW)
University of Vermont, VT (MW)
University of Wisconsin (Green Bay), WI (MW)

Western State College, CO (MW)
Whitman College, WA (MW)
Williams College, MA (MW)

Cycling

Marian College, IN (MW)

Dance

Aquinas College, MI (W)
Benedictine University, IL (W)
St. Ambrose University, IA (W)

Diving

Auburn University, AL (MW)
Austin College, TX (MW)
Boston College, MA (MW)
Boston University, MA (MW)
Brigham Young University, UT (MW)
California State University (Hayward), CA (MW)
Calvin College, MI (MW)
Cleveland State University, OH (MW)
Colgate University, NY (MW)
College of St. Benedict, MN (W)
College of Wooster, OH (MW)
Dartmouth College, NH (MW)
Davidson College, NC (M)
Denison University, OH (MW)
Diablo Valley Community College, CA (MW)
Drexel University, PA (MW)
George Washington University, DC (MW)
Hamline University, MN (MW)
Hiram College, OH (MW)
Keene State College, NH (MW)
Kenyon College, OH (MW)
Los Angeles Valley College, CA (W)
Louisiana State University (Baton Rouge), LA (MW)
Loyola College, MD (MW)
Manhattanville College, NY (W)
Mississippi Valley State University, MS (MW)
Monmouth College, NJ (MW)
Montgomery College, MD (MW)
New Mexico State University, NM (MW)
Oakland University, MI (MW)
Pfeiffer College, NC (W)
Queens College, NY (MW)
Rider College, NJ (W)

Saint Bonaventure University, NY (MW)
Saint John's University, MN (M)
Southern Methodist University, TX (MW)
Sweet Briar College, VA (W)
University of Arkansas (Fayetteville), AR (W)
University of Arkansas (Little Rock), AR (M)
University of California (Berkeley), CA (W)
University of Findlay, OH (MW)
University of Louisville, KY (MW)
University of Maine, ME (MW)
University of Nebraska (Kearney), NE (W)
University of Southern California, CA (M)
University of Texas (Austin), TX (W)
University of Wisconsin (Stevens Point), WI (MW)
Whittier College, CA (MW)
York College of Pennsylvania, PA (MW)
Youngstown State University, OH (MW)

Equestrian

Alfred University, NY (MW)
Becker College, MA (W)
Bucks County Community College, PA (MW)
California State University (Fresno), CA (W)
Centenary College, NJ (MW)
Colby-Sawyer College, NH (MW)
College of Charleston, SC (MW)
Columbus State Community College, OH (MW)
Converse College, SC (W)
Cornell University, NY (W)
Dartmouth College, NH (MW)
Drew University, NJ (MW)
Fairleigh Dickinson University, NJ (W)
Ferrum College, VA (MW)
Goucher College, MD (MW)
Hartwick College, NY (MW)
Lynchburg College, VA (MW)
Mary Washington College, VA (MW)
Molloy College, NY (W)
Moravian College, PA (MW)
Mount Holyoke College, MA (W)
Otterbein College, OH (MW)

Pace University, NY (W)
Park College, MO (MW)
Sacred Heart University, CT (MW)
Saint Andrews Presbyterian College, NC (MW)
Saint John's University, NY (M)
Saint Lawrence University, NY (MW)
Seton Hill College, PA (W)
Sierra Nevada College, NV (MW)
Skidmore College, NY (MW)
Smith College, MA (W)
Snow College, UT (MW)
State University of New York College at Potsdam, NY (MW)
Stonehill College, MA (MW)
Sweet Briar College, VA (W)
Teikyo Post University, CT (MW)
Texas A&M University, TX (W)
University of Detroit Mercy, MI (W)
West Texas State University, TX (W)
Wilson College, PA (W)

Fencing

Boston College, MA (MW)
Brandeis University, MA (MW)
California Institute of Technology, CA (MW)
California State University (Fullerton), CA (MW)
Case Western Reserve University, OH (MW)
City College of New York, NY (W)
Cleveland State University, OH (MW)
College of William and Mary, VA (M)
Columbia University, NY (MW)
Cornell University, NY (W)
Drew University, NJ (MW)
Duke University, NC (MW)
Fairleigh Dickinson University, NJ (W)
Harvard University, MA (MW)
Haverford College, PA (MW)
Hunter College of the City University of New York, NY (MW)
James Madison University, VA (W)
Johns Hopkins University, MD (MW)
Lafayette College, PA (MW)

Lawrence University, WI (MW)
Massachusetts Institute of Technology, MA (MW)
Michigan State University, MI (M)
Mississippi State University, MS (M)
New York University, NY (MW)
North Carolina State University, NC (MW)
Northwestern University, IL (MW)
Ohio State University, OH (MW)
Pace University, NY (M)
Pace University (White Plains Campus), NY (MW)
Pennsylvania State University, PA (MW)
Princeton University, NJ (M)
Rutgers, Newark College of Arts and Sciences, NJ (MW)
Sacred Heart University, CT (MW)
Saint John's University, NY (MW)
Saint Mary's College, MI (W)
Scottsdale Community College, AZ (W)
Stanford University, CA (MW)
Stevens Institute of Technology, NJ (MW)
St. Gregory's College, OK (MW)
Temple University, PA (W)
Trinity College, CT (MW)
Tufts University, MA (W)
University of California (San Diego), CA (MW)
University of Detroit Mercy, MI (M)
University of Illinois (Chicago), IL (M)
University of Massachusetts (Dartmouth), MA (MW)
University of North Carolina (Asheville), NC (MW)
University of North Carolina (Chapel Hill), NC (MW)
University of Notre Dame, IN (MW)
University of Pennsylvania, PA (MW)
Vassar College, NY (MW)
Wayne State University, MI (MW)
Wellesley College, MA (W)
William Patterson College, NJ (MW)
Yale University, CT (MW)
Yeshiva University, NY (MW)

Field Hockey

Albright College, PA (W)
Alvernia College, PA (W)
American University, DC (W)
Amherst College, MA (W)
Appalachian State University, NC (W)
Assumption College, MA (W)
Babson College, MA (W)
Ball State University, IN (W)
Bates College, ME (W)
Becker College, MA (W)
Bellarmine College, KY (W)
Bentley College, MA (W)
Bethany College, KS (W)
Bethany College, WV (W)
Bloomsburg University, PA (W)
Boston College, MA (W)
Boston University, MA (W)
Bowdoin College, ME (W)
Bridgewater College, VA (W)
Bridgewater State College, MA (W)
Brown University, RI (W)
Bryant College, RI (W)
Bryn Mawr College, PA (W)
Bucknell University, PA (W)
Cabrini College, PA (W)
Castleton State College, VT (W)
Catawba College, NC (W)
Catholic University of America, DC (W)
Central Michigan University, MI (W)
Clark University, MA (W)
Colgate University, NY (W)
The College of New Jersey, NJ (W)
College of Notre Dame of Maryland, MD (W)
College of William and Mary, VA (W)
College of Wooster, OH (W)
College of the Holy Cross, MA (W)
Columbia University, NY (W)
Connecticut College, CT (W)
Cornell University, NY (W)
Dartmouth College, NH (W)
Davidson College, NC (W)
Davis & Elkins College, WV (W)
Delaware Valley College, PA (W)
Denison University, OH (W)
De Pauw University, IN (W)
Dickinson College, PA (W)
Drew University, NJ (W)
Drexel University, PA (W)
Duke University, NC (W)
Earlham College, IN (W)
Eastern College, PA (W)

Eastern Connecticut State University, CT (W)
Eastern Mennonite College, VA (W)
East Stroudsburg University, PA (W)
Elizabethtown College, PA (W)
Elmira College, NY (W)
Essex Community College, MD (W)
Fairfield University, CT (W)
Fairleigh Dickinson University, NJ (W)
Fitchburg State College, MA (W)
Franklin & Marshall College, PA (W)
Georgetown University, DC (W)
Gettysburg College, PA (W)
Gordon College, MA (W)
Goucher College, MD (W)
Hamilton College, NY (W)
Hanover College, IN (W)
Harford Community College, MD (W)
Hartwick College, NY (W)
Harvard University, MA (W)
Haverford College, PA (W)
Herkimer County Community College, NY (W)
High Point University, NC (W)
Hofstra University, NY (W)
Hood College, MD (W)
Hope College, MI (W)
Houghton College, NY (W)
Indiana University of Pennsylvania, PA (W)
Ithaca College, NY (W)
James Madison University, VA (W)
Johns Hopkins University, MD (W)
Juniata College, PA (W)
Kean University, NJ (W)
Keene State College, NH (W)
Kent State University (Ashtabula), OH (W)
Kent State University (Kent), OH (W)
Kent State University (New Philadelphia), OH (W)
Kent State University (Warren), OH (W)
Kenyon College, OH (W)
Keystone Junior College, PA (W)
King's College, PA (W)
Kutztown University, PA (W)
Lafayette College, PA (W)
La Salle University, PA (W)
Lebanon Valley College, PA (W)
Lehigh University, PA (W)

Lock Haven University of Pennsylvania, PA (W)
Long Island University (C. W. Post Campus), NY (W)
Longwood College, VA (W)
Lycoming College, PA (W)
Lynchburg College, VA (W)
Manhattanville College, NY (W)
Mansfield University, PA (W)
Marietta College, OH (W)
Mary Baldwin College, VA (W)
Mary Washington College, VA (W)
Marywood College, PA (W)
Massachusetts Institute of Technology, MA (W)
Merrimack College, MA (W)
Messiah College, PA (W)
Miami University, OH (W)
Michigan State University, MI (W)
Middlebury College, VT (W)
Millersville University, PA (W)
Montclair State College, NJ (W)
Moravian College, PA (W)
Mount Holyoke College, MA (W)
Muhlenberg College, PA (W)
Nichols College, MA (W)
Northwestern University, IL (W)
Oberlin College, OH (W)
Ocean County College, NJ (W)
Ohio State University, OH (W)
Ohio University, OH (W)
Ohio Wesleyan University, OH (W)
Old Dominion University, VA (W)
Olivet College, MI (W)
Oswego State University (SUNY), NY (W)
Pennsylvania State University, PA (W)
Pfeiffer College, NC (W)
Philadelphia University, PA (W)
Plymouth State College, NH (W)
Princeton University, NJ (W)
Providence College, RI (W)
Quinnipiac University, CT (W)
Radford University, VA (W)
Randolph-Macon College, VA (W)
Rensselaer Polytechnic Institute, NY (W)
Rider College, NJ (W)
Roanoke College, VA (W)
Rowan University, NJ (W)
Sacred Heart University, CT (W)
Saint Joseph's University, PA (W)
Saint Lawrence University, NY (W)
Saint Louis University, MO (W)

Saint Michael's College, VT (W)
Salem State College, MA (W)
Shippensburg University of Pennsylvania, PA (W)
Siena College, NY (W)
Skidmore College, NY (W)
Slippery Rock University of Pennsylvania, PA (W)
Smith College, MA (W)
Southwest Missouri State University, MO (W)
Springfield College, MA (W)
Stanford University, CA (W)
State University of New York College (Brockport), NY (W)
State University of New York College (Cortland), NY (W)
State University of New York College at Geneseo, NY (W)
State University of New York College at New Paltz, NY (W)
Swarthmore College, PA (W)
Sweet Briar College, VA (W)
Syracuse University, NY (W)
Temple University, PA (W)
Towson State University, MD (W)
Transylvania University, KY (W)
Trinity College, CT (W)
Tufts University, MA (W)
Union College, NY (W)
University at Albany (SUNY), NY (W)
University at Buffalo (SUNY), NY (W)
University of California (Berkeley), CA (W)
University of Connecticut, CT (W)
University of Delaware, DE (W)
University of Iowa, IA (W)
University of Louisville, KY (W)
University of Maine, ME (W)
University of Maryland, MD (W)
University of Massachusetts (Amherst), MA (W)
University of Massachusetts (Dartmouth), MA (W)
University of Massachusetts (Lowell), MA (W)
University of Michigan, MI (W)
University of New Hampshire, NH (W)
University of North Carolina (Asheville), NC (W)
University of North Carolina (Chapel Hill), NC (W)
University of Pennsylvania, PA (W)
University of Rhode Island, RI (W)

University of Richmond, VA (W)
University of Scranton, PA (W)
University of the Pacific, CA (W)
University of Toledo, OH (W)
University of Vermont, VT (W)
University of Virginia, VA (W)
Ursinus College, PA (W)
Vassar College, NY (W)
Villanova University, PA (W)
Virginia Commonwealth University, VA (W)
Wake Forest University, NC (W)
Washington College, MD (W)
Wellesley College, MA (W)
Wesley College, DE (W)
Wesleyan University, CT (W)
West Chester University, PA (W)
Western Maryland College, MD (W)
Western New England College, MA (W)
Westfield State College, MA (W)
Wilkes College, NC (W)
Wilkes University, PA (W)
William Patterson College, NJ (W)
Wilson College, PA (W)
Worcester State College, MA (W)
Yale University, CT (W)
York College of Pennsylvania, PA (W)

Football

Abilene Christian University, TX (M)
Adams State College, CO (M)
Adrian College, MI (M)
Alabama A&M University, AL (M)
Alabama State University, AL (M)
Albany State University, GA (M)
Albion College, MI (M)
Albright College, PA (M)
Alcorn State University, MS (M)
Alfred University, NY (M)
Allegheny College, PA (M)
Alma College, MI (M)
American International College, MA (M)
Amherst College, MA (M)
Anderson University, IN (M)
Angelo State University, TX (M)
Anoka-Ramsey College, MN (M)
Appalachian State University, NC (M)
Apprentice School, VA (M)
Arizona State University, AZ (M)
Arkansas State University, AR (M)

Arkansas Tech University, AR (M)
Ashland College, OH (M)
Assumption College, MA (M)
Auburn University, AL (M)
Augsburg College, MN (M)
Augustana College, IL (M)
Augustana College, SD (M)
Aurora University, IL (M)
Austin College, TX (M)
Austin Peay State University, TN (M)
Avila College, MO (M)
Azusa Pacific University, CA (M)
Baker University, KS (M)
Ball State University, IN (M)
Bates College, ME (M)
Baylor University, TX (M)
Beloit College, WI (M)
Bemidji State University, MN (M)
Benedictine College, KS (M)
Benedictine University, IL (M)
Bethany College, KS (M)
Bethany College, WV (M)
Bethel College, KS (M)
Bethel College, MN (M)
Bethune-Cookman College, FL (M)
Black Hills State University, SD (M)
Blackburn College, IL (M)
Bloomsburg University, PA (M)
Bluffton College, OH (M)
Boise State University, ID (M)
Boston College, MA (M)
Bowdoin College, ME (M)
Bowie State University, MD (M)
Bowling Green State University, OH (M)
Brainerd Community College, MN (M)
Bridgewater College, VA (M)
Bridgewater State College, MA (M)
Brigham Young University, UT (M)
Brown University, RI (M)
Bryant College, RI (M)
Bucknell University, PA (M)
Buena Vista University, IA (M)
Buffalo State College, NY (M)
Butler University, IN (M)
Butte College, CA (M)
Cabrillo College, CA (M)
California Lutheran University, CA (M)
California Polytechnic State University, CA (M)
California State University (Fresno), CA (M)

California State University (Hayward), CA (M)
California State University (Northridge), CA (M)
California State University (Sacramento), CA (M)
California University, PA (M)
Cameron University, OK (M)
Campbellsville College, KY (M)
Canisius College, NY (M)
Capital University, OH (M)
Carleton College, MN (M)
Carnegie-Mellon University, PA (M)
Carroll College, MT (M)
Carroll College, WI (M)
Carson-Newman College, TN (M)
Carthage College, WI (M)
Case Western Reserve University, OH (M)
Catawba College, NC (M)
Catholic University of America, DC (M)
Cayuga Community College, NY (M)
Central College, IA (M)
Central Connecticut State University, CT (M)
Central Lakes College, MN (M)
Central Methodist College, MO (M)
Central Michigan University, MI (M)
Central Missouri State University, MO (M)
Central Washington University, WA (M)
Cerritos College, CA (M)
Chadron State College, NE (M)
Chaffey College, CA (M)
Chapman University, CA (M)
Cheyney University of Pennsylvania, PA (M)
Chowan College, NC (M)
Citadel, SC (M)
City College of San Francisco, CA (M)
Clarion University, PA (M)
Clark Atlanta University, GA (M)
Clemson University, SC (M)
Coahoma Junior College, MS (M)
Coe College, IA (M)
Coffeyville Community College, KS (M)
Colgate University, NY (M)
College of Mount St. Joseph, OH (M)

The College of New Jersey, NJ (M)
College of St. Francis, IL (M)
College of the Desert, CA (M)
College of the Holy Cross, MA (M)
College of the Redwoods, CA (M)
College of the Sequoias, CA (M)
College of William and Mary, VA (M)
College of Wooster, OH (M)
Colorado College, CO (M)
Colorado School of Mines, CO (M)
Colorado State University, CO (M)
Columbia University, NY (M)
Compton Community College, CA (M)
Concord College, WV (M)
Concordia College, MN (M)
Concordia University, MN (M)
Concordia University, NE (M)
Concordia University, IL (M)
Concordia University Wisconsin, WI (M)
Contra Costa College, CA (M)
Copiah-Lincoln Community College, MS (M)
Cornell College, IA (M)
Cornell University, NY (M)
Culver-Stockton College, MO (M)
Cumberland College, KY (M)
Curry College, MA (M)
Dakota State University, SD (M)
Dakota Wesleyan University, SD (M)
Dana College, NE (M)
Dartmouth College, NH (M)
Davidson College, NC (M)
Dean Junior College, MA (M)
De Anza College, CA (M)
Delaware State University, DE (M)
Delaware Valley College, PA (M)
Delta State University, MS (M)
Denison University, OH (M)
De Pauw University, IN (M)
Diablo Valley Community College, CA (M)
Dickinson College, PA (M)
Dickinson State University, ND (M)
Dixie College, UT (M)
Doane College, NE (M)
Dodge City Community College, KS (M)
Drake University, IA (M)
Duke University, NC (M)

Duquesne University, PA (M)
Earlham College, IN (M)
East Carolina University, NC (M)
East Central University, OK (M)
Eastern Illinois University, IL (M)
Eastern Kentucky University, KY (M)
Eastern Michigan University, MI (M)
Eastern New Mexico University, NM (M)
Eastern Oregon State College, OR (M)
Eastern Washington University, WA (M)
East Stroudsburg University, PA (M)
East Tennessee State University, TN (M)
East Texas Baptist University, TX (M)
Edinboro University of Pennsylvania, PA (M)
El Camino College, CA (M)
Elizabeth City State University, NC (M)
Elmhurst College, IL (M)
Elon College, NC (M)
Emory and Henry College, VA (M)
Emporia State University, KS (M)
Eureka College, IL (M)
Evangel College, MO (M)
Fairleigh Dickinson University, NJ (M)
Fairmont State College, WV (M)
Fayetteville State University, NC (M)
Fergus Falls Community College, MN (M)
Ferris State College, MI (M)
Ferrum College, VA (M)
Fitchburg State College, MA (M)
Florida A&M University, FL (M)
Florida Atlantic University, FL (M)
Florida State University, FL (M)
Football College, CA (M)
Fordham University, NY (M)
Fort Hays State University, KS (M)
Fort Lewis College, CO (M)
Fort Scott College, KS (M)
Fort Valley State University, GA (M)
Franklin & Marshall College, PA (M)
Fresno City College, CA (M)

Friends University, KS (M)
Fullerton College, CA (M)
Furman University, SC (M)
Gannon College, PA (M)
Garden City Community College, KS (M)
Gardner-Webb College, NC (M)
Geneva College, PA (M)
Georgetown College, KY (M)
Georgetown University, DC (M)
Georgia Institute of Technology, GA (M)
Georgia Military College, GA (M)
Georgia Southern University, GA (M)
Gettysburg College, PA (M)
Glendale Community College, AZ (M)
Glendale Community College, CA (M)
Glenville State College, WV (M)
Golden West College, CA (M)
Graceland College, IA (M)
Grambling State University, LA (M)
Grand Rapids Community College, MI (M)
Grand Valley State College, MI (M)
Grinnell College, IA (M)
Grove City College, PA (M)
Gustavus Adolphus College, MN (M)
Hamilton College, NY (M)
Hamline University, MN (M)
Hampden-Sydney College, VA (M)
Hampton University, VA (M)
Hanover College, IN (M)
Harding University, AR (M)
Harvard University, MA (M)
Haskell Indian Nations University, KS (M)
Hastings College, NE (M)
Heidelberg College, OH (M)
Henderson State University, AR (M)
Hibbing Community College, MN (M)
Highland Community College, KS (M)
Hillsdale College, MI (M)
Hinds Community College, MS (M)
Hiram College, OH (M)
Hofstra University, NY (M)
Holmes Junior College, MS (M)
Hope College, MI (M)
Howard Payne University, TX (M)

Howard University, DC (M)
Hudson Valley Community College, NY (M)
Humboldt State University, CA (M)
Huron University, SD (M)
Hutchinson College, KS (M)
Idaho State University, ID (M)
Illinois College, IL (M)
Illinois State University, IL (M)
Illinois Wesleyan University, IL (M)
Indiana State University, IN (M)
Indiana University, IN (M)
Indiana University of Pennsylvania, PA (M)
Inver Hills Community College, MN (M)
Iona College, NY (M)
Iowa State University of Science and Technology, IA (M)
Iowa Wesleyan College, IA (M)
Itawamba Community College, MS (M)
Ithaca College, NY (M)
Jackson State University, MS (M)
Jacksonville State University, AL (M)
James Madison University, VA (M)
Jamestown College, ND (M)
John Carroll University, OH (M)
Johnson C. Smith University, NC (M)
Jones County Junior College, MS (M)
Juniata College, PA (M)
Kalamazoo College, MI (M)
Kansas State University, KS (M)
Kansas Wesleyan College, KS (M)
Kean University, NJ (M)
Kent State University (Ashtabula), OH (M)
Kent State University (Kent), OH (M)
Kent State University (New Philadelphia), OH (M)
Kent State University (Warren), OH (M)
Kentucky State University, KY (M)
Kentucky Wesleyan College, KY (M)
Kenyon College, OH (M)
Kilgore College, TX (M)
King's College, PA (M)
Knox College, IL (M)
Kutztown University, PA (M)
Lafayette College, PA (M)

Lake Forest College, IL (M)
Lambuth University, TN (M)
Langston University, OK (M)
La Salle University, PA (M)
Lawrence University, WI (M)
Lebanon Valley College, PA (M)
Lees-McRae College, NC (M)
Lehigh University, PA (M)
Lenoir-Rhyne College, NC (M)
Lewis and Clark College, OR (M)
Liberty University, VA (M)
Linfield College, OR (M)
Livingstone College, NC (M)
Lock Haven University of Pennsylvania, PA (M)
Long Beach City College, CA (M)
Long Island University (C. W. Post Campus), NY (M)
Loras College, IA (M)
Los Angeles Pierce Junior College, CA (M)
Los Angeles Valley College, CA (M)
Los Medanos College, CA (M)
Louisiana College, LA (M)
Louisiana State University (Baton Rouge), LA (M)
Louisiana Tech University, LA (M)
Luther College, IA (M)
Lycoming College, PA (M)
Macalester College, MN (M)
Manchester College, IN (M)
Mankato State University, MN (M)
Mansfield University, PA (M)
Marietta College, OH (M)
Marist College, NY (M)
Marshall University, WV (M)
Mars Hill College, NC (M)
Maryville College, TN (M)
Massachusetts Institute of Technology, MA (M)
Mayville State College, ND (M)
McKendree College, IL (M)
McNeese State University, LA (M)
McPherson College, KS (M)
Mercyhurst College, PA (M)
Mesa Community College, AZ (M)
Mesa State College, CO (M)
Miami University, OH (M)
Michigan State University, MI (M)
Michigan Technological University, MI (M)
Mid-America Nazarene College, KS (M)

Middlebury College, VT (M)
Middle Tennessee State University, TN (M)
Midland Lutheran College, NE (M)
Miles College, AL (M)
Millersville University, PA (M)
Millikin University, IL (M)
Minot State, ND (M)
Mississippi College, MS (M)
Mississippi Delta Junior College, MS (M)
Mississippi Gulf Coast Junior College, MS (M)
Mississippi State University, MS (M)
Mississippi Valley State University, MS (M)
Missouri Southern State College, MO (M)
Missouri Valley College, MO (M)
Missouri Western State College, MO (M)
Modesto Junior College, CA (M)
Monmouth College, IL (M)
Monmouth College, NJ (M)
Montana College of Mineral Science and Technology, MT (M)
Montana State University, MT (M)
Montclair State College, NJ (M)
Moorhead State University, MN (M)
Moorpark College, CA (M)
Moravian College, PA (M)
Morehouse College, GA (M)
Morgan State University, MD (M)
Morningside College, IA (M)
Morris Brown College, GA (M)
Mount Union College, OH (M)
Mt. San Antonio College, CA (M)
Muhlenberg College, PA (M)
Murray State University, KY (M)
Muskingum College, OH (M)
Nassau Community College, NY (M)
Navarro College, TX (M)
Nebraska Wesleyan University, NE (M)
Newberry College, SC (M)
New Mexico Highlands University, NM (M)
New Mexico State University, NM (M)
Nicholls State University, LA (M)
Nichols College, MA (M)
Norfolk State University, VA (M)

North Carolina A & T State University, NC (M)
North Carolina Central University, NC (M)
North Carolina State University, NC (M)
North Central College, IL (M)
North Dakota State, ND (M)
North Dakota State University, ND (M)
Northeastern Illinois University, IL (M)
Northeast Louisiana University, LA (M)
Northeast Mississippi Community College, MS (M)
Northeast Missouri State University, MO (M)
Northern Arizona University, AZ (M)
Northern Illinois University, IL (M)
Northern Michigan University, MI (M)
Northern Montana College, MT (M)
Northern State University, SD (M)
North Greenville College, SC (M)
North Hennepin Community College, MN (M)
North Iowa Area Community College, IA (M)
Northland Community & Technical College, MN (M)
Northwestern College, IA (M)
Northwestern College, MN (M)
Northwestern Oklahoma State University, OK (M)
Northwestern State University of Louisiana, LA (M)
Northwestern University, IL (M)
Northwest Mississippi Community College, MS (M)
Northwest Missouri State University, MO (M)
Northwood Institute, MI (M)
Norwich University, VT (M)
Oberlin College, OH (M)
Occidental College, CA (M)
Ohio Northern University, OH (M)
Ohio State University, OH (M)
Ohio University, OH (M)
Ohio Wesleyan University, OH (M)
Oklahoma Panhandle State University, OK (M)
Oklahoma State University, OK (M)
Olivet College, MI (M)

Olivet Nazarene University, IL (M)
Orange Coast College, CA (M)
Oregon Institute of Technology, OR (M)
Oregon State University, OR (M)
Ottawa University, KS (M)
Otterbein College, OH (M)
Ouachita Baptist University, AR (M)
Pace University, NY (M)
Pacific Lutheran University, WA (M)
Palomar College, CA (M)
Pennsylvania State University, PA (M)
Peru State College, NE (M)
Phoenix College, AZ (M)
Pittsburg State University, KS (M)
Plymouth State College, NH (M)
Pomona-Pitzer Colleges, CA (M)
Portland State University, OR (M)
Prairie View A&M University, TX (M)
Presbyterian College, SC (M)
Princeton University, NJ (M)
Principia College, IL (M)
Purdue University, IN (M)
Quincy University, IL (M)
Ramapo College, NJ (M)
Randolph-Macon College, VA (M)
Ranetto Santiago College, CA (M)
Rensselaer Polytechnic Institute, NY (M)
Rice University, TX (M)
Ricks College, ID (M)
Ripon College, WI (M)
Riverside Community College, CA (M)
Robert Morris College, PA (M)
Rochester Community College, MN (M)
Rocky Mountain College, MT (M)
Rose-Hulman Institute of Technology, IN (M)
Rowan University, NJ (M)
Saddleback College, CA (M)
Saginaw Valley State University, MI (M)
Saint Ambrose University, IA (M)
Saint Anselm College, NH (M)
Saint Cloud State University, MN (M)
Saint Francis College, IN (M)
Saint Francis College, PA (M)

Saint John Fisher College, NY (M)
Saint John's University, MN (M)
Saint John's University, NY (MW)
Saint Joseph's College, IN (M)
Saint Lawrence University, NY (M)
Saint Mary College, KS (M)
Saint Mary's College of California, CA (M)
Saint Norbert College, WI (M)
Saint Olaf College, MN (M)
Saint Paul's College, VA (M)
Saint Peter's College, NJ (M)
Samford University, AL (M)
Sam Houston State University, TX (M)
San Bernardino Community College, CA (M)
San Diego Mesa College, CA (M)
San Diego State University, CA (M)
San Joaquin Delta College, CA (M)
San Jose State University, CA (M)
Santa Barbara City College, CA (M)
Santa Clara University, CA (M)
Santa Monico College, CA (M)
Santa Rosa Junior College, CA (M)
Savannah State College, GA (M)
Scottsdale Community College, AZ (M)
Shepherd College, WV (M)
Shippensburg University of Pennsylvania, PA (M)
Siena College, NY (M)
Sierra College, CA (M)
Simpson College, CA (M)
Sioux Falls College, SD (M)
Slippery Rock University of Pennsylvania, PA (M)
Snow College, UT (M)
Solano Community College, CA (M)
South Carolina State College, SC (M)
South Dakota School of Mines and Technology, SD (M)
South Dakota State University, SD (M)
Southeastern Oklahoma State University, OK (M)
Southeast Missouri State University, MO (M)
Southern Arkansas University, AR (M)

Southern Illinois University, IL (M)
Southern Methodist University, TX (M)
Southern Oregon State College, OR (M)
Southern University and A&M College, LA (M)
Southern Utah University, UT (M)
Southwest Baptist University, MO (M)
Southwestern College, CA (M)
Southwestern College, KS (M)
Southwest Missouri State University, MO (M)
Southwest State University, MN (M)
Southwest Texas State University, TX (M)
Spokane Community College, WA (M)
Springfield College, MA (M)
Stanford University, CA (M)
State University of New York College (Brockport), NY (M)
State University of New York College (Cortland), NY (M)
State University of New York Maritime College, NY (M)
State University of West Georgia, GA (M)
Stephen F. Austin State University, TX (M)
Sterling College, KS (M)
St. Mary of the Plains College, KS (M)
Stonehill College, MA (M)
Sul Ross State University, TX (M)
Swarthmore College, PA (M)
Syracuse University, NY (M)
Tabor College, KS (M)
Taft College, CA (M)
Tarleton State University, TX (M)
Teikyo Westmar University, IA (M)
Temple University, PA (M)
Tennessee State University, TN (M)
Tennessee Technological University, TN (M)
Tennessee Wesleyan College, TN (M)
Texas A&I University, TX (M)
Texas A&M Commerce, TX (M)
Texas A&M University, TX (M)
Texas Christian University, TX (M)
Texas Lutheran College, TX (M)

Texas Southern University, TX (M)
Texas Tech University, TX (M)
Thomas More College, KY (M)
Towson State University, MD (M)
Trinity College, CT (M)
Trinity University, TX (M)
Tri-State University, IN (M)
Troy State University, AL (M)
Tufts University, MA (M)
Tulane University, LA (M)
Tuskegee University, AL (M)
Tyler Junior College, TX (M)
Union College, KY (M)
Union College, NY (M)
University of Akron, OH (M)
University of Alabama (Birmingham), AL (M)
University of Alabama (Tuscaloosa), AL (M)
University of Albany (SUNY), NY (M)
University of Arizona, AZ (M)
University of Arkansas (Fayetteville), AR (M)
University of Arkansas (Monticello), AR (M)
University of Arkansas (Pine Bluff, AR (M)
University of Buffalo (SUNY), NY (M)
University of California (Berkeley), CA (M)
University of California (Davis), CA (M)
University of California (UCLA), CA (M)
University of Central Arkansas, AR (M)
University of Central Florida, FL (M)
University of Central Oklahoma, OK (M)
University of Chicago, IL (M)
University of Cincinnati, OH (M)
University of Colorado, CO (M)
University of Connecticut, CT (M)
University of Dayton, OH (M)
University of Delaware, DE (M)
University of Dubuque, IA (M)
University of Findlay, OH (M)
University of Florida, FL (M)
University of Georgia, GA (M)
University of Guam, PA (M)
University of Hawaii (Manoa), HI (M)
University of Houston, TX (M)
University of Idaho, ID (M)

University of Illinois (Chicago), IL (M)
University of Illinois (Urbana-Champaign), IL (M)
University of Indianapolis, IN (M)
University of Iowa, IA (M)
University of Kansas, KS (M)
University of Kentucky, KY (M)
University of La Verne, CA (M)
University of Louisiana at Lafayette, LA (M)
University of Louisville, KY (M)
University of Maine, ME (M)
University of Mary, ND (M)
University of Maryland, MD (M)
University of Massachusetts (Amherst), MA (M)
University of Massachusetts (Boston), MA (M)
University of Massachusetts (Lowell), MA (M)
University of Memphis, TN (M)
University of Miami, FL (M)
University of Michigan, MI (M)
University of Minnesota (Duluth), MN (M)
University of Minnesota (Minneapolis), MN (M)
University of Minnesota (Morris), MN (M)
University of Mississippi, MS (M)
University of Missouri, MO (M)
University of Missouri (Columbia), MO (M)
University of Missouri (Rolla), MO (M)
University of Montana, MT (M)
University of Nebraska, NE (M)
University of Nebraska (Kearney), NE (M)
University of Nebraska (Lincoln), NE (M)
University of Nevada, NV (M)
University of Nevada (Reno), NV (M)
University of New Hampshire, NH (M)
University of New Haven, CT (M)
University of New Mexico, NM (M)
University of North Alabama, AL (M)
University of North Carolina (Asheville), NC (M)
University of North Carolina (Chapel Hill), NC (M)
University of North Dakota, ND (M)

University of Northern Colorado, CO (M)
University of Northern Iowa, IA (M)
University of North Texas, TX (M)
University of Notre Dame, IN (M)
University of Oklahoma, OK (M)
University of Oregon, OR (M)
University of Pennsylvania, PA (M)
University of Pittsburgh, PA (M)
University of Puget Sound, WA (M)
University of Redlands, CA (M)
University of Rhode Island, RI (M)
University of Richmond, VA (M)
University of San Diego, CA (M)
University of South Carolina (Columbia), SC (M)
University of South Dakota, SD (M)
University of South Florida, FL (M)
University of Southern California, CA (M)
University of Southern Mississippi, MS (M)
University of St. Thomas, MN (M)
University of Stony Brook (SUNY), NY (M)
University of Tennessee, TN (M)
University of Tennessee (Knoxville), TN (M)
University of Tennessee (Martin), TN (M)
University of Texas (Austin), TX (M)
University of Texas (El Paso), TX (M)
University of Toledo, OH (M)
University of Tulsa, OK (M)
University of Utah, UT (M)
University of Virginia, VA (M)
The University of Virginia's College at Wise, VA (M)
University of Washington, WA (M)
University of West Alabama, AL (M)
University of Wisconsin (Eau Claire), WI (M)
University of Wisconsin (La Crosse), WI (M)
University of Wisconsin (Madison), WI (M)
University of Wisconsin (Oshkosh), WI (M)

University of Wisconsin (Platteville), WI (M)
University of Wisconsin (River Falls), WI (M)
University of Wisconsin (Stevens Point), WI (M)
University of Wisconsin (Stout), WI (M)
University of Wisconsin (Superior), WI (M)
University of Wyoming, WY (M)
Upper Iowa University, IA (M)
Ursinus College, PA (M)
Utah State University, UT (M)
Valdosta State University, GA (M)
Valley City State University, ND (M)
Valparaiso University, IN (M)
Vanderbilt University, TN (M)
Ventura College, CA (M)
Villanova University, PA (M)
Virginia Military Institute, VA (M)
Virginia Polytechnic Institute & State University, VA (M)
Virginia State University, VA (M)
Virginia Union University, VA (M)
Wabash College, IN (M)
Wake Forest University, NC (M)
Waldorf College, IA (M)
Walla Walla Community College, WA (M)
Wartburg College, IA (M)
Washburn University, KS (M)
Washington and Jefferson College, PA (M)
Washington State University, WA (M)
Washington University, MO (M)
Wayne State College, NE (M)
Wayne State University, MI (M)
Weber State College, UT (M)
Wesleyan University, CT (M)
Wesley College, DE (M)
West Chester University, PA (M)
Western Carolina University, NC (M)
Western Connecticut State University, CT (M)
Western Illinois University, IL (M)
Western Kentucky University, KY (M)
Western Maryland College, MD (M)
Western Michigan University, MI (M)
Western Montana College, MT (M)

Western New England College, MA (M)
Western New Mexico University, NM (M)
Western Oregon State College, OR (M)
Western State College, CO (M)
Western Washington University, WA (M)
West Liberty State College, WV (M)
Westfield State College, MA (M)
Westminster College, PA (M)
West Texas State University, TX (M)
West Virginia Institute of Technology, WV (M)
West Virginia University, WV (M)
West Virginia Wesleyan College, WV (M)
Wheaton College, IL (M)
Whittier College, CA (M)
Whitworth College, WA (M)
Wilberforce University, OH (M)
Wilkes College, NC (M)
Wilkes University, PA (M)
Willamette University, OR (M)
William Jewell College, MO (M)
William Patterson College, NJ (M)
William Penn College, IA (M)
William Rainey Harper College, IL (M)
Williams College, MA (M)
Williamson Trade School, PA (M)
Wilmington College, OH (M)
Wingate College, NC (M)
Winona State University, MN (M)
Winston-Salem State University, NC (M)
Wofford College, SC (M)
Worcester State College, MA (M)
Worthington Community College, MN (M)
Yakima Valley College, WA (M)
Yale University, CT (M)
Youngstown State University, OH (M)
Yuba Community College, CA (M)

Golf

Abilene Christian University, TX (M)
Adams State College, CO (M)
Adelphi University, NY (M)
Adirondack College, NY (M)

Adrian College, MI (MW)
Alabama A&M University, AL (M)
Alabama State University, AL (MW)
Albion College, MI (MW)
Albright College, PA (M)
Alcorn State University, MS (M)
Alfred University, NY (M)
Allegheny College, PA (M)
Allen County College, KS (M)
Allentown College of Saint Francis de Sales, PA (M)
Alma College, MI (MW)
Alvernia College, PA (M)
American International College, MA (M)
American University, DC (M)
Amherst College, MA (MW)
Anderson College, SC (M)
Anderson University, IN (MW)
Appalachian State University, NC (MW)
Apprentice School, VA (M)
Aquinas College, MI (MW)
Arizona State University, AZ (MW)
Arkansas College, AR (MW)
Arkansas State University, AR (MW)
Arkansas Tech University, AR (M)
Ashland College, OH (M)
Atlantic Community College, NJ (MW)
Auburn University, AL (MW)
Augusta State University, GA (M)
Augustana College, IL (MW)
Augustana College, SD (MW)
Aurora University, IL (MW)
Austin College, TX (M)
Austin Community College, MN (M)
Austin Peay State University, TN (M)
Averett College, VA (M)
Babson College, MA (M)
Baker University, KS (M)
Ball State University, IN (M)
Barry University, FL (MW)
Barton College, NC (M)
Barton County College, KS (M)
Bates College, ME (MW)
Baylor University, TX (M)
Becker College, MA (M)
Belhaven College, MS (M)
Bellarmine College, KY (MW)
Belmont Abbey College, NC (M)
Belmont College, TN (MW)
Beloit College, WI (M)

Bemidji State University, MN (MW)
Benedictine College, KS (MW)
Benedictine University, IL (MW)
Bergen Community College, NJ (M)
Berry College, GA (M)
Bethany College, KS (MW)
Bethany College, WV (MW)
Bethel College, IN (M)
Bethel College, MN (M)
Bethune-Cookman College, FL (MW)
Binghamton University (SUNY), NY (M)
Bismarck State College, ND (MW)
Blackburn College, IL (M)
Black Hawk College, IL (M)
Bluefield College, VA (M)
Bluefield State College, WV (M)
Bluffton College, OH (M)
Boise State University, ID (MW)
Boston College, MA (MW)
Boston University, MA (MW)
Bowdoin College, ME (MW)
Bowling Green State University, OH (MW)
Bradley University, IL (MW)
Brescia University, KY (MW)
Brevard Community College, FL (M)
Briar Cliff College, IA (MW)
Bridgewater College, VA (M)
Brigham Young University, UT (MW)
Broome Community College, NY (M)
Broward Community College, FL (MW)
Brown University, RI (MW)
Bryant College, RI (MW)
Bucknell University, PA (MW)
Bucks County Community College, PA (MW)
Buena Vista University, IA (MW)
Butler County Community College, KS (M)
Butler County Community College, PA (M)
Butler University, IN (MW)
Butte College, CA (M)
Cabrillo College, CA (M)
Cabrini College, PA (M)
California Baptist University, CA (M)
California Institute of Technology, CA (MW)
California Lutheran University, CA (M)
California State University at Bakersfield, CA (M)

California State University (Chico), CA (M)
California State University (Dominguez Hills), CA (M)
California State University (Fresno), CA (M)
California State University (Long Beach), CA (MW)
California State University (Northridge), CA (MW)
California State University (Sacramento), CA (MW)
California State University (San Bernardino), CA (M)
California State University (Stanislaus), CA (M)
Calvin College, MI (MW)
Cameron University, OK (M)
Campbellsville University, KY (M)
Campbell University, NC (MW)
Canisius College, NY (M)
Capital University, OH (M)
Carleton College, MN (MW)
Carroll College, WI (MW)
Carson-Newman College, TN (M)
Carthage College, WI (M)
Case Western Reserve University, OH (M)
Catawba College, NC (MW)
Cayuga County Community College, NY (M)
Cedarville College, OH (M)
Centenary College, LA (M)
Centenary College, NJ (MW)
Central Arizona College, AZ (M)
Central College, IA (M)
Central Christian College, KS (W)
Central Connecticut State University, CT (M)
Central Methodist College, MO (MW)
Central Missouri State University, MO (M)
Central Washington University, WA (M)
Central Wesleyan College, SC (M)
Cerritos College, CA (M)
Chadron State College, NE (W)
Chapman University, CA (M)
Charleston Southern University, SC (M)
Chicago State University, IL (MW)
Chowan College, NC (M)
Christopher Newport College, VA (M)
Citadel, SC (M)

Clarion University, PA (M)
Clark College, WA (M)
Clark State College, OH (M)
Clarkson University, NY (MW)
Clemson University, SC (M)
Cleveland State University, OH (MW)
Cloud County Community College, KS (M)
Coahoma Junior College, MS (M)
Coastal Carolina College, SC (MW)
Coastal Carolina Community College, NC (M)
Coe College, IA (MW)
Coffeyville Community College, KS (M)
Coker College, SC (M)
Colgate University, NY (M)
College of Allegheny County, PA (MW)
College of Charleston, SC (MW)
The College of New Jersey, NJ (M)
College of St. Francis, IL (MW)
College of the Desert, CA (M)
College of the Holy Cross, MA (M)
College of the Redwoods, CA (M)
College of the Sequoias, CA (M)
College of William and Mary, VA (MW)
College of Wooster, OH (M)
Colorado Christian University, CO (M)
Colorado School of Mines, CO (MW)
Colorado State University, CO (MW)
Columbia Basin Community College, WA (MW)
Columbia College, MO (M)
Columbia-Greene Community College, NY (M)
Columbia University, NY (M)
Columbus College, GA (M)
Columbus State Community College, OH (MW)
Community College of Rhode Island, RI (M)
Concord College, WV (M)
Concordia College, MN (MW)
Concordia Lutheran College, TX (MW)
Concordia University, NE (MW)
Concordia University, MN (M)
Concordia University Wisconsin, WI (MW)
Cornell College, IA (WM)

Cornell University, NY (M)
Cowley County Community College, KS (M)
Creighton University, NE (MW)
Culver-Stockton College, MO (MW)
Cumberland College, KY (MW)
Cuyahoga Community College, OH (M)
Dakota Wesleyan University, SD (MW)
Dallas Baptist University, TX (M)
Danville Area Community College, IL (M)
Dartmouth College, NH (MW)
Davidson College, NC (M)
Davis & Elkins College, WV (M)
Daytona Beach Community College, FL (W)
Defiance College, OH (M)
Delaware Valley College, PA (M)
Delta College, MI (M)
Delta State University, MS (M)
Denison University, OH (M)
DePaul University, IL (M)
De Pauw University, IN (MW)
Detroit College of Business, MI (M)
Dickinson College, PA (MW)
Dickinson State University, ND (M)
Doane College, NE (MW)
Dodge City Community College, KS (M)
Dominican College, NY (M)
Dominican University, IL (MW)
Dowling College, NY (MW)
Drake University, IA (M)
Drexel University, PA (M)
Drury College, MO (M)
Duke University, NC (MW)
Duquesne University, PA (M)
Dutchess Community College, NY (M)
East Carolina University, NC (M)
East Central University, OK (M)
Eastern Kentucky University, KY (MW)
Eastern Michigan University, MI (MW)
Eastern Montana College, MT (MW)
Eastern Washington University, WA (MW)
Eastern Wyoming College, WY (M)
Eastfield College, TX (M)
East Tennessee State University, TN (M)

East Texas Baptist University, TX (M)
Eckerd College, FL (M)
Edgewood College, WI (MW)
Edmonds Community College, WA (MW)
El Camino College, CA (M)
Elgin Community College, IL (MW)
Elizabethtown College, PA (M)
Elmhurst College, IL (M)
Elmira College, NY (M)
Elon College, NC (M)
Emerson College, MA (M)
Emory University, GA (M)
Emporia State University, KS (M)
Erskine College, SC (M)
Essex Community College, MD (M)
Eureka College, IL (M)
Everett Community College, WA (MW)
Fairfield University, CT (M)
Fairleigh Dickinson University (Madison), NJ (M)
Fairleigh Dickinson University (Teaneck), NJ (M)
Fayetteville State University, NC (MW)
Fergus Falls Community College, MN (MW)
Ferris State College, MI (MW)
Ferrum College, VA (MW)
Flagler College, FL (M)
Florida A&M University, FL (M)
Florida Atlantic University, FL (MW)
Florida International University, FL (W)
Florida Southern College, FL (MW)
Florida State University, FL (MW)
Foothill College, CA (MW)
Fordham University, NY (M)
Fort Hays State University, KS (M)
Fort Lewis College, CO (M)
Francis Marion University, SC (M)
Franklin & Marshall College, PA (MW)
Franklin Pierce College, NH (M)
Frederick Community College, MD (MW)
Freed-Hardeman College, TN (M)
Fresno City College, CA (MW)
Fullerton College, CA (M)
Furman University, SC (MW)

Gannon College, PA (M)
Gardner-Webb College, NC (M)
George C. Wallace Community College, AL (M)
George Mason University, VA (M)
Georgetown College, KY (MW)
Georgetown University, DC (M)
George Washington University, DC (M)
Georgia College State University, GA (M)
Georgia Institute of Technology, GA (M)
Georgia Southern University, GA (M)
Georgia State University, GA (MW)
Gettysburg College, PA (MW)
Glendale Community College, AZ (M)
Glen Oaks Community College, MI (MW)
Glenville State College, WV (M)
Golden West College, CA (MW)
Gonzaga University, WA (MW)
Goshen College, IN (M)
Grace College, IN (M)
Graceland College, IA (M)
Grambling State University, LA (MW)
Grand Canyon College, AZ (M)
Grand Rapids Baptist Seminary of Cornerstone University, MI (M)
Grays Harbor College, WA (MW)
Grayson County College, TX (M)
Greenfield Community College, MA (MW)
Green Mountain College, VT (MW)
Green River Community College, WA (MW)
Greensboro College, NC (M)
Greenville College, IL (M)
Grinnell College, IA (MW)
Grove City College, PA (MW)
Gustavus Adolphus College, MN (MW)
Hamilton College, NY (MW)
Hamline University, MN (M)
Hampden-Sydney College, VA (M)
Hampton University, VA (M)
Hannibal-Lagrange College, MO (M)
Hanover College, IN (MW)
Harding University, AR (M)

Hardin-Simmons University, TX (MW)
Hartwick College, NY (MW)
Harvard University, MA (MW)
Haskell Indian Nations University, KS (W)
Hastings College, NE (MW)
Heidelberg College, OH (MW)
Henderson State University, AR (M)
Herkimer County Community College, NY (MW)
High Point University, NC (M)
Hinds Community College, MS (M)
Hiram College, OH (M)
Hofstra University, NY (M)
Holy Family College, PA (M)
Holmes Junior College, MS (M)
Hope College, MI (M)
Houston Baptist University, TX (M)
Howard Payne University, TX (M)
Huntingdon College, AL (M)
Huntington College, IN (M)
Huron University, SD (MW)
Husson College, ME (M)
Huston-Tillotson College, TX (M)
Hutchinson College, KS (M)
Idaho State University, ID (M)
Illinois Central College, IL (M)
Illinois College, IL (MW)
Illinois State University, IL (MW)
Illinois Valley Community College, IL (M)
Illinois Wesleyan University, IL (M)
Indian Hills Community College, IA (M)
Indiana University, IN (MW)
Indiana University of Pennsylvania, PA (M)
Indiana University-Purdue University, IN (M)
Indiana Wesleyan University, IN (M)
Indian River Community College, FL (M)
Inver Hills Community College, MN (M)
Iona College, NY (M)
Iowa State University of Science and Technology, IA (MW)
Iowa Wesleyan College, IA (MW)
Itawamba Community College, MS (MW)
Jackson State University, MS (M)

Jacksonville University, FL (MW)
Jacksonville College, TX (M)
Jacksonville State University, AL (M)
James Madison University, VA (MW)
Jamestown College, ND (MW)
Jefferson Community College, NY (M)
John Carroll University, OH (M)
Johnson County Community College, KS (M)
Johnson C. Smith University, NC (M)
Jones County Junior College, MS (M)
Judson College, AL (W)
Kalamazoo College, MI (M)
Kalamazoo Valley Community College, MI (MW)
Kansas City Kansas Community College, KS (M)
Kansas Newman College, KS (MW)
Kansas State University, KS (MW)
Kean University, NJ (M)
Kennesaw State College, GA (M)
Kent State University (Ashtabula), OH (M)
Kent State University (East Liverpool), OH (M)
Kent State University (Kent), OH (M)
Kent State University (New Philadelphia), OH (M)
Kent State University (Warren), OH (M)
Kentucky State University, KY (M)
Kentucky Wesleyan College, KY (M)
Kenyon College, OH (M)
King College, TN (M)
King's College, PA (M)
Kirkwood Community College, IA (M)
Kishwaukee College, IL (M)
Knox College, IL (M)
Lackawanna Junior College, PA (M)
Lafayette College, PA (M)
Lake Michigan College, MI (M)
Lake Superior State University, MI (M)
Lamar Community College, CO (M)
Lamar University, TX (MW)
Lansing Community College, MI (MW)

La Roche College, PA (M)
La Salle University, PA (M)
Lawrence University, WI (M)
Lebanon Valley College, PA (M)
Lee College, TN (M)
Lehigh County Community College, PA (MW)
Lehigh University, PA (M)
Le Moyne College, NY (M)
Lenoir Community College, NC (M)
Lenoir-Rhyne College, NC (MW)
Letourneau College, TX (MW)
Lewis and Clark College, OR (M)
Lewis Clark State College, ID (MW)
Lewis University, IL (MW)
Liberty University, VA (M)
Limestone College, SC (M)
Lincoln College, IL (MW)
Lincoln Memorial University, TN (M)
Lincoln Trail College, IL (M)
Lincoln University, MO (M)
Linfield College, OR (M)
Livingstone College, NC (M)
Long Beach City College, CA (MW)
Long Island University (Brooklyn), NY (M)
Longwood College, VA (MW)
Loras College, IA (MW)
Louisburg College, NC (M)
Louisiana State University (Baton Rouge), LA (MW)
Louisiana Tech University, LA (M)
Lower Columbia College, WA (MW)
Loyola College, MD (M)
Loyola Marymount University, CA (M)
Loyola University, IL (MW)
Luther College, IA (MW)
Lycoming College, PA (M)
Lynchburg College, VA (M)
Lynn University, FL (MW)
Macalester College, MN (MW)
Macomb Community College, MI (M)
Madison Area Technical College, WI (MW)
Madonna University, MI (M)
Malone College, OH (M)
Manchester College, IN (M)
Manhattan College, NY (M)
Mankato State University, MN (MW)

Maple Woods Community College, MO (M)
Marian College, IN (M)
Marian College, WI (M)
Marietta College, OH (M)
Marion Military Institute, AL (M)
Marquette University, WI (M)
Marshall University, WV (M)
Mars Hill College, NC (M)
Marymount University, VA (M)
Massachusetts Institute of Technology, MA (M)
Master's College, CA (M)
McCook Community College, NE (M)
McKendree College, IL (MW)
McLennan Community College, TX (MW)
McNeese State University, LA (MW)
McPherson College, KS (MW)
Mercer University, GA (MW)
Mercy College, NY (MW)
Mercyhurst College, PA (M)
Merrimack College, MA (M)
Mesa Community College, AZ (MW)
Mesa State College, CO (W)
Messiah College, PA (M)
Miami University, OH (M)
Michigan State University, MI (MW)
Middlebury College, VT (M)
Middlesex County College, NJ (M)
Middle Tennessee State University, TN (M)
Midland College, TX (MW)
Midland Lutheran College, NE (MW)
Midwestern State University, TX (M)
Millersville University, PA (M)
Millikin University, IL (MW)
Minneapolis Community & Technical College, MN (MW)
Minot State, ND (M)
Mississippi College, MS (M)
Mississippi Gulf Coast Junior College, MS (M)
Mississippi State University, MS (MW)
Mississippi Valley State University, MS (MW)
Missouri Baptist College, MO (M)
Missouri Southern State College, MO (M)
Missouri Valley College, MO (MW)

Missouri Western State College, MO (M)
Mitchell College, CT (MW)
Mitchell Community College, NC (M)
Modesto Junior College, CA (MW)
Mohawk Valley Community College, NY (M)
Monmouth College, IL (MW)
Montana College of Mineral Science and Technology, MT (MW)
Montana State University, MT (W)
Montclair State College, NJ (M)
Montreat-Anderson College, NC (M)
Moorhead State University, MN (W)
Moravian College, PA (M)
Morehead State University, KY (M)
Morningside College, IA (W)
Morton College, IL (M)
Mott Community College, MI (M)
Mount Holyoke College, MA (W)
Mount Marty College, SD (MW)
Mount Mercy College, IA (MW)
Mount Olive College, NC (M)
Mount St. Mary College, MD (MW)
Mount Union College, OH (M)
Mt. San Antonio College, CA (MW)
Muhlenberg College, PA (MW)
Murray State University, KY (M)
Muskegon Community College, MI (M)
Muskingum College, OH (M)
Nassau Community College, NY (M)
Nazareth College, NY (MW)
Nebraska Wesleyan University, NE (M)
Newberry College, SC (M)
New Mexico Junior College, NM (M)
New Mexico State University, NM (MW)
New York University, NY (M)
Niagara University, NY (M)
Nicholls State University, LA (M)
Nichols College, MA (M)
North Carolina State University, NC (MW)
North Central College, IL (M)
North Dakota State, ND (MW)

North Dakota State University, ND (M)
Northeastern Illinois University, IL (M)
Northeastern State University, OK (MW)
Northeast Louisiana University, LA (M)
Northeast Mississippi Community College, MS (M)
Northeast Missouri State University, MO (MW)
Northern Arizona University, AZ (M)
Northern Illinois University, IL (MW)
Northern Kentucky University, KY (MW)
Northern Michigan University, MI (M)
Northern Montana College, MT (W)
Northern State University, SD (MW)
North Greenville College, SC (M)
North Hennepin Community College, MN (MW)
North Iowa Area Community College, IA (M)
Northland Community & Technical College, MN (M)
Northwest Mississippi Community College, MS (M)
Northwestern College, IA (MW)
Northwestern College, MN (M)
Northwestern Oklahoma State University, OK (MW)
Northwestern University, IL (M)
Northwood Institute, MI (M)
Northwood University (Texas Campus), TX (MW)
Norwich University, VT (MW)
Nova Southern University, FL (M)
Nyack College, NY (MW)
Oakland City University, IN (MW)
Oakland Community College, MI (M)
Oakland University, MI (M)
Oakton Community College, IL (M)
Occidental College, CA (M)
Ocean County College, NJ (MW)
Odessa College, TX (M)
Oglethorpe University, GA (MW)
Ohio Northern University, OH (MW)

Ohio State University, OH (MW)
Ohio University, OH (M)
Ohio Wesleyan University, OH (M)
Oklahoma City University, OK (M)
Oklahoma State University, OK (MW)
Old Dominion University, VA (M)
Olivet College, MI (MW)
Olivet Nazarene University, IL (M)
Olney Central College, IL (M)
Oral Roberts University, OK (MW)
Orange Coast College, CA (MW)
Orange County Community College, NY (M)
Oregon State University, OR (MW)
Oswego State University (SUNY), NY (M)
Otero Junior College, CO (MW)
Ottawa University, KS (MW)
Otterbein College, OH (M)
Pace University, NY (MW)
Pace University (White Plains Campus), NY (MW)
Pacific Lutheran University, WA (M)
Pacific University, OR (MW)
Paducah Community College, CA (M)
Palomar College, CA (M)
Paris Junior College, TX (M)
Parkland College, IL (M)
Penn State Abington College, PA (M)
Pennsylvania State University, PA (MW)
Penn State (Behrend College), PA (M)
Penn Valley Community College, MO (M)
Pepperdine University, CA (MW)
Pfeiffer College, NC (M)
Phoenix College, AZ (MW)
Pikeville College, KY (MW)
Pima Community College (West Campus), AZ (M)
Pittsburg State University, KS (M)
Point Loma Nazarene College, CA (M)
Pomona-Pitzer Colleges, CA (M)
Portland State University, OR (M)

Prairie View A&M University, TX (M)
Presbyterian College, SC (M)
Prince George's Community College, MD (M)
Princeton University, NJ (M)
Principia College, IL (MW)
Providence College, RI (M)
Purdue University, IN (MW)
Queens College, NY (M)
Queens College, NC (M)
Quincy University, IL (MW)
Quinnipiac University, CT (M)
Quinsigamond College, MA (MW)
Radford University, VA (M)
Ramapo College, NJ (M)
Randolph-Macon College, VA (M)
Ranetto Santiago College, CA (M)
Regis University, CO (M)
Rend Lake, IL (MW)
Rensselaer Polytechnic Institute, NY (M)
Rhode Island College, RI (M)
Rice University, TX (M)
Rider College, NJ (M)
Ripon College, WI (M)
Riverland Community College, MN (MW)
Riverside Community College, CA (M)
Roanoke College, VA (M)
Robert Morris College, PA (M)
Rochester Community College, MN (MW)
Rockland Community College, NY (M)
Rocky Mountain College, MT (MW)
Rollins College, FL (MW)
Roosevelt University, IL (M)
Rose-Hulman Institute of Technology, IN (M)
Rutgers, Newark College of Arts and Sciences, NJ (W)
Sacred Heart University, CT (MW)
Saddleback College, CA (MW)
Saginaw Valley State University, MI (M)
Saint Ambrose University, IA (MW)
Saint Andrews Presbyterian College, NC (M)
Saint Anselm College, NH (MW)
Saint Augustine's College, NC (M)
Saint Bonaventure University, NY (MW)

Saint Cloud State University, MN (MW)
Saint Edward's University, TX (M)
Saint Francis College, IN (M)
Saint Francis College, PA (MW)
Saint John Fisher College, NY (M)
Saint John's University, MN (M)
Saint John's University, NY (MW)
Saint Joseph's College, IN (M)
Saint Joseph's University, PA (M)
Saint Louis University, MO (M)
Saint Martin's College, WA (MW)
Saint Mary College, KS (M)
Saint Mary's College, IN (W)
Saint Mary's College of California, CA (M)
Saint Mary's University, TX (M)
Saint Michael's College, VT (MW)
Saint Norbert College, WI (MW)
Saint Olaf College, MN (MW)
Saint Peter's College, NJ (M)
Saint Thomas Aquinas College, NY (M)
Saint Thomas University, FL (M)
Salem State College, MA (M)
Salem-Teikyo University, WV (M)
Salve Regina College, RI (MW)
Samford University, AL (MW)
Sam Houston State University, TX (M)
San Diego State University, CA (MW)
San Joaquin Delta College, CA (M)
San Jose State University, CA (MW)
Santa Barbara City College, CA (MW)
Santa Clara University, CA (MW)
Santa Rosa Junior College, CA (M)
Sauk Valley College, IL (M)
Schoolcraft College, MI (M)
Scottsdale Community College, AZ (MW)
Seton Hall University, NJ (M)
Seton Hill College, PA (W)
Shawnee State University, OH (M)
Shelby State Community College, TN (M)
Shepherd College, WV (M)
Shorter College, GA (MW)

Siena College, NY (M)
Siena Heights College, MI (M)
Sierra College, CA (MW)
Simpson College, CA (MW)
Sinclair Community College, OH (M)
Skidmore College, NY (M)
Slippery Rock University of Pennsylvania, PA (M)
Snow College, UT (MW)
South Carolina State College, SC (MW)
South Dakota State University, SD (W)
Southeastern Community College, IA (M)
Southeastern Illinois College, IL (M)
Southeastern Louisiana University, LA (M)
Southeastern Oklahoma State University, OK (MW)
Southern Arkansas University, AR (M)
Southern Illinois University, IL (MW)
Southern Illinois University (Edwardsville), IL (M)
Southern Methodist University, TX (MW)
Southern University and A&M College, LA (M)
Southern Utah University, UT (M)
Southern Wesleyan University, SC (M)
South Plains Community College, TX (M)
Southwest Baptist University, MO (M)
Southwestern College, KS (MW)
Southwestern Oklahoma State University, OK (MW)
Southwestern University, TX (MW)
Southwest Missouri State University, MO (MW)
Southwest State University, MN (W)
Southwest Texas State University, TX (M)
Spartanburg Methodist, SC (M)
Spokane Community College, WA (MW)
Spring Hill College, AL (MW)
Stanford University, CA (MW)
State Fair Community College, MO (M)
State University of New York College at Brockport, NY (W)

State University of New York College (New Paltz), NY (M)
State University of New York Institute of Technology at Utica/Rome, NY (M)
State University of New York Maritime College, NY (M)
Stephen F. Austin State University, TX (M)
Stetson University, FL (MW)
St. Catherine College, KY (MW)
St. Gregory's College, OK (M)
Suffolk County Community College, NY (M)
Suffolk University, MA (M)
Sul Ross State University, TX (MW)
Swarthmore College, PA (M)
Tabor College, KS (M)
Taft College, CA (M)
Talledaga College, AL (M)
Teikyo Westmar University, IA (MW)
Temple Junior College, TX (M)
Temple University, PA (M)
Tennessee Technological University, TN (MW)
Tennessee Wesleyan College, TN (M)
Texas A&I University, TX (MW)
Texas A&M Commerce, TX (MW)
Texas A&M University, TX (MW)
Texas Christian University, TX (MW)
Texas Lutheran College, TX (MW)
Texas Tech University, TX (MW)
Texas Wesleyan College, TX (M)
Thomas College, ME (MW)
Three Rivers Community College, MO (M)
Toccoa Falls College, GA (M)
Towson State University, MD (M)
Transylvania University, KY (MW)
Trevecca Nazarene College, TN (MW)
Trinidad State Junior College, CO (MW)
Trinity College, CT (M)
Trinity University, TX (M)
Tri-State University, IN (MW)
Troy State University, AL (M)
Tufts University, MA (M)
Tulane University, LA (M)
Tusculum College, TN (M)
Tyler Junior College, TX (MW)
Union College, KY (MW)

Union College, NY (M)
Union County College, NJ (M)
Union University, TN (M)
University of Akron, OH (M)
University of Alabama (Birmingham), AL (MW)
University of Alabama (Huntsville), AL (M)
University of Alabama (Tuscaloosa), AL (MW)
University at Albany (SUNY), NY (W)
University of Arizona, AZ (MW)
University of Arkansas (Fayetteville), AR (MW)
University of Arkansas (Little Rock), AR (M)
University of Arkansas (Pine Bluff), AR (M)
University at Buffalo (SUNY), NY (M)
University of California (Berkeley), CA (MW)
University of California (Davis), CA (M)
University of California (Irvine), CA (M)
University of California (San Diego), CA (M)
University of California (Santa Barbara), CA (M)
University of California (UCLA), CA (MW)
University of Central Arkansas, AR (M)
University of Central Florida, FL (MW)
University of Central Oklahoma, OK (M)
University of Charleston, WV (M)
University of Cincinnati, OH (MW)
University of Colorado, CO (MW)
University of Colorado (Colorado Springs), CO (M)
University of Connecticut, CT (M)
University of Dallas, TX (M)
University of Dayton, OH (MW)
University of Delaware, DE (M)
University of Denver, CO (MW)
University of Detroit Mercy, MI (M)
University of Dubuque, IA (MW)
University of Evansville, IN (MW)
University of Findlay, OH (M)
University of Florida, FL (MW)

University of Georgia, GA (MW)
University of Hartford, CT (MW)
University of Hawaii (Hilo), HI (M)
University of Hawaii (Manoa), HI (MW)
University of Houston, TX (M)
University of Idaho, ID (MW)
University of Illinois (Chicago), IL (MW)
University of Illinois (Urbana-Champaign), IL (MW)
University of Incarnate Word, TX (M)
University of Indianapolis, IN (MW)
University of Iowa, IA (MW)
University of Kansas, KS (MW)
University of Kentucky, KY (MW)
University of La Verne, CA (M)
University of Louisiana at Lafayette, (LA) (M)
University of Louisville, KY (M)
University of Mary Hardin-Baylor, TX (M)
University of Maryland, MD (M)
University of Maryland (Baltimore County), MD (MW)
University of Maryland (Eastern Shore), MD (M)
University of Massachusetts (Dartmouth), MA (M)
University of Massachusetts (Lowell), MA (M)
University of Memphis, TN (MW)
University of Miami, FL (MW)
University of Michigan, MI (MW)
University of Minnesota (Minneapolis), MN (MW)
University of Minnesota (Morris), MN (MW)
University of Mississippi, MS (MW)
University of Missouri, MO (MW)
University of Missouri (Columbia), MO (MW)
University of Missouri (Kansas City), MO (MW)
University of Missouri (Rolla), MO (M)
University of Mobile, AL (MW)
University of Montana, MT (W)
University of Montevallo, AL (M)
University of Nebraska, NE (M)
University of Nebraska (Kearney), NE (M)

University of Nebraska (Lincoln), NE (MW)
University of Nevada, NV (M)
University of Nevada (Reno), NV (M)
University of New England, ME (M)
University of New Hampshire, NH (M)
University of New Mexico, NM (MW)
University of New Orleans, LA (M)
University of North Alabama, AL (M)
University of North Carolina (Asheville), NC (M)
University of North Carolina (Chapel Hill), NC (MW)
University of North Carolina (Charlotte), NC (M)
University of North Carolina (Greensboro), NC (M)
University of North Carolina (Pembroke), NC (M)
University of North Carolina (Wilmington), NC (MW)
University of North Dakota, ND (M)
University of Northern Colorado, CO (MW)
University of Northern Iowa, IA (MW)
University of North Florida, FL (M)
University of North Texas, TX (MW)
University of Notre Dame, IN (MW)
University of Oklahoma, OK (MW)
University of Oregon, OR (MW)
University of Portland, OR (M)
University of Puget Sound, WA (MW)
University of Redlands, CA (M)
University of Rhode Island, RI (M)
University of Richmond, VA (M)
University of San Diego, CA (M)
University of San Francisco, CA (MW)
University of Scranton, PA (M)
University of South Alabama, AL (MW)
University of South Carolina (Aiken), SC (M)
University of South Carolina (Columbia), SC (MW)
University of South Carolina (Myrtle Beach), SC (MW)

University of Southern California, CA (MW)
University of Southern Colorado, CO (M)
University of Southern Indiana, IN (MW)
University of Southern Mississippi, MS (MW)
University of South Florida, FL (MW)
University of St. Thomas, MN (MW)
University at Stony Brook (SUNY), NY (W)
University of Tampa, FL (M)
University of Tennessee, TN (M)
University of Tennessee (Knoxville), TN (MW)
University of Tennessee (Martin), TN (M)
University of Texas (Arlington), TX (M)
University of Texas (Austin), TX (MW)
University of Texas (El Paso), TX (MW)
University of Texas (Pan American), TX (M)
University of Texas (San Antonio), TX (M)
University of the Pacific, CA (M)
University of Toledo, OH (M)
University of Tulsa, OK (MW)
University of Utah, UT (M)
University of Vermont, VT (M)
University of Virginia, VA (M)
The University of Virginia's College at Wise, VA (M)
University of Washington, WA (MW)
University of West Florida, FL (M)
University of Wisconsin (Eau Claire), WI (M)
University of Wisconsin (Green Bay), WI (MW)
University of Wisconsin (La Crosse), WI (M)
University of Wisconsin (Madison), WI (MW)
University of Wisconsin (Oshkosh), WI (M)
University of Wisconsin (Platteville), WI (M)
University of Wisconsin (River Falls), WI (M)
University of Wisconsin (Stevens Point), WI (M)
University of Wisconsin (Superior), WI (M)

University of Wyoming, WY (MW)
Upper Iowa University, IA (MW)
Urbana University, OH (MW)
Ursinus College, PA (M)
U.S. International University, CA (MW)
Utah State University, UT (M)
Valdosta State University, GA (M)
Valley City State University, ND (M)
Valparaiso University, IN (M)
Vanderbilt University, TN (MW)
Ventura, College, CA (M)
Villanova University, PA (M)
Vincennes University, IN (M)
Virginia Commonwealth University, VA (M)
Virginia Military Institute, VA (M)
Virginia State University, VA (M)
Virginia Union University, VA (M)
Virginia Wesleyan College, VA (M)
Wabash College, IN (M)
Wabash Valley College, IL (M)
Wagner College, NY (M)
Wake Forest University, NC (MW)
Waldorf College, IA (MW)
Wallace State Community College, AL (M)
Walla Walla Community College, WA (MW)
Walsh College, OH (M)
Warner Southern College, FL (M)
Wartburg College, IA (MW)
Washburn University, KS (M)
Washington and Jefferson College, PA (M)
Washington State University, WA (MW)
Waubonsee College, IL (M)
Wayne State College, NE (MW)
Wayne State University, MI (M)
Webber College, FL (MW)
Weber State College, UT (MW)
Wesleyan University, CT (M)
Wesley College, DE (MW)
West Chester University, PA (M)
Western Carolina University, NC (M)
Western Illinois University, IL (M)
Western Kentucky University, KY (MW)
Western Maryland College, MD (M)

Western Montana College, MT (MW)
Western Nebraska Community College, NE (M)
Western New England College, MA (M)
Western State College, CO (M)
Western Texas College, TX (M)
Western Washington University, WA (MW)
West Liberty State College, WV (M)
Westminster College, PA (M)
West Texas State University, TX (MW)
West Virginia University Institute of Technology, WV (M)
West Virginia Wesleyan College, WV (M)
Wheaton College, IL (M)
Wheeling Jesuit College, WV (MW)
Whitman College, WA (M)
Whittier College, CA (M)
Wichita State University, KS (MW)
Wilkes College, NC (M)
Wilkes University, PA (M)
Willamette University, OR (M)
William Jewell College, MO (MW)
William Patterson College, NJ (M)
William Penn College, IA (MW)
William Rainey Harper College, IL (M)
Williams College, MA (M)
Wilmington College, OH (M)
Wingate College, NC (M)
Winona State University, MN (MW)
Winston-Salem State University, NC (M)
Winthrop University, SC (MW)
Wofford College, SC (M)
Worcester State College, MA (M)
Wright State University, OH (M)
Xavier University, OH (MW)
Yale University, CT (MW)
Yeshiva University, NY (M)
York College of Pennsylvania, PA (M)
Youngstown State University, OH (M)

Gymnastics

Arizona State University, AZ (W)
Auburn University, AL (W)
Ball State University, IN (W)

Boise State University, ID (W)
Bowling Green State University, OH (W)
Brigham Young University, UT (W)
Brown University, RI (W)
California State University (Fullerton), CA (W)
California State University (Sacramento), CA (W)
Centenary College, LA (W)
Central Michigan University, MI (W)
College of William and Mary, VA (MW)
Cornell University, NY (W)
Eastern Michigan University, MI (W)
Eastern Oklahoma State College, OK (MW)
George Washington University, DC (W)
Georgia College State University, GA (W)
Gustavus Adolphus College, MN (W)
Hamline University, MN (W)
Houston Baptist University, TX (MW)
Illinois State University, IL (W)
Iowa State University of Science and Technology, IA (MW)
Ithaca College, NY (W)
James Madison University, VA (MW)
Kent State University (Ashtabula), OH (MW)
Kent State University (Kent), OH (MW)
Kent State University (New Philadelphia), OH (MW)
Kent State University (Warren), OH (MW)
Long Island University (Brooklyn), NY (MW)
Louisiana State University (Baton Rouge), LA (W)
Massachusetts Institute of Technology, MA (MW)
Michigan State University, MI (MW)
Mississippi Valley State University, MS (M)
Montclair State College, NJ (W)
North Carolina State University, NC (MW)
Northern Illinois University, IL (W)
Ohio State University, OH (MW)
Oregon State University, OR (W)

Pennsylvania State University, PA (MW)
Radford University, VA (MW)
Rhode Island College, RI (W)
Rose State Junior College, OK (MW)
Salem State College, MA (W)
Samford University, AL (W)
San Jose State University, CA (W)
Seattle Pacific University, WA (W)
Southeast Missouri State University, MO (W)
Southern Connecticut State University, CT (M)
Southern Utah University, UT (W)
Springfield College, MA (MW)
Stanford University, CA (MW)
State University of New York College (Brockport), NY (W)
State University of New York College (Cortland), NY (W)
Temple University, PA (MW)
Texas Tech University, TX (MW)
Texas Woman's University, TX (W)
Towson State University, MD (W)
University of Alabama (Tuscaloosa), AL (W)
University of Alaska, AK (W)
University of Arizona, AZ (W)
University of Bridgeport, CT (W)
University of California (Berkeley), CA (MW)
University of California (Davis), CA (W)
University of California (Santa Barbara), CA (MW)
University of California (UCLA), CA (W)
University of Denver, CO (W)
University of Florida, FL (W)
University of Georgia, GA (W)
University of Illinois (Chicago), IL (MW)
University of Illinois (Urbana-Champaign), IL (MW)
University of Iowa, IA (MW)
University of Kentucky, KY (W)
University of Maryland, MD (W)
University of Massachusetts (Amherst), MA (MW)
University of Michigan, MI (MW)
University of Minnesota, MN (MW)
University of Missouri, MO (W)
University of Missouri (Columbia), MO (W)
University of Nebraska (Lincoln), NE (MW)

University of New Hampshire, NH (W)
University of New Mexico, NM (M)
University of North Carolina (Asheville), NC (W)
University of Oklahoma, OK (MW)
University of Pennsylvania, PA (W)
University of Pittsburgh, PA (W)
University of Rhode Island, RI (MW)
University of Utah, UT (W)
University of Vermont, VT (MW)
University of Washington, WA (W)
University of Wisconsin (Eau Claire), WI (W)
University of Wisconsin (La Crosse), WI (MW)
University of Wisconsin (Oshkosh), WI (MW)
University of Wisconsin (River Falls), WI (W)
University of Wisconsin (Stout), WI (W)
University of Wisconsin (Superior), WI (W)
Ursinus College, PA (W)
Utah State University, UT (W)
Ventura College, CA (W)
West Chester University, PA (W)
Western Michigan University, MI (MW)
West Virginia University, WV (W)
Winona State University, MN (W)
Yale University, CT (W)

Handball

Lake Forest College, IL (MW)
Pacific University, OR (MW)

Heavyweight Crew

Cornell University, NY (M)
Massachusetts Institute of Technology, MA (M)

Horse Judging

Frank Phillips College, TX (MW)

Ice Hockey

American International College, MA (M)
Amherst College, MA (M)

Assumption College, MA (M)
Augsburg College, MN (M)
Babson College, MA (M)
Bemidji State University, MN (MW)
Bentley College, MA (M)
Bethel College, MN (M)
Boston College, MA (M)
Boston University, MA (M)
Bowdoin College, ME (MW)
Bowling Green State University, OH (M)
Broome Community College, NY (M)
Brown University, RI (MW)
Buffalo State College, NY (MW)
Canisius College, NY (M)
Clarkson University, NY (M)
Colgate University, NY (MW)
College of St. Scholastica, MN (M)
College of the Holy Cross, MA (MW)
Colorado College, CO (M)
Community College of Rhode Island, RI (M)
Concordia College, MN (MW)
Connecticut College, CT (MW)
Cornell University, NY (MW)
Curry College, MA (M)
Dartmouth College, NH (MW)
Elmira College, NY (M)
Emerson College, MA (M)
Fairfield University, CT (M)
Ferris State College, MI (M)
Fitchburg State College, MA (M)
Fordham University, NY (M)
Gustavus Adolphus College, MN (MW)
Hamilton College, NY (MW)
Hamline University, MN (M)
Harvard University, MA (MW)
Hibbing Community College, MN (M)
Hudson Valley Community College, NY (M)
Iona College, NY (M)
Kean University, NJ (M)
Kent State University (Ashtabula), OH (M)
Kent State University (Kent), OH (M)
Kent State University (New Philadelphia), OH (M)
Kent State University (Warren), OH (M)
Lake Forest College, IL (M)
Lake Superior State University, MI (M)
Lawrence University, WI (M)

Lebanon Valley College, PA (M)
Lehigh University, PA (M)
Mankato State University, MN (M)
Massachusetts College of Liberal Arts, MA (M)
Massachusetts Institute of Technology, MA (MW)
Mercyhurst College, PA (M)
Merrimack College, MA (M)
Miami University, OH (M)
Michigan State University, MI (M)
Michigan Technological University, MI (M)
Middlebury College, VT (MW)
Minot State University (Bottineau), ND (M)
Mohawk Valley Community College, NY (M)
Moravian College, PA (M)
New Hampshire College, NH (M)
New Jersey Institute of Technology, NJ (M)
Niagara University, NY (MW)
Nichols College, MA (M)
North County Community College, NY (MW)
Northern Michigan University, MI (M)
Norwich University, VT (M)
Ocean County College, NJ (M)
Ohio State University, OH (M)
Oswego State University (SUNY), NY (M)
Pace University, NY (M)
Plattsburgh State University (SUNY), NY (M)
Plymouth State College, NH (M)
Princeton University, NJ (MW)
Providence College, RI (MW)
Quinnipiac University, CT (M)
Rainy River Community College, MN (M)
Rensselaer Polytechnic Institute, NY (M)
Rochester Institute of Technology, NY (MW)
Sacred Heart University, CT (MW)
Saint Anselm College, NH (M)
Saint Cloud State University, MN (M)
Saint John's University, MN (M)
Saint John's University, NY (M)
Saint Lawrence University, NY (MW)
Saint Michael's College, VT (M)
Saint Olaf College, MN (M)
Salem State College, MA (M)

Skidmore College, NY (MW)
State University of New York College (Brockport), NY (M)
State University of New York College (Cortland), NY (MW)
State University of New York College (Fredonia), NY (M)
State University of New York College (Geneseo), NY (M)
State University of New York College (Potsdam), NY (M)
State University of New York Maritime College, NY (M)
Stonehill College, MA (M)
Suffolk University, MA (M)
Trinity College, CT (M)
Tufts University, MA (M)
Union College, NY (MW)
University of Alabama (Huntsville), AL (M)
University of Alaska, AK (M)
University of Alaska (Fairbanks), AK (M)
University at Buffalo (SUNY), NY (M)
University of Connecticut, CT (M)
University of Denver, CO (M)
University of Lowell, MA (M)
University of Maine, ME (MW)
University of Massachusetts (Amherst), MA (M)
University of Massachusetts (Boston), MA (M)
University of Massachusetts (Dartmouth), MA (M)
University of Massachusetts (Lowell), MA (M)
University of Michigan, MI (M)
University of Minnesota (Duluth), MN (M)
University of Minnesota (Minneapolis), MN (MW)
University of New Hampshire, NH (MW)
University of North Dakota, ND (M)
University of Notre Dame, IN (M)
University of Rhode Island, RI (M)
University of Scranton, PA (M)
University of St. Thomas, MN (MW)
University of Tennessee (Knoxville), TN (M)
University of Vermont, VT (M)
University of Wisconsin (Eau Claire), WI (M)
University of Wisconsin (La Crosse), WI (M)

University of Wisconsin (Madison), WI (MW)
University of Wisconsin (River Falls), WI (M)
University of Wisconsin (Stevens Point), WI (M)
University of Wisconsin (Superior), WI (MW)
U.S. International University, CA (M)
Wesleyan University, CT (MW)
Western Michigan University, MI (M)
Western New England College, MA (M)
William Patterson College, NJ (M)
Williams College, MA (MW)
Worcester State College, MA (M)
Yale University, CT (MW)

Indoor Track

Abilene Christian University, TX (W)
Adams State College, CO (MW)
Alabama A&M University, AL (MW)
Alabama State University, AL (MW)
Alcorn State University, MS (M)
Alfred University, NY (MW)
Allegheny College, PA (MW)
Allentown College of Saint Francis de Sales, PA (MW)
Amherst College, MA (MW)
Anderson College, SC (M)
Anderson University, IN (MW)
Appalachian State University, NC (MW)
Aquinas College, MI (MW)
Arizona State University, AZ (MW)
Arkansas College, AR (M)
Arkansas State University, AR (MW)
Ashland College, OH (MW)
Auburn University, AL (MW)
Augsburg College, MN (MW)
Augustana College, SD (MW)
Austin Peay State University, TN (W)
Baker University, KS (MW)
Ball State University, IN (MW)
Baltimore City Community College, MD (MW)
Barber-Scotia College, NC (MW)
Barton County College, KS (MW)

Bates College, ME (MW)
Baylor University, TX (MW)
Beloit College, WI (MW)
Bemidji State University, MN (MW)
Benedict College, SC (M)
Benedictine College, KS (MW)
Benedictine University, IL (MW)
Bentley College, MA (MW)
Bethel College, KS (M)
Bethel College, MN (MW)
Bethune-Cookman College, FL (MW)
Black Hills State University, SD (M)
Boston College, MA (W)
Boston University, MA (MW)
Bowdoin College, ME (MW)
Bowie State University, MD (MW)
Brandeis University, MA (MW)
Brevard College, NC (MW)
Bridgewater College, VA (MW)
Brigham Young University, UT (MW)
Bronx Community College, NY (MW)
Brown University, RI (MW)
Bucknell University, PA (MW)
Buffalo State College, NY (MW)
Butler University, IN (MW)
California State University (Stanislaus), CA (W)
Canisius College, NY (MW)
Carleton College, MN (MW)
Carnegie-Mellon University, PA (MW)
Carroll College, WI (MW)
Carthage College, WI (MW)
Case Western Reserve University, OH (MW)
Cayuga County Community College, NY (MW)
Cedarville College, OH (MW)
Central College, IA (MW)
Central Connecticut State University, CT (MW)
Central Michigan University, MI (MW)
Central Missouri State University, MO (MW)
Chadron State College, NE (MW)
Charleston Southern University, SC (MW)
Chicago State University, IL (MW)
Christopher Newport College, VA (MW)
City College of New York, NY (MW)

Clemson University, SC (MW)
Cleveland State University, OH (MW)
Cloud County Community College, KS (MW)
Coastal Carolina College, SC (W)
Coe College, IA (MW)
Colby Community College, KS (MW)
Colgate University, NY (MW)
The College of New Jersey, NJ (W)
College of William and Mary, VA (MW)
College of Wooster, OH (MW)
College of the Holy Cross, MA (MW)
Colorado College, CO (MW)
Colorado School of Mines, CO (MW)
Colorado State University, CO (MW)
Columbia University, NY (MW)
Concordia University, NE (MW)
Coppin State College, MD (MW)
Cornell College, IA (MW)
Cornell University, NY (MW)
Dakota State University, SD (MW)
Danville Area Community College, IL (MW)
Dartmouth College, NH (MW)
Delaware State University (MW)
Delhi College of Technology (SUNY), NY (MW)
Denison University, OH (MW)
DePaul University, IL (MW)
Dickinson College, PA (MW)
Dickinson State University, ND (MW)
Doane College, NE (MW)
Drake University, IA (MW)
Drexel University, PA (M)
Duke University, NC (MW)
East Carolina University, NC (MW)
Eastern Illinois University, IL (MW)
Eastern Kentucky University, KY (MW)
Eastern Michigan University, MI (MW)
Eastern Oklahoma State College, OK (MW)
Eastern Washington University, WA (MW)
East Stroudsburg University, PA (MW)

East Tennessee State University, TN (MW)
Edward Waters College, FL (MW)
Elmhurst College, IL (MW)
Emporia State University, KS (MW)
Essex Community College, MD (M)
Everett Community College, WA (MW)
Fairleigh Dickinson University, NJ (MW)
Ferris State College, MI (MW)
Florida Memorial College, FL (MW)
Fordham University, NY (MW)
Fort Hays State University, KS (MW)
Franklin & Marshall College, PA (MW)
Fresno Pacific University, CA (MW)
Garden City Community College, KS (MW)
Geneva College, PA (MW)
George Mason University, VA (MW)
Georgia Institute of Technology, GA (M)
Georgia Southern University, GA (W)
Gettysburg College, PA (MW)
Gonzaga University, WA (MW)
Grambling State University, LA (W)
Grand Valley State College, MI (MW)
Grinnell College, IA (MW)
Gustavus Adolphus College, MN (MW)
Hagerstown Junior College, MD (MW)
Hamilton College, NY (MW)
Hamline University, MN (MW)
Hampton University, VA (MW)
Harding University, AR (MW)
Hartwick College, NY (MW)
Hastings College, NE (MW)
Haverford College, PA (MW)
Heidelberg College, OH (MW)
Henderson State University, AR (M)
Highland Community College, KS (MW)
Hillsdale College, MI (MW)
Hiram College, OH (MW)
Houston Baptist University, TX (MW)
Howard Payne University, TX (M)

Idaho State University, ID (MW)
Illinois College, IL (MW)
Illinois State University, IL (MW)
Illinois Wesleyan University, IL (MW)
Indiana State University, IN (M)
Indiana Wesleyan University, IN (MW)
Iona College, NY (MW)
Iowa Wesleyan College, IA (MW)
Ithaca College, NY (MW)
Jackson State University, MS (MW)
James Madison University, VA (MW)
Jamestown College, ND (MW)
John Carroll University, OH (MW)
Johns Hopkins University, MD (MW)
Johnson County Community College, KS (MW)
Johnson C. Smith University, NC (MW)
Kansas State University, KS (MW)
Kansas Wesleyan College, KS (MW)
Keene State College, NH (MW)
Kent State University, OH (MW)
Kentucky State University, KY (MW)
Kenyon College, OH (MW)
Knox College, IL (MW)
Kutztown University, PA (MW)
Lafayette College, PA (MW)
Lake Superior State University, MI (MW)
Lamar University, TX (MW)
La Salle University, PA (MW)
Lawrence University, WI (MW)
Liberty University, VA (MW)
Lincoln University, MO (M)
Long Island University (Brooklyn), NY (MW)
Loras College, IA (W)
Louisiana State University (Baton Rouge), LA (MW)
Louisiana Tech University, LA (MW)
Loyola University, IL (MW)
Lubbock Christian College, TX (MW)
Luther College, IA (MW)
Lynchburg College, VA (MW)
Macalester College, MN (MW)
Macomb Community College, MI (MW)
Malone College, OH (MW)

Manchester College, IN (MW)
Manhattan College, NY (MW)
Mankato State University, MN (MW)
Mansfield University, PA (MW)
Marietta College, OH (M)
Marist College, NY (MW)
Marquette University, WI (MW)
Marshall University, WV (MW)
Mary Washington College, VA (MW)
Massachusetts Institute of Technology, MA (MW)
McPherson College, KS (MW)
Mercer County Community College, NJ (MW)
Messiah College, PA (MW)
Mid-America Nazarene College, KS (MW)
Middle Tennessee State University, TN (MW)
Midland Lutheran College, NE (MW)
Millikin University, IL (M)
Milwaukee Area Technology College, WI (MW)
Minot State, ND (MW)
Mississippi State University, MS (MW)
Mississippi Valley State University, MS (MW)
Missouri Southern State College, MO (MW)
Missouri Valley College, MO (MW)
Mohawk Valley Community College, NY (MW)
Monmouth College, IL (MW)
Montana State University, MT (MW)
Montclair State College, NJ (MW)
Moravian College, PA (MW)
Morgan State University, MD (MW)
Mount Holyoke College, MA (W)
Mount St. Mary College, MD (MW)
Muhlenberg College, PA (MW)
Murray State University, KY (MW)
Muskingum College, OH (MW)
Nassau Community College, NY (MW)
New York Institute of Technology, NY (MW)
New York University, NY (MW)
Norfolk State University, VA (MW)
North Carolina A & T State University, NC (MW)

North Carolina Central University, NC (MW)
North Central College, IL (MW)
North Dakota State, ND (MW)
North Dakota State University, ND (MW)
Northeast Louisiana University, LA (MW)
Northern Arizona University, AZ (MW)
Northwest Missouri State University, MO (MW)
Northwestern College, IA (MW)
Northwestern University, IL (MW)
Northwood Institute, MI (MW)
Northwood Institute (Texas Campus), TX (MW)
Norwich University, VT (MW)
Oakton Community College, IL (MW)
Oberlin College, OH (MW)
Odessa College, TX (W)
Ohio Northern University, OH (MW)
Ohio State University, OH (MW)
Ohio University, OH (MW)
Oklahoma Christian University of Science & Art, OK (MW)
Oklahoma State University, OK (MW)
Oral Roberts University, OK (MW)
Otterbein College, OH (MW)
Pace University, NY (MW)
Parkland College, IL (MW)
Pennsylvania State University, PA (MW)
Pittsburg State University, KS (MW)
Plattsburgh State University (SUNY), NY (MW)
Prairie View A&M University, TX (MW)
Pratt Community College, KS (MW)
Purdue University, IN (MW)
Queens College, NY (MW)
Rensselaer Polytechnic Institute, NY (M)
Rhode Island College, RI (MW)
Rice University, TX (MW)
Ricks College, ID (MW)
Rider College, NJ (MW)
Ripon College, WI (MW)
Robert Morris College, PA (MW)
Roberts Wesleyan College, NY (MW)
Rochester Institute of Technology, NY (M)

Rose-Hulman Institute of Technology, IN (MW)
Saginaw Valley State University MI (MW)
Saint Cloud State University, MN (MW)
Saint Francis College, PA (MW)
Saint John's University, MN (M)
Saint John's University, NY (M)
Saint Joseph's University, PA (MW)
Saint Lawrence University, NY (MW)
Saint Norbert College, WI (MW)
Saint Olaf College, MN (MW)
Saint Paul's College, VA (M)
Saint Peter's College, NJ (MW)
Salve Regina College, RI (MW)
Samford University, AL (MW)
Seton Hall University, NJ (MW)
Shippensburg University of Pennsylvania, PA (MW)
Simpson College, CA (MW)
Smith College, MA (W)
South Carolina State College, SC (MW)
South Dakota State University, SD (MW)
Southeastern Louisiana University, LA (MW)
Southeast Missouri State University, MO (MW)
Southern Illinois University, IL (MW)
Southern Methodist University, TX (MW)
Southern Oregon State College, OR (MW)
Southern University and A&M College, LA (MW)
South Plains Community College, TX (M)
Southwestern College, KS (MW)
Southwest Missouri State University, MO (MW)
Spoon River College, IL (MW)
Spring Arbor College, MI (MW)
Springfield College, MA (MW)
St. Francis College, NY (MW)
State University of New York, NY (MW)
State University of New York College (Brockport), NY (MW)
State University of New York College (Cortland), NY (MW)
State University of New York College (Fredonia), NY (MW)
State University of New York College at Geneseo, NY (MW)
State University of New York at New Paltz, NY (MW)

Stephen F. Austin State University, TX (MW)
Stonehill College, MA (MW)
Swarthmore College, PA (MW)
Syracuse University, NY (MW)
Talladaga College, AL (MW)
Tarleton State University, TX (MW)
Teikyo Westmar University, IA (MW)
Tennessee State University, TN (MW)
Tennessee Technological University, TN (MW)
Texas A&I University, TX (MW)
Texas A&M University, TX (MW)
Texas Southern University, TX (M)
Texas Tech University, TX (MW)
Towson State University, MD (MW)
Trinity College, CT (MW)
Tri-State University, IN (MW)
Troy State University, AL (W)
Tufts University, MA (MW)
Union College, NY (MW)
University of Alabama (Tuscaloosa), AL (MW)
University at Albany (SUNY), NY (MW)
University of Arkansas (Fayetteville), AR (M)
University of Arkansas (Pine Bluff), AR (W)
University at Buffalo (SUNY), NY (MW)
University of Central Oklahoma, OK (MW)
University of Chicago, IL (MW)
University of Colorado, CO (MW)
University of Delaware, DE (MW)
University of Detroit Mercy, MI (MW)
University of Findlay, OH (MW)
University of Georgia, GA (MW)
University of Houston, TX (MW)
University of Idaho, ID (MW)
University of Illinois (Chicago) IL (MW)
University of Illinois (Urbana-Champaign), IL (MW)
University of Iowa, IA (M)
University of Kansas, KS (MW)
University of Kentucky, KY (MW)
University of Louisiana at Lafayette, LA (MW)

University of Louisville, KY (MW)
University of Mary, ND (MW)
University of Maryland, MD (MW)
University of Maryland (Baltimore County), MD (MW)
University of Maryland (Eastern Shore), MD (MW)
University of Massachusetts (Amherst), MA (MW)
University of Massachusetts (Boston), MA (MW)
University of Massachusetts (Dartmouth), MA (MW)
University of Massachusetts (Lowell), MA (MW)
University of Memphis, TN (MW)
University of Michigan, MI (MW)
University of Minnesota, MN (Duluth), MN (MW)
University of Minnesota (Minneapolis), MN (MW)
University of Mississippi, MS (M)
University of Missouri, MO (MW)
University of Missouri (Columbia), MO (MW)
University of Mobile, AL (MW)
University of Montana, MT (MW)
University of Nebraska, NE (M)
University of Nebraska (Lincoln), NE (MW)
University of Nevada, NV (W)
University of New Hampshire, NH (MW)
University of New Haven, CT (MW)
University of New Orleans, LA (MW)
University of North Carolina (Asheville), NC (M)
University of North Carolina (Chapel Hill), NC (MW)
University of North Dakota, ND (MW)
University of Northern Iowa, IA (MW)
University of North Florida, FL (MW)
University of North Texas, TX (MW)
University of Notre Dame, IN (MW)
University of Oklahoma, OK (MW)
University of Pennsylvania, PA (MW)

University of Pittsburgh, PA (MW)
University of Pittsburgh (Johnstown), PA (W)
University of Rhode Island, RI (MW)
University of Richmond, VA (MW)
University of South Alabama, AL (MW)
University of South Carolina, SC (W)
University of South Dakota, SD (MW)
University of Southern Mississippi, MS (MW)
University of South Florida, FL (MW)
University of St. Thomas, MN (MW)
University at Stony Brook (SUNY), NY (MW)
University of Tennessee, TN (MW)
University of Tennessee (Knoxville), TN (MW)
University of Texas (Arlington), TX (MW)
University of Texas (Austin), TX (M)
University of Texas (El Paso), TX (MW)
University of Texas (Pan American), TX (MW)
University of Texas (San Antonio), TX (MW)
University of Toledo, OH (MW)
University of Tulsa, OK (MW)
University of Utah, UT (MW)
University of Vermont, VT (MW)
University of Virginia, VA (MW)
University of Washington, WA (MW)
University of Wisconsin (Eau Claire), WI (MW)
University of Wisconsin (La Crosse), WI (MW)
University of Wisconsin (Madison), WI (MW)
University of Wisconsin (Milwaukee), WI (MW)
University of Wisconsin (Oshkosh), WI (MW)
University of Wisconsin (Platteville), WI (MW)
University of Wisconsin (River Falls), WI (MW)
University of Wisconsin (Stevens Point), WI (MW)
University of Wisconsin (Stout), WI (MW)

University of Wisconsin (Superior), WI (MW)
University of Wyoming, WY (MW)
Urbana University, OH (MW)
Ursinus College, PA (MW)
Utah State University, UT (MW)
Vanderbilt University, TN (W)
Vincennes University, IN (MW)
Virginia Commonwealth University, VA (MW)
Virginia Military Institute, VA (M)
Virginia Polytechnic Institute & State University, VA (MW)
Virginia State University, VA (MW)
Wagner College, NY (MW)
Wake Forest University, NC (MW)
Wartburg College, IA (MW)
Wayland Baptist University, TX (MW)
Wayne State College, NE (MW)
Wesleyan University, CT (MW)
West Chester University, PA (MW)
Western Carolina University, NC (MW)
Western Illinois University, IL (MW)
Western Kentucky University, KY (MW)
Western Michigan University, MI (MW)
Western Oregon State College, OR (MW)
Western Washington University, WA (MW)
Westfield State College, MA (MW)
West Virginia University, WV (MW)
Wheaton College, IL (MW)
Wichita State University, KS (MW)
Wilberforce University, OH (M)
Willamette University, OR (MW)
William Jewell College, MO (MW)
William Patterson College, NJ (MW)
William Penn College, IA (MW)
Williams College, MA (MW)
Winona State University, MN (W)
Winston-Salem State University, NC (MW)
Worcester State College, MA (MW)
York College (CUNY), NY (MW)

Judo

Cumberland College, KY (MW)
Polytechnic University (Brooklyn Campus), NY (MW)
Slippery Rock University of Pennsylvania, PA (MW)
University of Puerto Rico (Bayamon), PR (MW)

Lacrosse

Adelphi University, NY (M)
Alfred University, NY (MW)
Allegheny College, PA (W)
Allentown College of Saint Francis de Sales, PA (M)
Alvernia College, PA (MW)
American University, DC (W)
Amherst College, MA (MW)
Assumption College, MA (MW)
Babson College, MA (MW)
Ball State University, IN (W)
Bates College, ME (MW)
Bentley College, MA (MW)
Bloomfield College, NJ (M)
Bloomsburg University, PA (W)
Boston College, MA (MW)
Boston University, MA (W)
Bowdoin College, ME (MW)
Bridgewater College, VA (W)
Bridgewater State College, MA (W)
Broome Community College, NY (M)
Brown University, RI (MW)
Bryant College, RI (M)
Bryn Mawr College, PA (W)
Bucknell University, PA (MW)
Butler University, IN (M)
Cabrini College, PA (MW)
Canisius College, NY (M)
Castleton State College, VT (MW)
Catawba College, NC (M)
Catholic University of America, DC (MW)
Catonsville Community College, MD (MW)
Centenary College, NJ (MW)
City College of New York, NY (M)
Clark University, MA (M)
Clarkson University, NY (MW)
Colby-Sawyer College, NH (W)
Colgate University, NY (MW)
The College of New Jersey, NJ (W)
College of Notre Dame of Maryland, MD (W)
College of William and Mary, VA (W)

College of Wooster, OH (MW)
College of the Holy Cross, MA (MW)
Colorado College, CO (M)
Columbia University, NY (W)
Connecticut College, CT (MW)
Cornell University, NY (MW)
Curry College, MA (MW)
Dartmouth College, NH (MW)
Davidson College, NC (W)
Dean Junior College, MA (M)
Delhi College of Technology (SUNY), NY (M)
Denison University, OH (MW)
Dickinson College, PA (MW)
Dowling College, NY (M)
Drew University, NJ (MW)
Drexel University, PA (MW)
Duke University, NC (M)
Duquesne University, PA (W)
Earlham College, IN (W)
Eastern College, PA (W)
Eastern Connecticut State University, CT (MW)
East Stroudsburg University, PA (W)
Elmira College, NY (MW)
Essex Community College, MD (MW)
Fairfield University, CT (MW)
Fairleigh Dickinson University (Madison), NJ (M)
Fairleigh Dickinson University (Teaneck), NJ (M)
Finger Lakes Community College, NY (MW)
Fordham University, NY (M)
Franklin & Marshall College, PA (MW)
Georgetown University, DC (MW)
Gettysburg College, PA (MW)
Goucher College, MD (MW)
Green Mountain College, VT (M)
Hamilton College, NY (MW)
Hampden-Sydney College, VA (M)
Harford Community College, MD (MW)
Hartwick College, NY (MW)
Harvard University, MA (MW)
Haverford College, PA (MW)
Herkimer County Community College, NY (M)
Hofstra University, NY (MW)
Hood College, MD (W)
Howard University, DC (W)
Hudson Valley Community College, NY (M)

Indiana University of Pennsylvania, PA (W)
Ithaca College, NY (MW)
James Madison University, VA (W)
Jefferson Community College, NY (M)
Johns Hopkins University, MD (MW)
Kean University, NJ (M)
Keene State College, NH (MW)
Kenyon College, OH (MW)
King's College, PA (MW)
Lafayette College, PA (MW)
Lake Forest College, IL (M)
La Salle University, PA (W)
Lehigh University, PA (MW)
Le Moyne College, NY (M)
Limestone College, SC (MW)
Long Island University (C. W. Post Campus), NY (MW)
Long Island University (Southampton Campus), NY (M)
Longwood College, VA (W)
Loyola College, MD (MW)
Lycoming College, PA (MW)
Lynchburg College, VA (MW)
Manhattan College, NY (MW)
Manhattanville College, NY (M)
Marietta College, OH (M)
Marist College, NY (MW)
Marymount University, VA (M)
Mary Washington College, VA (W)
Massachusetts Institute of Technology, MA (MW)
Merrimack College, MA (M)
Messiah College, PA (MW)
Michigan State University, MI (M)
Middlebury College, VT (MW)
Millersville University, PA (W)
Mitchell College, CT (M)
Mohawk Valley Community College, NY (M)
Molloy College, NY (M)
Montclair State College, NJ (M)
Mount Holyoke College, MA (W)
Mount St. Mary College, MD (MW)
Mount Union College, OH (M)
Muhlenberg College, PA (W)
Nassau Community College, NY (M)
Nazareth College, NY (M)
New Hampshire College, NH (M)
Niagara University, NY (W)
Nichols College, MA (MW)
North Country Community College, NY (W)

Northwestern University, IL (W)
Northwood Institute, MI (M)
Norwich University, VT (M)
Oberlin College, OH (MW)
Ohio State University, OH (M)
Ohio Wesleyan University, OH (MW)
Old Dominion University, VA (W)
Oswego State University (SUNY), NY (M)
Pace University, NY (M)
Pace University (White Plains Campus), NY (M)
Pennsylvania State University, PA (MW)
Pfeiffer College, NC (M)
Philadelphia University, PA (W)
Plymouth State College, NH (MW)
Princeton University, NJ (MW)
Providence College, RI (MW)
Queens College, NY (M)
Quinnipiac College, CT (MW)
Radford University, VA (M)
Randolph-Macon College, VA (MW)
Regis University, CO (MW)
Rensselaer Polytechnic Institute, NY (M)
Rhode Island College, RI (W)
Roanoke College, VA (MW)
Rochester Institute of Technology, NY (M)
Rowan University, NJ (W)
Sacred Heart University, CT (W)
Saint Anselm College, NH (MW)
Saint Bonaventure University, NY (M)
Saint John's University, NY (M)
Saint Joseph's University, PA (MW)
Saint Lawrence University, NY (MW)
Saint Mary's College of California, CA (MW)
Saint Michael's College, VT (MW)
Saint Vincent College, PA (M)
Shippensburg University of Pennsylvania, PA (W)
Siena College, NY (M)
Skidmore College, NY (MW)
Smith College, MA (W)
Springfield College, MA (MW)
St. John Fisher College, NY (M)
State University of New York College (Cortland), NY (MW)
State University of New York College at Fredonia, NY (W)

State University of New York College at Geneseo, NY (MW)
State University of New York College at New Paltz, NY (W)
State University of New York College (Potsdam), NY (MW)
State University of New York Maritime College, NY (M)
Stevens Institute of Technology, NJ (M)
Swarthmore College, PA (MW)
Sweet Briar College, VA (W)
Syracuse University, NY (MW)
Temple University, PA (W)
Texas Tech University, TX (M)
Towson State University, MD (MW)
Trinity College, CT (MW)
Tufts University, MA (MW)
Union College, NY (MW)
Unity College, ME (M)
University at Albany (SUNY), NY (MW)
University of California (Berkeley), CA (W)
University of California (Davis), CA (W)
University of Connecticut, CT (W)
University of Delaware, DE (MW)
University of Denver, CO (MW)
University of Hartford, CT (M)
University of Maryland, MD (MW)
University of Maryland (Baltimore County), MD (MW)
University of Massachusetts (Amherst), MA (MW)
University of Massachusetts (Boston), MA (M)
University of New England, ME (MW)
University of New Hampshire, NH (MW)
University of New Haven, CT (M)
University of North Carolina (Asheville), NC (MW)
University of North Carolina (Chapel Hill), NC (MW)
University of Notre Dame, IN (W)
University of Pennsylvania, PA (MW)
University of Puget Sound, WA (W)
University of Redlands, CA (W)
University of Rhode Island, RI (M)
University of Richmond, VA (W)
University of Scranton, PA (MW)

University of Vermont, VT (MW)
University of Virginia, VA (MW)
Ursinus College, PA (W)
Vassar College, NY (MW)
Villanova University, PA (MW)
Virginia Military Institute, VA (M)
Wellesley College, MA (W)
Wesleyan University, CT (MW)
Wesley College, DE (MW)
West Chester University, PA (MW)
Western Connecticut State University, CT (W)
Western Maryland College, MD (MW)
Western New England College, MA (MW)
Whittier College, CA (M)
Willamette University, OR (M)
Williams College, MA (MW)
Yale University, CT (MW)

Lightweight Crew

Cornell University, NY (M)
Massachusetts Institute of Technology, MA (M)

Livestock Judging

Frank Phillips College, TX (MW)

Marathon

Vincennes University, IN (MW)

Martial Arts

Austin College, TX (W)
Cayuga County Community College, NY (M)
Cleveland State University, OH (MW)
Georgian Court College, NJ (W)
Loras College, IA (W)
Mississippi State University, MS (MW)
Mississippi Valley State University, MS (M)
Pontifical Catholic University of Puerto Rico, PR (MW)
Roosevelt University, IL (MW)

Nordic Skiing

Clarkson University, NY (MW)
Gustavus Adolphus College, MN (MW)
Macalester College, MN (MW)

Ping Pong

University of Puerto Rico (Bayamon), PR (MW)

Pistol

Massachusetts Institute of Technology, MA (M)

Polo

Cornell University, NY (MW)
Skidmore College, NY (MW)

Power Lifting

Bayamon Central University, PR (MW)
Cayuga County Community College, NY (M)
Lafayette College, PA (M)
Louisiana Tech University, LA (MW)
Mississippi State University, MS (MW)
Mississippi Valley State University, MS (M)
Northwestern Oklahoma State University, OK (M)
Snow College, UT (MW)

Racquetball

Broward Community College, FL (MW)
Butler County Community College, KS (M)
Butler County Community College, PA (M)
Cayuga County Community College, NY (MW)
Goldey-Beacom College, DE (W)
Louisiana Tech University, LA (MW)
Maple Woods Community College, MO (M)
Snow College, UT (MW)

Riflery

Canisius College, NY (MW)
Centenary College, LA (MW)
Citadel, SC (M)
Duquesne University, PA (MW)
Hardin-Simmons University, TX (MW)
Jacksonville State University, AL (MW)

King's College, PA (MW)
Marion Military Institute, AL (M)
Massachusetts Institute of Technology, MA (MW)
Mississippi State University, MS (MW)
Morehead State University, KY (M)
Murray State University, KY (MW)
New Jersey Institute of Technology, NJ (M)
North Carolina State University, NC (MW)
North Georgia College & State University, GA (MW)
Norwich University, VT (MW)
Ohio State University, OH (MW)
Rose-Hulman Institute of Technology, (MW)
Saint Louis University, MO (M)
State University of New York Maritime College, NY (M)
Texas A&I University, TX (MW)
Texas Christian University, TX (W)
Trinity University, TX (MW)
University of Akron, OH (M)
University of Alaska (Fairbanks), AK (MW)
University of Alaska Southeast, AK (MW)
University of Kentucky, KY (MW)
University of Mississippi, MS (W)
University of San Francisco, CA (MW)
University of Tennessee (Martin), TN (MW)
University of Texas (Arlington), TX (MW)
University of Texas (El Paso), TX (W)
University of Texas (San Antonio), TX (MW)
Virginia Military Institute, VA (M)
West Texas State University, TX (MW)
West Virginia University, WV (MW)
Xavier University, OH (MW)

Rodeo

Austin College, TX (MW)
Central Arizona College, AZ (MW)

Central Wyoming College, MY (MW)
Chadron State College, NE (M)
Colby Community College, KS (MW)
College of Southern Idaho, ID (MW)
Dakota Wesleyan University, SD (M)
Dawson Community College, MT (MW)
Dickinson State University, ND (MW)
Diné College, AZ (MW)
Eastern New Mexico University, NM (MW)
Eastern Oklahoma State College, OK (M)
Eastern Wyoming College, WY (MW)
Fort Scott College, KS (MW)
Frank Phillips College, TX (MW)
Laramie County Community College, WY (MW)
Lewis Clark State College, ID (MW)
Miles Community College, MT (MW)
Mississippi State University, MS (MW)
New Mexico Junior College, NM (MW)
North Central Texas College, TX (MW)
Northern Montana College, MT (MW)
Northwest Mississippi Community College, MS (MW)
Northwestern Oklahoma State Unversity, OK (M)
Odessa College, TX (MW)
Pratt Community College, KS (MW)
Sam Houston State University, TX (MW)
South Plains Community College, TX (MW)
Southwestern Oklahoma State University, OK (MW)
Sul Ross State University, TX (MW)
Tarleton State University, TX (MW)
Texas Tech University, TX (MW)
University of West Alabama, AL (MW)
Utah State University, UT (M)
Walla Walla Community College, WA (MW)
Weber State College, UT (MW)

Western Montana College, MT (MW)
Western Texas College, TX
Wharton County Junior College, TX (MW)

Rowing

Bates College, ME (MW)
California State University (Sacramento), CA (W)
College of the Holy Cross, MA (MW)
Duke University, NC (W)
Humboldt State University, CA (W)
Rollins College, FL (MW)
University of California (Davis), CA (W)
University of Cincinnati, OH (W)
University of Connecticut, CT (W)
University of Delaware, DE (W)
University of Iowa, IA (W)
University of Kansas, KS (W)
University of Michigan, MI (MW)
University of Notre Dame, IN (W)
University of Texas (Austin), TX (W)
University of Virginia, VA (W)
Vassar College, NY (MW)
Washington College, MD (MW)

Rugby

Fairfield University, CT (M)
Lafayette College, PA (M)
Manhattanville College, NY (M)
Mississippi State University, MS (M)
Norwich University, VT (MW)
Saint Mary's College of California, CA (M)
State University of New York Maritime College, NY (M)
Trinity College, CT (MW)
University of California (Berkeley), CA (M)
University of Rhode Island, RI (M)
University of Wisconsin (La Crosse), WI (M)
Utah State University, UT (M)

Sailing

Boston College, MA (MW)
Bowdoin College, ME (MW)

Brandeis University, MA (MW)
Broward Community College, FL (MW)
California Maritime Academy, CA (M)
Christopher Newport College, VA (MW)
Cleveland State University, OH (MW)
College of Charleston, SC (MW)
Connecticut College, CT (MW)
Dartmouth College, NH (MW)
Fairfield University, CT (W)
Franklin Pierce College, NH (MW)
Georgetown University, DC (MW)
Harvard University, MA (MW)
Lambuth University, TN (M)
Massachusetts Institute of Technology, MA (MW)
Mercer University, GA (W)
Mitchell College, CT (MW)
Norwich University, VT (MW)
Old Dominion University, VA (MW)
Orange Coast College, CA (MW)
Rollins College, FL (MW)
Salem State College, MA (MW)
Stanford University, CA (MW)
State University of New York Maritime College, NY (M)
Stonehill College, MA (MW)
Tufts University, MA (W)
University of California (Irvine), CA (MW)
University of Hawaii (Manoa), HI (MW)
University of Rhode Island, RI (MW)
University of Wisconsin (Green Bay), WI (MW)
Washington College, MD (MW)

Skiing

Green Mountain College, VT (MW)
Rocky Mountain College, MT (MW)
University of Denver, CO (MW)

Snowboarding

Sierra Nevada College, NV (MW)

Soccer

Adelphi University, NY (MW)
Adirondack College, NY (MW)
Adrian College, MI (MW)

Agnes Scott College, GA (W)
Alabama A&M University, AL (MW)
Albertson College of Idaho, ID (MW)
Albion College, MI (MW)
Albright College, PA (MW)
Alderson-Broaddus College, WV (M)
Alfred University, NY (MW)
Allegheny College, PA (MW)
Allen County College, KS (M)
Allentown College, PA (MW)
Alma College, MI (MW)
Alvernia College, PA (M)
American International College, MA (MW)
American University, DC (M)
Amherst College, MA (MW)
Anderson College, SC (MW)
Anderson University, IN (MW)
Andrew College, GA (MW)
Angelo State University, TX (W)
Appalachian State University
Apprentice School, VA (M)
Aquinas College, MI (MW)
Arizona State University, AZ (W)
Asbury College, KY (M)
Ashland College, OH (M)
Assumption College, MA (MW)
Atlantic Community College, NJ (M)
Atlantic Union College, MA (M)
Auburn University, AL (W)
Auburn University (Montgomery), AL (MW)
Augsburg College, MN (MW)
Augusta State University, GA (M)
Augustana College, IL (M)
Augustana College, SD (W)
Aurora University, IL (M)
Austin College, TX (MW)
Austin Community College, MN (M)
Averett College, VA (M)
Avila College, MO (MW)
Azusa Pacific University, CA (MW)
Babson College, MA (MW)
Baker University, KS (MW)
Bard College, NY (MW)
Barry University, FL (MW)
Bartlesville Wesleyan, OK (M)
Barton College, NC (MW)
Bates College, ME (MW)
Becker College, MA (MW)
Belhaven College, MS (MW)
Bellarmine College, KY (MW)
Belleville Area College, IL (M)
Bellevue Community College,

WA (MW)
Belmont Abbey College, NC (M)
Belmont College, TN (M)
Beloit College, WI (MW)
Bemidji State University, MN (W)
Benedictine College, KS (MW)
Benedictine University, IL (MW)
Bentley College, MA (M)
Bergen Community College, NJ (M)
Berry College, GA (MW)
Bethany College, KS (M)
Bethany College, WV (M)
Bethany Lutheran College, MN (M)
Bethel College, IN (M)
Bethel College, KS (MW)
Bethel College, MN (MW)
Binghamton University (SUNY), NY (MW)
Biola University, CA (M)
Birmingham-Southern College, AL (MW)
Blackburn College, IL (MW)
Bloomfield College, NJ (M)
Bloomsburg University, PA (MW)
Bluffton College, OH (MW)
Boise State University, ID (W)
Borough of Manhattan Community College (CUNY), NY (M)
Boston College, MA (MW)
Boston University, MA (MW)
Bowdoin College, ME (MW)
Bowling Green State University, OH (M)
Bradley University, IL (M)
Brandeis University, MA (MW)
Brescia University, KY (M)
Brevard College, NC (MW)
Brewton Parker College, GA (MW)
Briar Cliff College, IA (MW)
Bridgewater College, VA (M)
Bridgewater State College, MA (MW)
Brigham Young University, HI (M)
Brigham Young University, UT (MW)
Bronx Community College, NY (M)
Brooklyn College (CUNY), NY (MW)
Broome Community College, NY (MW)
Brown University, RI (MW)
Bryant College, RI (MW)
Bryn Mawr College, PA (W)
Bucknell University, PA (MW)

Bucks County Community College, PA (MW)
Buffalo State College, NY (MW)
Bunker Hill Community College, MA (MW)
Butler University, IN (MW)
Butte College, CA (W)
Cabrillo College, CA (MW)
Cabrini College, PA (M)
California Baptist University, CA (MW)
California Institute of Technology, CA (M)
California Lutheran University, CA (MW)
California Maritime Academy, CA (M)
California Polytechnic State University, CA (MW)
California State Polytechnic University, CA (MW)
California State University at Bakersfield, CA (MW)
California State University (Chico), CA (MW)
California State University (Dominguez Hills), CA (MW)
California State University (Fresno), CA (MW)
California State University (Fullerton), CA (M)
California State University (Hayward), CA (MW)
California State University (Long Beach), CA (W)
California State University (Los Angeles), CA (MW)
California State University (Northridge), CA (M)
California State University (Sacramento), CA (MW)
California State University (San Bernardino), CA (MW)
California State University (Stanislaus), CA (MW)
California University, PA (MW)
Calvin College, MI (MW)
Campbellsville University, KY (MW)
Campbell Unversity, NC (MW)
Canisius College, NY (MW)
Capital University, OH (M)
Cardinal Stritch University, WI (MW)
Carleton College, MN (MW)
Carlow College, PA (W)
Carnegie-Mellon University, PA (MW)
Carroll College, WI (MW)
Carson-Newman College, TN (MW)

Case Western Reserve University, OH (MW)
Castleton State College, VT (MW)
Catawba College, NC (MW)
Catholic University of America, DC (M)
Catonsville Community College, MD (MW)
Cecil Community College, MD (M)
Cedarville College, OH (M)
Centenary College, LA (MW)
Centenary College, NJ (MW)
Central Christian College, KS (MW)
Central College, IA (MW)
Central Community College, NE (M)
Central Connecticut State University, CT (M)
Central Methodist College, MO (MW)
Central Michigan University, MI (W)
Central Missouri State University, MO (W)
Central Wesleyan College, SC (M)
Cerritos College, CA (MW)
Champlain College, VT (MW)
Chapman University, CA (MW)
Charles County Community College, MD (MW)
Charleston Southern University, SC (M)
Chowan College, NC (MW)
Christian Brothers College, TN (MW)
Christopher Newport College, VA (M)
Citadel, SC (M)
City College of New York, NY (MW)
City College of San Francisco, CA (M)
Clarkson University, NY (MW)
Clark University, MA (MW)
Clemson University, SC (M)
Cleveland State University, OH (M)
Clinton Community College, NY (MW)
Cloud County Community College, KS (M)
Coastal Carolina College, SC (MW)
Cochise College, AZ (W)
Coe College, IA (MW)
Coker College, SC (MW)
Colby-Sawyer College, NH (MW)

Colgate University, NY (MW)
College of Charleston, SC (M)
College of Mount St. Joseph, OH (M)
The College of New Jersey, NJ (MW)
College of Notre Dame, CA (M)
College of Notre Dame of Maryland, MD (W)
College of St. Benedict, MN (W)
College of St. Francis, IL (MW)
College of St. Rose, NY (MW)
College of St. Scholastica, MN (MW)
College of the Desert, CA (MW)
College of the Holy Cross, MA (MW)
College of William and Mary, VA (MW)
College of Wooster, OH (MW)
Colorado Christian University, CO (MW)
Colorado College, CO (MW)
Colorado School of Mines, CO (M)
Columbia Christian College, OR (M)
Columbia-Green Community College, NY (MW)
Columbia Union College, MD (MW)
Columbia University, NY (MW)
Columbus College, GA (M)
Columbus State Community College, OH (M)
Community College of Philadelphia, PA (M)
Community College of Rhode Island, RI (M)
Concord College, WV (MW)
Concordia College (Moorhead), MI (M)
Concordia University (St. Paul), MN (M)
Concordia College, MN (MW)
Concordia College, NY (MW)
Concordia University, NE (MW)
Concordia University Wisconsin, WI (MW)
Connecticut College, CT (MW)
Copiah-Lincoln Community College, MS (MW)
Coppin State College, MD (M)
Cornell College, IA (MW)
Cornell University, NY (MW)
Cosumnes River College, CA (MW)
Covenant College, GA (MW)
Cuesta College, CA (W)
Cumberland College, KY (MW)

Curry College, MA (MW)
Cuyahoga Community College, OH (MW)
Dallas Baptist University, TX (M)
Dana College, NE (W)
Danville Area Community College, IL (M)
Dartmouth College, NH (MW)
Davidson College, NC (MW)
Davis & Elkins College, WV (M)
Dean Junior College, MA (MW)
De Anza College, CA (MW)
Defiance College, OH (M)
Delaware Valley College, PA (MW)
Delhi College of Technology (SUNY), NY (MW)
Delta College, MI (M)
Denison University, OH (MW)
DePaul University, IL (MW)
De Pauw University, IN (MW)
Detroit College of Business, MI (M)
Diablo Valley Community College, CA (W)
Dickinson College, PA (MW)
Doane College, NE (MW)
Dominican College, CA (MW)
Dominican College, NY (MW)
Dominican University, IL (MW)
Dowling College, NY (M)
Drake University, IA (M)
Drew University, NJ (M)
Drexel University, PA (M)
Drury College, MO (M)
Duke University, NC (M)
Dundalk Community College, MD (MW)
Duquesne University, PA (MW)
Dutchess Community College, NY (M)
Earlham College, IN (MW)
East Carolina University, NC (M)
East Central College, MO (M)
East Los Angeles College, CA (MW)
Eastern College, PA (MW)
Eastern Connecticut State University, Ct (MW)
Eastern Illinois University, IL (M)
Eastern Mennonite College, VA (M)
Eastern Michigan University, MI (MW)
Eastern Nazarene College, MA (M)
Eastern Washington University, WA (W)

East Stroudsburg University, PA (M)
East Texas Baptist University, TX (MW)
Eckerd College, FL (MW)
Edgewood College, WI (M)
Edinboro University of Pennsylvania, PA (M)
Edmonds Community College, WA (M)
El Camino College, CA (MW)
Elizabethtown College, PA (MW)
Elmira College, NY (MW)
Elon College, NC (MW)
Emerson College, MA (M)
Emory University, GA (MW)
Erskine College, SC (MW)
Everett Community College, WA (M)
Evergreen State College, WA (MW)
Fairfield University, CT (MW)
Fairleigh Dickinson University (Madison), NJ (M)
Fairleigh Dickinson University (Teaneck), NJ (M)
Ferris State College, MI (W)
Ferrum College, VA (MW)
Finger Lakes Community College, NY (MW)
Fisk University, TN (M)
Fitchburg State College, MA (M)
Flagler College, FL (MW)
Florida Atlantic University, FL (MW)
Florida Insitute of Technology, FL (M)
Florida International University, FL (MW)
Florida Southern College, FL (MW)
Florida State University, FL (W)
Foothill College, CA (MW)
Fordham University, NY (MW)
Fort Lewis College, CO (M)
Francis Marion University, SC (MW)
Franklin & Marshall College, PA (MW)
Franklin Pierce College, NH (MW)
Frederick Community College, MD (M)
Fresno City College, CA (MW)
Fresno Pacific University, CA (M)
Friends University, KS (M)
Fullerton College, CA (M)
Fulton-Montgomery Community College, NY (MW)

Furman University, SC (M)
Garden City Community College, KS (M)
Genesee Community College, KS (M)
Genesee Community College, NY (MW)
Geneva College, PA (MW)
George Fox College, OR (MW)
George Mason University, VA (MW)
Georgetown College, KY (MW)
Georgetown University, DC (MW)
George Washington University, DC (MW)
Georgia College State University, GA (M)
Georgia Southern University, GA (M)
Georgia State University, GA (MW)
Gettysburg College, PA (MW)
Glendale Community College, AZ (M)
Glendale Community College, CA (MW)
Gloucester County College, NJ (MW)
Golden West College, CA (MW)
Goldey-Beacom College, DE (MW)
Gonzaga University, WA (MW)
Gordon College, MA (MW)
Goshen College, IN (MW)
Goucher College, MD (MW)
Grace College, IN (MW)
Graceland College, IA (MW)
Grambling State University, LA (M)
Grand Canyon College, AZ (MW)
Grand Rapids Baptist Seminary of Cornerstone University, MI (MW)
Grand View College, IA (MW)
Grays Harbor College, WA (MW)
Greenfield Community College, MA (MW)
Green Mountain College, VT (MW)
Green River Community College, WA (MW)
Greensboro College, NC (M)
Greenville College, IL (M)
Grinnell College, IA (MW)
Grove City College, PA (MW)
Gustavus Adolphus College, MN (MW)
Hagerstown Junior College, MD (M)

Hamilton College, NY (MW)
Hamline University, MN (M)
Hampden-Sydney College, VA (M)
Hanover College, IN (MW)
Hardin-Simmons University, TX (MW)
Harding University, AR (MW)
Harford Community College, MD (M)
Harris-Stowe State College, MO (M)
Hartwick College, NY (MW)
Harvard University, MA (MW)
Hastings College, NE (MW)
Haverford College, PA (MW)
Hawaii Pacific University, HI (MW)
Heidelberg College, OH (MW)
Herkimer County Community College, NY (MW)
Hesser College, NH (M)
High Point University, NC (MW)
Hilbert College, NY (MW)
Hillsdale College, MI (MW)
Hiram College, OH (MW)
Hofstra University, NY (MW)
Holmes Junior College, MS (MW)
Holy Family College, PA (MW)
Hood College, MD (W)
Hope College, MI (M)
Houghton College, NY (MW)
Houston Baptist University, TX (MW)
Howard University, DC (MW)
Hudson Valley Community College, NY (MW)
Humboldt State University, CA (MW)
Hunter College of the City University of New York, NY (M)
Huntingdon College, AL (MW)
Huntington College, IN (MW)
Husson College, ME (M)
Idaho State University, ID (W)
Illinois College, IL (MW)
Illinois State University, IL (W)
Illinois Wesleyan University, IL (MW)
Indiana Institute of Technology, IN (MW)
Indiana University, IN (MW)
Indiana University of Pennsylvania, PA (MW)
Indiana University-Purdue University, IN (MW)
Indiana University-Purdue University (Fort Wayne), IN (MW)

Indiana Wesleyan University, IN (MW)
Iona College, NY (MW)
Iowa State University of Science and Technology, IA (W)
Iowa Wesleyan College, IA (MW)
Itawamba Community College, MS (MW)
Ithaca College, NY (MW)
Jacksonville State University, AL (W)
Jacksonville University, FL (MW)
James Madison University, VA (M)
Jamestown College, ND (W)
Jefferson Community College, NY (MW)
John Brown University, AR (M)
John Carroll University, OH (M)
Johns Hopkins University, MD (MW)
Johnson County Community College, KS (M)
Johnson State College, VT (MW)
Jones County Junior College, MS (MW)
Juniata College, PA (M)
Kalamazoo College, MI (MW)
Kansas City Kansas Community College, KS (MW)
Kansas Newman University, KS (MW)
Kean University, NJ (MW)
Kennesaw State College, GA (M)
Keene State College, NH (MW)
Kentucky Christian College, KY (M)
Kentucky Wesleyan College, KY (MW)
Kenyon College, OH (MW)
Keystone Junior College, PA (M)
King College, TN (MW)
King's College, PA (MW)
Kishwaukee College, IL (M)
Knox College, IL (MW)
Kutztown University, PA (MW)
Lafayette College, PA (M)
Lake Forest College, IL (MW)
Lambuth University, TN (W)
Lander College, SC (M)
La Roche College, PA (MW)
La Salle University, PA (MW)
Lawrence University, WI (MW)
Lebanon Valley College, PA (MW)
Lee College, TN (MW)
Lees-McRae College, NC (MW)
Lehigh University, PA (MW)
Le Moyne College, NY (MW)

Lenoir-Rhyne College, NC (MW)
LeTourneau College, TX (MW)
Lewis and Clark Community College, IL (MW)
Lewis University, IL (MW)
Liberty University, VA (MW)
Limestone College, SC (MW)
Lincoln Christian College, IL (M)
Lincoln College, IL (MW)
Lincoln Land Community College, IL (M)
Lincoln Memorial University, TN (MW)
Lincoln University, MO (M)
Lindenwood College, MO (MW)
Linfield College, OR (MW)
Lock Haven University of Pennsylvania, PA (M)
Long Beach City College, CA (MW)
Long Island University (Brooklyn), NY (M)
Long Island University (C. W. Post Campus), NY (M)
Long Island University (Southampton Campus), NY (MW)
Longwood College, VA (MW)
Loras College, IA (M)
Los Angeles Pierce Junior College, CA (M)
Los Medanos College, CA (M)
Louisiana College, LA (MW)
Louisiana State University (Baton Rouge), LA (W)
Loiusiana Tech University, LA (MW)
Lower Columbia College, WA (M)
Loyola College, MD (MW)
Loyola Marymount University, CA (MW)
Loyola University, IL (MW)
Lubbock Christian College, TX (MW)
Luther College, IA (MW)
Lycoming College, PA (MW)
Lynchburg College, VA (M)
Lyndon State College, VT (MW)
Lynn University, FL (MW)
Macalester College, MN (MW)
Macomb Community College, MI (M)
Madison Area Technical College, WI (M)
Malone College, OH (M)
Manchester College, IN (M)
Manchester Community Technical College, CT (MW)

Manhattan College, NY (W)
Manhattanville Community College, NY (M)
Marian College, IN (MW)
Marian College, WI (MW)
Marietta College, OH (M)
Marion Military Institute, AL (M)
Marist College, NY (MW)
Marquette University, WI (MW)
Marshall University, WV (M)
Mars Hill College, NC (MW)
Marycrest College, IA (M)
Marycrest International University, IA (MW)
Marymount University, VA (MW)
Maryville College, TN (M)
Maryville University, MO (MW)
Mary Washington College, VA (MW)
Marywood University, PA (MW)
Massachusetts Bay Community College, MA (MW)
Massachusetts College of Liberal Arts, MA (MW)
Massachusetts Institute of Technology, MA (MW)
Massasoit Community College, MA (MW)
Master's College, CA (MW)
McHenry County College, IL (M)
McKendree College, IL (MW)
McNeese State University, LA (W)
Mercer County Community College, NJ (MW)
Mercer University, GA (MW)
Mercy College, NY (MW)
Mercyhurst College, PA (MW)
Merrimack College, MA (MW)
Mesa Community College, AZ (MW)
Mesa State College, CO (W)
Messiah College, PA (MW)
Metropolitan State College, CO (MW)
Miami University, OH (W)
Miami-Dade Community College (North), FL (W)
Michigan State University, MI (MW)
Middlebury College, VT (MW)
Middlesex County College, NJ (MW)
Midland Lutheran College, NE (W)
Midwestern State University, TX (M)
Millersville University, PA (M)

Millikin University, IL (MW)
Milwaukee Area Technology College, WI (M)
Mississippi Gulf Coast Community College, MS (MW)
Mississippi State University, MS (MW)
Missouri Baptist College, MO (MW)
Missouri Southern State College, MO (M)
Missouri Valley College, MO (MW)
Mitchell College, CT (MW)
Modesto Junior College, CA (MW)
Mohawk Valley Community College, NY (MW)
Molloy College, NY (MW)
Monmouth College, IL (M)
Monmouth College, NJ (MW)
Montclair State College, NJ (M)
Montgomery College, MD (M)
Montreat-Anderson College, NC (MW)
Moody Bible Institute, IL (M)
Moorpark College, CA (MW)
Moraine Valley Community College, IL (MW)
Moravian College, PA (M)
Morehead State University, KY (W)
Morningside College, IA (W)
Morton College, IL (M)
Mount Holyoke College, MA (W)
Mount Marty College, SD (M)
Mount Mercy College, IA (MW)
Mount Olive College, NC (M)
Mount St. Mary College, MD (MW)
Mount Union College, OH (M)
Mount Vernon Nazarene College, OH (M)
Mt. San Antionio College, CA (MW)
Muhlenberg College, PA (MW)
Muskingum College, OH (MW)
Nassau Community College, NY (MW)
National-Louis University, IL (M)
Nazareth College, NY (MW)
New Hampshire College, NH (MW)
New Jersey Institute of Technology, NJ (M)
New York Institute of Technology, NY (M)
New York University, NY (MW)

Niagara County Community College, NY (MW)
Niagara University, NY (MW)
Nicholls State University, LA (W)
Nichols College, MA (MW)
North Carolina State University, NC (MW)
North Carolina Wesleyan College, NC (MW)
North Central College, IL (M)
North Central Missouri College, MO (W)
North Country Community College, NY (MW)
Northeastern Christian Junior College, PA (M)
Northeastern Junior College, CO (W)
Northeastern State University, OK (MW)
Northeast Louisiana University, LA (W)
Northeast Missouri State University, MO (MW)
Northern Arizona College, AZ (M)
Northern Illinois University, IL (MW)
Northern Kentucky University, KY (MW)
Northern Montana College, MT (W)
North Georgia College & State University, GA (MW)
North Greenville College, SC (MW)
North Idaho College, ID (W)
Northland College, WE (M)
Northwestern College, IA (MW)
Northwestern College, MN (M)
Northwestern State University of Louisiana, LA (W)
Northwestern University, IL (M)
Northwest Missouri State University, MO (W)
Northwest Nazarene University, ID (M)
Northwood Institute, MI (W)
Northwood University (Texas Campus), TX (MW)
Norwich University, VT (MW)
Notre Dame College of Ohio, OH (W)
Nova Southern University, FL (M)
Nyack College, NY (MW)
Oakland University, MI (M)
Oberlin College, OH (MW)
Occidental College, CA (MW)
Ocean County College, NJ (M)

Oglethorpe University, GA (MW)
Ohio Dominican College, OH (M)
Ohio Northern University, OH (MW)
Ohio State University, OH (M)
Ohio Wesleyan University, OH (M)
Oklahoma Christian University of Science & Art, OK (M)
Oklahoma City University, OK (M)
Old Dominion University, VA (M)
Olivet College, MI (MW)
Olivet Nazarene University, IL (MW)
Oral Roberts University, OK (MW)
Orange Coast College, CA (MW)
Orange County Community College, NY (MW)
Oswego State University (SUNY), NY (MW)
Ottawa University, KS (M)
Otterbein College, OH (MW)
Ouachita Baptist University, AR (MW)
Oxnard College, CA (MW)
Pace University, NY (M)
Pace University (White Plains Campus), NY (M)
Pacific Lutheran University, WA (MW)
Pacific University, OR (MW)
Palm Beach Atlantic College, FL (M)
Palomar College, CA (MW)
Pan American University, TX (M)
Park College, MO (MW)
Parkland College, IL (MW)
Passaic County Community College, NJ (M)
Penn State Abington College, PA (M)
Penn State Berks-Lehigh Valley College, PA (M)
Pennsylvania State University, PA (MW)
Penn State Behrend College, PA (M)
Pepperdine University, CA (W)
Pfeiffer College, NC (M)
Philadelphia University, PA (MW)
Phillips University, OK (M)
Phoenix College, AZ (MW)
Piedmont College, GA (MW)

Pierce College, WA (M)
Plattsburgh State University (SUNY), NY (MW)
Plymouth State College, NH (MW)
Point Loma Nazarene College, NH (MW)
Point Park College, PA (M)
Polytechnic University (Brooklyn Campus), NY (M)
Pomona-Pitzer Colleges, CA (MW)
Presbyterian College, SC (MW)
Prince George's Community College, MD (M)
Princeton University, NJ (MW)
Principia College, IL (MW)
Providence College, RI (MW)
Purchase College (SUNY), NY (M)
Purdue University, IN (W)
Queensborough Community College, NY (MW)
Queens College, NY (M)
Queens College, NC (MW)
Quincy University, IL (MW)
Quinnipiac University, CT (MW)
Radford University, VA (MW)
Ramapo College, NJ (M)
Randolph-Macon College, VA (MW)
Ranetto Santiago College, CA (M)
Regis College, MA (W)
Regis University, CO (MW)
Rensselaer Polytechnic Institute, NY (MW)
Rhode Island College, RI (M)
Rider College, NJ (MW)
Ripon College, WI (MW)
Riverland Community College, MN (MW)
Roanoke College, VA (M)
Robert Morris College, PA (MW)
Roberts Wesleyan College, NY (MW)
Rochester College, MI (M)
Rochester Community & Technical College, MN (W)
Rochester Institute of Technology, NY (MW)
Rockhurst College, MO (M)
Rockland Community College, NY (M)
Rocky Mountain College, MT (W)
Rollins College, FL (MW)
Roosevelt University, IL (M)
Rose-Hulman Institute of Technology, IN (MW)

Rowan University, NJ (M)
Rutgers, Camden College of Arts and Sciences, NJ (MW)
Sacred Heart University, CT (MW)
Saginaw Valley State University, MI (MW)
Saint Ambrose University, IA (MW)
Saint Andrews Presbyterian College, NC (M)
Saint Anselm College, NH (MW)
Saint Augustine's College, NC (M)
Saint Bonaventure University, NY (MW)
Saint Edward's University, TX (MW)
Saint Francis College, IN (MW)
Saint Francis College, NY (M)
Saint Francis College, PA (MW)
Saint John Fisher College, NY (MW)
Saint John's University, MN (M)
Saint John's University, NY (M)
Saint Joseph's College, IN (MW)
Saint Joseph's University, PA (M)
Saint Lawrence University, NY (MW)
Saint Leo University, FL (M)
Saint Louis University, MO (M)
Saint Mary College, KS (MW)
Saint Mary's College, IN (W)
Saint Mary's College, MI (W)
Saint Mary's College of California, CA (MW)
Saint Mary's University, TX (M)
Saint Michael's College, VT (MW)
Saint Norbert College, WI (MW)
Saint Olaf College, MN (MW)
Saint Peter's College, NJ (MW)
Saint Thomas Aquinas College, NY (MW)
Saint Thomas University, FL (MW)
Saint Vincent College, PA (M)
Saint Xavier University, IL (M)
Salem State College, MA (MW)
Salem-Teikyo University, WV (M)
Salve Regina College, RI (MW)
Sam Houston State University, TX (M)
Samford University, AL (W)
San Diego City College, CA (MW)
San Diego Mesa College, CA (MW)

San Diego State University, CA (MW)
San Francisco State University, CA (MW)
San Joaquin Delta College, CA (M)
San Jose State University, CA (M)
Santa Barbara City College, CA (MW)
Santa Clara University, CA (MW)
Santa Monica College, CA (M)
Santa Rosa Junior College, CA (MW)
Schoolcraft College, MI (MW)
Schreiner College, TX (MW)
Scottsdale Community College, AZ (MW)
Seattle Pacific University, WA (M)
Seattle University, WA (MW)
Seton Hall University, NJ (MW)
Seton Hill College, PA (W)
Shawnee State University, OH (MW)
Shepherd College, WV (MW)
Shippensburg University of Pennsylvania, PA (MW)
Shoreline Community College, WA (MW)
Siena College, NY (MW)
Siena Heights College, MI (MW)
Sierra Nevada College, NV (MW)
Sioux Falls College, SD (MW)
Skagit Valley College, WA (M)
Skidmore College, NY (MW)
Skyline College, CA (M)
Slippery Rock University of Pennsylvania, PA (MW)
Smith College, MA (W)
Snow College, UT (MW)
South Carolina State College, SC (W)
Southeast Missouri State University, MO (M)
Southeastern Louisiana University, LA (W)
Southern California College, CA (M)
Southern Connecticut State University, CT (MW)
Southern Illinois University (Edwardsville), IL (MW)
Southern Methodist University, TX (MW)
Southern Nazarene University, OK (M)
Southern Oregon State College, OR (MW)

Southern Wesleyan University, SC (M)
Southwest, NM (MW)
Southwestern College, CA (M)
Southwest Baptist University, MO (MW)
Southwest Missouri State University, MO (MW)
Southwest State University, MN (W)
Southwestern Oklahoma State University, OK (MW)
Spartanburg Methodist, SC (MW)
Spokane Community College, WA (MW)
Spring Arbor College, MI (MW)
Spring Hill College, AL (MW)
Springfield College, MA (MW)
Springfield Technical Community College, MA (MW)
Stanford University, CA (MW)
State Fair Community College, MO (W)
State University of New York College (Brockport), NY (MW)
State University of New York College (Cortland), NY (MW)
State University of New York College (Fredonia), NY (MW)
State University of New York College (Geneseo), NY (MW)
State University of New York College (New Paltz), NY (MW)
State University of New York College (Potsdam), NY (MW)
State University of New York Institute of Technology at Utica/Rome (MW)
State University of New York Maritime College, NY (M)
Sterling College, KS (MW)
Stetson University, FL (MW)
Stevens Institute of Technology, NJ (M)
St. Catherine College, KY (MW)
St. Louis Community College (Florissant Valley), MO (M)
St. Louis Community College (Forest Park), MO (M)
Stonehill College, MA (MW)
Suffolk County Community College, NY (M)
Suffolk University, MA (M)
Swarthmore College, PA (MW)
Sweet Briar College, VA (W)
Syracuse University, NY (MW)
Tabor College, KS (M)
Teikyo Post University, CT (MW)

Teikyo Westmar University, IA (MW)

Temple Baptist Seminary, TN (M)

Temple University, PA (MW)

Tennessee Wesleyan College, TN (MW)

Texas A&I University, TX (W)

Texas A&M Commerce, TX (W)

Texas A&M University, TX (W)

Texas Christian University, TX (MW)

Texas Lutheran College, TX (MW)

Texas Southern University, TX (M)

Texas Tech University, TX (M)

Texas Wesleyan University, TX (MW)

Thomas College, ME (MW)

Thomas More College, KY (MW)

Tiffin University, OH (M)

Toccoa Falls College, GA (MW)

Towson State University, MD (MW)

Transylvania University, KY (MW)

Trevecca Nazarene College, TN (MW)

Trinity Christian College, IL (M)

Trinity College, CT (MW)

Trinity College, IL (M)

Trinity University, TX (MW)

Tri-State University, IN (MW)

Triton College, IL (M)

Truett-McConnell Junior College, GA (MW)

Tufts University, MA (MW)

Tusculum College, TN (M)

Tyler Junior College, TX (M)

Union College, KY (MW)

Union College, NY (MW)

Union County College, NJ (M)

Union University, TN (M)

Unity College, ME (MW)

University of Akron, OH (M)

University of Alabama (Birmingham), AL (MW)

University of Alabama (Huntsville), AL (MW)

University of Alabama (Tuscaloosa), AL (W)

University of Albany (SUNY), NY (MW)

University of Arizona, AZ (W)

University of Arkansas (Fayetteville), AR (W)

University of Arkansas (Little Rock), AR (W)

University of Bridgeport, CT (MW)

University of Buffalo (SUNY), NY (MW)

University of California (Berkeley), CA (MW)

University of California (Davis), CA (MW)

University of California (Irvine), CA (MW)

University of California (San Diego), CA (MW)

University of California (Santa Barbara), CA (MW)

University of California (Santa Cruz), CA (MW)

University of California (UCLA), CA (MW)

University of Central Arkansas, AR (MW)

University of Central Florida, FL (MW)

University of Charleston, WV (MW)

University of Cincinnati, OH (MW)

University of Colorado, CO (W)

University of Colorado (Colorado Springs), CO (M)

University of Connecticut, CT (MW)

University of Dallas, TX (MW)

University of Dayton, OH (MW)

University of Delaware, DE (MW)

University of Denver, CO (MW)

University of Detroit Mercy, MI (MW)

University of Evansville, IN (MW)

University of Findlay, OH (MW)

University of Georgia, GA (W)

University of Hartford, CT (MW)

University of Hawaii (Manoa), HI (W)

University of Houston, TX (W)

University of Idaho, ID (W)

University of Illinois (Urbana-Champaign), IL (W)

University of Incarnate Word, TX (MW)

University of Indianapolis, IN (MW)

University of Iowa, IA (W)

University of Kansas, KS (W)

University of Kentucky, KY (MW)

University of La Verne, CA (M)

University of Louisville, KY (MW)

University of Maine, ME (M)

University of Maine, (Fort Kent), ME (W)

University of Maine (Machias), ME (MW)

University of Maine (Presque Isle), ME (MW)

University of Mary Hardin-Baylor, TX (M)

University of Maryland, MD (MW)

University of Maryland (Baltimore County), MD (MW)

University of Massachusetts (Amherst), MA (MW)

University of Massachusetts (Boston), MA (MW)

University of Massachusetts (Dartmouth), MA (M)

University of Massachusetts (Lowell), MA (M)

University of Memphis, TN (MW)

University of Miami, FL (W)

University of Minnesota, MN (W)

University of Mississippi, MS (W)

University of Missouri (Rolla), MO (MW)

University of Mobile, AL (MW)

University of Montana, MT (W)

University of Nevada, NV (M)

University of New England, ME (MW)

University of New Hampshire, NH (MW)

University of New Haven, CT (MW)

University of New Mexico, NM (M)

University of North Alabama, AL (W)

University of North Carolina (Asheville), NC (MW)

University of North Carolina (Chapel Hill), NC (MW)

University of North Carolina (Charlotte), NC (MW)

University of North Carolina (Greensboro), NC (M)

University of North Carolina (Pembroke), NC (M)

University of North Carolina (Wilmington), NC (M)

University of Northern Colorado, CO (W)

University of North Texas, TX (W)

University of Notre Dame, IN (MW)

University of Oklahoma, OK (W)

University of Pennsylvania, PA (M)
University of Pittsburgh, PA (MW)
University of Pittsburgh (Bradford), PA (M)
University of Pittsburgh (Johnstown), PA (M)
University of Portland, OR (MW)
University of Puerto Rico, PR (M)
University of Puget Sound, WA (MW)
University of Redlands, CA (MW)
University of Rhode Island, RI (MW)
University of Richmond, VA (M)
University of Rio Grande, OH (M)
University of San Diego, CA (MW)
University of San Francisco, CA (MW)
University of Scranton, PA (MW)
University of South Alabama, AL (MW)
University of South Carolina, SC (MW)
University of South Carolina (Aiken), SC (MW)
University of South Carolina (Spartanburg), SC (MW)
University of South Dakota, SD (W)
University of Southern California, CA (W)
University of Southern Colorado, CO (MW)
University of Southern Indiana, IN (MW)
University of Southern Mississippi, MS (W)
University of South Florida, FL (MW)
University of St. Thomas, MN (MW)
University of Stony Brook (SUNY), NY (MW)
University of Tampa, FL (M)
University of Tennessee, TN (MW)
University of Tennessee (Knoxville), TN (MW)
University of Texas (Austin), TX (W)
University of Texas (El Paso), TX (W)
University of Texas (Pan American), TX (M)

University of Texas (San Antonio), TX (M)
University of the Pacific, CA (W)
University of Tulsa, OK (MW)
University of Vermont, VT (MW)
University of Virginia, VA (MW)
University of Washington, WA (M)
University of West Florida, FL (MW)
University of Wisconsin (Eau Claire), WI (W)
University of Wisconsin (Green Bay), WI (M)
University of Wisconsin (Madison), WI (MW)
University of Wisconsin (Milwaukee), WI (MW)
University of Wisconsin (Oshkosh), WI (M)
University of Wisconsin (Platteville), WI (M)
University of Wisconsin (Stevens Point), WI (W)
University of Wisconsin (Stout), WI (W)
University of Wyoming, WY (W)
University of the District of Columbia, DC (M)
Ursinus College, PA (M)
U.S. International University, CA (M)
Valley Forge Christian College, PA (M)
Valparaiso University, IN (MW)
Vanderbilt University, TN (MW)
Vassar College, NY (MW)
Villanova University, PA (MW)
Vincennes University, IN (M)
Virginia Commonwealth University, VA (M)
Virginia Military Institute, VA (M)
Virginia Polytechnic Institute & State University, VA (MW)
Virginia Wesleyan College, VA (MW)
Viterbo College, WI (M)
Wabash College, IN (M)
Wake Forest University, NC (M)
Waldorf College, IA (MW)
Wallace State Community College, AL (M)
Walla Walla Community College, WA (MW)
Walsh College, OH (M)
Warner Pacific College, OR (M)
Warner Southern College, FL (MW)
Warren Wilson College, NC (MW)

Wartburg College, IA (MW)
Washington and Jefferson College, PA (MW)
Washington College, MD (MW)
Washington State University, WA (W)
Washington University, MO (M)
Waubonsee College, IL (M)
Wayne State College, NE (W)
Weber State College, UT (W)
Webber College, FL (MW)
Webster University, MO (M)
Wellesley College, MA (W)
Wesleyan University, CT (MW)
Wesley College, DE (MW)
West Chester University, PA (MW)
Western Connecticut State University, CT (MW)
Western Illinois University, IL (MW)
Western Kentucky University, KY (M)
Western Maryland College, MD (MW)
Western Michigan University, MI (M)
Western New England College, MA (MW)
Western Washington University, WA (MW)
Westfield State College, MA (MW)
West Liberty State College, WV (W)
Westminster College, PA (MW)
Westmont College, CA (MW)
West Texas State University, TX (MW)
West Virginia University, WV (MW)
West Virginia Wesleyan College, WV (M)
Wheaton College, IL (MW)
Wheeling Jesuit College, WV (MW)
Whitman College, WA (MW)
Whittier College, CA (MW)
Whitworth College, WA (MW)
Wilkes College, NC (M)
Wilkes University, OR (M)
Willamette University, OR (M)
William Jewell College, MO (MW)
William Patterson College, NJ (M)
William Rainey Harper College, IL (M)
Williams College, MA (MW)
Williamson Trade School, PA (M)

William Woods College, MO (W)
Wilmington College, OH (MW)
Wingate College, NC (M)
Winona State University, MN
(W)
Winthrop University, SC (MW)
Wofford College, SC (MW)
Wright State University, OH
(MW)
Xavier University, OH (MW)
Yale University, CT (MW)
Yavapai College, AZ (M)
York College (CUNY), NY (M)
York College of Pennsylvania, PA
(M)
Youngstown State University,
OH (M)

Softball

Adams State College, CO (W)
Adelphi University, NY (W)
Adirondack College, NY (W)
Adrian College, MI (W)
Alabama A&N University, AL
(W)
Alabama State University, AL
(W)
Albion College, MI (W)
Albright College, PA (W)
Alfred University, NY (W)
Alice Lloyd College, KY (W)
Allegheny College, KY (W)
Allen County College, KS (W)
Allentown College, PA (W)
Alma College, MI (W)
Alvernia College, PA (W)
American International College,
MA (W)
Anderson-Broaddus College, WV
(W)
Anderson College, SC (W)
Anderson University, IN (W)
Anoka-Ramsey College, MN (W)
Apprentice School, VA (W)
Aquinas College, MI (W)
Arizona State University, AZ (W)
Armstrong Atlantic State Univer-
sity, GA (W)
Asbury College, KY (W)
Ashland College, OH (W)
Assumption College, MA (W)
Athens State College, AL (W)
Auburn University, AL (W)
Augsburg College, MN (W)
Augusta State University, GA
(W)
Augustana College, IL (W)
Augustana College, SD (W)
Aurora University, IL (W)
Austin College, TX (W)

Austin Community College, MN
(W)
Austin Peay State University, TN
(W)
Averett College, VA (W)
Avila College, MO (W)
Azusa Pacific University, CA (W)
Babson College, MA (W)
Bacone Junior College, OK (W)
Baker University, KS (W)
Ball State University, IN (W)
Barber-Scotia College, NC (W)
Bard College, NY (W)
Barry University, FL (W)
Barton College, NC (W)
Barton County College, KS (W)
Bates College, ME (W)
Baylor University, TX (W)
Becker College, MA (W)
Belhaven College, MS (W)
Bellarmine College, KY (W)
Belleville Area College, IL (W)
Bellevue College, NE (W)
Bellevue Community College,
WA (W)
Belmont College, TN (W)
Beloit College, WI (W)
Bemidji State University, MN
(W)
Benedict College, SC (W)
Benedictine College, KS (W)
Benedictine University, IL (W)
Bentley College, MA (W)
Bergen Community College, NJ
(W)
Bethany College, KS (W)
Bethany College, WV (W)
Bethany Lutheran College, MN
(W)
Bethel College, IN (W)
Bethel College, MN (W)
Bethune-Cookman College, FL
(W)
Big Bend Community College,
WA (W)
Binghamton University (SUNY),
NY (W)
Black Hawk College, IL (W)
Bloomfield College, NJ (W)
Bloomsburg University, PA (W)
Bluefield State College, WV (W)
Bluffton College, OH (W)
Boston College, MA (W)
Boston University, MA (W)
Bowdoin College, ME (W)
Bowie State University, MD (W)
Bowling Green State University,
OH (W)
Bradley University, IL (W)
Brainerd Community College,
MN (W)

Brandeis University, MA (W)
Brescia University, KY (W)
Brevard Community College, FL
(W)
Brewton Parker College, GA
(W)
Briar Cliff College, IA (W)
Bridgewater College, VA (W)
Brigham Young University, HI
(W)
Brigham Young University, UT
(W)
Bronx Community College, NY
(W)
Brooklyn College (CUNY), NY
(W)
Broome Community College,
NY (W)
Broward Community College,
FL (W)
Brown University, RI (W)
Bryant College, RI (W)
Bucknell University, PA (W)
Bucks County Community Col-
lege, PA (W)
Buena Vista University, IA (W)
Buffalo State College, NY (W)
Bunker Hill Community College,
KS (W)
Butler County Community Col-
lege, KS (W)
Butler County Community Col-
lege, PA (W)
Butler University, IN (W)
Butte College, CA (W)
Cabrillo College, CA (W)
Cabrini College, PA (W)
California Baptist University, CA
(W)
California Lutheran University,
CA (W)
California Polytechnic State Uni-
versity, CA (W)
California State Polytechnic Uni-
versity, CA (W)
California State University at
Bakersfield, CA (W)
California State University
(Chico), CA (W)
California State University
(Dominguez Hills), CA (W)
California State University
(Fresno), CA (W)
California State University
(Fullerton), CA (W)
California State University (Hay-
ward), CA (W)
California State University (Long
Beach), CA (W)
California State University
(Northridge), CA (W)

California State University (Sacramento), CA (W)
California State University (San Bernardino), CA (W)
California State University (Stanislaus), CA (W)
Calvin College, MI (W)
Cameron University, OK (W)
Campbell University, NC (W)
Campbellsville University, KY (W)
Capital University, OH (W)
Cardinal Stritch College, WI (W)
Carlow College, PA (W)
Carson-Newman College, TN (W)
Carthage College, WI (W)
Castleton State College, VT (W)
Catawba College, NC (W)
Catholic University of America, DC (W)
Catonsville Community College, MD (W)
Cayuga County Community College, NY (W)
Cecil Community College, MD (W)
Cedarville College, OH (W)
Centenary College, LA (W)
Centenary College, NJ (W)
Central Arizona College, AZ (W)
Central Christian College, KS (W)
Central College, IA (W)
Central Connecticut State University, CT (W)
Central Florida Community College, FL (W)
Central Lakes College, MN (W)
Central Methodist College, MO (W)
Central Michigan University, MI (W)
Central Missouri State University, MO (W)
Central Wesleyan College, SC (W)
Cerritos College, CA (W)
Chaffey College, CA (W)
Chaminade University of Honolulu, HI (W)
Chapman University, CA (W)
Charleston Southern University, SC (W)
Chattahoochee Valley Community College, AL (W)
Chipola Junior College, FL (W)
Chowan College, NC (W)
Christian Brothers College, TN (W)
Christopher Newport College, VA (W)

Clackamas Community College, OR (W)
Clarion University, PA (W)
Clark University, MA (W)
Cleveland State University, OH (W)
Clinton Community College, NY (W)
Cloud County Community College, KS (W)
Coahoma Junior College, MS (W)
Coastal Carolina College, SC (W)
Coastal Carolina Community College, NC (W)
Coastal Georgia Community College, GA (W)
Coe College, IA (W)
Coker College, SC (W)
Colby Community College, KS (W)
Colgate University, NY (W)
College of Allegheny County, PA (W)
College of Charleston, SC (W)
College of Mount St. Joseph, OH (W)
The College of New Jersey, NJ (W)
College of New Rochelle, NY (W)
College of Notre Dame, CA (W)
College of Notre Dame of Maryland, MD (W)
College of Saint Mary, NE (W)
College of St. Benedict, MN (W)
College of St. Francis, IL (W)
College of St. Mary, NE (W)
College of St. Rose, NY (W)
College of St. Scholastica, MN (W)
College of the Desert, CA (W)
College of the Holy Cross, MA (W)
College of the Redwoods, CA (W)
College of the Sequoias, CA (W)
Colorado College, CO (W)
Colorado Northwestern Community College, CO (W)
Colorado School of Mines, CO (W)
Colorado State University, CO (W)
Columbia College, MO (W)
Columbia-Greene Community College, NY (W)
Columbia Union College, MD (W)
Columbus College, GA (W)

Columbus State Community College, OH (W)
Community College of Allegheny County (Allegheny Campus), PA (W)
Community College of Philadelphia, PA (W)
Community College of Rhode Island, RI (W)
Concord College, WV (W)
Concordia College, WV (W)
Concordia College (Duluth), MN (W)
Concordia University (St. Paul), MN (W)
Concordia College, NY (W)
Concordia University, IL (W)
Concordia University, NE (W)
Concordia University Wisconsin, WI (W)
Connors State College, OK (W)
Copiah-Lincoln Community College, MS (W)
Cornell College, IA (W)
Cornell University, NY (W)
Cosumnes River College, CA (W)
Cowley County Community College, KS (W)
Creighton University, NE (W)
Crowder College, MO (W)
Cuesta College, CA (W)
Culver-Stockton College, MO (W)
Cumberland College, KY (W)
Curry College, MA (W)
Cuyahoga Community College (Metropolitan Campus), OH (W)
Cuyahoga Community College (Western Campus), OH (W)
Dakota State University, SD (W)
Dakota Wesleyan University, SD (W)
Dana College, NE (W)
Danville Area Community College, IL (W)
Davis & Elkins College, WV (W)
Dawson Community College, MT (W)
Daytona Beach Community College, FL (W)
Dean Junior College, MA (W)
Defiance College, OH (W)
Delaware County Community College, PA (W)
Delaware State University, DE (W)
Delaware Valley College, PA (W)
Delta College, MI (W)
Delta State University, MS (W)

Denison University, OH (W)
DePaul University, IL (W)
De Pauw University, IN (W)
Des Moines Area Community
College, IA (W)
Diablo Valley Community College, CA (W)
Dickinson College, PA (W)
Dixie College, UT (W)
Doane College, NE (W)
Dodge City Community College,
KS (W)
Dominican College, NY (W)
Dominican University, IL (W)
Dowling College, NY (W)
Drake University, IA (W)
Drexel University, PA (W)
Dundalk Community College,
MD (W)
Dutchess Community College,
NY (W)
East Carolina University, NC
(W)
East Central College, MO (W)
Eastern College, PA (W)
Eastern Connecticut State University, CT (W)
Eastern Illinois University, IL
(W)
Eastern Kentucky University, KY
(W)
Eastern Mennonite College, VA
(W)
Eastern Michigan University, MI
(W)
Eastern Nazarene College, MA
(W)
Eastern New Mexico University,
NM (W)
Eastern Oregon State College,
OR (M)
Eastfield College, TX (W)
East Stroudsburg University, PA
(W)
East Texas Baptist University, TX
(W)
Eckerd College, FL (W)
Edgewood College, WI (W)
Edinboro University of Pennsylvania, PA (W)
Edmonds Community College,
WA (W)
Edward Waters College, FL (W)
El Camino College, CA (W)
Elgin Community College, IL
(W)
Elizabeth City State University,
NC (W)
Elizabethtown College, PA (W)
Elmhurst College, IL (W)
Elmira College, NY (W)

Elon College, NC (W)
Emerson College, MA (W)
Emory University, GA (W)
Emporia State University, KS
(W)
Enterprise State Junior College,
AL (W)
Erskine College, SC (W)
Essex Community College, MD
(M)
Eureka College, IL (W)
Fairfield University, CT (W)
Fairleigh Dickinson University
(Madison), NJ (W)
Fairleigh Dickinson University
(Teaneck), NJ (W)
Faulkner University, AL (W)
Fayetteville State University, NC
(W)
Fergus Falls Community College, MN (W)
Ferris State College, MI (W)
Ferrum College, VA (W)
Fitchburg State College, MA
(W)
Florida Institute of Technology,
FL (W)
Florida Southern College, FL
(W)
Foothill College, CA (W)
Fordham University, NY (W)
Fort Hays State University, KS
(W)
Fort Lewis College, CO (W)
Fort Scott College, KS (W)
Fort Valley State University, GA
(W)
Francis Marion University, SC
(W)
Franklin & Marshall College, PA
(W)
Franklin Pierce College, NH (W)
Freed-Hardeman College, TN
(W)
Fresno City College, CA (W)
Friends University, KS (W)
Fullerton College, CA (W)
Fulton-Montgomery Community
College, NY (W)
Furman University, SC (W)
Gadsden State Community College, AL (W)
Gannon College, PA (W)
Garden City Community College, KS (W)
Gardner-Webb College, NC (W)
Garrett Community College,
MD (W)
Genesee Community College,
NY (W)
Geneva College, PA (W)

George C. Wallace Community
College, AL (W)
George Fox College, OR (W)
George Mason University, VA
(W)
Georgetown College, KY (W)
Georgia College State University,
GA (W)
Georgia Institute of Technology,
GA (W)
Georgian Court College, NJ (W)
Georgia Southern University, GA
(W)
Georgia Southwestern State University, GA (W)
Georgia State University, GA
(W)
Gettysburg College, PA (W)
Glen Oaks Community College,
MI (W)
Glendale Community College,
AZ (W)
Glendale Community College,
CA (W)
Gloucester County College, NJ
(W)
Golden West College, CA (W)
Goldey-Beacom College, DE
(W)
Gordon College, MA (W)
Goshen College, IN (W)
Grace College, IN (W)
Graceland College, IA (W)
Grambling State University, LA
(W)
Grand Rapids Baptist Seminary
of Cornerstone University, MI
(W)
Grand Rapids Community College, MI (W)
Grand Valley State College, MI
(W)
Grand View College, IA (W)
Grays Harbor College, WA (W)
Grayson County College, TX (W)
Greenfield Community College,
MA (W)
Green Mountain College, VT
(W)
Green River Community College, WA (W)
Greensboro College, NC (W)
Greenville College, IL (W)
Grinnell College, IA (W)
Grove City College, PA (W)
Gulf Coast Community College,
FL (W)
Gustavus Adolphus College, MN
(W)
Hagerstown Junior College, MD
(W)

Hamilton College, NY (W)
Hamline University, MN (W)
Hannibal-Lagrange College, MO (W)
Hanover College, IN (W)
Harford Community College, MD (W)
Harvard University, MA (W)
Haskell Indian Nations University, KS (W)
Hastings College, NE (W)
Haverford College, PA (W)
Hawaii Pacific University, HI (W)
Heidelberg College, OH (W)
Henderson State University, AR (W)
Herkimer County Community College, NY (W)
Hesser College, NH (W)
Hibbing Community College, MN (W)
Highland Community College, KS (W)
Hilbert College, NY (W)
Hillsborough Community College, FL (W)
Hillsdale College, MI (W)
Hinds Community College, MS (W)
Hiram College, OH (W)
Hiwassee College, TN (W)
Hofstra University, NY (W)
Holy Family College, PA (W)
Hope College, MI (W)
Hudson Valley Community College, NY (W)
Humboldt State University, CA (W)
Hunter College of the City University of New York, NY (W)
Huntingdon College, AL (W)
Huntington College, IN (W)
Husson College, ME (W)
Hutchinson College, KS (W)
Illinois Benedictine College, IL (W)
Illinois Central College, IL (W)
Illinois College, IL (W)
Illinois State University, IL (W)
Illinois Valley Community College, IL (W)
Illinois Wesleyan University, IL (W)
Indian Hills Community College, IA (W)
Indiana Institute of Technology, IN (W)
Indiana State University, IN (W)
Indiana University, IN (W)

Indiana University of Pennsylvania, PA (W)
Indiana University-Purdue University, IN (W)
Indiana University-Purdue University (Fort Wayne), IN (W)
Indiana University Southeast, IN (W)
Indiana Wesleyan University, IN (W)
Inver Hills Community College, MN (W)
Iona College, NY (W)
Iowa State University of Science and Technology, IA (W)
Iowa Wesleyan College, IA (W)
Itawamba Community College, MS (W)
Ithaca College, NY (W)
Jackson State University, MS (W)
Jacksonville State University, AL (W)
Jamestown College, ND (W)
Jefferson Community College, NY (W)
Jefferson Davis Junior College, AL (W)
Jefferson State Community College, AL (W)
John Carroll University, OH (W)
John C. Calhoun Community College, AL (W)
Johnson County Community College, KS (W)
Johnson C. Smith University, NC (W)
Johnson State College, VT (W)
Jones County Junior College, MS (W)
Judson College, AL (W)
Juniata College, PA (W)
Kalamazoo College, MI (W)
Kalamazoo Valley Community College, MI (W)
Kankakee Community College, IL (W)
Kansas City Kansas Community College, KS (W)
Kansas Newman University, KS (W)
Kansas Wesleyan College, KS (W)
Kaskaskia Community College, IL (W)
Kean University, NJ (W)
Kennesaw State College, GA (W)
Keene State College, NH (W)
Kent State University (Ashtabula), OH (W)

Kent State University (Kent), OH (W)
Kent State University (New Philadelphia), OH (W)
Kent State University (Warren), OH (W)
Kentucky State University, KY (W)
Kentucky Wesleyan College, KY (W)
Kenyon College, OH (W)
Keystone Junior College, PA (W)
King College, TN (W)
King's College, PA (W)
Kirkwood Community College, IA (W)
Kishwaukee College, IL (W)
Knox College, IL (W)
Kutztown University, PA (W)
Labette Community College, KS (W)
Lackawanna Junior College, PA (W)
Lafayette College, PA (W)
Lake Erie College, OH (W)
Lake Forest College, IL (W)
Lake Land College, IL (W)
Lake Michigan College, MI (W)
Lake-Sumter Community College, FL (W)
Lake Superior State University, MI (W)
Lamar Community College, CO (W)
Lambuth University, TN (W)
Lander College, SC (W)
Lansing Community College, MI (W)
La Roche College, PA (W)
La Salle University, PA (W)
Lawrence University, WI (W)
Lebanon Valley College, PA (W)
Lee College, TN (W)
Lees Junior College, KY (W)
Lehigh University, PA (W)
Le Moyne College, NY (W)
Lenoir-Rhyne College, NC (W)
Letourneau College, TX (W)
Lewis and Clark College, OR (W)
Lewis University, IL (W)
Liberty University, VA (W)
Limestone College, SC (W)
Lincoln College, IL (W)
Lincoln Land Community College, IL (W)
Lincoln Memorial University, TN (W)
Lincoln Trail College, IL (W)
Lincoln University, MO (W)
Lindenwood College, IL (W)

Linfield College, OR (W)
Long Beach City College, CA (W)
Long Island University (Brooklyn), NY (W)
Long Island University (C. W. Post Campus), NY (W)
Long Island University (Southampton Campus), NY (W)
Longwood College, VA (W)
Loras College, VA (W)
Los Angeles Pierce Junior College, CA (W)
Los Angeles Valley College, CA (W)
Los Medanos College, CA (W)
Louisiana College, LA (W)
Louisiana State University (Baton Rouge), LA (W)
Louisiana Tech University, LA (W)
Lower Columbia College, WA (W)
Loyola Marymount University, CA (W)
Loyola University, IL (W)
Luther College, IA (W)
Lycoming College, PA (W)
Lynchburg College, VA (W)
Lyndon State College, VT (W)
Macalester College, MN (W)
Macomb Community College, MI (W)
Madison Area Technical College, WI (W)
Madonna University, MI (W)
Malone College, OH (W)
Manchester College, OH (W)
Manchester Community Technical College, CT (W)
Manhattan College, NY (W)
Manhattanville College, NY (W)
Mankato State University, MN (W)
Mansfield University, PA (W)
Marian College, IN (W)
Marian College, WI (W)
Marietta College, OH (W)
Marist College, NY (W)
Mars Hill College, NC (W)
Mary Holmes College, MS (W)
Marycrest International University, IA (W)
Maryville College, TN (W)
Maryville University, MO (W)
Mary Washington College, VA (W)
Marywood College, PA (W)
Massachusetts Bay Community College, MA (W)
Massachusetts College of Liberal Arts, MA (W)

Massachusetts Institute of Technology, MA (W)
Massasoit Community College, MA (W)
Master's College, CA (W)
Mayville State College, ND (W)
McHenry County College, IL (W)
McKendree College, IL (W)
McLennan Community College, TX (W)
McNeese State University, LA (W)
Mercer County Community College, NJ (W)
Mercer University, GA (W)
Mercy College, NY (W)
Mercyhurst College, PA (W)
Merrimack College, MA (W)
Mesa Community College, AZ (W)
Mesa State College, CO (W)
Messiah College, PA (W)
Miami-Dade Community College (South Campus), FL (W)
Miami University, OH (W)
Michigan State University, MI (W)
Mid-America Nazarene College, KS (W)
Middlesex County College, NJ (W)
Middle Tennessee State University, TN (W)
Midland College, TX (W)
Midland Lutheran College, NE (W)
Miles College, AL (W)
Millersville University, PA (W)
Milligan College, TN (W)
Millikin University, IL (W)
Mississippi College, MS (W)
Mississippi Delta Junior College, MS (W)
Mississippi Gulf Coast Junior College, MS (W)
Mississippi State University, MS (W)
Mississippi University For Women, MS (W)
Mississippi Valley State University, MS (W)
Missouri Baptist College, MO (W)
Missouri Southern State College, MO (W)
Missouri Valley College, MO (W)
Missouri Western State College, MO (W)
Mitchell College, CT (W)
Modesto Junior College, CA (W)

Mohawk Valley Community College, NY (W)
Molloy College, NY (W)
Monmouth College, IL (W)
Monmouth College, NJ (W)
Montclair State College, NJ (W)
Montreat-Anderson College, NC (W)
Moorhead State University, MN (W)
Moorpark College, CA (W)
Moraine Valley Community College, IL (W)
Morehead State University, KY (W)
Morgan State University, MO (W)
Morningside College, IA (W)
Morton Collge, IL (W)
Mott Community College, MI (W)
Mount Holyoke College, MA (W)
Mount Marty College, SD (W)
Mount Mercy College, IA (W)
Mount Olive College, NC (W)
Mount St. Mary College, MD (W)
Mount Union College, OH (W)
Mount Vernon Nazarene College, OH (W)
Mt. San Antonio College, CA (W)
Mt. Wachusett Community College, MA (W)
Muhlenberg College, PA (W)
Muskegon Community College, MI (W)
Muskingum College, OH (W)
Nassau Community College, NY (W)
National-Louis University, IL (W)
Navarro College, TX (W)
Nebraska Wesleyan University, NE (W)
Newberry College, SC (W)
New Hampshire College, NH (W)
New Jersey Institute of Technology, NJ (W)
New Mexico Highland University, NM (W)
New Mexico State University, NM (W)
Niagara County Community College, NY (W)
Niagara University, NY (W)
Nicholls State University, LA (W)
Nichols College, MA (W)

Norfolk State University, VA (W)
North Arkansas College, AR (W)
North Carolina A & T State University, NC (W)
North Carolina Central University, NC (W)
North Central College, IL (W)
North Central Texas College, TX (W)
North County Community College, NY (W)
North Dakota State University, ND (W)
North Florida Junior College, FL (W)
Northeastern Illinois University, IL (W)
Northeastern Junior College, CO (W)
Northeastern State University, OK (W)
Northeast Louisiana University, LA (W)
Northeast Mississippi Community College, MS (W)
Northeast Missouri State University, OK (W)
Northern Illinois University, IL (W)
Northern Kentucky University, KY (W)
Northern State University, SD (W)
North Georgia College & State University, GA (W)
North Greenville College, SC (W)
North Hennepin Community College, MN (W)
North Idaho College, ID (W)
North Iowa Area Community College, IA (W)
Northwest Shoals Community College, AL (W)
Northwestern College, IA (W)
Northwestern College, MN (W)
Northwestern State University of Louisiana, LA (W)
Northwestern University, IL (W)
Northwest Mississippi Community College, MS (W)
Northwest Missouri State University, MO (W)
Northwood Institute, MI (W)
Northwood Institute (Texas Campus), TX (W)
Norwich University, VT (W)
Notre Dame College of Ohio, OH (W)
Nyack College, NY (W)
Oakland City University, IN (W)

Oakland Community College, MI (W)
Oakton Community College, IL (W)
Oberlin College, OH (W)
Ocean County College, NJ (W)
Ohio Dominican College, OH (W)
Ohio Northern University, OH (W)
Ohio State University, OH (W)
Ohio University, OH (W)
Ohio Valley College, WV (W)
Oklahoma Baptist University, OK (W)
Oklahoma City University, OK (W)
Oklahoma State University, OK (W)
Olivet College, MI (W)
Olivet Nazarene University, IL (W)
Olney Central College, IL (W)
Olympic College, WA (W)
Orange Coast College, CA (W)
Orange County Community College, NY (W)
Oregon Institute of Technology, OR (W)
Oregon State University, OR (W)
Oswego State University (SUNY), NY (W)
Otero Junior College, CO (W)
Otterbein College, OH (W)
Pace University, NY (W)
Pace University (White Plains Campus), NY (W)
Pacific Lutheran University, WA (W)
Pacific University, OR (W)
Paducah Community College, CA (W)
Paine College, GA (W)
Palm Beach Community College, FL (W)
Palomar College, CA (W)
Paris Junior College, TX (W)
Parkland College, IL (W)
Penn State Abington College, PA (W)
Pennsylvania State University, PA (W)
Penn State Behrend College, PA (W)
Penn State Berks-Lehigh Valley College, PA (W)
Peru State College, NE (W)
Pfeiffer College, NC (W)
Philadelphia University, PA (W)
Phoenix College, AZ (W)
Piedmont College, GA (W)

Pierce College, WA (W)
Pikeville College, KY (W)
Pima Community College (West Campus), AZ (W)
Pittsburg State University, KS (W)
Plymouth State College, NH (W)
Point Park College, PA (W)
Pomona-Pitzer Colleges, CA (W)
Pontifical Catholic University of Puerto Rico, PR (W)
Portland State University, OR (W)
Pratt Community College, KS (W)
Prince George's Community College, MD (W)
Principia College, IL (W)
Providence College, RI (MW)
Purdue University, IN (W)
Queensborough Community College, NY (W)
Queens College, NY (W)
Quincy University, IL (W)
Quinnipiac University, CT (W)
Quinsigamond College, MA (W)
Ramapo College, NJ (W)
Randolph-Macon College, VA (W)
Ranetto Santiago College, CA (W)
Regis College, MA (W)
Regis University, CO (W)
Rend Lake, IL (W)
Rensselaer Polytechnic Institute, NY (W)
Rhode Island College, RI (W)
Ricks College, ID (W)
Rider College, NJ (W)
Ripon College, WI (W)
Riverland Community College, MN (W)
Riverside Community College, CA (W)
Roane State Community College, TN (W)
Robert Morris College, PA (W)
Roberts Wesleyan College, NY (W)
Rochester College, MI (W)
Rochester Community College, MN (W)
Rochester Institute of Technology, NY (W)
Rockland Community College, NY (W)
Rollins College, FL (W)
Rose-Hulman Institute of Technology, IN (W)
Rowan College of New Jersey, NJ (W)

Rutgers, Newark College of Arts and Sciences, NJ (W)
Sacred Heart University, CT (W)
Saddleback College, CA (W)
Saginaw Valley State University, MI (W)
Saint Ambrose University, IA (W)
Saint Andrews Presbyterian College, NC (W)
Saint Anselm College, NH (W)
Saint Augustine's College, NC (W)
Saint Bonaventure University, NY (W)
Saint Cloud State University, MN (W)
Saint Edward's University, TX (W)
Saint Francis College, IN (W)
Saint Francis College, NY (W)
Saint Francis College, PA (W)
Saint John Fisher College, NY (W)
Saint John's University, NY (W)
Saint Joseph's College, IN (W)
Saint Joseph's University, PA (W)
Saint Leo University, FL (W)
Saint Louis University, MO (W)
Saint Mary College, IN (W)
Saint Mary's College, IN (W)
Saint Mary's College, MI (W)
Saint Mary's College of California, CA (W)
Saint Mary's University, TX (W)
Saint Norbert College, MN (W)
Saint Olaf College, WI (W)
Saint Paul's College, VA (W)
Saint Peter's College, NJ (W)
Saint Thomas Aquinas College, NY (W)
Saint Thomas University, FL (W)
Saint Vincent College, PA (W)
Saint Xavier University, IL (W)
Salem State College, MA (W)
Salem-Teikyo University, WV (W)
Salve Regina College, RI (W)
Samford University, AL (W)
Sam Houston State University, TX (W)
San Bernardino Community College, CA (W)
San Diego City College, CA (W)
San Diego Mesa College, CA (W)
San Diego State University, CA (W)
San Francisco State University, CA (W)

San Joaquin Delta College, CA (W)
San Jose State University, CA (W)
Santa Clara University, CA (W)
Santa FE Community College, FL (W)
Santa Monica College, CA (W)
Santa Rosa Junior College, CA (W)
Sauk Valley College, IL (W)
Scottsdale Community College, AZ (W)
Seminole Community College, FL (W)
Seton Hall University, NJ (W)
Seton Hill College, PA (W)
Seward County Community College, KS (W)
Shawnee State University, OH (W)
Shepherd College, WV (W)
Shippensburg University of Pennsylvania, PA (W)
Shoreline Community College, WA (W)
Siena College, NY (W)
Siena Heights College, MI (W)
Sierra College, CA (W)
Simpson College, CA (W)
Sioux Falls College, SD (W)
Skagit Valley College, WA (W)
Skyline College, CA (W)
Slippery Rock University of Pennsylvania, PA (W)
Smith College, MA (W)
Snead State Community College, AL (W)
Solano Community College, CA (W)
South Carolina State College, SC (W)
South Dakota State University, SD (W)
Southeast Community College, NE (W)
Southeastern Community College, IN (W)
Southeastern Illinois College, IL (W)
Southeastern Louisiana University, LA (W)
Southeast Missouri State University, MO (W)
Southern Arkansas University, AR (W)
Southern California College, CA (W)
Southern Connecticut State University, CT (W)
Southern Illinois University, IL (W)

Southern Illinois University (Edwardsville), IL (W)
Southern Union State Community College, AL (W)
Southern Utah University, UT (W)
Southern Wesleyan University, SC (W)
Southwest Baptist University, MO (W)
Southwestern College, CA (W)
Southwestern Michigan Junior College, MI (W)
Southwestern Oklahoma State University, OK (W)
Southwest Missouri State University, MO (W)
Southwest State University, MN (W)
Southwest Texas State University, TX (W)
Spartanburg Methodist, SC (W)
Spokane Community College, WA (W)
Spoon River College, IL (W)
Spring Arbor College, MI (W)
Springfield College, MA (W)
Springfield Technical Community College, MA (W)
Spring Hill College, AL (W)
Stanford University, CA (W)
State University of New York College (Brockport), NY (W)
State University of New York College (Cortland), NY (W)
State University of New York College at Fredonia, NY (W)
State University of New York College (Geneseo), NY (W)
State University of New York College (New Paltz), NY (W)
State University of New York College at Potsdam, NY (W)
State University of New York Institute of Technology at Utica/Rome, NY (W)
State University of New York Maritime College, NY (W)
State University of West Georgia, GA (W)
Stephen F. Austin State University, TX (W)
Sterling College, KS (W)
Stetson University, FL (W)
St. Catherine College, KY (W)
St. Johns River Community College, FL (W)
St. Louis Community College (Florissant Valley), MO (W)
St. Louis Community College (Forest Park), MO (W)

St. Mary of the Plains College, KS (W)
Stonehill College, MA (W)
St. Petersburg Junior College, FL (W)
Suffolk County Community College, NY (W)
Suffolk University, MA (W)
Swarthmore College, PA (W)
Syracuse University, NY (W)
Tabor College, KS (W)
Taft College, CA (W)
Tarleton State University, TX (W)
Teikyo Post University, CT (W)
Teikyo Westmar University, IA (W)
Temple Baptist Seminary, TN (W)
Temple College, TX (W)
Temple University, PA (W)
Tennessee State University, TN (W)
Tennessee Technological University, TN (W)
Tennessee Wesleyan College, TN (W)
Texarkana College, TX (W)
Texas A&I University, TX (W)
Texas A&M University, TX (W)
Texas Lutheran College, TX (W)
Texas Wesleyan University, TX (W)
Texas Woman's University, TX (W)
Thomas College, ME (W)
Thomas More College, KY (W)
Towson State University, MD (W)
Transylvania University, KY (W)
Trevecca Nazarene College, TN (W)
Trinity Christian College, IL (W)
Trinity College, CT (W)
Trinity College, IL (W)
Trinity University, TX (W)
Tri-State University, IN (W)
Triton College, IL (W)
Troy State University, AL (W)
Tufts University, MA (W)
Tusculum College, TN (W)
Tuskegee University, AL (W)
Union College, KY (W)
Union College, NY (W)
Union County College, NJ (W)
Union University, TN (W)
Unity College, ME (W)
University of Akron, OH (W)
University of Alabama (Birmingham), AL (W)
University at Albany (SUNY), NY (W)

University of Arizona, AZ (W)
University of Arkansas (Fayetteville), AR (W)
University of Arkansas (Monticello), AR (W)
University of Arkansas (Pine Bluff), AR (W)
University of Bridgeport, CT (W)
University at Buffalo (SUNY), NY (W)
University of California (Berkeley), CA (W)
University of California (Davis), CA (W)
University of California (Riverside), CA (W)
University of California (San Diego), CA (W)
University of California (Santa Barbara), CA (W)
University of California (UCLA), CA (W)
University of Central Arkansas, AR (W)
University of Central Oklahoma, OK (W)
University of Charleston, WV (W)
University of Chicago, IL (W)
University of Colorado (Colorado Springs), CO (W)
University of Connecticut, CT (W)
University of Dayton, OH (W)
University of Delaware, DE (W)
University of Detroit Mercy, MI (W)
University of Dubuque, IA (W)
University of Evansville, IN (W)
University of Findlay, OH (W)
University of Georgia, GA (W)
University of Hartford, CT (W)
University of Hawaii (Manoa), HI (W)
University of Illinois (Urbana-Champaign), IL (W)
University of Incarnate Word, TX (W)
University of Indianapolis, IN (W)
University of Iowa, IA (W)
University of Kansas, KS (W)
University of Kentucky, KY (W)
University of La Verne, CA (W)
University of Louisiana at Lafayette, LA (W)
University of Maine (Presque Isle), ME (W)
University of Mary, ND (W)

University of Mary Hardin-Baylor, TX (W)
University of Maryland (Baltimore County), MD (W)
University of Massachusetts (Amherst), MA (W)
University of Massachusetts (Boston), MA (W)
University of Massachusetts (Dartmouth), MA (W)
University of Massachusetts (Lowell), MA (W)
University of Memphis, TN (W)
University of Michigan, MI (W)
University of Minnesota (Duluth), MN (W)
University of Minnesota (Mineapolis), MN (W)
University of Minnesota (Morris), MN (W)
University of Missouri, MO (W)
University of Missouri (Columbia), MO (W)
University of Missouri (Rolla), MO (W)
University of Mobile, AL (W)
University of Alabama (Huntsville), AL (W)
University of Alabama (Tuscaloosa), AL (W)
University of Nebraska (Kearney), NY (W)
University of Nebraska (Lincoln), NE (W)
University of Nevada, NV (W)
University of New England, ME (W)
University of New Haven, CT (W)
University of New Mexico, NM (W)
University of North Alabama, AL (W)
University of North Carolina (Asheville), NC (W)
University of North Carolina (Chapel Hill), NC (W)
University of North Carolina (Charlotte), NC (W)
University of North Carolina (Greensboro), NC (W)
University of North Carolina (Pembroke), NC (W)
University of North Carolina (Wilmington), NC (W)
University of North Dakota, ND (W)
University of North Florida, FL (W)
University of Northern Colorado, CO (W)

University of Northern Iowa, IA (W)
University of Notre Dame, IN (W)
University of Oklahoma, OK (W)
University of Oregon, OR (W)
University of Pennsylvania, PA (W)
University of Pittsburgh, PA (W)
University of Puerto Rico, PR (M)
University of Puget Sound, WA (W)
University of Redlands, CA (W)
University of Rhode Island, RI (MW)
University of Rio Grande, OH (W)
University of San Diego, CA (W)
University of Scranton, PA (W)
University of South Carolina, SC (W)
University of South Carolina (Aiken), SC (W)
University of South Carolina (Spartanburg), SC (W)
University of South Dakota, SD (W)
University of Southern Colorado, CO (W)
University of Southern Indiana, IN (W)
University of Southern Mississippi, MS (W)
University of South Florida, FL (W)
University of St. Thomas, MN (W)
University at Stony Brook (SUNY), NY (W)
University of Tampa, FL (W)
University of Tennessee (Martin), TN (W)
University of Texas (Arlington), TX (W)
University of Texas (Austin), TX (W)
University of Texas (San Antonio), TX (W)
University of the Pacific, CA (W)
University of Toledo, OH (W)
University of Tulsa, OK (W)
University of Utah, UT (W)
University of Vermont, VT (W)
University of Virginia, VA (W)
The University of Virginia's College at Wise, VA (W)
University of Washington, WA (MW)
University of West Alabama, AL (W)

University of West Florida, FL (W)
University of Wisconsin (Eau Claire), WI (W)
University of Wisconsin (Green Bay), WI (W)
University of Wisconsin (La Crosse), WI (W)
University of Wisconsin (Madison), WI (W)
University of Wisconsin (Oshkosh), WI (W)
University of Wisconsin (Platteville), WI (W)
University of Wisconsin (River Falls), WI (W)
University of Wisconsin (Stevens Point), WI (W)
Upper Iowa University, IA (W)
Urbana University, OH (W)
Ursinus College, PA (W)
U.S. International University, CA (W)
Utah State University, UT (W)
Valdosta State University, GA (W)
Valley City State University, ND (W)
Valparaiso University, IN (W)
Ventura College, CA (W)
Villanova University, PA (W)
Virginia State University, VA (W)
Virginia Union University, VA (W)
Virginia Wesleyan College, VA (W)
Viterbo College, WI (W)
Wabash Valley College, IL (W)
Wagner College, NY (W)
Waldorf College, IA (W)
Wallace Community College (Selma), AL (W)
Wallace State Community College, AL (W)
Walla Walla Community College, WA (W)
Walsh College, OH (W)
Warner Pacific College, OR (W)
Warner Southern College, FL (W)
Warren Wilson College, NC (W)
Wartburg College, IA (W)
Washburn University, KS (W)
Washington and Jefferson College, PA (W)
Washington University, MO (W)
Waubonsee College, IL (W)
Wayne State College, NE (W)
Wayne State University, MI (W)
Webber College, FL (W)
Wesleyan University, CT (W)

Wesley College, DE (W)
West Chester University, PA (W)
West Liberty State College, WV (W)
Western Connecticut State University, CT (W)
Western Illinois University, IL (W)
Western Maryland College, MD (W)
Western Michigan University, MI (W)
Western New England College, MA (W)
Western New Mexico University, NM (W)
Western Oregon State College, OR (W)
Western Washington University, WA (W)
Westfield State College, MA (W)
Westminster College, PA (W)
West Virginia Institute of Technology, WV (W)
West Virginia Wesleyan College, WV (W)
Wheaton College, IL (W)
Whittier College, CA (W)
Wichita State University, KS (W)
Wilkes College, NC (W)
Wilkes University, PA (W)
Willamette University, OR (W)
William Jewell College, MO (W)
William Patterson College, NJ (W)
William Penn College, IA (W)
William Rainey Harper College, IL (W)
Williams College, MA (W)
William Woods College, MO (W)
Wilmington College, DE (W)
Wilmington College, OH (W)
Wilson College, PA (W)
Wingate College, NC (W)
Winona State University, MN (W)
Winston-Salem State University, NC (W)
Winthrop University, SC (W)
Worcester State College, MA (W)
Wright State University, OH (W)
Yakima Valley College, WA (W)
Yale University, CT (W)
York College of Pennsylvania, PA (W)
Youngstown State University, OH (W)
Yuba Community College, CA (W)

Spirit Squads

Concordia University, IL (W)

Sprint Football

Cornell University, NY (M)

Squash

Amherst College, MA (MW)
Atlantic Community College, NJ
    (W)
Bates College, ME (MW)
Bowdoin College, ME (MW)
Brown University, RI (W)
Claflin College, SC (W)
Connecticut College, CT (M)
Cornell University, NY (M)
Dartmouth College, NH (MW)
Franklin & Marshall College, PA
    (MW)
Hamilton College, NY (MW)
Harvard University, MA (MW)
Haverford College, PA (MW)
Johns Hopkins University, MD
    (W)
Massachusetts Institute of Tech-
    nology, MA (M)
Middlebury College, VT (W)
Mount Holyoke College, MA
    (W)
North Carolina Wesleyan Col-
    lege, NC (W)
Princeton University, NJ (MW)
Smith College, MA (W)
State University of New York
    (Stony Brook), NY (M)
Stevens Institute of Technology,
    NJ (M)
Trinity College, CT (MW)
Tufts University, MA (MW)
University of Pennsylvania, PA
    (MW)
Vassar College, NY (MW)
Wellesley College, MA (W)
Wesleyan University, CT (MW)
Williams College, MA (MW)
Yale University, CT (MW)

Swimming

Adelphi University, NY (MW)
Agnes Scott College, GA (W)
Albright College, PA (MW)
Asbury College, KY (MW)
Auburn University, AL (MW)
Babson College, MA (MW)
Bentley College, MA (MW)
Bloomsburg University, PA (W)

Boston University, MA (MW)
Bradley University, IL (MW)
Brevard Community College, FL
    (MW)
Bridgewater State College, MA
    (MW)
Brigham Young University, UT
    (MW)
Brooklyn College (CUNY), NY
    (W)
Bryn Mawr College, PA (W)
Bucknell University, PA (MW)
Butler University, IN (MW)
California Polytechnic State Uni-
    versity, CA (MW)
California State University
    (Fresno), CA (W)
California State University (Hay-
    ward), CA (MW)
Calvin College, MI (MW)
Campbellsville University, KY
    (MW)
Canisius College, NY (W)
Carnegie-Mellon University, PA
    (MW)
Carroll College, WI (MW)
Carthage College, WI (MW)
Catawba College, NC (W)
Catholic University of America,
    DC (MW)
Chapman University, CA (MW)
Cleveland State University, OH
    (MW)
Colgate University, NY (MW)
College of New Rochelle, NY
    (W)
College of Notre Dame of Mary-
    land, MD (W)
College of St. Benedict, MN
    (W)
College of Wooster, OH (MW)
Concordia College, MN (W)
Connecticut College, CT (MW)
Creighton University, NE (MW)
Cumberland College, KY (MW)
Dartmouth College, NH (MW)
Davidson College NC (M)
Denison University, OH (MW)
Diablo Valley Community Col-
    lege, CA (MW)
Dickinson College, PA (MW)
Drexel University, PA (MW)
Duquesne University, PA (MW)
Eastern Connecticut State Uni-
    versity, CT (W)
Eastern Illinois University, MI
    (MW)
Eastern Oklahoma State College,
    OK (MW)
Evergreen State College, WA
    (MW)

Florida A&M University, FL
    (MW)
Franklin & Marshall College, PA
    (MW)
Genesee Community College,
    NY (MW)
George Washington University,
    DC (MW)
Gettysburg College, PA (MW)
Goucher College, MD (MW)
Herkimer County Community
    College, NY (MW)
Hillsdale College, MI (W)
Hiram College, OH (MW)
Hood College, MD (W)
Howard University, DC (MW)
Hunter College of the City Uni-
    versity of New York, NY (W)
Illinois Benedictine College, IL
    (MW)
Iowa State University of Science
    and Technology, IA (M)
Iowa Wesleyan College, IA (MW)
John Brown University, AR
    (MW)
Keene State College, NH (MW)
Kent State University (Ashta-
    bula), OH (MW)
Kenyon College, OH (MW)
Lebanon Valley College, PA
    (MW)
Lewis University, IL (MW)
Lincoln College, OR (MW)
Linfield College, OR (MW)
Long Beach City College, CA
    (M)
Los Angeles Valley College, CA
    (MW)
Louisiana State University
    (Baton Rouge), LA (MW)
Loyola College, MD (MW)
Loyola Marymount University,
    CA (W)
Manhattanville College, NY (W)
Mansfield University, PA (W)
Marymount University, VA
    (MW)
Mary Washington College, VA
    (MW)
Metropolitan State College, CO
    (MW)
Millikin University, IL (M)
Mississippi Valley State Univer-
    sity, MS (M)
Monmouth College, NJ (MW)
Montgomery College, MD (MW)
New Mexico State University,
    NM (MW)
North Central College, IL (MW)
Northeast Louisiana University,
    LA (MW)

Oakland University, MI (MW)
Old Dominion University, VA
  (MW)
Ouachita Baptist University, AR
  (MW)
Pacific Lutheran University, WA
  (MW)
Pepperdine University, CA (W)
Pfeiffer College, NC (W)
Pontifical Catholic University of
  Puerto Rico, PR (MW)
Queens College, NY (MW)
Randolph Macon College, VA
  (MW)
Rice University, TX (W)
Rider College, NJ (W)
Rollins College, FL (MW)
Roosevelt University, IL (MW)
Sacred Heart University, CT
  (MW)
Saint Bonaventure University,
  NY (MW)
Saint John's University, MN (M)
Salem State College, MA (MW)
Salem-Teikyo University, WV
  (MW)
San Diego State University, CA
  (W)
San Francisco State University,
  CA (MW)
San Joaquin Delta College, CA
  (MW)
San Jose State University, CA
  (W)
Santa Monica College, CA
  (MW)
Santa Rosa Junior College, CA
  (MW)
Shippensburg University of
  Pennsylvania, PA (MW)
Snow College, UT (MW)
South Dakota State University,
  SD (MW)
Southern Arkansas University,
  AR (MW)
Southern Methodist University,
  TX (MW)
Southern Oregon State College,
  OR (MW)
Southwest Missouri State Uni-
  versity, MO (W)
State University of New York
  College (Brockport), NY
  (MW)
State University of New York
  Maritime College, NY (M)
Swarthmore College, PA (MW)
Tennessee State University, TN
  (M)
Transylvania University, KY
  (MW)

Tri-State University, IN (MW)
Tufts University, MA (MW)
Tulane University, LA (MW)
University of Arkansas (Fayet-
  teville), AR (W)
University of Arkansas (Little
  Rock), AR (MW)
University of California (Berke-
  ley), CA (W)
University of Charleston, WV
  (MW)
University of Findlay, OH (MW)
University of Louisville, KY
  (MW)
University of Maine, ME (MW)
University of Missouri (Rolla),
  MO (M)
University of Nebraska (Kear-
  ney), NE (W)
University of Nevada (Reno),
  NV (W)
University of New Mexico, NM
  (MW)
University of North Florida, FL
  (W)
University of Puerto Rico (Baya-
  mon), PR (MW)
University of Puerto Rico
  (Cayey), PR (M)
University of Puget Sound, WA
  (MW)
University of Redlands, CA
  (MW)
University of San Diego, CA (W)
University of Scranton, PA
  (MW)
University of Southern Califor-
  nia, CA (MW)
University of Tampa, FL (MW)
University of Texas (Austin), TX
  (W)
University of the Pacific, CA (MW)
University of Wisconsin (Stevens
  Point), WI (MW)
Ursinus College, PA (MW)
Ventura College, CA (MW)
Virginia Military Institute, VA
  (M)
Warren Wilson College, NC
  (MW)
Washington College, MD (MW)
Washington State University, WA
  (W)
Wesleyan University, CT (MW)
Western Connecticut State Uni-
  versity, CT (W)
Western Maryland College, MD
  (MW)
Westminster College, PA (MW)
West Virginia Wesleyan College,
  WV (MW)

Wheaton College, IL (MW)
Whittier College, CA (MW)
Whitworth College, WA (MW)
Winston-Salem State University,
  NC (MW)
Xavier University, OH (MW)
York College of Pennsylvania, PA
  (MW)
Youngstown State University,
  OH (MW)

Swimming-Diving

Albion College, MI (MW)
Alfred University, NY (MW)
Allegheny College, PA (MW)
Alma College, MI (MW)
American University, DC (MW)
Amherst College, MA (MW)
Arizona State University, AZ
  (MW)
Ashland College, OH (MW)
Augustana College, IL (MW)
Ball State University, IN (MW)
Bates College, ME (MW)
Beloit College, WI (MW)
Benedictine University, IL (MW)
Bethany College, KS (MW)
Bethany College, WV (MW)
Binghamton University (SUNY),
  NY (MW)
Bloomsburg University, PA
  (MW)
Boston College, MA (MW)
Bowdoin College, ME (MW)
Bowling Green State University,
  OH (MW)
Brandeis University, MA (MW)
Broward Community College,
  FL (MW)
Brown University, RI (MW)
Buena Vista University, IA (MW)
Buffalo State College, NY (MW)
Cabrillo College, CA (MW)
California Baptist University, CA
  (MW)
California Institute of Technol-
  ogy, CA (MW)
California State University at
  Bakersfield, CA (MW)
California State University
  (Chico), CA (W)
California State University (Hay-
  ward), CA (MW)
California State University
  (Northridge), CA (MW)
Carleton College, MN (MW)
Case Western Reserve University,
  OH (MW)
Central Connecticut State Uni-
  versity, CT (MW)

Central Washington University, WA (MW)
Cerritos College, CA (MW)
Chaffey College, CA (MW)
Clarion University, PA (MW)
Clarkson University, NY (MW)
Clark University, MA (MW)
Clemson University, SC (MW)
Cleveland State University, OH (MW)
Coe College, IA (MW)
College of Charleston, SC (MW)
The College of New Jersey, NJ (MW)
College of St. Rose, NY (MW)
College of the Holy Cross, MA (MW)
College of the Sequoias, CA (MW)
College of William and Mary, VA (MW)
Colorado College, CO (MW)
Colorado School of Mines, CO (MW)
Colorado State University, CO (W)
Columbia University, NY (MW)
Concordia University, NE | (MW)
Cornell University, NY (MW)
Cuesta College, CA (MW)
Davidson College, NC (W)
Delta State University, MS (MW)
Delhi College of Technology (SUNY), NY (MW)
De Pauw University, IN (MW)
Drexel University, PA (MW)
Drury College, MO (M)
Duke University, NC (MW)
Duquesne University, PA (MW)
East Carolina University, NC (MW)
Eastern Illinois University, IL (MW)
Eastern Michigan University, MI (MW)
East Stroudsburg University, PA (W)
Edinboro University of Pennsylvania, PA (MW)
El Camino College, CA (MW)
Elizabethtown College, PA (MW)
Emory University, GA (MW)
Eureka College, IL (MW)
Fairfield University, CT (MW)
Fairmont State College, WV (MW)
Florida Atlantic University, FL (MW)

Florida State University, FL (MW)
Foothill College, CA (MW)
Fordham University, NY (MW)
Fullerton College, CA (MW)
Furman University, SC (MW)
Gannon College, PA (MW)
George Mason University, VA (MW)
Georgetown University, DC (MW)
Georgia Southern University, GA (W)
Golden West College, CA (MW)
Grand Rapids Community College, MI (MW)
Grand Valley State College, MI (MW)
Grinnell College, IA (MW)
Grove City College, PA (MW)
Gustavus Adolphus College, MN (MW)
Hamilton College, NY (MW)
Hamline University, MN (MW)
Hartwick College, NY (MW)
Harvard University, MA (MW)
Henderson State University, AR (MW)
Hope College, MI (MW)
Illinois Institute of Technology, IL (MW)
Illinois State University, IL (W)
Illinois Wesleyan University, IL (MW)
Indian River Community College, FL (MW)
Indiana University, IN (MW)
Indiana University-Purdue University, IN (MW)
Iona College, NY (MW)
Ithaca College, NY (MW)
James Madison University, VA (MW)
John Carroll University, OH (MW)
Johns Hopkins University, MD (MW)
Kalamazoo College, MI (MW)
Kean University, NJ (W)
Kent State University (Ashtabula), OH (MW)
Kent State University (New Philadelphia), OH (MW)
Kent State University (Warren), OH (MW)
King's College, PA (MW)
Knox College, IL (MW)
Kutztown University of Pennsylvania, PA (MW)
Lafayette College, PA (MW)
Lake Forest College, IL (MW)

La Salle University, PA (MW)
Lawrence University, WI (MW)
Lehigh University, PA (MW)
Lewis and Clark College, OR (MW)
Lincoln College, IL (MW)
Long Beach City College, CA (W)
Loras College, IA (MW)
Los Angeles Pierce Junior College, CA (MW)
Luther College, IA (MW)
Lycoming College, PA (MW)
Macalester College, MN (MW)
Manhattanville College, NY (W)
Mankato State University, MN (MW)
Marist College, NY (MW)
Mary Baldwin College, VA (W)
Massachusetts Institute of Technology, MA (MW)
Miami University, OH (MW)
Michigan State University, MI (MW)
Middlebury College, VT (MW)
Millersville University, PA (W)
Millikin University, IL (W)
Modesto Junior College, CA (MW)
Montclair State College, NJ (MW)
Mount Holyoke College, MA (W)
Mount Union College, OH (MW)
Mt. San Antonio College, CA (MW)
Nazareth College, NY (MW)
New York University, NY (MW)
Niagara University, NY (MW)
North Carolina State University, NC (MW)
Northeast Missouri State University, MO (MW)
Northern Arizona University, AZ (MW)
Northern Illinois University, IL (MW)
Northern Michigan University, MI (W)
Northwestern University, IL (MW)
Norwich University, VT (MW)
Oberlin College, OH (MW)
Occidental College, CA (MW)
Ocean County College, NJ (MW)
Ohio Northern University, OH (MW)
Ohio State University, OH (MW)

Ohio University, OH (MW)
Ohio Wesleyan University, OH (MW)
Olivet College, MI (MW)
Orange Coast College, CA (MW)
Oregon State University, OR (W)
Oswego State University (SUNY), NY (MW)
Palomar College, CA (MW)
Pennsylvania State University, PA (MW)
Pfeiffer College, NC (W)
Plattsburgh State University (SUNY), NY (MW)
Plymouth State College, NH (W)
Pomona-Pitzer Colleges, CA (MW)
Princeton University, NJ (MW)
Principia College, IL (MW)
Providence College, RI (MW)
Purdue University, IN (MW)
Ranetto Santiago College, CA (MW)
Regis College, MA (W)
Rensselaer Polytechnic Institute, NY (MW)
Rice University, TX (M)
Rider College, NJ (M)
Ripon College, WI (MW)
Riverside Community College, CA (MW)
Roanoke College, VA (W)
Rochester Institute of Technology, NY (MW)
Rose-Hulman Institute of Technology, IN (MW)
Rose State Junior College, OK (MW)
Rowan University, NJ (MW)
Saddleback College, CA (MW)
Saint Bonaventure University, NY (MW)
Saint Cloud State University, MN (MW)
Saint Francis College, NY (MW)
Saint John's University, NY (MW)
Saint Lawrence University, NY (MW)
Saint Louis University, MO (MW)
Saint Mary's College, IN (W)
Saint Mary's College, MI (W)
Saint Michael's College, VT (MW)
Saint Olaf College, MN (MW)
Saint Peter's College, NJ (MW)
San Diego Mesa College, CA (MW)
Seton Hall University, NJ (MW)

Siena College, NY (W)
Sierra College, CA (MW)
Skidmore College, NY (W)
Slippery Rock University of Pennsylvania, PA (MW)
Smith College, MA (W)
Solano Community College, CA (MW)
Southern Connecticut State University, CT (MW)
Southern Illinois University, IL (MW)
Southern Methodist University, TX (MW)
Southwest Missouri State University, MO (M)
Springfield College, MA (MW)
Stanford University, CA (MW)
State University of New York College (Brockport), NY (MW)
State University of New York College (Cortland), NY (MW)
State University of New York College (Geneseo), NY (MW)
State University of New York College (New Paltz), NY (MW)
State University of New York College (Potsdam), NY (MW)
Sweet Briar College, VA (W)
Syracuse University, NY (MW)
Texas A&I University, TX (MW)
Texas A&M University, TX (MW)
Texas Christian University, TX (MW)
Towson State University, MD (MW)
Trinity College, CT (MW)
Trinity College, IL (MW)
Trinity University, TX (MW)
Triton College, IL (MW)
Union College, KY (MW)
Union College, NY (MW)
University of Alabama (Tuscaloosa), AL (MW)
University of Alaska, AK (M)
University of Arizona, AZ (MW)
University at Buffalo (SUNY), NY (MW)
University of California (Berkeley), CA (MW)
University of California (Davis), CA (MW)
University of California (Irvine), CA (MW)
University of California (Riverside), CA (MW)
University of California (San Diego), CA (MW)

University of California (Santa Barbara), CA (MW)
University of California (Santa Cruz), CA (W)
University of California (UCLA), CA (W)
University of Chicago, IL (MW)
University of Cincinnati, OH (MW)
University of Connecticut, CT (MW)
University of Delaware, DE (MW)
University of Denver, CO (MW)
University of Evansville, IN (MW)
University of Florida, FL (MW)
University of Georgia, GA (MW)
University of Hawaii (Manoa), HI (MW)
University of Houston, TX (W)
University of Illinois (Chicago), IL (MW)
University of Illinois (Urbana-Champaign), IL (W)
University of Indianapolis, IN (MW)
University of Iowa, IA (MW)
University of Kansas, KS (MW)
University of Kentucky, KY (MW)
University of Maryland, MD (MW)
University of Maryland (Baltimore County), MD (MW)
University of Massachusetts (Amherst), MA (MW)
University of Massachusetts (Dartmouth), MA (MW)
University of Massachusetts (Lowell), MA (M)
University of Miami, FL (MW)
University of Michigan, MI (MW)
University of Minnesota, MN (MW)
University of Missouri, MO (MW)
University of Missouri (Columbia), MO (MW)
University of Nebraska, NE (W)
University of Nebraska (Lincoln), NE (MW)
University of Nevada, NV (MW)
University of New Hampshire, NH (MW)
University of New Orleans, LA (MW)
University of North Carolina (Asheville), NC (MW)

University of North Carolina (Chapel Hill), NC (MW)
University of North Carolina (Wilmington), NC (MW)
University of North Dakota, ND (MW)
University of North Texas, TX (W)
University of Northern Colorado, CO (W)
University of Northern Iowa, IA (MW)
University of Notre Dame, IN (MW)
University of Pennsylvania, PA (MW)
University of Pittsburgh, PA (MW)
University of Rhode Island, RI (MW)
University of Richmond, VA (MW)
University of Southern California, CA (W)
University of South Carolina, SC (MW)
University of South Dakota, SD (MW)
University of St. Thomas, MN (MW)
University at Stony Brook (SUNY), NY (MW)
University of Tennessee, TN (MW)
University of Tennessee (Knoxville), TN (MW)
University of Texas (Austin), TX (M)
University of Toledo, OH (M)
University of Utah, UT (MW)
University of Vermont, VT (MW)
University of Virginia, VA (MW)
University of Washington, WA (MW)
University of Wisconsin (Eau Claire), WI (MW)
University of Wisconsin (Green Bay), WI (MW)
University of Wisconsin (La Crosse), WI (MW)
University of Wisconsin (Madison), WI (MW)
University of Wisconsin (Milwaukee), WI (MW)
University of Wisconsin (Oshkosh), WI (MW)
University of Wisconsin (River Falls), WI (MW)
University of Wyoming, WY (MW)
Valparaiso University, IN (MW)

Vassar College, NY (MW)
Villanova University, PA (MW)
Vincennes University, IN (MW)
Wabash College, IN (M)
Washington and Jefferson College, PA (MW)
Washington University, MO (MW)
Wayne State University, MI (MW)
Wellesley College, MA (W)
West Chester University of Pennsylvania, PA (MW)
Western Illinois University, IL (MW)
Western Kentucky University, KY (W)
Western State College, CO (W)
Westfield State College, MA (W)
West Virginia University, WV (MW)
Whitman College, WA (MW)
Whittier College, CA (MW)
Willamette University, OR (MW)
William Patterson College, NJ (MW)
William Rainey Harper College, IL (MW)
Williams College, MA (MW)
William Woods College, MO (W)
Wright State University, OH (MW)
Yale University, CT (MW)
York College of Pennsylvania, PA (MW)

Synchronized Swimming

Canisius College, NY (W)
Hinds Community College, MS (MW)
Ohio State University, OH (W)
Saint John's University, NY (W)
University of Alabama (Birmingham), AL (W)
University of Richmond, VA (W)
Walsh College, OH (W)

Table Tennis

Morehouse College, GA (M)

Tennis

Abilene Christian University, TX (MW)
Adelphi University, NY (MW)
Adirondack College, NY (MW)
Adrian College, MI (MW)
Agnes Scott College, GA (W)
Alabama A&M University, AL (M)

Alabama State University, AL (MW)
Albany State University, GA (W)
Albion College, MI (MW)
Albright College, PA (MW)
Alcorn State University, MS (W)
Alfred University, NY (MW)
Alice Lloyd College, KY (M)
Allegheny College, PA (MW)
Allentown College, PA (MW)
Alma College, MI (MW)
Alvernia College, PA (MW)
American International College, MA (MW)
American University, DC (MW)
Amherst College, MA (MW)
Anderson College, SC (MW)
Anderson University, IN (MW)
Andrew College, GA (MW)
Angelo State University, TX (W)
Appalachian State University, NC (MW)
Apprentice School, VA (M)
Aquinas College, MI (MW)
Assumption College, MA (MW)
Arizona State University, AZ (MW)
Arkansas State University, AR (W)
Arkansas Tech University, AR (W)
Armstrong Atlantic State University, GA (MW)
Asbury College, KY (MW)
Ashland College, OH (MW)
Atlantic Community College, NJ (MW)
Auburn University, AL (MW)
Auburn University (Montgomery), AL (MW)
Augusta State University, GA (MW)
Augustana College, IL (MW)
Augustana College, SD (MW)
Aurora University, IL (MW)
Austin College, TX (MW)
Austin Community College, MN (MW)
Austin Peay State University, TN (MW)
Averett College, VA (MW)
Azusa Pacific University, CA (MW)
Babson College, MA (MW)
Baker University, KS (MW)
Ball State University, IN (MW)
Barber-Scotia College, NY (MW)
Bard College, NY (MW)
Barry University, FL (MW)
Barstow College, CA (MW)

Barton College, NC (MW)
Barton County College, KS (W)
Bates College, ME (MW)
Baylor University, TX (MW)
Becker College, MA (M)
Belhaven College, MS (MW)
Bellarmine College, KY (MW)
Belleville Area College, IL (MW)
Bellevue Community College, WA (W)
Belmont Abbey College, NC (MW)
Belmont College, TN (MW)
Beloit College, WI (MW)
Bemidji State University, MN (W)
Benedict College, SC (MW)
Benedictine College, KS (MW)
Benedictine University, IL (MW)
Bentley College, MA (MW)
Berry College, GA (MW)
Bethany College, KS (MW)
Bethany College, WV (MW)
Bethel College, IN (MW)
Bethel College, KS (MW)
Bethel College, MN (MW)
Bethune-Cookman College, FL (MW)
Binghamton University (SUNY), NY (MW)
Biola University, CA (W)
Birmingham-Southern College, AL (MW)
Blackburn College, IL (W)
Bloomsburg University, PA (MW)
Bluefield State College, WV (MW)
Blue Mountain College, MS (W)
Blue Moutain College, OR (MW)
Bluffton College, OH (MW)
Boise State University, ID (MW)
Boston College, MA (MW)
Boston University, MA (MW)
Bowdoin College, ME (MW)
Bowling Green State University, OH (MW)
Bradley University, IL (MW)
Brainerd Community College, MN (MW)
Brandeis University, MA (MW)
Brenau Women's University, GA (W)
Brescia University, KY (W)
Brevard College, NC (MW)
Brevard Community College, FL (W)
Brewton Parker College, GA (MW)
Bridgewater College, VA (MW)

Bridgewater State College, MA (MW)
Brigham Young University, HI (MW)
Brigham Young University, UT (MW)
Brooklyn College (SUNY), NY (MW)
Broome Community College, NY (M)
Broward Community College, FL (MW)
Brown University, RI (MW)
Bryant College, RI (MW)
Bryn Mawr College, PA (W)
Bucknell University, PA (MW)
Bucks County Community College, PA (MW)
Buena Vista University, IA (MW)
Buffalo State College, NY (W)
Butler County Community College, KS (MW)
Butler County Community College, PA (MW)
Butler University, IN (MW)
Butte College, CA (MW)
Cabrillo College, CA (MW)
Cabrini College, PA (MW)
California Institute of Technology, CA (MW)
California Lutheran University, CA (MW)
California Polytechnic State University, CA (MW)
California State Polytechnic University, CA (MW)
California State University at Bakersfield, CA (W)
California State University (Chico), CA (W)
California State University (Fresno), CA (MW)
California State University (Fullerton), CA (W)
California State University (Hayward), CA (MW)
California State University (Long Beach), CA (W)
California State University (Los Angeles), CA (MW)
California State University (Northridge), CA (W)
California State University (Sacramento), CA (MW)
California State University (San Bernardino), CA (W)
California University, PA (M)
Calvin College, MI (MW)
Cameron University, OK (W)
Campbellsville University, KY (MW)

Campbell University, NC (MW)
Canisius College, NY (MW)
Capital University, OH (MW)
Carleton College, MN (MW)
Carlow College, PA (W)
Carnegie-Mellon University, PA (MW)
Carroll College, WI (MW)
Carson-Newman College, TN (MW)
Carthage College, WI (MW)
Case Western Reserve University, OH (MW)
Castleton State College, VT (MW)
Catawba College, NC (MW)
Catholic University of America, DC (MW)
Catonsville Community College, MD (W)
Cayuga County Community College, NY (MW)
Cecil Community College, MD (W)
Cedarville College, OH (MW)
Centenary College, LA (MW)
Central College, IA (MW)
Central Christian College, KS (W)
Central Connecticut State University, CT (MW)
Central Florida Community College, FL (W)
Central Lakes College, MN (MW)
Central Methodist College, MO (MW)
Central Washington University, WA (MW)
Cerritos College, CA (MW)
Chaminade University of Honolulu, HI (MW)
Chapman University, CA (MW)
Charles County Community College, MD (M)
Charleston Southern University, SC (MW)
Cheyney University of Pennsylvania, PA (MW)
Chicago State University, IL (MW)
Chowan College, NC (MW)
Christian Brothers College, TN (W)
Christopher Newport College, VA (MW)
Citadel, SC (M)
City College of New York, NY (MW)
City College of San Francisco, CA (MW)

Clarion University, PA (W)
Clark Atlanta University, GA (MW)
Clark College, WA (W)
Clarkson University, NY (MW)
Clark University, MA (MW)
Clemson University, SC (MW)
Cleveland State University, OH (MW)
Cloud County Community College, KS (MW)
Coastal Carolina College, SC (MW)
Coastal Carolina Community College, NC (MW)
Coe College, IA (MW)
Coffeyville Community College, KS (MW)
Coker College, SC (MW)
Colby-Sawyer College, NH (MW)
Colgate University, NY (MW)
College of Allegheny County, PA (W)
College of Charleston, SC (MW)
College of Mount St. Joseph, OH (MW)
The College of New Jersey, NJ (MW)
College of New Rochelle, NY (W)
College of St. Benedict, MN (W)
College of St. Francis, IL (MW)
College of St. Mary, NY (W)
College of St. Scholastica, MN (MW)
College of the Desert, CA (MW)
College of the Holy Cross, MA (MW)
College of the Sequoias, CA (MW)
College of William and Mary, VA (MW)
College of Wooster, OH (MW)
Colorado Christian University, CO (MW)
Colorado College, CO (MW)
Colorado School of Mines, CO (MW)
Colorado State University, CO (W)
Columbia Basin Community College, WA (MW)
Columbia College, SC (W)
Columbia Union College, MD (W)
Columbia University, NY (MW)
Columbus College, GA (MW)
Community College of Philadelphia, PA (MW)
Community College of Rhode Island, RI (MW)

Concord College, WV (MW)
Concordia College, MN (MW)
Concordia College, NY (MW)
Concordia Lutheran College, TX (MW)
Concordia Seminary, MO (MW)
Concordia University, NE (MW)
Concordia University, IL (MW)
Concordia University, MN (MW)
Concordia University Wisconsin, WI (MW)
Connecticut College, CT (MW)
Cannors State College, OK (MW)
Contra Costa College, CA (MW)
Converse College, SC (W)
Copiah-Lincoln Community College, MS (MW)
Coppin State College, MD (MW)
Cornell College, IA (MW)
Cornell University, NY (MW)
Consumnes River College, CA (MW)
Cowley County Community College, KS (MW)
Creighton University, NE (MW)
Cuesta College, CA (W)
Culver-Stockton College, MO (MW)
Cumberland College, KY (MW)
Curry College, MA (MW)
Dartmouth College, NH (MW)
Davidson College, NC (MW)
Davis & Elkins College, WV (MW)
Dean Junior College, MA (M)
Defiance College, OH (M)
Delaware County Community College, PA (M)
Delaware State University, DE (MW)
Delhi College of Technology (SUNY), NY (MW)
Delta College, MI (M)
Delta State University, MS (MW)
Denison University, OH (MW)
DePaul University, IL (MW)
De Pauw University, IN (MW)
Diablo Valley Community College, CA (M)
Dickinson College, PA (MW)
Dickinson State University, ND (MW)
Dixie College, UT (M)
Doane College, NE (MW)
Dominican College, CA (MW)
Dominican University, IL (MW)
Dowling College, NY (MW)

Drake University, IA (MW)
Drew University, NJ (MW)
Drexel University, PA (MW)
Drury College, MO (M)
Duke University, NC (MW)
Duquesne University, PA (MW)
Dutchess College, NY (MW)
Earlham College, IN (MW)
East Carolina University, NC (MW)
East Central University, OK (MW)
Eastern College, PA (MW)
Eastern Illinois University, IL (MW)
Eastern Kentucky University, KY (MW)
Eastern Michigan University, MI (MW)
Eastern Montana College, MT (MW)
Eastern Nazarene College, MA (MW)
Eastern New Mexico University, NM (W)
Eastern Oklahoma State College, OK (MW)
Eastern Washington University, WA (MW)
Eastfield College, TX (MW)
East Stroudsburg University, PA (MW)
East Tennessee State University, TN (MW)
Eckerd College, FL (MW)
Edgewood College, WI (MW)
Edinboro University of Pennsylvania, PA (MW)
El Camino College, CA (MW)
Elgin Community College, IL (MW)
Elizabethtown College, PA (MW)
Elmhurst College, IL (MW)
Elmira College, NY (MW)
Elon College, NC (MW)
Emerson College, MA (W)
Emory University, GA (MW)
Emory and Henry College, VA (MW)
Emporia State University, KS (MW)
Erskine College, SC (MW)
Essex Community College, MD (MW)
Eureka College, IL (MW)
Evangel College, MO (W)
Everett Community College, WA (MW)
Evergreen State College, WA (MW)

Fairfield University, CT (MW)
Fairleigh Dickinson University
(Madison), NJ (MW)
Fairleigh Dickinson University
(Teaneck), NJ (MW)
Fashion Institute of Technology,
NY (MW)
Ferris State College, MI (MW)
Ferrum College, VA (MW)
Flagler College, FL (MW)
Florida A&M University, FL
(MW)
Florida Atlantic University, FL
(MW)
Florida International University,
FL (W)
Florida Southern College, FL
(MW)
Florida State University, FL (MW)
Foothill College, CA (M)
Fordham University, NY (MW)
Fort Hays State University, KS
(MW)
Fort Valley State University, GA
(MW)
Francis Marion University, SC
(MW)
Franklin & Marshall College, PA
(MW)
Franklin Pierce College, NH
(MW)
Freed-Hardeman College, TN
(MW)
Fresno City College, CA (MW)
Fullerton College, CA (MW)
Furman University, SC (MW)
Gannon College, PA (MW)
Gardner-Webb College, NC
(MW)
Geneva College, PA (MW)
George Fox University, OR
(MW)
George Mason University, VA
(MW)
Georgetown College, KY (MW)
Georgetown University, DC
(MW)
George Washington University,
DC (MW)
Georgia College State University,
GA (MW)
Georgia Institute of Technology,
GA (MW)
Georgia Military College, GA
(M)
Georgia Southern University, GA
(MW)
Georgia Southwestern State Uni-
versity, GA (MW)
Georgia State University, GA
(MW)

Gettysburg College, PA (MW)
Glen Oaks Community College,
MI (W)
Glendale Community College,
AZ (MW)
Glendale Community College,
CA (MW)
Gloucester County College, NJ
(MW)
Golden West College, CA (MW)
Gonzaga University, WA (MW)
Gordon College, MA (MW)
Goshen College, IN (MW)
Goucher College, MD (MW)
Grace College, IN (MW)
Graceland College, IA (MW)
Grambling State University, LA
(MW)
Grand Canyon College, AZ
(MW)
Grand Rapids Baptist Seminary
of Cornerstone University, MI
(M)
Grand Rapids Community Col-
lege, MI (MW)
Grand View College, IA (MW)
Greensboro College, NC (MW)
Green Mountain College, VT
(MW)
Green River Community Col-
lege, WA (MW)
Greenville College, IL (MW)
Grinnell College, IA (MW)
Grove City College, PA (MW)
Gustavus Adolphus College, MN
(MW)
Hamilton College, NY (MW)
Hampden-Sydney College, VA
(M)
Hampton University, VA (M)
Hanover College, IN (MW)
Harding University, AR (MW)
Hardin-Simmons University, TX
(MW)
Harford Community College,
MD (MW)
Hartwick College, NY (MW)
Harvard University, MA (MW)
Hastings College, NE (MW)
Haverford College, PA (MW)
Hawaii Pacific University, HI
(MW)
Heidelberg College, OH (MW)
Henderson State University, AR
(MW)
Herkimer County Community
College, NY (MW)
Highland Park Community Col-
lege, MI (M)
High Point University, NC
(MW)

Hillsborough Community Col-
lege, FL (W)
Hillsdale College, MI (MW)
Hiram College, OH (MW)
Hofstra University, NY (MW)
Holmes Junior College, MS
(MW)
Hood College, MD (W)
Hope College, MI (MW)
Houston Baptist University, TX
(M)
Howard Payne University, TX
(W)
Howard University, DC (MW)
Hudson Valley Community Col-
lege, NY (W)
Hunter College of the City Uni-
versity of New York, NY (MW)
Huntingdon College, AL (MW)
Hungtington College, IN (MW)
Huston-Tillotson College, TX
(MW)
Hutchinson College, KS (MW)
Idaho State University, ID (W)
Illinois College, IL (MW)
Illinois State University, IL
(MW)
Illinois Valley Community Col-
lege, IL (MW)
Illinois Wesleyan University, IL
(MW)
Indiana State University, IN
(MW)
Indiana University, IN (MW)
Indiana University of Pennsylva-
nia, PA (W)
Indiana University-Purdue Uni-
versity, IN (MW)
Indiana University-Purdue Uni-
versity (Fort Wayne), IN (MW)
Indiana University Southeast, IN
(MW)
Indiana Wesleyan University, IN
(MW)
Indian River Community Col-
lege, FL (MW)
Iona College, NY (MW)
Iowa State University of Science
and Technology, IA (W)
Itawamba Community College,
MS (MW)
Ithaca College, NY (MW)
Jackson State University, MS
(MW)
Jacksonville State University, AL
(MW)
Jacksonville University, FL
(MW)
James Madison University, VA
(MW)
Jefferson College, MO (M)

Jefferson Davis Junior College, AL (MW)
Jefferson State Community College, AL (MW)
John Brown University, AR (MW)
John Carroll University, OH (MW)
Johns Hopkins University, MD (MW)
Johnson County Community College, KS (MW)
Johnson C. Smith University, NC (M)
Johnson State College, VT (MW)
Jones County Junior College, MS (MW)
Judson College, AL (W)
Juniata College, PA (W)
Kalamazoo College, MI (MW)
Kalamazoo Valley Community College, MI (MW)
Kankakee Community College, IL (M)
Kansas State University, KS (W)
Kaskaskia Community College, IL (M)
Kean University, NJ (MW)
Kent State University, OH (MW)
Kentucky Christian College, KY (MW)
Kentucky State University, KY (MW)
Kentucky Wesleyan College, KY (MW)
Kenyon College, OH (MW)
Keystone Junior College, PA (M)
King College, TN (MW)
King's College, PA (MW)
Kishwaukee College, IL (W)
Knox College, IL (MW)
Kutztown University, PA (MW)
Labette Community College, KS (W)
Lafayette College, PA (MW)
Lake Forest College, IL (MW)
Lake Land College, IL (M)
Lake Superior State University, MI (MW)
Lamar University, TX (MW)
Lambuth University, TN (MW)
Lander College, SC (MW)
La Roche College, PA (W)
La Salle University, PA (MW)
Lawrence University, WI (MW)
Lebanon Valley College, PA (MW)
Lee College, TN (MW)
Lees-McRae College, NC (MW)
Lehigh University, PA (MW)

Le Moyne College, NY (MW)
Le Tourneau College, TX (MW)
Lewis and Clark College, OR (MW)
Lewis and Clark Community College, IL (MW)
Lewis Clark State College, ID (MW)
Lewis University, IL (MW)
Liberty University, VA (M)
Limestone College, SC (MW)
Lincoln Memorial University, TN (MW)
Lincoln Trail College, IL (MW)
Lincoln University, MO (MW)
Linfield College, OR (MW)
Livingstone College, NC (MW)
Long Beach City College, CA (MW)
Long Island University (Brooklyn), NY (MW)
Long Island University (C.W. Post Campus), NY (W)
Longwood College, VA (MW)
Loras College, IA (MW)
Los Angeles Pierce Junior College, CA (MW)
Louisiana College, LA (W)
Louisiana State University (Baton Rouge), LA (MW)
Louisiana Tech University, LA (W)
Loyola College, MD (MW)
Loyola Marymount University, CA (MW)
Luther College, IA (MW)
Lycoming College, PA (MW)
Lynchburg College, VA (MW)
Lyndon State College, VT (MW)
Lynn University, FL (MW)
Macalester College, MN (MW)
Macomb Community College, MI (MW)
Madison Area Technical College, WI (MW)
Malone College, OH (MW)
Manchester College, IN (MW)
Manhattan College, NY (MW)
Manhattanville College, NY (MW)
Mankato State University, MN (MW)
Marian College, IN (MW)
Marian College, WI (MW)
Marietta College, OH (MW)
Marist College, NY (MW)
Marquette University, WI (MW)
Marshall University, WV (W)
Mars Hill College, NC (MW)
Mary Baldwin College, VA (W)
Marymount College, CA (MW)

Marymount University, VA (MW)
Maryville College, TN (MW)
Maryville University, MO (MW)
Mary Washington College, VA (MW)
Marywood College, PA (MW)
Massachusetts College of Liberal Arts, MA (MW)
Massachusetts Institute of Technology, MA (MW)
McHenry County College, IL (MW)
McKendree College, IL (MW)
McNeese State University, LA (W)
McPherson College, KS (MW)
Mercer County Community College, NJ (M)
Mercer University, GA (MW)
Mercy College, NY (M)
Mercyhurst College, PA (MW)
Merrimack College, MA (MW)
Mesa Community College, AZ (MW)
Mesa State College, CO (MW)
Messiah College, PA (MW)
Metropolitan State College, CO (MW)
Miami University, OH (W)
Michigan State University, MI (MW)
Michigan Technological University, MI (MW)
Middlebury College, VT (MW)
Middlesex County College, NJ (MW)
Middle Tennessee State University, TN (MW)
Midland Lutheran College, NE (MW)
Midwestern State University, TX (MW)
Millersville University, PA (MW)
Milligan College, TN (MW)
Millikin University, IL (MW)
Minot State, ND (MW)
MiraCosta College, CA (M)
Mississippi College, MS (MW)
Mississippi Delta Junior College, MS (W)
Mississippi Gulf Coast Junior College, MS (MW)
Mississippi State University, MS (MW)
Mississippi University For Women, MS (W)
Mississippi Valley State University, MS (MW)
Missouri Southern State College, MO (W)

Missouri Western State College, MO (W)
Mitchell College, CT (MW)
Mitchell Community College, NC (M)
Modesto Junior College, CA (MW)
Mohawk Valley Community College, NY (MW)
Molloy College, NY (W)
Monmouth College, NJ (M)
Montana State University, MT (MW)
Montclair State College, NJ (MW)
Montgomery College, MD (MW)
Montreat-Anderson College, NC (MW)
Moorhead State University, MN (W)
Moorpark College, CA (MW)
Moraine Valley Community College, IL (MW)
Moravian College, PA (MW)
Morehead State University, KY (MW)
Morehouse College, GA (M)
Morgan State University, MD (MW)
Morningside College, IA (W)
Morris Brown College, GA (MW)
Mount Holyoke College, MA (W)
Mount Olive College, NC (MW)
Mount St. Mary College, MD (MW)
Mount Union College, OH (MW)
Mount Vernon Nazarene College, OH (M)
Mt. San Antonio College, CA (M)
Mt. Wachusett Community College, MA (MW)
Muhlenberg College, PA (MW)
Murray State University, KY (MW)
Muskingum College, OH (MW)
Nassau Community College, NY (MW)
Nazareth College, NY (MW)
Nebraska Wesleyan University, NE (MW)
Newberry College, SC (MW)
New Hampshire College, NH (MW)
New Jersey Institute of Technology, NJ (MW)
New Mexico State University, NM (MW)

New York University, NY (MW)
Niagara University, NY (MW)
Nicholls State University, LA (W)
Nichols College, MA (MW)
North Carolina A & T State University, NC (MW)
North Carolina Central University, NC (MW)
North Carolina State University, NC (MW)
North Carolina Wesleyan College, NC (M)
North Central College, IL (MW)
North Central Texas College, TX (W)
North Dakota State, ND (MW)
Northeastern Illinois University, IL (MW)
Northeastern State University, OK (MW)
Northeast Louisiana University, LA (M)
Northeast Mississippi Community College, MS (MW)
Northeast Missouri State University, MO (MW)
Northern Arizona University, AZ (MW)
Northern Illinois University, IL (MW)
Northern Kentucky University, KY (MW)
Northern Michigan University, MI (W)
Northern State University, SD (MW)
North Georgia College & State University, GA (MW)
North Greenville College, SC (MW)
North Hennepin Community College, MN (MW)
Northwestern College, IA (MW)
Northwestern College, MN (M)
Northwestern Oklahoma State University, OK (MW)
Northwestern State University of Louisiana, LA (W)
Northwestern University, IL (MW)
Northwest Mississippi Community College, MS (MW)
Northwest Missouri State University, MO (MW)
Northwest Nazarene University, ID (W)
Northwood Institute, MI (M)
Northwood Institute (Texas Campus), TX (M)
Notre Dame College of Ohio, OH (W)

Nova Southern University, FL (W)
Oakland Community College, MI (MW)
Oakland University, MI (MW)
Oakton Community College, IL (MW)
Oberlin College, OH (MW)
Occidental College, CA (MW)
Ocean County College, NJ (MW)
Oglethorpe University, GA (MW)
Ohio Northern University, OH (MW)
Ohio State University, OH (MW)
Ohio University, OH (MW)
Ohio Wesleyan University, OH (MW)
Okaloosa-Walton Community College, FL (MW)
Oklahoma Baptist University, OK (M)
Oklahoma Christian University of Science & Art, OK (M)
Oklahoma City University, OK (MW)
Oklahoma State University, OK (MW)
Old Dominion University, VA (MW)
Olivet College, MI (MW)
Olivet Nazarene University, IL (MW)
Olney Central College, IL (MW)
Oral Roberts University, OK (MW)
Orange Coast College, CA (MW)
Orange County Community College, NY (MW)
Oregon State University, OR (W)
Oswego State University (SUNY), NY (MW)
Ottawa University, KS (MW)
Otterbein College, OH (MW)
Ouachita Baptist University, AR (MW)
Pace University, NY (MW)
Pace University, NY (MW)
Pace University (White Plains Campus), NY (MW)
Pacific Lutheran University, WA (MW)
Pacific University, OR (MW)
Paducah Community College, CA (MW)
Palm Beach Community College, FL (MW)
Palomar College, CA (MW)

Parkland College, IL (MW)
Penn State Abington College, PA (MW)
Penn State Berks-Lehigh Valley College, PA (MW)
Pennsylvania State University, PA (MW)
Penn State (Behrend College), PA (MW)
Pepperdine University, CA (MW)
Pfeiffer College, NC (MW)
Philadelphia University, PA (MW)
Phillips University, OK (M)
Piedmont College, GA (MW)
Pikesville College, KY (MW)
Pima Community College (West Campus), AZ (MW)
Plattsburgh State University (SUNY), NY (MW)
Plymouth State College, NH (MW)
Point Loma Nazarene College, CA (MW)
Polytechnic University (Brooklyn Campus), NY (M)
Pomona-Pitzer Colleges, CA (MW)
Pontifical Catholic University of Puerto Rico, PR (MW)
Portland State University, OR (W)
Prairie View A&M University, TX (MW)
Pratt Community College, KS (MW)
Presbyterian College, SC (MW)
Prince George's Community College, MD (MW)
Princeton University, NJ (MW)
Principia College, IL (MW)
Providence College, RI (MW)
Purdue University, IN (MW)
Queensborough Community College, NY (MW)
Queens College, NY (MW)
Queens College, NC (MW)
Quincy University, IL (MW)
Quinnipiac University, CT (MW)
Radford University, VA (MW)
Ramapo College, NJ (MW)
Randolph-Macon College, VA (MW)
Ranetto Santiago College, CA (MW)
Regis College, MA (W)
Regis University, CO (W)
Rend Lake College, IL (MW)
Rensselaer Polytechnic Institute, NY (MW)

Rhode Island College, RI (MW)
Rice University, TX (MW)
Rider College, NJ (MW)
Ripon College, WI (MW)
Riverland Community College, MN (MW)
Riverside Community College, CA (MW)
Roanoke College, VA (MW)
Robert Morris College, PA (MW)
Roberts Wesleyan College, NY (MW)
Rochester Institute of Technology, NY (MW)
Rockland Community College, NY (MW)
Rollins College, FL (MW)
Roosevelt University, IL (MW)
Rose-Hulman Institute of Technology, IN (MW)
Rose State Junior College, OK (MW)
Rowan University, NJ (MW)
Rust College, MS (MW)
Sacred Heart University, CT (W)
Saddleback College, CA (MW)
Saginaw Valley State University, MI (W)
Saint Ambrose University, IA (MW)
Saint Andrews Presbyterian College, NC (MW)
Saint Anselm College, NH (MW)
Saint Augustine's College, NC (M)
Saint Bonaventure University, NY (MW)
Saint Cloud State University, MN (MW)
Saint Edward's University, TX (MW)
Saint Francis College, IN (MW)
Saint Francis College, NY (MW)
Saint Francis College, PA (MW)
Saint John Fisher College, NY (MW)
Saint John's University, MN (M)
Saint John's University, NY (MW)
Saint Joseph's College, IN (MW)
Saint Joseph's University, PA (MW)
Saint Lawrence University, NY (MW)
Saint Leo University, FL (MW)
Saint Louis University, MO (MW)
Saint Mary College, KS (M)
Saint Mary's College, IN (W)

Saint Mary's College, MI (W)
Saint Mary's College of California, CA (MW)
Saint Mary's University, TX (MW)
Saint Michael's College, VT (MW)
Saint Norbert College, WI (MW)
Saint Olaf College, MN (MW)
Saint Peter's College, NJ (MW)
Saint Thomas University, FL (MW)
Saint Vincent College, PA (M)
Salem State College, MA (MW)
Salem-Teikyo University, WV (MW)
Salve Regina College, RI (MW)
Sam Houston State University, TX (MW)
Samford University, AL (MW)
San Bernardino Community College, CA (MW)
San Diego City College, CA (MW)
San Diego Mesa College, CA (MW)
San Diego State University, CA (MW)
San Francisco State University, CA (W)
San Joaquin Delta College, CA (MW)
San Jose State University, CA (MW)
Santa Barbara City College, CA (MW)
Santa Clara University, CA (MW)
Santa Monica College, CA (MW)
Santa Rosa Junior College, CA (MW)
Sauk Valley College, IL (W)
Savannah State College, GA (W)
Schreiner College, TX (MW)
Scottsdale Community College, AZ (MW)
Seattle University, WA (MW)
Seminole Community College, FL (MW)
Seton Hall University, NJ (MW)
Seton Hill College, PA (W)
Seward County Community College, KS (MW)
Shawnee State University, OH (W)
Shepherd College, WV (MW)
Shippensburg University of Pennsylvania, PA (W)
Shoreline Community College, WA (MW)

Shorter College, GA (MW)
Siena College, NY (MW)
Siena Heights College, MI (MW)
Sierra College, CA (MW)
Simpson College, CA (MW)
Sinclair Community College,
OH (MW)
Sioux Falls College, SD (MW)
Skagit Valley College, WA (MW)
Skidmore College, NY (MW)
Slippery Rock University of
Pennsylvania, PA (W)
Smith College, MA (W)
Snow College, UT (MW)
South Carolina State College,
SC (MW)
South Dakota School of Mines
and Technology, SD (M)
Southeastern Louisiana Univer-
sity, LA (MW)
Southeastern Oklahoma State
University, OK (MW)
Southern Arkansas University,
AR (W)
Southern California College, CA
(MW)
Southern Polytechnic State Uni-
versity, GA (M)
Southern Illinois University, IL
(MW)
Southern Illinois University
(Edwardsville), IL (MW)
Southern Methodist University,
TX (MW)
Southern Oregon State College,
OR (MW)
Southern University and A&M
College, LA (MW)
South Plains Community Col-
lege, TX (MW)
Southwest Baptist University,
MO (MW)
Southwestern College, CA (W)
Southwestern College, KS (MW)
Southwestern University, TX
(MW)
Southwest Missouri State Uni-
versity, MO (MW)
Southwest State University, MN
(W)
Southwest Texas State University,
TX (MW)
Spartanburg Methodist, SC (W)
Spokane Community College,
WA (MW)
Spring Arbor College, MI (MW)
Springfield College, MA (MW)
Spring Hill College, AL (MW)
Stanford University, CA (MW)
State University of New York
College (Brockport), NY (W)

State University of New York
College (Cortland), NY (W)
State University of New York
College (Fredonia), NY (MW)
State University of New York
College at Geneseo, NY (W)
State University of New York
College (New Paltz), NY
(MW)
State University of New York
College (Potsdam), NY (W)
State University of New York
Maritime College, NY (MW)
State University of West Georgia,
GA (MW)
Sterling College, KS (MW)
Stetson University, FL (MW)
Stevens Institute of Technology,
NJ (MW)
St. Gregory's College, OK (MW)
Stonehill College, MA (MW)
Suffolk County Community Col-
lege, NY (MW)
Suffolk University, MA (MW)
Sul Ross State University, TX
(MW)
Swarthmore College, PA (MW)
Sweet Briar College, VA (W)
Syracuse University, NY (W)
Tabor College, KS (MW)
Tarleton State University, TX
(W)
Teikyo Westmar University, IA
(M)
Temple Junior College, TX
(MW)
Temple University, PA (MW)
Tennessee Technological Univer-
sity, TN (MW)
Tennesee Wesleyan College, TN
(MW)
Texas A&I University, TX (MW)
Texas A&M University, TX
(MW)
Texas Christian University, TX
(MW)
Texas Lutheran College, TX
(MW)
Texas Tech University, TX (MW)
Texas Wesleyan University, TX
(MW)
Texas Woman's University, TX
(W)
Thomas College, ME (MW)
Thomas More College, KY
(MW)
Towson State University, MD
(MW)
Transylvania University, KY
(MW)
Trinity College, CT (MW)

Trinity University, TX (MW)
Tri-State University, IN (MW)
Troy State University, AL (MW)
Tufts University, MA (MW)
Tulane University, LA (MW)
Tusculum College, TN (MW)
Tuskegee University, AL (MW)
Tyler Junior College, TX (MW)
Union College, NY (MW)
Union University, TN (MW)
University of Akron, OH (MW)
University of Alabama (Birming-
ham), AL (M)
University of Alabama
(Huntsville), AL (MW)
University of Alabama
(Tuscaloosa), AL (MW)
University at Albany (SUNY),
NY (MW)
University of Arizona, AZ (MW)
University of Arkansas (Fayet-
teville), AR (MW)
University of Arkansas (Little
Rock), AR (MW)
University of Arkansas (Pine
Bluff), AR (M)
University at Buffalo (SUNY),
NY (MW)
University of California (Berke-
ley), CA (MW)
University of California (Davis),
CA (MW)
University of California (Irvine),
CA (MW)
University of California (River-
side), CA (MW)
University of California (San
Diego), CA (MW)
University of California (Santa
Barbara), CA (MW)
University of California (Santa
Cruz), CA (MW)
University of California (UCLA),
CA (MW)
University of Central Arkansas,
AR (MW)
University of Central Florida, FL
(MW)
University of Central Oklahoma,
OK (MW)
University of Charleston, WV
(MW)
University of Chicago, IL (MW)
University of Cincinnati, OH
(W)
University of Colorado, CO
(MW)
University of Colorado (Col-
orado Springs), CO (MW)
University of Connecticut, CT
(MW)

University of Dallas, TX (MW)
University of Dayton, OH (MW)
University of Delaware, DE (MW)
University of Denver, CO (MW)
University of Detroit Mercy, MI (MW)
University of Dubuque, IA (MW)
University of Evansville, IN (MW)
University of Findlay, OH (MW)
University of Florida, FL (MW)
University of Georgia, GA (MW)
University of Hartford, CT (MW)
University of Hawaii (Hilo), HI (MW)
University of Hawaii (Manoa), HI (MW)
University of Houston, TX (W)
University of Idaho, ID (MW)
University of Illinois (Chicago), IL (MW)
University of Illinois (Urbana-Champaign), IL (MW)
University of Incarnate Word, TX (MW)
University of Indianapolis, IN (MW)
University of Iowa, IA (MW)
University of Kansas, KS (MW)
University of Kentucky, KY (MW)
University of La Verne, CA (MW)
University of Louisiana at Lafayette, LA (MW)
University of Louisville, KY (MW)
University of Mary, ND (MW)
University of Mary Hardin-Baylor, TX (MW)
University of Maryland, MD (MW)
University of Maryland (Baltimore County), MD (MW)
University of Maryland (Eastern Shore), MD (MW)
University of Massachusetts (Amherst), MA (MW)
University of Massachusetts (Boston), MA (MW)
University of Massachusetts (Dartmouth), MA (MW)
University of Massachusetts (Lowell), MA (MW)
University of Memphis, TN (MW)
University of Miami, FL (MW)

University of Michigan, MI (MW)
University of Minnesota (Duluth), MN (MW)
University of Minnesota (Minneapolis), MN (MW)
University of Minnesota (Morris), MN (MW)
University of Mississippi, MS (MW)
University of Missouri (Columbia), MO (MW)
University of Missouri (Kansas City), MO (MW)
University of Montana, MT (MW)
University of Nebraska, NE (MW)
University of Nebraska (Kearney), NE (MW)
University of Nebraska (Lincoln), NE (MW)
University of Nevada, NV (MW)
University of Nevada (Reno), NV (MW)
University of New Hampshire, NH (MW)
University of New Haven, CT (W)
University of New Mexico, NM (MW)
University of New Orleans, LA (W)
University of North Alabama, AL (MW)
University of North Carolina (Asheville), NC (MW)
University of North Carolina (Chapel Hill), NC (MW)
University of North Carolina (Charlotte), NC (MW)
University of North Carolina (Greensboro), NC (MW)
University of North Carolina (Wilmington), NC (MW)
University of Northern Colorado, CO (MW)
University of Northern Iowa, IA (MW)
University of North Florida, FL (MW)
University North Texas, TX (W)
University Notre Dame, IN (MW)
University of Oklahoma, OK (MW)
University of Oregon, OR (MW)
University of Pennsylvania, PA (MW)
University of Pittsburg, PA (W)
University of Portland, OR (MW)

University of Puerto Rico, PR (MW)
University of Puerto Rico (Bayamon), PR (MW)
University of Puerto Rico (Ponce), PR (MW)
University of Puget Sound, WA (MW)
University of Redlands, CA (MW)
University of Rhode Island, RI (MW)
University of Richmond, VA (MW)
University of San Diego, CA (MW)
University of San Francisco, CA (MW)
University of Scranton, PA (MW)
University of South Alabama, AL (MW)
University of South Carolina, SC (MW)
University of South Carolina (Aiken), SC (M)
University of South Carolina (Spartanburg), SC (MW)
University of South Dakota, SD (MW)
University of Southern California, CA (MW)
University of Southern Colorado, CO (MW)
University of Southern Indiana, IN (MW)
University of Southern Mississippi, MS (MW)
University of South Florida, FL (MW)
University of St. Thomas, MN (MW)
University at Stony Brook (SUNY), NY (MW)
University of Tampa, FL (MW)
University of Tennessee, TN (MW)
University of Tennessee (Knoxville), TN (MW)
University of Tennessee (Martin), TN (MW)
University of Texas (Arlington), TX (MW)
University of Texas (Austin), TX (MW)
University of Texas (El Paso), TX (W)
University of Texas (Pan American), TX (MW)
University of Texas (San Antonio), TX (MW)

University of the District of Columbia, DC (MW)
University of the Pacific, CA (MW)
University of Toledo, OH (MW)
University of Tulsa, OK (MW)
University of Utah, UT (MW)
University of Vermont, VT (MW)
University of Virginia, VA (MW)
The University of Virginia's College at Wise, VA (MW)
University of Washington, WA (MW)
University of West Florida, FL (MW)
University of Wisconsin (Eau Claire), WI (MW)
University of Wisconsin (Green Bay), WI (MW)
University of Wisconsin (La Crosse), WI (MW)
University of Wisconsin (Madison), WI (MW)
University of Wisconsin (Milwaukee), WI (W)
University of Wisconsin (Oshkosh), WI (MW)
University of Wisconsin (Platteville), WI (MW)
University of Wisconsin (River Falls), WI (MW)
University of Wisconsin (Stevens Point), WI (MW)
University of Wisconsin (Stout), WI (W)
University of Wyoming, WY (W)
Upper Iowa University, IA (MW)
Ursinus College, PA (MW)
U.S. International University, CA (MW)
Utah State University, UT (M)
Valdosta State University, GA (MW)
Valley City State University, ND (MW)
Valparaiso University, IN (MW)
Vanderbilt University, TN (MW)
Vassar College, NY (MW)
Ventura College, CA (MW)
Villanova University, PA (MW)
Vincennes University, IN (M)
Virginia Commonwealth University, VA (MW)
Virginia Intermont College, VA (MW)
Virginia Military Institute, VA (M)
Virginia State University, VA (MW)
Virginia Union University, VA (M)

Virginia Wesleyan College, VA (MW)
Wabash College, IN (M)
Wabash Valley College, IL (MW)
Wagner College, NY (MW)
Wake Forest University, NC (MW)
Wallace Community College (Selma), AL (MW)
Wallace State Community College, AL (MW)
Walla Walla Community College, WA (MW)
Walsh College, OH (MW)
Walters State Community College, TN (M)
Warner Southern College, FL (MW)
Wartburg College, IA (MW)
Washburn University, KS (MW)
Washington and Jefferson College, PA (MW)
Washington State University, WA (MW)
Washington University, MO (MW)
Waubonsee College, IL (MW)
Wayne State University, MI (MW)
Webber College, FL (MW)
Weber State College, UT (MW)
Webster University, MO (MW)
Wellesley College, MA (W)
Wesleyan University, CT (MW)
Wesley College, DE (MW)
West Chester University, PA (MW)
Western Carolina University, NC (MW)
Western Connecticut State University, CT (MW)
Western Illinois University, IL (MW)
Western Kentucky University, KY (MW)
Western Maryland College, MD (MW)
Western Michigan University, MI (MW)
Western New England College, MA (MW)
Western Washington University, WA (MW)
Western Wyoming Community College, WY (MW)
West Liberty State College, WV (M)
Westminster College, PA (MW)
Westmont College, CA (MW)
West Texas State University, TX (MW)

West Virginia Institute of Technology, WV (MW)
West Virginia State College, WV (MW)
West Virginia University, WV (MW)
West Virginia Wesleyan College, WV (MW)
Wharton County Junior College, TX (MW)
Wheaton College, IL (MW)
Whitman College, WA (MW)
Whittier College, CA (MW)
Whitworth College, WA (MW)
Wichita State University, KS (MW)
Wilkes College, NC (MW)
Wilkes University, PA (MW)
Willamette University, OR (MW)
William Jewell College, MO (MW)
William Patterson College, NJ (W)
William Penn College, IA (MW)
William Rainey Harper College, IL (MW)
Williams College, MA (MW)
William Woods College, MO (W)
Wilmington College, OH (MW)
Wilson College, PA (W)
Wingate College, NC (MW)
Winona State University, MN (MW)
Winston-Salem State University, NC (MW)
Winthrop University, SC (MW)
Wofford College, SC (MW)
Worcester State College, MA (MW)
Wright State University, OH (MW)
Xavier University, OH (MW)
Yakima Valley College, WA (MW)
Yale University, CT (MW)
Yeshiva University, NY (MW)
York College (CUNY), NY (M)
York College of Pennsylvania, PA (MW)
Youngstown State University, OH (MW)
Yuba Community College, CA (MW)

Timber Sports

Finger Lakes Community College, NY (MW)

Track&Field

Abilene Christian University, TX (MW)
Adams State College, CO (MW)

Adrian College, MI (MW)
Alabama A&M University, AL (MW)
Alabama State University, AL (MW)
Albany State University, GA (MW)
Albion College, MI (MW)
Albright College, PA (MW)
Alcorn State University, MS (MW)
Alfred University, NY (MW)
Allegheny College, PA (MW)
Allen County College, KS (MW)
Allentown College of Saint Francis de Sales, PA (MW)
Alma College, MI (MW)
American University, DC (MW)
Amherst College, MA (MW)
Anderson College, SC (M)
Anderson University, IN (MW)
Angelo State University, TX (MW)
Appalachian State University, NC (MW)
Apprentice School, VA (MW)
Aquinas College, MI (MW)
Arizona State University, AZ (MW)
Arkansas State University, AR (MW)
Ashland College, OH (MW)
Auburn University, AL (MW)
Augsburg College, MN (MW)
Augustana College, IL (MW)
Augustana College, SD (MW)
Austin College, TX (M)
Austin Peay State University, TN (MW)
Azusa Pacific University, CA (MW)
Bacone Junior College, OK (MW)
Baker University, KS (MW)
Ball State University, IN (MW)
Baltimore City Community College, MD (MW)
Barber-Scotia College, NC (MW)
Barton County College, KS (MW)
Bates College, ME (MW)
Bayamon Central University, PR (MW)
Baylor University, TX (MW)
Bellarmine College, KY (MW)
Belmont College, TN (MW)
Beloit College, WI (MW)
Bemidji State University, MN (MW)
Benedict College, SC (MW)

Benedictine College, KS (MW)
Benedictine University, IL (MW)
Bentley College, MA (MW)
Bergen Community College, NJ (MW)
Bethany College, KS (MW)
Bethany College, WV (MW)
Bethel College, KS (MW)
Bethel College, MN (MW)
Bethune-Cookman College, FL (MW)
Binghamton University (SUNY), NY (MW)
Biola University, CA (M)
Black Hills State University, SD (MW)
Bloomsburg University, PA (MW)
Blue Mountain College, OR (MW)
Bluffton College, OH (MW)
Boston College, MA (MW)
Boston University, MA (MW)
Bowdoin College, ME (MW)
Bowie State University, MD (MW)
Bowling Green State University, OH (MW)
Brandeis University, MA (MW)
Brevard College, NC (MW)
Briar Cliff College, IA (MW)
Bridgewater College, VA (MW)
Bridgewater State College, MA (MW)
Brigham Young University, UT (MW)
Bronx Community College, NY (MW)
Brooklyn College (CUNY), NY (MW)
Brown University, RI (MW)
Bryant College, RI (MW)
Bryn Mawr College, PA (W)
Bucknell University, PA (MW)
Buena Vista University, IA (MW)
Buffalo State College, NY (MW)
Butler University, IN (MW)
Butte College, CA (MW)
Cabrini College, PA (MW)
California Baptist University, CA (MW)
California Institute of Technology, CA (MW)
California Lutheran University, CA (MW)
California Polytechnic State University, CA (MW)
California State Polytechnic University, CA (MW)
California State University at Bakersfield, CA (MW)

California State University (Chico), CA (MW)
California State University (Fresno), CA (MW)
California State University (Fullerton), CA (MW)
California State University (Hayward), CA (MW)
California State University (Long Beach), CA (MW)
California State University (Los Angeles), CA (MW)
California State University (Northridge), CA (MW)
California State University (Sacramento), CA (MW)
California State University (Stanislaus), CA (MW)
California University, PA (MW)
Calvin College, MI (MW)
Campbell University, NC (MW)
Canisius College, NY (MW)
Carleton College, MN (MW)
Carnegie-Mellon University, PA (MW)
Carroll College, WI (MW)
Carson-Newman College, TN (MW)
Carthage College, WI (MW)
Case Western Reserve University, OH (MW)
Catholic University of America, DC (MW)
Cayuga County Community College, NY (MW)
Cedarville College, OH (MW)
Central Arizona College, AZ (MW)
Central College, IA (MW)
Central Connecticut State University, CT (MW)
Central Methodist College, MO (MW)
Central Michigan University, MI (MW)
Central Missouri State University, MO (MW)
Central Washington University, WA (MW)
Cerritos College, CA (MW)
Chadron State College, NE (MW)
Chapman University, CA (W)
Charleston Southern University, SC (MW)
Chemeketa Community College, OR (MW)
Cheyney University of Pennsylvania, PA (MW)
Chicago State University, IL (MW)

Christopher Newport College, VA (MW)
Citadel, SC (M)
City College of New York, NY (MW)
City College of San Francisco, CA (MW)
Clackamas Community College, OR (MW)
Claflin College, SC (MW)
Clarion University, PA (MW)
Clark Atlanta University, GA (MW)
Clemson University, SC (MW)
Cleveland State University, OH (MW)
Cloud County Community College, KS (MW)
Coahoma Junior College, MS (M)
Coastal Carolina College, SC (MW)
Coe College, IA (W)
Coffeyville Community College, KS (MW)
Colby Community College, KS (MW)
Colby-Sawyer College, NH (MW)
Colgate University, NY (MW)
The College of New Jersey, NJ (MW)
College of Notre Dame, CA (MW)
College of St. Francis, IL (W)
College of the Holy Cross, MA (MW)
College of the Redwoods, CA (MW)
College of the Sequoias, CA (MW)
College of William and Mary, VA (MW)
College of Wooster, OH (MW)
Colorado College, CO (MW)
Colorado School of Mines, CO (MW)
Colorado State University, CO (MW)
Columbia Union College, MD (MW)
Columbia University, NY (MW)
Compton Community College, CA (MW)
Concord College, WV (MW)
Concordia College, MN (MW)
Concordia College (Moorhead), MN (MW)
Concordia University (St. Paul), MN (MW)
Concordia University, NE (MW)
Concordia University, IL (MW)

Concordia University Wisconsin, WI (MW)
Connecticut College, CT (MW)
Contra Costa College, CA (MW)
Copiah-Lincoln Community College, MS (M)
Coppin State College, MD (MW)
Cornell College, IA (MW)
Cornell University, NY (MW)
Consumnes River College, CA (MW)
Cuesta College, CA (MW)
Cumberland College, KY (MW)
Cuyahoga Community College, OH (MW)
Dakota State University, SD (MW)
Dakota Wesleyan University, SD (MW)
Dana College, NE (MW)
Danville Area Community College, IL (MW)
Dartmouth College, NH (MW)
Davidson College, NC (MW)
Defiance College, OH (MW)
Delaware State University, DE (MW)
Delaware Valley College, PA (MW)
Delhi College of Technology (SUNY), NY (MW)
Denison University, OH (MW)
DePaul University, IL (MW)
De Pauw University, IN (MW)
Diablo Valley Community College, CA (MW)
Dickinson College, PA (MW)
Dickinson State University, ND (MW)
Doane College, NE (MW)
Dodge City Community College, KS (MW)
Drake University, IA (MW)
Drexel University, PA (M)
Duke University, NC (MW)
Duquesne University, PA (W)
Earlham College, IN (MW)
East Carolina University, NC (MW)
East Central University, OK (M)
Eastern Connecticut State University, CT (MW)
Eastern Illinois University, IL (MW)
Eastern Kentucky University, KY (MW)
Eastern Mennonite College, VA (MW)
Eastern Michigan University, MI (MW)

Eastern Oklahoma State College, OK (MW)
Eastern Washington University, VA (MW)
East Stroudsburg University, PA (MW)
East Tennessee State University, TN (MW)
Edinboro University of Pennsylvania, PA (MW)
Edward Waters College, FL (MW)
El Camino College, CA (MW)
Elizabeth City State University, NC (MW)
Elizabethtown College, PA (MW)
Elmhurst College, IL (MW)
Elon College, NC (M)
Emory and Henry College, VA (MW)
Emory University, GA (MW)
Emporia State University, KS (MW)
Essex Community College, MD (MW)
Eureka College, IL (MW)
Everett Community College, WA (MW)
Fairleigh Dickinson University, NJ (MW)
Ferris State College, MI (MW)
Fisk University, TN (MW)
Fitchburg State College, MA (MW)
Florida A&M University, FL (MW)
Florida Memorial College, FL (MW)
Florida State University, FL (MW)
Foothill College, CA (MW)
Fordham University, NY (MW)
Fort Hays State University, KS (MW)
Fort Scott College, KS (M)
Fort Valley State University, GA (MW)
Francis Marion University, SC (MW)
Franklin & Marshall College, PA (MW)
Fresno City College, CA (MW)
Fresno Pacific University, CA (MW)
Fullerton College, CA (MW)
Furman University, SC (M)
Garden City Community College, KS (MW)
Gardner-Webb College, NC (M)
Geneva College, PA (MW)

George Fox College, OR (MW)
George Mason University, VA (MW)
Georgetown University, DC (MW)
Georgia Institute of Technology, GA (MW)
Georgia Southern University, GA (W)
Georgia State University, GA (W)
Gettysburg College, PA (MW)
Glendale Community College, AZ (MW)
Glendale Community College, CA (MW)
Glenville State College, WV (MW)
Gloucester County College, NJ (MW)
Golden West College, CA (MW)
Gonzaga University, WA (MW)
Goshen College, IN (MW)
Goucher College, MD (MW)
Grace College, IN (MW)
Graceland College, IA (MW)
Grand Rapids Baptist Seminary of Cornerstone University, MI (MW)
Grand Valley State College, MI (MW)
Grand View College, IA (MW)
Greenville College, IL (MW)
Grinnell College, IA (MW)
Grove City College, PA (MW)
Gustavus Adolphus College, MN (MW)
Hagerstown Junior College, MD (MW)
Hamilton College, NY (MW)
Hamline University, MN (MW)
Hampton University, VA (MW)
Hanover College, IN (MW)
Harding University, AR (MW)
Harris-Stowe State College, MO (W)
Hartwick College, NY (MW)
Harvard University, MA (MW)
Haskell Indian Nations University, KS (MW)
Hastings College, NE (MW)
Haverford College, PA (MW)
Heidelberg College, OH (MW)
Herkimer County Community College, NY (MW)
Highland Community College, KS (MW)
High Point University, NC (M)
Hillsdale College, MI (MW)
Hinds Community College, MS (M)

Hiram College, OH (MW)
Holmes Junior College, MS (MW)
Hope College, MI (MW)
Houghton College, NY (MW)
Houston Baptist University, TX (MW)
Howard University, DC (MW)
Humboldt State University, CA (MW)
Hunter College of the City University of New York, NY (MW)
Huntington College, IN (MW)
Hutchinson College, KS (MW)
Idaho State University, ID (MW)
Illinois College, IL (MW)
Illinois State University, IL (MW)
Illinois Wesleyan University, IL (MW)
Indiana State University, IN (MW)
Indiana University, IN (MW)
Indiana University of Pennsylvania, PA (MW)
Indiana Wesleyan University, IN (MW)
Inver Hills Community College, MN (MW)
Iona College, NY (MW)
Iowa State University of Science and Technology, IA (MW)
Iowa Wesleyan College, IA (MW)
Ithaca College, NY (MW)
Jackson State University, MS (MW)
James Madison University, VA (MW)
Jamestown College, ND (MW)
John Carroll University, OH (MW)
Johns Hopkins University, MD (MW)
Johnson County Community College, KS (MW)
Johnson C. Smith University, NC (MW)
Jones County Junior College, MS (M)
Juniata College, PA (MW)
Kansas City Kansas Community College, KS (MW)
Kansas State University, KS (MW)
Kansas Wesleyan College, KS (MW)
Kennesaw State College, GA (MW)
Keene State College, NH (MW)
Kent State University (Ashtabula), OH (MW)

Kent State University (Kent), OH (MW)
Kent State University (New Philadelphia), OH (MW)
Kent State University (Warren), OH (MW)
Kentucky State University, KY (MW)
Kenyon College, OH (MW)
Knox College, IL (MW)
Kutztown University, PA (MW)
Lafayette College, PA (MW)
Lake Superior State University, MI (MW)
Lamar University, TX (MW)
Lane Community College, OR (MW)
Langston University, OK (MW)
La Salle University, PA (MW)
Lawrence University, WI (MW)
Lebanon Valley College, PA (MW)
Lehigh University, PA (M)
LeMoyne-Owen College, TN (M)
Lewis and Clark College, OR (MW)
Lewis University, IL (MW)
Liberty University, VA (MW)
Lincoln University, MO (MW)
Linfield College, OR (MW)
Livingstone College, NC (MW)
Long Beach City College, CA (MW)
Long Island University (Brooklyn), NY (MW)
Long Island University (C.W. Post Campus), NY (MW)
Loras College, IA (MW)
Los Angeles Valley College, CA (MW)
Louisiana State University (Baton Rouge), LA (MW)
Louisiana Tech University, LA (MW)
Loyola University, IL (MW)
Lubbock Christian College, TX (MW)
Luther College, IA (MW)
Lycoming College, PA (MW)
Lynchburg College, VA (MW)
Macalester College, MN (MW)
Macomb Community College, MI (MW)
Madison Area Technical College, WI (MW)
Malone College, OH (MW)
Manchester College, IN (MW)
Manhattan College, NY (MW)
Mankato State University, MN (MW)

Mansfield University, PA (MW)
Marian College, IN (MW)
Marietta College, OH (MW)
Marist College, NY (MW)
Marquette University, WI (MW)
Marshall University, WV (MW)
Maryville University, MO (MW)
Mary Washington College, VA (MW)
Massachusetts Institute of Technology, MA (MW)
McKendree College, IL (MW)
McNeese State University, LA (MW)
Mercer County Community College, NJ (MW)
Mesa Community College, AZ (MW)
Messiah College, PA (MW)
Miami-Dade Community College (South Campus), FL (M)
Miami University, OH (MW)
Michigan State University, MI (MW)
Michigan Technological University, MI (MW)
Mid-America Nazarene College, KS (MW)
Middlebury College, VT (MW)
Middlesex County College, NJ (MW)
Middle Tennessee State University, TN (MW)
Midland Lutheran College, NE (MW)
Midwestern State University, TX (MW)
Miles College, AL (MW)
Millersville University, PA (MW)
Millikin University, IL (MW)
Milwaukee Area Technology College, WI (MW)
Minot State, ND (MW)
MiraCosta College, CA (W)
Mississippi College, MS (M)
Mississippi Delta Junior College, MS (M)
Mississippi Gulf Coast Junior College, MS (M)
Mississippi State University, MS (MW)
Mississippi Valley State University, MS (MW)
Missouri Southern State College, MO (MW)
Missouri Valley College, MO (MW)
Modesto Junior College, CA (MW)
Mohawk Valley Community College, NY (MW)

Monmouth College, IL (MW)
Monmouth College, NJ (M)
Montana State University, MT (MW)
Montclair State College, NJ (MW)
Moorhead State University, MN (MW)
Moorpark College, CA (MW)
Moravian College, PA (M)
Morehead State University, KY (MW)
Morehouse College, GA (M)
Morgan State University, MD (MW)
Morningside College, IA (MW)
Morris Brown College, GA (MW)
Mount Holyoke College, MA (W)
Mount Marty College, SD (MW)
Mount Mercy College, IA (MW)
Mount St. Mary College, MD (MW)
Mount Union College, OH (MW)
Mt. San Antonio College, CA (MW)
Muhlenberg College, PA (MW)
Murray State University, KY (MW)
Muskingum College, OH (MW)
Nassau Community College, NY (MW)
Nebraska Wesleyan University, NE (MW)
New Mexico State University, NM (MW)
New York Institute of Technology, NY (M)
New York University, NY (MW)
Nicholls State University, LA (MW)
Norfolk State University, VA (MW)
North Carolina A & T State University, NC (MW)
North Carolina Central University, NC (MW)
North Carolina State University, NC (MW)
North Central College, IL (MW)
North Dakota State, ND (MW)
North Dakota State University, ND (MW)
Northeast Louisiana University, LA (MW)
Northeast Missouri State University, MO (MW)
Northern Arizona University, AZ (MW)

North Idaho College, ID (MW)
Northwestern College, IA (MW)
Northwestern College, MN (MW)
Northwestern State University of Louisiana, LA (MW)
Northwestern University, IL (MW)
Northwest Missouri State University, MO (MW)
Northwest Nazarene University, ID (MW)
Northwood Institute, MI (MW)
Northwood Institute (Texas Campus), TX (MW)
Norwich University, VT (MW)
Oakton Community College, IL (MW)
Oberlin College, OH (MW)
Occidental College, CA (MW)
Ocean County College, NJ (MW)
Odessa College, TX (MW)
Oglethorpe University, GA (MW)
Ohio Northern University, OH (MW)
Ohio State University, OH (MW)
Ohio University, OH (MW)
Ohio Wesleyan University, OH (MW)
Oklahoma Baptist University, OK (M)
Oklahoma Christian University of Science & Art, OK (MW)
Oklahoma Panhandle State University, OK (MW)
Oklahoma State University, OK (MW)
Olivet College, MI (MW)
Olivet Nazarene University, IL (MW)
Orange Coast College, CA (MW)
Oregon State University, OR (MW)
Oswego State University (SUNY), NY (MW)
Ottawa University, KS (MW)
Otterbein College, OH (MW)
Pace University, NY (MW)
Pacific Lutheran University, WA (MW)
Pacific University, OR (MW)
Paine College, GA (MW)
Park College, MO (MW)
Parkland College, IL (MW)
Pennsylvania State University, PA (MW)

Penn State Behrend College, PA (MW)
Phoenix College, AZ (MW)
Pima Community College (West Campus), AZ (MW)
Pittsburg State University, KS (MW)
Plattsburgh State University (SUNY), NY (MW)
Point Loma Nazarene College, CA (MW)
Pomona-Pitzer Colleges, CA (MW)
Pontifical Catholic University of Puerto Rico, PR (MW)
Portland State University, OR (MW)
Prairie View A&M University, TX (MW)
Pratt Community College, KS (MW)
Presbyterian College, SC (M)
Princeton University, NJ (MW)
Principia College, IL (MW)
Providence College, RI (MW)
Purdue University, IN (MW)
Queensborough Community College, NY (MW)
Queens College, NY (MW)
Ramapo College, NJ (MW)
Ranetto Santiago College, CA (MW)
Rensselaer Polytechnic Institute, NY (M)
Rhode Island College, RI (MW)
Rice University, TX (MW)
Ricks College, ID (MW)
Rider College, NJ (MW)
Ripon College, WI (MW)
Riverside Community College, CA (MW)
Roanoke College, VA (M)
Robert Morris College, PA (MW)
Roberts Wesleyan College, NY (MW)
Rochester College, MI (MW)
Rochester Institute of Technology, NY (MW)
Roosevelt University, IL (MW)
Rose-Hulman Institute of Technology, IN (MW)
Rowan University, NJ (MW)
Rust College, MS (MW)
Rutgers Camden College of Arts and Sciences, NJ (MW)
Sacred Heart University, CT (MW)
Saddleback College, CA (MW)
Saginaw Valley State University, MI (MW)

Saint Ambrose University, IA (MW)
Saint Andrews Presbyterian College, NC (MW)
Saint Augustine's College, NC (MW)
Saint Cloud State University, MN (MW)
Saint Francis College, IN (MW)
Saint Francis College, PA (MW)
Saint John Fisher College, NY (MW)
Saint John's University, MN (M)
Saint John's University, NY (MW)
Saint Joseph's College, IN (MW)
Saint Joseph's University, PA (MW)
Saint Lawrence University, NY (MW)
Saint Mary's College, IN (W)
Saint Mary's College, MI (W)
Saint Norbert College, WI (MW)
Saint Olaf College, MN (MW)
Saint Paul's College, VA (MW)
Saint Peter's College, NJ (MW)
Salem State College, MA (MW)
Salve Regina College, RI (MW)
Samford University, AL (MW)
Sam Houston State University, TX (W)
San Bernardino Community College, CA (MW)
San Diego Mesa College, CA (MW)
San Diego State University, CA (W)
San Francisco State University, CA (MW)
San Joaquin Delta College, CA (MW)
San Jose State University, CA (M)
Santa Barbara City College, CA (MW)
Santa Monica College, CA (MW)
Santa Rosa Junior College, CA (MW)
Savannah State College, CA (M)
Scottsdale Community College, AZ (MW)
Seattle Pacific University, WA (MW)
Seminole Community College, FL (M)
Seton Hall University, NJ (MW)
Shippensburg University of Pennsylvania, PA (MW)
Siena Heights College, MI (MW)
Simpson College, CA (MW)

Sioux Falls College, SD (MW)
Skyline College, CA (MW)
Slippery Rock University of Pennsylvania, PA (MW)
Smith College, MA (W)
South Carolina State College, SC (MW)
South Dakota School of Mines and Technology, SD (MW)
South Dakota State University, SD (MW)
Southeastern Louisiana University, LA (MW)
Southeastern Oklahoma State University, OK (MW)
Southeast Missouri State University, MO (MW)
Southern Arkansas University, AR (MW)
Southern Illinois University, IL (MW)
Southern Illinois University (Edwardsville), IL (MW)
Southern Methodist University, TX (MW)
Southern Oregon State College, OR (MW)
Southern University and A&M College, LA (MW)
Southern Utah University, UT (MW)
South Plains Community College, TX (M)
Southwestern College, CA (MW)
Southwestern College, KS (MW)
Southwestern Oregon Community College, OR (MW)
Southwest Missouri State University, MO (MW)
Southwest Texas State University, TX (MW)
Spokane Community College, WA (MW)
Spoon River College, IL (MW)
Spring Arbor College, MI (MW)
Springfield College, MA (MW)
St. Francis College, NY (MW)
Stanford University, CA (MW)
State University of New York College (Brockport), NY (MW)
State University of New York College (Cortland), NY (MW)
State University of New York College (Fredonia), NY (MW)
State University of New York College (Geneseo), NY (MW)
State University of New York at New Paltz, NY (MW)
Stephen F. Austin State University, TX (MW)

Sterling College, KS (MW)
Stonehill College, MA (MW)
Sul Ross State University, TX (MW)
Swarthmore College, PA (MW)
Syracuse University, NY (MW)
Tabor College, KS (MW)
Taft College, CA (MW)
Talledaga College, AL (MW)
Tarleton State University, TX (MW)
Teikyo Westmar University, IA (MW)
Temple University, PA (MW)
Tennessee State University, TN (MW)
Texas A&I University, TX (MW)
Texas A&M Commerce, TX (MW)
Texas A&M University, TX (MW)
Texas Christian University, TX (MW)
Texas Lutheran College, TX (W)
Texas Southern University, TX (M)
Texas Tech University, TX (MW)
Tougaloo College, MS (MW)
Towson State University, MD (MW)
Trinity Christian College, IL (MW)
Trinity College, CT (MW)
Trinity University, TX (MW)
Tri-State University, IN (MW)
Troy State University, AL (MW)
Tufts University, MA (MW)
Tulane University, LA (MW)
Umpqua College, OR (MW)
Union College, NY (MW)
University of Akron, OH (MW)
University of Alabama (Birmingham), AL (MW)
University of Alabama (Tuscaloosa), AL (MW)
University at Albany (SUNY), NY (MW)
University of Arizona, AZ (MW)
University of Arkansas (Fayetteville), AR (MW)
University of Arkansas (Pine Bluff), AR (MW)
University at Buffalo (SUNY), NY (MW)
University of California (Berkeley), CA (MW)
University of California (Davis), CA (MW)
University of California (Irvine), CA (MW)
University of California (Riverside), CA (MW)

University of California (San Diego), CA (MW)
University of California (Santa Barbara), CA (MW)
University of California (UCLA), CA (MW)
University of Central Florida, FL (W)
University of Central Oklahoma, OK (MW)
University of Chicago, IL (MW)
University of Cincinnati, OH (M)
University of Colorado, CO (MW)
University of Connecticut, CT (MW)
University of Dallas, TX (MW)
University of Delaware, DE (MW)
University of Detroit Mercy, MI (MW)
University of Dubuque, IA (MW)
University of Findlay, OH (MW)
University of Florida, FL (MW)
University of Georgia, GA (MW)
University of Hartford, CT (MW)
University of Houston, TX (MW)
University of Idaho, ID (MW)
University of Illinois (Chicago), IL (MW)
University of Illinois (Urbana-Champaign), IL (MW)
University of Indianapolis, IN (MW)
University of Iowa, IA (MW)
University of Kansas, KS (MW)
University of Kentucky, KY (MW)
University of La Verne, CA (MW)
University of Louisiana at Lafayette, LA (MW)
University of Louisville, KY (MW)
University of Maine, ME (MW)
University of Mary, ND (MW)
University of Maryland, MD (M)
University of Maryland (Baltimore County), MD (MW)
University of Maryland (Eastern Shore), MD (MW)
University of Massachusetts (Amherst), MA (MW)
University of Massachusetts (Boston), MA (MW)
University of Massachusetts (Dartmouth), MA (MW)

University of Massachusetts (Lowell), MA (MW)
University of Memphis, TN (M)
University of Miami, FL (W)
University of Michigan, MI (MW)
University of Minnesota, MN (MW)
University of Mississippi, MS (MW)
University of Missouri, MD (MW)
University of Missouri (Columbia), MO (MW)
University of Mobile, AL (MW)
University of Montana, MT (MW)
University of Nebraska, NE (MW)
University of Nebraska (Kearney), NE (MW)
University of Nebraska (Lincoln), NE (MW)
University of Nevada, NV (W)
University of Nevada (Reno), NV (MW)
University of New Hampshire, NH (MW)
University of New Haven, CT (MW)
University of New Mexico, NM (MW)
University of New Orleans, LA (MW)
University of North Carolina (Asheville), NC (MW)
University of North Carolina (Chapel Hill), NC (MW)
University of North Carolina (Charlotte), NC (MW)
University of North Carolina (Pembroke), NC (M)
University of North Carolina (Wilmington), NC (MW)
University of North Dakota, ND (MW)
University of Northern Colorado, CO (MW)
University of Northern Iowa, IA (MW)
University of North Florida, FL (MW)
University of North Texas, TX (MW)
University of Notre Dame, IN (MW)
University of Oklahoma, OK (MW)
University of Oregon, OR (MW)
University of Pennsylvania, PA (MW)

University of Pittsburgh, PA (MW)

University of Pittsburgh (Johnstown), PA (MW)

University of Portland, OR (MW)

University of Puerto Rico, PR (MW)

University of Puerto Rico (Bayamon), PR (MW)

University of Puerto Rico (Ponce), PR (MW)

University of Puget Sound, WA (MW)

University of Redlands, CA (MW)

University of Rhode Island, RI (MW)

University of Richmond, VA (MW)

University of Rio Grande, OH (MW)

University of South Alabama, AL (MW)

University of South Carolina, SC (MW)

University of South Dakota, SD (MW)

University of Southern California, CA (MW)

University of Southern Mississippi, MS (MW)

University of South Florida, FL (MW)

University of St. Thomas, MN (MW)

University at Stony Brook (SUNY), NY (MW)

University of Tennessee, TN (MW)

University of Tennessee (Knoxville), TN (MW)

University of Tennessee (Martin), TN (MW)

University of Texas (Arlington), TX (MW)

University of Texas (Austin), TX (MW)

University of Texas (El Paso), TX (MW)

University of Texas (Pan American), TX (MW)

University of Texas (San Antonio), TX (MW)

University of Toledo, OH (MW)

University of Tulsa, OK (MW)

University of Utah, UT (MW)

University of Vermont, VT (MW)

University of Virginia, VA (MW)

University of Washington, WA (MW)

University of Wisconsin (Eau Claire), WI (MW)

University of Wisconsin (La Crosse), WI (MW)

University of Wisconsin (Madison), WI (MW)

University of Wisconsin (Milwaukee), WI (MW)

University of Wisconsin (Oshkosh), WI (MW)

University of Wisconsin (Platteville), WI (MW)

University of Wisconsin (River Falls), WI (MW)

University of Wisconsin (Stevens Point), WI (MW)

University of Wisconsin (Stout), WI (MW)

University of Wisconsin (Superior), WI (MW)

University of Wyoming, WY (MW)

Upper Iowa University, IA (MW)

Urbana University, OH (MW)

Ursinus College, PA (MW)

U.S. International University, CA (MW)

Utah State University, UT (M)

Valley City State University, ND (MW)

Valparaiso University, IN (MW)

Vanderbilt University, TN (W)

Ventura College, CA (MW)

Vincennes University, IN (MW)

Virginia Commonwealth University, VA (MW)

Virginia Military Institute, VA (M)

Virginia Polytechnic Institute & State University, VA (MW)

Virginia State University, VA (W)

Virginia Union University, VA (MW)

Wabash College, IN (M)

Wagner College, NY (MW)

Wallace State Community College, AL (MW)

Walsh College, OH (MW)

Wartburg College, IA (MW)

Washington and Jefferson College, PA (M)

Washington State University, WA (M)

Washington University, MO (MW)

Wayland Baptist University, TX (MW)

Wayne State College, NE (MW)

Weber State College, UT (MW)

Wesleyan University, CT (MW)

West Chester University, PA (MW)

West Liberty State College, WV (MW)

Western Carolina University, NC (MW)

Western Illinois University, IL (MW)

Western Kentucky University, KY (MW)

Western Maryland College, MD (MW)

Western Michigan University, MI (MW)

Western New Mexico University, NM (MW)

Western Oregon State College, OR (MW)

Western State College, CO (MW)

Westfield State College, MA (MW)

Westminster College, PA (M)

Westmont College, CA (MW)

West Virginia State College, WV (MW)

West Virginia University, WV (MW)

West Virginia Wesleyan College, WV (MW)

Wheaton College, IL (MW)

Whitman College, WA (MW)

Whittier College, CA (MW)

Whitworth College, WA (MW)

Wichita State University, KS (MW)

Wilberforce University, OH (M)

Willamette University, OR (MW)

William Jewell College, MO (MW)

William Patterson College, NJ (MW)

William Penn College, IA (MW)

William Rainey Harper College, IL (MW)

Williams College, MA (MW)

Wilmington College, OH (MW)

Winona State University, MN (W)

Winston-Salem State University, NC (MW)

Winthrop University, SC (MW)

Worcester State College, MA (MW)

Yale University, CT (MW)

York College (CUNY), NY (MW)

York College of Pennsylvania, PA (M)

Youngstown State University, OH (MW)

Yuba Community College, CA (MW)

Volleyball

Abilene Christian University, TX (W)
Adams State College, CO (W)
Adelphi University, NY (W)
Adirondack College, NY (W)
Adrian College, MI (W)
Agnes Scott College, GA (W)
Alabama A&M University, AL (W)
Alabama State University, AL (W)
Albany State University, GA (W)
Albertson College of Idaho, ID (W)
Albion College, MI (W)
Albright College, PA (W)
Alcorn State University, MS (W)
Alderson-Broaddus College, WV (W)
Alfred University, NY (W)
Allegheny College, PA (W)
Allen County College, KS (W)
Allentown College, PA (W)
Alma College, MI (W)
Alvernia College, PA (MW)
American International College, MA (W)
American University, DC (W)
Amherst College, MA (W)
Anderson College, SC (W)
Anderson University, IN (W)
Angelo State University, TX (W)
Anoka-Ramsey College, MN (W)
Appalachian State University, NC (W)
Apprentice School, VA (W)
Aquinas College, MI (W)
Arizona State University, AZ (W)
Arkansas College, AR (W)
Arkansas State University, AR (W)
Arkansas Tech University, AR (W)
Armstrong Atlantic State University, GA (W)
Asbury College, KY (W)
Ashland College, OH (W)
Assumption College, MA (W)
Atlantic Union College, MA (W)
Auburn University, AL (W)
Augusta State University, GA (W)
Augustana College, IL (W)
Augustana College, SD (W)
Aurora University, IL (W)
Austin College, TX (W)
Austin Community College, MN (W)
Austin Peay State University, TN (W)

Averett College, VA (W)
Avila College, MO (W)
Azusa Pacific University, CA (W)
Babson College, MA (W)
Baker University, KS (W)
Ball State University, IN (MW)
Baptist Bible College, MO (W)
Barber-Scotia College, NC (W)
Bard College, NY (MW)
Barry University, FL (W)
Barstow College, CA (W)
Barton College, NC (W)
Barton County College, KS (W)
Bates College, ME (W)
Bayamon Central University, PR (MW)
Baylor University, TX (W)
Becker College, MA (W)
Belhaven College, MS (W)
Bellarmine College, KY (W)
Belleville Area College, IL (W)
Bellevue College, NE (W)
Bellevue Community College, WA (W)
Belmont Abbey College, NC (W)
Belmont College, TN (W)
Beloit College, WI (W)
Bemidji State University, MN (W)
Benedict College, SC (W)
Benedictine College, KS (W)
Benedictine University, IL (W)
Bentley College, MA (W)
Bergen Community College, NJ (W)
Bethany College, KS (W)
Bethany College, WV (W)
Bethany Lutheran College, MN (W)
Bethel College, IN (W)
Bethel College, KS (W)
Bethel College, MN (W)
Bethune-Cookman College, FL (W)
Big Bend Community College, WA (W)
Binghamton University (SUNY), NY (W)
Biola University, CA (W)
Birmingham-Southern College, AL (W)
Bismarck State College, ND (W)
Blackburn College, IL (W)
Black Hawk College, IL (W)
Black Hills State University, SD (W)
Bloomfield College, NJ (W)
Blue Mountain College, OR (W)
Bluffton College, OH (W)
Boise State University, ID (W)
Boston College, MA (W)

Bowdoin College, ME (W)
Bowie State University, MD (W)
Bowling Green State University, OH (W)
Bradley University, IL (W)
Brainerd Community College, MN (W)
Brescia University, KY (W)
Brevard Community College, FL (W)
Briar Cliff College, IA (W)
Bridgewater State College, MA (W)
Brigham Young University, HI (W)
Brigham Young University, UT (MW)
Bronx Community College, NY (W)
Brooklyn College-City University of New York, NY (MW)
Broome Community College, NY (W)
Broward Community College, FL (MW)
Brown University, RI (W)
Bryant College, RI (W)
Bryn Mawr College, PA (W)
Bucknell University, PA (W)
Buena Vista University, IA (W)
Buffalo State College, NY (W)
Butler County Community College, KS (W)
Butler County Community College, PA (W)
Butler University, IN (W)
Butte College, CA (W)
Cabrillo College, CA (W)
Cabrini College, PA (W)
Caldwell College, NJ (W)
California Baptist University, CA (MW)
California Institute of Technology, CA (W)
California Lutheran University, CA (W)
California Maritime Academy, CA (M)
California Polytechnic State University, CA (W)
California State Polytechnic University, CA (W)
California State University at Bakersfield, CA (W)
California State University (Chico), CA (W)
California State University (Dominguez Hills), CA (W)
California State University (Fresno), CA (W)

California State University (Fullerton), CA (W)
California State University (Hayward), CA (W)
California State University (Long Beach), CA (MW)
California State University (Los Angeles), CA (W)
California State University (Northridge), CA (MW)
California State University (Sacramento), CA (W)
California State University (San Bernardino), CA (W)
California State University (Stanislaus), CA (W)
California University, PA (M)
Calvin College, MI (W)
Cameron University, OK (W)
Campbell University, NC (W)
Campbellsville University, KY (W)
Canisius College, NY (W)
Capital University, OH (W)
Cardinal Stritch University, WI (MW)
Carleton College, MN (MW)
Carlow College, PA (W)
Carnegie-Mellon University, PA (W)
Carroll College, MT (W)
Carroll College, WI (W)
Carson-Newman College, TN (W)
Carthage College, WI (W)
Case Western Reserve University, OH (W)
Catawba College, NC (W)
Catholic University of America, DC (W)
Catonsville Community College, MD (W)
Cayuga County Community College, NY (W)
Cecil Community College, MD (W)
Cedarville College, OH (W)
Centenary College, LA (W)
Centenary College, NJ (W)
Central Arizona College, AZ (W)
Central College, IA (W)
Central Christian College, KS (W)
Central Community College, NE (W)
Central Connecticut State University, CT (W)
Central Lakes College, MN (W)
Central Methodist College, MO (MW)

Central Michigan University, MI (W)
Central Missouri State University, MO (W)
Central Washington University, WA (W)
Central Wesleyan College, SC (W)
Central Wyoming College, WY (W)
Cerritos College, CA (W)
Chadron State College, NE (W)
Chaffey College, CA (W)
Chaminade University of Honolulu, HI (W)
Chapman University, CA (W)
Charles County Community College, MD (W)
Charleston Southern University, SC (W)
Chemeketa Community College, OR (W)
Cheyney University of Pennsylvania, PA (W)
Chicago State University, IL (W)
Chowan College, NC (W)
Christian Brothers College, TN (W)
Christopher Newport College, VA (W)
City College of New York, NY (MW)
City College of San Francisco, CA (W)
Clackamas Community College, OR (W)
Clarion University, PA (W)
Clark Atlanta University, GA (W)
Clark College, WA (W)
Clarkson University, NY (W)
Clark State College, OH (W)
Clark University, MA (W)
Clemson University, SC (W)
Cleveland State University, OH (W)
Clinton Community College, IA (W)
Cloud County Community College, KS (W)
Coastal Carolina College, SC (W)
Coe College, IA (W)
Coffeyville Community College, KS (W)
Coker College, SC (W)
Colby Community College, KS (W)
Colby-Sawyer College, NH (W)
Colgate University, NY (W)
College of Charleston, SC (W)

College of Mount St. Joseph, OH (W)
College of New Rochelle, NY (W)
College of Notre Dame, CA (W)
College of Notre Dame of Maryland, MD (W)
College of Saint Mary, NE (W)
College of Southern Idaho, ID (W)
College of St. Benedict, MN (W)
College of St. Francis, IL (W)
College of St. Mary, NE (W)
College of St. Rose, NY (W)
College of St. Scholastica, MN (W)
College of the Desert, CA (W)
College of the Holy Cross, MA (W)
College of the Ozarks, MO (W)
College of the Redwoods, CA (W)
College of the Sequoias, CA (W)
College of William and Mary, VA (W)
College of Wooster, OH (W)
Colorado Christian University, CO (W)
Colorado College, CO (W)
Colorado School of Mines, CO (W)
Colorado State University, CO (W)
Columbia Basin Community College, WA (W)
Columbia Christian College, OR (W)
Columbia College, MO (W)
Columbia College, SC (W)
Columbia Union College, MD (W)
Columbia University, NY (W)
Columbus State Community College, OH (W)
Community College of Allegheny County (South Campus), PA (W)
Community College of Philadelphia, PA (W)
Community College of Rhode Island, RI (W)
Concord College, WV (W)
Concordia College, MI (W)
Concordia College (Moorhead), MN (W)
Concordia University (St. Paul), MN (W)
Concordia College, NY (MW)
Concordia Lutheran College, TX (W)
Concordia University, NE (W)

Concordia University, IL (W)
Concordia University Wisconsin,
    WI (W)
Connecticut College, CT (W)
Converse College, SC (W)
Coppin State College, MD (W)
Cornell College, IA (W)
Cornell University, NY (W)
Consumnes River College, CA
    (W)
Covenant College, GA (W)
Cowley County Community Col-
    lege, KS (W)
Cuesta College, CA (W)
Culver-Stockton College, MO
    (W)
Cumberland College, KY (W)
Cuyahoga Community College
    (Metropolitan Campus), OH
    (W)
Dakota State University, SD (W)
Dakota Wesleyan University, SD
    (W)
Dallas Baptist University, TX
    (W)
Dana College, NE (W)
Davidson College, NC (W)
Dean Junior College, MA (W)
Defiance College, OH (W)
Delaware State University, DE
    (W)
Delaware Valley College, PA (W)
Delhi College of Technology
    (SUNY), NY (W)
Delta College, MI (W)
DePaul University, IL (W)
De Pauw University, IN (W)
Diablo Valley Community Col-
    lege, CA (W)
Dickinson College, PA (W)
Dickinson State University, ND
    (W)
Diné College, AZ (W)
Dixie College, UT (W)
Doane College, NE (W)
Dodge City Community College,
    KS (W)
Dominican College, CA (MW)
Dominican College, NY (W)
Dominican University, IL (MW)
Dowling College, NY (W)
Drake University, IA (W)
Drexel University, PA (W)
Drury College, MO (M)
Duke University, NC (W)
Duquesne University, PA (W)
Dutchess College, NY (W)
D'Youville College, NY (W)
Earlham College, IN (W)
East Carolina University, NC
    (W)

East Central College, MO (W)
Eastern College, PA (W)
Eastern Connecticut State Uni-
    versity, CT (W)
Eastern Illinois University, IL
    (W)
Eastern Kentucky University, KY
    (W)
Eastern Mennonite College, VA
    (W)
Eastern Michigan University, MI
    (W)
Eastern Montana College, MT
    (MW)
Eastern Nazarene College, MA
    (W)
Eastern New Mexico University,
    NM (W)
Eastern Oregon State College,
    OR (W)
Eastern Washington University,
    WA (W)
Eastern Wyoming College, WY
    (W)
Eastfield College, TX (W)
East Stroudsburg University, PA
    (MW)
East Texas Baptist University, TX
    (W)
Eckerd College, FL (W)
Edgewood College, WI (W)
Edinboro University of Pennsyl-
    vania, PA (M)
Edmonds Community College,
    WA (W)
El Camino College, CA (MW)
Elgin Community College, IL
    (W)
Elizabethtown College, PA (W)
Elmhurst College, IL (W)
Elmira College, NY (W)
Elon College, NC (W)
Emerson College, MA (W)
Emory and Henry College, VA
    (W)
Emory University, GA (W)
Emporia State University, KS
    (W)
Erskine College, SC (W)
Essex Community College, MD
    (W)
Eureka College, IL (W)
Evangel College, MO (W)
Everett Community College, WA
    (W)
Fairfield University, CT (W)
Fairleigh Dickinson University,
    NJ (W)
Fashion Institute of Technology,
    NY (W)
Faulkner University, AL (W)

Fayetteville State University, NC
    (W)
Fergus Falls Community Col-
    lege, MN (W)
Ferris State College, MI (W)
Ferrum College, VA (W)
Fisk University, TN (W)
Fitchburg State College, MA
    (W)
Flagler College, FL (W)
Florida A&M University, FL
    (W)
Florida Atlantic University, FL
    (W)
Florida College, FL (W)
Florida Institute of Technology,
    FL (W)
Florida International University,
    FL (W)
Florida Memorial College, FL
    (W)
Florida Southern College, FL
    (W)
Florida State University, FL (W)
Foothill College, CA (W)
Fordham University, NY (MW)
Fort Hays State University, KS
    (W)
Fort Lewis College, CO (W)
Fort Scott College, KS (W)
Fort Valley State College, GA
    (W)
Francis Marion University, SC
    (W)
Franklin & Marshall College, PA
    (W)
Frank Phillips College, TX (W)
Freed-Hardeman College, TN
    (W)
Fresno City College, CA (W)
Fresno Pacific University, CA
    (W)
Friends University, KS (W)
Fullerton College, CA (W)
Fulton-Montgomery Community
    College, NY (W)
Furman University, SC (W)
Gannon College, PA (W)
Garden City Community Col-
    lege, KS (W)
Gardner-Webb College, NC (W)
Garrett Community College,
    MD (W)
Genesee Community College,
    NY (MW)
Geneva College, PA (MW)
George Fox College, OR (W)
George Mason University, VA
    (MW)
Georgetown College, KY (W)
Georgetown University, DC (W)

George Washington University, DC (W)
Georgia Institute of Technology, GA (W)
Georgian Court College, NJ (W)
Georgia Southern University, GA (W)
Georgia Southwestern State University, GA (W)
Georgia State University, GA (W)
Glendale Community College, AZ (W)
Glendale Community College, CA (W)
Glenville State College, WV (W)
Glen Oaks Community College, MI (W)
Golden West College, CA (W)
Goldey-Beacom College, DE (W)
Gonzaga University, WA (W)
Gordon College, MA (W)
Goshen College, IN (W)
Goucher College, MD (W)
Grace College, IN (W)
Graceland College, IA (MW)
Grambling State University, LA (W)
Grand Canyon College, AZ (W)
Grand Rapids Baptist Seminary of Cornerstone University, MI (W)
Grand Rapids Community College, MI (W)
Grand Valley State College, MI (W)
Grand View College, IA (W)
Grays Harbor College, WA (W)
Greenfield Community College, MA (MW)
Green Mountain College, VT (W)
Green River Community, College, WA (W)
Greensboro College, NC (W)
Greenville College, IL (W)
Grinnell College, IA (W)
Grove City College, PA (W)
Gulf Coast Community College, FL (W)
Gustavus Adolphus College, MN (W)
Hagerstown Junior College, MD (W)
Hamilton College, NY (W)
Hamline University, MN (W)
Hampton University, VA (W)
Hannibal-Lagrange College, MO (W)
Hanover College, IN (W)

Harding University, AR (W)
Hardin-Simmons University, TX (W)
Harris-Stowe State College, MO (W)
Harvard University, MA (MW)
Hastings College, NE (W)
Haverford College, PA (W)
Hawaii Pacific University, HI (W)
Heidelberg College, OH (W)
Henderson State University, AR (W)
Henry Ford Community College, MI (W)
Herkimer County Community College, NY (W)
Hesser College, NH (W)
Hibbing Community College, MN (W)
Highland Community College, KS (W)
High Point University, NC (W)
Hilbert College, NY (W)
Hillsborough Community College, FL (W)
Hillsdale College, MI (W)
Hiram College, OH (W)
Hofstra University, NY (W)
Hood College, MD (W)
Hope College, MI (W)
Houghton College, NY (W)
Houston Baptist University, TX (W)
Howard Payne University, TX (W)
Howard University, DC (W)
Hudson Valley Community College, NY (W)
Humboldt State University, CA (W)
Hunter College of the City University of New York, NY (MW)
Huntingdon College, AL (W)
Huntington College, IN (W)
Huron University, SD (W)
Husson College, ME (W)
Huston-Tillotson College, TX (W)
Hutchinson College, KS (W)
Idaho State University, ID (W)
Illinois Benedictine College, IL (W)
Illinois Central College, IL (W)
Illinois College, IL (W)
Illinois Institute of Technology, IL (W)
Illinois State University, IL (W)
Illinois Valley Community College, IL (W)
Illinois Wesleyan University, IL (W)

Indian Hills Community College, IA (W)
Indiana State University, IN (W)
Indiana University, IN (W)
Indiana University of Pennsylvania, PA (W)
Indiana University-Purdue University, IN (W)
Indiana University-Purdue University (Fort Wayne), IN (MW)
Indiana Wesleyan University, IN (W)
Indian River Community College, FL (W)
Inver Hills Community College, MN (W)
Iona College, NY (W)
Iowa State University of Science and Technology, IA (W)
Iowa Wesleyan College, IA (W)
Ithaca College, NY (W)
Jackson State University, MS (W)
Jacksonville College, TX (W)
Jacksonville State University, AL (W)
Jacksonville University, FL (W)
James Madison University, VA (W)
Jamestown College, ND (W)
Jefferson College, MO (W)
Jefferson Community College, NY (W)
Jefferson Davis Junior College, AL (W)
John Brown University, AR (W)
John Carroll University, OH (W)
Johns Hopkins University, MD (W)
Johnson County Community College, KS (W)
Judson College, AL (W)
Juniata College, PA (MW)
Kalamazoo College, MI (W)
Kalamazoo Valley Community College, MI (W)
Kankakee Community College, IL (W)
Kansas City Kansas Community College, KS (W)
Kansas Newman University, KS (W)
Kansas State University, KS (W)
Kansas Wesleyan College, KS (W)
Kaskaskia Community College, IL (W)
Kean University, NJ (W)
Keene State College, NH (W)
Kent State University (Ashtabula), OH (W)

Kent State University (East Liverpool), OH (W)
Kent State University (Kent), OH (W)
Kent State University (New Philadelphia), OH (W)
Kent State University (Warren), OH (W)
Kentucky Christian College, KY (W)
Kentucky State University, KY (W)
Kentucky Wesleyan College, KY (W)
Kenyon College, OH (W)
King College, TN (W)
King's College, PA (W)
Kirkwood Community College, IA (W)
Kishwaukee College, IL (W)
Knox College, IL (W)
Kutztown University, PA (W)
Labette Community College, KS (W)
Lackawanna Junior College, PA (W)
Lafayette College, PA (W)
Lake Erie College, OH (W)
Lake Forest College, IL (W)
Lake Land College, IL (W)
Lake Michigan College, MI (W)
Lake Region State College, ND (W)
Lake-Sumter Community College, FL (W)
Lake Superior State University, MI (W)
Lamar Community College, CO (W)
Lamar University, TX (W)
Lambuth University, TN (W)
Lansing Community College, MI (W)
La Roche College, PA (W)
La Salle University, PA (W)
Lawrence University, WI (W)
Lebanon Valley College, PA (W)
Lee College, TN (W)
Lee College, TX (W)
Lees-McRae College, NC (W)
Lehigh County Community College, PA (W)
Lehigh University, PA (W)
Le Moyne College, NY (W)
Lenoir-Rhyne College, NC (W)
Letourneau College, TX (W)
Lewis and Clark College, OR (W)
Lewis and Clark Community College, IL (W)
Lewis Clark State College, ID (W)

Lewis University, IL (MW)
Liberty University, VA (W)
Limestone College, SC (W)
Lincoln Christian College, IL (W)
Lincoln College, IL (W)
Lincoln Land Community College, IL (W)
Lincoln Memorial University, TN (W)
Lincoln Trail College, IL (W)
Lincoln University, MO (W)
Linfield College, OR (W)
Long Beach City College, CA (MW)
Long Island University (C.W. Post Campus), NY (W)
Long Island University (Southampton Campus), NY (MW)
Loras College, CA (W)
Los Angeles Pierce Junior College, CA (M)
Louisburg College, NC (W)
Louisiana State University (Baton Rouge), LA (W)
Louisiana Tech University, LA (W)
Lower Columbia College, WA (W)
Loyola College, MD (W)
Loyola Marymount University, CA (MW)
Loyola University, IL (WM)
Lubbock Christian College, TX (W)
Luther College, IA (W)
Lycoming College, PA (W)
Lynchburg College, VA (W)
Macalester College, MN (W)
Macomb Community College, MI (W)
Madison Area Technical College, WI (W)
Madonna University, MI (W)
Malone College, OH (W)
Manchester College, IN (W)
Manhattan College, NY (W)
Manhattanville College, NY (W)
Mankato State University, MN (W)
Marian College, IN (W)
Marian College, WI (W)
Marietta College, OH (W)
Marist College, NY (W)
Marquette University, WI (W)
Marshall University, WV (W)
Mars Hill College, NC (W)
Mary Baldwin College, VA (W)
Marycrest College, IA (W)
Marycrest International University, IA (M)

Marymount University, VA (W)
Maryville College, TN (W)
Maryville University, MO (W)
Mary Washington College, VA (W)
Marywood College, PA (W)
Massachusetts College of Liberal Arts, MA (W)
Massachusetts Institute of Technology, MA (MW)
Master's College, CA (W)
Mayville State College, ND (W)
McCook Community College, NE (W)
McHenry County College, IL (W)
McKendree College, IL (W)
McNeese State University, LA (W)
McPherson College, KS (W)
Mercer University, GA (W)
Mercy College, NY (W)
Mercyhurst College, PA (W)
Merrimack College, MA (W)
Mesa Community College, AZ (W)
Mesa State College, CO (W)
Messiah College, PA (W)
Metropolitan State College, CO (W)
Miami-Dade Community College (North Campus), FL (W)
Miami-Dade Community College (South Campus), FL (W)
Miami University, OH (W)
Michigan State University, MI (W)
Michigan Technological University, MI (W)
Mid-America Nazarene College, KS (W)
Middle Tennessee State University, TN (W)
Midland Lutheran College, NE (W)
Mid-Plains Community College, NE (W)
Midwestern State University, TX (W)
Miles College, AL (W)
Millersville University, PA (W)
Milligan College, TN (W)
Millikin University, IL (W)
Mineral Area College, MO (W)
Minneapolis Community & Technical College, MN (W)
Minot State, ND (W)
Mississippi College, MS (W)
Mississippi State University, MS (W)

Mississippi University For Women, MS (MW)
Mississippi Valley State University, MS (W)
Missouri Baptist College, MO (W)
Missouri Southern State College, MO (W)
Missouri Valley College, MO (W)
Missouri Western State College, MO (W)
Mitchell College, CT (W)
Modesto Junior College, CA (W)
Mohawk Valley Community College, NY (W)
Molloy College, NY (W)
Monmouth College, IL (W)
Montana College of Mineral Science and Technology, MT (W)
Montana State University, MT (W)
Montgomery College, MD (W)
Montreat-Anderson College, NC (W)
Moody Bible Institute, IL (MW)
Moorhead State University, MN (W)
Moorpark College, CA (MW)
Moraine Valley Community College, IL (MW)
Moravian College, PA (W)
Morehead State University, KY (W)
Morgan State University, MD (W)
Morningside College, IA (W)
Morris Brown College, GA (W)
Morton College, IL (W)
Mott Community College, MI (W)
Mount Holyoke College, MA (W)
Mount Marty College, SD (W)
Mount Mercy College, IA (W)
Mount Olive College, NC (W)
Mount Union College, OH (W)
Mount Vernon Nazarene College, OH (W)
Mt. San Antonio College, CA (MW)
Muhlenberg College, PA (W)
Multnomah School of the Bible, OR (W)
Murray State University, KY (W)
Muskegon Community College, MI (W)
Muskingum College, OH (W)
Nassau Community College, NY (W)
National-Louis University, IL (W)

Navarro College, TX (W)
Nazareth College, NY (W)
Nebraska Wesleyan University, NE (W)
Newberry College, SC (W)
New Hampshire College, NH (W)
New Jersey Institute of Technology, NJ (M)
New Mexico Highlands University, NM (W)
New Mexico State University, NM (W)
New York Institute of Technology, NY (M)
New York University, NY (MW)
Niagara County Community College, NY (W)
Niagara University, NY (W)
Nicholls State University, LA (W)
North Carolina A & T State University, NC (W)
North Carolina Central University, NC (W)
North Carolina State University, NC (W)
North Carolina Wesleyan College, NC (W)
North Central College, IL (W)
North Central Texas College, TX (W)
North Dakota State, ND (W)
North Dakota State University, ND (W)
Northeastern Illinois University, IL (W)
Northeastern Junior College, CO (W)
Northeast Louisiana University, LA (W)
Northeast Missouri State University, MO (W)
Northern Arizona University, AZ (W)
Northern Illinois University, IL (W)
Northern Kentucky University, KY (W)
Northern Michigan University, MI (W)
Northern Montana College, MT (W)
Northern State University, SD (W)
North Greenville College, SC (W)
North Hennepin Community College, MN (W)
North Idaho College, ID (W)

North Iowa Area Community College, IA (MW)
Northland College, WI (W)
Northland Community & Technical College, MN (W)
Northwest College, WY (W)
Northwestern College, IA (W)
Northwestern College, MN (W)
Northwestern State University of Louisiana, LA (W)
Northwestern University, IL (W)
Northwest Missouri State University, MO (W)
Northwest Nazarene University, ID (W)
Northwood Institute, MI (W)
Northwood Institute (Texas Campus), TX (W)
Notre Dame College of Ohio, OH (W)
Nova Southern University, FL (W)
Nyack College, NY (W)
Oakland City University, IN (W)
Oakland Community College, MI (W)
Oakland University, MI (W)
Oakton Community College, IL (W)
Oberlin College, OH (W)
Occidental College, CA (W)
Oglethorpe University, GA (W)
Ohio Dominican College, OH (W)
Ohio Northern University, OH (W)
Ohio State University, OH (MW)
Ohio University, OH (W)
Ohio Valley College, WV (W)
Ohio Wesleyan University, OH (W)
Olivet College, MI (W)
Olivet Nazarene University, IL (W)
Olney Central College, IL (W)
Olympic College, WA (W)
Oral Roberts University, OK (W)
Orange Coast College, CA (MW)
Orange County Community College, NY (W)
Oregon Institute of Technology, OR (W)
Oregon State University, OR (W)
Oswego State University (SUNY), NY (W)
Otero Junior College, CO (W)
Ottawa University, KS (W)
Otterbein College, OH (W)
Ouachita Baptist University, AR (W)

Pace University, NY (MW)
Pace University (White Plains Campus), NY (W)
Pacific Lutheran University, WA (W)
Pacific University, OR (W)
Palm Beach Atlantic College, FL (W)
Palomar College, CA (W)
Panola College, TX (W)
Park College, MO (MW)
Parkland College, IL (W)
Pennsylvania State University, PA (MW)
Penn State Abington College, PA (MW)
Penn State Behrend College, PA (MW)
Penn State Berks-Lehigh Valley College, PA (W)
Penn Valley Community College, MO (W)
Pensacola Junior College, FL (W)
Pepperdine University, CA (MW)
Peru State College, NE (W)
Pfeiffer College, NC (W)
Philadelphia University, PA (W)
Phoenix College, AZ (W)
Piedmont College, GA (W)
Pierce College, WA (W)
Pikeville College, KY (W)
Pima Community College (West Campus), AZ (W)
Pittsburg State University, KS (W)
Plattsburgh State University (SUNY), NY (W)
Plymouth State College, NH (W)
Polk Community College, FL (W)
Polytechnic University (Brooklyn Campus), NY (W)
Pomona-Pitzer Colleges, CA (W)
Pontifical Catholic University of Puerto Rico, PR (MW)
Portland State University, OR (W)
Prairie View A&M University, TX (W)
Pratt Community College, KS (W)
Presbyterian College, SC (W)
Prince George's Community College, MD (W)
Princeton University, NJ (W)
Principia College, IL (W)
Providence College, RI (W)
Purchase College (SUNY), NY (W)
Purdue University, IN (W)

Purdue University (Calumet), IN (W)
Queens College, NY (MW)
Queens College, NC (W)
Queensborough Community College, NY (W)
Quincy University, IL (MW)
Quinnipiac University, CT (W)
Radford University, VA (W)
Rainy River Community College, MN (W)
Ramapo College, NJ (MW)
Randolph-Macon College, VA (W)
Ranetto Santiago College, CA (W)
Regis College, MA (W)
Regis University, CO (W)
Rend Lake College, IL (W)
Rhode Island College, RI (W)
Rice University, TX (W)
Ricks College, ID (W)
Rider College, NJ (W)
Ripon College, WI (W)
Riverland Community College, MN (W)
Roanoke College, VA (W)
Robert Morris College, PA (W)
Roberts Wesleyan College, NY (W)
Rochester College, MI (W)
Rochester Community College, MN (W)
Rochester Institute of Technology, NY (W)
Rockhurst College, MO (W)
Rockland Community College, NY (W)
Rocky Mountain College, MT (W)
Rollins College, FL (W)
Roosevelt University, IL (W)
Rose-Hulman Institute of Technology, IN (W)
Rutgers, Newark College of Arts and Sciences, NJ (M)
Sacred Heart University, CT (MW)
Saddleback College, CA (W)
Sage Junior College of Albany, NY (W)
Saginaw Valley State University, MI (W)
Saint Ambrose University, IA (MW)
Saint Andrews Presbyterian College, NC (W)
Saint Augustine's College, NC (W)
Saint Bonaventure University, NY (W)

Saint Cloud State University, MN (W)
Saint Edward's University, TX (W)
Saint Francis College, IN (W)
Saint Francis College, NY (W)
Saint Francis College, PA (MW)
Saint John Fisher College, NY (W)
Saint Joseph's College, IN (W)
Saint Lawrence University, NY (W)
Saint Leo University, FL (W)
Saint Louis University, MO (W)
Saint Martin's College, WA (W)
Saint Mary College, KS (W)
Saint Mary's College, IN (W)
Saint Mary's College, MI (W)
Saint Mary's College of California, CA (W)
Saint Mary's University, TX (W)
Saint Michael's College, VT (W)
Saint Norbert College, WI (W)
Saint Olaf College, MN (W)
Saint Paul's College, VA (W)
Saint Peter's College, NJ (W)
Saint Thomas Aquinas College, NY (W)
Saint Thomas University, FL (W)
Saint Vincent College, PA (W)
Saint Xavier University, IL (W)
Salem State College, MA (W)
Salem-Teikyo University, WV (W)
Samford University, AL (W)
Sam Houston State University, TX (W)
San Bernardino Community College, CA (W)
San Diego City College, CA (W)
San Diego Mesa College, CA (MW)
San Diego State University, CA (MW)
San Francisco State University, CA (W)
San Joaquin Delta College, CA (W)
San Jose State University, CA (W)
Santa Barbara City College, CA (MW)
San Clara University, CA (W)
Santa Monica College, CA (MW)
Santa Rosa Junior College, CA (W)
Sauk Valley College, IL (W)
Savannah State College, GA (W)
Schoolcraft College, MI (W)

Schreiner College, TX (W)
Scottsdale Community College, AZ (W)
Seattle Pacific University, WA (W)
Seminole Community College, FL (W)
Seton Hall University, NJ (W)
Seton Hill College, PA (W)
Seward County Community College, KS (W)
Shawnee State University, OH (W)
Shepherd College, WV (W)
Sheridan College, WY (W)
Shippensburg University of Pennsylvania, PA (W)
Shoreline Community College, WA (W)
Siena College, NY (W)
Siena Heights College, MI (W)
Sierra College, CA (W)
Simpson College, CA (W)
Sinclair Community College, OH (W)
Sioux Falls College, SD (W)
Skagit Valley College, WA (W)
Skidmore College, NY (W)
Skyline College, CA (W)
Slippery Rock University of Pennsylvania, PA (W)
Smith College, MA (W)
Snow College, UT (W)
Solano Community College, CA (W)
South Carolina State College, SC (W)
South Dakota School of Mines and Technology, SD (W)
South Dakota State University, SD (W)
Southeast Community College, NE (W)
Southeastern Community College, IA (W)
Southeastern Illinois College, IL (W)
Southeastern Louisiana University, LA (W)
Southeast Missouri State University, MO (W)
Southern Arkansas University, AR (W)
Southern California College, CA (W)
Southern Connecticut State University, CT (W)
Southern Illinois University, IL (W)
Southern Nazarene University, OK (W)

Southern Oregon State College, OR (W)
Southern University and A&M College, LA (W)
Southern Union State Community College, AL (MW)
Southern Utah University, UT (W)
Southern Wesleyan University, SC (W)
South Florida Community College, FL (W)
Southwest Baptist University, MO (W)
Southwestern College, CA (W)
Southwestern College, KS (W)
Southwestern Oregon Community College, OR (W)
Southwestern University, TX (W)
Southwest Missouri State University, MO (W)
Southwest State University, MN (W)
Southwest Texas State University, TX (W)
Spartanburg Methodist, SC (W)
Spokane Community College, WA (W)
Spoon River College, IL (W)
Spring Arbor College, MI (W)
Springfield College, MA (MW)
Stanford University, CA (MW)
State University of New York College (Brockport), NY (W)
State University of New York College (Cortland), NY (W)
State University of New York College (Fredonia), NY (W)
State University of New York College (Geneseo), NY (W)
State University of New York College (New Paltz), NY (MW)
State University of New York College (Potsdam), NY (W)
State University of New York Institute of Technology at Utica/Rome, NY (W)
State University of New York Maritime College, NY (MW)
State University of West Georgia, GA (W)
Stephen F. Austin State University, TX (W)
Sterling College, KS (W)
Stetson University, FL (W)
Stevens Institute of Technology, NJ (MW)
St. Louis Community College (Florissant Valley), MO (W)

St. Louis Community College (Forest Park), MO (W)
St. Mary of the Plains College, KS (W)
St. Petersburg Junior College, FL (W)
Stonehill College, MA (W)
St. Philip's College, TX (W)
Suffolk County Community College, NY (W)
Suffolk University, MA (W)
Sul Ross State University, TX (W)
Swarthmore College, PA (W)
Sweet Briar College, VA (W)
Syracuse University, NY (W)
Tabor College, KS (W)
Taft College, CA (W)
Talledaga College, AL (W)
Tarleton State University, TX (W)
Teikyo Westmar University, IA (W)
Temple Baptist Seminary, TN (W)
Temple University, PA (W)
Tennessee Technological University, TN (W)
Texas A&I University, TX (W)
Texas A&M Commerce, TX (W)
Texas A&M University, TX (W)
Texas Christian University, TX (W)
Texas Lutheran College, TX (W)
Texas Southern University, TX (M)
Texas Tech University, TX (W)
Texas Wesleyan College, TX (W)
Texas Woman's University, TX (W)
Thomas More College, KY (W)
Three Rivers Community College, MO (W)
Tiffin University, OH (W)
Toccoa Falls College, GA (W)
Towson State University, MD (W)
Trevecca Nazarene College, TN (W)
Trinidad State Junior College, CO (W)
Trinity Christian College, IL (W)
Trinity College, CT (W)
Trinity College, IL (W)
Trinity University, TX (W)
Tri-State University, IN (MW)
Triton College, IL (W)
Troy State University, AL (W)
Tufts University, MA (W)
Tulane University, LA (W)
Tusculum College, TN (W)

Tuskegee University, AL (W)
Tyler Junior College, TX (W)
Umpqua College, OR (W)
Union College, KY (W)
Union College, NY (W)
Union University, TN (W)
Unity College, ME (W)
University of Akron, OH (W)
University of Alabama (Birming-
ham), AL (MW)
University of Alabama
(Huntsville), AL (W)
University of Alabama
(Tuscaloosa), AL (W)
University of Alaska, AK (W)
University of Alaska (Fairbanks),
AK (W)
University at Albany (SUNY),
NY (W)
University of Arizona, AZ (W)
University of Arkansas (Fayet-
teville), AR (W)
University of Arkansas (Little
Rock), AR (W)
University of Arkansas (Pine
Bluff), AR (W)
University of Bridgeport, CT
(MW)
University at Buffalo (SUNY),
NY (W)
University of California (Berke-
ley), CA (W)
University of California (Davis),
CA (W)
University of California (Irvine),
CA (MW)
University of California (River-
side), CA (MW)
University of California (San
Diego), CA (MW)
University of California (Santa
Barbara), CA (M)
University of California (Santa
Cruz), CA (MW)
University of California (UCLA),
CA (MW)
University of Central Arkansas,
AR (W)
University of Central Florida, FL
(W)
University of Central Oklahoma,
OK (W)
University of Charleston, WV
(W)
University of Chicago, IL (W)
University of Cincinnati, OH
(W)
University of Colorado (Col-
orado Springs), CO (W)
University of Connecticut, CT
(W)

University of Dallas, TX (W)
University of Dayton, OH (W)
University of Delaware, DE (W)
University of Denver, CO (W)
University of Dubuque, IA (W)
University of Evansville, IN (W)
University of Findlay, OH (W)
University of Florida, FL (W)
University of Georgia, GA (W)
University of Guam, PA (MW)
University of Hartford, CT (W)
University of Hawaii (Hilo), HI
(W)
University of Hawaii (Manoa),
HI (MW)
University of Houston, TX (W)
University of Idaho, ID (W)
University of Illinois (Chicago),
IL (W)
University of Illinois (Urbana-
Champaign), IL (W)
University of Incarnate Word, TX
(W)
University of Indianapolis, IN
(W)
University of Iowa, IA (W)
University of Kansas, KS (W)
University of Kentucky, KY (W)
University of La Verne, CA
(MW)
University of Louisiana at
Lafayette, LA (W)
University of Louisville, KY (W)
University of Maine, ME (W)
University of Maine (Fort Kent),
ME (W)
University of Maine (Machias),
ME (W)
University of Mary, ND (W)
University of Mary Hardin-Bay-
lor, TX (W)
University of Maryland, MD (W)
University of Maryland (Balti-
more County), MD (W)
University of Maryland (Eastern
Shore), MD (W)
University of Massachusetts
(Amherst), MA (W)
University of Massachusetts
(Boston), MA (W)
University of Massachusetts
(Dartmouth), MA (MW)
University of Massachusetts
(Lowell), MA (W)
University of Memphis, TN (W)
University of Minnesota
(Duluth), MN (W)
University of Minnesota (Min-
neapolis), MN (W)
University of Minnesota (Mor-
ris), MN (W)

University of Mississippi, MS
(W)
University of Missouri, MO (W)
University of Missouri (Colum-
bia), MO (W)
University of Montana, MT (W)
University of Montevallo, AL
(W)
University of Nebraska, NE (W)
University of Nebraska (Kear-
ney), NE (W)
University of Nebraska (Lin-
coln), NE (W)
University of Nevada (Reno),
NV (W)
University of New England, ME
(W)
University of New Haven, CT
(W)
University of New Mexico, NM
(W)
University of New Orleans, LA
(W)
University of North Alabama, AL
(W)
University of North Carolina
(Asheville), NC (W)
University of North Carolina
(Chapel Hill), NC (W)
University of North Carolina
(Charlotte), NC (W)
University of North Carolina
(Greensboro), NC (W)
University of North Carolina
(Pembroke), NC (W)
University of North Carolina
(Wilmington), NC (W)
University of North Dakota, ND
(W)
University of North Florida, FL
(W)
University of Northern Col-
orado, CO (W)
University of Northern Iowa, IA
(W)
University of North Texas, TX
(W)
University of Notre Dame, IN
(W)
University of Oklahoma, OK (W)
University of Oregon, OR (W)
University of Pennsylvania, PA
(W)
University of Pittsburgh, PA (W)
University of Pittsburgh (Brad-
ford), PA (W)
University of Pittsburgh (John-
stown), PA (W)
University of Portland, OR (W)
University of Puerto Rico, PR
(MW)

University of Puerto Rico (Bayamon), PR (MW)
University of Puerto Rico (Ponce), PR (MW)
University of Puget Sound, WA (W)
University of Redlands, CA (W)
University of Rhode Island, RI (MW)
University of Rio Grande, OH (W)
University of San Diego, CA (W)
University of San Francisco, CA (W)
University of Scranton, PA (W)
University of South Alabama, AL (W)
University of South Carolina, SC (W)
University of South Carolina (Aiken), SC (W)
University of South Carolina (Spartanburg), SC (W)
University of South Dakota, SD (W)
University of Southern California, CA (MW)
University of Southern Colorado, CO (W)
University of Southern Indiana, IN (W)
University of Southern Mississippi, MS (W)
University of South Florida, FL (W)
University of St. Thomas, MN (W)
University at Stony Brook (SUNY), NY (W)
University of Tampa, FL (W)
University of Tennessee, TN (W)
University of Tennessee (Knoxville), TN (W)
University of Tennessee (Martin), TN (W)
University of Texas (Arlington), TX (W)
University of Texas (Austin), TX (W)
The University of Texas at Brownsville and Texas Southmost College, TX (W)
University of Texas (El Paso), TX (W)
University of Texas (Pan American), TX (W)
University of Texas (San Antonio), TX (MW)
University of the District of Columbia, DC (W)

University of the Pacific, CA (MW)
University of Toledo, OH (W)
University of Tulsa, OK (W)
University of Utah, UT (W)
University of Vermont, VT (W)
University of Virginia, VA (W)
University of Washington, WA (W)
University of West Alabama, AL (W)
University of Wisconsin (Eau Claire), WI (W)
University of Wisconsin (Green Bay), WI (W)
University of Wisconsin (La Crosse), WI (W)
University of Wisconsin (Madison), WI (W)
University of Wisconsin (Milwaukee), WI (W)
University of Wisconsin (Oshkosh), WI (W)
University of Wisconsin (Platteville), WI (W)
University of Wisconsin (River Falls), WI (W)
University of Wisconsin (Stevens Point), WI (W)
University of Wisconsin (Stout), WI (W)
University of Wisconsin (Superior), WI (W)
University of Wyoming, WY (W)
Upper Iowa University, IA (W)
Ursinus College, PA (W)
U.S. International University, CA (W)
Utah State University, UT (W)
Valdosta State University, GA (W)
Valley City State University, ND (W)
Valley Forge Christian College, PA (W)
Valparaiso University, IN (W)
Vassar College, NY (MW)
Ventura College, CA (W)
Villanova University, PA (W)
Vincennes University, IN (W)
Virginia Commonwealth University, VA (W)
Virginia Polytechnic Institute & State University, VA (W)
Virginia State University, VA (W)
Virginia Union University, VA (W)
Viterbo College, WI (W)
Wabash Valley College, IL (W)
Wagner College, NY (W)
Waldorf College, IA (W)

Walla Walla Community College, WA (W)
Walsh College, OH (W)
Warner Pacific College, OR (W)
Warner Southern College, FL (W)
Wartburg College, IA (W)
Washburn University, KS (W)
Washington and Jefferson College, PA (W)
Washington College, MD (W)
Washington State University, WA (W)
Washington University, MO (W)
Waubonsee College, IL (W)
Wayne State College, NE (W)
Wayne State University, MI (W)
Webber College, FL (W)
Weber State College, UT (W)
Webster University, MO (W)
Wellesley College, MA (W)
Wesleyan University, CT (W)
West Chester University, PA (W)
Westark Community College, AR (W)
Western Carolina University, NC (W)
Western Connecticut State University, CT (W)
Western Illinois University, IL (W)
Western Kentucky University, KY (W)
Western Maryland College, MD (W)
Western Michigan University, MI (W)
Western Montana College, MT (W)
Western Nebraska Community College, NE (W)
Western New England College, MA (MW)
Western New Mexico University, NM (W)
Western Oregon State College, OR (W)
Western State College, CO (W)
Western Washington University, WA (MW)
Western Wyoming Community College, WY (W)
Westfield State College, MA (W)
West Liberty State College, WV (W)
Westminster College, PA (W)
Westmont College, CA (W)
West Texas State University, TX (W)
West Virginia Institute of Technology, WV (W)

West Virginia University, WV (W)
West Virginia Wesleyan College, WV (W)
Wharton County Junior College, TX (W)
Wheaton College, IL (W)
Wheeling Jesuit College, WV (W)
Whitman College, WA (W)
Whittier College, CA (W)
Whitworth College, WA (W)
Wichita State University, KS (W)
Wilberforce University, OH (M)
Wilkes College, NC (W)
Willamette University, OR (W)
William Jewell College, MO (W)
William Patterson College, NJ (W)
William Penn College, IA (W)
William Rainey Harper College, IL (W)
Williams College, MA (MW)
William Woods College, MO (W)
Wilmington College, DE (W)
Wilmington College, OH (W)
Wilson College, PA (W)
Wingate College, NC (W)
Winona State University, MN (W)
Winston-Salem State University, NC (W)
Winthrop University, SC (W)
Wofford College, SC (W)
Worcester State College, MA (W)
Worthington Community College, MN (W)
Wright State University, OH (W)
Xavier University, OH (W)
Yakima Valley College, WA (W)
Yale University, CT (W)
Yavapai College, AZ (W)
Yeshiva University, NY (M)
York College (CUNY), NY (MW)
York College of Pennsylvania, PA (W)
Youngstown State University, OH (W)
Yuba Community College, CA (W)

Water Polo

Austin College, TX (M)
Boston College, MA (M)
Brown University, RI (MW)
Bucknell University, PA (MW)
Cabrillo College, CA (MW)
California Baptist University, CA (MW)
California Institute of Technology, CA (MW)

California Maritime Academy, CA (M)
California State University at Bakersfield, CA (M)
California State University (Long Beach), CA (MW)
California State University (San Bernardino), CA (W)
Cerritos College, CA (MW)
Chaffey College, CA (M)
Chaminade University of Honolulu, HI (M)
Chapman University, CA (MW)
Cleveland State University, OH (M)
College of the Sequoias, CA (M)
Cosumnes River College, CA (W)
Cuesta College, CA (MW)
Diablo Valley Community College, CA (MW)
El Camino College, CA (M)
Foothill College, CA (MW)
Fordham University, NY (M)
Fullerton College, CA (M)
George Washington University, DC (M)
Golden West College, CA (MW)
Grove City College, PA (MW)
Hartwick College, NY (W)
Harvard University, MA (MW)
Hope College, MI (M)
Indiana University, IN (W)
Johns Hopkins University, MD (M)
Long Beach City College, CA (MW)
Los Angeles Pierce Junior College, CA (M)
Los Angeles Valley College, CA (MW)
Loyola Marymount University, CA (MW)
Lynchburg College, VA (M)
Marist College, NY (W)
Massachusetts Institute of Technology, MA (M)
Modesto Junior College, CA (MW)
Montclair State College, NJ (M)
Mt. San Antonio College, CA (MW)
Occidental College, CA (M)
Orange Coast College, CA (MW)
Paine College, GA (W)
Palomar College, CA (M)
Pepperdine University, CA (M)
Pomona-Pitzer Colleges, CA (MW)
Queens College, NY (M)

Ranetto Santiago College, CA (M)
Riverside Community College, CA (MW)
Saddleback College, CA (MW)
Saint Francis College, NY (MW)
Salem-Teikyo University, WV (MW)
San Diego Mesa College, CA (MW)
San Diego State University, CA (W)
San Joaquin Delta College, CA (M)
Santa Clara University, CA (M)
Santa Monica College, CA (M)
Santa Rosa Junior College, CA (MW)
Sierra College, CA (M)
Slippery Rock University of Pennsylvania, PA (MW)
Solano Community College, CA (M)
Southern Oregon State College, OR (MW)
Stanford University, CA (M)
Trinity College, CT (MW)
University of California (Berkeley), CA (MW)
University of California (Davis), CA (MW)
University of California (Irvine), CA (M)
University of California (Riverside), CA (MW)
University of California (San Diego), CA (MW)
University of California (Santa Barbara), CA (M)
University of California (Santa Cruz), CA (MW)
University of California (UCLA), CA (MW)
University of Dayton, OH (M)
University of Hawaii (Manoa), HI (W)
University of Massachusetts (Amherst), MA (MW)
University of Puerto Rico, PR (M)
University of Redlands, CA (M)
University of Rhode Island, RI (M)
University of Richmond, VA (M)
University of Southern California, CA (MW)
University of the Pacific, CA (MW)
Ventura College, CA (M)
Villanova University, PA (W)

Washington and Jefferson College, PA (MW)
Whittier College, CA (MW)

Water Skiing

Mississippi State University, MS (MW)
Rollins College, FL (MW)

Weightlifting

Bayamon Central University, PR (MW)
Broward Community College, FL (MW)
Community College of Rhode Island, RI (MN)
Johnson County Community College, KS (M)
Lafayette College, PA (M)
Mississippi State University, MS (MW)
North Iowa Area Community College, IA (M)
Pontifical Catholic University of Puerto Rico, PR (M)
Roosevelt University, IL (M)
Rose State Junior College, OK (MW)
Snow College, UT (MW)
University of Puerto Rico (Bayamon), PR (MW)
University of Puerto Rico (Cayey), PR (M)
University of Puerto Rico (Ponce), PR (MW)
Willamette University, OR (M)

Wrestling

Adams State College, CO (M)
Albright College, PA (M)
American University, DC (M)
Anderson College, SC (M)
Anoka-Ramsey College, MN (M)
Appalachian State University, NC (M)
Apprentice School, VA (M)
Arizona State University, AZ (M)
Ashland College, OH (M)
Augsburg College, MN (M)
Augustana College, IL (M)
Augustana College, SD (M)
Bergen Community College, NJ (M)
Binghamton University (SUNY), NY (M)
Bloomsburg University, PA (M)
Boise State University, ID (M)
Boston College, MA (M)

Boston University, MA (M)
Briar Cliff College, IA (M)
Bridgewater State College, MA (M)
Brown University, RI (M)
Bucknell University, PA (M)
Buena Vista University, IA (M)
California Polytechnic State University, CA (M)
California State University at Bakersfield, CA (M)
California State University (Chico), CA (M)
California State University (Fresno), CA (M)
California State University (Fullerton), CA (M)
Campbell University, NC (M)
Capital University, OH (M)
Carleton College, MN (M)
Carroll College, WI (M)
Carson-Newman College, TN (M)
Case Western Reserve University, OH (M)
Centenary College, NJ (M)
Central College, IA (M)
Central Connecticut State University, CT (M)
Central Michigan University, MI (M)
Central Missouri State University, MO (M)
Central Washington University, WA (M)
Cerritos College, CA (M)
Chadron State College, NE (M)
Cheyney University of Pennsylvania, PA (M)
Citadel, SC (M)
Clackamas Community College, OR (M)
Clarion University, PA (M)
Clemson University, SC (M)
Cleveland State University, OH (M)
Coe College, IA (M)
Colby Community College, KS (M)
College of Mount St. Joseph, OH (M)
The College of New Jersey, NJ (M)
College of William and Mary, VA (M)
Colorado School of Mines, CO (M)
Columbia University, NY (M)
Concordia College, MN (M)
Concordia University, MN (M)
Coppin State College, MD (M)

Cornell College, IA (M)
Cornell University, NY (M)
Cuesta College, CA (M)
Cumberland College, KY (W)
Cuyahoga Community College (Metropolitan Campus), OH (M)
Dakota Wesleyan University, SD (M)
Dana College, NE (M)
Delaware State University, DE (M)
Delaware Valley College, PA (M)
De Pauw University, IN (M)
Diablo Valley Community College, CA (M)
Dickinson State University, ND (M)
Drexel University, PA (M)
Duke University, NC (M)
Duquesne University, PA (M)
Eastern Illinois University, IL (M)
Eastern Michigan University, MI (M)
East Stroudsburg University, PA (M)
Edinboro University of Pennsylvania, PA (M)
Elizabethtown College, PA (M)
Elmhurst College, IL (M)
Emerson College, MA (M)
Fordham University, NY (M)
Fort Hays State University, KS (M)
Fort Lewis College, CO (M)
Franklin & Marshall College, PA (M)
Fresno City College, CA (M)
Furman University, SC (M)
Gannon College, PA (M)
Garden City Community College, KS (M)
George Mason University, VA (M)
Georgia State University, GA (M)
Gettysburg College, PA (M)
Gloucester County College, NJ (M)
Golden West College, CA (M)
Grand Rapids Community College, MI (M)
Hamline University, MN (M)
Hampton University, VA (M)
Harvard University, MA (M)
Heidelberg College, OH (M)
Hofstra University, NY (M)
Howard University, DC (M)
Humboldt State University, CA (M)

Hunter College of the City University of New York, NY (M)
Huron University, SD (M)
Illinois College, IL (M)
Indiana University, IN (M)
Iowa State University of Science and Technology, IA (M)
Ithaca College, NY (M)
James Madison University, VA (M)
Jamestown College, ND (M)
John Carroll University, OH (M)
Johns Hopkins University, MD (M)
Kean University, NJ (M)
Kent State University (Ashtabula), OH (M)
Kent State University (Kent), OH (M)
Kent State University (New Philadelphia), OH (M)
Kent State University (Warren), OH (M)
King's College, PA (M)
Knox College, IL (M)
Kutztown University, PA (M)
Labette Community College, KS (M)
Lafayette College, PA (M)
Lawrence University, WI (M)
Lebanon Valley College, PA (M)
Lehigh University, PA (M)
Lincoln College, IL (M)
Linfield College, OR (M)
Livingstone College, NC (M)
Lock Haven University of Pennsylvania, PA (M)
Longwood College, VA (M)
Loras College, IA (M)
Lower Columbia College, WA (M)
Luther College, IA (M)
Lycoming College, PA (M)
Madison Area Technical College, WI (M)
Mankato State University, MN (M)
Marquette University, WI (M)
Massachusetts Institute of Technology, MA (M)
Mayville State College, ND (M)
Mesa State College, CO (M)
Messiah College, PA (M)
Michigan State University, MI (M)
Middlesex County College, NJ (M)
Millersville University, PA (M)
Millikin University, IL (M)
Modesto Junior College, CA (M)
Montclair State College, NJ (M)

Moorhead State University, MN (M)
Moorpark College, CA (M)
Moravian College, PA (M)
Mount Union College, OH (M)
Mt. San Antonio College, CA (M)
Muhlenberg College, PA (M)
Muskegon Community College, MI (M)
Muskingum College, OH (M)
Nassau Community College, NY (M)
New York University, NY (M)
Niagara County Community College, NY (M)
Norfolk State University, VA (M)
North Carolina A & T State University, NC (M)
North Carolina State University, NC (M)
North Central College, IL (M)
North Dakota State University, ND (M)
Northern Illinois University, IL (M)
Northern Montana College, MT (M)
Northern State University, SD (M)
North Idaho College, ID (M)
Northwest College, WY (M)
Northwestern College, IA (M)
Northwestern College, MN (M)
Northwestern University, IL (M)
Norwich University, VT (M)
Oakton Community College, IL (M)
Ohio Northern University, OH (M)
Ohio State University, OH (M)
Ohio University, OH (M)
Oklahoma State University, OK (M)
Old Dominion University, VA (M)
Olivet College, MI (M)
Oregon Institute of Technology, OR (M)
Oregon State University, OR (M)
Oswego State University (SUNY), NY (M)
Pacific Lutheran University, WA (M)
Pacific University, OR (M)
Palomar College, CA (M)
Pennsylvania State University, PA (M)
Pfeiffer College, NC (M)
Pima Community College (West Campus), AZ (M)

Plymouth State College, NH (M)
Pontifical Catholic University of Puerto Rico, PR (M)
Portland State University, OR (M)
Princeton University, NJ (M)
Purdue University, IN (M)
Ranetto Santiago College, CA (M)
Rhode Island College, RI (M)
Ricks College, ID (M)
Rider College, NJ (M)
Rochester Community College, MN (M)
Rochester Institute of Technology, NY (M)
Rose-Hulman Institute of Technology, IN (M)
Rutgers, Newark College of Arts and Sciences, NJ (M)
Sacred Heart University, CT (M)
Saint Cloud State University, MN (M)
Saint John's University, MN (M)
Saint Lawrence University, NY (M)
Saint Olaf College, MN (M)
San Bernardino Community College, CA (M)
San Francisco State University, CA (M)
San Joaquin Delta College, CA (M)
San Jose State University, CA (M)
Santa Rosa Junior College, CA (M)
Seton Hall University, NJ (M)
Shippensburg University of Pennsylvania, PA (M)
Sierra College, CA (M)
Simpson College, CA (M)
Skyline College, CA (M)
Slippery Rock University of Pennsylvania, PA (M)
South Dakota State University, SD (M)
Southern Illinois University (Edwardsville), IL (M)
Southern Oregon State College, OR (M)
Southwest State University, MN (M)
Springfield College, MA (M)
Stanford University, CA (M)
State University of New York College (Brockport), NY (M)
State University of New York College (Cortland), NY (M)

Stevens Institute of Technology, NJ (M)

St. Louis Community College (Florissant Valley), MO (M)

St. Louis Community College (Forest Park), MO (M)

Swarthmore College, PA (M)

Syracuse University, NY (M)

Teikyo Westmar University, IA (M)

Trinity College, CT (M)

Trinity College, IL (M)

Triton College, IL (M)

University at Buffalo (SUNY), NY (M)

University of California (Davis), CA (M)

University of Central Oklahoma, OK (M)

University of Chicago, IL (M)

University of Dayton, OH (M)

University of Dubuque, IA (M)

University of Findlay, OH (M)

University of Illinois (Chicago), IL (M)

University of Illinois (Urbana-Champaign), IL (M)

University of Indianapolis, IN (M)

University of Iowa, IA (M)

University of La Verne, CA (M)

University of Mary, ND (M)

University of Maryland, MD (M)

University of Massachusetts (Boston), MA (M)

University of Massachusetts (Lowell), MA (M)

University of Michigan, MI (M)

University of Minnesota (Duluth), MN (M)

University of Minnesota (Minneapolis), MN (M)

University of Minnesota (Morris), MN (M)

University of Missouri, MO (M)

University of Missouri (Columbia), MO (M)

University of Nebraska, NE (M)

University of Nebraska (Kearney), NE (M)

University of Nebraska (Lincoln), NE (M)

University of New Hampshire, NH (M)

University of New Mexico, NM (M)

University of North Carolina (Asheville), NC (M)

University of North Carolina (Chapel Hill), NC (M)

University of North Carolina (Pembroke), NC (M)

University of North Dakota, ND (M)

University of Northern Colorado, CO (M)

University of Northern Iowa, IA (M)

University of Oklahoma, OK (M)

University of Oregon, OR (M)

University of Pennsylvania, PA (M)

University of Pittsburgh, PA (M)

University of Pittsburgh (Johnstown), PA (M)

University of Puerto Rico, PR (M)

University of Puerto Rico (Bayamon), PR (M)

University of Rhode Island, RI (M)

University of Scranton, PA (M)

University of Southern Colorado, CO (M)

University of St. Thomas, MN (M)

University of Toledo, OH (M)

University of Virginia, VA (M)

University of Wisconsin (Eau Claire), WI (M)

University of Wisconsin (La Crosse), WI (M)

University of Wisconsin (Madison), WI (M)

University of Wisconsin (Oshkosh), WI (M)

University of Wisconsin (Plat-teville), WI (M)

University of Wisconsin (River Falls), WI (M)

University of Wisconsin (Stevens Point), WI (M)

University of Wisconsin (Superior), WI (M)

University of Wyoming, WY (M)

Upper Iowa University, IA (M)

Ursinus College, PA (M)

Utah State University, UT (M)

Valparaiso University, IN (M)

Virginia Military Institute, VA (M)

Virginia Polytechnic Institute & State University, VA (M)

Wabash College, IN (M)

Wagner College, NY (M)

Waldorf College, IA (M)

Wartburg College, IA (M)

Washington and Jefferson College, PA (M)

Waubonsee College, IL (M)

Wesleyan University, CT (M)

Western Maryland College, MD (M)

Western New England College, MA (M)

Western State College, CO (M)

West Liberty State College, WV (M)

West Virginia University, WV (M)

Wheaton College, IL (M)

Wilkes College, NC (M)

William Penn College, IA (M)

William Rainey Harper College, IL (M)

Williams College, MA (M)

Williamson Trade School, PA (M)

Wilmington College, OH (M)

Winston-Salem State University, NC (M)

Worthington Community College, MN (M)

Yeshiva University, NY (M)

York College of Pennsylvania, PA (M)

INDEX